INTERNAL
CORPORATE
INVESTIGATIONS

SECOND EDITION

**Brad D. Brian and
Barry F. McNeil,
Editors**

Section of Litigation

Defending Liberty
Pursuing Justice

Cover design by Gray Cat Design

07 06 05 04 03   5 4 3 2 1

Library of Congress Cataloging-in-Publication Data

Internal corporate investigations / Brad D. Brian, Barry F. McNeil, editors.—2d ed.
    p. cm.
  Includes index.
  ISBN 1-59031-038-1
  1. Corporation law—United States—Criminal provisions. 2. Governmental investigations—United States. I. Brian, Brad D., 1952- . II. McNeil, Barry F., 1944- .

KF1416 .I573 2002
345. 73'0268—dc21   2002007851

About the Editors

Brad D. Brian

Mr. Brian, a partner in the Los Angeles firm of Munger, Tolles & Olson LLP, is a Fellow in the American College of Trial Lawyers and is listed in *The Best Lawyers in America* (S. Naifeh & G. Smith) in both the business litigation and criminal defense categories. Mr. Brian was selected by the *National Law Journal* as one of the top ten trial lawyers of 1994 and was listed by *California Law Business* in 1998, 1999, 2000, and 2001 as one of the 100 most influential lawyers in California. He has conducted more than 100 internal corporate investigations in the areas of securities regulation, environmental compliance, government contracts, the Foreign Corrupt Practices Act, the False Claims Act, bribery, and other matters. He has been active in the leadership of the American Bar Association Litigation Section since 1986 and has taught trial advocacy at the University of Southern California Law Center, Harvard Law School's trial advocacy program, and the National Institute for Trial Advocacy. Mr. Brian graduated magna cum laude in 1977 from the Harvard Law School, where he served as managing editor of the *Harvard Law Review*. He later served as an assistant U.S. attorney in Los Angeles.

Barry F. McNeil

Mr. McNeil, a partner in the Dallas office of Haynes & Boone, LLP, is a Fellow in the American College of Trial Lawyers and a former chair of the Litigation Section of the American Bar Association. Mr. McNeil was recently ranked as one of the 15 top litigators in the trial bar by *International Commercial Litigation* and as one of the top three antitrust lawyers in Dallas, Texas, by *D Magazine*. Mr. McNeil has more than 30 years of experience as a trial lawyer, first with the Antitrust Division of the Department of Justice and now in private practice. He has defended companies and senior officers before juries throughout the country in class actions and in civil and criminal fraud cases. In *The National Law Journal*'s "Biggest Defense Verdict of 1999" (May 22, 2000), Mr. McNeil led the successful defense of a national healthcare provider, winning a "slam-dunk defense verdict."

Contents

CHAPTER 6   **Employees' Rights and Duties During an Internal Investigation** 169

JOSEPH F. COYNE, JR.

CHARLES F. BARKER

CHAPTER 11 **Report of the Investigation** 335

EDWIN G. SCHALLERT

NATALIE R. WILLIAMS

CHAPTER 14 **Internal Investigations in Health Care:
Unique Enforcement Environment and the
Dilemma of Disclosure** 431

STACY L. BRAININ

CHAPTER 15 **An Overview of Internal Investigations from
the In-house Perspective** 449

H. LOWELL BROWN

Foreword to Second Edition

Great companies are built upon two fundamental foundations of integrity: complete and honest financial reporting and compliance with the law and ethical standards. As this new edition goes to press, questions about both dimensions of corporate integrity dominate not just the business news, but also the national news. Public confidence in corporations and the people who manage them has reached low ebb. The capital markets have responded with punishing sell-offs, regulators have launched a record number of investigative proceedings, and Congress has enacted legislation that imposes new oversight regulation on the accounting profession and stiff new penalties for fraud and other forms of corporate crime. In this superheated environment—one in which executives are led off in handcuffs for deterrent effect—the strength and stability of a company's compliance program have never been more critical to the trustworthiness and credibility of the enterprise and the people who manage it.

This book focuses on a central element of any corporate compliance program: the company's willingness and ability to conduct an honest and searching internal investigation. The need for an internal investigation typically arises in two contexts. The company may receive notice of potential wrongdoing from a regulator or law enforcement authority: That news may arrive in the form of a phone call from an official, an article in the press, or a subpoena. Alternatively, and more frequently, allegations of potential misconduct may surface through one of a number of different internal channels: a visit from a concerned employee to an ombudsperson or compliance officer; an anonymous e-mail; a phone call to a corporate "hotline"; an exit interview with a departing employee; or a posting on an intranet bulletin board.

Whether an allegation of misconduct originates from outside the company or through one of its internal channels, management and company counsel must launch an internal investigation to accomplish three objectives. First, they must find out if the allegations are true. Second, if misconduct is substantiated, the company must assess its legal exposure and formulate a strategy for dealing with regulators and law enforcement authorities (often by making appropriate disclosure). Third, management must impose appropriate discipline and systematically address the institutional failures that may have contributed to the misconduct.

Particularly when allegations surface through one of the internal channels, company counsel and management must recognize that later they will be judged on how they responded *from the moment* the allegations came to their attention. At General Electric, when we teach compliance to our managers, we warn them that three fundamental questions will be asked in the aftermath of a compliance failure: *What did they know? When did they know it? What did they do about it?* It is not enough for the senior managers of a company just to ensure that an internal investigation is done; they also must ensure that it is done well. Officers, directors, audit committees, and counsel will be held accountable by regulators, shareholders, and the public for the thoroughness and probity of an investigation, its independence from the wrongdoers, the care with which evidence was preserved, and the speed with which the investigation was conducted. The investigation will be viewed by the public and regulators alike as a reflection of the integrity of the company's compliance program and, ultimately, of the character of the company and its senior management.

Where the allegation originates with the government, the company's ability to conduct a thorough, independent investigation—and its reputation for integrity—are important factors that can constructively shape the interactions between the government and the company. The company with an esteemed reputation—and the technical ability to carry out an independent, comprehensive investigation—is more likely to be able to obtain time to conduct its own investigation before official proceedings are commenced. The company's cooperation may reap short-term benefits—for example, the orderly production of documents and witnesses, rather than through the execution of search warrants or other highly disruptive evidence-gathering mechanisms. Most important, the company's searching and effective cooperation may contribute to more lenient charging decisions by law enforcement authorities. And even if the company and the government have opposing views of the conduct in question, and the context is fiercely adversarial, the company's ability to conduct a privileged internal investigation that faces the facts—and their implications—with brutal honesty will sharpen its ability to defend itself in negotiations with the government and any subsequent proceedings.

To conduct an internal investigation effectively, lawyers must understand the ramifications of the steps they take at each stage of the investigation. In the multifaceted contexts in which these matters can arise—public and rapid inquiries in different countries, subject to different bodies of law, under the shadow of parallel regulatory, judicial and legislative proceedings—strategic decisions have far-reaching and sometimes unforeseen consequences. This revised edition provides a comprehensive guide to this complex landscape. Brad Brian and Barry McNeil have assembled an outstanding group of lawyers who address in practical and comprehensive terms the key issues in the lifespan of an investigation: the initial step of determining who will conduct the investigation; the careful measures that must be taken to preserve evidence, gather facts, and prevent charges of obstruction; the art of conducting an employee interview; the complexities associated with maintaining privileges; the decision to write a report; and many other important issues.

Those of us who counsel companies daily and have lived through a number of public and highly charged internal investigations understand that they are draining, sometimes devastating, experiences for employees and leaders who are swept up in them. Yet these searching inquiries are essential to the health of any company that is committed to integrity. To preserve that commitment, management and its counsel must promptly and thoroughly investigate allegations of misconduct and then take the tough, effective action necessary to prevent a recurrence. There has never been a more urgent need for lawyers to understand the importance of internal investigations and to master the intricacies of conducting them. This book shows them how to do it.

Ben W. Heineman, Jr., GE General Counsel
Brackett B. Denniston III, GE Senior Counsel, Litigation and Legal Policy
E. Scott Gilbert, GE Counsel, Litigation and Legal Policy
Fairfield, Connecticut

Foreword to First Edition

Internal or special investigations in the business world are like brain surgeries in the world of medical trauma—delicate, fraught with unsuspected complications, and even when quite successful, serious aftereffects may remain. This book provides the very best advice on internal investigations from the very best practitioners. No corporate general counsel and no law firm representing business clients should be without it.

The opening question—whether to conduct an internal investigation—is made especially difficult because it is almost always asked during an emergency or crisis that precludes reasonable time, reasonable reflection, and thorough analysis. The heated focus is on finding the sources of the problems so that management can deal with them effectively. The atmosphere is such that the company is scandalized or about to be seriously damaged by the disaster or calamity or by public charges of wrongdoing. No small wonder investigations are begun without any idea of where they may lead or end.

The objective of the choice of an internal investigation—to find the facts and remedy the problems, including blunting public speculation of the degree and extent of wrongdoing—is worthy. But alone and without guidance through the minefield of consequences of such investigations, management may soon find that the merits or the objectives are not themselves enough to justify a decision to begin.

These chapters, written by the country's most experienced lawyers in this field (and excellent trial lawyers, too), explore and explain succinctly the issues necessary to evaluate an investigation and clearly describe the methods and alternatives available to achieve the objectives. But this book does more. It guides the businessperson and counsel to reasoned choices and away from the pitfalls of expediency. These authors explain fact finding, legal standards, duty of disclosure, attorney-client privilege protection, the rights and effects of regulatory and legislative bodies, and possible hearings and findings. The list of subjects is comprehensive and the treatment uniformly understandable.

Because the editors, Brad Brian and Barry McNeil, collected these outstanding lawyers to contribute to this unique exposition and then pulled no punches in vigorous editing, I believe it has achieved a function that may or may not have been intended. It serves the public interest. It provides the information and assessments by which we all may judge the good faith and efficiency of internal and special investigations. For that reason alone I could commend this book, but because of all the other reasons touched on, I am pleased to write this short note.

Benjamin R. Civiletti
Venable, Baetjer, Howard & Civiletti
Baltimore, Maryland

Contributors

Scott N. Auby is a partner in the Washington, D.C., office of Debevoise & Plimpton.

Charles F. Barker is a partner in the law firm of Sheppard, Mullin, Richter & Hampton LLP in Los Angeles, California.

Nancy E. Barton is a senior vice president, general counsel, and secretary at General Electric Capital Corporation, Stamford, Connecticut.

Judah Best is a senior partner in the Washington, D.C., office of Debevoise & Plimpton.

Dennis J. Block is a senior partner at Cadwalader, Wickersham & Taft, New York, New York.

Stacy L. Brainin is a partner in Haynes and Boone, L.L.P. in Dallas, Texas.

Brad D. Brian is a partner at Munger, Tolles & Olson LLP in Los Angeles, California.

H. Lowell Brown is the former assistant general counsel, Northrop Grumman Corporation, and now practices law in Washington, D.C., and California.

Christopher H. Buckley, Jr. is a partner in the Washington, D.C., office of Gibson, Dunn & Crutcher LLP.

Michele C. Coyle is a partner in the Los Angeles office of Hogan & Hartson L.L.P.

Joseph F. Coyne, Jr. is a partner in the law firm of Sheppard, Mullin, Richter & Hampton LLP in Los Angeles, California.

Lawrence J. Fox is a partner at Drinker, Biddle & Reath in Philadelphia, Pennsylvania.

David S. Frankel is a partner in the law firm of Kramer Levin Naftalis & Frankel LLP in New York, New York.

Larry A. Gaydos is a partner in Haynes and Boone in Dallas, Texas.

Thomas E. Holliday is a partner at Gibson Dunn & Crutcher LLP in Los Angeles, California.

Barry F. McNeil is a partner at Haynes and Boone in Dallas, Texas.

Gary P. Naftalis is a partner in the law firm of Kramer Levin Naftalis & Frankel LLP in New York, New York.

Edwin G. Schallert is a partner in Debevoise & Plimpton in New York, New York.

Michael Shepard is a partner at Heller Ehrman White & McAuliffe LLP in San Francisco, California.

Charles J. Stevens is a partner at Stevens & O'Connell LLP in Sacramento, California.

Randall J. Turk is a partner at Baker Botts, LLP in Washington, D.C.

Michael Waldman is a partner at the law firm of Fried, Frank, Harris, Shriver & Jacobson in Washington, D.C.

Natalie R. Williams is deputy chief of the civil rights bureau of the Office of the New York State Attorney General in New York, New York.

Overview: Initiating an Internal Investigation and Assembling the Investigative Team

1

by Brad D. Brian & Barry F. McNeil*

---

* Brad D. Brian is a partner at Munger, Tolles & Olson LLP in Los Angeles, California. Barry F. McNeil is a partner at Haynes and Boone in Dallas, Texas.

1

I. INTRODUCTION

IN THE WAKE OF highly publicized corporate shake-ups, internal investigations have gained national prominence and have established themselves as an important tool of management. An internal investigation is often the first step employed by senior management to uncover wrongdoing and to rid the corporation of the wrongdoers. More and more companies are vesting lawyers with a broad mandate to investigate internal corruption and fashion remedial actions.

With the recent passage of the Sarbanes-Oxley Act of 2002,[1] the need for internal corporate investigations has increased dramatically. Aimed at eliminating accounting fraud and implemented as an attempt to restore confidence in corporations, the Act has had an immediate effect on public companies in the United States, as well as the accounting, legal, and investment banking community.

Given the volume of the Act's requirements, the Act will not be addressed in detail here. It is important to note, however, that the Act places new restraints and duties on corporate officers and directors, requires a host of reporting and disclosure requirements,[2] and imposes new responsibilities on legal counsel. The Act directs the SEC to issue rules requiring that a lawyer report evidence of a "material violation" of the securities law or a breach of fiduciary duty to the chief legal counsel

---

1. Pub. L. No. 107-204, 116 Stat. 745 (2002).

2. The Act immediately required that each periodic report filed by a public company include a certification by the company's chief executive officer and chief financial officer that the report fully complies with periodic reporting requirements of the Securities Exchange Act of 1934 and that the information presented in all material respects fairly presents the financial condition and result of the company's operations. Additionally, public companies must now disclose to the public on a "rapid and current basis" such additional information concerning material changes in the financial condition or operations of the company, in plain English, as the SEC determines is necessary or useful for the protection of investors. Each financial report that contains financial statements and is filed with the SEC must also reflect all material correcting adjustments identified by the company's accounting firm.

The Act also requires faster disclosure of insider transactions. The Act requires reports of changes in beneficial ownership to be filed with SEC by the end of the second business day following the transaction by insiders. Previously, insiders did not have to report trades until the tenth day of the month following the month in which the trade occurred, meaning that an insider trade could go unreported for as long as 40 days.

or the chief executive officer of the company. If the chief legal counsel or the chief executive officer does not appropriately respond to the evidence, the lawyer must then report the evidence to the audit committee or to the full board of directors. These rules appear to apply to both inside and outside counsel advising a reporting company.

While the precise standards governing the lawyer's reporting obligation are far from clear, on November 6, 2002 (as this publication goes to press), the SEC proposed rules for implementing the standards affecting professional conduct of attorneys.[3] Within the SEC's proposal is an additional obligation that a reporting attorney, if not satisfied with the company's response, must make a "noisy withdrawal." The proposed rules will certainly be the subject of considerable comment by lawyers and bar associations in the coming weeks.

The Act leaves many of the critical details and the implementation of the Act to the rule-making authority of the SEC. While we all await various regulations that will determine how the Act will be interpreted, it is clear that Sarbanes-Oxley will have significant and far-reaching effects not only on how public companies operate but also on how their auditors and lawyers investigate and report possible wrongdoings.[4]

In this book, various authors provide advice on the skills involved in conducting internal investigations and, in the process, give insights into avoiding the many traps that can appear. While it is impossible to predict every trap, close adherence to the ground rules set forth in this book will enable the reader to address even problems not anticipated at the outset of the investigation.

The chapters of this book are organized so as to take each aspect of the investigation and, for each, to provide the full body of applicable law as well as numerous practical tips. The book begins with a detailed discussion of the attorney-client privilege and work-product doctrine. A lawyer should never commence an investigation without first carefully considering issues of privilege.

---

3. *See* United States Securities and Exchange Commission Press Release 2002-158, Nov. 6, 2002.

4. The chapters contained in this book were written before the Sarbanes-Oxley Act was passed. While the Act does not affect the bulk of the recommendations set forth in those chapters, particular attention will need to be paid in the future to the internal and external reporting and disclosure obligations of companies and their lawyers. These obligations will be addressed in future revisions or supplements to this book.

Chapter 11 of this book addresses the final phase of the internal investigation—the report to management. In that chapter, the authors provide valuable advice on communicating the contents of the report to the client in a way that provides management with the fullest possible information, yet limits dissemination to the narrowest possible audience, and thus minimizes concerns such as leaks and defamation suits. Between these two chapters, other authors discuss the remaining components of an internal investigation. These authors—all highly acknowledged lawyers in this field—provide important practical tips and legal insights into the key elements of internal investigations, including:

- conducting employee interviews,
- avoiding charges of witness intimidation or obstruction of justice during the investigation,
- organizing and reviewing documents pertinent to the internal investigation,
- understanding employees' rights and obligations throughout the investigation,
- coordinating parallel criminal and civil proceedings that may arise in connection with, or in response to, the internal investigation, and
- deciding whether and what to disclose to government agencies.

In addition, four chapters address internal investigations in the context of specialized circumstances—shareholder litigation, environmental actions, securities cases, and government contract investigations. There are, of course, many other subjects that are equally specialized. These were chosen not because they are the only specialized subjects, but because they illustrate the use of internal investigations in specialized areas. With this overview in mind, some of the more significant issues that arise at the outset of internal investigations are addressed.

II. DIFFERENT TYPES OF INTERNAL INVESTIGATIONS

Internal investigations may arise in a variety of ways and uncover a wide band of problems. To use an overworked metaphor, internal investigations do not take place on a single playing field against a single opponent. Underlying many internal investigations is corporate conduct that can trigger confrontations on a number of fields, each with different opponents, different rules, and different referees. A company's illegal conduct may result in federal and state prosecutions, administrative actions, private litigation, and, many times, difficult dealings with the news media. A lawyer's failure to recognize this reality at the outset will greatly diminish the overall effectiveness of the investigation.

As a consequence, there are several types of internal investigations. One is purely reactive, arising in response to some external event—for example, a grand jury subpoena, a document request by the Inspector General of a government agency, an administrative audit, or a private lawsuit. Another is proactive—the company conducts the internal investigation on its own initiative to determine whether any wrongdoing has occurred and, if so, to take remedial steps. Finally, many internal investigations fit into neither category but are a mixture of both.

Counsel's role in connection with the internal investigation will vary depending upon the type of investigation under way. For example, if the investigation is triggered by some government action (e.g., grand jury subpoena or administrative audit), counsel may be retained for one or more of three purposes: first, to conduct the investigation; second, to advise the company of its legal rights and potential liabilities; and third, to represent the company in a lawsuit or other proceeding brought against the company by the government or a private litigant. Having a single counsel perform all three roles can be a prudent (and less costly) decision under many circumstances. However, in other circumstances—for example, where the company is likely to waive the attorney-client privilege otherwise protecting the investigation—the company may be better served by retaining one law firm to conduct the investigation and provide legal advice to the company, and a second firm to conduct all later legal procedures.

The type of internal investigation will likewise determine the scope of the assignment. If the investigation is a reaction to a government initiative, the internal investigation may be limited to the allegations under scrutiny. But if the investigation is proactive, management may instruct counsel to look into a variety of issues within a broad subject matter. The result could be a far different internal investigation, with different questions regarding the attorney-client privilege, the team assembled to conduct the investigation, and the supervision by company management.

III. THE INITIAL MEETING

Experience teaches that a crucial event in an internal investigation is the initial meeting between management and the lawyer who will conduct the internal investigation. The lawyer learns for the first time the conduct at issue and, together with management, begins exploring the steps involved to marshal the facts and analyze their legal consequences. Decisions must be made in this first session, and the judgments underlying those decisions are ones that both the company and counsel must live with throughout the ensuing inquiry. A modest but acceptable agenda for the initial meeting will include discussion along the following lines:

- The starting point: deciding whether or not to conduct an investigation.
- Defining the scope of the investigation.
- Applying the attorney-client privilege and the attorney work-product doctrine.
- Assembling the team to conduct the internal investigation.
- Anticipating what can go wrong.
- Agreeing on lines of reporting and supervision.

A. *The Starting Point: Whether to Conduct an Investigation*

The starting point is rather obvious: Should the company conduct any investigation at all? Why should the company investigate claims that, if true, will subject the company to criminal or civil lawsuits? This impulse—Isn't the company better off not knowing?—is not irrational and should be addressed head-on at the outset.

Probably the most important factor in deciding whether to conduct an internal investigation is the existence or nonexistence of a government investigation or private lawsuit. If the Justice Department or other prosecuting agency has served a grand jury subpoena or is otherwise conducting an investigation, the company effectively has no choice but to conduct its own internal investigation. The same reasoning applies if a former employee has complained to the government about misconduct allegedly constituting a crime.

The harder question arises when the government has not initiated its own investigation, but the company is aware of internal allegations of wrongdoing. Here, management may be more tempted not to conduct its own internal investigation, hoping that the allegations will never become public. Although there is no blanket rule, the better course more often than not favors beginning an investigation. A company should not remain blind to its own conduct, not wishing to know its improprieties. It is criminally liable for its employees' illegal conduct, as long as the employees acted within the scope of their employment, and as long as they intended, at least in part, to benefit the corporation.[5] The law's reach alone is enough to compel self-analysis and correction. Add to that the heavy overlay of government regulation and the severe financial consequences accompanying findings of liability, and the usual result is that management should not choose to remain ignorant of allegations of employee misconduct.

Conducting an internal investigation also will enable the company to decide whether to disclose to the government the allegations and the company's findings in response to those allegations.[6] Under some circumstances, disclosing the results of an internal investigation might enable the company to avoid an enforcement action—either because the allegations are unfounded or because, as a result of the company's cooperation, the government chooses not to prosecute the company.[7] If the government decides to prosecute the company, under the federal Sentencing Guidelines the company's monetary fine can be reduced by the voluntary disclosure and cooperation.[8]

Internal investigations provide another significant advantage to the company—that of enabling the company to formulate its defenses at an early stage in anticipation of later criminal or civil proceedings. For example, while a corporation generally is liable for its employee's acts, such liability might not attach where the employee has acted for personal benefit contrary to the corporation's diligent efforts to prevent such misconduct.[9] In addition, while a company is legally respon-

---

5. *See* United States v. Beusch, 596 F.2d 871 (9th Cir. 1979); Standard Oil Co. v. United States, 307 F.2d 120 (5th Cir. 1962).

6. The topic of disclosure is addressed in detail in chapter 8, "Disclosure of Results of Internal Investigations to the Government or Other Third Parties."

7. DEPARTMENT OF JUSTICE MANUAL, Principles of Federal Prosecution, § 230 at 9-506–9-508 (citing a company's voluntary disclosure and cooperation as factors influencing the decision whether to pursue criminal charges).

8. *See* chapter 8, "Sentencing of Organizations," Roger W. Haines et al., FEDERAL SENTENCING GUIDELINES MANUAL (1997), § 8C2.5 (g).

9. *See, e.g.,* United States v. Beusch, 596 F.2d at 878 (due diligence is a factor to be weighed by the jury in determining whether the individual actor intended to benefit the corporation).

sible for some acts of misconduct, it is not necessarily liable for the full scope of employee misconduct. A properly conducted investigation will enable the company and its counsel to place the misconduct in its best light, to assert defenses where appropriate, and to argue mitigation.

Often an internal investigation also will ease the daily disruption to the company that is caused by a government investigation. Government investigations are, by nature, disruptive, and considerable groundwork can be done before the government's investigation has begun or has accelerated.

Finally, although a corporation generally is not required to disclose a prior crime,[10] in many instances disclosure may be the only means of preventing future criminal conduct. For example, in the field of government contracting, companies are often called upon to certify financial statements, to make accurate financial records available for audit, or otherwise to represent the company's prior conduct. Under these circumstances, disclosing prior misconduct may be the only practical method of preventing the occurrence of another criminal act that will expose the company—and perhaps its individual officers—to further criminal liability.

B. *Defining the Scope of the Internal Investigation*

In the initial meeting, company management and counsel also should reach agreement on the scope of the investigation. That scope should correspond to the severity of the matter under investigation. There is a wide difference between suspicion that a bookkeeper has embezzled funds, on the one hand, and public allegations of widespread bribery in government procurement procedures, on the other.

If the internal investigation results from a recently commenced government inquiry, the scope of the internal investigation is somewhat preordained—one will likely mirror the other. The question of scope becomes more difficult, however, where the allegations of misconduct arise within the company and there is, as yet, no known government investigation.

There are numerous instances where a company may elect to review internal practices solely for corrective action, and not in immi-

---

10. *See* chapter 8, "Disclosure of Results of Internal Investigations to the Government or Other Third Parties."

nent fear of litigation. A hospital corporation may wish to review and institute new tracking systems in light of recently instituted government regulations; a company may analyze pricing practices in connection with an annual antitrust compliance program; management may be concerned about possible kickbacks by its purchasing department; or a company may suspect drug abuse in the workplace and wish to formulate a remedial plan.

In any of these instances, counsel and management should reach a clear understanding of the scope of the inquiry and should strictly conform all services to the agreed-upon parameters. Such an approach helps to ensure that the results of the investigation are fully protected from unwanted disclosure. If, for example, counsel veers beyond the agreed-upon scope—gathering information and giving advice outside the understood areas of concern—the risk of disclosure increases.[11] Additionally, a clear articulation of the engagement—and thus of counsel's role to obtain facts and render legal advice—makes less likely any challenge to the investigation on grounds that counsel acted as a business advisor, not a lawyer.

Counsel should confirm in writing the scope of the investigation. Whether or not in the form of an engagement letter, the document should state that counsel has been asked to investigate certain allegations; that the investigation is being conducted to enable counsel to advise the company regarding its legal rights, obligations, and potential liabilities; and that all communications with counsel are protected by the attorney-client privilege and thus intended to remain confidential. In some cases, it may be wise to circulate this memorandum among the employees to be interviewed.

C. *Applying the Attorney-Client Privilege and Work-Product Doctrine*

Chapter 2 deals at length with the application to internal investigations of the attorney-client privilege and the attorney work-product doctrine. While not repeating that entire discussion here, certain points do bear emphasis.

---

11. While the attorney-client privilege presumably protects all client communications, the work product privilege may not attach to the lawyer's efforts outside the scope of the engagement (other than client communications) when those efforts are unrelated to the prospect of future litigation. Third-party interviews are one example of this concern.

First, there can be no greater risk in commencing an investigation than to treat issues of privilege carelessly. Upon the conclusion of the investigation, the company might decide to disclose the results, but this decision should be one of choice, not the product of carelessness or ignorance.

Thus, before commencing the investigation, both management and its counsel should be versed in fundamental principles of privilege. Under the United States Supreme Court's decision in *Upjohn Co. v. United States*,[12] counsel's communications with company employees will be protected by the company's attorney-client privilege under certain described circumstances.[13] Federal and state law give added work product protection if counsel's work is "in anticipation of litigation or for trial."[14]

The initial engagement is important to the question of privilege. When management chooses to investigate its own conduct and no legal proceeding is under way, counsel must carefully consider whether its role—the gathering of data, the analysis, the conclusions—will be protected from later, unwanted disclosure. Is management seeking business advice or legal advice? Is counsel performing an investigative service or a legal service? Are employees clearly informed that their communications with company counsel are intended to remain confidential? The answers to all these questions will affect the degree to which the internal investigation can be protected from unwanted disclosure, and should promptly be discussed with management to alleviate later claims of surprise.

D. *Assembling the Investigative Team*

There may be no more delicate task than determining who should conduct the internal investigation. The choice often is between a lawyer and a nonlawyer—for example, in-house security personnel. Except in relatively insignificant matters (e.g., petty theft), lawyers are the better choice to conduct the investigation. This conclusion is arrived at for two reasons.

---

12. 449 U.S. 383 (1981).

13. *Upjohn* protects these communications if challenged in a federal proceeding; state law, both statutory and common law, provides guidance for protection should the assertion be challenged in a state proceeding.

14. FED. R. CIV. P. 26(b)(3). State laws vary in their protections afforded the lawyer's work product, though presumably all states have some form of protection.

First, having counsel conduct the internal investigation better enables the company to protect the entire investigation pursuant to the attorney-client privilege and the attorney work-product doctrine. Although an investigation by a nonlawyer may conceivably come within some work product protection, far greater protection comes where a lawyer has conducted the investigation consistent with all available legal privileges.[15]

Second, the internal investigation inevitably will lead to an analysis of the company's legal rights, obligations, and potential liabilities. Only a lawyer can address these ultimate issues.

Although nonlawyers should not supervise the internal investigation, they can perform valuable roles. Many internal investigations deal with complex questions of accounting, engineering, testing procedures, and the like. Auditors, engineers, and other nonlawyer specialists can provide invaluable assistance in these areas. Because many of these individuals can be found within the company, their participation might have the added benefit of reducing the cost of the internal investigation.

Once the company decides to have a lawyer conduct the investigation, the next question is whether that lawyer should be a member of the company's inside law department or retained from outside the company. There is no simple answer to this question, except to say that it depends upon all the circumstances, including cost. In almost all circumstances, it will be less expensive to have the investigation conducted in-house than to retain outside counsel.

Cost considerations, however, should not control the determination. Indeed, financial concerns often quickly give way to the more important factor of comparative independence of counsel conducting the investigation. Although the government will not perceive outside counsel as totally independent, outside counsel surely is more independent than inside counsel. Inside counsel, after all, has only one client—the company—whereas outside counsel has many.

This question of independence comes sharply into focus when considering the interview process. If inside counsel both interviews key employees and provides them with legal advice, counsel may find it difficult to approach the investigation with total independence.

---

15. *See* chapter 2, "Implications of the Attorney-Client Privilege and the Work-Product Doctrine."

Additionally, under some circumstances, lawyers employed by the company may themselves be witnesses to the underlying conduct, thus disqualifying themselves from the role of counsel. This potentiality is certainly not remote and should be examined at the outset to prevent future problems during the investigation.

Moreover, if pertinent employees have previously relied on inside counsel for legal advice, they might regard counsel as their personal lawyer during the course of their interviews. Although all witnesses should be told that the company's counsel does not represent them personally, a prior legal relationship between a witness and an inside lawyer could obscure this admonition and create at least a factual dispute over the witness's understanding at the time of the interview.[16]

E. *Anticipating What Can Go Wrong*

At the outset, investigative counsel should address management's instinctive judgment that an investigation may generate more bad than good. Counsel should anticipate this instinct and should use it as an opportunity to educate the client on the pitfalls of internal investigations. Counsel may wish to provide the client with concrete examples of the risks associated with even the best-conceived and properly conducted internal investigation.

Possibly the most serious risk is the potential for inadvertent disclosure of the results of the investigation. If the company cannot be confident that its results will be disclosed only when it chooses to do so, the undertaking becomes a perilous one indeed. This risk requires a strict adherence to all legal privileges.

A second concern involves employee interviews. Chapter 3 is devoted to this topic and sets forth practical tips. It is sufficient here to say that a sloppy interview can create a passel of later problems. Investigative counsel must approach the interview process along carefully drawn lines. They must clearly define their role—whom they represent and whom they do not. They must set out equally clearly the nature of the investigation and the employee's obligation to maintain the confidentiality of the interview. To do otherwise will unnecessarily cause confusion and invite later problems.

Third, defamation actions are far from theoretical in the aftermath

---

16. *See* chapter 3, "The Interview Process," for a more complete discussion of this issue.

of internal investigations. Investigations yield information, and that information must be reported in one form or another within the company, and possibly to outsiders. It is often difficult to achieve the proper balance between the company's need to act upon the information and its desire not to incur defamation charges from employees or third parties. This topic is discussed in detail in chapter 11, "Report of the Investigation," and will not be repeated here. This concern is a vital one, however, and should be flagged earlier in the investigation, so that both management and counsel are sensitive to it.

Finally, it is wise to emphasize to the client that during the internal investigation, employees should not create new documents discussing the allegations, except under the strict supervision of counsel. It is also wise to point out that despite this advice, employees might go ahead and create evidence in the midst of the investigation. Nevertheless, experience shows that mistakes do occur. Clear written instructions to employees at all levels will help to minimize this risk. The instructions can be included in a memorandum setting out the nature of the investigation and the documents sought, and providing assistance on responding to any outstanding discovery request.

F. *Agreeing to Lines of Reporting and Supervision*

Will counsel report to the general counsel? To senior management? To the chief executive officer? Or to an audit or special committee? What if senior management is itself responsible for the practices under investigation and yet demands full reports?

These questions involve both practical and political problems. Management is vitally interested in the investigation, its progress, and its discoveries. Indeed, it must have *some* information regarding the underlying conduct to meet its responsibilities. Yet steps must be taken, on the one hand, to shield management from unwanted information, and on the other, to protect management and the company from allegations of witness tampering. These subjects are also addressed in detail in chapter 11, "Report of the Investigation," and in chapter 4, "Perjury, Obstruction of Justice, and the Victim and Witness Protection Act."

Experience teaches that the best course is to confront all difficult problems early on, and to resolve them to the mutual satisfaction of management and counsel. Failure to do so only defers these hard questions and makes for a more difficult resolution at later stages in the investigation, when emotions are high (with the possible onset of government action) and objectivity is short.

IV. PRELIMINARY STEPS TO PREPARE FOR GOVERNMENT INVESTIGATIONS

Chapter 7 addresses at length the issues that arise in parallel civil and criminal investigations of the allegations under scrutiny. These government investigations heighten the company's concern and complicate the issues facing company counsel. At the outset of an internal investigation, it is impossible to predict each of the issues that will arise in the event of later government investigations. But counsel should take immediate steps to prepare management for certain key events that could occur during the course of a criminal investigation.

The first potential event is a search warrant. Not long ago, business litigators had only to concern themselves with the case law surrounding grand jury subpoenas *duces tecum*.[17] Increasingly, federal investigators are making use of search warrants as an alternative method of obtaining documents from a company.

The growing use of warrants poses unique concerns to the company and its counsel. By their very nature, search warrants are sudden and without notice. Also, by using warrants, government agents put themselves in a position (arguably improperly) to obtain statements from witnesses before they have reviewed any documents, before they have consulted with counsel if they choose to do so, and before they understand their legal rights.

Moreover, a well-planned and executed search can be a spectacle. When government agents descend upon a company in the midst of its workday—occasionally fully armed—the trauma to the individual employees and the company can be enormous. This procedure can pose enormous costs to the company's treasury and to the employees' morale. At the outset of an internal investigation, therefore, counsel should warn management of the potential use of search warrants and should apprise employees of the procedures to be followed in the event of a search. A written memorandum could prove helpful.

The company should also be warned of the potential for government agents' *ex parte* contacts with company employees. As explained more fully below, in 1989 the Attorney General published a memorandum an-

---

17. FED. R. CRIM. P. 17(c).

nouncing the Justice Department's view that it is permitted to conduct investigative interviews of company employees whether or not the company is represented by counsel.[18]

The company, and employees thought to be affected, should be apprised of this policy and of the employees' rights and obligations in the event they are contacted. Employees should *not* be told they cannot speak with government agents. But they can be told what their rights are—they have the right to talk or not to talk, they can consult with counsel before deciding whether to talk, and they can have company counsel present at any interview if they choose. Moreover, there is nothing improper in advising employees that, in view of the strict penalties flowing from enforcement of federal criminal laws and in view of the breadth of case law regarding corporate liabilities, management would prefer to have its counsel attend any interviews of company employees.

V. CONCLUSION

Without doubt, internal investigations pose significant risks to the corporate client. Unexpected turns can occur, mistakes can be made, and, more fundamentally, misconduct will be uncovered. Yet, clearly the bias favors commencing the investigation and learning of the underlying activity, for good or bad. How else can the company adequately defend itself in any ensuing civil or criminal proceeding?

---

18. *See* chapter 7, "The Practitioner's Guide to Parallel Proceedings."

Implications of the Attorney-Client Privilege and Work-Product Doctrine

2

by Dennis J. Block & Nancy E. Barton*

  * Dennis J. Block is a senior partner at Cadwalader, Wickersham & Taft, New York, New York, and Nancy E. Barton is a senior vice president, general counsel, and secretary at General Electric Capital Corporation, Stamford, Connecticut. The substantial assistance of Simon C. Roosevelt, an associate at Cadwalader, Wickersham & Taft, Beth J. Jacobwitz and Laura A. Cooper, trial counsel, Division of Enforcement, New York Stock Exchange, Inc., is gratefully acknowledged. The views expressed in this chapter are those of the authors and do not necessarily reflect the views of General Electric Capital Corporation and the New York Stock Exchange, Inc.

I. INTRODUCTION

THE GOAL OF PROVIDING maximum protection of the investigative record requires consideration of the elements of both the attorney-client privilege and the work-product doctrine—which are distinct and provide separate but overlapping protections—and to comport the investigative process as closely as practicable to these requisites.[1]

---

1. *See* Parts II and III, *infra.* Another privilege, called the "self-critical analysis privilege" or "self-evaluative privilege," could possibly be available to protect corporate internal investigations from discovery. This privilege was first recog-

There are essential differences between the attorney-client privilege and the work-product doctrine. The court in *Scourtes v. Fred W. Albrecht Grocery Co.*[2] distinguished them as follows:

> The purpose of the attorney-client privilege is to encourage full disclosure of information between a lawyer and his client by guarantying the inviolability of their confidential communications. The "work product of the attorney," on the other hand, is accorded protection for the purpose of preserving our adversary system of litigation by assuring a lawyer that his

---

nized in *Bredice v. Doctor's Hospital, Inc.*, 50 F.R.D. 249 (D.D.C. 1970), *aff'd mem.*, 479 F.2d 920 (D.C. Cir. 1973), in the context of a medical staff's evaluation of potential improvements in procedures. The application of the self-critical analysis privilege requires that the following three criteria be met:

> First, the information contained in the document must result from an internal investigation or review conducted to evaluate or improve a party's procedures or products; second, the party must originally have intended that the information remain confidential and demonstrate a strong interest in preserving the free flow of the type of information sought; finally, the information contained in the documents must be of a type whose flow would be curtailed if discovery were allowed.

Etienne v. Mitre Corp., 146 F.R.D. 145, 147 (E.D. Va. 1993) (citations and internal quotations omitted). While some courts have discussed the applicability of this privilege to corporate internal investigations, no court has yet upheld a claim of privilege on this basis. *See, e.g.,* Federal Trade Comm'n v. TRW, Inc., 628 F.2d 207, 210 (D.C. Cir. 1980) (self-evaluative privilege does not apply in the context of governmental subpoena); Westmoreland v. CBS, Inc., 97 F.R.D. 703, 706 (S.D.N.Y. 1983) (internal study for self-evaluation not protected where relied upon in public statements); Lloyd v. Cessna Aircraft Co., 74 F.R.D. 518, 521 (E.D. Tenn. 1977) (internal problem list not protected by self-evaluative privilege). Indeed, other courts have entirely rejected the self-critical analysis privilege. *See, e.g.,* Griffith v. Davis, 161 F.R.D. 687, 701 (C.D. Cal. 1995) (the Ninth Circuit does not recognize the privilege of "self-critical analysis"); Aramburu v. Boeing Co., 885 F. Supp. 1434, 1440-41 (D. Kan. 1995) (rejecting "self-critical analysis privilege" in Title VII cases). *See also In re* Application of Federation Internationale de Basketball, 2000 WL 1585682, *3 (S.D.N.Y. Oct. 24, 2000) (declining to consider whether there is a self-evaluative privilege and noting that the issue has not been decided by the Supreme Court or the Second Circuit).

2. 15 F.R.D. 55, 58 (N.D. Ohio 1953).

private files shall, except in unusual circumstances, remain free from the encroachments of opposing counsel.[3]

Because of the difference in the underlying rationale for each doctrine, the attorney-client privilege and the work-product doctrine differ in the circumstances under which the protection may be waived and the extent to which exceptions will override the protection.[4]

II. ATTORNEY-CLIENT PRIVILEGE

The principal means for preserving the confidentiality of counsel's investigative record is the attorney-client privilege.

A. Definition of the Attorney-Client Privilege

The attorney-client privilege is defined in the often-cited case of *United States v. United Shoe Mach. Corp.*:[5]

The privilege applies only if (1) the asserted holder of the privilege is or sought to become a client; (2) the person to whom the communication was made (a) is a member of the bar of a court, or his subordinate and (b) in connection with this communication is acting as a lawyer; (3) the communication relates to a fact of which the attorney was informed (a) by his client (b) without the presence of strangers (c) for the purpose of securing primarily either (i) an opinion on law or (ii) legal services or (iii) assistance in some legal proceeding, and not (d) for the purpose of committing a crime or tort; and (4) the privilege has been (a) claimed and (b) not waived by the client.[6]

The burden of establishing a claim of privilege is on the party claiming it.[7]

---

3. *Id.* at 58.
4. *See* Parts II and III, *supra.*
5. 89 F. Supp. 357 (D. Mass. 1950).
6. *Id.* at 358-59.
7. Von Bulow v. Von Bulow, 811 F.2d 136, 146 (2d Cir.), *cert. denied*, 481 U.S. 1015 (1987).

The attorney-client privilege is an evidentiary rule.[8] The federal courts have a bifurcated approach to the applicability of the attorney-client privilege, depending upon whether the cause of action that is the subject of the litigation arises under federal or state law. Federal Rule of Evidence 501 provides, in relevant part:

> Except as otherwise required by [federal law] . . . the privilege of a witness, person, government, State or political subdivision thereof shall be governed by the principles of the common law as they may be interpreted by the courts of the United States in the light of reason and experience. However, in civil actions and proceedings with respect to an element of a claim or defense as to which State law supplies the rule of decision, the privilege of a witness, person, government, State or political subdivision thereof shall be determined in accordance with State law.

In adopting the Federal Rules of Evidence, Congress deleted proposed rule 503, which would have provided a uniform federal definition of the attorney-client privilege. Although the proposed rule was rejected by Congress, some federal courts have relied on the formulation of the proposed rule to define the federal common-law privilege to be applied under rule 501.[9]

Many states have statutes governing the privilege. For example, a New York statute provides, in relevant part:

> Unless the client waives the privilege, a lawyer or his employee, or any person who obtains without the knowledge of the client evidence of a confidential communication made between the

---

8. United States v. Rogers, 751 F.2d 1074, 1077 (9th Cir. 1985); *In re* Grand Jury Proceedings (John Doe), 575 F. Supp. 197, 204 (N.D. Ohio 1983), *aff'd*, 754 F.2d 154 (6th Cir. 1985). The confidentiality of clients' communications with counsel is also mandated by the professional codes governing the practice of law. *See* ABA MODEL RULES OF PROF'L CONDUCT R. 1.6; ABA MODEL CODE OF PROF'L RESPONSIBILITY DR 4-101.

9. *See, e.g., In re* Feldberg, 862 F.2d 622, 626 (7th Cir. 1988); Diversified Indus. Inc. v. Meredith, 572 F.2d 596, 605 n.1, 610 (8th Cir. 1973) (en banc); United States v. McPartin, 595 F.2d 1321, 1336-37 (7th Cir.), *cert. denied*, 444 U.S. 833 (1979).

attorney or his employee and the client in the course of professional employment, shall not disclose, or be allowed to disclose such communication, nor shall the client be compelled to disclose such communication, in any action, disciplinary trial or hearing, or administrative action, proceeding or hearing conducted by or on behalf of any state, municipal or local government agency or by the legislature or any committee or body thereof. . . . [10]

In developing a federal common law of privilege, courts may seek guidance from state law.[11] One court has articulated four factors that should be weighed in determining whether to apply a state privilege to a federal claim:

[F]irst, the federal government's need for the information being sought in enforcing its substantive and procedural policies; second, the importance of the relationship or policy sought to be furthered by the state rule of privilege and the probability that the privilege will advance that relationship or policy; third, in the particular case, the special need for the information sought to be protected; and fourth, in the particular case, the adverse impact on the local policy that would result from non-recognition of the privilege.[12]

Where the claim is based on state law, the privilege is a "substantive" matter to be governed by state law.[13]

B. *Elements of Attorney-Client Privilege*

Simply stated, the elements of attorney-client privilege are: (1) a

---

10. N.Y.C.P.L.R. 4503(a) (McKinney Supp. 1997). *See also* CAL. EVID. CODE 950-62; D.I. Chadbourne, Inc. v. Superior Ct., 60 Cal. 2d 723, 36 Cal. Rptr. 723 (1964) (setting forth criteria for applicability of the privilege in the corporate context).

11. *See, e.g.*, Los Angeles Memorial Coliseum Comm'n v. National Football League, 89 F.R.D. 489, 492 (C.D. Cal. 1981).

12. United States v. King, 73 F.R.D. 103, 105 (E.D.N.Y. 1976).

13. Republic Gear Co. v. Borg-Warner Corp., 381 F.2d 551, 556 n.2 (2d Cir. 1967). *See* FED. R. EVID. 501.

client, (2) a lawyer, (3) a retainer for the purpose of rendering legal advice, (4) a communication between them, and (5) an intent that the communication be confidential.

1. The Client

A client may be an individual or a corporation,[14] and a corporate client may include subsidiaries and affiliates.[15] A lawyer representing a corporation represents the *corporate entity*, not its shareholders, officers, or directors.[16]

It has been long established that a corporate client, like an individual client, may assert the attorney-client privilege.[17] However, since a corporate client can act only through its human constituents, a lawyer communicating with a corporate client must be mindful of which corporate agents sufficiently personify the corporation so their communications with counsel will be privileged.

Prior to the Supreme Court's 1981 decision in *Upjohn Co. v. United States*,[18] the United States Courts of Appeals had split on the appropriate test for determining which employee communications were protected. The Third and Sixth Circuits embraced the so-called "control group" test, which would protect only the communications of senior management; the Seventh and Eighth Circuits adopted a broader test, the so-called "subject matter" test, which would encompass certain communications of lower-level employees.

The control group test, as enunciated in *City of Philadelphia v.*

---

14. Commodity Futures Trading Comm'n v. Weintraub, 471 U.S. 343, 348 (1985) ("It is by now well established . . . that the attorney-client privilege attaches to corporations"); Bell v. Maryland, 378 U.S. 226, 263 (1964) ("A corporation, like any other 'client,' is entitled to the attorney-client privilege"); Radiant Burners, Inc. v. American Gas Ass'n, 320 F.2d 314, 322-23 (7th Cir.), *cert. denied*, 375 U.S. 929 (1963).

15. *See, e.g.*, United States v. United Shoe Mach. Corp., 89 F. Supp. 357, 359 (D. Mass., 1950); Duplan Corp. v. Deering Milliken, Inc., 397 F. Supp. 1146, 1184-85 (D.S.C. 1975).

16. *Diversified Indus.*, 572 F.2d at 611 n.5; *see also* ABA MODEL RULES OF PROF'L CONDUCT R. 1.13; ABA MODEL CODE OF PROF'L RESPONSIBILITY EC 5-18.

17. *Weintraub*, 471 U.S. at 348; Radiant Burners, Inc. v. American Gas Ass'n, 320 F.2d 314, 322-23 (7th Cir. 1963).

18. 449 U.S. 383 (1981) (discussed *infra*).

Westinghouse Electric Corp.,[19] requires that the person making the communication be "in a position to control or even to take a substantial part in a decision about any action which the corporation may take upon the advice of the attorney," or be "an authorized member of a body or group which has that authority."[20] This control group test has been widely criticized by commentators as being too restrictive, particularly when the advice is complex, because the lower-level employees most likely to have detailed factual knowledge are also least likely to be in a control position.[21] As one commentator pointed out, counsel is faced with a difficult choice—required to proceed without benefit of the privilege if full factual development is to be accomplished, or to proceed without necessary factual background if the privilege is to be maintained.[22]

In recognition of the deficiencies of the control group test, a number of courts developed tests that account more realistically for the practicalities of corporate existence. The first attempt was made in *Harper & Row Publishers, Inc. v. Decker*,[23] where the Seventh Circuit concluded that communications with counsel by noncontrolling employees are privileged when "the employee makes the communications at the direction of his superiors in the corporation and where the subject matter upon which the attorney's advice is sought by the cor-

---

19. 210 F. Supp. 483 (E.D. Pa. 1962), *mandamus and prohibition denied sub nom.*, General Elec. Co. v. Kirkpatrick, 312 F.2d 742 (3d Cir.), *cert. denied*, 372 U.S. 943 (1963).

20. 210 F. Supp. at 485.

21. *E.g.*, Block & Barton, *Internal Corporate Investigations: Maintaining the Confidentiality of a Corporate Client's Communications with Investigative Counsel*, 35 Bus. Law 5, 13-17 (1979); Kobak, *The Uneven Application of the Attorney-Client Privilege to Corporations in the Federal Courts*, 6 Ga. L. Rev. 339, 362-71 (1972); Note, *Privileged Communications—Inroads on the "Control Group" Test in the Corporate Area*, 22 Syr. L. Rev. 759 (1971); Comment, *The Application in the Federal Courts of the Attorney-Client Privilege to the Corporation*, 39 Fordham L. Rev. 281, 290-93 (1970); Weinschel, *Corporate Employee Interviews and the Attorney-Client Privilege*, 12 B.C. Ind. & Comm. L. Rev. 873 (1970). *But see* Note, *Attorney-Client Privilege for Corporate Clients: The Control Group Test*, 84 Harv. L. Rev. 424 (1970).

22. Weinschel, *supra* note 21, at 876.

23. 423 F.2d 487 (7th Cir. 1970), *aff'd* by an equally divided Court, 400 U.S. 348 (1971).

poration and dealt with in the communication is the performance by the employee of the duties of his employment."[24]

Subsequent decisions approved in concept the greater flexibility afforded by the *Harper & Row* test, but suggested additional criteria designed to curb its potential abuse, which might occur if employee communications were routinely funneled through counsel. Thus, in *Diversified Industries, Inc. v. Meredith*,[25] the court made explicit a requirement (undoubtedly implicit in *Harper & Row*) that the communications directed by corporate superiors and made by the lower-level employee be for the corporation to secure legal advice.[26]

Notwithstanding the criticisms of the control group test, the Third Circuit in *In re Grand Jury Investigation*[27] and the Sixth Circuit in *United States v. Upjohn Co.*[28] adopted the control group test, explicitly rejecting the subject matter test formulated by the Seventh and Eighth Circuits.[29]

In *Upjohn Co. v. United States*,[30] the Supreme Court rejected the strict control group test, but declined to establish a bright-line test of its own. Instead, the Court held that the privilege should be determined on a case-by-case basis.[31] On the facts of *Upjohn*, the Court held the following factors to be persuasive in establishing the validity of the privilege:

- The communications were made by employees to corporate counsel in order for the corporation to secure legal advice.
- The employees were cooperating with corporate counsel at the direction of corporate superiors.
- The communications concerned matters within the employees' scope of employment.
- The information was not available from upper-echelon management.[32]

---

24. *Id.* at 491-92.
25. 572 F.2d 596 (8th Cir. 1978) (en banc).
26. *Id.* at 605.
27. 599 F.2d 1224 (3d Cir. 1979).
28. 600 F.2d 1223 (6th Cir. 1979), *rev'd,* 449 U.S. 383 (1981).
29. 599 F.2d at 1237; 600 F.2d at 1225.
30. 449 U.S. 383 (1981).
31. *Id.* at 396.
32. 449 U.S. at 394.

This formulation is remarkably similar to the subject-matter test the Court declined to adopt.[33] In light of *Upjohn*, corporate counsel undertaking an internal investigation should document the fact that the corporation is seeking legal advice from its counsel and that the cooperation of corporate employees is expressly requested regarding matters within their scope of employment.

2. The Attorney

Investigative counsel also should ensure that legal services are rendered only by qualified personnel. When the attorney is admitted to practice in a state or nation, membership in the bar where the services are performed "is not a *sine qua non*."[34] The prevailing view is that membership in the bar where the services are performed is "merely one factor to be considered in determining whether counsel was acting in a legal capacity."[35]

The involvement of the corporation's inside counsel in an internal investigation does not vitiate privilege, since the attorney-client privilege also applies to a corporation's house counsel:

> [T]he apparent factual differences between these house counsel and outside counsel are that the former are paid annual salaries, occupy offices in the corporation's buildings, and are employees rather than independent contractors. These are not sufficient differences to distinguish the two types of counsel for purposes of the attorney-client privilege. And this is appar-

---

33. *See id.* at 391-92.

34. Zenith Radio Corp. v. Radio Corp. of Am., 121 F. Supp. 792, 794 (D. Del. 1954) (Bar membership should properly be of the court for the area wherein the services are rendered, but this is not a sine qua non, e.g., visiting counsel, long-distance services by correspondence, pro hac vice services, "house counsel" who practice law only for the corporate client and its affiliates and not for the public generally, for which local authorities do not insist on admission to the local bar). *But see* United States v. United Shoe Mach. Corp., 89 F. Supp. 357, 360 (D. Mass. 1950) ("The fact that [house patent counsel], though resident of Massachusetts and regularly working here, have never received a license to practice law here shows that these regular employees are not acting as attorneys for United.").

35. Paper Converting Mach. Co. v. FMC Corp., 215 F. Supp. 249, 251 (E.D. Wis. 1963); *see also* Georgia-Pacific Plywood Co. v. United States Plywood Corp., 18 F.R.D. 463, 466 (S.D.N.Y. 1956).

ent when attention is paid to the realities of modern corporate law practice. The type of service performed by house counsel is substantially like that performed by many members of the large urban law firms. The distinction is chiefly that the house counsel gives advice to one regular client, the outside counsel to several regular clients.[36]

In addition, agents and subordinates working under the direct supervision and control of the lawyer are included within the scope of the attorney-client privilege.[37] Courts have recognized that a lawyer's effectiveness depends on the ability to rely on the assistance of various aides, including "secretaries, file clerks, telephone operators, messengers, clerks not yet admitted to the bar, and aides of other sorts."[38] However, merely denominating persons as "agents" will not necessarily make them so for purposes of preserving the privilege.[39]

The attorney-client privilege has also been found to protect communications to and from outside experts retained to assist the lawyer, such as accountants or private investigators.[40] Statements made to and

---

36. United Shoe Mach. Corp., 89 F. Supp. at 360; O'Brien v. Board of Educ., 86 F.R.D. 548, 549 (S.D.N.Y. 1980) (fact that document was authored by in-house counsel rather than by independent counsel was "of no significance"); *see also* Shelton v. American Motors Corp., 805 F.2d 1323, 1326 n.3 (8th Cir. 1986); Valente v. PepsiCo. Inc., 68 F.R.D. 361, 367 (D. Del. 1975); *but see* United States v. Ackert, 169 F.3d 136, 139 (2d Cir. 1999) (communications between in-house tax counsel and an investment banker regarding an investment proposal for the corporation not privileged).

37. Zenith Radio Corp., 121 F. Supp. at 794; FTC v. TRW, Inc., 749 F. Supp. 160, 163 n.7 (D.D.C. 1979) (citing 8 WIGMORE, EVIDENCE § 2301, at 583; § 2317, at 618), *aff'd*, 628 F.2d 207 (D.C. Cir. 1980); Caremark, Inc. v. Affiliated Computer Serv., Inc., 192 F.R.D. 263 (N.D. Ill. 2000) (attorney-client privilege applies to communications between attorney and his agent who has "express authority to coordinate legal review of contracts and service relationships for the purpose of renegotiating its terms").

38. *See, e.g.*, United States v. Korvel, 296 F.2d 918, 921 (2d Cir. 1961). At least one court has held that communications between a lawyer and the agent are privileged only to the extent that disclosure would reveal a confidence of the client. United States v. Covington & Burling, 430 F. Supp. 1117, 1120-21 (D.D.C. 1977).

39. *See* Burlington Indus. v. Exxon Corp., 65 F.R.D. 26, 40 (D. Md. 1974).

40. Materials prepared by "Investigators or other agents [of the attorney] in the compilation of material in preparation for trial" are also protected from discovery

from these assistants are generally considered to be privileged if the communication is made in confidence for the purpose of obtaining legal advice from a lawyer.[41] Thus, "information provided to [an] accountant by the client at the behest of his lawyer for the purposes of the interpretation and analysis" would be protected by the attorney-client privilege "to the extent that it is imparted in connection with the legal representation."[42] Similarly, statements made by a client to a detective hired by a lawyer are protected by the attorney-client privilege.[43]

It should make no difference whether the accountant was hired by the lawyer or the client, as long as the accountant's role is to assist the lawyer in rendering legal advice; however, it may be more difficult as a practical matter to establish the requisites for invocation of the privilege when the accountant is retained by the client independent of a request by the lawyer.[44]

---

by the work-product doctrine. United States v. Nobles, 422 U.S. 225, 238-39 (1975); *see also In re* Grand Jury Subpoena, 599 F.2d 504, 513 (2d Cir. 1979). *See* Part III, *infra*.

41. *See* United States v. Cote, 456 F.2d 142, 144-45 (8th Cir. 1972) (the test is "whether the accountant's services are a necessary aid to the rendering of effective legal services to the client"); *see also* United States v. Randall, 194 F.R.D. 369, 372 (D. Mass. 1999) (attorney-client privilege "extends to communications made by the client to certain agents of the attorney, including an accountant, hired to assist the attorney in providing legal advice").

42. United States v. Schwimmer, 392 F.2d 237, 243 (2d Cir. 1989), *quoting* United States v. Kovel, 296 F.2d at 922; *see also* Summit v. Levy, 111 F.R.D. 40, 41 (S.D.N.Y. 1986); *see also In re* Grand Jury Proceedings, 220 F.3d 568, 571 (7th Cir. 2000) ("material transmitted to accountants may fall under the attorney-client privilege if the accountant is acting as an agent of an attorney for the purpose of assisting with the provision of legal advice"); United States v. Ackert, 169 F.3d 136 (2d Cir. 1999) (noting that "Kovel [*supra*,] recognized that an accountant can play a role analogous to an interpreter in helping the attorney understand financial information passed to the attorney by the client"); Ampa, Ltd. v. Kentfield Capital LLC, 2000 WL 1156860, *1 (S.D.N.Y. Aug. 16, 2000) (presence of outside accountant, uninvolved in the legal issue discussed, waives privilege).

43. Clark v. City of Munster, 115 F.R.D. 609, 615 (N.D. Ind. 1987); *cf.* Duplan Corp., 397 at 1163.

44. *Compare* United States v. Judson, 322 F.2d 460, 465-66 (9th Cir. 1963) (privilege applied to net worth statement prepared for IRS investigation by accountant hired by client at the request of the lawyer) *with* United States v. Adlman,

Investigative counsel and their clients who retain such outside experts should take appropriate steps to document the fact that the expert is being retained to assist in the rendition of legal advice.

3. Legal Advice

A central issue for counsel in connection with an internal investigation is whether counsel has been employed to perform legal services. The question of what functions are included under the rubric of "legal advice" is governed by some general rules that do not translate readily into principles for the conduct of an internal investigation. In general, for the privilege to apply, the lawyer must have been consulted in a professional legal capacity.[45] Where counsel's activities are

---

68 F.3d 1495, 1500 n.1 (2d Cir. 1995) (attorney-client privilege was inapplicable to written analysis of tax consequences of a proposed corporate reorganization where the analyses were prepared by the company's regular outside accountants, and there was no evidence that the accountants were hired to render legal advice or to assist in-house counsel in rendering legal advice); United States v. Adlman, No. 96-6095, 1998 WL 74092, at *10 (2d Cir. Feb. 13, 1998) (remanding to the district court for a determination as to whether the work product privilege protected the accountant's analysis of the litigation risks of the proposed corporate reorganization; if the district court finds that the analysis "would not have been prepared but for [the company's] anticipation of litigation," it is protected); United States v. Brown, 478 F.2d 1038, 1040 (7th Cir. 1973) (privilege inapplicable to accountant's notes of meeting between client and lawyer where the accountant's presence was requested by the client and not the lawyer). *See also* United States v. Covington & Burling, 430 F. Supp. 1117, 1121 (D.D.C. 1977) (communications between the lawyer and an accounting firm used as a consultant in preparing a negotiating position for the client were deemed privileged only to the extent that they revealed client confidences). *See also* discussion of Adlman *infra*, Point IV, A.1.b.

45. *See, e.g.*, United States v. Dakota, 197 F.3d 821, 825 (6th Cir. 1999) (because client contacted tribal attorney for individual legal advice not relating to corporate matters, no attorney-client privilege existed); United States v. Randall, 194 F.R.D. 369, 372 (D. Mass. 1999) (communications with an accountant referred by an attorney retained as a tax preparer, not for legal advice, did not trigger attorney-client privilege); *In re* Kinoy, 326 F. Supp. 400, 403-05 (S.D.N.Y. 1970) (communication to attorney-parent not privileged where court concluded communication would have been made even if parent were not a lawyer); Modern Woodmen of Am. v. Watkins, 132 F.2d 352, 354 (5th Cir. 1942) (communication to a lawyer as a personal friend not privileged); United States v. Fisher, 692 F. Supp. 488, 492 (E.D. Pa. 1988) (mere eligibility for prepaid legal services by virtue of union membership is insufficient to establish the attorney-client relationship; the

"business rather than legal in nature," the resulting communications are not privileged.[46] Where legal and business advice is mixed, the communication is not privileged unless "the communication is designed to meet problems which can fairly be characterized as predominantly legal."[47] Conversely, business advice will not be protected simply because legal considerations are also involved.[48]

---

relationship will only arise when legal advice is actually sought); *see also* United States v. Tedder, 801 F.2d 1437, 1442 (4th Cir. 1986) (admissions of perjury made by a lawyer to a colleague who had no professional involvement in the case were not privileged), *cert. denied*, 480 U.S. 938 (1987); *but see* Montgomery County v. Microvote Corp., 175 F.3d 296, 303 (3d Cir. 1999) (client's mere reference to its attorney as a "consultant" does not render the communications unprivileged).

46. E.I. du Pont de Nemours & Co. v. Forma-Pack, Inc., 351 Md. 422, 718 A.2d 1129, 1141-42 (Md. 1998) (communications between corporation and debt collection agency hired by the corporation's legal department are not privileged because agency was hired for the business of debt collection, not for the purposes of litigation); F.H. Krear & Co. v. 19 Named Trustees, 90 F.R.D. 102, 103 (S.D.N.Y. 1981) (lawyer's contacts were business, not legal, communications and thus not privileged); *In re* Grand Jury Subpoena Duces Tecum Dated Sept. 15, 1983, 731 F.2d 1032, 1037 (2d Cir. 1984) ("the privilege is triggered only by a client's request for legal, as contrasted with business, advice"); United States v. International Business Machines Corp., 66 F.R.D. 206, 210 (S.D.N.Y. 1974).

47. *See, e.g.*, Neuder v. Battelle Pac. N.W. Nat'l Lab., 194 F.R.D. 289, 292 (D.D.C. 2000) ("[w]here business and legal advice are intertwined, the legal advice must predominate for the communication to be protected"); Lloyds v. Fidelity & Cas. Co. of N.Y., No. 89 Civ. 0876, 1997 WL 769467 at *2 (N.D. Ill. Dec. 9, 1997) (conducting a document-by-document review of whether legal advice was "the predominant element in the communication"); *see also* 3 J. WEINSTEIN & M. BERGER, WEINSTEIN'S EVIDENCE 503, 13(3)(c) at 503-38, *quoted in* Cuno, Inc. v. Pall Corp., 121 F.R.D. 198, 204 (E.D.N.Y. 1988). *See, e.g.*, Spectrum Sys. Int'l Corp. v. Chemical Bank (must be "primarily or predominantly of a legal character"), *rev'g* 157 A.D. 2d 444, 558 N.Y.S. 2d 486 (1st Dep't 1990) ("primarily if not solely" standard); United Shoe Mach. Corp., 89 F. Supp. at 359 ("the privilege of nondisclosure is not lost merely because relevant nonlegal considerations are expressly stated in a communication which also includes legal advice").

48. *See, e.g.*, Neuder, 194 F.R.D. at 292 (quoting Great Plains Mutual Ins. Co., Inc. v. Mutual Reins. Bureau, 150 F.R.D. 193, 197 (D. Kan. 1993) and stating that where the giving of legal advice is incidental to the giving of business advice, the privilege is not triggered); Georgia-Pacific Corp. v. GAF Roofing Mfg. Corp., 1996 WL 29392, at *4 (S.D.N.Y. Jan. 25, 1996) (attorney negotiating portion of acquisition agreement was not "exercising a lawyer's traditional function"); United States v. Loften, 518 F. Supp. 839, 846 (S.D.N.Y. 1981) (even if "little bits of legal advice were ... buried within discussions of primarily business matters" in reports, those communications

Matters that can be handled by laymen as easily as lawyers may not be privileged.[49] Similarly, a lawyer's ministerial or clerical duties may not be privileged.[50] However, when the professional training of a lawyer is necessary, the fact that some tasks might be characterized as nonlegal is not dispositive.[51]

The leading authority on the existence of legal advice in the context of internal investigations is *Diversified Industries, Inc. v. Meredith*,[52] in which the Eighth Circuit (en banc) held that this element was present when counsel had been retained in connection with the investigation of a possible "slush fund" used to bribe purchasing agents. Although the majority suggested initially that the retention of "a professional legal adviser" resulted in a prima facie assumption that the purpose

---

would not qualify as privileged), *aff'd*, 819 F.2d 1130 (2d Cir. 1987); Federal Sav. & Loan Ins. Corp. v. Fielding, 343 F. Supp. 537, 546 (D. Nev. 1972) ("When the attorney and the client get in bed together as business partners, their relationship is a business relationship, not a professional one, and their confidences are business confidences unprotected by a professional privilege"); Hardy v. New York News, Inc., 114 F.R.D. 633, 643-44 (S.D.N.Y. 1987) (discussing SCM Corp. v. Xerox Corp., 70 F.R.D. 508, 517 (D. Conn.), *appeal dismissed*, 534 F.2d 1031 (2d Cir. 1976)).

49. *See, e.g.*, Marsh v. Safir, 2000 WL 460580, at *12 (S.D.N.Y. Apr. 20, 2000) ("[a]n attorney's performance of a function that is normally performed by a non-attorney is not covered by the attorney-client privilege"); SEC v. Gulf & Western Indus., 518 F. Supp. 675, 683 (D.D.C. 1981) (lawyer was merely acting as scribe); Bird v. Penn Cent. Co., 61 F.R.D. 43, 46 n.3 (E.D. Pa. 1973) (lawyer acted as a "lay claims investigator"); Merrin Jewelry Co. v. St. Paul Fire & Marine Ins. Co., 49 F.R.D. 54, 57 (S.D.N.Y. 1970) (same); Georgia-Pacific Plywood Co. v. United States Plywood Corp., 18 F.R.D. 463, 464 (S.D.N.Y. 1956), *quoted in* Underwater Storage, Inc. v. U.S. Rubber Co., 314 F. Supp. 546, 548 (D.D.C. 1970).

50. *See, e.g.*, Puerto Rico v. S.S. Zoe Colocotroni, 61 F.R.D. 653, 660 (D.P.R. 1974); Duplan Corp., 397 F. Supp. at 1168 (lawyer served merely as "conduit" for transmission of patent applications); *see also In re* Grand Jury Testimony of Attorney X, 621 F. Supp. 590, 592 (E.D.N.Y. 1985); United States v. Wilson, 798 F.2d 509, 513 (1st Cir. 1986); United States v. Palmer, 536 F.2d 1278, 1281 (9th Cir. 1976) (attorney acted as "transfer shipping agent"); Covington & Burling, 430 F. Supp. at 1121-22 (lawyer assisted in nonlegal aspects of contract negotiations); Underwater Storage, Inc. v. U.S. Rubber Co., 314 F. Supp. 546, 549 (D.D.C. 1970) (determining patentability, drafting patent specifications, and preparing and processing applications did not constitute legal advice).

51. *See* Diversified Indus., 572 F.2d at 610.

52. *Id.*

for the retention was securing legal advice,[53] the remainder of the opinion focused more specifically upon elements that would justify this conclusion. The court described the authorization given to counsel as including the conduct of an investigation, the retention of accounting assistance, and the conduct of interviews of employees with knowledge of the facts. These steps were designed specifically to enable counsel "to analyze the accounting data, to evaluate and draw conclusions as to the propriety of past actions and to make recommendations for possible future courses of action."[54] Thus, counsel was utilizing "the training, skills, and background necessary to make the independent analysis and recommendations that the Board felt essential to the future welfare of the corporation," which could not be provided by accountants or lay investigators.[55]

One dissenting judge parted company with his colleagues on this point, on the basis of his belief that counsel had been retained "to make a factual investigation and business recommendations,"[56] which could just as well have been performed by lay investigators or accountants. In so concluding, the dissenting judge relied in part upon the minutes of the board meeting at which the retention of counsel was authorized as indicating the purpose of the retention was investigative, not legal.[57] He also pointed out that counsel's report of the investigation consisted principally of a description of the investigation and its factual findings, with recommendations that could have been made by lay investigators, accountants, bankers "or, for that matter, by any person possessing ordinary common sense and business prudence."[58]

The Supreme Court's decision in *Upjohn Co. v. United States*,[59] which involved a fact pattern similar to *Diversified Industries*, accepted without much discussion the premise that the corporation had retained counsel "in order to secure legal advice."[60] The concurring opinion was more explicit in defining the legal functions that must underlie the assertion of privilege:

---

53. *Id.*
54. *Id.*
55. Diversified Indus., 572 F.2d at 610.
56. *Id.* at 614.
57. *Id.* at 614-15.
58. *Id.*
59. 449 U.S. 383 (1981).
60. *Id.* at 394.

The attorney must be one authorized by the management to inquire into the subject and must be seeking information to assist counsel in performing any of the following functions: (a) evaluating whether the employee's conduct has bound or would bind the corporation; (b) assessing the legal consequences, if any, of that conduct; or (c) formulating appropriate legal responses to actions that have been or may be taken by others with regard to that conduct.[61]

The New York Court of Appeals has held the attorney-client privilege applicable to a lawyer-conducted internal investigation into allegations of fraud in the business relationship between certain employees of a bank and outside vendors. In *Spectrum Systems International Corp. v. Chemical Bank*,[62] the court reiterated its previous holding in *Rossi v. Blue Cross and Blue Shield*[63] that, in order for the privilege to apply, the communication from lawyer to client must be made "for the purpose of facilitating the rendition of legal advice or services in the course of a professional relationship." While acknowledging that certain functions of the retained lawyers were "investigative" in nature, the court nevertheless held "[t]hat nonprivileged information is included in an otherwise privileged lawyer's communication to its client—while influencing whether the document would be protected in whole or only in part—does not destroy the immunity." The court recognized that "[i]n transmitting legal advice and furnishing legal services it will often be necessary for a lawyer to refer to nonprivileged matter." The court held that "[t]he critical inquiry is whether, viewing the lawyer's communication in its full content and context, it was made in order to render legal advice or services to the client."

After reviewing the document in question and the undisputed facts in the record, the court found counsel's report offered "no recommendations for desirable future business procedures or corruption prevention measures, or employee discipline. . . . Rather, the narration relates and integrates the facts with the law firm's assessment of the client's legal position and evidences the lawyer's motivation to convey legal advice."

---

61. *Id.* at 403 (Burger, C.J., concurring).
62. 78 N.Y.2d 371, 581 N.E.2d 1055, 575 N.Y.S.2d 809 (1991).
63. 73 N.Y.2d 588, 540 N.E.2d 703, 542 N.Y.S.2d 508 (1989).

The *Spectrum* court further found that the fact that counsel's report may have been "inconclusive, looking toward future discussion" was "without significance," recognizing that "[l]egal advice often begins—and may end—with a preliminary evaluation and a range of options. More than that may not be possible upon an initial investigation." Likewise, the absence of legal research in the lawyer's communication was held "not determinative of privilege, as long as the communication reflects the attorney's professional skills and judgments." The Court of Appeals expressly recognized that "[l]egal advice may be grounded 'in experience as well as research.'"

Documentation of the purpose of the retention of investigative counsel should clearly reflect that the intended role is broader than simply ascertaining the relevant facts, since a court may later conclude that this was a layperson's function. Additional purposes commonly identified in the documentation surrounding internal corporate investigations include analyzing and advising with respect to the corporation's own potential liabilities; analyzing and advising with respect to the corporation's claims against third parties or, possibly, its own employees; preparing to defend the corporation in the virtually inevitable litigation likely to ensue from the underlying situation; and making recommendations to the corporation as to other kinds of future legal action, such as improved compliance programs.

4. Communication

The attorney-client privilege protects only the communication between the attorney and the client; it does not protect underlying facts from disclosure. As the Supreme Court stated in *Upjohn v. United States*:[64]

> [T]he protection of the privilege extends only to communications and not to facts. A fact is one thing and a communication concerning that fact is an entirely different thing. The client cannot be compelled to answer the question, "what did you say or write to the attorney?" but may not refuse to disclose any relevant fact within his knowledge merely because he in-

---

64. 449 U.S. 383 (1981).

corporated a statement of such fact into his communication to his attorney.[65]

The privilege plainly protects communications from the client to the lawyer, and should also protect communications from the lawyer to the client.[66] However, some courts have held that a lawyer's communications will not be privileged unless they are based on or relate to a client's confidences, or would reveal such confidences if disclosed.[67]

---

65. *Id.* at 395-96 (citations omitted). *See also* United States v. O'Malley, 786 F.2d 786, 794 (7th Cir. 1986). Thus, absent special circumstances, a client's identity, date of consultation, and fee information are not privileged. *See In re* Grand Jury Subpoena Served upon John Doe, Esq., 781 F.2d 238, 247 (2d Cir.) (en banc), *cert. denied*, 475 U.S. 1106 (1986); *In re* Grand Jury Subpoena (Shargel), 742 F.2d 61, 63 & n.3 (2d Cir. 1984). However, "[a] client's identity and the nature of that client's fee arrangements may be privileged where the person invoking the privilege can show that a strong probability exists that disclosure of such information would implicate that client in the very criminal activity for which legal advice was sought." United States v. Hodge & Zweig, 548 F.2d 1347, 1353 (9th Cir. 1977) (citing Baird v. Koerner, 279 F.2d 623, 630 (9th Cir. 1960)). Later Ninth Circuit cases have largely limited the *Baird v. Koerner* exception to its facts. *See, e.g., In re* Grand Jury Subpoenas (Hirsch), 803 F.2d 493, 497-98 (9th Cir. 1986), *modified* 817 F.2d 64 (9th Cir. 1987).

66. *See* Allen v. West Point-Pepperell Inc., 848 F. Supp. 423, 431 (S.D.N.Y. 1994) (barring defendants from "inquir[ing] as to the legal advice rendered" by attorney); Spectrum Sys., 78 N.Y.2d at 377 ("the privilege extends as well to communications from attorney to client") (applying New York law); Natta v. Hogan, 392 F.2d 686, 692-93 (10th Cir. 1968); Schwimmer v. United States, 232 F.2d 855, 863 (8th Cir.), *cert. denied*, 352 U.S. 833 (1956); 8 in 1 Pet Products, Inc. v. Swift & Co., 218 F. Supp. 253 (S.D.N.Y. 1963); American Optical Corp. v. Medtronic, Inc., 56 F.R.D. 426, 430 (D. Mass. 1972); *see also* Upjohn, 449 U.S. at 390 ("[t]he privilege exists to protect not only the giving of professional advice to those who can act on it but also the giving of information to the lawyer to enable him to give sound and informed advice.").

67. *See, e.g.*, Rehling v. City of Chicago, 207 F.3d 1009, 1019 (7th Cir. 2000) ("statements made by the lawyer to the client will be protected in circumstances where those communications rest on confidential information obtained from the client [citation omitted] or where those communications would reveal the substance of a confidential communication by the client [citation omitted]"); *see also* United States v. Motorola, Inc., 1999 WL 552553, at *2 (D.D.C. 1999) (stating that communications from attorney to client are privileged to the extent that they reveal client confidences); American Standard Inc. v. Pfizer Inc., 828 F.2d 734, 745 (Fed. Cir. 1987); Brinton v. Department of State, 636 F.2d 600, 603 (D.C. Cir. 1980), *cert. denied*, 452 U.S. 905 (1981); Mead Data Cent. Inc. v. United States, 566 F.2d

This approach has been criticized,[68] and recent cases hold that counsel's advice is privileged, whether or not the advice would tend to disclose a confidence of the client.[69]

Counsel in jurisdictions that do not clearly protect the lawyer's communications to the client should take special care to ensure the confidentiality of their advice, particularly in written materials, by making explicit (rather that implicit) the interrelationship between the client's confidences and the lawyer's advice.

Another issue faced by investigative counsel is that documents that do not themselves represent confidential communications to a lawyer do not become privileged merely by transmitting them to a lawyer.[70] Thus, the underlying corporate documents examined by coun-

---

242, 254 (D.C. Cir. 1977); United States v. International Business Machines Corp., 66 F.R.D. 206, 212 (S.D.N.Y. 1974); Burlington Indus., 65 F.R.D. at 37; *Bird*, 61 F.R.D. at 46; *see also* United States v. Under Seal, 748 F.2d 871, 874 (4th Cir. 1984), *vacated as moot*, 757 F.2d 600 (4th Cir. 1985).

68. *See In re* LTV Sec. Litig., 89 F.R.D. 595, 601-03 (N.D. Tex. 1981).

69. *See, e.g.*, Spectrum Sys., 78 N.Y.2d at 378 (rejecting the "cramped view" of the privilege espoused by cases such as Mead Data Central, 566 F.2d 242; United States v. Amerada Hess Corp., 619 F.2d 980, 986 (3d Cir. 1980); United States v. Ramirez, 608 F.2d 1261, 1268 n.12 (9th Cir. 1979); Mead Data, 566 F.2d at 254 n.25).

70. *See, e.g.*, American Med. Sys., Inc. v. National Union Fire Ins. Co. of Pittsburgh, Inc., 1999 WL 970341 (E.D. La. Oct. 22, 1999) ("[l]etters that merely transmit documents to or from an attorney, even at the attorney's request for purposes of rendering legal advice to a client, are neither privileged nor attorney work-product"); United States v. Frederick, 182 F.3d 496, 500 (7th Cir. 1999) (information of the type normally furnished to an accountant does not become privileged merely because an attorney is the tax preparer); United States v. Doe, 959 F.2d 1158, 1165 (2d Cir. 1992) (law firm in possession of client's telephone bills must produce them to the grand jury because "[d]ocuments created by and received from an unrelated third party and given by the client to his attorney in the course of seeking legal advice do not thereby become privileged"); Fisher v. United States, 425 U.S. 391, 403-04 (1976) ("preexisting documents which could have been obtained by court process from the client when he was in possession may also be obtained from the attorney by similar process following transfer by the client in order to obtain more informed legal advice"); SCM Corp., 70 F.R.D. at 523 ("[l]egal departments are not citadels in which public, business or technical information may be placed to defeat discovery and thereby ensure confidentiality"), *appeal dismissed and mandamus denied*, 534 F.2d 1031 (2d Cir. 1976); IT Corp. v. United Tel. Co., 60 F.R.D. 177, 185 (M.D. Fla. 1973); Air-Shield, Inc. v. Air Reduction Co., 46 F.R.D. 96, 97 (N.D. Ill. 1968).

sel are not themselves protected from discovery, although counsel's own assembly and organization of documents that counsel deemed relevant are probably protected by the work-product doctrine.[71]

In addition, the mere presence of a lawyer at corporate meetings, including meetings of the board of directors, will not render the meetings or the minutes privileged.[72] Communications made during corporate meetings will be considered privileged only where they relate to the request for or rendition of legal advice and are intended to be confidential and privileged.[73] Where the purpose of the meeting, attended only by parties within the attorney-client relationship, is to plan legal strategy, or where disclosure would reveal the contents of privileged communications, that portion of the meeting and minutes may be privileged.[74] Accordingly, the records of corporate meetings, particularly board minutes, should reflect plainly on their face that legal advice has been sought or rendered.

Finally, it is important for counsel to appreciate the fact that a lawyer's own files are not necessarily privileged. As the Supreme Court noted in *Hickman v. Taylor:*[75]

> Nor does [the attorney-client] privilege concern the memoranda, briefs, communications, and other writings prepared by counsel for his own use in prosecuting his client's case; and it is equally unrelated to writings which reflect a lawyer's mental impressions, conclusions, opinions, or legal theories.[76]

A lawyer's internal memorandum may not be a communication directed to anyone for purposes of legal advice, and it does not neces-

---

71. *See* Part III, *infra.*

72. *See, e.g.,* Neuder, 194 F.R.D. at 293 (attorney's attendance at committee meeting did not render documents produced during the meeting subject to the attorney-client privilege); United States v. Motorola, Inc., 1999 WL 552553, at *4 (D.D.C. 1999) (ordering production of minutes of meeting of board of directors despite an attorney's presence); Diversified Indus. v. Meredith, 572 F.2d 596, 611 (8th Cir. 1978) (en banc).

73. *E.g.,* International Tel. & Tel. Co. v. United Tel. Co., 60 F.R.D. 177, 185 (M.D. Fla. 1973).

74. *See, e.g.,* Diversified Indus., 572 F.2d at 611 (8th Cir. 1978) (en banc).

75. 329 U.S. 495 (1947).

76. *Id.* at 508 (dictum).

sarily reflect either a communication from a client or an intention to communicate confidentially with a client.[77] These documents may constitute work product;[78] however, the work-product doctrine may be overcome by an adversary's showing of substantial need and undue hardship,[79] and therefore it is prudent to ensure that the documents are privileged by expressly intertwining the client's communications with the lawyer's conclusions.

5. Confidentiality

Investigative counsel also should ensure that privileged material is treated with the appropriate degree of confidentiality. The privilege protects only those communications made in confidence, and any information a client gives to a lawyer is presumed to be confidential.[80] However, communications made in the presence of others are not deemed to be confidential if the third parties are not part of the attorney-client relationship.[81]

Communications meant to be transmitted to third parties do not ordinarily fall under the protection of the privilege.[82] There is a split of authority regarding whether information disclosed to a lawyer with

---

77. *See* Sneider v. Kimberly-Clark Corp., 91 F.R.D. 1, 6 (N.D. Ill. 1980). *See also* SCM Corp., 70 F.R.D. at 523 (lawyer's opinions and legal theories, even if never transmitted to client, may be privileged if they reveal confidences from the client), *appeal dismissed and mandamus denied*, 534 F.2d 1031 (2d Cir. 1976); Cedrone v. Unity Sav. Ass'n, 103 F.R.D. 423, 429 (E.D. Pa. 1984) (any oral or written communication between lawyers concerning the representation of a client is protected by the attorney-client privilege as long as it utilizes client confidences).

78. *See* Part III, *infra.*

79. *See* Part III.D, *infra.*

80. Analytica, Inc. v. NPD Research, Inc., 708 F.2d 1263, 1267 (7th Cir. 1983).

81. *See, e.g.,* Johnson v. United States, 542 F.2d 941, 942 (5th Cir. 1976), *cert. denied*, 430 U.S. 934 (1977); Ampa, Ltd. v. Kentfield Capital LLC, 2000 WL 1156860, at *1 (S.D.N.Y. Aug. 16, 2000) (privilege waived with respect to minutes of board meeting at which an accountant, unrelated to the legal issue discussed, was present).

82. Lorenz v. Valley Forge Ins. Co., 815 F.2d 1095, 1098 (7th Cir. 1987); United States v. Aronson, 781 F.2d 1580, 1581 (11th Cir. 1986); Radio Corp. of Am. v. Rauland Corp., 18 F.R.D. 440, 443 (N.D. Ill. 1955); Rediker v. Warfield, 11 F.R.D. 125, 128 (S.D.N.Y. 1951) (no privilege exists if the communication is made "with the understanding that it is to be imparted to a third party").

the intention that the lawyer draft a document to be released to third parties is protected by the attorney-client privilege.[83] However, most courts hold that the mere intent to disclose the substance of communications between a lawyer and a client does not vitiate the privilege; rather, actual disclosure is required to breach the confidentiality.[84] Thus, investigative counsel should exercise caution in the preparation and preservation of drafts of documents such as press releases, SEC filings, and similar papers.

C. *Practical Problems of Employee Interviews*

As difficult as the application of the attorney-client privilege already is in the context of internal corporate investigations, a further layer of complexity is added by the process of conducting employee interviews.

1. Potential Conflicts of Interest Warnings to Employees

A lawyer representing a corporation represents the corporate entity, not its employees.[85] In conducting an internal corporate investigation, counsel runs the risk that corporate personnel may mistakenly believe corporate counsel represents the employees individually, in addition to the corporation. If this occurs, counsel may face the possibility of disqualification in a later litigation against an employee.

---

83. Schenet v. Anderson, 678 F. Supp. 1280, 1282 (E.D. Mich. 1988) (discussing the various views).

84. *In re* Grand Jury Subpoena Duces Tecum Dated Sept. 15, 1983, 731 F.2d 1032, 1037 (2d Cir. 1984) ("although some of the documents appear to be drafts of communications the final version of which might eventually be sent to other persons, and as distributed would not be privileged, we see no basis in the record for inferring that [appellant] did not intend that the drafts . . . be confidential. . . we see no indication that a waiver has yet occurred"); *see also* United States v. Schlegel, 313 F. Supp. 177, 179 (D. Neb. 1970) (the client intends only as much information to be conveyed to third parties as is actually conveyed; all other information remains privileged). *But see In re* Grand Jury Proceedings (John Doe), 727 F.2d 1352, 1356 (4th Cir. 1984) (statements made by a client to an attorney with the intention that they be communicated to a third party are not privileged even if the intended publication does not occur).

85. ABA Model Rules of Prof'l Conduct R. 1.13; ABA Model Code of Prof'l Responsibility EC 5-18.

One former federal judge dubbed the introductory advice to corporate employees as "Adnarim" warnings ("Miranda" spelled backward), and set them forth, in stark terms, as follows:

> I am not your lawyer, I represent the corporation. It is the corporation's interests I have been retained to serve. You are entitled to have your own lawyer. If you cannot afford a lawyer, the corporation may, or may not, pay his fee. You may wish to consult with him before you confer with me. Among other things, you may wish to claim the privilege against self-incrimination. You may wish not to talk to me at all.
>
> What you tell me, if it relates to the performance of your duties, and is confidential, will be privileged. The privilege, however, requires explanation. It is not your privilege to claim. It is the corporation's privilege. Thus, not only can I tell, I must tell, others in the corporation what you have told me, if it is necessary to enable me to provide the legal services to the corporation it has retained me to provide.
>
> Moreover, the corporation can waive its privilege and thus, the president, or I, or someone else, can disclose to the authorities what you tell me if the corporation decides to waive its privilege.
>
> Also, if I find wrongdoing, I am under certain obligations to report it to the Board of Directors and perhaps the stockholders.
>
> Finally, the fact that our conversation is privileged does not mean that what you did, or said, is protected from disclosure just because you tell me about it. You may be subpoenaed, for example, and required to tell what you did, or said or observed, even though you told me about it.
>
> Do you understand?[86]

While so dire a warning is likely to frighten an employee, and thus to be counterproductive, it is necessary that employees are provided enough information, in a clear enough manner, to understand that corporate investigative counsel does not represent the employee.

---

86. Remarks by Frederick B. Lacey, formerly a U.S. district judge for the District of New Jersey, reprinted with permission.

ABA Model Rule 1.13(d) provides some guidance on this issue, stating that "[i]n dealing with an organization's directors, officers [and] employees... a lawyer shall explain the identity of the client when it is apparent that the organization's interests are adverse to those of the [organization's] constituents with whom the lawyer is dealing." Further, the comment to this Model Rule suggests that

> care must be taken to assure that the individual understands that, when there is such adversity of interest, the lawyer for the organization cannot provide legal representation for that constituent individual, and that discussions between the lawyer for the organization and the individual may not be privileged. Whether such a warning should be given may turn on the facts of each case.

Apart from professional considerations, the impetus to provide appropriate disclosure to employees may be found in a seminal decision, *E.F. Hutton & Co. v. Brown*,[87] in which corporate counsel was disqualified as a result of a corporate officer's lack of understanding of counsel's role. In *Brown*, counsel for Hutton conducted an internal investigation, which included interviewing various Hutton personnel regarding certain specified transactions. Shortly thereafter, Hutton's lawyer accompanied one of Hutton's officers to two hearings regarding those transactions. During both hearings, the employee informed the judge that he was represented by the counsel for the corporation, and counsel did not take any action to correct this mistake.[88]

In a subsequent litigation by Hutton against the officer arising out of the same transactions, Hutton's counsel was disqualified. The court rationalized that the corporate officer reasonably believed that both he and Hutton were jointly represented by Hutton's counsel. The court stated that a lawyer's appearance on behalf of a corporate employee individually at a judicial proceeding raises a presumption of individual representation, which the corporation did not overcome.[89] Consequently, because of the subsequent conflicting interests between the

---

87. 305 F. Supp. 371 (S.D. Tex. 1969).
88. *Id.* at 390-91.
89. *Id.* at 391.

employee and the corporation, the court required the lawyer to with-draw from the litigation.[90]

The court was careful to note that "not all corporate counsel ap-pearing with corporate officers who are called to testify will risk dis-qualification. Only those counsel who permit the officer to believe that they represent him individually will disable themselves from ap-pearing in subsequent litigation. And it is eminently proper to dis-qualify these, for they are persons who are in a position, and have the obligation to ensure that there is no misunderstanding by the officer."[91]

2. Counsel's Communications with Former Employees

It is not unusual for investigative counsel to need to interview former employees of the corporation. The opinion of the Court in *Upjohn* did not address the issue of whether the attorney-client privilege ex-tends to communications between counsel and former employees. How-ever, in the concurring opinion, Chief Justice Burger noted his approval of a rule that would treat communications between counsel and former employees as privileged in situations where "a former employee speaks at the direction of the management with a lawyer regarding conduct or proposed conduct within the scope of employment."[92]

The extension of the attorney-client privilege to include former employees serves to promote honest communication between the former employees and corporate counsel. Accordingly, most courts have adhered to the view that these communications are privileged.[93]

---

90. *Id.*

91. Brown, 305 F. Supp. at 398. Another case, *United States v. Keplinger*, 776 F.2d 678 (7th Cir. 1985), *cert. denied*, 476 U.S. 1183 (1986), followed the same type of analysis as *Brown*, but reached the opposite conclusion, holding that the individual corporate employees were not represented by the corporate counsel. The court based its conclusion on the fact that defendants did not seek individual legal advice, did not inquire regarding individual representation, and did not indicate their belief that such a relationship existed. Moreover, the mere fact that the corporation's lawyer accompanied one of the defendants to a meeting did not support a finding that the defendant had a reasonable basis for believing that he was being represented individually.

92. Upjohn Co. v. United States, 449 U.S. 399 (1981) (Burger, C.J., concur-ring).

93. *See In re* Coordinated Pretrial Proceedings in Petroleum Prod. Antitrust Litig., 658 F.2d 1355, 1361 n.7 (9th Cir. 1981) ("Former employees, as well as

3. Adversary's Communications with Current or Former Employees

Assuming that counsel's interview with a current or former employee was privileged at the time it was held, it is important to caution the employee not to discuss the interview with anyone else. The traditional waiver problems inherent in the employee's discussions with third parties[94] are exacerbated by the developing law in some jurisdictions that an adversary's counsel may interview current and former corporate employees without notifying the corporation's counsel.[95]

The ABA Code of Professional Responsibility provides that "[d]uring the course of his representation of a client a lawyer shall not . . . communicate or cause another to communicate on the subject of the representation with a party he knows to be represented by a lawyer in that matter unless he has the prior consent of the lawyer representing such other party or is authorized by law to do so."[96] The ABA Model Rules of Professional Conduct contain a similar provision.[97]

In the context of a corporate client, it may be difficult to determine which corporate employees are considered to be a party with

---

current employees, may possess the relevant information needed by corporate counsel to advise the client with respect to actual or potential difficulties"), *cert. denied*, 455 U.S. 990 (1982); Command Transp., Inc. v. Y.S. Line (USA) Corp., 116 F.R.D. 94, 97 (D. Mass. 1987) (where the court noted that "a formalistic distinction based solely on the timing of the interview cannot make a difference if the goals of the privilege outlined in *Upjohn* are to be achieved"). *See also* Admiral Ins. v. United States Dist. Ct. for Dist. of Ariz., 881 F.2d 1486, 1493 (9th Cir. 1989) (noting that communications between former employees and corporate counsel would be privileged if the employee possesses information critical to the representation of the corporation and the communications concern matters within the scope of employment); Connolly Data Sys. v. Victor Tech., Inc., 114 F.R.D. 89, 92 (S.D. Cal. 1987). *But see* Barrett Indus. Trucks, Inc. v. Old Republic Ins. Co., 129 F.R.D. 515, 517 (N.D. Ill. 1990) (where court refused to extend the attorney-client privilege to cover former employees).

94. *See* Part IV.A *infra*.

95. *See, e.g.*, Thorn v. Sunstrand Corp., No. 95 Civ. 50099, 1997 WL 627607, at *2-3 (N.D. Ill. Oct. 10, 1997) (plaintiff's counsel was permitted to interview a management employee of the corporate defendant who had retired subsequent to being deposed in the litigation and finding that the retiree's statements could no longer bind the company).

96. DR 7-104(A)(1).

97. Model Code of Prof'l Responsibility R. 4.2.

whom *ex parte* communication by opposing counsel is prohibited. Some courts have taken the view that the term "party" in litigation involving corporations includes only employees who have the legal authority to bind the corporation.[98] The New York Court of Appeals has added that the prohibition also includes "the corporate employees responsible for actually effectuating the advice of counsel in the matter."[99] Finally, the comments to the ABA Model Rules state that the prohibition against *ex parte* contact applies to employees with "managerial responsibility," those whose acts or omissions may be imputed to the corporation for purposes of criminal or civil liability, and those whose statements might constitute admissions of the corporation.[100]

A minority of courts has taken a different approach. For example, in *Mompoint v. Lotus Development Corp.*,[101] the court permitted the plaintiff's counsel to hold *ex parte* interviews with corporate employees in the context of a sexual harassment suit, but only after inquiry into whether the interview would deal with questions within the scope of the employee's employment, and therefore be likely to result in evidence admissible against the corporation. In addition, the court held that it was necessary to consider the need, according to the circumstances of each case, for the corporation to have its counsel present to ensure "effective representation" of the corporation.[102]

The Committee on Professional Ethics of the Association of the Bar of the City of New York reached an even broader conclusion, determining that the "corporation's right to effective representation can be guarded adequately only by viewing all present employees of a corporation as 'parties' for purposes of DR 7-104 where the proposed interview concerns matters within the scope of the employees' employment."[103] The Massachusetts Bar Association has also adopted this approach.[104]

---

98. *See* Wright v. Group Health Hosp., 691 P.2d 564, 569 (Wash. 1984); Niesig v. Team I, 76 N.Y.2d 363, 374, 559 N.Y.S.2d 493, 498, 558 N.E.2d 1030, 1035 (1990).

99. Niesig, 76 N.Y.2d at 374.

100. 858 F.2d 834 (2d Cir. 1988), *cert. denied*, 498 U.S. 871.

101. 110 F.R.D. 414 (D. Mass. 1986).

102. *Id.* at 418.

103. Opinion 80-46 of the Committee on Professional Ethics of the Association of the Bar of the City of New York.

104. Committee of Professional Ethics of the Massachusetts Bar Formal Opinion No. 82-7.

The authorities seem to be in agreement that the ethical rules do not restrain counsel from communication with former employees.[105] One court has noted, however, that former employees "are 'barred from discussing privileged information to which they are privy.'"[106]

The application of these ethical rules to federal prosecutors is unclear. In *United States v. Hammad*,[107] the Second Circuit ruled that DR 7-104(A)(1) was applicable to criminal prosecutions,[108] but left open the possibility that certain investigative techniques, particularly those involving informants, may be permissible, even though these techniques would involve the prosecutor's indirect communication with an adverse party represented by counsel.[109] The Attorney General has issued an instruction to Justice Department lawyers that "contact with a represented individual in the course of authorized law enforcement does not violate DR 7-104."[110] The Attorney General relies on the Supremacy Clause as mandating that the federal interest in maintaining effective investigation is paramount to the state interests in regulating the legal profession.[111] However, it is far from clear whether the "guideline" issued by the Attorney General can supersede the Second Circuit's contrary ruling.

---

105. *See, e.g.*, Davidson Supply Co. v. P.P.E., Inc., No. Civ. S 97-905, 1997 WL 778353, at *2 (D. Md. Dec. 16, 1997) (ethical rules did not prohibit plaintiff's counsel from contacting a former employee); Thorn, 1997 WL 627607, at *3 (Rule 4.2 of the Rules of Professional Conduct for the Northern District of Illinois does not prohibit contact with a former manager); *but see* Camden v. State of Md., 910 F. Supp. 1115, 1123 (D. Md. 1996) (holding that plaintiff's contact with the former employee who conducted the internal corporate investigation into plaintiff's discrimination claims was prohibited by Rule 4.2); Zachair, Ltd. v. Driggs, 965 F. Supp. 741, 754 (D. Md. 1997) (contact with former in-house counsel was prohibited by Rule 4.2); Niesig, 76 N.Y.2d at 374-75.

106. Thorn, 1997 WL 627607, at *3 (finding that a retired management employee of a corporate defendant had not disclosed any privileged information to plaintiff and approving of plaintiff's warning to the retiree at the beginning of the interview not to disclose privileged information) (quoting Orlowski v. Dominick's Finer Foods, 937 F. Supp. 723, 728 (N.D. Ill. 1996)).

107. 858 F.2d 834 (2d Cir. 1988), *cert. denied*, 498 U.S. 871 (1990).

108. *Id.* at 837-38.

109. *Id.* at 838-40.

110. Memorandum From Office of the Attorney General to All Justice Department Litigators (June 8, 1989).

111. *Id.*

The Attorney General also promulgated a rule which provides that "[a] communication with a current employee [of a represented party] shall be considered to be a communication with the organization. . . only if the employee is a controlling individual."[112] The rule defines "controlling individual" as "a current high level employee who is known by the government to be participating as a decision maker in the determination of the organization's legal position in the proceeding or investigation of the subject matter."[113]

The Eighth Circuit, in *United States v. O'Keeffe*,[114] recently held that the above-quoted rule was invalid because there was no statutory authority for the Attorney General to promulgate such a rule.[115] The Eighth Circuit affirmed the district court's holding that the government was barred from having *ex parte* communications with current employees under Missouri Supreme Court Rule 4-4.2, which prohibits, inter alia, *ex parte* communications with "persons having the managerial responsibility on behalf of the organization, and with any other person whose act or omission in connection with that matter may be imputed to the organization. . . or whose statement may constitute an admission on the part of the organization," when the organization is represented by counsel and such counsel's consent to the contact has not been obtained.[116]

Since both current and former employees may have privileged information—including what they discussed with investigative counsel—the cases permitting *ex parte* contact with these employees and the Attorney General's position create an enormous potential hole in the attorney-client privilege. Accordingly, investigative counsel would be wise to request that employees refrain from cooperating with adversaries, at least until investigative counsel can be present to protect the corporation's interests.[117]

---

112. 28 C.F.R. § 77.10(a).

113. *Id.*

114. 132 F.3d 1252 (8th Cir. 1998).

115. *Id.* at 1252-56.

116. *Id.* at 1252; *see also* State *ex rel.* Pitts v. Roberts, 857 S.W.2d 200, 202 (Mo. 1993) (adopting the above-quoted language as part of Missouri's ethical rules) (en banc).

117. Such a request is permissible under ABA Model Rule 3.4(f), where the person so requested is an employee or other agent of the corporation and "the lawyer reasonably believes that the person's interests will not be adversely affected by refraining from giving such information."

III. WORK PRODUCT PROTECTION

A related but independent basis for potentially preserving the confidentiality of counsel's investigative record is the work-product doctrine.

A. *Work-Product Doctrine Defined*

Rule 26(b)(3) of the Federal Rules of Civil Procedure provides, in relevant part:

> Subject to the provisions of subdivision (b)(4) of this rule, a party may obtain discovery of documents and tangible things otherwise discoverable under subdivision (b)(1) of this rule and prepared in anticipation of litigation or for trial by or for another party or by or for that other party's representative (including the other party's attorney, consultant, surety, indemnitor, ensurer, or agent) only upon a showing that the party seeking discovery has substantial need of the materials in the preparation of the party's case and that the party is unable without undue hardship to obtain the substantial equivalent of the materials by other means. In ordering discovery of such materials when the required showing has been made, the court shall protect against disclosure of the mental impressions, conclusions, opinions, or legal theories of a lawyer or other representative of a party concerning the litigation.

Similarly, rule 16(b)(2) of the Federal Rules of Criminal Procedure provides, in relevant part:

> Except as to scientific or medical reports, this subdivision does not authorize the discovery or inspection of reports, memoranda, or other internal defense documents made by the defendant, or the defendant's attorneys or agents in connection with the investigation or defense of the case, or of statements made by the defendant, or by government or defense witnesses, or by prospective government or defense witnesses, to the defendant, the defendant's agents or attorneys.

These federal rules are a codification of the United States Supreme Court's definition of attorney work product set forth in the seminal case of *Hickman v. Taylor*.[118]

The promulgation of rule 26(b)(3) of the Federal Rules of Civil Procedure resolved varying judicial interpretations of *Hickman* by protecting all materials, including legal theories, research, and factual materials prepared in anticipation of trial, whether prepared by a lawyer, a party, or an agent of a party.[119] Work product protection is available in both civil actions and criminal actions, including grand jury proceedings.[120] The work-product doctrine does not protect discovery of the underlying facts of a dispute as opposed to the attorney's mental impressions, conclusions, opinions or legal theories.[121]

In contrast with the attorney-client privilege, federal courts resolve questions involving the work-product doctrine by reference to the federal rules and federal common law.[122] Many states also have enacted

---

118. 329 U.S. 495 (1947).

119. United States v. Skeddle, 989 F. Supp. 912, 914-15 (N.D. Ohio 1997) (in criminal action against certain officers, corporation had standing to assert the work product privilege over materials obtained by a firm hired to investigate misconduct by the corporation's officers); Hawkins v. District Ct. In and For the Fourth Judicial District, 638 P.2d 1372, 1376 (Col. 1982) (en banc).

120. United States v. Jacques Dessange, Inc., 2000 WL 310345, at *3 (S.D.N.Y. March 27, 2000) (noting that the same principles are generally applicable regardless of whether the litigation is civil or criminal); *In re* Doe, 662 F.2d 1073, 1078 (4th Cir. 1981), *cert. denied*, 455 U.S. 1000 (1982); Skeddle, 1997 WL 661440, at *1; *see also* United States v. Nobles, 422 U.S. 225, 236 (1975); *In re* Grand Jury Proceedings, 473 F.2d 840, 842-43 (8th Cir. 1975).

121. *See* Moore U.S.A. Inc. v. The Standard Register Co., 2000 WL 876884, at *6 (W.D.N.Y. May 26, 2000) (work-product doctrine does not protect the identity of the people who provided information to counsel that led to the initiation of suit); Thomas & Betts Corp. v. Panduit Corp., No. 93 Civ. 4017, 1997 WL 603880, at *6 (N.D. Ill. Sept. 23, 1997) (holding that the identity of distributors contacted during plaintiff corporation's massive internal investigation into defendant's misappropriation of plaintiff's confidential business information was not protected by the work-product doctrine); *but see In re* Grand Casinos, Inc., 181 F.R.D. 615, 622 (D. Minn. 1998) (where lawyer prepared documents that collated or categorized facts, such documents where held privileged because they "properly reflected their counsel's thought processes or mental impressions").

122. *See, e.g.*, Baker v. General Motors Corp., 209 F.3d 1051, 1053-54 (8th Cir. 2000); Estate of Chopper v. R.J. Reynolds Tobacco Co., 195 F.R.D. 648, 650 (N.D. Iowa 2000); Railroad Salvage of Conn., Inc. v. Japan Freight Consolidators (U.S.A.) Inc., 97 F.R.D. 37, 40-41 (E.D.N.Y. 1983), *aff'd*, 779 F.2d 38 (2d Cir. 1985).

statutes protecting attorney work product; these statutes can differ significantly from the federal rule, and the practitioner is cautioned to consult the appropriate state's law.[123]

B. *Factual Versus Opinion Work Product*

The rules and the common law distinguish between "factual" and "opinion" work product. Factual work product encompasses documents or exhibits prepared in anticipation of litigation, while opinion work product includes mental impressions, opinions, or legal theories.[124] There is also a distinction between written statements prepared by witnesses and oral statements made by witnesses to the lawyer:

> But as to oral statements made by witnesses to [the attorney], whether presently in the form of his mental impressions or memoranda, we do not believe that any showing of necessity can be made under the circumstances of this case so as to justify production.[125]

While general work product may be discovered upon the requisite showing of substantial need and undue hardship, "[i]n ordering discovery of such [work product] materials when the required showing has been made, the court shall protect against disclosure of the mental impressions, conclusions, opinions, or legal theories of a lawyer or other representative of a party concerning the litigation."[126]

C. *Elements of the Work-Product Doctrine*

Whether the work product is classified as ordinary or opinion, it is necessary that it be prepared in anticipation of litigation or for trial by a lawyer, a party, or a party's representative.[127] As with the attorney-

---

123. *See, e.g.*, N.Y.C.P.L.R. § 3101; ILL. STAT. ANN. ch. 110 § 101.19-5; CAL. CODE CIV. PROC. § 2018.

124. *See* Hickman, 329 U.S. at 508.

125. *Id.* at 512-13.

126. FED. R. CIV. P. 26(b)(3).

127. *Id.*

client privilege, the underlying facts incorporated into the work product are not protected from discovery.[128]

1. Anticipation of Litigation

The attorney work-product doctrine attaches only to materials prepared for use in a pending litigation or in contemplation of future litigation.[129] For material to be considered prepared "in anticipation of litigation," the prospect of litigation must be identifiable, though litigation need not have already commenced.[130] Some articulable claim must exist,[131] however, and a remote possibility of litigation is insufficient.[132]

---

128. *See, e.g., In re* International Sys. & Control Corp. Sec. Litig., 91 F.R.D. 552, 561 (S.D. Tex. 1981) ("It has consistently been held that the work product privilege does not shield from discovery the underlying facts the party's representative learned, the persons from who he learned such facts, or the existence of certain documents"), *vacated on other grounds*, 693 F.2d 1235 (5th Cir. 1982).

129. FED. R. CIV. P. 26(b)(3). *See* United States v. Adlman, 134 F.3d 1194, 1196-1202 (2d Cir. 1998) (interpreting "in anticipation of litigation" to mean "if 'in light of the nature of the document and the factual situation in the particular case, the document can fairly be said to have been prepared or obtained *because of* the prospect of litigation'") (quoting CHARLES A. WRIGHT, ARTHUR R. MILLER & RICHARD L. MARCUS, 8 FEDERAL PRACTICE & PROCEDURE § 2024, at 343 (1994)); Garrett v. Metropolitan Life Ins. Co., No. 95 Civ. 2406 (PKL), 1996 WL 324725, at *3 (S.D.N.Y. June 12, 1996) ("Regulatory investigations by outside agencies present more than a mere possibility of future litigation, and provide reasonable grounds for anticipating litigation"); Martin v. Monfort, Inc., 150 F.R.D. 172, 173 (D. Colo. 1993) (investigation by the Department of Labor "presents more than a remote prospect of future litigation, and provides reasonable grounds for anticipating litigation sufficient to trigger application of the work-product doctrine"); *see also In re* Grand Jury Proceedings, 219 F.3d 175, 190 (2d Cir. 2000); General Elec. Capital Corp. v. Direct TV, Inc., 1998 WL 849389, at *7 (D. Conn. July 30, 1998); Prebena Wire Bending Mach. Co. v. Transit Worldwide Corp., 1999 WL 1063216 at * 1 (S.D.N.Y. Nov. 23, 1999); Taylor v. Temple & Cutler, 192 F.R.D. 522, 560 (E.D. Mich. 1999); Jaroslawicz Englehard Corp., 115 F.R.D. 515, 517 (D.N.J. 1987) (the compilation of documents for an SEC investigation is sufficient to constitute preparation for litigation).

130. *In re* Grand Jury Subpoenas, 959 F.2d 1158, 1166 (2d Cir. 1992); Panter v. Marshall Field & Co., 80 F.R.D. 718, 725 n.6 (N.D. Ill. 1978); Stix Prods., Inc. v. United Merchants & Mfrs., Inc., 47 F.R.D. 334, 338 (S.D.N.Y. 1969); *accord*, Hercules, Inc. v. Exxon Corp., 434 F. Supp. 136, 151 (D. Del. 1977).

131. Coastal States Gas Corp. v. Department of Energy, 617 F.2d 854, 864-65 (D.C. Cir. 1980); Garfinkle v. Arcata Nat'l Corp., 64 F.R.D. 688, 690 (S.D.N.Y. 1974).

132. *See, e.g.*, Garfinkle, 64 F.R.D. at 690; Burlington Indus. v. Exxon Corp., 65 F.R.D. 26, 33 (D. Md. 1974).

The Second Circuit, in *United States v. Adlman*,[133] recently addressed the appropriate test for the phrase "in anticipation of litigation" under Rule 26(b)(3) of the Federal Rules of Civil Procedure. Specifically, the Second Circuit addressed the issue of "whether Rule 26(b)(3) is inapplicable to a litigation analysis prepared by a party or its representative in order to inform a business decision which turns on the party's assessment of the likely outcome of litigation expected to result from the transaction."[134]

Adlman involved the preparation of a memorandum by an Arthur Andersen & Co. accountant and lawyer that contained a detailed legal analysis of likely IRS challenges, defenses to an IRS action, and alternative transactions to the corporation's proposed reorganization and merger of two of its wholly owned subsidiaries.[135] The reorganization resulted in the company being able to claim a tax refund, which the IRS challenged. The IRS served a subpoena on the accountant/lawyer, seeking the memorandum. The corporation objected to its production, claiming that the memorandum was protected by the attorney-client and work product privileges.[136] The district court first held that the memorandum was not protected by the attorney-client privilege, finding that the corporation had not consulted the accountant in order to obtain legal advice.[137] The Second Circuit affirmed the district court's first holding, but remanded for a determination as to whether the memorandum was protected from disclosure to the IRS under the work-product doctrine.[138] On remand, the district court rejected the work product claim.[139]

The corporation appealed the district court's second decision. The Second Circuit first noted that some courts, in following a line of Fifth Circuit cases,[140] had interpreted the phrase "in anticipation

---

133. 134 F.3d 1194 (2d Cir. 1998).

134. *Id.* at 1197.

135. *Id.* at 1193.

136. *Id.* at 1193-94.

137. United States v. Adlman, No. M-18-304, 1994 WL 191869, at *2 (S.D.N.Y. May 16, 1994).

138. United States v. Adlman, 68 F.3d 1495, 1501 (2d Cir. 1995).

139. United States v. Adlman, No. M-18-304, 1996 WL 84502, at *1 (S.D.N.Y. Feb. 27, 1996).

140. *See* United States v. Davis, 636 F.2d 1028 (5th Cir.) (holding that documents created during the course of preparing tax returns were not protected by the work-product doctrine), *cert. denied*, 454 U.S. 862 (1981); United States v. El Paso

of litigation" to mean "'primarily or exclusively to assist in litigation'—a formulation that would potentially exclude documents containing analysis of expected litigation, if their primary, ultimate, or exclusive purpose is to assist in making a business decision."[141] In the Second Circuit's view, "[n]othing in the Rule (26(b)(3)] states or suggests that documents prepared 'in anticipation of litigation' with the purpose of assisting in the making of a business decision do not fall within its scope."[142] Further, Rule 26(b)(3) "takes pains to grant special protection to the type of materials at issue in this case—documents setting forth legal analysis."[143] Specifically, Rule 26(b)(3) "generally withholds protection for documents prepared in anticipation of litigation" where the adverse party demonstrates a "substantial need" for the documents; but Rule 23(b)(3) also "directs that 'the court *shall* protect against disclosure of the mental impressions, conclusions, opinions or legal theories'" of a party or its representative concerning the litigation.[144] According to the Second Circuit, given this special level of protection over lawyers' thought processes, opinions, and legal theories, "it would oddly undermine [Rule 26(b)(3)'s] purposes if such documents were excluded from protection merely because they were prepared to assist in the making of a business decision expected to result in the litigation."[145] The Second Circuit found that "a document created because of anticipated litigation, which tends to reveal mental impressions, conclusions, opinions or

---

Co., 682 F.2d 530 (5th Cir. 1982) (holding that documents prepared to establish and justify reserves on the company's financial statements were not protected by the work-product doctrine), *cert. denied*, 466 U.S. 944 (1984).

141. United States v. Adlman, 134 F.3d 1194, 1196-2000 (2d Cir. 1998) (collecting cases).

142. *Id.* at 1198; *see In re* Grand Jury Proceedings, 604 F.2d 798, 803 (3d Cir. 1979); National Union Fire Ins. Co. v. Murray Sheet Metal Co., Inc., 967 F.2d 980, 984 (4th Cir. 1992); Banks Mfg. Co. v. National Presto Indus., Inc., 709 F.2d 1109, 1118-19 (7th Cir. 1983); Simon v. G.D. Searle & Co., 816 F.2d 397, 401 (8th Cir.), *cert. denied*, 484 U.S. 917 (1987); Senate of Puerto Rico v. United States Dep't of Justice, 823 F.2d 574, 586 n. 42 (D.C. Cir. 1987); *see also* CHARLES A. WRIGHT, ARTHUR R. MILLER & RICHARD L. MARCUS, 8 FEDERAL PRACTICE & PROCEDURE § 2024, at 343 (1994).

143. Adlman, 134 F.3d at 1198.

144. *Id.* (quoting Rule 26(b)(3) (emphasis in original)).

145. *Id.*

theories concerning the litigation, does not lose work product protection merely because it is intended to assist in the making of a business decision influenced by the likely outcome of the anticipated litigation."[146]

Other courts, the Second Circuit observed, "ask whether the documents were "prepared 'because of' existing or expected litigation—a formulation that would include such documents."[147] The Second Circuit determined that the "because of" formulation conforms to the plain language of Rule 26(b)(3) and the purposes underlying the work product rule. The Second Circuit concluded that "[t]he fact that a document's purpose is business related appears irrelevant to the question of whether it should be protected under Rule 26(b)(3)."[148] "Conversely, it should be emphasized that the 'because of' formulation . . . withholds protection from documents that are prepared in the ordinary course of business or that would have been created in essentially similar form irrespective of the litigation."[149]

The Second Circuit provided the following hypothetical scenarios in rejecting the "primarily or exclusively to assist in litigation" and adopting the "because of" formulation:

> (i) A company contemplating a transaction recognizes that the transaction will result in litigation; whether to undertake the transaction and, if so, how to proceed with the transaction may well be influenced by the company's evaluation of the likelihood of

---

146. *Id.* at 1194; *see also* Granite Partners, L.P. v. Bear, Stearns & Co. Inc., 184 F.R.D. 49, 52 (S.D.N.Y. 1999).

147. Adlman, 134 F.3d at 1197, 1201-02.

148. *Id.* at 1200.

149. *Id.* at 1202; Tayler v. Travelers Ins. Co., 183 F.R.D. 67, 69-70 (N.D.N.Y. 1998) ("there is no work product immunity for documents prepared in the ordinary course of business prior to the commencement of litigation"); United States v. Ernstoff, 183 F.R.D. 148, 156 (D.N.J. 1998) (same); *see also* Advisory Committee Note to FED. R. CIV. P. 26(b)(3) (1970); Simon v. G.D. Searle & Co., 816 F.2d 397, 401 (8th Cir.), *cert. denied*, 484 U.S. 917 (1987); Montgomery County v. Microvote Corp., 175 F.3d 296, 302 (3d Cir. 1999); Pfizer v. Advanced Monobloc Corp., 1999 WL 743868, at *4 (Del. Super. Sept. 20, 1999); CBS Corp. v. Northrop Grumman Corp., 1999 WL 4931, at *1 (S.D.N.Y. Jan. 5, 1999).

success in litigation. Thus, a memorandum may be prepared in expectation of litigation with the primary purpose of helping the company decide whether to undertake the contemplated transaction. An example would be a publisher contemplating publication of a book where the publisher has received a threat of suit from a competitor purporting to hold exclusive publication rights. The publisher commissions its attorneys to prepare an evaluation of the likelihood of success in the litigation, which includes the attorneys' evaluation of various legal strategies that might be pursued. If the publisher decides to go ahead with the publication and is sued, under the "primarily to assist in litigation" formulation the study will likely be disclosed to the opposing lawyers because its principal purpose was not to assist in litigation but to inform the business decision whether to publish. We can see no reason under the words or policies of the Rule why such a document should not be protected. *See United States v. Adlman*, 69 F.3d at 1501.

(ii) A company is engaged in, or contemplates, some kind of partnership, merger, joint undertaking, or business association with another company; the other company reasonably requests that the company furnish a candid assessment by the company's attorneys of its likelihood of success in existing litigations. For instance, the company's bank may request such a report from the company's attorneys concerning its likelihood of success in an important litigation to inform its lending policy toward the company. Or a securities underwriter contemplating a public offering of the company's securities may wish to see such a study to decide whether to go ahead with the offering without waiting for the termination of the litigation. Such a study would be created to inform the judgment of the business associate concerning its business decisions. No part of its purpose would be to aid in the conduct of the litigation. Nonetheless it would reveal the attorneys' most intimate strategies and assessments concerning the litigation. We can see no reason why, under the Rule, the litigation adversary should have access to it. But under the Fifth Circuit's "to assist" test, it would likely be discoverable by the litigation adversary.

(iii) A business entity prepares financial statements to assist its executives, stockholders, prospective investors, business partners, and others in evaluating future courses of action. Financial statements include reserves for projected litigation. The company's independent auditor requests a memorandum prepared by the company's attorneys estimating the likelihood of success in litigation and an accompanying analysis of the company's legal strategies and options to assist it in estimating what should be reserved for litigation losses.[150]

The Second Circuit concluded that the work product protection should be accorded to each of the reports described above.[151] Notably, the Second Circuit did not address whether the corporation may have waived the work product protection by producing the documents described in hypotheticals (ii) and (iii) to other companies, banks, underwriters or accountants.

The Second Circuit remanded the action to the district court for a determination of whether the work product privilege protected the Arthur Andersen memorandum with the following instructions:

> If the district court concludes that substantially the same Memorandum would have been prepared in any event—as part of the ordinary course of business of undertaking the restructuring—then the court should conclude the Memorandum was not prepared because of expected litigation and should adhere to its prior ruling denying the protection of the rule.
>
> On the other hand, if the court finds the Memorandum would not have been prepared but for [the corporation's] anticipation of litigation with the IRS over losses generated by the restructuring, then judgment should be entered in favor of [the corporation].[152]

The Second Circuit further concluded that the IRS had not made a sufficient showing of substantial need and unavailability to overcome the work product protection.[153]

---

150. 134 F.3d at 1199-1200.
151. *Id.* at 1202.
152. *Id.* at 1204.
153. *Id.*

In a dissent, Judge Kearse disagreed with "the majority's expansion of the work product privilege to afford protections to documents not prepared in anticipation of litigation but instead prepared in order to permit the client to determine whether to undertake a business transaction, where there will be no anticipation of litigation unless the transaction is undertaken."[154]

The Second Circuit's decision in *Adlman* calls into question a number of New York district court decisions holding that to invoke the work product privilege, the "primary motivating purpose" in creating the materials must be to assist in pending or impending litigation.[155]

---

154. Adlman, 134 F.3d at 1205 (Kearse, J., dissenting).

155. *See, e.g.*, *In re* Subpoena Duces Tecum Served on Willkie Farr & Gallagher, No. M8-85, 1997 U.S. Dist. LEXIS 2927 (S.D.N.Y. Mar. 14, 1997) (counsel's report of internal corporate investigation held not to constitute work product even though shareholder suit had been filed and the SEC had begun an informal inquiry, since litigation must be the "primary motivation" for retaining counsel and creating the report; here, the court found that the company had commissioned the investigation to address its accounting practices, a potential "business problem," and to obtain a clean bill of health from its auditors); Garrett v. Metropolitan Life Ins. Co., No. 95 Civ. 2406 (PKL), 1996 WL 325725, at *4 (S.D.N.Y. June 12, 1996) ("work product applies if the 'primary motivating purpose' behind the performance of the work was to assist in the pending or impending litigation'"); *In re* Kidder Peabody, No. 94 Civ. 3954 (BSJ), 1996 WL 263030 at *5, 6 (S.D.N.Y. May 17, 1996) ("inapplicability of the work product rule follows ...from the existence of pressing non-litigation reasons for the creation of the interview documents" and noting that it was "painfully evident that the Jett scandal presented Kidder not only with a serious legal problem, but also a major business crisis"; holding the internal investigation was not protected by the work-product doctrine, as it constituted "a crucial aspect of Kidder's public relations strategy ...[that] would have been undertaken regardless of whether litigation was threatened"); Sackman v. The Liggett Group, Inc., 920 F. Supp. 357, 366 (E.D.N.Y. 1996) (to receive work product protection, the "primary motivating purpose" in creating the materials must be to assist in pending or impending litigation); *In re* Leslie Fay, Inc. Sec. Litig., 161 F.R.D. 274, 280-81 (S.D.N.Y. 1995) (investigation and report used to make decisions on firing responsible personnel, to implement new internal controls, and to reassure creditors was not work product). The Second Circuit cited with approval the decision in *In re* Woolworth Corp. Sec. Litig., No. 94 Civ. 2217 (RO), 1996 WL 306576, at *3 (S.D.N.Y. June 7, 1996) (affording work product protection to internal investigation report where "a distinction between 'anticipation of litigation' and 'business purposes' is in this case artificial, unrealistic and the line between is here essentially blurred to oblivion"). Other courts have also applied the "primary motivat-

2. Subsequent Litigation

A dispute exists among the circuits regarding whether the work product protection lapses once a litigation ends.[156] Some courts have held that the protection applies only if the materials were prepared in anticipation of the suit before the court, and the documents prepared for one case are freely discoverable in another.[157] Other courts have held that work product from a terminated action retains its qualified immunity from disclosure even in subsequent unrelated litigation, and that documents prepared in one case may never be disclosed in a subsequent case.[158] The third, intermediate approach depends upon "whether the first action was complete and upon the relationship between the first and second actions,"[159] and extends work product protection to subsequent cases only where they are related to the first action.[160] The intermediate approach has been criticized because, as noted by the Eighth

---

ing purpose" formulation. *See, e.g.*, Stout v. Illinois Farmers Ins. Co., 150 F.R.D. 594, 604 (S.D. Ind. 1993) ("[i]f a document or thing would have been created for non-litigation uses regardless of its intended use in litigation preparation, it should not be accorded work product protection"), *aff'd*, 852 F. Supp. 704 (S.D. Ind. 1994).

156. Levingston v. Allis-Chalmers Corp., 109 F.R.D. 546, 552 (S.D. Miss. 1985) (outlining the three views); *see also* Frontier Ref., Inc. v. Gorman-Rupp Co., Inc., 136 F.3d 695, 703 (10th Cir. 1998) (declining to decide whether subsequent litigation must be closely related to action for which protected material was prepared).

157. *See, e.g.*, United States v. International Bus. Mach. Corp., 66 F.R.D. 154, 178 (S.D.N.Y. 1974); Honeywell, Inc. v. Piper Aircraft Corp., 50 F.R.D. 117, 119 (M.D. Pa. 1970); Hanover Shoe, Inc. v. United Shoe Mach. Corp., 207 F. Supp. 407, 410 (M.D. Pa. 1962); Gulf Constr. Co. v. St. Joe Paper Co., 24 F.R.D. 411, 415 (S.D. Tex. 1959); Tobacco & Allied Stocks, Inc. v. Transamerica Corp., 16 F.R.D. 534, 537 (D. Del. 1954).

158. *See, e.g.*, *In re* Murphy, 560 F.2d 326, 334 (8th Cir. 1977); Duplan Corp. v. Moulinage et Retorderie de Chavanoz, 487 F.2d 480, 484-85 (4th Cir. 1973); *accord, In re* International Sys. & Controls Corp. Sec. Litig., 91 F.R.D. 552, 557 (S.D. Tex. 1981), *vacated on other grounds*, 693 F.2d 1235 (5th Cir. 1982); SCM Corp. v. Xerox Corp., 70 F.R.D. 508, 516 (D. Conn.), *appeal dismissed and mandamus denied*, 534 F.2d 1031 (2d Cir. 1976); Burlington Indus. v. Exxon Corp., 65 F.R.D. 26, 43 (D. Md. 1974).

159. 4 J. MOORE, FEDERAL PRACTICE § 26-64(2) at 26-415 (2d ed. 1979).

160. *See, e.g.*, Garrett v. Metropolitan Life Ins. Co., No. 95 Civ. 2406 (PKL), 1996 WL 325725 at *4 (S.D.N.Y. June 12, 1996) ("[d]ocuments prepared for one litigation that would have been shielded retain the protection in a second litigation if the two actions are closely related in parties or subject matter"); Hercules, Inc. v. Exxon Corp., 434 F. Supp. 136, 153 (D. Del. 1977) (parties or subject matter must be

Circuit, "[t]he unrelatedness of the subsequent litigation provides an insufficient basis for disregarding the privilege articulated in *Hickman* and incorporated in rule 26(b)(3)."[161]

Although the United States Supreme Court has not directly addressed the issue, the Court has indicated, in dictum, that as long as the material was initially prepared by a party in anticipation of litigation, it remains privileged in subsequent litigations.[162]

3. Materials Prepared by Corporate Employees

There is no distinction between materials prepared by lawyers and material prepared by nonlawyers. Rule 26(b)(3) explicitly extends the protection to materials prepared "by or for another party or by or for that other party's representative." As the Advisory Committee Note to rule 26(b)(3) explains, the rule "reflects the trend of the cases by requiring a special showing not merely as to materials prepared by a lawyer, but also as to the materials prepared . . . by or for a party or any representative acting on his behalf."[163] Both opinion and factual work product are protected.[164]

---

closely related); *In re* Grand Jury Proceedings (FMC Corp.), 604 F.2d 798, 803 (3d Cir. 1979) (identity of subject matter and temporal connection found to exist, no decision on whether relatedness required); Puerto Rico v. S.S. Zoe Colocotroni, 61 F.R.D. 653, 659 (D.P.R. 1974) (confined work product from previous litigation to where first action not completed or bears a substantial relationship with present litigation, or in which same counsel exists on either side); Republic Gear Co. v. Borg-Warner Corp., 381 F.2d 551, 557 (2d Cir. 1967).

161. *In re* Murphy, 560 F.2d at 335 (8th Cir. 1977).

162. FTC v. Grolier Inc., 462 U.S. 19, 25 (1983) ("the literal language of [rule 26(b)(3)] protects material for any litigation or trial as long as they were prepared by or for a party to the subsequent litigation") (dictum) (emphasis by the Court); Walsh v. Seaboard Surety Co., 184 F.R.D. 494, 497 (D. Conn. 1999); *In re* Sharonda B, 1998 WL 341801, at *6 (N.D. Ill. June 11, 1998).

163. 48 F.R.D. 487, 502 (1970); *see also* Atlantic Richfield Co. v. Current Controls, Inc., No. 93-CV-0950E(H), 1997 WL 538876, at *3 (W.D.N.Y. Aug. 21, 1997) ("it is of no consequence that most of the subject documents were prepared by non-attorneys . . . the work product privilege applies also to documents prepared by a 'party' and 'representatives' of that party, including consultants, sureties, indemnitors, insurers and agents") (collecting cases); J. MOORE, FEDERAL PRACTICE 26.64[3] ("under the new language . . . there will be no technical distinction between materials prepared by the attorney in the case and those that are prepared by a claim agent, insurer, or other agent of the party, or by the party himself").

164. Duplan Corp. v. Deering Milliken, Inc., 540 F.2d 1215, 1219 (4th Cir. 1976)

D. *Overcoming the Qualified Immunity*

Rule 26(b)(3) provides that a party may obtain discovery of work product materials only (1) upon a showing that the party seeking discovery has substantial need of the materials in the preparation of the party's case, and (2) that the party is unable without undue hardship to obtain the substantial equivalent of the materials by other means.

In *Hickman v. Taylor*,[165] the Court wrote that "[w]here relevant and non-privileged facts remain hidden in a lawyer's file and where production of those facts is essential to the preparation of one's case, discovery may properly be had."[166] The Court added that the "burden rests on the one who would invade that privacy to establish adequate reasons to justify production through a subpoena or court order."[167] The clearest case for ordering production of non-opinion work product is when crucial information is in the exclusive control of the opposing party.[168] In *Hickman v. Taylor*, Justice Murphy indicated that written statements within the work-product doctrine might be discovered if it appeared that "the witnesses [were] no longer available or [could] be reached only with difficulty."[169] The published decisions show considerable variation in the liberality of the lower courts in deciding how much "difficulty" will suffice, and in granting motions to produce.[170]

(citations omitted) ("opinion work product immunity now applies equally to lawyers and nonlawyers alike").

165. 329 U.S. 495 (1947).

166. *Id.* at 511.

167. *Id.* at 512. *See also In re* Sealed Case, 676 F.2d 793, 809 (D.C. Cir. 1982); *In re* Murphy, 560 F.2d at 334.

168. *See, e.g.*, Loctite Corp. v. Fel-Pro, Inc., 667 F.2d 577, 582 (7th Cir. 1981); S.S. Zoe Colocotroni, 61 F.R.D. at 658-59.

169. 329 U.S. at 511.

170. *See, e.g.*, Loctite Corp., 667 F.2d at 582-83 (where court ordered the production of non-opinion work product when crucial information is in the exclusive control of the opposing party); *but see* Southern Ry v. Lanham, 403 F.2d 119, 130 (5th Cir. 1968) (where court rejected "rigid rule that the moving party must always show he has been unable to obtain statements of his own"); *see also* Skeddle, 989 F. Supp. at 914 (ordering production of interview notes of an investigator of the interviewees whom the government will be calling at trial on the grounds that

E. *Protection of a Lawyer's Mental Impressions*

The decision in *Hickman v. Taylor* is based in large measure on protecting the thought processes of counsel:

> Historically, a lawyer is an officer of the court and is bound to work for the advancement of justice while faithfully protecting the rightful interests of his clients. In performing his various duties, however, it is essential that a lawyer work with a certain degree of privacy, free from unnecessary intrusion by opposing parties and their counsel. Proper preparation of a client's case demands that he assemble information, sift what he considers to be the relevant from the irrelevant facts, prepare his legal theories, and plan his strategy without undue and needless interference. That is the historical and the necessary way in which lawyers act within the framework of our system of jurisprudence to promote justice and protect their client's interests.[171]

Courts, having this rationale in mind, have protected the mental impressions and legal theories of a lawyer.[172]

In *Upjohn Co. v. United States*,[173] the Court stated that the draftsmen of rule 26(b)(3) regarded "opinion" work product as "deserving special attention."[174] As the Court noted, "[f]orcing a lawyer to disclose notes and memoranda of witnesses' oral statements is particularly disfavored because it tends to reveal a lawyer's mental processes."[175] However, the Court expressly declined to specify what, if any, showing of necessity would be sufficient to compel disclosure.[176]

Rule 26(b)(3) also recognizes that ordinary or factual work prod-

---

"[o]nce such individual has been called as a witness, his or her version of the pertinent facts becomes publicly known; as a result, there is little reason to protect fact work product").

171. 329 U.S. at 510-11.

172. Nguyen v. Excel Corp., 197 F.3d 200, 210 (5th Cir. 1999); *see, e.g.,* Duplan Corp., 509 F.2d at 734-35; *see also* Berkey Photo, Inc. v. Eastman Kodak Co., 74 F.R.D. 613, 616 (S.D.N.Y. 1977).

173. 449 U.S. 383 (1981).

174. *Id.* at 400.

175. *Id.* at 399.

176. *Id.* at 401.

uct may also contain opinion work product. Thus, the rule provides that even when a court finds substantial need and undue hardship sufficient to require discovery of ordinary work product, "the court shall protect against disclosure of the mental impressions, conclusions, opinions, or legal theories of a lawyer or other representative of a party concerning the litigation."[177] There is some disagreement among the courts as to whether opinion work product is absolutely privileged,[178] or whether the party seeking discovery of these materials simply must meet a higher burden.[179]

In light of the high-level protection afforded to opinion work product, investigative counsel can maximize the likelihood the work-product doctrine will apply by making explicit the mental impressions and legal theories that ordinarily are implicit in many documents relating to the investigation. In particular, investigative counsel should carefully consider the benefits and detriments of the several ways of eliciting information from corporate employees and others. The use of questionnaires or other written witness statements may be more efficient when there are numerous witnesses involved, but these documents are more likely to be classified as factual work product, subject to discovery upon the requisite showing of substantial need and undue hardship.[180] The conduct of oral interviews and preparation of

---

177. Fed. R. Civ. P. 26(b)(3).

178. *See, e.g.*, Duplan Corp., 509 F.2d at 734-35 (absolutely immune in subsequent litigation); *In re* Grand Jury Proceedings (Duffy), 473 F.2d 840, 848 (8th Cir. 1973) (absolute protection); *see also* Laxalt v. C.K. McClatchy, 116 F.R.D. 438, 441 (D. Nev. 1987) ("opinion work product [not reduced to a tangible form] enjoys an almost absolute immunity from discovery").

179. *See, e.g.*, Office of Thrift Supervision v. Vinson & Elkins, LLP, 124 F.3d 1304, 1307-08 (1st Cir. 1997) ("[o]pinion work product ...is virtually undiscoverable" and holding that the OTS had not demonstrated a "substantial need" for lawyers' notes of employee interviews where the OTS had obtained notes from the FDIC's lawyers of those same interviews); City of Springfield v. Rexnord Corp., 196 F.R.D. 7, 10 (D. Mass. 2000) (noting that opinion work product afforded special protection); *In re* Sealed Case, 676 F.2d at 809-10 (document not discoverable unless extraordinary showing made); *In re* Grand Jury Investigation (Sun Co.), 599 F.2d 1224, 1231 (3d Cir. 1979) (memorandum not absolutely protected). *But see* Donovan v. Fitzsimmons, 90 F.R.D. 583, 588 (N.D. Ill. 1981) (no showing beyond the substantial need/undue hardship standard required to discover opinion work product).

180. *See* Hickman v. Taylor, 329 U.S. at 511; *In re* John Doe Corp., 675 F.2d 482,

extensive file memoranda is far more time-consuming, but is more likely to generate documents that will be classified as opinion work product.[181] Of course, a personal interview is a far preferable method for eliciting complete and candid information, apart from work product considerations. In a complex investigation involving numerous witnesses, a cost/benefit analysis may result in the use of questionnaires for less significant witnesses, while the key personnel are interviewed personally.

IV. OVERCOMING THE ATTORNEY-CLIENT PRIVILEGE AND WORK-PRODUCT DOCTRINE

The corporation and its investigative counsel must be cognizant of the fact that, despite their best efforts, the investigative record may still be subject to discovery. One way otherwise protected materials become discoverable is through waiver, intentional or otherwise.[182] In addition, exceptions to the attorney-client privilege and the work-product doctrine may come into play when a crime or fraud is involved or in connection with shareholder litigation.[183] Thus, investigative counsel should take care in the preparation of documents, even if they are intended to be privileged or work product, because they may become discoverable.

A. *Waiver*

Investigative counsel must take steps to ensure that the attorney-client privilege and the work-product doctrine are not inadvertently waived, through disclosure or otherwise. Because the attorney-client privilege and the work-product doctrine derive from separate and distinct policies, the actions that will result in waiver are also distinct.

---

492 (2d Cir. 1982); *In re* Grand Jury Investigation, 599 F.2d 1224, 1230-32 (3d Cir. 1979); Connelly v. Dun & Bradstreet, Inc., 96 F.R.D. 339, 342-43 (D. Mass. 1982).

181. *See* Upjohn Co., 449 U.S. at 399.

182. *See* Part IV.A, *infra.*

183. *See* Parts IV.B and IV.C, *infra.*

1. Waiver of the Attorney-Client Privilege

An essential element of the attorney-client privilege is the confidentiality of the communication.[184] If a communication ordinarily within the privilege is not intended to be confidential, or the "cloak of confidence" has been lifted, the privilege is waived.[185] The attorney-client privilege may be waived intentionally; in addition, through various actions by the client, the privilege may be waived by implication. In the context of internal investigations and the typically ensuing legal proceedings, waiver of privilege is an ever-present concern. While an intentional waiver of privilege is generally the subject of debate and deliberation,[186] it must be recognized that an unintentional or implied waiver might well be the consequence of certain conduct.

a. Voluntary Disclosure and Disclosure to Government Authorities. The voluntary disclosure of a communication to a third party generally effects a waiver of the privilege.[187] The option to waive the

---

184. United States v. Kelsey-Hayes Wheel Co., 15 F.R.D. 461, 464 (E.D. Mich. 1954).

185. *See, e.g.*, Dunn Chem. Co. v. Sybron Corp., 1975-2 Trade Cas. (CCH) ¶ 60,561, at 67,463 (S.D.N.Y.).

186. One possible consequence of the disclosure of results of an internal investigation that should be considered is the likelihood of litigation against the corporation or investigative counsel by corporate employees (or third parties) whose conduct is criticized. *See Bell Suit Fallout: Outside Probers Want Protection*, LEGAL TIMES, July 27, 1988. If libel, negligence or other claims are a likely prospect, the corporation and its investigative counsel should consider ways to minimize such claims—such as deletion of the names and other identifying information concerning people whose conduct is criticized—and appropriate provision for the indemnification of counsel in the event that litigation occurs.

187. *See, e.g.*, PaineWebber Group, Inc. v. Zinsmeyer Trusts Partnership, 187 F.3d 988, 992 (8th Cir. 1999) ("attorney-client privilege is waived by the voluntary disclosure of privileged communications, and courts typically apply such a waiver to all communications on the same subject matter"); United States v. Dakota, 197 F.3d 821, 825 (6th Cir. 1999) (corporation may waive attorney-client privilege via voluntary disclosure to third parties); National Education Training Corp. v. Skillsoft Corp., 1999 WL 378337, at *3 (S.D.N.Y. June 10, 1999); *In re* John Doe Corp., 675 F.2d 482, 489 (2d Cir. 1982); Bower v. Weisman, 669 F. Supp. 602, 604 (S.D.N.Y. 1987); Eigenheim Bank v. Halpern, 598 F. Supp. 988, 991 (S.D.N.Y. 1984); Teachers Ins. & Annuity Ass'n v. Shamrock Broadcasting Co., 521 F. Supp. 638, 641 (S.D.N.Y. 1981).

attorney-client privilege belongs to the client.[188] When the client is a corporation, the power to waive the corporation's privilege rests with the corporate decision maker at the time the waiver determination is made,[189] whether it be the corporation's management,[190] its board of directors,[191] or a trustee or other successor to the corporation.[192]

The lawyer generally is not entitled to waive the privilege without the consent of the client or the permission of the court. However, where a client is aware that the lawyer intends to disclose confidential communications, the client must take affirmative action to preserve the confidentiality of the communications to retain the privilege.[193]

Traditionally, disclosure of privileged communications to a government agency, in the course of an investigation or proceeding by the agency, was held to be a waiver of the privilege for all future cases or proceedings regarding all communications on the same subject matter.[194]

In *In re Steinhardt Partners,*[195] the Second Circuit held that voluntary production to the SEC of an investigation report waived the work

---

188. See ABA Model Rules of Prof'l Conduct R. 1.6 and ABA Model Code of Professional Responsibility DR 4-101, delineating the circumstances in which counsel may unilaterally disclose otherwise privileged communications.

189. Normally, the corporate decision-maker will be a person or group of people who are part of the "control group," despite the fact that lower-level employees may act for the corporate client sufficiently to invoke the privilege in the first instance.

190. See CFTC v. Weintraub, 471 U.S. 343, 349 (1985).

191. See United States v. DeLillo, 448 F. Supp. 840, 842-43 (E.D.N.Y. 1978).

192. See In re Bevill, Bresler & Schulman Asset Mgmt. Corp., 805 F.2d 120, 124-25 (3d Cir. 1986).

193. Id.

194. See, e.g., United States v. Massachusetts Inst. of Tech., 129 F.3d 681, 688 (1st Cir. 1997); Genentech, Inc. v. United States Int'l Trade Comm'n, 122 F.3d 1409, 1417 (Fed. Cir. 1997); In re Steinhardt Partners, L.P., 9 F.3d 230, 235 (2d Cir. 1993); Westinghouse Elec. Corp. v. Republic of the Philippines, 951 F.2d 1414, 1424 (3d Cir. 1991); In re Martin Marietta Corp., 856 F.2d 619, 623-24 (4th Cir. 1988), cert. denied, 490 U.S. 1011 (1989); In re the Leslie Fay Co. Inc. Sec. Litig., 161 F.R.D. 274, 283-84 (S.D.N.Y. 1995); Trans World Airlines v. Hughes, 332 F.2d 602, 615 (2d Cir. 1964), cert. dismissed, 380 U.S. 248 (1965); United States v. Kelsey-Hayes Wheel Co., 15 F.R.D. 461, 464-65 (E.D. Mich. 1954); In re Penn. Cent. Comm'l Paper Litig., 61 F.R.D. 453, 463-67 (S.D.N.Y. 1973).

195. 9 F.3d 230 (2d Cir. 1993).

product protection with respect to the report in subsequent litigation.[196] The *Steinhardt* court, however, "decline[d] to adopt a *per se* rule that all voluntary disclosures to the government waive work product protection" and noted that "[e]stablishing a rigid rule would fail to anticipate situations in which the disclosing party and the government may share a common interest in developing legal theories and analyzing information, or situations in which the SEC and the disclosing party have entered into an explicit agreement that the SEC will maintain the confidentiality of the disclosed materials."[197]

Some courts have come to recognize a "limited" waiver,[198] due to policy considerations such as "facilitating the settlement of litigation, permitting full cooperation among joint defendants, expediting discovery, and encouraging voluntary disclosure to regulatory agencies."[199]

The scope of this "limited" waiver has varied.[200] Several courts have limited the waiver to the facts actually disclosed.[201] One court went even further, holding that voluntary compliance with a subpoena issued by a government agency does not constitute a waiver as to subsequent civil litigation.[202]

---

196. *Id.* at 236; *see also* Information Resources, Inc. v. Dun & Bradstreet Corp., 999 F. Supp. 591 (S.D.N.Y. 1998).

197. *Id.; see also In re* the Leslie Fay Co., 161 F.R.D. at 284 (finding no waiver because "the disclosure of privileged information to the government may not constitute a waiver if the government agrees to maintain the confidentiality of the disclosed materials").

198. *See* United States v. Upjohn Co., 600 F.2d 1223, 1227 n.12 (6th Cir. 1979), *rev'd on other grounds*, 449 U.S. 383 (1981); Diversified Indus., 572 F.2d at 611; Nutramax Laboratories, Inc. v. Twin Laboratories, Inc. 183 F.R.D. 458, 467 (D. Md. 1998) (documents consisting of opinion work product, which were put to testimonial use in litigation, were subject to a limited waiver of the documents themselves, but not to a broad subject matter waiver); *see generally* Dennis J. Block & Jonathan M. Hoff, *Selective Waiver of Attorney-Client Privilege*, 211 N.Y.L.J. 96, 5 col. 1 (1994).

199. *In re* Martin Marietta Corp., 856 F.2d at 623.

200. *See* Block & Barton, *Waiver of the Attorney-Client Privilege by Disclosure to the SEC*, 10 SEC. REG. L.J. 170 (1982).

201. *See e.g.*, United States v. Upjohn Co., 600 F.2d 1223, 1227 n.12 (6th Cir. 1979), *rev'd on other grounds*, 449 U.S. 383 (1981); *In re* the Leslie Fay Co., 161 F.R.D. at 284.

202. Diversified Indus., 572 F.2d at 611.

Other courts have rejected the "limited waiver" concept entirely,[203] on the theory that such a rule would not further the interest of promoting frank discussions between lawyer and client.[204]

Another issue is whether disclosure of corporate investigative reports, which themselves were based in part on privileged documents, results in a waiver of privilege regarding the documents referred to in the report and/or the entire investigative file. The Supreme Court, in *Upjohn Co. v. United States*,[205] held that employees' responses to a questionnaire designed to investigate an allegation of certain questionable payments to government officials and notes reflecting re-

---

203. The First, Second, Third, Fourth, Seventh, D.C., and Federal Circuits have rejected the selective waiver doctrine. *See, e.g.*, Massachusetts Inst. of Tech., 129 F.3d at 685 (stating "... the general principle that disclosure normally negates the privilege is worth maintaining.... Following the Eighth Circuit's approach would require, at the very least, a new set of difficult line-drawing exercises that would consume time and increase uncertainty"); *In re* Steinhardt Partners, 9 F.3d at 235 (quoting Permian Corp. v. United States, 665 F.2d 1214, 1220-21 (D.C. Cir. 1981) and stating "[t]he client cannot be permitted to choose among his opponent, waiving the privilege for some and resurrecting the claim of confidentiality to obstruct others, or to invoke the privilege as to communications whose confidentiality he has already compromised for his own benefit"); Westinghouse Elec. Corp., 951 F.2d at 1424-26 (rejecting Eighth Circuit rule espoused in *Diversified* and adopting the D.C. Circuit rule); *In re* Martin Marietta Corp., 856 F.2d at 623-24; United States v. Hamilton, 19 F.3d 350, 353 (7th Cir. 1994); Permian Corp., 665 F.2d at 1221; Genentech, Inc., 122 F.3d at 1417. *But see In re* Perrigo, 128 F.3d 430 (6th Cir. 1997) (neither adopting nor rejecting the selective waiver doctrine); *In re* Columbia/HCA Healthcare Corp., 192 F.R.D. 575, 579 (M.D. Tenn. 2000) (noting that the Sixth Circuit has neither adopted nor rejected the selective waiver doctrine and declining to adopt it); *In re* Sealed Case, 676 F. 2d 793, 824 (D.C. Cir. 1982) (company voluntarily submitted report of investigative counsel to SEC); *In re* Subpoena Duces Tecum, 738 F.2d 1367, 1370 (D.C. Cir. 1984) (privilege waived where client willingly sacrificed confidentiality by voluntarily disclosing the material to the SEC in an effort to convince them that a formal investigation was not warranted); Neal v. Honeywell, Inc., No. 93 Civ. 1143, 1995 WL 591461 at *7 n.2 (N.D. Ill. Oct. 4, 1995) (collecting cases); Teachers Ins. & Annuity Ass'n v. Shamrock Broadcasting Co., 521 F. Supp. 638, 646 (S.D.N.Y. 1981) (no limited waiver absent an express reservation of rights, stipulation or protective order).

204. *See, e.g.*, Massachusetts Inst. of Tech., 129 F.3d at 685 (rejecting the reasoning of the Eighth Circuit in *Diversified* that selective waiver doctrine encourages "the frank exchange between attorney and client in future cases").

205. 449 U.S. 383 (1981).

sponses to the questionnaire were communications protected by the attorney-client privilege.[206] Further, the Court held that in-house counsel's notes and memoranda of employees' oral statements during interviews were protected by the work-product doctrine.[207] In *Upjohn*, the company had filed the investigative report as part of a Form 8-K with the SEC and produced it to the IRS.[208] Using a list of employees produced by the company, the IRS interviewed all of the same employees who answered the questionnaire and who were interviewed during the corporation's investigation.[209]

The *Upjohn* Court held that "[w]hile it would probably be more convenient for the Government to secure the results of [the company's] internal investigation by simply subpoenaing the questionnaires and notes taken by petitioner's attorneys," such convenience could not overcome the attorney-client privilege, and the IRS had not demonstrated "substantial need and inability to obtain the equivalent without undue hardship" necessary to overcome the work product privilege.[210] The Supreme Court did not address whether the production to the IRS and filing the report as part of a Form 8-K with the SEC constituted a waiver of the attorney-client and work product privileges over the responses to the questionnaires and notes of interviews.

Several years after *Upjohn*, the Second Circuit held, in *In re von Bulow*, that a voluntary waiver of the attorney-client privilege with respect to one document may result in a waiver as to all communications made about the same subject between the attorney and the client.[211] This subject matter waiver will be found if "the privilege-holder has attempted to use the privilege as both 'a sword' and 'a shield' or where the . . . party [challenging the privilege] has been prejudiced at

---

206. *Id.* at 396.

207. *Id.* at 401.

208. *Id.* at 387.

209. Upjohn, 449 U.S. at 387.

210. *Id.* at 396, 401. *But see In re* Martin Marietta Corp., 856 F.2d at 623-24 (holding that the company's submission of a position paper to the U.S. attorney discussing the conclusions of an internal investigation into certain allegations of fraud waived the work product and attorney-client privileges as to the investigation documents on the same subject as the position paper in an action brought by a former employee of the company).

211. *In re* von Bulow, 828 F.2d 94, 103 (2d Cir. 1987).

trial."[212] These conditions are satisfied when the privilege holder not only discloses a privileged communication, but affirmatively makes use of the disclosure.

Two district courts have recently applied the *von Bulow* principle in the internal investigation context where the company had published the investigative report. In *In re Kidder Peabody Sec. Litig.*,[213] the court concluded that where Kidder had made repeated affirmative use in several litigations and agency proceedings and investigations of a report prepared by counsel that summarized the factual findings and recommendations of counsel's internal investigation, to show that Kidder was the victim and Joseph Jett was the wrongdoer, Kidder had waived the attorney-client privilege for those portions of the underlying interview documents that contain the substance of any of the statements used in the final report.[214]

The court in *In re the Leslie Fay Companies Inc. Sec. Litig.*[215] adopted a similar approach. The court held that, where the final report was disclosed to the SEC and the findings of the report were being used in the class-action litigation to establish the liability of the company's outside auditors and co-defendants, any privilege covering the subject matters discussed in the report was waived and withholding such information would prejudice the co-defendant auditors.[216] The court held, however, that "an equitable piercing of the attorney-client privilege should be narrowly tailored to address the potential prejudice to the party attacking the privilege" and, thus, concluded that the waiving party was entitled to withhold from discovery any documents containing "legal advice or advice not contained or discussed in" the report.[217]

---

212. *Id.*

213. 168 F.R.D. 459 (S.D.N.Y. 1996).

214. *Id.* at 474. In *Kidder*, the report had been disclosed to the SEC and also used affirmatively by Kidder in pending lawsuits and arbitrations. *Id.*

215. 161 F.R.D. 274 (S.D.N.Y. 1995).

216. *Id.* at 284.

217. *Id.*; *but see* Peterson v. Wallace Computer Serv., Inc., 984 F. Supp. 821, 824-26 (D. Vt. 1997) (where corporate defendant asserted as a defense that it had conducted an adequate internal investigation into plaintiff's hostile work environment claim, and had agreed that the director of human resources and other employees would testify to the scope and substance of the investigation, the court held that the company waived the attorney-client privilege over the investigative notes and memoranda and that plaintiff had demonstrated a substantial need for such material necessary to overcome the work product privilege).

A contrary result was reached in *In re Woolworth Corp. Sec. Class Action Litig.*[218] In refusing to order the production of interview notes and other memoranda used to prepare an internal investigation report that the company had published and produced to the class-action plaintiffs, the *Woolworth* court rejected the subject matter waiver argument on public policy grounds because "[a] finding that publication of an internal investigative report constitutes waiver might well discourage corporations from taking the responsible step of employing outside counsel to conduct an investigation when wrongdoing is suspected."[219] The *Woolworth* court relied on *Upjohn*,[220] which the *Woolworth* court found to be directly on point.[221] The *Woolworth* court rejected plaintiffs' contention that the company was using the attorney-client privilege over the underlying notes and memoranda of outside counsel as both a "sword and a shield" because "[p]laintiffs are free to depose all of the employees [who] Paul, Weiss interviewed (and plaintiffs had, to a large extent, done so) in order to glean facts not sufficiently set forth in the [r]eport."[222]

Counsel advising corporations in the context of internal investigations must be aware of the *Steinhardt, von Bulow, Kidder, Leslie Fay,* and *Woolworth* precedents.[223] Voluntary disclosure of an investigative

---

218. No. 94 Civ. 2217 (RO), 1996 WL 306576, at *2 (S.D.N.Y. June 7, 1996).

219. *Id.*

220. 449 U.S. 383 (1980).

221. *Id.* at 390.

222. Woolworth, 1996 WL 306576, at *2.

223. *See also* Pittman v. Frazer, 129 F.3d 983, 987-88 (8th Cir. 1997) (holding that the company's use of photographs taken by investigator as trial exhibits did not waive the work product protection with respect to the investigator's entire file); Falise et al. v. American Tobacco Co. et al., 193 F.R.D. 73, 84-85 (E.D.N.Y. 2000) (rejecting plaintiff's claim that broad subject matter waiver occurred because defendants were ordered to produce certain documents in a former proceeding); *In re* Subpoena Duces Tecum Served on Willkie Farr & Gallagher, 1997 U.S. Dist. LEXIS 2927 (S.D.N.Y. Mar. 14, 1997) (disclosure by investigative counsel of paraphrased statements from employee interviews, and its assessment as to employees' credibility to company's auditors to obtain an unqualified audit opinion, waived the attorney-client privilege as to specific items disclosed to auditors); *see generally* Dennis J. Block & Jonathan M. Hoff, *Selective Waiver of Attorney-Client Privilege*, 211 N.Y.L.J. 96, 5 col. 1 (1994) (noting that courts have suggested that where disclosures to the government are conditioned upon an express agreement of confidentiality, the attorney-client privilege may be preserved over such information in subsequent private litigation).

report to a government agency, without the agency's agreement to keep the report confidential, coupled with affirmative use of the report in subsequent litigation may result in waiver of the attorney-client and work product privileges over not only the report, but the underlying interview notes and memoranda as well.

b. Reliance on Advice of Counsel. Another circumstance that dictates waiver of the attorney-client privilege is where a party places its privileged communications at issue. The privilege is "intended as a shield, not a sword."[224] Thus, where a party raises an issue to which an effective rebuttal would require inquiry into privileged communications, the privilege may be deemed waived.[225] Ordinarily, the mere filing of a complaint or answer will not be deemed a waiver.[226] However, there may be cases where the opposing party cannot defend itself without inquiry into privileged matters.[227]

In the context of internal investigations, the otherwise privileged communications between counsel and the client may be placed at issue by an assertion of reliance on "advice of counsel" as the basis for a claim or defense. This reliance waives the privilege of communications and documents relating to the advice.[228] The assertion of this

---

224. 8 WIGMORE, EVIDENCE § 2327, at 638.

225. *See, e.g.*, Robinson v. Time Warner, Inc., 187 F.R.D. 144, 146 (S.D.N.Y. 1999) (attorney-client privilege may be waived where a defendant places privileged matters at issue); Sealy v. Gruntal & Company et al., 1998 U.S. Dist. LEXIS 15654, at *14-15 (S.D.N.Y. 1998) (reliance for affirmative defense upon an internal corporate investigation of a civil rights claim will result in waiver of the privilege); Gorzegno v. Maguire, 62 F.R.D. 617, 621-22 (S.D.N.Y. 1973); *but see* Baker v. General Motors Corp., 209 F.3d 1051, 1055 (8th Cir. 2000) (declining to extend "at issue waiver" where "a party has used witness testimony and made factual representations that were allegedly contrary to what the privileged documents will reveal").

226. *See* Mendenhall v. Barber-Greene Co., 531 F. Supp. 948, 950 (N.D. Ill. 1981).

227. *See generally* Hearn v. Rhay, 68 F.R.D. 574, 581 (E.D. Wash. 1975). Various assertions can result in a waiver of privilege. *See* United States v. Exxon Corp., 94 F.R.D. 246, 247-49 (D.D.C. 1981) (good faith); Sedco Int'l, S.A. v. Cory, 683 F.2d 1201, 1206 (8th Cir.), *cert. denied*, 459 U.S. 1017 (1982) (estoppel or equitable reliance); Russell v. Curtin Matheson Scientific, Inc., 493 F. Supp. 456, 458 (S.D. Tex. 1980) (equitable tolling of the statute of limitations); Pitney-Bowes, Inc. v. Mestre, 86 F.R.D. 444, 447 (S.D. Fla. 1980) (intent of the parties to a contract).

228. *See* Sealy v. Guntal & Co., 1998 U.S. Dist. LEXIS 15654 (S.D.N.Y. Oct. 7,

defense may also waive the attorney's work product privilege for the document relied upon.[229] Similarly, when the party holding the privilege seeks to demonstrate good-faith reliance on the advice of counsel, the issue of whether counsel was fully informed of all relevant facts, unbiased, and competent may also become relevant.[230] In this situation, the mental processes of counsel would then become a discoverable issue in the case.[231]

c. Testimony. Generally, a client may testify in his or her own behalf without waiving the attorney-client privilege.[232] But where the client testifies regarding the substance of privileged communications, or fails to object to such testimony by others, the privilege is waived.[233]

1998) (reliance for affirmative defense upon an internal corporate investigation of plaintiff's allegations of discrimination waives attorney-client privilege with respect to communications associated with the investigation); Panter v. Marshall Field & Co., 80 F.R.D. 718, 721-23 (N.D. Ill. 1978); Refuse & Environmental Sys. v. Industrial Servs. of Am., 120 F.R.D. 8, 11 (D. Mass. 1988); SEC v. Forma, 117 F.R.D. 516, 523 (S.D.N.Y. 1987); Handgards, Inc. v. Johnson & Johnson, 413 F. Supp. 926, 929 (N.D. Cal. 1976); Garfinkle v. Arcata Nat'l Corp., 64 F.R.D. 688, 689 (S.D.N.Y. 1974).

229. Panter, 80 F.R.D. at 721-22.

230. Axler v. Scientific Ecology Group, Inc., et al., 196 F.R.D. 210, 212 (D. Mass. 2000) (in order to pursue its statute of limitations defense, "defendants are entitled to discovery from plaintiffs' counsel concerning what investigation they conducted, what information they received, and when they received it"); Durkin v. Shields (*In re* Imperial Corp. of America), 179 F.R.D. 286, 290 (S.D. Cal. 1998) ("party alleging reliance on his attorney's investigation to discover certain causes of action and overcome the statute of limitations bar, impliedly waived the attorney-client privilege and work-product protection that might apply regarding the investigation and its findings and conclusions"); Draney v. Wilson, 592 F. Supp. 9, 11 (D. Ariz. 1984); SEC v. Scott, 565 F. Supp. 1513, 1534 (S.D.N.Y. 1983), *aff'd*, 734 F.2d 118 (2d Cir. 1984); United States v. Stirling, 571 F.2d 708, 735 (2d Cir.), *cert. denied*, 439 U.S. 824 (1978).

231. Handgards, Inc., 413 F. Supp. at 932 ("While an attorney's private thoughts are most certainly deserving of special protections, I believe that the concern for a lawyer's privacy must give way when the advice of counsel is directly at issue.").

232. *See* People v. Shapiro, 306 N.Y. 453, 459, 126 N.E.2d 559, 562 (1955).

233. *See, e.g.,* IMC Chemicals, Inc. v. Niro Inc., 2000 WL 1466495, at *16 (D. Kan. July 19, 2000) ("When a party or its attorney discloses privileged communications upon deposition, fairness generally dictates that the privilege is waived as to all communications related to the disclosed matters."); Ampa Ltd. v. Kentfield

Using a privileged document to refresh the recollection of a witness may present special problems. Federal Rule of Evidence 612 provides, in pertinent part:

> [I]f a witness uses a writing to refresh memory for the purpose of testifying, either –
> (1) while testifying, or
> (2) before testifying,
> if the court in its discretion determines it is necessary in the interests of justice, an adverse party is entitled to have the writing produced at the hearing, to inspect it, to cross-examine the witness thereon, and to introduce in evidence those portions which relate to the testimony of the witness.

The rule applies not only to witnesses at trial, but also to testimony at a deposition.[234]

Some courts have assumed that any material consulted by a witness prior to testifying loses its privileged status—i.e., that it is *always* necessary, "in the interests of justice," to require production.[235] Ac-

---

Capital LLC, et al., 2000 WL 1156860 (S.D.N.Y. Aug. 16, 2000) (where counsel marked a document as an exhibit and asked a question about it during deposition, privilege was waived). United States v. Skeddle, 989 F. Supp 905, 915-16 (N.D. Ohio 1997) (where the corporation's lawyer testified as to communications with management concerning negotiations with respect to outsourcing the company's computer department, sale of certain gas wells, and an agreement to lease robotics equipment, the attorney-client privilege was waived as to communications regarding those transactions; the in-house counsel's testimony, however, did not waive the attorney-client privilege as to communications during the corporation's internal investigations into the alleged wrongdoing in connection with such underlying transactions); Ferrignon v. Bergen Brunswig Corp., 77 F.R.D. 455, 460 (N.D. Cal. 1978); United States v. Gurtner, 474 F.2d 297, 299 (9th Cir. 1973).

234. *See, e.g.*, S & A Painting Co. v. O.W.B. Corp., 103 F.R.D. 407, 409 (W.D. Pa. 1984); IMC Chemicals, Inc., 2000 WL 1466495, at *16 (D. Kan. July 19, 2000); Nutramax Laboratories, Inc. v. Twin Laboratories Inc. et al., 183 F.R.D. 458, 467 (D. Md. 1998) (applying Federal Rule of Evidence 612 in the context of a deposition).

235. *See, e.g.*, Marshall v. United States Postal Serv., 88 F.R.D. 348, 350 (D.D.C. 1980) ("once a document is used to refresh the recollection of a witness, privileges as to that document have been waived"); Wheeling-Pittsburgh Steel v. Underwriters Labs., 81 F.R.D. 8, 9 (N.D. Ill. 1978); Berkey Photo, Inc. v. Eastman Kodak Co.,

ceptance of an unqualified rule requiring production whenever a privileged document has been used to refresh recollection, however, has not been universal. A leading commentator has criticized as theoretically unsound a rule imputing waiver whenever a witness uses a privileged document to refresh his recollection.[236]

Some courts have adopted a middle course, holding that the discoverability of privileged material used before testifying is subject to the discretion of the court.[237] Even where privileged information is used to refresh recollection while testifying, the waiver may be limited to only those documents actually used to refresh.[238]

d. Inadvertent Disclosure. Clients traditionally bear the risk of inadvertent disclosure of communications because "the means of preserving secrecy of communication are entirely in the client's hands and since the privilege is a derogation from the general testimonial duty and should be strictly construed."[239] Some courts have held that

---

74 F.R.D. 613, 616 (S.D.N.Y. 1977); R.J. Hereley & Son Co. v. Stotler & Co., 87 F.R.D. 358, 359 (N.D. Ill. 1980); Bailey v. Meister Brau, Inc. 57 F.R.D. 11, 13 (N.D. Ill. 1972); *see also* James Julian, Inc. v. Raytheon Co., 93 F.R.D. 138, 145 (D. Del. 1982). *But see* Joseph Schlitz Brewing Co. v. Muller & Phipps (Hawaii), Ltd., 85 F.R.D. 118, 120 (W.D. Mo. 1980) (where deponent testified that he had "looked at" his correspondence file of 39 documents prior to testifying, court held that actual use of any of the documents had not been established to invoke Rule 612).

236. 4 J. WEINSTEIN & M. BERGER, WEINSTEIN'S EVIDENCE 612(04) (1997).

237. *See, e.g.*, Smith & Wesson v. United States, 782 F.2d 1074, 1083 (1st Cir. 1986) (no abuse of discretion where trial court ruled that disclosure of an unredacted copy of a report was not necessary "in the interests of justice" (citing United States v. Massachusetts Maritime Academy, 762 F.2d 142, 157 (1st Cir. 1985)); Derderian v. Polaroid Corp., 121 F.R.D. 13, 15 (D. Mass. 1988) (personal notes kept by employment discrimination plaintiff were protected from discovery by attorney-client privilege and work-product doctrine, even though the employee reviewed the notes before the deposition, absent showing that disclosure of the notes was necessary in the interests of justice; employer had full access to agents or employees in order to obtain evidence about meetings or communications allegedly recorded in notes, employer had knowledge of the dispute since its inception, and the lapse of time was not great between making of the notes and plaintiff's deposition).

238. *See, e.g.*, S & A Painting Co., 103 F.R.D. at 409.

239. 8 WIGMORE, EVIDENCE § 2326.

the privilege is destroyed whenever communications have been intercepted, i.e., by eavesdroppers, or where privileged documents have been lost or stolen.[240] This approach has been criticized, and the current trend is to examine whether the client took reasonable precautions to ensure the confidentiality of the communications.[241]

The courts are in agreement that the privilege may be lost when otherwise privileged documents are accessible to third persons,[242] or where they are indiscriminately mingled with other documents.[243] Courts are split on what inadvertent acts and circumstances constitute a "waiver" of the privilege.

Some federal courts follow the "Wigmore rule": "the risk of insufficient precautions [against unintended disclosure of privileged material] is upon the client," and "[t]here is always the objective consideration that when [a privileged person's] conduct touches a certain point of disclosure, fairness requires that his immunity shall cease whether he intended that result or not."[244] These courts have held that the simple act of disclosure waives the privilege.[245]

---

240. *See, e.g.*, Suburban Sew 'n Sweep, Inc. v. Swiss Bernina, Inc., 914 F.R.D. 254, 258 (N.D. Ill. 1981) (citing cases).

241. *See* Mendenhall, 531 F. Supp. at 955 n.8; Kenyatta v. Kelly, 375 F. Supp. 1175, 1177 (E.D. Pa. 1974) (privilege could still be asserted despite fact that stolen documents had been copied and widely disseminated). In *United States v. Zolin*, 309 F.2d 1411, 1417 (9th Cir. 1987), *aff'd in part, vacated in part*, 109 S. Ct. 2619 (1989), the court held that, where an agent of the holder of the privilege erroneously discloses privileged material, such disclosure will not amount to a waiver of the privilege; *but see* Transonic Systems, Inc. v. Non-Invasive Medical Tech., 192 F.R.D. 710, 715-16 (D. Utah 2000) (stating that the voluntary production, during discovery, of a document labeled "attorneys' eyes only" did not constitute inadvertent disclosure).

242. *See, e.g.*, *In re* Victor, 422 F. Supp. 475, 476 (S.D.N.Y. 1976) (documents found in public hallway outside lawyer's office).

243. *See In re* Horowitz, 482 F.2d 72, 81-82 (2d Cir.), *cert. denied*, 414 U.S. 867 (1973). *But see* James Julian, Inc., 93 F.R.D. at 142 (filing of documents in general file did not destroy privilege because it was impractical to have separate files and screen each employee requiring access).

244. 8 WIGMORE, EVIDENCE §§ 2325, 2327 (McNaughton, *rev.* 1961).

245. *See, e.g.*, *In re* Grand Jury Investigation of Ocean Transp., 604 F.2d 672, 674-75 (D.C. Cir.), *cert. denied*, 444 U.S. 915 (1979); Underwater Storage, Inc. v. U.S. Rubber Co., 314 F. Supp. 546, 549 (D.D.C. 1970) (document inadvertently produced pursuant to consent order "entered the public domain" and destroyed basis for privilege); Thomas v. Pansy Ellen Prods., 672 F. Supp. 237, 243 (W.D.N.C.

Other courts have held that an evidentiary privilege is not waived absent some intention to waive.[246] For example, in *Manufacturers & Traders Trust Co. v. Servotronics, Inc.*,[247] the New York Appellate Division expressly rejected the Wigmore rule, noting that no New York state court had previously addressed the question of waiver with respect to inadvertent disclosure of documents. The court stated that "intent must be the primary component of any waiver test," but held that a party would be required to demonstrate its intent by objective evidence.[248] In the case before it, the court found that the party asserting the privilege demonstrated its intent to keep the documents in question confidential, despite the documents' inadvertent disclosure during discovery. Reasonable precautions had been taken to ensure their confidentiality, including, inter alia, the precaution of having qualified personnel screen the documents before producing them.[249] One of the factors used by the *Servotronics* court to assess whether an inadvertent disclosure would waive the attorney-client privilege was whether the client promptly objected to the disclosure after discovering it, the court noting that "[a]n objection entered promptly upon learning of a disclosure suggests that a genuine intent to preserve confidentiality existed before disclosure."[250] Other courts have also declined to find waiver when the disclosure was found to be "inadvertent" under the circumstances.[251]

1987) ("voluntary production, even where inadvertent, effects a waiver of privilege," quoting *Underwater Storage*); *accord* Duplan Corp., 397 F. Supp. at 1162.

246. *See, e.g.*, Dunn Chem. Co. v. Sybron Corp., 1975-2 Trade Cas. (CCH) 160, 561, at 67, 463 (S.D.N.Y.); Connecticut Mut. Life Ins. Co. v. Shields, 18 F.R.D. 448, 451 (S.D.N.Y. 1955).

247. 132 A.D.2d 392, 522 N.Y.S.2d 999 (4th Dep't 1987).

248. 132 A.D.2d at 399.

249. *Id.; see* Bras v. Atlas Constr. Corp., 153 A.D.2d 914, 915, 545 N.Y.S.2d 723, 724 (2d Dep't 1989) (finding privilege waived where screening procedure utilized by attorney prior to production of documents was "not reasonably designed or executed so as to prevent the inadvertent disclosure").

250. Manufacturers & Traders Trust Co., 132 A.D.2d at 400.

251. *See* United States v. United Tech. Corp., 979 F. Supp 108, 116 (D. Conn. 1997) (setting forth five factors to consider when determining whether inadvertent waiver constituted an irrevocable waiver of the attorney-client privilege and holding that no waiver had occurred where the company had "made a reasonable effort to sift through a huge volume of documents" to withhold privileged docu-

Even where the initial production may have been inadvertent, a delay in claiming the privilege can result in a waiver.[252] While a single act of disclosure may not destroy the privilege, that disclosure may compromise a client's position should there be an inadvertent disclosure in the future.[253]

e. Non-Waiver Stipulations. The voluntary surrender of potentially privileged documents in exchange for a non-waiver stipulation may not be consistent with an intent to preserve properly the confidentiality of those documents. Several courts have held that the voluntary disclosure of documents pursuant to a non-waiver agreement in a previous litigation effected a waiver of the attorney-client privilege. In *Chubb Integrated Systems v. National Bank*,[254] the court characterized this agreement as "merely a contract between two parties to refrain from raising the issue of waiver or from otherwise utilizing the information disclosed."[255] Noting that "[c]onfidentiality is the dispositive factor in deciding whether a communication is privileged,"[256] the court rejected the argument that the privilege should still

---

ments; only one privileged document was inadvertently disclosed; the company had listed the document on its privilege log; and the company immediately demanded the document's return); Lois Sportswear, U.S.A., Inc. v. Levi Strauss & Co., 104 F.R.D. 103, 105 (S.D.N.Y. 1985), *aff'd*, 799 F.2d 867 (2d Cir. 1986) (no waiver when 22 documents out of 16,000 were inadvertently disclosed); Standard Chartered Bank v. Ayala Int'l Holdings, 111 F.R.D. 76, 85 (S.D.N.Y. 1986) (same, regarding one sentence in a five-page document produced among over 1,000 pages and where counsel took care to withhold all other allegedly privileged documents); Eisenberg v. Gagnon, 766 F.2d 770, 778 (3d Cir.), *cert. denied*, 474 U.S. 946 (1985) (the privilege was not waived when information came into the hands of opposing counsel where the party divulging the information believed the disclosure to be in camera).

252. Baxter Travenol Labs. v. Abbott Labs., 117 F.R.D. 119, 121 (N.D. Ill. 1987) (unfair and unrealistic to uphold the privilege where documents have been examined and used by the opposing party prior to assertion of the privilege); *In re* Grand Jury Investigation of Ocean Transp., 604 F.2d at 674-75.

253. *See* Eigenheim Bank v. Halpern, 598 F. Supp. 988, 991-92 (S.D.N.Y. 1984) (after second "inadvertent" disclosure, privilege found waived due to inadequate procedures followed to maintain confidentiality of documents).

254. 103 F.R.D. 52 (D.D.C. 1984).

255. *Id.* at 67-68.

256. *Id.* at 67.

attach, inasmuch as "[p]laintiff has no genuine claim of confidentiality to the documents it produced" in the previous litigation.[257]

Even a litigant who discloses documents to its adversary pursuant to a court-ordered non-waiver stipulation may find that another court will refuse to accept the inadvertent waiver position adopted by the previous judge. In *United States v. International Business Machines Corp.*,[258] the government challenged IBM's claim of privilege, arguing that IBM had waived any privilege it might have claimed by previously disclosing the documents in question to the Control Data Corporation in other antitrust litigation in Minnesota.[259] The New York court ordered IBM to produce the documents, despite IBM's arguments that (1) the earlier disclosure was made under compulsion of discovery orders issued by the Minnesota district court, (2) the documents were produced under what IBM believed to be a non-waiver order expressly protecting the right of its privilege in the documents, and (3) any disclosure of privileged information was "inadvertent."[260]

By contrast, in *Transamerica Computer Co. v. International Business Machines Corp.*,[261] the court affirmed the district court's denial of the plaintiff's motion to compel IBM to disclose those very same documents produced to Control Data in the Minnesota litigation. The *Transamerica* court characterized IBM's court-ordered production in Minnesota as "compelled," not voluntary, and found that no waiver had occurred.[262]

---

257. *Id.* at 68; *see also* Republic of Philippines v. Westinghouse Electric Corp., 132 F.R.D. 384, 390 (D.N.J. 1998) ("once information is disclosed to an adversary . . . a future adversary in a related proceeding may have access to the information"); Republic Gear Co. v. Borg-Warner Corp., 381 F.2d 551, 558 n.5 (2d Cir. 1967) (an "estoppel certificate" offered by plaintiff agreeing not to use any privileged information against any of the nonparty foreign clients was characterized as "illusory," insofar as the court might not have the jurisdiction to interfere in other future litigation).

258. 60 F.R.D. 658 (S.D.N.Y.), *appeal dismissed*, 493 F.2d 112 (2d Cir. 1973), *appeal dismissed and cert. denied*, 416 U.S. 976 (1974).

259. *See* United States v. International Bus. Mach. Corp., 471 F.2d 507, 508-11 (2d Cir. 1972), *rev'd on jurisdictional grounds*, 480 F.2d 293 (2d Cir. 1973) (en banc), *cert. denied*, 416 U.S. 979, 980 (1974).

260. *See* Pretrial Order No. 5, *quoted in* 471 F.2d at 508.

261. 573 F.2d 646 (9th Cir. 1978).

262. *Id.* at 651.

f. Joint Defense Agreements. Communication between joint defendants and their respective counsel does not necessarily result in loss of the attorney-client or work product privileges merely by reason of the presence of those persons.[263] In a "proper case," the privilege may apply to joint consultations even where the parties are not immediately anticipating litigation.[264] Under the joint defense doctrine, when two or more parties have a common interest, communications by one party to a lawyer in the presence of the other party are not discoverable by third parties; however, in a subsequent dispute between the two parties, either can compel the disclosure of the confidential communications that passed between them and their respective lawyers.[265]

263. United States v. McPartlin, 595 F.2d 1321, 1336-37 (7th Cir.) *cert. denied*, 444 U.S. 833 (1979); Hunydee v. United States, 355 F.2d 183, 185 (9th Cir. 1965); Continental Oil Co. v. United States, 330 F.2d 347, 350 (9th Cir. 1964); *see also* United States v. United Tech. Corp., 979 F. Supp. 108, 111-12 (D. Conn. 1997) (holding that "the attorney-client privilege, as extended by the common interest rule, protects from disclosure" all of the documents containing the legal advice of counsel to members of a consortium) (collecting cases); IBJ Whitehall Bank & Trust Co. v. Cory & Associates, Inc., 1999 WL 617842, at *3 (N.D. Ill. Aug. 12, 1999); United States v. Henke, 222 F.3d 633, 637 (9th Cir. 2000). *See also* discussion of the requirement that communications be confidential in order for the attorney-client privilege to apply, Part III.C.5, *supra*.

264. United States v. Furst, 886 F.2d 558, 578 (3d Cir. 1989), *cert. denied*, 493 U.S. 1662 (1990); United Coal Cus. v. Powell Constr. Co., 839 F.2d 958, 965 (3d Cir. 1988); SCM Corp., 70 F.R.D. at 513 (dicta) (discussions among joint venturers negotiating terms among themselves were not protected, but privilege might apply to protect discussions aimed at exploiting common interest in patents); *see also* Burlington Indus., 65 F.R.D. at 43-45 (privilege applied to confidences shared among joint licensors of patents) (citing cases). More than one court has held that the privilege applies only to an identical legal, not commercial, interest. *See* Sneider, 91 F.R.D. at 8; *In re* Eastern Transmission Corp., 1990 WL 139403, at *2 (E.D.Pa. Sept. 19, 1990).

265. *See* Securities Investor Protection Corp. v. Stratton Oakmont, Inc., 213 B.R. 433, 439 (S.D.N.Y. Bankr. 1997) (in connection with an action by the SEC, a brokerage firm and its individual officers who were represented by counsel separate from the broker's counsel entered into a joint defense agreement and exchanged information protected by the attorney-client and work product privileges; the bankruptcy court held that in the liquidation proceedings of the broker, the trustee became an adversary to the individual officers and the privilege was waived as to material previously exchanged under the joint defense agreement); Medcom Holding Co. v. Baxter Travenol Labs., 698 F. Supp. 841, 844 (N.D. Ill.1988); McCORMICK, EVIDENCE § 91, at 190-91 (Cleary ed., 1972). Similarly, a lawyer who represents two parties with respect to a single matter may not assert the

A corporation and its counsel conducting the internal investigation should not assume automatically that a "joint defense" privilege will protect communications with the alleged wrongdoers or their counsel. On the contrary, the actual or potential conflicts of interest between the corporation and these persons may preclude the assertion of a "common interest."

2. Waiver of the Work-Product Doctrine

Like the attorney-client privilege, work product protection can be waived.[266] However, because protecting client confidences is not the primary purpose of the work-product doctrine, disclosures to a third party do not automatically waive the protection. Rather, the general test is whether the materials at issue have been disclosed in a manner inconsistent with maintaining their secrecy vís-a-vìs the adversary.[267]

---

privilege in a later dispute between the clients. Quintel Corp., J.N.V. v. Citibank, N.A., 567 F. Supp. 1357, 1364 (S.D.N.Y. 1983).

266. *See, e.g.*, United States v. Nobles, 422 U.S. 225, 239 (1975) (protection waived as to portion of investigator's report when defense decided to present him as witness); Shields v. Sturm, Ruger & Co., 864 F.2d 379, 382 (5th Cir. 1989) (work product protection waived when lawyer requests the witness to disclose the information, or when the lawyer discloses the information to the court voluntarily or makes no objection when it is offered (citing Fox v. Taylor Diving & Salvage Co., 694 F.2d 1349, 1356 (5th Cir. 1983)); Grumman Aerospace Corp. v. Titanium Metals Corp., 91 F.R.D. 84, 89 (E.D.N.Y. 1981) (disclosure of report to defendant, although in hopes of settlement, waived work product protection); Electronic Memories & Magnetics Corp. v. Control Data Corp., 20 Fed. R. Serv. 2d 705, 706 (N.D. Ill. 1975) (work product waived where attorney himself is witness).

267. *See, e.g., In re* Steinhardt Partners, 9 F.3d at 236 (refusing to adopt "a *per se* rule that all voluntary disclosures to the government waive work product protection; crafting rules relating to privilege in matters of governmental investigations must be done on a case-by-case basis"); Dennis J. Block & Jonathan M. Hoff, *Selective Waiver of Attorney-Client Privilege*, 211 N.Y.L.J. 96, 5 col. 1 (1994) (collecting cases in which courts appear prepared to protect privileged information from disclosure to private litigants where the disclosure to the government is conditioned upon an express agreement of confidentiality or where the corporation can articulate some shared investigatory common interest with the government); *see also* United States v. American Tel. & Tel. Co., 642 F.2d 1285, 1299 (D.C. Cir. 1980) (no waiver by producing document to government because government was not an adversary in that particular litigation); Peralta v. Cendant Corp., 190 F.R.D. 38, 40 (D. Conn. 1999) (communication with defendant's counsel relating to "former employee's conduct or knowledge" during his or her employment is privileged); Gucci America, Inc. v. Costco Cos., 2000 WL 60209, at *4

The broad subject matter waiver of the attorney-client privilege, requiring the production of all related privileged materials, may not be fully applicable to the work-product doctrine. More than one court has declined to impose a broad subject matter waiver in the context of an inadvertent waiver relating to opinion work product.[268] Another court has held that the voluntary disclosure of factual work product resulted in a subject matter waiver, but, as to opinion work product, the waiver would be limited only to the documents actually disclosed.[269]

Finally, under Federal Rule of Evidence 612, work product protection may be waived where otherwise protected material is used to refresh a witness's recollection and disclosure is necessary "in the interests of justice."[270]

B. *The Crime/Fraud Exception*

Another important issue that arises in connection with internal in-

---

(S.D.N.Y. Jan. 24, 2000) (fact that attorney discussed interview with employees does not constitute waiver because "it did not substantially increase the likelihood that [plaintiff] would secure the [privileged] information"); B.C.F. Oil Refining Inc. v. Consolidated Edison Co., 168 F.R.D. 161 (S.D.N.Y. 1996) (sending a written transcript of internal investigation interview to employee interviewed does not constitute waiver). *In re* International Sys. & Controls Corp. Sec. Litig., 91 F.R.D. 552, 556 (S.D. Tex. 1981), *vacated on other grounds*, 693 F.2d 1235 (5th Cir. 1982); Burlington Indus., 65 F.R.D. at 46.

268. *See* Duplan Corp., 540 F.2d at 1222-23 (court noting the "harsh results" of applying the concept to Rule 26(b)(3), including the reluctance of lawyers to produce work product, especially where opinion work product was involved and the waiver was inadvertent); *In re* United Mine Workers of Am. Employee Benefit Plans Litig., 159 F.R.D. 307, 310-12 n.2 (D.D.C. 1994); Corp. for Public Broadcasting v. American Auto Centennial Comm., 1999 WL 1815561, at *2 (D.D.C. Feb. 2, 1999) (documents "outside the scope of the subject matter" remain privileged and are not subject to disclosure).

269. *In re* Martin Marietta Corp., 856 F.2d at 624-26.

270. *See, e.g.*, James Julian, Inc., 93 F.R.D. at 145-46; Bailey v. Meister Brau, Inc., 57 F.R.D. 11, 13 (N.D. Ill. 1972); Berkey Photo, Inc., 74 F.R.D. at 616; *In re* Comair Air Disaster Litig., 100 F.R.D. 350, 353 (E.D. Ky. 1983) (where material is used to refresh recollection, "[FED R. EVID.] 612 weighs the balance in favor of finding that the 'substantial need' exists [under FED. R. CIV. P. 26(b)(3)], because of the policy in favor of effective cross-examination"). *But see* Bogosian v. Gulf Oil Corp., 738 F.2d 587, 595 n.3 (3d Cir. 1984) ("Rule 612...does not displace the protections of FED. R. CIV P. 26(b)(3)," suggesting that Rule 612 should be construed narrowly in order to respect the protections of work product material embodied in Rule 26(b)(3)).

vestigations is whether it may later be alleged that the attorney-client privilege or the work-product doctrine is pierced by the crime/fraud exception. The crime/fraud exception to the attorney-client privilege and the work-product doctrine allows discovery of materials that would otherwise be protected where the communication or document involves the furtherance of criminal or fraudulent activity. Application of this exception to the two doctrines requires several distinctions.

1. Application to the Attorney-Client Privilege

The attorney-client privilege does not protect communications "made in furtherance of contemplated or ongoing criminal or fraudulent conduct."[271] The crime or fraud need not have occurred for this exception to apply; it need only have been the objective of the client's communication.[272] The exception will apply even if the lawyer is unaware that advice is sought in furtherance of such an improper purpose.[273]

Mere allegations of fraud are not sufficient to pierce the privilege.[274] Corporate documents are not discoverable under the crime/fraud exception merely upon a showing that the client corporation communicated with counsel while the client was engaged in criminal activity. Rather, the party seeking discovery must establish probable cause to believe that the communication was intended, in some way, to facilitate or conceal the criminal activity.[275]

The courts apply a two-prong test to establish whether the crime/fraud exception applies. First, there must be a prima facie showing that the client was engaged in or planning criminal or fraudulent activities when the advice of counsel was sought, or that the client committed a fraud or crime subsequent to obtaining counsel's advice.[276] Second, there

---

271. *In re* Grand Jury Subpoena Duces Tecum Dated Sept. 15, 1983, 731 F.2d 1032, 1038 (2d Cir. 1984); *see also In re* John Doe Corp., 675 F.2d 482, 491-92 (2d Cir. 1982).

272. *In re* Grand Jury Subpoena, 731 F.2d at 1039.

273. *Id.*; United States v. Laurins, 857 F.2d 529, 540 (9th Cir. 1988), *cert. denied*, 109 S. Ct. 3215 (1989).

274. Ward v. Succession of Freeman, 854 F.2d 780, 790 (5th Cir. 1988), *cert. denied*, 109 S. Ct. 2064 (1989).

275. *In re* Grand Jury Subpoenas Duces Tecum (Corp. Grand Jury Witness), 798 F.2d 32, 34 (2d Cir. 1986).

276. *In re* Grand Jury Investigation (Schroeder), 842 F.2d 1223, 1226 (11th Cir. 1987).

must be a showing that the lawyer's assistance was obtained in furtherance of the criminal or fraudulent act, or was closely related to it.[277]

In *United States v. Zolin*,[278] the Supreme Court rejected a long line
of cases requiring that a prima facie showing of the existence of the
crime/fraud exception be established by evidence independent of the
contested communication. The Court also held that in appropriate circumstances, in camera review of allegedly privileged attorney-client
communications may be used to determine whether the communications fall within the crime/fraud exception.[279] Such in camera review is
not automatic; before a district court may engage in in camera review at
the request of the party opposing the privilege, that party must present
evidence sufficient to support a reasonable belief that the review may
reveal evidence that establishes the exception's applicability.[280] The party
opposing the privilege may use any relevant nonprivileged evidence,
lawfully obtained, to counter that threshold showing, even if its evidence is not "independent" of the contested communications.[281]

2. Application to the Work-Product Doctrine

The crime/fraud exception to the attorney-client privilege also
applies to the work-product doctrine.[282] The crime/fraud exception
applies both to factual work product and to opinion work product,[283]
but a distinction between the two types of work product is made for
purposes of discovery under the crime/fraud exception.

---

277. *Id.*

278. 491 U.S. 554 (1989).

279. *Id.* at 574.

280. *Id.* at 574-75; *see also* United States v. Martin Marietta Corp., 886 F. Supp.
1243, 1246-47 (D. Md. 1995); IMC Chemicals Inc. v. Niro Inc., 2000 WL 1466495,
at *26 (D. Kan. July 19, 2000); First Union Nat'l Bank of Fla. v. Whitener, 715 So.
2d 979, 984 (Fla. Dist. Ct. App., June 12, 1998).

281. Zolin, 491 U.S. at 574.

282. *See, e.g., In re* International Sys. & Controls Corp. Sec. Litig., 693 F.2d
1235, 1242 (5th Cir. 1982); *In re* Sealed Case, 676 F.2d 793, 812 (D.C. Cir. 1982);
In re John Doe Corp., 675 F.2d 482, 489 (2d Cir. 1982); *In re* Grand Jury Proceed-
ings (FMC Corp.), 604 F.2d 798, 802-03 (3d Cir. 1979); Hercules, Inc. v. Exxon
Corp., 434 F. Supp. 136, 155 (D. Del. 1977); Olson v. Accessory Controls and
Equipment Corp., 757 A.2d 14, 30, 254 Conn. 145, 173 (Conn. 1999).

283. *See In re* Doe, 662 F.2d 1073, 1081 (4th Cir. 1981), *cert. denied*, 455 U.S.
1000 (1982); *see also In re* Sealed Case, 676 F.2d 793, 311 (D.C. Cir. 1982) (un-

For factual work product, as with the attorney-client privilege, the attorney's knowledge of the client's activities or motive is irrelevant, and ongoing criminal or fraudulent activity by the client results in a waiver of work product protection for facts recorded by the lawyer.[284] This is a much lesser showing than is required for discovery of opinion work product.

To obtain discovery of opinion work product, the party seeking discovery must establish that (1) the client was engaged in or planning a criminal or fraudulent scheme when seeking the advice of counsel to further the scheme, and (2) the documents containing the lawyer's opinion work product must bear a close relationship to the client's existing or future scheme to commit a crime.[285] In cases where the fraud is that of the client, the retention of the immunity to protect the lawyer's privacy may be appropriate,[286] and the party seeking discovery of the lawyer's mental impressions or other opinion work product may be required to make a prima facie showing that the lawyer knowingly participated in the crime or fraud.[287] However, some courts hold that a guilty client should not be able to assert the work product immunity of an innocent lawyer.[288] Nor should the lawyer be permitted to invoke the immunity to cover the lawyer's own crime or fraud.[289]

---

necessary to show extraordinary necessity when crime/fraud exception being applied); Chaudhry v. Gallerizzo, 174 F.3d 394, 406 (4th Cir. 1999).

284. *In re* Antitrust Grand Jury (Advance Publication), 305 F.2d 155, 163 (6th Cir. 1986).

285. *See In re* Murphy, 560 F.2d 326, 338 (8th Cir. 1977); *In re* Sealed Case, 676 F.2d at 814-15; *In re* Grand Jury Proceedings (FMC Corp.), 604 F.2d at 803; *Hercules, Inc.*, 434 F. Supp. at 155-56.

286. *See In re* Grand Jury Proceedings, 604 F.2d 795, 801 (D.C. Cir. 1981); *In re* Special Sept. 1978 Grand Jury (II), 640 F.2d 49, 63 (7th Cir. 1980).

287. *In re* International Sys. & Controls Corp. Sec. Litig., 91 F.R.D. 552, 559-60 (S.D. Tex. 1981), *vacated on other grounds*, 693 F.2d 1235 (5th Cir. 1982).

288. *See In re* Sealed Case, 676 F.2d at 812.

289. *See In re* Doe, 662 F.2d 1073, 1078 (4th Cir. 1981), *cert. denied*, 455 U.S. 1000 (1982). Where the very act of litigating is alleged to be in furtherance of a fraud, the party seeking disclosure of material subject to the work product privilege, under the crime-fraud exception, must show probable cause that the litigation or an aspect thereof had little or no legal or factual basis and was carried on substantially for the purpose of furthering the crime or fraud. *See In re* Richard Roe, Inc., 168 F.3d 69, 71 (1999).

3. Application to Internal Corporate Investigations

An internal investigation frequently deals with underlying conduct that may be characterized as criminal or fraudulent. In addition, one aspect of an internal investigation may be to determine whether, and to what extent, the underlying conduct must be disclosed, either publicly or to an adversely affected third party, a determination that itself carries overtones of ongoing fraudulent conduct. Accordingly, investigative counsel must remain vigilant concerning the client's conduct and apparent intentions to ensure that counsel does not become enmeshed in criminal or fraudulent conduct of the client and thereby jeopardize the attorney-client privilege and work-product doctrine (or suffer more serious consequences).

C. *Shareholder Litigation*

Public disclosure of the existence of an internal corporate investigation, or the results of such an investigation, frequently gives rise to shareholder litigation. Ironically, it is this predictable consequence of investigative activity that renders the attorney-client privilege most vulnerable. This weakness is created by the *Garner* rule,[290] pursuant to which otherwise privileged communications between counsel and their corporate clients may be discovered by plaintiffs in shareholder actions upon a showing of good cause. The *Garner* rule rests on the principle that a corporation owes a fiduciary duty to its shareholders and therefore should not be allowed to assert the attorney-client privilege against its "beneficiaries."[291]

The court in *Garner* enumerated certain "indicia" of good cause:

> [1] the number of shareholders [calling for the information] and the percentage of stock they represent; [2] the bona fides of the shareholders; [3] the nature of [the] claim and whether

---

290. *See* Garner v. Wolfinbarger, 430 F.2d 1093 (5th Cir. 1970), *cert. denied*, 401 U.S. 974 (1971).

291. *Id.* at 1101-02. The *Garner* rule is not limited to the corporate arena; it has been applied in various fiduciary relationships. *See, e.g.,* Aquinaga v. John Morrell & Co., 112 F.R.D. 671, 680-82 (D. Kan. 1986) (*Garner* doctrine applied to union members and officers); Quintel Corp. N.V. v. Citibank N.A., 567 F. Supp. 1357, 1363 (S.D.N.Y. 1983) (*Garner* rule applied to investment advisor in real estate transaction); Donovan v. Fitzsimmons, 90 F.R.D. 583, 586-87 (N.D. Ill. 1981) (*Garner* rationale applied to pension fund trustee).

it is obviously colorable; [4] the apparent necessity or desirability of the shareholders having the information and the availability of it from other sources; [5] whether, if the shareholders' claim is of wrongful action by the corporation, it is of action criminal, or illegal but not criminal, or of doubtful legality; [6] whether the communication related to past or to prospective actions; [7] whether the communication is advice concerning the litigation itself; [8] the extent to which the communication is identified versus the extent to which the shareholders are blindly fishing; and [9] the risk of revelation of trade secrets or other information in whose confidentiality the corporation has an interest for independent reasons.[292]

The *Garner* doctrine has been followed in numerous cases, although in most of these cases the courts denied the discovery sought on the ground that the plaintiff had failed to demonstrate good cause.[293] Some courts, however, have squarely rejected the *Garner* rule and held that there is "no extraordinary avenue . . . available to [shareholders] to pierce the [corporation's] privilege."[294]

The rationale for the *Garner* rule rests upon the "joint defense" doctrine,[295] and should thus be limited to derivative actions, where the interests of the corporation and its shareholders are theoretically the same. However, many courts have applied the *Garner* rule in shareholder class actions as well as derivative actions,[296] although the inter-

---

292. 430 F.2d at 1104.

293. *See, e.g.*, Cohen v. Uniroyal, Inc., 80 F.R.D. 480, 484-85 (E.D. Pa. 1978); *In re* Transocean Tender Offer Sec. Litig., 78 F.R.D. 692, 696-97 (N.D. Ill. 1978). *But see* Sandberg v. Virginia Bankshares, Inc., 979 F.2d 332, 351-54 (4th Cir. 1992) (plaintiffs did not show good cause); *In re* Bairnco Corp. Sec. Litig., 148 F.R.D. 91, 99 (S.D.N.Y. 1993); Quintel Corp., 567 F. Supp. at 1374 (plaintiff did show good cause).

294. *See* Milroy v. Hanson, 875 F. Supp. 646, 651-52 (D. Neb. 1995); Tail of the Pup, Inc. v. Webb, 528 So. 2d 506, 507 (Fla. Dist. Ct. App. 1988); Lefkowitz v. Duquesne Light Co., 1988 WL 169273, at *5-6 (W.D. Pa. June 14, 1988); Shirvani v. Capital Investing Corp., 112 F.R.D. 389, 391 (D. Conn. 1986). *See generally* D. Block & A. Prussin, *After* Upjohn, *the Garner Rule Still Creates Uncertainty in the Area of Corporate Attorney-Client Privilege*, 3 Bus. Advoc. 5 (Spring 1981).

295. *See* Part II.B.5, *supra*.

296. *See, e.g., In re* Transocean Tender Offer Sec. Litig., 78 F.R.D. 692, 696-97 (N.D. Ill. 1978); Bailey v. Meister Brau, Inc. 55 F.R.D. 211, 214 (N.D. Ill. 1972). *But*

ests of the plaintiff shareholder (sometimes a former shareholder) and the defendant corporation are unquestionably inconsistent.

Some courts have limited the *Garner* doctrine to discovery of the legal advice preceding the allegedly wrongful conduct, while protecting discussions between the corporation and its counsel after the alleged wrongdoing or in connection with subsequent litigation.[297] Since communications with investigative counsel normally occur in the period following the alleged wrongdoing, this line of cases should protect the investigative report from discovery under the *Garner* rule. Moreover, some courts have held that the *Garner* rule does not apply to materials protected by the work-product doctrine, because the rules for disclosure of work product are contained in the Federal Rules of Civil Procedure, which reject a good cause standard in favor of the substantial need/undue hardship test.[298]

The Sixth Circuit's decision in *In re Perrigo Co.*[299] addressed the issue of disclosure of an investigation report in parallel shareholder derivative and class actions. The report in *Perrigo* was prepared with the assistance of outside counsel after a four-month investigation undertaken following a demand by the shareholders in the derivative action that Perrigo sue certain officers and directors. The report concluded that maintenance of the derivative action was not in Perrigo's best interests.[300] A shareholder class action was filed alleging violations of the securities laws based on substantially the same facts and against the same defendants as alleged in the derivative action.[301]

Defendants moved to dismiss the derivative action pursuant to a Michigan statute that provides in relevant part that the court "shall dismiss a derivative proceeding if . . . the court finds that" "all disin-

---

see Weil v. Investment Indicators, Research & Mgmt., Inc., 647 F.2d 18, 23 (9th Cir. 1981) (holding that *Garner* rule was inapplicable to class-action suit by former shareholders).

297. *In re* LTV Securities Litigation, 89 F.R.D. at 606-08; Panter, 80 F.R.D. at 723-24.

298. *See In re* Celotex Corp., 196 B.R. 596, 600 n.3 (M.D. Fla. Bankr. 1996) ("*Garner* decision does not apply to material protected by the work-product doctrine"); *In re* International Systems & Controls Corp., 693 F.2d at 1240; *In re* Dayco Corp. Sec. Litig., 99 F.R.D. 616, 620-21 (S.D. Ohio 1983). *See* Part III.D. *supra*.

299. 128 F.3d 430 (6th Cir. 1997).

300. *Id.* at 433.

301. *Id.* at 432.

terested independent directors" "have made a determination in good faith after conducting a reasonable investigation . . . that the maintenance of the derivative proceeding is not in the best interests of the corporation" and "the plaintiff shall have the burden of proving that the determination was not made in good faith or that the investigation was not reasonable."[302] Perrigo did not use the report or disclose any of its contents in its motion to dismiss and claimed that the attorney-client and work product privileges protected the report from disclosure.[303]

The district court held that the derivative plaintiffs had demonstrated substantial need and undue hardship in obtaining the information in the report from other sources and compelled defendants to produce the report.[304] Specifically, because the derivative plaintiffs bear the burden under the Michigan statute to demonstrate that the independent directors' decision was not in good faith and the investigation was not reasonable, the derivative plaintiffs should be given access to the report.[305]

The district court held in the class action, however, that plaintiffs had not demonstrated a substantial need or undue hardship and thus were not entitled to the report.[306] The district court entered a protective order prohibiting disclosure of the report, but to the extent either party to the derivative action used any portion of the report in its papers "to induce the court's reliance," the report would become a part of the publicly available record.[307]

The Sixth Circuit upheld the district court's ruling that Perrigo would be compelled to produce the report to the derivative plaintiffs, but not to the class-action plaintiffs, because, "[a]s a matter of fairness and practicality, the derivative plaintiffs (unlike the class

---

302. MICH. COMP. LAWS § 450.1495.

303. *In re* Perrigo Co., 128 F.3d at 438.

304. Kearney v. Jandernoa, 949 F. Supp. 510, 511 (W.D. Mich. 1996).

305. *Id.*

306. Picard Chemical Inc. Plan v. Perrigo Co., 951 F. Supp. 679 (W.D. Mich. 1996); *but see* non-derivative cases in which courts have compelled disclosure of protected information, albeit with a heightened burden on plaintiffs to show the "good cause" required by *Garner*: Fausek v. White, 965 F.2d 126, 130 (6th Cir.), *cert. denied*, 506 U.S. 1034 (1992); Ward, 854 F.2d at 786; Miller, 1994 WL 698287, at *1. (S.D.N.Y. Dec. 13, 1994).

307. 951 F. Supp. at 691.

action plaintiffs) will need the report in order" to rebut the presumption that the independent directors acted in good faith.[308] With respect to the protective order, the Sixth Circuit upheld that portion of the district court's order that prohibited general disclosure of the report, on the ground that Perrigo had not "utterly waived its privilege" and that "fairness considerations simply do not require public disclosure."[309]

The Sixth Circuit granted mandamus, however, to reverse the district court's order allowing public disclosure of any portions of the report that might be filed in connection with court proceedings.[310] The Sixth Circuit observed that as a result of the district court's decisions, "Perrigo was faced with the choice of waiving the protection of the Report or withdrawing its motion to dismiss" in the derivative action, and held that "such a result would be contrary to Michigan law, which holds that 'it is not within the power of the court or any party to waive the privilege for [the client].'"[311] The district court was directed to conduct an in camera review of the report and "weigh the interests of Perrigo in maintaining its privilege" against the interests of the public to inspect judicial records before unsealing the report.[312]

The *Garner* doctrine poses potential problems for a corporation and its counsel in the context of an internal investigation. The matters giving rise to an investigation frequently engender both shareholder derivative actions on behalf of the corporation and shareholder class or individual actions against the corporation—often framed alternatively in the same complaint or joined in consolidated actions. At the same time, the corporation may be subject to civil or criminal claims by government authorities. In these circumstances, the preservation of the corporation's attorney-client privilege may be critical. *Perrigo* poses one solution, although not without flaws: that the internal investigation be kept under court-ordered seal.

---

308. 128 F.3d at 438.
309. *Id.* at 439.
310. *Id.* at 440.
311. *Id.* at 440, 438 (quotation omitted).
312. Perrigo, 128 F.3d at 438.

The Interview Process | 3

by Randall J. Turk*

---

* Randall J. Turk is a partner at Baker Botts, LLP in Washington, D.C.

I. INTRODUCTION

THE WITNESS INTERVIEW may be the most important task during an internal investigation. The significance of witness interviews is reflected throughout the investigation and post-investigation process:

- Witness interviews enable counsel to gather facts necessary to determine whether any wrongdoing has occurred.
- Witness interviews enable the lawyer to lay the foundation for the application to the internal investigation of the attorney-client privilege and the attorney work product doctrine.
- Throughout the interview process, counsel is able to meet and assess the credibility of the individuals who may be the most significant witnesses in any later litigation or government investigation.

Despite the importance of this process, lawyers too often treat witness interviews as a casual exercise not requiring substantial preparation or expertise. Too often, witnesses are interviewed by untrained personnel or before the lawyer has fully considered the purposes of the interview or even of the internal investigation, has determined the key factual and legal issues, or has reviewed the critical documents.

Indeed, one of the most common mistakes in internal investigations is to conduct all the witness interviews at the outset of the investigation before any groundwork has been performed. Although this course may be necessary when one or more witnesses receive a subpoena to give testimony within a short time period, it is usually preferable to postpone most of the critical or detailed witness interviews until after the key preliminary steps have been taken.

The singular importance of the witness interview cannot be overstated. The better prepared the lawyer is in advance of the interview, the more productive the interview will be.

II. ASSESSING THE PURPOSE OF THE INVESTIGATION

The nature of the interview process is determined by the purpose and timing of the internal investigation. Before scheduling witness interviews, a lawyer should ask several questions:

- What is the purpose of the internal investigation?
- What legal questions—including the assessment of both legal vulnerabilities and defenses—will be addressed at the end of the investigation?
- What are the potential uses of the investigation's findings and the investigator's work product?
- Is there a risk that certain inquiries could stir the interest of the company's potential adversaries and thus foster litigation adverse to the company?

The answers to these questions frequently will influence the pace, structure, content, and order of the witness interviews. For instance, witness interviews may well proceed in an entirely different order if they are being conducted in response to a government investigation rather than in response to a management request for an investigation of alleged employee misconduct. In the former situation, the order of witness interviews may be determined by the order in which the government seeks to interview employees, or even the order in which grand jury subpoenas are served. In the latter situation, by contrast, the lawyer conducting the internal investigation will have more control over the sequence and pace of the employee interviews.

Before undertaking detailed witness interviews, the lawyer conducting the investigation should attempt to ascertain the legal issues to be answered during the investigation, and to conduct at least preliminary legal research of those issues. Too often, internal investigations consist of an unfocused gathering of facts, or focus on only one side of an issue, finding fault without assessing defenses, or documenting defenses without adequately assessing vulnerabilities. The more the interviewer knows at the outset about what the possible vulnerabilities and legal defenses might be, the more useful the interviews will be.

Knowing beforehand whether the investigation is likely to lead to a voluntary disclosure also can influence the way the interviews are recorded. For example, although it is always preferable for two people to attend each interview (as a precaution in the event that the interviewee later denies something he or she said during the interview), if a voluntary disclosure is contemplated, only one person should take notes, and only one memorandum of the interview should be prepared. (This may also be an advisable course for interviews conducted in other contexts.) Similarly, a single report should be prepared upon the conclusion of the investigation, so there will be no inconsistency between the findings provided to company management and the findings relayed to whomever the disclosure will be made.

Finally, the lawyer conducting the investigation must be conscious of the risk that the investigation itself might prompt employees or others to initiate litigation against the company. Such a risk can influence the scope of the investigation, the number of employees interviewed, and even whether disgruntled former employees are interviewed at all. Any decision to limit the scope of the investigation should, of course, be made by management, not by the lawyer retained to conduct the investigation. But the lawyer should be aware of the risks in order to provide advice upon which management can make such a decision.

Each of the questions above can directly and substantially impact the type of investigation conducted. The answers to these questions can vary greatly depending upon the circumstances of each case. But addressing these questions at the outset will enable the lawyer to conduct the witness interviews in a logical, organized manner.

The lawyer's initial plan, however, should not be etched in stone. It can, and often should, be modified or even replaced as new facts come to light. Throughout the investigation, the lawyer must continually readdress the questions and make necessary adjustments.

III. CATEGORIZING THE INVESTIGATION

Most internal investigations fall into one of the following five categories.

A. *Minor Compliance Problems*

Most companies address minor compliance problems by having a corporate employee—often, but not always, a lawyer—speak with the relevant personnel and review relevant documents. Frequently, no record of the inquiry is made, and the result is an oral report followed by corrective action. Because the purpose of this inquiry is usually to guide a management decision—as opposed to developing a precise report upon which formal action can be taken—the order of witness interviews is usually less important, and the interviews are usually less structured, than would be the case in a more formal investigation.

B. *Routine Internal Investigations*

The most common approach to more significant compliance problems is the internal investigation designed to inform management of the facts necessary to assess responsibility and address the problem. Many of these investigations are handled by outside counsel, although some larger companies and those in heavily regulated industries are developing the in-house capability to conduct the investigations alone or, more commonly, in conjunction with outside counsel. Usually, while notes are taken and summarized for management, there is no formal report. Because such investigations not only are designed to assess corporate compliance with the law and the need for any corrective action, but also raise the possibility of litigation against the company, it is important to consider with care who should be interviewed and in what sequence, and to employ skilled interview techniques and preparation.

C. *Major Investigations*

A full-scale investigation is most frequently provoked by serious compliance concerns or threatened shareholder action addressed to possible management misfeasance. These investigations are usually undertaken by outside counsel—frequently assisted by inside or outside auditors—who maintain a record of their inquiry and present a formal report. Frequently, board decisions are made based on the report. Again, it is important to conduct the interviews in the proper sequence and to use skilled interviewing and recordkeeping techniques.

D. *Response to a Criminal or Other Enforcement Action*

An investigation in response to an enforcement action is driven by the schedule and pace of the government inquiry. Frequently, the investigation cannot proceed in the most orderly fashion—with document review preceding interviews, and interviews scheduled in the order to best ascertain the facts. Rather, investigations are often propelled by a desire to interview witnesses before the government does. Moreover, the recordkeeping aspect of the process is quite different, as the purpose is to gather key facts as quickly as possible and in support of a defense, rather than to amass all of the facts in a methodical fashion, make a record of the inquiry and develop a report on which management or the board can act.

E. *Voluntary Disclosure*

Companies hoping that a voluntary disclosure of corporate misconduct will blunt the consequences to the corporation of a government inquiry also may not have the luxury of proceeding in an ordinary fashion because disclosure, to be voluntary, must occur before the conduct at issue comes to light. Thus, investigations intended to lead to voluntary disclosures can sometimes be "quick-and-dirty," designed to obtain a rough but accurate idea of the facts in a relatively short period of time. After initial disclosure, a full-scale internal investigation is often undertaken.

IV. KEY PRINCIPLES

Though there are exceptions, several general organizing principles guide the conduct of interviews in internal investigations. First, it is best to gather and analyze all relevant documents before beginning witness interviews. Documents can be used to refresh a witness's recollections, structure interviews, and help determine whether a witness is being truthful. In addition, the interviews can be useful in resolving any inconsistencies or ambiguities in the documents. Since it is best to assume the interviewer will have access to a witness only once—though it is often possible to have more than one interview—it is important to be ready to ask all questions in the first instance.

Second, except in unusual circumstances or to learn answers to routine questions, the lawyer should avoid using written questionnaires in lieu of face-to-face interviews. Though the response to a questionnaire circulated by counsel is protected by the attorney-client privilege,[1] questionnaires often create more problems than they solve. The responses to questionnaires are not protected as work product because they do not reflect the lawyer's mental impressions.[2] Thus, should there be a waiver of the attorney-client privilege—or if the privilege is later deemed never

---

1. Upjohn Co. v. United States, 449 U.S. 383, 397 (1981).
2. *See In re* Grand Jury Investigations, 599 F.2d 1224, 1240 (3d Cir. 1978).

to have attached—these responses cannot be protected. This is particularly problematic because the answers are presented in a manner over which the lawyer has no control. If those answers turn out to be incorrect or misleading, the use of a questionnaire can have caused significant problems.

The one useful purpose of a questionnaire is to determine answers to basic questions that will help organize an investigation and identify persons to be interviewed, such as who in a company has done business with a particular competitor or who has sold particular products to a particular foreign country. Therefore, we recommend that questionnaires, if used at all, should be used only for the limited purpose of defining or narrowing the pool of potential witnesses. The lawyer must still gather the facts from these witnesses by conducting face-to-face interviews.

Third, if possible, counsel should seek to interview witnesses before an adverse party does. When a witness's recollection is refreshed after he or she has already been interviewed by the other side, it is often difficult to correct the record with maximum credibility. In part this is because witnesses are often reluctant to change their testimony—particularly if their first interview was given to government agents—even if they become aware of new facts later that conflict with their earlier recollection. Contacting the witnesses before they are approached by the other side also gives counsel the opportunity to inform the witnesses of their right to decide whether to be interviewed or to have counsel present to avoid overbearing interview techniques by the other side.

Fourth, if time permits, it is best to interview lower-level employees first and work up to higher-level employees. When time is of the essence, the interviewer may have to go directly to the person who—based upon events and documents—is most likely to be knowledgeable. This is especially true when there is a danger that subsequent events will diminish the likelihood that key witnesses will agree to be interviewed. In any event, interviews should not be undertaken without a clear understanding of the corporate hierarchy and the interrelationships among personnel.

Fifth, if possible, witnesses with knowledge of the same aspect of a transaction or subject of inquiry should be interviewed by the same person. While witness interview memoranda can summarize the facts gathered in an interview, they rarely communicate all the facts, and they are inadequate to communicate the witness's effect or quality of memory— factors that may be important to the ultimate conclusions reached in an investigation.

V. BEFORE THE INTERVIEW

Once an agency or grand jury inquiry is under way, many companies notify the relevant company employees in a written memorandum. The memorandum should state that a government investigator may wish to interview them and that the investigator may suggest that an interviewee can avoid a grand jury or other formal appearance if they consent to an informal interview, usually at their home in the evening. The memorandum should state that employees have the right to decide whether or not to be interviewed, that they are not required to consent to an interview, that they are entitled to seek legal advice before deciding whether to proceed with the interview, and that if they intend to proceed with an interview they are entitled to have counsel present. If the company intends to advance counsel fees to employees, employees should be informed and told whom to contact in the company to make these arrangements.

In order to protect the interviews under the attorney-client privilege, it is critical that prospective witnesses be informed by management that the company requires information from the witness so the company may obtain legal advice based upon an accurate understanding of the facts. This and other important points for prospective witnesses can be made in a written request for an interview directed to the employee by the relevant manager or inside counsel. If a written request is sent, it should state that the company has asked counsel to investigate a specific matter and that the company requests the employee's cooperation in counsel's inquiry. Whether this advice is written or oral, counsel needs to indicate clearly that the lawyer represents the company and not the individual employee. Counsel should state specifically that the interview is protected by the attorney-client privilege, but that the privilege belongs to the company, and that only the company—not the employee—can waive the privilege, and that it can do so at any time without the consent of the witness. If this advice is given in writing, it can also be used as an opportunity to reiterate instructions to employees not to destroy any relevant documents.

VI. THE MECHANICS

Interviews should generally be undertaken by two people, one of whom can serve as a witness at some subsequent time in the event the interviewee backs away from any testimony given during the interview. That person should also be the note-taker. Both individuals should be familiar with the documents and the result of other witness interviews.

All personnel engaged in the interview process—whether corporate employees, outside auditors, or law firm employees—should take their instructions from and report to counsel responsible for the inquiry and only to counsel. Where responsibility for an inquiry is assigned to a non-lawyer, that person must operate under counsel's direction and report to counsel in order to maintain the attorney-client privilege and the work product protection.[3] All relevant documents should be easily accessible. Interviews should be conducted in quiet, comfortable surroundings, usually apart from the individual's work environment. The setting should be designed to put the witness at ease. Frequently, this means that interviews should be undertaken on-site rather than in the offices of outside counsel.

VII. WARNINGS TO WITNESSES

As more and more internal investigations have been undertaken, legal and ethical issues have arisen regarding what warnings the investigating lawyer should give the witness at the outset of the interview. If the investigation is undertaken by counsel pursuant to a company's attorney-client privilege, the employee must be advised that the interviewer represents the company, not the individual employee. The employee should also be told that the interview is being conducted pursuant to the company's attorney-client privilege, and that this privilege can be waived by the company—and only the company—at any time, and without the employee's consent. These admonitions are essential, not only to maximize the company's choices in deciding what to do with the investigative results, but also to ensure that employees understand they are not speaking to their own lawyers.[4]

The underpinnings of the work product protection and the attorney-

---

3. *See In re* John Doe Corp., 675 F.2d 482 (2d Cir. 1982) (investigation by accounting firm as part of its audit not privileged); *In re* Grand Jury Subpoena, 599 F.2d 504, 510 (2d Cir. 1979) (investigation conducted by management not privileged).

4. Waggoner v. Snow, Becker, Kroll, Klaris & Krauss, 991 F.2d 1501, 1505-06 (9th Cir. 1993) (warnings defeat corporate officer's claim of an attorney-client relationship with corporate counsel); United States v. Calhoon, 859 F. Supp. 1496, 1497-98 (M.D. Ga. 1994) (same).

client privilege also must be established at the outset of the interview. It must be clear that the interview is intended to gather facts the company needs so counsel can provide the company with legal advice in anticipation of litigation. This is particularly important when an informal internal review is being undertaken. An investigation—particularly one undertaken in-house by a non-lawyer—may well be held to be unprotected because it is not focused on possible litigation.[5] It must be clear that the information is sought and will be maintained in confidence. The following is an example of introductory remarks designed to advise employees of the interviewer's representation of the company and of the company's attorney-client privilege.

> As you know, [your management] has asked you to meet with us as part of our inquiry into [the matter]. The purpose of our meeting is so that we can gather the information that we need, as counsel, to develop the legal advice that the company has sought and to prepare for possible litigation involving this matter.
>
> I am a lawyer and I represent the company. I do not represent you or any other employee personally. This inquiry is being undertaken pursuant to the company's attorney-client privilege, but the company may decide to waive the privilege at some point in the future. You cannot waive the attorney-client privilege as applied to this interview. If the company decides to waive its attorney-client privilege, it can do so without getting your consent and without even consulting with you. To allow the company to maintain the privileged protection of the information we gather, it is important that you not discuss the substance of this interview with anyone.
>
> Do you have any questions before we begin?

In order to secure the work product protection, it is wise to describe the "matter" broadly enough to encompass a range of consequences—for example, government investigation, parallel civil litigation, suit by a competitor, etc.—so the interview notes will be protected in a wide range of resulting litigation. It may also be useful to confirm these warnings at the end of the interview.

---

5. *In re* Grand Jury Subpoena, 599 F.2d at 510; Shulton v. Optel Corp., No. 85-2925 (D.N.J. 1987), 87 U.S. Dist., LEXIS 10097.

There does not seem to be much debate that the warnings described above must be given to employees at the outset of the interviews. The debate begins with whether the interviewer is obligated either to warn the witness that his statements may be used against him or to advise the witness to retain separate counsel.

As noted in chapter 2, "Internal Corporate Investigations: Implications of the Attorney-Client Privilege and Work Product Doctrine," former U.S. District Judge Frederick B. Lacey recommends that employees be given full "Adnarim" warnings (Miranda spelled backwards). According to Judge Lacey, employees should be told that they have a right to their own lawyers and that they may decide not to talk to the company's counsel.

We do not believe that existing case law requires these additional admonitions. Indeed, advising employees that they need not speak with company counsel may conflict with the employees' duty to cooperate, implicit in the employee's duty of loyalty found in some case law.[6] Although there surely are occasions where employees should be advised to retain counsel, company counsel should not assume this additional responsibility in every instance, particularly in advance of interviewing the employee to ascertain what he or she knows and whether retention of separate counsel is either required or advisable.

A legal obligation to warn that statements can be used against the employee would arise only if the employer's investigation could be construed as the action of the government. It is well established that the government may not force one of its employees to choose between his constitutional rights—here, the right to remain silent—and his job.[7] This principle has also been applied to non-government employers whose actions can be construed as state action.[8] A finding of state action can be based upon pervasive government regulation, public funding, or a "symbiotic" relationship and interdependence between the government and the private employer. To date, the ordinary government contractor has not been held to be a state actor.[9] But it is certainly conceivable that the disclosure made pursuant to an agreement with the government—for example,

---

6. *See, e.g.,* Goth v. Loft, Inc., 5 A.2d 503 (Del. Sup. Ct. 1939); *but see* discussion *infra* at 103. Also, see the discussion of employees' duties in chapter 6.

7. Garrity v. New Jersey, 385 U.S. 493 (1967).

8. *See* Lefkowitz v. Turley, 414 U.S. 70 (1973).

9. *See* Rendell-Baker v. Kohn, 457 U.S. 830, 840-43 (1982).

an administrative agreement arising out of a threatened debarment—could be construed as state action because the government's coercive power is brought to bear, indirectly, on the contractor's employee.

With respect to the question of separate counsel, the Model Rules of Professional Conduct, which have now been adopted in some form in most jurisdictions, discuss the corporate lawyer's obligation when handling a corporate employee. Model Rule of Professional Conduct 1.13(d) provides:

> In dealing with an organization's directors, officers, employees, members, shareholders or other constituents, a lawyer shall explain the identity of the client when it is apparent that the organization's interests are adverse to those of the constituents with whom the lawyer is dealing.

The annotations to that rule note that a "failure to clarify the nature of [the lawyer's] role in representing the organization may lead a constituent dealing with the lawyer to conclude that the lawyer jointly represents the constituent as well as the organization."[10] For this reason, a lawyer must be sensitive to the circumstances in which an employee could believe that the lawyer represents the employee personally. Model Rule 4.3, "Dealing With Unrepresented Person," provides, inter alia:

> When the lawyer knows or reasonably should know that the unrepresented person misunderstands the lawyer's role in the matter, the lawyer shall make reasonable efforts to correct the misunderstanding.[11]

In the District of Columbia, the version of the rules adopted by the court of appeals appears to go further. The Commentary section, entitled "Clarifying the Lawyer's Role," states that

---

10. AMERICAN BAR ASSOCIATION, ANNOTATED MODEL RULES OF PROF'L CONDUCT at 210 (3d ed. 1996); *see* Waggoner v. Snow, Becker, Kroll, Klaris & Krauss, *supra* note 4; United States v. Calhoon, *supra* note 4; *but see* In the Matter of Bevill, Bresler & Schulman Asset Mgmt. Corp., 805 F.2d 120, 125 (3d Cir. 1986) (corporate officer does not have a personal attorney-client privilege with respect to communications with corporate counsel made in his role as a corporate officer); *In re* Grand Jury Subpoena Duces Tecum (Vesco), 391 F. Supp. 1029, 1034 (S.D.N.Y. 1975) (same).

11. *See In re* Baron, 342 S.2d 505 (Fla. 1977).

... when the organization's interest[s] ... become adverse to those of one or more of its constituents. . . the lawyer should advise any constituent, whose interest the lawyer finds adverse to that of the organization, of the conflict or potential conflict of interest, that the lawyer cannot represent such constituent, and that such person may wish to obtain independent representation.[12]

It appears that this commentary would impose on corporate counsel, who determined that an employee's interests may diverge from the company's, the additional obligation to advise that employee to obtain individual representation. While this obligation has been suggested by some ethics experts, few reported judicial decisions have imposed an equivalent responsibility.[13] The best course is for corporate counsel to assess the employee's situation following an initial interview, which will provide the factual basis for an opinion.

A related ethical issue that frequently arises in internal investigations relates to the representation by counsel that the witness's statement is protected by the corporation's attorney-client privilege. Model Rule of Professional Conduct 4.1(a) prohibits counsel from knowingly making a false statement of material fact. If the company has a statutory or other obligation to disclose to the government the substance of the interview—for example, where there is a commitment to make a voluntary disclosure of the witness's statement or where there are allegations falling within the Anti-Kickback Act or the various mandatory reporting requirements found in the federal environmental laws—the employee should be informed of these obligations or the likelihood that the privilege will be waived. Otherwise, the witness might be left with the erroneous impression that the company intends to protect the interview by asserting the company's attorney-client privilege.

---

12. DISTRICT OF COLUMBIA BAR ASSOCIATION, DISTRICT OF COLUMBIA RULES OF PROF'L CONDUCT at I-28 (1990).

13. *Cf.* Gregory v. Gregory, 92 Cal. App. 2d 343, 206 P.2d 1122 (1949) (opposing party should be advised of right to independent counsel).

VIII. CONDUCTING THE INTERVIEW

There are as many interviewing styles as there are interviewers, but some principles can be applied to most interviews. Generally, it is important to treat the witness with respect, regardless of what may have been done or how abusive the witness may be (some corporate employees resent the intrusion of a lawyer into what they believe to be a business matter). It is generally not helpful for counsel to inject their own personality or personal views into the interview itself, to become engaged in an argument or discussion with the witness on the matter under investigation, to use the occasion to advise the witness on how he or she should have handled the situation in issue, or to disclose how the investigation is proceeding (although some sharing of information is often necessary for a productive interview).

Interviews should be planned and structured so that the easy, less contentious issues arise first. So-called "nondirective" interviewing—relying on open-ended questions—is best used at the beginning of an interview to get the witness's version of events in an unfettered manner. This can be followed by a step-by-step, pointed review of the facts, utilizing documents or a time line, in which more precise answers are sought.

Effective interviewing, like effective cross-examination, requires the pursuit of two occasionally inconsistent goals: (1) following up on leads provided by the witness's responses to questions, and (2) ensuring that the witness has answered the questions propounded. Rigid pursuit of the second goal can cause the interviewer to miss key pieces of information referred to by the witness but not directly responsive to the question. Failure to pursue the second goal will undermine a comprehensive review of the critical facts. Counsel must listen to the answers and pursue leads offered by the witness, but always ensure that the witness has responded to the immediate question.

We believe that a written outline is useful in structuring the interview and ensuring that key points are covered. However, we caution counsel against scripting the interview on a question-by-question basis. This "wedding" between interviewer and outline often causes the interviewer to focus on the next question on his outline rather than listening to the witness's answer. The result is a failure to ask follow-up questions. Therefore, we would suggest using a checklist of key topics to be covered in the interview rather than a detailed outline of questions.

IX. TYPICAL PROBLEMS ARISING DURING THE INTERVIEW

A number of situations may arise during the interview that require the interviewer to proceed with caution. The more common scenarios are discussed below.

A. *The Employee Who Asks for Legal Advice*

Even when an employee has been given the warnings discussed *supra* at page 98, it is not uncommon for him or her to request legal advice or to otherwise suggest that he or she is looking to the interviewer as personal legal counsel. These situations must be dealt with quickly and clearly. The interviewer must repeat that he or she is representing the company and cannot provide the employee with any legal advice. The employee should be instructed to direct all such questions to the company's general counsel. These points must be discussed until the employee has a clear understanding of them. If the interview is memorialized, the memorandum should state that the interviewer repeated the warnings and the employee understood them.

B. *The Reluctant Employee*

It is not uncommon for an employee to express a desire not to be interviewed. While we believe that the better view of the law is that an employee has a duty to cooperate with the internal investigation, a lawyer may certainly court trouble by appearing to bully the employee into agreeing to an interview.[14] Therefore, we would suggest that counsel and the company weigh the need for the employee's cooperation against the potential exposure from forcing the issue before seeking to force an employee to cooperate. If the interview is essential, the client may very well conclude that it is appropriate to commence disciplinary proceedings against the employee if he or she refuses to cooperate.

---

14. *See* Shepherd v. American Broadcasting Cos., Inc., 62 F.3d 1469, 1483-84 (D.C. Cir. 1995) (reversing district court finding that outside counsel had harassed company employee by attempting to interview her at the company's offices after she had refused to be interviewed); Department of Veterans Affairs Med. Ctr. v. Federal Labor Relations Auth., 16 F.3d 1526, 1534-36 (9th Cir. 1994) (hospital committed unfair labor practice under the Federal Service Labor-Management Relations Statute by failing to inform interviewee that she could refuse to be interviewed without fear of reprisal).

C. *The Employee Who Places Conditions on the Interview*

An employee may also insist that an interview take place under certain conditions. These typically include (1) the participation of employee's counsel; (2) the interview is recorded or transcribed; (3) certain topics are avoided; or (4) the company will not disclose the content of the interview without the employee's consent.

This situation also requires counsel and management to weigh the need for the information possessed by the employee against the burdens imposed by the proposed conditions. In those situations where the employee's testimony is essential, counsel may very well recommend that the company agree to the conditions. If so, the understanding between the company and the employee should be reduced to writing and signed by all parties. In those situations where counsel has in effect waived any claim of privilege that might otherwise have attached to the interview, counsel must proceed on the assumption that every question and document used during the interview will be made public by the interviewee and conduct the interview accordingly.

X. INTERVIEWING FORMER COMPANY EMPLOYEES

The Supreme Court, in *Upjohn Co. v. United States*,[15] declined to address whether the attorney-client privilege protects communications between corporate counsel and a former employee, but the logic of *Upjohn* suggests no meaningful distinction between present and former employees.[16]

As with employee interviews, management should request the former employee's assistance, explaining that the purpose of the interview is to secure legal advice for the company and asking that the interview be kept confidential. Again, both in the letter and at the outset of the interviews, the former employee should be told that the interviewer represents the company, not the former employee personally. Every effort

---

15. 449 U.S. 383, 394 n.3 (1981).

16. *See In re* Coordinated Pretrial Proceedings in Petroleum Prods. Antitrust Litig., 658 F.2d 1355, 1361 (9th Cir. 1981), *cert. denied*, California v. Standard Oil Co., 455 U.S. 990 (1982); *but see In re* Grand Jury Subpoena Dated July 13, 1979, 478 F. Supp. 368, 374-75 (E.D. Wis. 1979). This issue is addressed in more detail in the chapter, "Internal Corporate Investigations: Implications of the Attorney-Client Privilege and the Work Product Doctrine," *supra*.

should be made to ensure that the interview memorandum is a protected work product.

XI. RECORDKEEPING

In an internal investigation of significant scope, it is impossible to find facts and reach conclusions if counsel does not memorialize witness interviews in some fashion. The challenge is to do so in the way that is most likely to protect the content of those interviews. Each member of an internal investigation team must try to use the same format and rules for the maintenance of interview records.

The work product of counsel produced in anticipation of litigation is protected from forced disclosure during discovery.[17] It is important to establish on the face of any document or memorandum that litigation is anticipated. This is made more difficult—though not impossible—when the investigation is handled in-house because litigation is more likely to be handled by outside counsel, and in-house counsel have other business responsibilities.[18] A documentary record should establish the potential for litigation and, particularly, that all non-lawyer work in the investigation is performed at the direction of counsel in contemplation of litigation.[19] Work product protection has been denied where the anticipated litigation has been found to be too remote.[20]

Work product protection will protect interview notes.[21] Because courts give the greatest protection to work product reflecting counsel's impressions, analysis, and opinions, the interview memorandum should be

---

17. See FED. R. CIV. P. 26.

18. *See In re* Sealed Case (Tesoro Petroleum), 676 F.2d 793 (D.C. Cir. 1982); *In re* John Doe Corp. (Southland), 675 F.2d 482 (2d Cir. 1982).

19. *Compare* Southern Bell Tel. & Tel. Co. v. Deason, 632 So. 2d 1377, 1384-85 (Fla. 1994) (internal audits conducted by company employees at the request of counsel are work product) *with* United States v. Rosenthal, 142 F.R.D. 389, 392 (S.D.N.Y. 1992) (accounting firm's report not protected work product where engagement letter ambiguous as to whether work was related to the seeking of legal advice).

20. Diversified Indus., Inc. v. Meredith, 572 F.2d 596, 604 (8th Cir. 1977); Scott Paper Co. v. Celocote Co., 103 F.R.D. 591, 596 (D. Me. 1984).

21. *In re* Grand Jury Subpoena, 478 F. Supp. 368, 374 (E.D. Wis. 1979), *In re* Woolworth Corp. Sec. Litig., 1996 U.S. Dist. LEXIS 7773 at *10 (S.D.N.Y. 1996).

couched in these terms to the greatest extent possible.[22] We recommend that an interview memorandum always include a statement that it reflects the thoughts, impressions, and opinion of counsel. Extraneous factual recitations should be avoided, and statements of fact should always be interspersed with statements of counsel's mental impressions and strategies.

No tape recordings or verbatim transcripts of witness interviews should be made unless the witness is potentially adverse, and then only with great caution. Verbatim records may not qualify as work product, and, under the "Reverse Jencks" rule applicable to criminal cases, the government may later be able to obtain their discovery.[23] This rule arguably extends to counsel's notes of witness interviews if they are "substantially verbatim" statements. Under this rule, if a witness other than the defendant is called by the defense, all prior statements—including a statement "adopted" or signed by the witness, or a "substantially verbatim recital" contemporaneously transcribed—must be made available to the government.

Unless the witness is someone who may not later be available or who may be adverse, the benefits of a verbatim statement are usually outweighed by the vulnerability to discovery of these statements. But when there is a witness whose testimony must be "locked in," a written statement or transcript is appropriate. A great deal of thought and preparation must go into this document because it may take on a life of its own,[24] and because the circumstances of its creation frequently become an issue.

---

22. *See* Upjohn Co. v. United States, 449 U.S. 383, 400 (1981) (noting that FED. R. CIV. P. 26 accords "special protection" to work product revealing the attorney's mental processes); Hickman v. Taylor, 329 U.S. 495, 511-13 (1947); *In re* Sealed Case (Foster), 124 F.3d 230, 236-37 (D.C. Cir.) (those portions of client interview memorandum that are "purely factual" afforded less protection under the work product doctrine than those portions of the memorandum reflecting counsel's mental impressions), *cert. pending*, 66 U.S.L.W. 3492 (1997); *In re* Martin Marietta *(*United States v. Pollard*)*, 856 F.2d 619 (4th Cir. 1988), *cert. denied*, 490 U.S. 1011 (1989) finding waiver of work product protection in attorneys' notes other than those reflecting pure opinion).

23. FED. R. CRIM. P. 26.2; *see* United States v. Nobles, 422 U.S. 225, 230-32 (1975).

24. Such a document or recording can be especially problematic if the witness's testimony changes later after recollection has been refreshed by facts developed after the original verbatim statement was given.

The memorandum of an interview always should reflect the advice to the witness that provides the underpinning for an assertion of the attorney-client privilege. Specifically, the memorandum should reflect that the witness was told the company has sought legal advice and the witness's testimony is necessary for counsel to have a factual basis upon which to render advice.[25] The memorandum should further reflect that the witness was asked to keep the substance of the interview confidential. The memorandum also should reflect the admonition to the employee that the interviewer represents the company, not the employee personally.

All memoranda should be labeled as attorney-client privilege. If the investigation is undertaken by in-house counsel, there must be documentation that the inquiry is within the scope of legal duties assigned to counsel and that the inquiry is not just a factual investigation conducted as part of the business duties of the lawyer.[26]

To minimize the danger of waiver regarding witness interviews, interview memoranda should not be distributed to anyone outside the core group to whom the lawyer is reporting. The disclosure of particularized facts memorialized in those memoranda should similarly be limited.[27]

XII. OBSTRUCTION OF JUSTICE

Whenever an internal investigation precedes or shadows a government investigation, the government will be looking for conduct by corporate counsel that was intended to, or did, affect the tenor and shape of the witness's testimony. During witness interviews, lawyers should use extreme care to avoid any possible false or misleading conduct. This topic is addressed in detail in the chapter titled "Perjury, Obstruction of Justice, and the Victim and Witness Protection Act." It is mentioned briefly here because of its significance.

The witness-tampering statute, 18 U.S.C. § 1512, prohibits one from engaging in "misleading conduct" with intent to influence the testimony of a person in an official proceeding. The statute contains no requirement

---

25. *See* Independent Petrochem. Corp. v. Aetna Cas. & Surety Co., 654 F. Supp. 1334, 1364-65, *reconsideration denied*, 672 F. Supp. 1 (D.D.C. 1986).

26. Spectrum Sys. Int'l Corp. v. Chemical Bank, 157 A.D.2d 444, 558 N.Y.S.2d 486 (1990). *Accord, In re* Grand Jury Subpoena, 599 F.2d 504, 510-11 (2d Cir. 1979).

27. *See In re* Sealed Case, 676 F.2d 793, 823 (D.C. Cir. 1982).

of corrupt intent. While section 1512 provides for an affirmative defense when the defendant's actions "consisted solely of lawful conduct" and the "sole intent was to cause truthful testimony" to be given, that defense must be supported by a preponderance of the evidence.

A lawyer who interviews a witness prior to the witness's grand jury appearance may attempt to test the witness's memory or to refresh the witness's recollection with documents or other facts. "Misleading conduct" is broadly defined to include concealing a material fact or making a false statement. Depending on the circumstances, a lawyer's suggestion to a witness of an alternative, non-incriminating interpretation of a transaction could subject the lawyer to liability.[28] The burden would then be on the lawyer to establish the affirmative defense of a lack of corrupt intent. Thus, in conducting witness interviews, the lawyer can ask about various interpretations, seek to refresh the witness's recollection, and expose the witness to other witnesses' accounts of the same transaction (though the lawyer should be careful here not to omit other more incriminating accounts of the same transaction). Overall, a lawyer should use caution in engaging in conduct that has the appearance of suggesting facts to the witness.

---

28. *See* United States v. Gabriel, 125 F.3d 89, 102 (2d Cir. 1997) (defendant violated § 1512 by attempting to mislead a prospective grand jury witness by providing him with the defendant's recollection of key events).

Perjury, Obstruction of Justice, and the Victim and Witness Protection Act

4

by Gary P. Naftalis & David S. Frankel*

* Gary P. Naftalis and David S. Frankel are engaged in the defense of white-collar criminal cases, SEC enforcement actions, and other administrative agency proceedings at Kramer Levin Naftalis & Frankel LLP in New York, New York.

I. INTRODUCTION

Lawyers conducting internal investigations must be aware of the federal criminal statutes that potentially apply to interviewing and preparing witnesses. These statutes include those covering perjury and subornation of perjury, misprision of felony, and obstruction of justice. Although these statutes are most important when the internal investigation is in response to a government investigation, their terms and prohibitions should be examined in conducting any internal investigation.

In the pages that follow, we review the statutory elements and controlling judicial interpretations of each statute, and then suggest some of the principles that might guide counsel in the course of an internal company investigation. Of special concern are two broad obstruction of justice statutes, 18 U.S.C. § 1512, the witness-tampering provision added by the Victim and Witness Protection Act of 1982, and 18 U.S.C. § 1510(b), enacted as part of the Financial Institution Reform, Recovery, and Enforcement Act of 1989. Both provisions, if applied literally, could substantially augment the scope of federal criminal liability for obstruction of justice, and both could influence counsel's conduct during internal company investigations.

II. PERJURY AND SUBORNATION OF PERJURY

Perjury is covered by two sections of the criminal code, 18 U.S.C. §§ 1621 and 1623. Section 1621 is the older and more general perjury statute, proscribing willfully false testimony given under oath "in any case in which a law of the United States authorizes an oath to be administered." Section 1623 applies only to false declarations made in proceedings either "before or ancillary to any court or grand jury."[1] However, section 1623 contains provisions designed to relax the government's evidentiary

---

1. The Supreme Court has construed the term "ancillary proceeding" to mean pretrial depositions in criminal cases as authorized by Fed. R. Crim. P. 15 and 18 U.S.C. § 3503. Dunn v. United States, 442 U.S. 100, 107-13 (1979).

burden by eliminating certain proof requirements applicable in section 1621 prosecutions.

Section 1622 is the federal subornation of perjury statute, which makes it a crime to "procure[ ] another to commit any perjury."

A. *Perjury Under Section 1621: Essential Elements*

In a prosecution for perjury under section 1621, the government must prove that the defendant knowingly and willfully made a material false statement.[2] In addition to perjurious assertions of fact, a witness's materially false avowal of not remembering may be punished as an act of perjury.[3]

The requirement that the false testimony be willfully, as well as knowingly, false is sometimes construed to mean that the defendant must have acted corruptly or with intent to deceive the tribunal.[4] More typically, the dual mens rea requirements are considered without any real differentiation.[5] The inquiry reduces to whether the defendant "subjectively knew

---

2. *E.g.,* United States v. Lighte, 782 F.2d 367 (2d Cir. 1986); United States v. Makris, 483 F.2d 1082 (5th Cir. 1973), *cert. denied*, 415 U.S. 914 (1974); United States v. Stone, 429 F.2d 138 (2d Cir. 1970); Vitello v. United States, 425 F.2d 416 (9th Cir.), *cert. denied*, 400 U.S. 822 (1970). Section 1621 provides in its entirety:

Whoever—
> (1) having taken an oath before a competent tribunal, officer or person, in any case in which a law of the United States authorizes an oath to be administered, that he will testify, declare, depose, or certify truly, or that any written testimony, declaration, deposition, or certificate by him subscribed, is true, willfully and contrary to such oath states or subscribes any material matter which he does not believe to be true; or
> (2) in any declaration, certificate, verification, or statement under penalty of perjury as permitted under section 1746 of title 28, United States Code, willfully subscribes as true any material matter which he does not believe to be true; is guilty of perjury and shall, except as otherwise expressly provided by law, be fined not more than $2,000 or imprisoned not more than five years, or both. This section is applicable whether the statement or subscription is made within or without the United States.

Thus, as a threshold matter, the government must also prove either (1) that the false statement was made under a properly administered oath, or (2) that the false statement was made in a writing under penalty of perjury as permitted pursuant to 28 U.S.C. § 1746.

3. *In re* Battaglia, 653 F.2d 419 (9th Cir. 1981).

4. *See, e.g.,* United States v. Laurelli, 187 F. Supp. 30 (M.D. Pa. 1960), *aff'd,* 293 F.2d 830 (3d Cir. 1961), *cert. denied,* 368 U.S. 961 (1962); United States v. Rose, 215 F.2d 617 (3d Cir. 1954).

that [the] statements were false."⁶ Implicit in this analysis is the notion that false statements made knowingly are, by definition, not the product of accident or negligence. In that sense, they are "willfully"—that is, purposely or intentionally—made.⁷

The element of "materiality" is broadly defined. In the case of perjury before the grand jury, it is sufficient under one frequently cited formulation that the false statement have the "natural effect or tendency . . . to influence, impede or dissuade further investigation," and that the "further investigation" is itself material to the grand jury's task. That is, if a truthful answer had been given, it "would have been of sufficient probative importance to the inquiry so that, at a minimum, further fruitful investigation would have occurred."⁸

Other cases describe the materiality requirement in similar fashion. For example, in *United States v. Berardi,*⁹ the Second Circuit stated that materiality is established "if the question posed is such that a truthful answer could help the inquiry, or a false response hinder it, and these effects are weighed in terms of potentiality rather than probability." In *United States v. Makris,*¹⁰ the court stated:

> The test of materiality is whether the false statement was capable of influencing the tribunal on the issue, or whether the false testimony would have the natural effect or tendency to influence, impede, or dissuade [the investigatory body] from pursuing its investigation.¹¹

---

5. *See, e.g.,* United States v. Sweig, 441 F.2d 114, 117 (2d Cir.), *cert. denied,* 403 U.S. 932 (1971) (rejecting contention, in prosecution under section 1621, that government had failed to prove "essential element of knowledge or willfulness").

6. *Id.*

7. *See also* United States v. Norris, 300 U.S. 564 (1937). In *Norris* the Court rejected the claim that recantation on the day following the false testimony, while the proceedings were still pending, constituted a defense to a perjury charge. The Court defined perjury as "the telling of a deliberate lie by a witness," as distinguished from "an innocent mistake." *Id.* at 576. The requisite mens rea was described by the Court as the "willful intent to swear falsely." A "corrupt" state of mind is an element of certain obstruction of justice statutes discussed *infra.*

8. United States v. Freedman, 445 F.2d 1220, 1226-27 (2d Cir. 1971).

9. 629 F.2d 723, 728 (2d Cir.), *cert. denied,* 449 U.S. 995 (1980).

10. 483 F.2d 1082 (5th Cir. 1973), *cert. denied,* 415 U.S. 914 (1974).

11. *Id.* at 1088 (citations omitted). *Accord* United States v. Wesson, 478 F.2d 1180, 1181 (7th Cir. 1973); United States v. Stone, 429 F.2d 138 (2d Cir. 1970). Materiality does appear to be somewhat more difficult to establish outside the grand jury context.

For the element of materiality to be satisfied, the allegedly perjurious statement need not relate to the central subject before the tribunal.[12] Nor must the false answer actually impede the investigation for it to be material.[13] In fact, a false answer to a grand jury that knows the witness is lying may still be material.[14]

B. *Burden of Proof and the Two-Witness Rule*

Courts traditionally have recognized the potential unfairness in permitting a perjury conviction on the basis of a single witness's uncorroborated testimony.[15] This has led some courts to state that perjury must be made out by a quantum of proof greater than the reasonable doubt standard usually mandated in criminal cases.[16]

See, e.g., United States v. Martinez, 855 F.2d 621 (9th Cir. 1988) (use of alias under which defendant had been living for seven years not material to hearing where only issue was financial eligibility for appointment of counsel); United States v. Qaisi, 779 F.2d 346 (6th Cir. 1985) (false statement regarding future viability of marriage immaterial in visa application hearing where validity of marriage at its inception had some bearing on outcome).

12. *E.g.,* United States v. Moreno Morales, 815 F.2d 725 (1st Cir. 1987); United States v. Wesson, 478 F.2d 1180 (7th Cir. 1973).

13. United States v. McComb, 744 F.2d 555 (7th Cir. 1984); United States v. Wesson, 478 F.2d 1180 (7th Cir. 1973).

14. United States v. Lee, 509 F.2d 645 (2d Cir.), *cert. denied,* 422 U.S. 1044 (1975). Until the Supreme Court's decision in *United States v. Gaudin,* 515 U.S. 506 (1995), courts had usually deemed materiality to be an issue for the court. In *Gaudin,* the Court ruled that the trial court's refusal to submit the question of materiality to the jury violated the Fifth and Sixth Amendments. It is thus now clear that the materiality element is for the jury. *Gaudin* involved a conviction under the federal false statement statute, 18 U.S.C. § 1001. However, courts have generally found that the analysis is the same under the federal perjury statutes and § 1001 regarding the defendant's right to have the jury decide the issue of materiality. *See, e.g.,* United States v. Littleton, 76 F.3d 614, 617 (4th Cir. 1996) (in a § 1623 prosecution, the defendant is entitled to a jury determination on the issue of the materiality of the allegedly false statement, and the government must prove the element of materiality beyond a reasonable doubt); *see generally* A. Saad, *Perjury,* 34 Am. Crim. L. Rev. 857, 874 (1997).

15. *See* Weiler v. United States, 323 U.S. 606 (1945) (discussing the need "to protect honest witnesses from hasty and spiteful retaliation in the form of unfounded perjury prosecutions," and the possibility that "equally honest witnesses may well have differing recollections of the same event").

16. *See* LaRocca v. United States, 337 F.2d 39 (8th Cir. 1964) ("substantial evidence excluding every other hypothesis than that of guilt"; "clear, convincing and

In practice, however, this stricter standard of proof has meant only that the government must prove the falsity of testimony in a perjury case under section 1621 either by the testimony of two witnesses or by the testimony of one witness plus independent corroborative evidence.[17] In *LaRocca v. United States*, for example, the court found no error in the use of a standard reasonable doubt jury charge, because other instructions were given to the effect that the jury could not convict unless it found independent evidence corroborating the testimony of the government's chief witness.[18] Similarly, in *United States v. Makris*, the court recited the supposed "moral certainty" burden of proof,[19] and then upheld perjury convictions because the proof was sufficient beyond a reasonable doubt.[20]

The corroborative evidence must be inconsistent with the innocence of the defendant, although it need not, standing alone, be sufficient to support a conviction. Instead, "such evidence must tend to substantiate . . . the testimony of the principal prosecution witness. . . . "[21]

C. *True Answers and Ambiguous Questions*

In *Bronston v. United States*,[22] the Supreme Court held that the general perjury statute does not reach a literally true but nonresponsive an-

---

direct evidence to a moral certainty and beyond a reasonable doubt that the defendant committed willful and corrupt perjury"); United States v. Brandyberry, 438 F.2d 226 (9th Cir.), *cert. denied,* 404 U.S. 842 (1971) (same).

17.   *E.g.,* Hammer v. United States, 271 U.S. 620 (1926); United States v. Collins, 272 F.2d 650 (2d Cir. 1959); United States v. Neff, 212 F.2d 297 (3d Cir. 1954).

18.   337 F.2d at 43-44.

19.   483 F.2d at 1085.

20.   *Id.* at 1087-88.

21.   United States v. Weiner, 479 F.2d 923, 927-28 (2d Cir. 1973). *Accord* United States v. Brandyberry, 438 F.2d 226 (9th Cir.), *cert. denied,* 404 U.S. 842 (1971) (numerous phone records and other documentary evidence tending to suggest defendant knew or had met with various persons, contrary to his denials in the grand jury); Arena v. United States, 226 F.2d 227, 236 (9th Cir. 1955), *cert. denied,* 350 U.S. 954 (1956) (corroborative evidence sufficient if it "tends to establish the defendant's guilt, and if such evidence together with the direct evidence is 'inconsistent with the innocence of the defendant'") (emphasis in original); United States v. Neff, 212 F.2d at 307 (evidence that defendant was member of Communist Party and paid party dues that were collected at her place of employment neither proves nor tends to prove that she ever attended a party meeting).

22.   409 U.S. 352 (1973).

swer, even one that was arguably misleading by negative implication.[23] Bronston had testified as a witness at a bankruptcy hearing and had been asked first whether he had any bank accounts in Swiss banks, to which he answered, truthfully, "No, sir." He was then asked whether he had ever had any Swiss bank accounts. He answered that his "company had an account there for about six months, in Zurich."[24] Bronston did not disclose that he had had a personal Swiss bank account also, for a period of about five years, in the early 1960s.

The government claimed that the answer regarding the corporate account was perjurious because it was designed to mislead the questioner, especially in light of the immediately preceding question and answer, by implying that Bronston, unlike his company, had not ever had a Swiss account. The Supreme Court rejected this argument:

> Beyond question, [Bronston's] answer to the crucial question was not responsive if we assume, as we do, that the first question was directed at personal bank accounts [rather than corporate accounts, or both corporate and personal accounts]. There is, indeed, an implication in the answer to the second question that there was never a personal bank account; in casual conversation this interpretation might reasonably be drawn. But we are not dealing with casual conversation and the statute does not make it a criminal act for a witness to willfully state any material matter that implies any material matter that he does not believe to be true.[25]

Any incompleteness in the witness's answer, which might be wholly in-

---

23. *Bronston* has since been held to apply to prosecutions under section 1623 also. *See, e.g.,* United States v. Boone, 951 F.2d 1526, 1536 (9th Cir. 1991) (literally true statement not actionable under section 1623); United States v. Reveron Martinez, 836 F.2d 684, 689 (1st Cir. 1988); United States v. Tonelli, 577 F.2d 194, 198 (3d Cir. 1978); United States v. Kehoe, 562 F.2d 65, 68 (1st Cir. 1977). It also applies to 18 U.S.C. § 1001 (false material statements to an agency or department of the United States). *E.g.,* United States v. Mandanici, 729 F.2d 914, 921 (2d Cir. 1984). *See also* United States v. Attick, 649 F.2d 61, 63 (1st Cir.), *cert denied,* 454 U.S. 861 (1981) (one cannot be convicted under 18 U.S.C. § 1014, prohibiting material false statements to a federally insured bank, "if the statement claimed to be false is, in fact, literally true").

24. *Id.* at 354.

25. *Id.* at 357-58.

nocent, or even purposeful evasion, is thus to be remedied by additional questioning by the lawyer.[26] As long as the answer is literally true, however, there can be no perjury.[27] On the other hand, where an answer is both responsive—therefore not signaling the need for further questioning—and materially false in context, it is perjurious "even if [it] could be literally true in isolation."[28]

Whether an answer is literally true is an issue of fact for the jury, provided the questions put to the witness were fairly susceptible of only one interpretation.[29] However, if a line of questioning is so vague that it is "fundamentally ambiguous," then the issue becomes one of legal sufficiency, and a perjury conviction may not be permitted to stand.[30]

---

26. *Id.* at 358-59.

27. *E.g.,* United States v. Hairston, 46 F.3d 361, 375 (4th Cir. 1995) (conviction for violation of section 1623 cannot be based on evasive answers or even misleading answers so long as such answers are literally true); United States v. Dean, 55 F.3d 640, 662 (D.C. Cir. 1995) (misleading but literally true statement does not constitute perjury as defined in section 1621); United States v. Chaplin, 25 F.3d 1373, 1380 (7th Cir. 1994) (literal truth of statement is complete defense to section 1621 perjury charge); United States v. Reveron Martinez, 836 F.2d 684, 689 (1st Cir. 1988) (reversing conviction based on plainly nonresponsive but literally true answer not further explored by questioner).

28. United States v. Shafrick, 871 F.2d 300, 305 (2d Cir. 1989).

29. United States v. Yasak, 884 F.2d 996, 1000-01 (7th Cir. 1989); United States v. Lighte, 782 F.2d 367, 372-73 (2d Cir. 1986).

30. *See, e.g.,* United States v. Ryan, 828 F.2d 1010 (3d Cir. 1987) (credit card application form asking for "Previous Address (Last 5 Years)" fundamentally ambiguous because term "address" might equally well refer to domicile or residence or mailing address, and because question could be read to call for one or more than one previous address—or even no previous address if the applicant did not live there within the last five years); United States v. Lighte, 782 F.2d at 375-76 (reversing conviction because undefined use of the pronoun "you" made it impossible for witness to know whether questioned in a personal capacity or as trustee of trust bank account; in effect, the answers were necessarily literally true); United States v. Bell, 623 F.2d 1132 (5th Cir. 1980) (asking grand jury witness whether he had records that were requested in subpoena could have meant "whether he had brought the records with him [to the grand jury] that day," just as plausibly as whether he had the records in his possession "at his office or anywhere else in the world"). *Compare* United States v. Glantz, 847 F.2d 1 (1st Cir. 1988) (literal truth defense not available where testimony read as a whole made it clear who was meant by "them" in question "Did you ever tell anyone that money was passed on to them?" and evidence established falsity of defendant's answer "Absolutely not.").

D. *Perjury Under Section 1623: Differences*

Section 1623 applies only to false material declarations made in a proceeding before or ancillary to a federal court or grand jury.[31] This limitation would appear to mean that SEC depositions, conducted pursuant to a private formal order of investigation issued by the commission or other administrative agency, cannot give rise to a perjury prosecution under section 1623. On the other hand, interviews conducted in the prosecutor's office, under oath, may come within the meaning of the term "ancillary proceeding."[32]

Whether section 1623 is available to a prosecutor contemplating a perjury case can have significant ramifications. Section 1623 was enacted

---

31. Section 1623 applies not only to false oral and written testimony, but also to the use of documentary evidence containing a false declaration. Specifically, 18 U.S.C. § 1623(a) provides:

> Whoever under oath (or in any declaration, certificate, verification, or statement under penalty of perjury as permitted under section 1746 of title 28, United States Code) in any proceeding before or ancillary to any court or grand jury of the United States knowingly makes any false material declaration or makes or uses any other information, including any book, paper, document, record, recording, or other material, knowing the same to contain any false material declaration, shall be fined not more than $10,000 or imprisoned not more than five years, or both.

At least one court has affirmed a section 1623(a) conviction based upon supplying false and forged documents to the grand jury in response to a subpoena, and then identifying those documents before the grand jury (although the opinion does not make clear what the defendants said in "identifying" the documents as business records). United States v. Norton, 755 F.2d 1428 (11th Cir. 1985). The court stated that "each document, which defendants had affirmatively presented to the Grand Jury, was displayed to them during their testimony. These documents were falsely identified as business records... when they were not actual business records.... The false documents were identified as depicting events and records that were in reality nonexistent." *Id.* at 1430-31.

32. United States v. Krogh, 366 F. Supp. 1255, 1256 (D.D.C. 1973) (holding that sworn deposition taken in the office of an Assistant U.S. Attorney General was a proceeding ancillary to a grand jury investigation); Dunn v. United States, 442 U.S. 100, 111 n.10 (1979) (distinguishing interview in private lawyer's office from situation in *Krogh*, without commenting on whether *Krogh* was rightly decided). Under one reading of *Dunn*, only testimony taken by deposition would come within the term "ancillary proceeding." *See* 442 U.S. at 109-13 (arguably suggesting that sworn affidavits and certifications are not statements accompanied by sufficient procedural safeguards ever to be regarded as possessing the "'degree of formality' required by § 1623").

in 1970 "to facilitate perjury prosecutions."[33] The statute eliminates several of the strict common-law evidentiary requirements for establishing falsity, which remain applicable in a prosecution under section 1621:

- The two-witness (or direct corroboration) rule is abolished, and proof beyond a reasonable doubt "is sufficient for conviction."[34] The two-witness rule remains applicable in section 1621 prosecutions.[35]

- Where the defendant has testified inconsistently in more than one proceeding, "to the degree that one of [his declarations] is necessarily false," the government need not allege or prove the falsity of either. Both declarations must be "material to the point in question," and the government must prove that they are "irreconcilably contradictory."[36]

---

33. Dunn v. United States, 442 U.S. at 107.

34. 18 U.S.C. § 1623(e).

35. United States v. Diggs, 560 F.2d 266 (7th Cir.), *cert. denied,* 434 U.S. 925 (1977); United States v. Ruggiero, 472 F.2d 599 (2d Cir.), *cert. denied,* 412 U.S. 939 (1973). A prosecutor's election to proceed under section 1623 rather than section 1621, where both are available, is not an equal protection violation. United States v. Ruggiero, 472 F.2d at 599.

36. 18 U.S.C. § 1623(c). Apparently recognizing that with the passage of time a witness's understanding of the true facts might change, Congress explicitly made it a defense in a section 1623 prosecution based on inconsistent declarations "that the defendant at the time he made each declaration believed the declaration was true." Section 1623 also specifically makes recantation a defense. The recantation must occur in "the same continuous court or grand jury proceeding in which [the false] declaration is made," and it must occur before the perjury has "substantially affected the proceeding" and before it "become[s] manifest [to the perjurer] that [the perjury] has been or will be exposed." 18 U.S.C. § 1623(d). *See* United States v. Denison, 663 F.2d 611 (5th Cir. 1981); United States v. Moore, 613 F.2d 1029 (D.C. Cir. 1979), *cert. denied,* 446 U.S. 954 (1980). The elimination of the common-law rule that recantation is not a defense to perjury is the only respect in which section 1623 is more lenient toward defendants than section 1621. However, it appears that unless recantation is immediate or nearly so, the government may well succeed in a claim that the original perjury was already manifest or had substantially affected the proceeding. *See* United States v. Tucker, 495 F. Supp. 607, 613-14 (E.D.N.Y. 1980); United States v. McAfee, 8 F.3d 1010, 1016 (5th Cir. 1993) (recantation by witness during a second deposition of testimony provided during a prior deposition held not to satisfy section 1623(d) because the false testimony and recantation did not take place in the same proceeding).

■ The mens rea requirement under section 1623 is "knowingly," rather than the willfulness standard of section 1621, although as described above this may have little practical effect.

E. *Subornation of Perjury*

18 U.S.C. § 1622 provides:

> Whoever procures another to commit any perjury is guilty of subornation of perjury, and shall be fined not more than $2,000 or imprisoned not more than five years, or both.

"Procuring" means inducing or instigating in any fashion.[37] In a prosecution under section 1622, the perjury must be proved to have occurred, and all the essential elements of the perjury must be proved as well as its "procurement."[38] This means that subornation of a section 1621 perjury requires proof of the perjury by two witnesses or one witness plus direct corroboration. In a prosecution for subornation of perjury before a court or grand jury, on the other hand, the two-witness rule is abrogated.[39] In any event, proof of the inducement to testify perjuriously may come from a single uncorroborated witness.[40]

Most of the reported decisions under section 1622 involve obvious misbehavior by the defendant—usually telling the witness to lie or, worse, to conceal their joint wrongdoing, which has become the subject of inves-

---

Moreover, the adequacy of the recantation defense has been held to be a question of law for the court to decide. United States v. Fornaro, 894 F.2d 508, 511 (2d Cir. 1990); United States v. Goguen, 723 F.2d 1012, 1017 (1st Cir. 1983) ("the issue whether an effective and timely recantation has been made is one of law to be decided by the court"). Additionally, a valid recantation may be found only in those instances where both an outright retraction and repudiation has occurred. *See, e.g.,* United States v. Scivola, 766 F.2d 37, 45 (1st Cir. 1985) (mere implicit admission of false testimony not sufficient to recant under section 1623; outright retraction and repudiation of prior false testimony is required).

37. *E.g.,* Petite v. United States, 262 F.2d 788 (4th Cir. 1959).

38. *E.g.,* United States v. Brumley, 560 F.2d 1268 (5th Cir. 1977); United States v. Tanner, 471 F.2d 128 (7th Cir.), *cert. denied,* 409 U.S. 949 (1972).

39. United States v. Gross, 511 F.2d 910 (3d Cir.), *cert. denied,* 423 U.S. 924 (1975).

40. United States v. Cravero, 530 F.2d 666 (5th Cir. 1976).

tigation.[41] These cases, even though they involve extreme circumstances, do provide some guidance on the type of conduct that should be avoided in interviewing and preparing witnesses in the course of an internal investigation.

In *United States v. Sarantos*,[42] the defendant, Sarantos, was a lawyer convicted of aiding and abetting the making of false statements to the Immigration and Naturalization Service (INS) in connection with a sham marriage scheme designed to obtain permanent U.S. residence for male Greek aliens.[43] Sarantos was not involved in arranging the sham marriages; his role was to assist in the filing of a petition with the INS stating that the parties were living together as husband and wife. He also instructed wives who were called before the INS to say that they were living with their husbands, but not to mention that they had received payment for agreeing to marry.[44]

The government offered no evidence that Sarantos was ever specifically told the couples were not living together. It did, however, present powerful circumstantial evidence that Sarantos must have known that to be the case. For example, the government proved that the couples sometimes required an interpreter because they shared no common language, and that divorce papers were sometimes executed "simultaneously with immigration papers."[45]

Sarantos objected to the trial court's jury charge, which permitted a conviction for aiding and abetting the making of materially false statements if "he knew . . . [the statements] were false and . . . willfully and knowingly participated in furthering the conduct." In defining "knowingly and willfully," the judge further charged:

[I]f you find that Mr. Sarantos acted with reckless disregard of

---

41. One circuit court has held, however, that a jury could reasonably infer that the gesture of a nod of the head by the defendant toward a witness who was testifying during a hearing was sufficient to conclude the defendant was encouraging the witness to commit perjury in violation of section 1622. *See* United States v. Flint, 993 F.2d 885 (9th Cir. 1993).

42. 455 F.2d 877 (2d Cir. 1972).

43. Sarantos was convicted of aiding and abetting a violation of 18 U.S.C. § 1001 (false statements to government agency) rather than subornation of perjury, but the principles are analogous.

44. *Id.* at 879-80.

45. *Id.* at 880.

whether the statements made were true or with a conscious effort to avoid learning the truth, this requirement is satisfied, even though you may find that he was not specifically aware of the facts which would establish the falsity of the statements.[46]

On appeal, Sarantos argued that when a lawyer is charged with aiding and abetting a false statement, the standard of scienter must be higher than reckless disregard of falsity. Otherwise, Sarantos contended, the attorney-client relationship would be "radically alter[ed]," as the lawyer effectively would be made "an investigative arm of the government."[47]

The Second Circuit rejected this argument, noting that the purpose of construing the term "knowingly" to include willful blindness to the existence of a fact "[i]s to prevent an individual like Sarantos from circumventing criminal sanctions merely by deliberately closing his eyes to the obvious risk that he is engaging in unlawful conduct." As for the claim that such a rule unduly infringes on the lawyer's role, the court stated:

> We have not held, as appellant contends, that a lawyer must investigate the truth of his client's assertions or risk going to jail. We have held, and continue to hold, that he cannot counsel others to make statements in the face of obvious indications of which he is aware that those assertions are not true.[48]

In *In re Grand Jury Subpoena (Legal Services Center)*,[49] the court was asked to enforce subpoenas calling for production of a lawyer's legal files relating to representation of clients before the INS. The government's theory was the same as in *Sarantos*: that "by 'turning a blind eye' to what the government considers obvious indications of the fraudulent character of their clients' marriages, [the attorneys] committed offenses against the United States including aiding and abetting, 18 U.S.C. § 2; suborning perjury, 18 U.S.C. § 1622; and conspiracy to commit an offense or defraud the United States, 18 U.S.C. § 371."[50]

The court quashed the subpoenas, finding that the government had

---

46. *Id.*
47. *Id.* at 880-81.
48. *Id.* at 881.
49. 615 F. Supp. 958 (D. Mass. 1985).
50. *Id.* at 967.

failed to make a sufficient showing that the lawyers were in possession of information clearly establishing their clients' fraud. The court noted the tension between a lawyer's obligation of zealous representation and any requirement that a lawyer investigate the truth or falsity of a client's assertions. In an effort to accommodate both interests, the court concluded that "[s]o long as the attorney does not have obvious indications of the client's fraud or perjury, the attorney is not obligated to undertake an independent determination before advancing his client's position."[51]

The lawyers in *Sarantos* and *In re Grand Jury Subpoena* were representing individuals and, at least in the latter case, arguably did not have access to information beyond what their clients told them. By contrast, counsel conducting an internal investigation normally will have interviewed a number of employees and reviewed corporate documents, providing additional perspective into whether an employee's proposed testimony is truthful. This means, in many cases, that counsel will have an independent basis for judging the testimony. To the extent there is good reason to mistrust the employee's version of the events, at least corporate counsel may not encourage the employee to testify to them.[52] Depending on the circumstances, it may also be appropriate for the employee to be separately represented.

III. MISPRISION OF A FELONY

During the course of an internal investigation, counsel may become aware of a crime previously committed. If so, counsel should be sensitive to the federal misprision of felony statute, 18 U.S.C. § 4. The essential elements of 18 U.S.C. § 4 are as follows: (i) the principal committed and completed the felony alleged; (ii) the defendant had full knowledge of that fact; (iii) the defendant failed to notify the authorities; and (iv) the defendant took an affirmative step to conceal the crime.[53]

---

51. *Id.* at 969.

52. *See also* Tedesco v. Mishkin, 629 F. Supp. 1474, 1479-80 (S.D.N.Y. 1986) (lawyer violated 18 U.S.C. § 1622 by failing to advise a witness, after hearing proposed testimony and knowing it to be false, against testifying in that manner; under all the circumstances, including repeated prior statements by lawyer indicating harmfulness of truthful testimony, witness understood lawyer's silence to signify agreement that witness should give proposed perjurious testimony).

53. United States v. Ciambrone, 750 F.2d 1416 (9th Cir. 1984); United States v. Baez, 732 F.2d 780 (10th Cir. 1984).

Mere silence, without some affirmative act of concealment, does not make out misprision of a felony.[54] Misprision of felony, like subornation of perjury, should raise few concerns for the lawyer conducting an internal investigation, as long as there is no solicitation of false testimony or suppression of evidence.[55] However, in some cases counsel conducting the internal investigation might be asked whether the company can destroy records apparently evidencing a crime. Destruction of documentary evidence can, under some circumstances, meet the affirmative concealment element of 18 U.S.C. § 4. Although we have found no reported cases directly on point, the applicability of 18 U.S.C. § 4 may depend upon whether the documents are destroyed pursuant to the company's normal practice of retaining records for a certain time period or whether the documents are being destroyed to conceal the earlier crime. The former situation would seem not to violate 18 U.S.C. § 4, but the latter clearly does.

Similarly, in the government contracting industry, findings in an internal company investigation may lead the company to adjust its accounting records in order to repay money owed to the government (e.g., by adjusting the company's overhead account). Corporate counsel, if asked to review this adjustment, should ensure that the adjustment accurately reflects

---

54. *See, e.g.,* United States v. Daddano, 432 F.2d 1119 (7th Cir. 1970), *cert. denied,* 402 U.S. 905 (1971) (affirmative act of concealment found where one robbery defendant arranged to give lie detector tests to the other participants in the bank robbery, on the theory that the tests, which included the question, "Did you give information to the authorities?" were designed to keep everybody quiet by impressing on them the risk of retaliation should they report the crime to the authorities); Bratton v. United States, 73 F.2d 795, 797 (10th Cir. 1934) (language in misprision statute requiring proof of nondisclosure and concealment means government must show something beyond mere failure to disclose, such as suppression of evidence, harboring of a fugitive, intimidation of witnesses or some "other positive act designed to conceal from the authorities the fact that a crime had been committed").

55. Although corruptly endeavoring to persuade a witness to invoke the Fifth Amendment privilege can amount to an obstruction of justice, advising a witness in good faith to exercise the privilege (or getting him an attorney who does so) cannot be either obstruction of justice or misprision of a felony. *See* United States v. Fayer, 523 F.2d 661, 662-64 (2d Cir. 1975) (defendant's counsel may suggest to witness that witness might wish to invoke Fifth Amendment privilege); *cf.* United States v. Jennings, 603 F.2d 650 (7th Cir. 1979) (Fifth Amendment protection against misprision prosecution for failure to disclose and concealing a crime operates whenever the disclosure might tend to show the defendant has committed a crime).

the necessary change and that it is not designed to conceal any prior misconduct.

IV. OBSTRUCTION OF JUSTICE AND THE VICTIM AND WITNESS PROTECTION ACT

Three of the general obstruction of justice statutes are relevant in the context of interviewing and preparing witnesses during an internal corporate investigation.[56] 18 U.S.C. § 1512, the witness-tampering provision enacted in 1982 as part of the Victim and Witness Protection Act (VWPA), is the most important of the three. It substantially expands the range of activities deemed illegal forms of witness tampering and eases the government's burden of proof. Sections 1503 and 1505 prohibit (in slightly different terms) "corrupt" efforts to interfere with the "due administration of justice." These sections may still be applicable to certain forms of witness tampering.

A. *Witness Tampering Under Section 1512*

Prior to enactment of section 1512, section 1503 contained a specific witness-tampering clause. It proscribed "corruptly, or by threats or force, or by any threatening letter or communication, endeavor[ing] to influence, intimidate or impede any witness...." Section 1505 contained a comparable provision relating to administrative and congressional proceedings. The term "corruptly" was defined in the cases to mean acting purposefully with the specific intent to obstruct justice.[57] These witness-

---

56. Also relevant, where the company is a financial institution, is the obstruction of justice statute enacted as part of the Financial Institution Reform, Recovery, and Enforcement Act of 1989 and codified at 18 U.S.C. § 1510(b). That statute is discussed *infra*. Various forms of obstruction of justice are prohibited by a series of statutes collected at 18 U.S.C. § 1501 *et seq*. Most of these plainly have no bearing upon the conduct of an internal investigation—for example, those prohibiting retaliation against witnesses involving bodily injury (section 1513(a)), obstruction of court orders (section 1509), obstruction of criminal investigations by bribery (section 1510(a)), etc.

57. *See, e.g.,* United States v. Carleo, 576 F.2d 846 (10th Cir.), *cert. denied,* 439 U.S. 850 (1978) (in section 1503 case, based on defendant's efforts to persuade the witness to leave town and remain silent, prosecution was required to prove corrupt intention to obstruct justice, and to that end was permitted to adduce evidence of

tampering clauses were deleted by the VWPA, which gathered all of the express witness-tampering provisions in section 1512.

However, in addition to the traditional forms of witness tampering (that is, corrupt, violent, and otherwise coercive behavior), section 1512 added new offenses. A broader range of conduct may now be susceptible to criminal prosecution. Under section 1512(b), it is now a crime to "engage[ ] in misleading conduct toward another person"[58] with the intent to "influence, delay, or prevent" a witness's testimony, or to "cause or induce any person" to "withhold" testimony or documents. Unlike a prosecution under either section 1503 or section 1505, the government need only prove the defendant acted knowingly with intent to bring about one of the enumerated results, and not specifically with the intent to obstruct justice. Moreover, once the government has established the defendant's intent under section 1512(b), the defendant has the burden of proving, by way of affirmative defense, that his "conduct consisted solely of lawful conduct and that [his] sole intention was to encourage, induce, or cause the other person to testify truthfully."[59]

---

prior incident in which defendant had beaten a man in presence of this witness and stated "that's what happened to snitches"). *See also* United States v. Ryan, 455 F.2d 728, 734 (9th Cir. 1971) ("[t]he word 'corrupt' in the statute means for an evil or wicked purpose," meaning a "specific intent to impede the administration of justice"). It is clear that, after passage of the VWPA, sections 1503 and 1505 continue to require intent to obstruct justice. *E.g.*, United States v. Barber, 881 F.2d 345 (7th Cir. 1989), *cert. denied*, 110 S. Ct. 1956 (1990) (submission of forged letters to sentencing judge was done with the corrupt purpose of obstructing justice and thus was proper basis for prosecution under 18 U.S.C. § 1503); United States v. Jeter, 775 F.2d 670, 675-76 (6th Cir. 1985) (section 1503 "contains a clear *mens rea* requirement that limits its scope to those who 'corruptly' or intentionally seek to obstruct the due administration of justice"); United States v. Laurins, 857 F.2d 529 (9th Cir. 1988), *cert. denied.* 492 U.S. 906 (1990) ("corruptly" in 18 U.S.C. § 1505 has same meaning as in 18 U.S.C. § 1503: "the act must be done with the purpose of obstructing justice").

58. Courts have interpreted the term "person" to include potential witnesses, United States v. Romero, 54 F.3d 56, 62 (2d Cir. 1995), *cert. denied*, 116 S. Ct. 1449 (1996); grand jury witnesses, United States v. Schmidt, 935 F.2d 1440, 1452 (4th Cir. 1991); and excused witnesses, United States v. Risken, 788 F.2d 1361, 1369 (8th Cir. 1986).

59. 18 U.S.C. § 1512(d). The Second Circuit has rejected an argument that the affirmative defense provision is a nullity on the grounds that a defendant cannot possess both the intent to cause a witness to withhold evidence and the "sole intent" to encourage truthful testimony. United States v. Johnson, 968 F.2d 208, 213 (2d Cir.

It is now also a crime (albeit a misdemeanor) to "harass" another person to the effect that "any person" is hindered, prevented, dissuaded, or even so much as delayed from attending or testifying in an official proceeding, or from providing information to law enforcement authorities.[60]

1. Misleading Conduct

"Misleading conduct" is defined in 18 U.S.C. § 1515(3) as follows:

(A) knowingly making a false statement; (B) intentionally omitting information from a statement and thereby causing a portion of such statement to be misleading, or intentionally concealing a material fact, and thereby creating a false impression by such statement; (C) with intent to mislead, knowingly submitting or inviting reliance on a writing or recording that is false, forged, altered, or otherwise lacking in authenticity; (D) with intent to mislead, knowingly submitting or inviting reliance on a sample, specimen, map, photograph, boundary mark, or other object that is misleading in a material respect; or (E) knowingly using a trick, scheme, or device with intent to mislead.

Before enactment of section 1512, a lawyer could reasonably have assumed his or her behavior was within the bounds of legitimate advocacy as long as it did not go beyond urging the persuasiveness of a witness's innocent explanation and seek to have the witness testify falsely.[61]

1992). The court held that once the government met its burden of proof beyond a reasonable doubt that the defendant intended to cause the witness to withhold testimony, the intent prong of the affirmative defense to section 1512 could still be satisfied by proving, by a preponderance of the evidence, that the testimony he wanted the witness to withhold was false. *Id.* Such a reading of section 1512(d) was deemed by the court to comport with the Senate Judiciary Committee's view of the affirmative defense as being "intended primarily to avoid the possibility that a [judge or other officer of the court] would violate this statute by threatening a witness or potential witness with a perjury or false statement prosecution if he testifies falsely." *Id.* (quoting S. REP. No. 532, 97th Cong., 2d Sess. 9, *reprinted in* 1982 U.S. CODE CONG. & ADMIN. NEWS 2515, 2525).

60. 18 U.S.C. § 1512(c).

61. *See, e.g.,* United States v. Brand, 775 F.2d 1460 (11th Cir. 1985) (reversing section 1503 conviction based on attempt to secure statement from witness to convince government to dismiss indictment).

There was some question in *Brand* whether the defendants first attempted to have the witness sign a false statement exculpating them. But the court concluded there was a sufficient basis for defendants to believe that the first proffered statement was true, and "[w]hen finally advised by [the witness] that he would refuse to sign the requested statement, [the defendants] accepted as an alternative the true statement signed by [the witness]."[62] Moreover, the defendants "made [no] effort to alter [the witness's] testimony, or influence it in any manner."[63] Endeavoring corruptly to persuade a witness to invoke the privilege against self-incrimination, or not to testify, also was, and is, punishable as an obstruction of justice.[64] But section 1512, by its terms, punishes misleading conduct that merely seeks to "influence" testimony, and eliminates the requirement that the government prove a corrupt purpose to obstruct justice. These changes conceivably could reach conduct that until now had been deemed legitimate.

The most obviously troublesome provision for counsel conducting an internal investigation is 18 U.S.C. § 1515(a)(3)(B). Especially in the early stages of an investigation, counsel may not have learned all relevant facts, and will not be in a position to share them in witness interviews. Later, with the benefit of hindsight and a fuller record, the government could conceivably claim that counsel had been acting intentionally in omitting information from a statement to a prospective witness.

More significantly, counsel may have legitimate reason to omit or conceal information in the course of employee interviews. From the corporation's point of view—and this is true not only at the outset but throughout the investigation—it is usually counterproductive to divulge all the facts to each potential witness. After all, the basic purpose of the

---

62. 775 F.2d at 1469.

63. *Id.* Hall v. United States, 419 F.2d 582, 584-85 (5th Cir. 1969) (no basis for section 1503 witness-tampering charge where defendant believed potential government witness would exonerate him, and so visited the witness to try to persuade him to testify truthfully at trial); Cole v. United States, 329 F.2d 437, 439 (9th Cir. 1964), *cert. denied,* 377 U.S. 954 (1965) (section 1503 "cannot proscribe criminal acts consistent with the due administration of justice, such as influencing a witness to tell the truth"); *cf.* United States v. St. Clair, 552 F.2d 57, 59 (2d Cir.), *cert. denied,* 433 U.S. 909 (1977) (18 U.S.C. § 1510 violated "whenever an individual induces or attempts to induce another person to make a material misrepresentation to a criminal investigator").

64. *E.g.,* United States v. Capo, 791 F.2d 1054 (2d Cir. 1986); United States v. Cioffi, 493 F.2d 1111, 1119 (2d Cir.), *cert. denied,* 419 U.S. 917 (1974).

internal investigation is to uncover possible or suspected wrongdoing. Some employees who are interviewed may be guilty of wrongdoing, or of a subpar job performance, which they wish to conceal. Counsel will want an opportunity to test their statements against those of other witnesses (and against the government's version of the facts, to the extent it is known), without first describing what everyone has so far said. This is true even where the employee being interviewed is not suspected of any misbehavior. Lawyers know that witnesses tend to take their cue in describing events from the lawyer doing the questioning. Thus, there is a risk—especially where a lawyer is acting on behalf of the witness's employer in criminal or administrative investigation—that innocent employees will tailor their testimony (wittingly or otherwise) to provide what they believe are the *right* answers.

Moreover, if some of the information gleaned in the course of the investigation is harmful to the corporation, counsel will not want to add to the number of witnesses who know the information. Although the corporation has no Fifth Amendment right against self-incrimination, it and its counsel also have no duty to reveal incriminating evidence learned in the course of an internal review. Depending on the extent of its understanding of the conduct under investigation, the government might or might not know enough to seek to question employees who do possess evidence of possible wrongdoing. Requiring counsel, in interviewing and preparing witnesses, to reveal inculpatory information they have learned, or face potential prosecution under section 1512, would unfairly undercut counsel's ability to protect the client.

Accordingly, we do not believe that Congress intended section 1515(3)(B) to require counsel, in conducting internal interviews, to disclose all relevant facts or risk criminal prosecution. Such a rigidly literal interpretation is contrary to the public policy underlying the statutory amendment. That public policy, although designed to expand the prosecutor's arsenal against obstruction of justice, was not intended to curtail a company's internal fact gathering even in response to a government investigation.

Section 1515(3)(A) presents problems also, notwithstanding that, unlike subsection (B), it requires that the defendant "knowingly mak[e] a false statement." For example, corporate counsel may have an adequate basis for suggesting to a witness that her recollection of events is mistaken. Other witnesses, perhaps more directly involved in the conduct at issue, may have given conflicting statements. Or perhaps there is documentary evidence contradicting this witness's testimony. Counsel may choose to share these items with the witness in an effort to suggest an alternative and innocent explanation of the events. Should the government conclude that the exculpatory version is false, it might seek to prosecute the lawyer under section 1512, contending that the lawyer "knew" the exculpatory version to be false at the time it was conveyed to the witness.

As a practical matter, the prosecutor often will not be in a position to learn what corporate counsel said to witnesses in the course of the investigation. But disclosure may occur under various scenarios, including the unhappy and voluble employee or former employee. Unlike sections 1503 and 1505, section 1512 does not require that there be a judicial proceeding (for example, a grand jury investigation) pending at the time of the alleged obstruction.[65] This means that section 1512 could reach even the very early efforts of corporate counsel in conducting an internal investigation, before the government has begun any inquiry (and before counsel has any clear idea of the true state of affairs).

Where a proceeding has begun, if corporate counsel's role continues to the point of participating in witness preparation, counsel should have section 1512 in mind during the course of such preparation. The following techniques are relatively common in witness preparation: refreshing recollection with documentary evidence or with the statements of other witnesses; noting that it is the responsibility of the questioning lawyer to pose the necessary questions, and advising that the witness not volunteer or offer speculation; advising that the witness not necessarily accept the assumptions or characterizations included in the examiner's questions; explaining the legal ramifications of differing emphases on the facts, all equally true; organizing the testimony to diminish the damage caused by adverse information; suggesting how to respond to anticipated questions, including possibly the volunteering of an explanatory gloss going beyond the literal terms of the question; and advising the witness as to demeanor.

---

65. *Compare* Pettibone v. United States, 148 U.S. 197 (1873) (reversing convictions under predecessor obstruction of justice statute because defendants were not aware of pending proceedings), and United States v. McComb, 744 F.2d 555, 560 (7th Cir. 1984) (pendency of a judicial proceeding is required to satisfy "administration of justice" element of section 1503; grand jury investigation is such a proceeding), *with* 18 U.S.C. § 1512(e)(1) ("an official proceeding need not be pending or about to be instituted at the time of the offense").

We do not believe that section 1512 was intended to prohibit any of these legitimate techniques. But the definition of the term "misleading" in section 1515(3)(B) is vague and potentially far-reaching. Lawyers conducting internal company investigations must be aware of sections 1512 and 1515(3)(B) to ensure that they do not engage in behavior that could be considered illegal.

2. Harassment

The harassment provision of section 1512 provides as follows:

Whoever intentionally harasses another person and thereby hinders, delays, prevents, or dissuades any person from—

1. attending or testifying in an official proceeding;
2. reporting to a law enforcement officer or judge of the United States the commission or possible commission of a Federal offense or a violation of conditions of probation, parole, or release pending judicial proceedings;
3. arresting or seeking the arrest of another person in connection with a Federal offense; or
4. causing a criminal prosecution, or a parole or probation revocation proceeding, to be sought or instituted, or assisting in such prosecution or proceeding;

or attempts to do so, shall be fined not more than $25,000 or imprisoned not more than one year, or both.[66]

On its face, the prohibition against harassment would appear to reach conduct not intended to have an impact on a witness's testimony. But this is surely the product of poor draftsmanship; it makes no sense to conclude that Congress meant section 1512(c) to reach intentionally harassing behavior toward a witness carried out for some purpose other than hindering testimony. The legislative history supports the imposition of this intent requirement, and in the few reported harassment cases, courts appear to have agreed.[67]

---

66. 18 U.S.C. § 1512(c).

67. *See* United States v. Wilson, 796 F.2d 55 (4th Cir. 1986) (nasty remarks to prospective government witnesses waiting outside courtroom were within the statute even though two of the witnesses did testify; section 1512(c)(1) applies to endeavors

3. Legislative History

Notwithstanding the apparent broad sweep of section 1512's literal language, there is evidence the statute was never intended to encroach on the legitimate exercise of the lawyer's role. Thus, courts should not interpret section 1512 to be used as broadly as some of its language literally would suggest.

Although the legislative history is slim, it seems clear that the principal purpose of enacting section 1512 was to reach subtle varieties of intimidation, usually carried out by prospective defendants for the purpose of securing false testimony or suppressing testimony entirely. The Senate Report accompanying the VWPA characterizes section 1512 as "an intimidation offense."[68]

In delineating the scope of section 1512, the report repeatedly refers to the problem of witness intimidation, and never to mere "influence" without a corrupt purpose.[69]

Indeed, in describing the first prohibited purpose in section 1512(b)(1), influencing testimony, the Senate Report explicitly notes that the statutory language is taken from section 1503:

> [Influence] is the broadest word used in 18 U.S.C. § 1503, and the Committee intends that it also receive an expansi[ve] interpretation in this section. The fact that the section requires that force, threat, intimidation, or deception be employed, suffices to narrow the offense to clearly culpable conduct.[70]

There is no question that Congress meant to reduce the intent requirement in the new legislation. But this emphasis on the safeguard provided by the relatively limited number of prohibited methods of influencing testimony—all of them inherently corrupt, including "deception," if by

---

to dissuade testimony, whether or not successful); United States v. Tison, 780 F.2d 1569 (11th Cir. 1986) (civil injunction action under section 1514; "attempting to intimidate a witness from providing accurate information to federal law officials is exactly the kind of harassment this legislation was designed to eliminate").

68. S. REP. No. 532, 97th Cong., 2d Sess. 14, *reprinted in* 1982 U.S. CODE CONG. & ADMIN. NEWS 2515, 2520.

69. *Id.* at 14-15, 1982 U.S. CODE CONG. & ADMIN. NEWS at 2520-21.

70. *Id.* at 16, 1982 U.S. CODE CONG. & ADMIN. NEWS at 2522.

deception is meant fraud[71]—suggests that Congress did not intend section 1512 to be applied to appropriate behavior by a lawyer in interviewing and preparing witnesses.

This is further reflected in the description of the loophole Congress understood itself to be mending. The principal perceived problem with the existing witness-tampering statutes was that they did not reach

> the most common form of intimidation—verbal harassment. Testimony given to the ABA [in public hearings relating to victim and witness intimidation] suggested that sometimes innocent acts, such as telephoning a victim to say hello, coming to his home, or even driving a motorcycle by, may be extremely effective in preventing a victim or witness from testifying. This type of activity is not covered by section 1503 which requires corruption, threats or force for an offense.[72]

This premise seems incorrect. Otherwise "innocent" behavior designed to intimidate a witness into not testifying, or changing the testimony—which is what these examples amount to—would have been covered by prior law. Sections 1503 and 1505 both made punishable "corrupt" endeavors to intimidate a witness, and courts have recognized that less than overt threats may, because of their effect on the witness, meet this definition.[73] Indeed, going even further, courts have recognized that even wholly

---

71. Although referred to here as "deception," and denominated "misleading conduct" in the enacted legislation (defined broadly), the witness-tampering behavior Congress principally sought to control was fraud. *See* S. Rep. No. 532, 97th Cong., 2d Sess. 17, *reprinted in* 1982 U.S. Code Cong. & Admin. News 2515, 2523 ("subsection [(b)] is confined to the traditional means of tampering involving the use of force, threat, intimidation, or fraud").

72. *Id.* at 15, 1982 U.S. Code Cong. & Admin. News at 2521.

73. *See e.g.*, United States v. Carlson, 547 F.2d 1346, 1359 & n.13 (8th Cir. 1976), *cert. denied*, 431 U.S. 914 (1977) (although witness refuses to describe the statements by defendant that caused him to refuse to testify, court finds evidence of "threats and intimidating overtures"); United States v. De Stefano, 476 F.2d 324 (7th Cir. 1973) (although confrontation clause violation requires reversal, court makes clear that simple question, "Have you done any fishing lately?" can be rendered intimidating conduct toward witness because of witness's and defendant's shared understanding of the underworld meaning of the phrase); *cf.* United States v. Lazzerini, 611 F.2d 940, 941-42 (1st Cir. 1979) (prosecution for endeavoring corruptly to influence a juror under 18 U.S.C. § 1503; no matter how "subtle or circui-

non-coercive behavior designed to obstruct or impede judicial proceedings is corrupt within the meaning of the omnibus clauses.[74]

Genuine inadequacies in sections 1503, 1505 and 1510 included the relatively narrow definition of "witness" as someone expected to testify in a judicial proceeding, the requirement that the anticipated testimony would have been admissible in court, and the requirement that the proceeding be pending and the defendant be aware of it.[75]

Although neither section 1512 nor section 1515 contains a definition of "harassment," section 1514, establishing a civil action "to restrain an offense under section 1512," does. It defines "harassment" as a course of conduct directed at a specific person that—

(A) causes substantial emotional distress in such person; and

(B) serves no legitimate purpose.[76]

Comments made in the course of the House's consideration of the legislation demonstrate a congressional intent that the harassing behavior not only serve no legitimate purpose, but also be intended to interfere with testimony:

> [T]he Senate amendment adds a new subsection describing a misdemeanor offense of intentionally harassing another person and thereby intentionally preventing any person from attending or testifying in an official proceeding.... The Senate language will

---

tous[,] . . . [i]f reasonable jurors could conclude, from the circumstances of the conversation, that the defendant had sought, however cleverly and with whatever cloaking of purpose, to influence improperly a juror, the offense was complete").

74. United States v. Gates, 616 F.2d 1103 (9th Cir. 1980) (upholding conviction based on providing a witness with a false story to recite in the grand jury). *See generally* United States v. Howard, 569 F.2d 1331, 1333-37 (5th Cir.), *cert. denied sub nom.,* Ritter v. United States, 439 U.S. 834 (1978) (omnibus clause of 18 U.S.C. § 1503 designed to reach acts that are similar in result, whatever the means, to the conduct set out in the first part of the statute).

75. *See generally* S. Rep. No. 532, 97th Cong., 2d Sess. 14-15, *reprinted in* 1982 U.S. Code Cong. & Admin. News 2520-21; Note, *Defining Witness Tampering Under 18 U.S.C. Section* 1512, 86 Colum. L. Rev. 1417, 1419-21 (1986); United States v. DiSalvo, 631 F. Supp. 1398, 1402 (E.D. Pa. 1986).

76. 18 U.S.C. § 1514(c)(1).

reach thinly-veiled threats that create justifiable apprehension in a victim or witness.[77]

This begins to sound like Congress was thinking in terms of behavior intended to obstruct or impair the functioning of the criminal justice system, even as it was eliminating the corrupt-intent requirement of prior law.[78]

Although the term "misleading conduct" is not discussed in the legislative history, the Senate Report does list fraud as one of the prohibited methods under section 1512 (along with force, threats, and intimidation), even though fraud is not mentioned in the statute. As one commentator pointed out, section 1512 was modeled on the witness-tampering provision of what was then the latest version of a proposed new Federal Criminal Code, and that provision prohibited fraud that obstructs or impairs the due administration of justice in a judicial proceeding. "Fraud" was defined identically to "misleading conduct" in section 1512.[79]

As its only example of fraud, the Senate Report accompanying the VWPA mentions deceiving a law enforcement officer about the meeting place with an informant, thereby hindering or preventing the communication of information relating to commission of a crime that would be punishable under 18 U.S.C. § 1512(b)(3).[80] Once again, this is conduct meant to obstruct the workings of the criminal justice system.

The Congress that considered the proposed Federal Criminal Code recognized the dangers in applying the fraud provision to actions of counsel.[81] That code included a defense that "the actor was a lawyer, and the

---

77. 128 CONG. REC. H8469 (daily ed. Oct. 1, 1982) (statement of Rep. Rodino).

78. *See also* S. Rep. No. 532, 97th Cong. 2d Sess. 17, *reprinted in* 1982 U.S. CODE CONG. & ADMIN. NEWS 2515, 2523 (describing Senate bill's version of harassment provision as "cover[ing] any conduct that maliciously hinders, delays, prevents or dissuades a witness or victim from fulfilling his societally desirable role with reference to attending or testifying in an official proceeding, or reporting or taking other action in relation to an offense or possible offense, if the conduct is done with intent to intimidate, harass, harm, or injure another person").

79. *See* Jeffress, *The New Federal Witness Tampering Statute*, 22 AM. CRIM. L. REV. 1, 2-3, 14 (1984).

80. S. Rep. No. 532, 97th Cong., 2d Sess. 16, *reprinted in* 1982 U.S. CODE CONG. & ADMIN. NEWS 2515, 2522.

81. Section 1512 did not receive anything like the careful committee review to which the Code provision was subjected. Jeffress, *supra* note 79, 22 AM. CRIM. L. REV. at 2-3 ("The VWPA was introduced on April 22, 1982, and enacted after a flurry of amendments on October 1, 1982. It was the subject of a single brief committee

conduct in which the actor engaged constituted an ethical representation of a client's interests." The proposed defense, unlike the affirmative defense in 18 U.S.C. § 1512(d), was required to be disproved by the government beyond a reasonable doubt.

The absence of comparable protection in section 1512 may make it susceptible to challenge on constitutional overbreadth grounds should it be applied to normal and innocent lawyering.[82] To the extent courts have rejected constitutional challenges to the statute, they have been examining traditional criminal behavior that plainly may be subject to punishment (and could have been prosecuted under section 1503)—for example, threatening to murder a witness.[83]

4. Safeguards

We have found no reported cases applying 18 U.S.C. § 1512 to the activities of lawyers in circumstances where there is no corrupt endeavor to obstruct justice. Indeed, the reported cases under section 1512 generally involve the same kind of culpable behavior previously prosecuted using 18 U.S.C. § 1503.[84]

This may reflect a narrower, and we believe more correct, interpretation of section 1512 than its own language might suggest, or it may reflect a sensitivity on the part of prosecutors to the dangers of interfering with the lawyer-witness relationship, absent a clear and corrupt effort to impede the judicial process. Or, it may simply result from the fact that much of what goes on between lawyer and witness is protected by privilege or otherwise not readily available to the prosecutor.

---

hearing, a single committee report, and extremely limited debate in the end-of-a-session frenzy during which it was enacted.").

82. *See, e.g.,* United States v. Clemons, 843 F.2d 741, 749-55 (3d Cir. 1988), *cert. denied,* 488 U.S. 835 (1988) (noting "doubts concerning the constitutionality of § 1512(c)," but finding any error harmless beyond a reasonable doubt on the facts of the case, which included uncontradicted testimony of threats of physical harm to the prospective witness); State v. Cohen, 568 So. 2d 49 (Fla. 1990) (holding that identical Florida state provision unconstitutionally vague).

83. *E.g.,* United States v. Wilson, 565 F. Supp. 1416, 1429-31 (S.D.N.Y. 1983).

84. *E.g.,* United States v. Maggitt, 784 F.2d 590 (5th Cir. 1986) (threat to murder witness); United States v. Rodolitz, 786 F.2d 77 (2d Cir. 1986) (upholding conviction under "misleading conduct" provision of 18 U.S.C. § 1512; defendant lied to witness to persuade witness that giving grand jury testimony which they both knew to be false was justified).

In any event, there are a number of cautions that a lawyer should consider implementing to further minimize risk of the behavior being challenged under section 1512. Certainly, counsel may not say or intimate—although this was true under prior law—that anything adverse will occur if the witness tells the story a certain way. To the contrary, it is important to emphasize that the employee's duty to cooperate with corporate counsel conducting an internal investigation implies nothing more than an obligation to be candid, and if the witness ultimately testifies, the truth must be told.

The employee should be advised that counsel is representing the corporation, not the employee, and the scope of the company's attorney-client privilege should be explained. Under some circumstances, it may be appropriate to refer to the possibility of separate representation. If counsel requests that the employee not discuss the investigation or the interview with others, counsel should state clearly that this is not meant to suggest that the employee will be precluded from testifying fully and honestly at some later point. To ensure against potential misunderstandings, counsel should have another lawyer or paralegal present as a witness to the interview.

B. *Omnibus Clauses of Sections 1503 and 1505*

In enacting the VWPA, Congress eliminated the specific witness-tampering clauses of sections 1503 and 1505. Left in place, however, were the so-called "omnibus clauses." Section 1503 did, and still does, apply to a person who "corruptly or by threats of force, or by any threatening letter or communication, influences, obstructs, or impedes, or endeavors to influence, obstruct or impede, the due administration of justice." Section 1505 applies to this behavior in relation to "the due and proper administration of the law under which any pending proceeding is being had before any department or agency of the United States, or the due and proper exercise of the power of [congressional investigation]."

Most courts that have considered the issue have concluded that the omnibus clauses of sections 1503 and 1505 still may be used to prosecute witness tampering, at least with respect to those offenses not explicitly covered by section 1512.[85] One court appears to have held that both sections may be used to prosecute the same conduct.[86]

The specific-intent requirement of sections 1503 and 1505 limits the range of potentially culpable conduct. With respect to the normal activities of a lawyer in conducting an internal investigation, the government would be required to demonstrate that counsel corruptly endeavored to persuade the witness to testify falsely. Thus, usual and necessary interviewing techniques create no risk simply by virtue of reflecting an intent to "influence" the witness. Prophylactic measures of the sort suggested above—above all, explicitly instructing witnesses that they are obligated to tell the truth should they be called upon to testify—should effectively eliminate any real danger of prosecution under either section.

In addition to a corrupt state of mind, in a prosecution under the omnibus clause of either section 1503 or section 1505, the government must prove (i) an "endeavor" (ii) to influence, obstruct or impede the due administration of justice.[87]

---

85. *E.g.,* United States v. Aguilar, 21 F.3d 1475, 1485-86 (9th Cir. 1994) (concluding that Congress did not intend by enacting section 1512 to preclude all charges of obstruction of justice involving witnesses under section 1503); United States v. Kenny, 973 F.2d 339, 342 (4th Cir. 1992) (discussing the ramifications of the 1982 amendment to section 1503, the court determined that section 1512 is not the only vehicle for prosecution of witness tampering); *accord,* United States v. Moody, 977 F.2d 1420, 1424 (11th Cir. 1992); United States v. Lester, 749 F.2d 1288, 1292-95 (9th Cir. 1984) (upholding section 1503 conviction based on hiding witness to prevent testimony, and noting that refusal to apply omnibus clause of section 1503 would mean that corrupt but noncoercive witness tampering would fall outside reach of both that section and 18 U.S.C. § 1512); United States v. King, 762 F.2d 232, 236-38 (2d Cir. 1985) (urging witness to lie may be a crime under section 1503, but it is not punishable under section 1512 because it is not one of that section's enumerated offenses); United States v. Arnold, 773 F.2d 823, 831-32 (7th Cir. 1985) (corruptly influencing a witness to invoke Fifth Amendment privilege properly prosecuted under omnibus clause of post-1982 section 1503).

86. *See* United States v. Wesley, 748 F.2d 962, 964 (5th Cir. 1984), *cert. denied,* 471 U.S. 1130 (1985) ("no indication that Congress intended that threats against witnesses would fall exclusively under section 1512 and [a]re exempt from prosecution under section 1503").

87. *E.g.,* Smith v. United States, 234 F.2d 385 (5th Cir. 1956) (filing of false affidavits prepared and presented to affiants by defendant). "Endeavor" has been defined as something less than an attempt:

The due administration of justice element of the statute requires that a judicial proceeding be pending, and the defendant be aware of it, at the time of the endeavor.[88]

V. FINANCIAL INSTITUTION REFORM, RECOVERY, AND ENFORCEMENT ACT OF 1989

The Financial Institution Reform, Recovery, and Enforcement Act of 1989 (FIRREA), the statute principally designed to deal with the financial crisis of the thrift industry and the Federal Savings and Loan Insurance Corporation, also added a new subsection to 18 U.S.C. § 1510, which previously covered obstruction of criminal investigations by bribery.

The word of the section is "endeavor," and by using it the section got rid of the technicalities which might be urged as besetting the word "attempt," and it describes any effort or essay to do or accomplish the evil purpose that the section was enacted to prevent. . . . The section . . . is not directed at success in corrupting a juror, but at the "endeavor" to do so. Experimental approaches to the corruption of a juror are the "endeavor" of the section.

United States v. Russell, 255 U.S. 138, 143 (1921). In practice, this standard requires very little to be proved to determine an endeavor. For example, in *United States v. Buffalano*, 727 F.2d 50 (2d Cir. 1984), the Second Circuit concluded an endeavor had been established where a lawyer falsely told a criminal defendant not his client that he could bribe the sentencing judge to ensure a lenient sentence. In fact, the lawyer had no intention of paying any bribe, and took no steps remotely connected with one; he simply put the money in his pocket. Nevertheless, his actions were held to constitute an endeavor capable of obstructing the judicial process on the ground that he falsely lulled the defendant into a belief that he would receive a light sentence, and the defendant was thereby deterred from taking actions on his own behalf to mitigate the sentence (such as cooperating with the government in another investigation, presenting mitigating material to the court drawn from his own life, and so on). *See also* United States v. Washington Water Power Co., 793 F.2d 1079 (9th Cir. 1986) (upholding convictions of company and one of its supervisors for assisting an employee in finding employment overseas, after the employee requested their help in moving to avoid service of expected subpoena).

88. Pettibone v. United States, 148 U.S. 197 (1893); United States v. McComb, 744 F.2d 555, 560 (7th Cir. 1984) (also rejecting the claim that only an FBI investigation was ongoing because the FBI and the prosecutor, rather than the grand jury, actually made the decision to issue subpoenas).

Like sections 1503 and 1505, section 1510 was amended in 1982 by the VWPA. The pre-1982 section 1510 prohibited endeavors to obstruct the communication of information to criminal investigators not only by means of bribery, but also by intimidation, force, threats or misrepresentation.

New section 1510(b) provides as follows:

> (b)(1) Whoever, being an officer of a financial institution, with the intent to obstruct a judicial proceeding, directly or indirectly notifies any other person about the existence or contents of a subpoena for records of that financial institution, or information that has been furnished to the grand jury in response to that subpoena, shall be fined under this title or imprisoned not more than 5 years, or both.
>
> (2) Whoever, being an officer of a financial institution, directly or indirectly notifies–
>
> (A) a customer of that financial institution whose records are sought by a grand jury subpoena;
>
> (B) any other person named in that subpoena;
>
> about the existence of that subpoena or information that has been furnished to the grand jury in response to that subpoena, shall be fined under this title or imprisoned not more than one year, or both.[89]

Notably, the term "officer of a financial institution" is defined to include not only officers and directors, but also an "employee, agent or attorney of or for a financial institution."[90] The section covers federal grand jury subpoenas relating to violations of various criminal banking statutes, as well as mail and wire fraud "affecting a financial institution." Pursuant to section 962(e) of FIRREA, "financial institution" is now defined at 18 U.S.C. § 20 to cover a variety of federally insured banks and bank holding companies. The felony provision in section 1510(b) requires, as do sections 1503 and 1505, a specific intent to obstruct justice. It also necessarily requires that a judicial proceeding be pending and that

---

89. Pub. L. No. 101-73, § 962(c), Fed. Banking L. Rep. (CCH) No. 1298, at ¶ 2962 (Aug. 18, 1989).

90. 18 U.S.C. § 1510(b)(b3)(A).

the defendant be aware of its pendency, given that disclosure of facts relating to grand jury subpoenas is the only prohibited activity.[91]

Counsel conducting an internal investigation may, in the course of interviews, "indirectly notif[y]" employees of the existence or contents of a subpoena (although explicit mention of the subpoena can presumably be avoided). But the requirement of a specific corrupt intent should eliminate the risk that notification will become a problem under subsection (b)(1), as long as counsel does not solicit or suggest obstructive behavior.

The misdemeanor provision, by contrast, requires only that the "notification" be made "'knowingly,' [which] incorporates the concept of 'willful blindness.'"[92] This may mean that corporate counsel is foreclosed from interviewing persons named in the subpoena, in order not to be accused of having "indirectly" provided them with notice of its existence. Arguably, any interviews could become a practical impossibility, for counsel would have to consider the risk that the mere dissemination of information about the investigation might result in a charge of indirect notification. Once again, however, counsel could refrain from explicit reference to the existence of the subpoena or its contents. Moreover, it may be possible to argue that use of the term "notify" (rather than the more usual "disclose,"[93] generally prohibiting disclosure of grand jury matters) was meant to require more purposeful behavior than incidental "notification" as a result of wholly proper lawyering activities.

---

91. Although the plain language of 18 U.S.C. § 1510(b) would appear to address only a subpoena seeking bank records, and not one calling for any testimony, the government may subpoena both documents and testimony, "thereby arguably bringing the testimony within the scope of 'information that has been furnished to the grand jury in response to the subpoena,' and placing individuals at risk for disclosing their testimony." R. Morvillo & J. Agostini, *Liability for Banking Crimes: Recent Developments*, 640 PLI/Comm 407 (1992) (citing B. ZISMAN, BANKS AND THRIFTS: GOVERNMENT ENFORCEMENT AND RECEIVERSHIP § 10.07 (1991)).

92. *See Joint Explanatory Statement of the Committee of Conference*, Fed. Banking L. Rep. (CCH) No. 1297, at 450-51 (Aug. 14, 1989).

93. *See, e.g.,* FED. R. CRIM. P. 6(e).

Gathering and Organizing Relevant Documents: An Essential Task in Any Investigation

5

by Larry A. Gaydos*

---

  * Larry A. Gaydos is a partner in Haynes & Boone in Dallas, Texas, and is the leader of the White Collar Defense and Antitrust practice group.

I. INTRODUCTION

THIS CHAPTER FOCUSES ON document gathering, processing, and review, one of the least glamorous aspects of legal practice. Although tedious and time-consuming, the identification and review of corporate records remain the keystone of every successful internal investigation. Documents are a window to the past—often the best window, sometimes the only window.

The facts underlying an internal inquiry cannot be reconstructed through employee interviews alone. Witnesses are reluctant to supply information voluntarily, especially when it implicates their own misconduct or that of a co-worker. Thus, selective use of key records is often the only means of achieving an effective interview. Similarly, poor memories can often be refreshed through the use of key documents. Finally, because scienter is a component of virtually all government prosecutions, motive, knowledge, and intent can be established, or defeated, by turning to company files.

Thus, investigative counsel is advised to regard this phase of the undertaking with considerable attention and advance planning. Documents may or may not reflect reality, but routinely they are the best available means of attempting to understand reality (through historical reconstruction), occasionally themselves becoming reality when examined in the artificial light of an adversary proceeding.

Before setting out proper procedures for document retention and review, the reader is reminded of the extreme perils of sloppy performance and inadequate organization in the document stage of the investigation: pleadings stricken for failure to comply with required productions;[1] waiver of attorney-client privilege or work product protection because of an inadvertently produced document;[2] and individuals convicted of obstructing justice because of alteration or concealment of documents under subpoena.[3]

At the outset of any internal investigation, the learning curve is great, and thousands of documents may have potential relevance. Ultimately, this curve must be mastered through education or through reasonable assumptions, or both. Once this is done, the universe of relevant documents can often be reduced to no more than several three-inch binders of "hot documents." These "hot documents" will include records essential to an understanding of past events and those critical to presenting an affirmative case for the company. And, inevitably, this binder will contain "bad documents," which are either problematic or susceptible to a problematic interpretation. Most every organization, no matter how moral, ethical, well-managed, or careful, will have bad documents in their files, and counsel should never assume otherwise.

Investigative counsel will find that the major objectives of the document portion of the internal investigation are to:

---

1. *See* Fed. R. Civ. P. 37(b)(2)(C).

2. *See In re* Sealed Case, 877 F.2d 976, 980 (D.C. Cir. 1989) (the traditional view is that the privilege is lost as to particular documents or even as to the whole subject matter without analysis of the client's intent); Suburban Sew 'N' Sweep, Inc. v. Swiss Bernina, Inc., 91 F.R.D. 254, 260 (N.D. Ill. 1981) (waiver found where the client threw documents into the trash and a snooping adversary recovered them); *but see* Mendenhall v. Barber-Greene Co., 531 F. Supp. 951, 955 (N.D. Ill. 1982) (holding that the client had not waived the attorney-client privilege where disclosure was the result of lawyer's negligence and not the client's). Other courts have found a good cause exception to the rule in extensive document production schedules provided reasonable precautions were taken to preserve the privilege. *See* Kansas-Nebraska Natural Gas Co. v. Marathon Oil Co., 109 F.R.D. 12, 21 (D. Neb. 1985).

3. *See* 18 U.S.C. § 1512(b)(2)(B) (West Supp. 1997).

- ensure a comprehensive review;
- work with minimal disruption of a client's business and maximum cost efficiency;
- preserve the original integrity of all documents;
- protect all applicable privileges, confidences, and proprietary secrets; and
- avoid unnecessary duplication of effort in the event the investigation ends in criminal or civil litigation.

With these objectives in mind, the five typical phases of the documentary portion of the internal investigation are:

- Organization and planning
- Gathering
- Processing and review
- Preparation of internal summaries, chronologies, binders
- Production of documents to government or civil litigants.

II. ORGANIZATION AND PLANNING

A. *Initial Dialogue with Management*

Some clients tend to view document review as costly, intrusive, and, at least to some extent, unnecessary. They appreciate neither the organization nor planning required to orchestrate an efficient and comprehensive document review, nor the importance of the effort.

Thus, counsel must, throughout all strategy sessions, explain the importance of this phase of the investigation to key management personnel. A checklist for the initial organizational meeting would look something like this:

- discuss the basics of investigative procedure;
- learn the company's organization and recordkeeping system;
- discuss the scope of the investigation;
- discuss the steps necessary to preserve privilege;
- discuss document retention/destruction policies;
- agree on the ground rules for dealing with lower-level employees necessarily involved in the document-gathering process; and
- agree on the best way to go about locating all relevant documents.

Another initial issue is the extent to which client personnel will participate in the document gathering, review, or processing. There are many factors to consider, and there is no single, correct approach.[4] When the internal investigation parallels a criminal investigation, control and integrity of documents take on added importance. Company counsel often find it beneficial to have an outside lawyer fully control the process and thereby serve as the corporate witness on subpoena compliance.[5]

B. *The Investigating Team*

The composition of the investigating team reflects the scope of the possible misconduct, but large inquiries will often be staffed by the partner in charge of the overall investigation; a junior partner or senior associate in charge of the document gathering, processing, and review; a number of junior associates for gathering, reviewing, and processing; a legal assistant in charge of gathering documents and client coordination; a legal assistant in charge of processing documents and support services coordination; and additional legal assistants or case clerks as needed for indexing, copying, numbering, data entry, and privilege logs.

It is important to have *one* lawyer who oversees the production, making decisions regarding privilege, and testifying if necessary on the production methodology and steps taken to preserve the integrity of the documents.

Also, when two or more teams are proceeding simultaneously, it is necessary to have an on-site gathering team, as well as a centralized processing and review team. Time-sensitive investigations permit only a general on-site review, targeting but not closely reviewing relevant files. The more detailed review occurs at the central location.

Finally, the value of talented legal assistants cannot be overstated.

---

4. The factors include relative cost savings, ability of client personnel to be available to counsel without impairing the business operation, the expertise client personnel can lend to the process (especially in highly technical areas), the degree to which the independence of the investigation could be called into question, the ability to preserve privilege, relative efficiency or inefficiency of client personnel in dealing with documents, and finally, the context of the investigation.

5. In large document productions pursuant to government subpoena, the investigating authority will usually want assurances that the company has complied with the terms of the subpoena. These assurances typically involve either sworn witness testimony before the investigating body or a sworn certification of compliance.

Throughout the investigation, they will coordinate support services, handle client inquiries, and respond to client requests for documents.

C. *Initial On-Site Walk-Through*

Since corporate-level managers often do not know the location, state, or condition of many relevant documents, counsel should consider an early series of brief visits to each field location to speak with on-site managers for guidance in collecting documents. Thus, at the initial management meeting, these on-site points of contact will be identified, an agenda developed, and an understanding reached concerning how much lower-level employees should be told regarding the investigation.

The initial field trips should often be seen as an opportunity, not to gather all pertinent documents, but to learn of their likely locations. The visit can also prepare company employees for the next phase—the gathering of pertinent documents. To the extent counsel will need documents used daily by employees, the initial visit is an excellent opportunity to begin the process of seeking copies of these documents without disrupting ongoing business activities. Documents typically falling in this category are calendars, appointment books, telephone/address books, daily activity logs, rolodexes, business card collections, current customer correspondence files, current customer or supplier files, and current year operational reports.

III. DOCUMENT GATHERING

A. *Ensuring Comprehensiveness*

There is an art to document gathering, and the methodology chosen varies with the level of comfort desired concerning the completeness of the search process. Depending on the complexity of the investigation and its overall significance to the company, here are several tips on maximizing the likelihood of locating the full range of requested documents.

- Provide employees with a *written*, understandable description of relevant documents broken down into well-defined categories.
- When practical, talk with each employee about the request, and show them examples of responsive documents.

■ In certain instances, counsel may wish to review and pull documents directly from the location—for example, each desk drawer, file cabinet, storage box, closet, and so forth.

Although this latter approach may seem overreaching, the fact remains that many employees simply forget archived locations and often do not know that responsive documents still exist. Experienced counsel have heard numerous instances of "I forgot I had those files"; "I've been looking for that"; "I didn't know my secretary had kept those old calendars"; "I didn't realize you wanted those"; and "I don't think you're going to find anything useful in there, just old drafts." These remarks, while benign, occur all too often and, if not dealt with, make for problems later on down the line.

B. *Ensuring Integrity and Control*

To standardize and memorialize the gathering of documents, counsel should prepare a search checklist and an index and have them available throughout the process. The checklist should be prepared for each location, listing the categories of documents, the key points of inquiry, and the topics to discuss with each employee. Appendix A is an example of a checklist used in an antitrust compliance investigation.

Where large amounts of documents are collected, the gathering phase should be separate from the review phase. Certainly, an on-site review and culling is necessary, but the focus is at the *file* level rather than on individual documents, thus minimizing disruption of business activity.

Because original files are collected and sent off site, a strictly enforced system must be in place for the comfort of the client and counsel. Each file (though not necessarily each document) should be assigned a number and indexed on site, contemporaneous with the gathering, to ensure the source location is preserved. Although counsel will wish to control the dissemination of the index, it may be appropriate to leave a copy with the document custodian to memorialize the files removed and aid in responding to the client's future requests for copies of selected documents. A sample index can be found at the end of this chapter as Appendix B.

After relevant documents are identified and numbered, the original index should be supplemented to reflect the numbered documents coming from each file. Ideally, documents required for day-to-day business should be identified in advance, so that working copies can be made and retained. If this is not practical, essential documents can be copied during the gathering process or copies can be made and returned to the client. The index should reflect the files that are retained, or copied and returned, in the event it becomes necessary to reinspect files for some reason in the future—for example, subsequent document request in litigation or grand jury subpoena *duces tecum*. A sample of this index is included at the end of this chapter as Appendix C.

The files that are gathered should be boxed as they are indexed. To ensure proper delivery and prevent inadvertent loss of documents, the on-site team should tape the boxes, apply preprinted shipping labels, and arrange for prompt shipment by a reliable service.

C. *Electronic Document Gathering*

Counsel should expect discovery requests to specifically seek information stored on an electronic medium. Electronic copies of information can contain important data not contained on a hard copy, including filenames, updates, when the information was accessed, and who most recently accessed the information.[6] Information stored on an electronic medium is more easily managed than information in hard copy and may actually be the preferred choice by lawyers making document requests.[7]

Finally, to ensure comprehensiveness when gathering documents, counsel must remain mindful that information may automatically be backed up on a default directory or permanently archived on an electronic medium even if the author or receiver of the information believes it has been deleted.[8]

IV. DOCUMENT PROCESSING

A. *Overview*

There are five separate functions that logically fit under the rubric "document processing": (1) numbering; (2) copying; (3) reviewing for producible, privileged, and "hot documents"; (4) indexing; and (5) coding/creation of a database.

---

6. *See* Armstrong v. Executive Office of the President, 1 F.3d 1274 (D.C. Cir. 1993); Lawrence R. Youst & Haejung Lisa Koh, *Management and Discovery of Electronically Stored Information*, 2 COMP. L. REV. AND TECH. J. 73, 74 (1997).

7. *See* Youst & Koh, at 74.

8. *See id.*, at 75.

The first three functions are mandatory in *every* investigation. The last two—indexing and coding—may or may not occur, depending on the nature of the investigation and cost considerations. Although numbering and copying can be costly, they are necessary to maintain the integrity of the documents. In an investigation of significance, proper numbering, copying, and review must take place under controlled procedures. The real question should not be *if*, but rather *when* and *by whom*.

There are many commercial services available to assist in the processing of documents. These litigation support companies provide basic services such as numbering and copying, as well as the more sophisticated indexing, coding, or computerization. Most large law firms now have a comparable capability. Commercial litigation support services may have greater efficiencies and thus a preferable cost structure, but with them there is some loss of control. Some investigations are highly sensitive, and the client may prefer that document review and processing take place solely within the law firm.

B. *Numbering*

Numbering can be done at a low level on a cost-efficient basis, as long as appropriate supervision is available. The numbers must be legible and consistent in their placement (generally the bottom-right corner), and must not obscure any of the document's content.

Bates stamping is the traditional method used, but in the last several years it has given way to more advanced forms such as preprinted labels, reproduction machines with automatic numbering, or bar codes. The Bates stamp can create user fatigue and is limited to alphanumeric codes. Labels can be removable or non-removable, and, while slightly more expensive (about $30 per thousand, or $50 per thousand pages with labor), are more versatile and faster (a skilled clerk can number 700-800 pages per hour). In addition, removable labels allow easy correction of mistakes, documents to be renumbered for subsequent productions, and important original documents to be returned to their original condition.

The future of numbering may reside in programmable reproduction machines, which can number copies (but not originals) as they are being reproduced. Finally, technological advances may allow "numbering" by placing bar codes on each page (or each document) similar to the pricing codes used at grocery stores. These codes allow the producing party to retrieve information about a document simply by scanning the code. Theoretically, opposing counsel can be denied access to the codes, although courts have not yet addressed the disclosure issues associated with this type of numbering, or the permissibility of altering the face of documents produced to opposing counsel with something more than an identifying number.

Alphanumeric codes are preferable to a simple numerical sequence. Often, a three-letter prefix tied to the geographic source of the document can facilitate interview preparation. For example, DAL 00246 indicates the document came from the client's Dallas office. Similarly, alphabetic or numeric prefixes can be linked to the subject matter or type of document. For example, DAL 30000 can refer to Dallas location documents regarding Contract X and DAL 40000 documents can refer to Dallas location documents regarding Contract Y. Alphanumeric codes likewise disclose information to adversaries, but this disadvantage is often outweighed by the convenience to the producing party. This coding is also useful when documents must be produced by category, rather than as maintained in the ordinary course of business.

C. *Copies*

How many copies are enough? The answer, it seems, is never enough, particularly when criminal and civil litigation await an internal investigation. At a minimum, every investigation should generate four distinct groups of documents: (1) the original files that may contain either numbered or unnumbered documents, or both; (2) a working set of all numbered documents; (3) a set of privileged documents; and (4) a set of "hot documents." If portions of the gathered files are subsequently produced in litigation, or to the government, counsel should retain a copy of the production set and possibly a working copy of the production set.

Needless to say, the copying process should be closely supervised. Despite the best of efforts, pages will be missed, some documents mistakenly copied, and so forth. To minimize embarrassing and compromising incidents, quality controls should include a page-by-page check of returned copies to ensure that instructions were followed, privileged documents not placed in production sets, and all pages legibly copied.

D. *Review*

During the document review stage, the real challenge is to identify the crucial documents early on, for rarely will investigative counsel have the luxury of a comprehensive document review before under taking the interview phase.

Several steps can be taken to help meet this challenge.

- The document review should take place in a central location to allow a full sharing of information and thus mutual education of the reviewing team.
- Precede the review process by thorough briefings to the review team of the conduct under investigation, the client's organization, the definition of "hot documents," and expected areas of privileged documents.
- Provide the review team with a list of key names, names likely to appear in privileged documents, a chronology of key events, and a priority list indicating the order in which boxes should be reviewed.
- Supervise the review closely for the first several days. The supervising lawyer should conduct frequent status meetings to ensure consistency and help prevent the "forest for the trees" myopia that can develop in the drudgery of reviewing thousands of documents.

E. *Indexing and Coding*

In every investigation some means of prompt retrieval must be available. The form may be nothing more than the annotated index created during the document-gathering process (see Appendix C), and the preparation of a "hot document" binder. The binder simply collects, by subject, by date, or by some other indicator, the important documents that counsel refers to time and again throughout the inquiry and wants to have at each witness interview. Indeed, the binder may well be the single most important tool at trial, for both direct and cross-examination.

In complex investigations, a more detailed index is often required, and many times a database must be created that allows for automated and sophisticated search techniques. Creation of a database requires standardized "coding," and is often an expensive process. Before rushing headlong into a costly process that may have only marginal returns, counsel should consider other alternatives.

When automated retrieval becomes necessary, counsel should consider the following suggestions:

- Defer the coding process until the document universe is known and key issues are best understood.

- Do not delegate coding to legal assistants without extensive lawyer input and supervision.
- Active lawyer involvement is essential to create a meaningful database.

Issue coding can, of course, be multidimensional and extremely sophisticated. Appendix D at the end of this chapter provides one example of an issue coding sheet.

Finally, counsel must take certain steps to ensure that any database created by counsel is protected from pretrial discovery.[9] To gain such protection under the work-product doctrine, counsel should primarily, or solely, control the database.[10] Courts are more inclined to protect computer databases from discovery if the database organizes information in a way that reveals the thought processes of the creating attorneys.[11]

F. *Computer Imaging of Documents*

As a companion to indexing and coding, computer imaging of documents can be an easy and cost-effective way to organize a large-scale document production. Imaging entails copying or scanning documents onto an electronic medium so that the documents can be accessed by computer.[12]

Computer-imaged documents on an electronic medium allow counsel to more accurately search the documents through the use of particular words and phrases or certain characteristics and then immediately review the responsive documents directly on the computer or retrieve a hard copy.[13] It is usually more cost-effective to copy and transport documents when they are imaged.[14] Bar codes and Bates labels can be avoided, since

---

9. *See* Philip J. Schworer, *Problems Arising From the Creation of a Computer-Based Litigation Support System*, 14 N. Ky. L. Rev. 263, 265 (1987).

10. *See id.*, at 266; *see also* Fauteck v. Montgomery Ward Co., 91 F.R.D. 393 (N.D. Ill. 1980) (court ordered discovery of database created by testifying experts).

11. *See* Santiago v. Miles, 121 F.R.D. 636 (W.D.N.Y. 1988); James H.A. Pooley & David M. Shaw, *The Emerging Law of Computer Networks: Finding Out What's There: Technical and Legal Aspects of Discovery*, 4 Tex. Intell. Prop. L.J. 57, 68 (1995).

12. *See* Robert L. Haig & Steven P. Caley, *Does a Good Result Beat a Cheap Legal Fee?*, 1996 WL 595744.

13. *See id.*

14. *See* Mariam J. Naini, *Cost-Effective Technology in the Management of Complex Litigation: A Stage-by-Stage Review*, 11 No.5 Inside Litig. 12, 13 (1997).

the computer can automatically add consecutive bar codes to the imaged documents.[15] Duplicate sets of photocopies can also be avoided, since the documents can be provided on CD-ROM disks.

Disadvantages of computer imaging include the possibility of working with lawyers who are uncomfortable with new technology and who may require special assistance in accessing the computer imaging system. Counsel must use special computer programs to group or organize the documents into files and show the beginning and ending of a document.[16] Finally, cross-checking an image with the original document would require the numbering of the original to match the imaged documents.[17]

G. *Inadvertent Waiver of Privilege*

Throughout the document-processing phase, counsel must keep uppermost in mind that these same documents may later be produced in adversarial proceedings. Counsel must therefore avoid at all costs waiver of privilege because of inadvertent production, a subject given uneven treatment by the courts. Some courts allow continued assertion of privilege after an inadvertent production, in order to avoid a drastic result.[18] Other courts take a balancing approach and weigh different factors in determining whether a party has waived the attorney-client privilege or work-product immunity doctrine.[19] Many courts, however, adopt a harsher stance and find waiver where a mistaken production, made without objection, has provided a windfall of privileged material to the opponent.[20] These courts reason that once a document has been produced, it enters the

---

15. *See id.*

16. *See id.*

17. *See id.*

18. *See, e.g.,* Kansas-Nebraska Natural Gas v. Marathon Oil Co., 109 F.R.D. 12, 21 (D. Neb. 1985).

19. The five factors most commonly used are "reasonableness of the precautions to prevent inadvertent disclosure, the time taken to rectify the error, the scope of the discovery . . . the extent of the disclosure [and the] overreaching issue of fairness[.]" *E.g.,* Lois Sportswear, U.S.A., Inc. v. Levi Strauss & Co., 104 F.R.D. 103, 105 (S.D.N.Y. 1985).

20. *See, e.g.,* Thomas v. Pansy Ellen Prods., Inc., 672 F. Supp. 237, 243 (W.D.N.C. 1987) ("voluntary production, even where inadvertent, effects a waiver of privilege"); Parkway Gallery v. Kittinger/Pennsylvania House Group, Inc., 116 F.R.D. 46, 50-51 (M.D.N.C. 1987).

"public domain" and confidentiality is destroyed.[21] *Parkway Gallery*[22] is particularly instructive to illustrate the harshness awaiting negligent counsel. In that case, the defendants produced 12,000 pages of documents at their offices for the plaintiff's review. For two weeks before the production, a lawyer and three assistants checked all files for questionable material. During the actual production itself, lead counsel for the defendants was hospitalized and unable to attend. Despite all precautions, the plaintiff obtained twenty privileged, inadvertently produced documents. At a later hearing, the court found that the defendants simply failed to protect the attorney-client privilege and therefore waived it, stating that "mere inadvertence, standing alone, is not sufficient to counter the strong policy that disclosure constitutes waiver."[23]

To make matters worse, some courts treat waiver of privileged information broadly and hold that all materials and information dealing with the same subject matter as the mistakenly produced material must also be provided in discovery once the privilege has been breached.[24]

In view of these bitter consequences, counsel may wish to reach an agreement with opposing counsel that inadvertent production of a privileged document will not be asserted as grounds to argue complete subject matter waiver. Such an agreement benefits both parties, facilitates expeditious production of documents, and avoids overly broad assertions of privilege. These agreements may require return of inadvertently produced privileged documents and a stipulation of nonuse.

Attorneys should not overlook the possibility that ethical considerations may require counsel to return inadvertently produced documents.[25] A few courts have even disqualified or considered disqualifying attorneys who have received privileged materials from an adverse party.[26]

---

21. *See, e.g.,* Underwater Storage, Inc. v. United States Rubber Co., 314 F. Supp. 546, 549 (D.D.C. 1970).

22. 116 F.R.D. 46 (M.D.N.C. 1987).

23. *Id.* at 51.

24. *See, e.g.,* Smith v. Alyeska Pipeline Service Co., 538 F. Supp. 977, 980-82 (D. Del. 1982), *aff'd*, 758 F.2d 668 (D.C. Cir. 1984).

25. *See* ABA Comm. on Ethics and Prof'l Responsibility, Formal Op. 382 (1994) (discusses receiving privileged material belonging to adverse party intentionally sent from an unauthorized source); ABA Comm. on Ethics and Prof'l Responsibility, Formal Op. 368 (1992) (discusses inadvertently receiving privilege material belonging to adverse party).

26. *See* Milford Power Ltd. v. New England Power Co., 896 F. Supp. 53 (D. Mass. 1995); Resolution Trust Corp. v. First of America Bank, 868 F. Supp. 217 (W.D. Mich.

V. PREPARATION OF INTERNAL SUMMARIES, CHRONOLOGIES, BINDERS

Important information contained in key documents must be organized into a useful, accessible form, regardless of the size and scope of the inquiry, and regardless of the sophistication or simplicity of the indexing system chosen by counsel. Although there are many ways to approach this, the most common tools are the hot document binder and the hot document chronology.

A. *Hot Document Chronology*

Arranging the hot documents in chronological order and creating a standardized summary is a valuable process separate and apart from the usefulness of the end product. Thinking sequentially about events while familiarizing oneself with the body of facts is the best available substitute for reenactment of the conduct in question.

A chronology is a living document; as more facts emerge, the document will be supplemented and annotated, for example, with excerpts of key witness testimony. Below is a sample page from a hot document chronology.

83/06/20	DE-159 - Exhibit 188—Jones memo to Sam Wilson (Pres. CEO) (cc: Jim Neal, Leo King, Jerry Johnson) re: tests of product produced by Wexlar system; duplication of formula was developed by careful trial and error and analysis

- "Duplication of the competitor's formula has been developed by careful trial and error:
- Used Wexlar testing (disclosed in European patent) *Mills Deposition*
- — Sandi Samuels was responsible for Wexlar testing

83/06/27	Exhibit 6445—Patent Searchers & Co. letter to Ramsey re: Patent Study; confirms Ramsey instruction to take no further action re: inspecting Patent No. 4,222,111
83/06/28	DE-183 - Exhibit 287—Sam Wilson memo to distribution (Neal, King, others) (cc: Samuels, Johnson) re: revised criti-

---

1994); Conley, Lott, Nichols Mach. Co. v. Brooks, 948 S.W.2d 345 (Tex. Ct. App. 1997).

cal paths for product X to be distributed on need-to-know basis

- Market date scheduled for third week of September
  Wilson Deposition
— Had settled on process going to use but not necessarily formulation, some refining work to be done (Wilson, Vol. II, p. 112)

There are four points to note about this sample. First, it is best to have a standard format for similar entries. This sample follows the format "date, document number, author(s), document type, recipient, copies, subject." Key points from the document are bullet points under the identifier entries and interview or testimony excerpts are placed below the key points.

Second, several copies of each document included in the chronology should be put into a separate folder. The folders should be prominently labeled and placed in chronological order. This will greatly facilitate interviews. Third, special attention should be paid to handwritten notes, so authenticity can be part of each interview. Finally, even in complex cases, a hot document chronology can ordinarily be captured in less than 100 pages, making for a manageable tool to use when preparing for and conducting interviews.

B. *Summaries*

Investigations that are not amenable to chronological organization require more creative organizational approaches along issue lines. This approach is effective only if there are several clearly identifiable issues or a manageable universe of documents.

VI. PRODUCTION OF DOCUMENTS TO GOVERNMENT OR CIVIL LITIGANTS

A. *Destruction of Documents*

When incriminating documents are uncovered in the midst of investigation, and there is no ongoing criminal or civil proceeding, counsel may be asked whether the documents can be destroyed. There are three important considerations that bear on this decision:

- Local ethics rules, statutes, or procedural rules may preclude destruction.[27]
- Destruction of *all* copies of any document may be impossible in this age of word-processing disks and reproduction machines.
- It is often less difficult to explain a "bad" document than to justify its destruction later. Destruction carries with it the blackest presumption imaginable.

Accordingly, the presumption will likely be against destroying problematic documents.

B. *Production Abuses*

Litigation lore is filled with stories about document productions on hot summer days in rat-infested warehouses without benefit of chairs, desks, or air conditioning. While this scenario may be more fiction than fact, document productions do bring out the worst behavior in some trial lawyers, all in the name of tactical advantage. Hopefully, courts are moving to sanction abuses, such as "shuffling" documents before production, or burying important documents amid a mass of irrelevant material. Certainly any counsel or client who attempts such tactics when responding to a government agency's subpoena *duces tecum* risks loss of credibility at a minimum, and possibly severe sanctions, including obstruction of justice charges.[28]

---

27. *See, e.g.,* Tex. Disciplinary R. Prof'l Conduct 3.04(a), *reprinted in* Tex. Gov't Code Ann. tit. 2, subtit. G app. A (Vernon Supp. 1997) (Tex. State Bar R. art. X § 9).

A lawyer shall not . . . unlawfully obstruct another party's access to evidence; in anticipation of a dispute unlawfully alter, destroy, or conceal a document or other material that a competent lawyer would believe has potential or actual evidentiary value, or counsel or assist another person to do any such act.

28. Fed. R. Civ. P. 37; 18 U.S.C. § 1512(b)(2)(B) (West Supp. 1997); United States v. Laurins, 857 F.2d 529 (9th Cir. 1988) (concealing documents falls within definition of specific intent required for obstruction of justice); United States v. Gravely, 840 F.2d 1156 (4th Cir. 1988) (stating that in order for defendant to be convicted of obstructing justice for destroying documents, the documents do not have to be under subpoena, if the defendant is aware that a grand jury will likely seek the documents in its investigation); *but see* Richmark Corp. v. Timber Falling Consultants, Inc., 730 F. Supp. 1525 (D. Or. 1990) (holding that "obstruction of justice" did not include alleged concealment or withholding of discovery documents in a civil case).

C. *Advocacy Considerations*

While abusive tactics are generally counterproductive, there are legitimate advocacy considerations involved in deciding the methodology for producing documents.

1. Ordinary Course versus Extraordinary Measures

Recipients of document requests from civil litigants or the government are accustomed to lengthy introductory paragraphs containing procedural "guidance" about how the documents must be produced. Most of these directives are properly viewed as requests for extraordinary measures that generally are not compelled by any court or reviewing authority. In 1980, Federal Rule of Civil Procedure 34(b) was amended to permit the party producing documents for inspection to make them available either "as they are kept in the usual course of business" or "organized and labeled to correspond with the categories in the request." This amendment was aimed at forestalling discovery abuses such as the deliberate shuffling of documents or hiding important documents in a mass of irrelevant ones.[29] The parties seeking discovery may elect one of the two methods in which the documents are to be produced.

Some experts argue that rule 34(b) as amended is ambiguous and should not be read as giving the responding party an absolute option to produce records as they are kept in the usual course of business. Wright and Miller argue that the producing party "should be required to produce them in a form that will make reasonable use of them possible."[30]

2. Overloading the Opposition versus Narrowing Scope of Request

Document requests are often broadly worded, so a reasonable interpretation could lead to a production of most, if not all, documents within the organization's control. One common reaction is to produce everything asked for, again on tactical grounds. While this strategy may occasionally work, it must not be undertaken lightly, and without regard to the types of documents maintained by the client.

---

29. *See, e.g.,* Board of Educ. v. Admiral Heating & Ventilating, Inc., 104 F.R.D. 23, 36 (N.D. Ill. 1984).

30. *See* 8 CHARLES ALAN Wright & ARTHUR R. Miller, FEDERAL PRACTICE AND PROCEDURE § 2213 (2d ed. 1991).

More times than not, this tactic will be unsuccessful and generate unnecessary expense. A client with 200 boxes of inventory records or old computer printouts that are of marginal relevance gains nothing by piling them on top of the production of otherwise relevant documents. To the extent these boxes of documents can be readily identified, they also can be quickly ignored and discarded by the opposition. A more reasonable approach is to negotiate the request in an attempt to narrow its scope. The process of narrowing not only saves cost in the copying and processing phases, but also starts a dialogue that can lead to information about the opposition's case, strategies, and goals.

3. On-Site Inspection versus Production of Complete Set

Another important consideration is whether an on-site inspection should be permitted, or demanded. One advantage is that it may provide important insights about the opponent's case and objectives. An on-site inspection may impose actual or psychological pressures, causing the opponent to overlook important records. Additionally, cost-conscious opponents will not copy irrelevant documents, and costs for both sides may be reduced. In fact, prohibitive cost may be the overriding factor in requesting an on-site inspection of documents.[31] Companies that have been involved in recurring litigation on the same or similar issues may have the universe of potentially relevant documents centrally assembled. In these cases on-site inspection may be the only reasonable approach.

If a client allows an on-site inspection at its facility, the documents should be segregated in an area away from employees, and steps should be taken to ensure that the adversary is not given the opportunity to gain otherwise unavailable information. On-site inspections must always be closely supervised.

By producing a complete set of documents without an inspection, the opponent remains away from the client's facility and the risk of snooping is eliminated. Additionally, if a set of documents is provided, the opponent may never give a proper, thorough review of the documents. An on-site inspection may promote an early intensive focus on your documents.

---

31. *See* Petruska v. Johns-Manville, 83 F.R.D. 32, 36 (E.D. Pa. 1979).

4. Confidentiality Agreements

Counsel must consider not only the process of discovery, but the nature of the information produced and the need to retain the confidentiality of certain information. Confidentiality agreements, or agreed protective orders, are essential in civil litigation where sensitive information—operational or financial—will likely be disclosed during the course of litigation. This order can have multiple levels of confidentiality, depending on the nature of the information and the persons viewing it. Confidentiality orders and agreements can take many forms, but items typically addressed include:

- Definition of "confidential information." In some cases it may be appropriate to have "confidential," "highly confidential," and perhaps other designations for extremely sensitive documents, with each classification having its own restrictions concerning who is "qualified" to have access to the information.
- Definition of "qualified persons" to have access to sensitive information. This can be as narrow or broad as needed depending on the sensitivity of the information reviewed. Persons qualified to review the information should be specifically defined by group. "Qualified persons" may include outside counsel and their employees, general counsel, or designated associate general counsel for a party, consultants, expert witnesses, or investigators.
- Whether information disclosed at a deposition can be designated as "confidential information" by indicating on the record that the testimony is so designated and subject to the provisions of the order. The portions of the deposition containing confidential information can be separately bound.
- Procedures for introducing confidential information at any hearing conducted in the litigation. For example, prior notification, exclusion of non-qualified personnel from the hearing, and designation of the hearing transcript as "confidential."
- Procedures for disclosing confidential information to a deponent or prospective trial witness, such as requiring prior written agreement to be bound by the terms of the confidentiality order.
- Restrictions on attendance at depositions where confidential information is disclosed.

■ Whether inadvertent disclosure of confidential information constitutes waiver of any confidentiality claim.

■ Procedures for sealing affidavits, briefs, memoranda of law or other papers containing confidential information that are filed in court.

■ Notification procedures in the event a non-party demands confidential information by subpoena or other legal process.

■ Disposition of confidential documents at the conclusion of the litigation (and appeals).

5. Personal versus Business Records

The distinction between a "personal" document and a "corporate" one often is important in federal cases, particularly in the context of a witness or defendant in a criminal case asserting a Fifth Amendment privilege against self-incrimination. The importance of this distinction stems from a line of Supreme Court cases holding that the privilege against self-incrimination protects a person from producing his personal papers, but not from producing corporate documents held in a representative capacity, even if the production is personally incriminating.[32] The rationale for this holding is that the privilege against self-incrimination is "purely a personal one," applicable only to "natural individuals."[33] The privilege against self-incrimination cannot be invoked by a corporation or other collective entity.[34] Despite the importance of the "personal-corporate" distinction, there is relatively little judicial interpretation of these terms. The courts that have addressed the issue generally have considered similar factors, including who produced the document in question and for what purpose, the nature of its contents, who has possession of and access to the document, and whether the document was necessary to or helpful in the conduct of the corporation's business.[35] Courts also consider whether the party resisting production holds the documents in an individual or representative capacity.[36]

The Supreme Court has held that a person cannot claim the Fifth

---

32. *See, e.g.,* Hale v. Henkel, 201 U.S. 43 (1901); Wilson v. United States, 221 U.S. 361, 382 (1911).

33. *See* United States v. White, 322 U.S. 694, 698-99 (1944).

34. *See id.,* at 699.

35. *See* Wilson, 221 U.S. at 380; *see also In re* Grand Jury Subpoena Duces Tecum Dated April 23, 1981, 522 F. Supp. 977, 984 (S.D.N.Y. 1981).

36. *See* Bellis v. United States, 417 U.S. 85, 92 (1974).

Amendment's protection on the basis of the content of the items demanded.[37] These rulings indicate that the distinction between personal and corporate documents may become less important in coming years.[38] The Supreme Court has apparently shifted to a new framework of analysis for documentary subpoenas, under which the validity of a subpoena no longer turns on the contents of the documents demanded, but rather on whether the act of producing them entails testimonial self-incrimination.[39] The most recent analysis under this new framework holds that "a person may not claim the [Fifth] Amendment's protections based upon the incrimination that may result from the contents or nature of the thing demanded."[40]

VII. CONCLUSION

Despite the lack of glamour and inescapable drudgery, document gathering, processing, and review are the foundations of internal investigations and complex litigation. Cases may not be won at this stage of a proceeding, but cases *can* be lost if serious missteps occur. Like most other legal endeavors, the keys to success are early planning, organization, attention to detail and follow-through.

---

37. *See* Fisher v. United States, 425 U.S. 391 (1976); *see also* United States v. Doe, 465 U.S. 605 (1984).
38. *See* Baltimore City Dep't of Social Servs. v. Bouknight, 493 U.S. 549 (1990).
39. *See* Fisher, 452 U.S. at 399.
40. Bouknight, 493 U.S. at 555.

APPENDIX A

Document Review Checklist

Date: _____

Name: _____

Location: _____

I. Preliminary
   - ❏ Represent the company, not the individual
   - ❏ Purpose and status of investigation
   - ❏ Purpose and procedures regarding document gathering
   - ❏ Must review all files
   - ❏ Will be indexed and preserved (retrievable)
   - ❏ Let us know if need copies now
   - ❏ Let us know if privileged documents in files
   - ❏ No altering or destroying documents

II. Walk-through
   - ❏ Show us files and generally describe
   - ❏ Any archived or storage documents
   - ❏ Computer databases
   - ❏ Secretary files

III. Documents
   - ❏ Calendars   1990   1989   1988   1987
   - ❏ Telephone/Address lists _____
   - ❏ Daily planners/notebooks _____
   - ❏ Mileage logs, travel and expense reports _____
   - ❏ Price lists _____
   - ❏ Competitor files _____
   - ❏ Marketing information _____
   - ❏ Customer files _____
   - ❏ Correspondence/Reading files _____
   - ❏ Customer entertainment files _____
   - ❏ Inventory files _____
   - ❏ Bid files _____
   - ❏ Other _____

IV. Areas Inspected
- ❏ Desk _____
- ❏ Credenza _____
- ❏ Book shelves _____
- ❏ File cabinets _____
- ❏ Closet _____
- ❏ Briefcase _____
- ❏ Secretary area _____
- ❏ Other _____

V. Final Remarks
- ❏ Provide business card
- ❏ Limit discussion about investigation
- ❏ Procedure if need document returned/copied
- ❏ Let us know if contacted, hear anything
- ❏ Optional—provide copy of index

APPENDIX B

File Control #	Location	Custodian	File Title or Description	Comments
DAL 0001	Dallas Area Office Mgr file cabinet	Sarah Jones	Profit Plans - 1990	Copies made and left in files
DAL 0002	Dallas Area Office Secretary desk	Sarah Jones	Appointment book - Jan	
DAL 0003	Dallas Area Office Secretary desk	Sarah Jones	Appointment book - Jan Jones; 1987	Original retained; copy made for investigation
AUS 0001	Austin District Office Bill Smith's desk	Bill Smith	Sales reports - FW 1989	Hot documents
AUS 0002	Austin District Office hall closet # 2	Bob Walker	Telephone/ address book (Betty Brown - 1984)	Storage - former employee files
AUS 0003	Austin District Office main file cabinet	Jim Stanley	Sales Meetings 1987-1990	Copies made and left in files *Hot documents

APPENDIX C

File Control #	Location	Custodian	File Title or Description	Comments
DAL 0001 0001-0084	Dallas Area Office Mgr file cabinet	Sarah Jones	Profit Plans - 1990	Copies made and left in files
DAL 0002 0085-0593	Dallas Area Office Secretary desk	Sarah Jones	Appointment book - Jan Jones; 1987	
DAL 0003 0514-1139	Dallas Area Office Secretary desk	Sarah Jones	Appointment book - Jan Jones; 1987	Original retained; copy made for investigation
AUS 0001 1140-1444	Austin District Office Bill Smith's desk	Bill Smith	Sales reports - FW 1989	Hot documents
AUS 0002 Not produced	Austin District Office hall closet # 2	Bob Walker	Telephone/ address book (Betty Brown - 1984)	Storage - former employee files
AUS 0003 1445-2218	Austin District Office main file cabinet	Jim Stanley	Sales Meetings 1987-1990	Copies made and left in files *Hot documents

APPENDIX D
ABC Equipment v. Jones Enterprises

CONFIDENTIAL & PRIVILEGED—PREPARED BY AND FOR COUNSEL

DOCUMENT NO.: _____ - _____   REVIEWED BY: _____
           Beginning   Ending   Attorney/Legal Assistant

DOC. DATE: _____   FILE NAME:_____   SOURCE:_____

DOCUMENT TYPE: [Circle appropriate letter(s)]

B Bond	H Handwritten notes	M Memo
E Exhibit (other proceeding)	L Letter	P Pleading
Hot Document: ❏ Yes ❏ No	Marginalia: ❏ Yes ❏ No	❏ Other

Attachments: _____

KEY ISSUES: [Circle Appropriate Number(s)]

01 ABC Negotiations	10 Jones Negotiations
02 ABC Computer Procedures	11 Jones Agreement
03 ABC Bankruptcy Approval	12 Jones Scheduling
04 ABC Schedule	13 Jones Startup
05 ABC Startup	14 Jones Contract Services
06 ABC Agreement	15 Jones Pricing
07 ABC Marketing	16 Jones Performance
08 ABC Expansion	17 Jones Competition
09 ABC Contract Services	18 Jones/NE Computer Services

Other: _____ _____ _____

AUTHOR(S): (1) _____   (2) _____   (3) _____

RECIPIENTS	COPIES	MENTIONED
_____	_____	_____
_____	_____	_____
_____	_____	_____

INTERNAL CORPORATE INVESTIGATION

Description: _____
_____
_____
_____
_____

Employees' Rights and Duties During an Internal Investigation

6

by Joseph F. Coyne, Jr. & Charles F. Barker*

---

* Joseph F. Coyne, Jr., and Charles F. Barker are partners in the law firm of Sheppard, Mullin, Richter & Hampton LLP in Los Angeles, California.

I. INTRODUCTION

Every lawyer performing an internal investigation on behalf of a company faces the same dilemma. The lawyer must implement the company's legitimate right and duty to make an exhaustive investigation of all pertinent facts, while at the same time respecting the rights of employees.[1]

Many of the rights and obligations of employees and employers participating in an internal investigation are not entirely clear. In some cases, these rights and obligations will vary depending on the applicable state statute, the corporation's bylaws, the lawyer's ethical considerations and the facts of the case. In other cases, these rights and obligations have not been clearly defined. As a consequence, this chapter does not set forth a list of "do's" and "don'ts" to be rigidly followed under all circumstances. Rather, lawyers conducting internal investigations must be flexible enough to adapt their conduct to the unique circumstances confronting them. With this background, this chapter addresses the rights and obligations of employees and employers during an internal investigation. We will proceed in the following order:

- employees' obligations,
- employees' rights,
- company's rights, and
- company's obligations.

II. EMPLOYEES' DUTY TO COOPERATE

A duty to cooperate exists in every employer/employee relationship,[2] and

---

1. For convenience, the term "employee" within this chapter includes officers, directors, and employees of the company.

2.. Some courts refer to the "Duty to Cooperate" as the Duty of Loyalty.

most states have statutes defining the scope of this duty. For example, California Labor Code section 2856 states:

> An employee shall substantially comply with all the directions of his employer concerning the service on which he is engaged, except where such obedience is impossible or unlawful, or would impose new and unreasonable burdens upon the employee.[3]

Even in states that have not codified the employee's "duty to cooperate," the courts have concluded that the employee's duty to cooperate is implicit or implied by law in every employer/employee relationship.[4] Because of the duty to cooperate, an employee is obligated to comply with all lawful, reasonable directions from an employer during an internal investigation. The issue of whether the directions are reasonable depends upon the basic duties for which the employee was hired. For example, asking a vice president of finance to review and comment on accounting records would seem to be reasonable within the scope of the duties for this position. But ordering that same vice president to review manufacturing records may be unreasonable.

The more fundamental question is whether the duty to cooperate obligates an employee to consent to an interview by the company's lawyer during an internal investigation. Subject to the employee's rights, we believe the answer to this question is "yes," as long as the interview addresses matters within the scope of employment duties. If the employee refuses to consent to an interview, the company may be entitled to terminate employment.[5]

As a practical matter, the company should consider providing a memorandum directing the employee to participate in the investigation. This memorandum would provide the basis for the company to

---

3. CAL. LABOR CODE § 2856 (West 1989).

4. *See, e.g.*, Thomas Blaney v. Commonwealth of Pennsylvania, Unemployment Comp. Bd. of Review, 58 Pa. Comwlth. 260, 427 A.2d 1242 (1981) (employee had a position of responsibility and was expected to cooperate with employer).

5. This issue is discussed in detail in the section of this chapter titled, "Company Rights in an Internal Investigation: Terminating Employees for Failing to Cooperate," *infra* at 186.

assert that the employee has a duty to cooperate in the internal investigation.[6]

III. EMPLOYEES' RIGHTS IN THE INTERNAL INVESTIGATION

Even though the duty to cooperate places an obligation on the employee to comply with all reasonable directions in a corporate internal investigation, the employee has certain rights that may affect the extent of the obligations. Rights of employees generally vary in each case depending upon the employee's contract, any applicable statutes, and constitutional provisions.[7] Prior to starting any internal investigation, it is imperative for the lawyer to determine the employees' rights so the company will not be exposed to suits for wrongful termination or other torts arising out of actions of the corporate counsel during the internal investigation.

A. *Contractual Rights*

The employee may have contractual rights that limit the ability of the company to demand full cooperation in an investigation. For example, an employee may be a union member governed by a collective bargaining agreement that requires notice to a union representative before the interview. Union employees also have the right to demand that a union representative be present if the investigatory interview may result in discipline.[8]

Some employees have written agreements that may identify their specific duties and responsibilities. Such an agreement may implicitly limit the level of the required cooperation in an investigation. Counsel should be aware of any contracts before demanding, under threat of discipline, that the employee cooperate in the investigation.

---

6. This memorandum should also preserve the attorney-client privilege, which is discussed in chapter 2, "Implications of the Attorney-Client Privilege and the Work Product Doctrine," *infra* at Chapter 2.

7. This article only addresses the right of private employees in an internal investigation and does not address the rights of public employees in internal investigations.

8. N.L.R.B. v. J. Weingarten, Inc., 420 U.S. 251, 95 S. Ct. 959, 43 L. Ed. 2d 171 (1975).

B. *Protection of Whistle-Blowing Activities*

Many federal and state laws encourage workers to report misconduct and improper acts to the government by providing protection from retaliatory action. Indeed, the federal False Claims Act,[9] which offers a bounty to employees to report improprieties to the government, specifically protects these employees from any adverse employment action "because of lawful acts done by the employee" in support of a claim under the False Claims Act.[10] Many states have similar whistle-blower protection laws that protect employees from retaliatory actions by their employers. For example, Michigan's Whistleblower Law states:

> An employer shall not discharge, threaten, or otherwise discriminate against an employee regarding the employee's compensation, terms, conditions, location, or privileges of employment because the employee, or a person acting on behalf of the employee, reports or is about to report, verbally or in writing, a violation or a suspected violation of a law or regulation or rule promulgated pursuant to law of this state, a political subdivision of this state, or the United States to a public body, unless the employee knows that the report is false, or because an employee is requested by a public body to participate in an investigation, hearing, or inquiry held by that public body, or a court action.[11]

Because of these heightened statutory protections for whistle-blowers, a lawyer should proceed cautiously when dealing with a whistle-blower in an internal investigation.

C. *Employees' Rights Against Self-Incrimination*

The general rule is that the United States Constitution does not limit the powers of private employers in conducting internal corporate investigations.[12] Consequently, private employers generally are not liable under

---

9. *See* 31 U.S.C. § 3729 *et seq.*

10. *See* 31 U.S.C. § 3730(h).

11. Mich. Comp. Laws § 15.362.

12. *See* Gallagher, *Legal and Professional Responsibility of Corporate Counsel to Employees During an Internal Investigation for Corporate Misconduct*, 6 Corp. L.R. 3, 12 (1983); Pearlman, *The Attorney-Client Privilege: A Look at Its Effect on the Corporate Client and the Corporate Executive*, 55 Ind. L.J. 407, 408 n.6 (1989).

federal or state law for violating the employees' constitutional rights because there is no state action in corporate internal investigations.[13] The actions of a regulated entity, however, may be considered state action when there is a sufficient nexus between the government and the regulated entity that its actions can be treated as the actions of the government itself. When this occurs, the constitutional protections are implicated and apply to the private entity.[14]

In *Skinner v. Railway Labor Executives Ass'n*,[15] the Supreme Court held that a private railroad acted as an agent for the government when it complied with the provisions of the Federal Railroad Administration Act in administering drug tests to its employees. As an agent of the government, the private railroad was held to the strictures of the Fourth Amendment.[16] As the Court stated:

> Whether a private party should be deemed an agent or instrument of the Government for Fourth Amendment purposes necessarily turns on the degree of the Government's participation in the private party's activities, *cf. Lustig v. United States*, 338 U.S. 74, 78-79, 69 S. Ct. 1372, 1373-74, 92 L. Ed. 1819 (1949) (plurality opinion); *Byars v. United States*, 272 U.S. 28, 32-33, 47 S. Ct. 248, 249-250, 71 L. Ed. 520 (1972), a question that can only be resolved "in light of all the circumstances." *Coolidge v. New Hampshire*, 403 U.S. at 443, 91 S. Ct. at 2026. The fact that the Government has not compelled a private party to perform a search does not, by itself, establish that the search is a private one. Here, specific features of the regulations combine to convince us that the Government did more than adopt a passive position toward the underlying private conduct.[17]

The Court then enumerated those "specific features" it considered important in turning the private urinalysis and breath test into state action

---

13. "State action" is a term used to describe any action by a local, state or federal government that triggers constitutional rights.

14. *See* Skinner v. Railway Labor Executives Ass'n, 489 U.S. 602, 109 S. Ct. 1402, 103 L. Ed. 2d 639 (1989).

15. *Id.*

16. *Id.* at 1411.

17. *Id.*

subject to the Fourth Amendment. In particular, the Court emphasized that (1) the regulations preempted state laws, rules, or regulations covering the subject matter and superseded collective bargaining agreements and arbitration awards; (2) the regulations permitted the Federal Railroad Administration to receive biological samples and test results procured by the private railroads; (3) the railroad was required to administer the test to protect the public safety; and (4) employees who refused to take the test would lose their position.[18]

Today, with many corporations conducting internal investigations in accordance with federal laws like the Securities Exchange Act of 1934,[19] the Foreign Corrupt Practices Act of 1977,[20] and the Department of Defense Voluntary Disclosure Program, an issue is raised as to whether the corporation's internal investigation could be considered state action. Although we believe there is no state action in private corporate internal investigations, under some circumstances the Supreme Court's ruling in *Skinner* could support a contrary argument.

For example, under the Department of Defense Voluntary Disclosure Program, an argument can be made that the government is implicitly mandating the company to perform an internal investigation. Because, under certain circumstances, the Voluntary Disclosure Program requires the company to disclose the results of its investigation, the employee might assert that the corporation is acting as an agent for the government. If an employee can prove that a private employer is acting as an agent of the government, the employee will be protected by all the rights afforded under the U.S. Constitution, according to the rationale set forth in *Skinner*.

Additionally, a few states have expanded private employees' rights to include protections for certain constitutional violations. One of the broadest rules is the Connecticut law, which provides that:

> [A]ny employer . . . who subjects any employee to discipline or discharge on account of the exercise of such employee of rights guaranteed by the First Amendment to the U.S. Constitution, or Section 3, 4 or 14 of Article I of the constitution of the state, provided such activity does not substantially or materially inter-

---

18. *Id.* at 1411-12.
19. 15 U.S.C. §§ 77b-78hh (1982).
20. 5 U.S.C. §§ 78m(b), 78dd, 78ff(a) (1982).

fere with the employee's bona fide job performance or the working relationship between the employee and the employer, shall be liable to such employee for damages caused by such discipline or discharge, including punitive damages, and for reasonable attorneys' fees as part of the cost of any such action for damages.[21]

Most notably, Connecticut's law does not protect the employee in asserting the Fifth Amendment Right Against Self-Incrimination and the Sixth Amendment Right to Counsel, which are the two most controversial rights of employees in internal investigations. Additionally, employees have started to claim that the federal and state constitutions embody public policies that can be enforced through tort actions against employers.[22] For example, private employees have asserted that the principles or protections of the United States Constitution or state constitution, especially those regarding the right against self-incrimination and the right to counsel, are public policies that the company must not violate by taking adverse action against them when they assert those rights. Although these assertions by employees are tenuous, counsel conducting an internal investigation should be careful in dealing with employees who assert their constitutional rights.

Absent state action, an employee has no constitutional right against self-incrimination in an internal investigation by a private employer. Indeed, a lawyer should be able to inquire into any facts regarding the employee's performance of his or her duties.[23] For practical reasons, though, a lawyer performing an internal investigation may be hard-pressed to force an employee to make self-incriminating statements. Consequently, the more practical question is whether the company may rightfully discharge an employee who asserts the right of self-incrimination and thereby fails to cooperate in the internal investigation.

Two arbitrations arising under collective bargaining agreements have illustrated the arguments for and against the employee's right against self-incrimination in internal investigations. In *Exact Weight Scale Company*,[24]

---

21. Conn. Gen. Stat. § 31-51q.

22. Employees who are discharged in violation of public policy may have a claim for wrongful termination. See *infra* page 173.

23. *See* TRW, Inc. v. Superior Court, 25 Cal. App. 4th 1834 (1994); some commentators, however, have argued that an employee in an internal investigation should be granted a right akin to the right against self-incrimination. *See* Gallagher, *supra* note 12.

24. 50 Lab. Arb. Rep. (BNA) 8 (1967).

an arbitrator examined whether an employer was justified in discharging an employee for refusing to admit or deny that he was violating a newly promulgated rule against working for competitors. The arbitrator concluded that the employer was not justified in discharging the employee and could not force the employee to make incriminating statements. As the arbitrator stated:

> I know of no principle, or decided case, upholding a company's right to compel an employee, under pain of discharge, to admit or deny a rule violation or other offense. Such a principle would contradict all our Anglo-American principles, particularly the one that a man is presumed innocent until he is proved guilty, and the burden of proof is on the one alleging an offense.[25]

In the alternative, an arbitrator in *Simonize Company*[26] ruled that an employee who properly asserted the right of self-incrimination in a criminal proceeding could be rightfully discharged by the corporation for asserting that right. Although this case does not examine the employee's right against self-incrimination in the context of an internal investigation, the policy reasons for dismissing the employee apply with equal force. As the arbitrator stated:

> We cannot say, in addition to the guarantee, that the person invoking the Fifth Amendment has the right to this advantage in a criminal proceeding, and also has a right to be completely free from any financial, social, or other possible loss which he may suffer, indirectly, as a result of exercising his constitutional right.
>
> Employers properly have a higher standard for employee qualifications than mere freedom from a criminal conviction. Employers have a right to absolute honesty, as well as a reasonable amount of cooperation, from their employees.
>
> The Fifth Amendment does not guarantee that a person who invokes it will not be subject to any unfavorable inference and does not guarantee that a person who invokes it shall be continued in employment.[27]

---

25. *Id.* at 8.
26. 44 LAB. ARB. REP. (BNA) 658 (1964).
27. *Id.* at 663 (emphasis added).

D. *Employees' Rights to Counsel*

The employee's right to counsel in an internal investigation depends upon the facts of the employee's particular circumstance. Absent state action or a special statute, the Sixth Amendment right to counsel does not apply to private employees in internal investigations. Thus, in these circumstances, an employee would not be entitled to have counsel present for an investigatory interview.[28] Ethical obligations and practical considerations, however, may mandate that an employee have separate counsel under some circumstances.

In all internal investigations, the corporation's lawyer must be aware of Ethical Consideration 5-18 of the Model Code, which states in pertinent part:

> A lawyer employed or retained by a corporation... owes his allegiance to the [corporation] and not to a stockholder, director, officer, employee, representative, or other person connected with ...[it]...Occasionally a lawyer is requested by a stockholder, director, officer, employee, representative, or other person connected with the...[corporation] to represent him in an individual capacity; in such case the lawyer may serve the individual only if the lawyer is convinced that differing interests are not present.

The newer Model Rules attempt to clarify this issue by defining potential conflicts of interest in the corporate setting in Rules 1.13(d) and (e), which provide:

(d) In dealing with an organization's directors, officers, employees, members, shareholders or other constituents, a lawyer shall explain the identity of the client when it is apparent that the organization's interests are adverse to those of the constituents with whom the lawyer is dealing.

(e) A lawyer representing an organization may also represent any of its directors, officers, employees, members, shareholders or other constituents, subject to the provisions of Rule 1.7 [conflicts of interest]. If the organization's consent to the dual representation is required by Rule 1.7, the consent shall be given

---

28. *See* TRW, Inc. v. Superior Court, 25 Cal. App. 4th 1834 (1994).

by an appropriate official of the organization other than the individual who is to be represented, or by the shareholder.

These strictures, and common sense, mean investigative lawyers must proceed cautiously with all employees of the corporation, even very senior managers and officers. At any moment in the investigation, the lawyer may learn that the person being interviewed is part of the problem, and not just a friendly source of information.

For these reasons, it is imperative that the lawyer performing the internal investigation only represent the corporation. If the lawyer attempts to perform dual representation of the employee and the corporation, the lawyer jeopardizes the relationship to both clients. Moreover, dual representation could create a conflict of interest to such an extent that the lawyer might be forced to withdraw from the internal investigation. Consequently, at the outset of the interview, it must be stated with emphasis that the lawyer represents the corporation and not the individual employee. If, after the initial interview, or even during the initial interview, the lawyer concludes that the employee may be in jeopardy, the lawyer should consider recommending that the employee consult separate counsel.

An issue exists regarding how to treat the employee once separate counsel is retained. The employee, as an individual, always has the right to consult a personal lawyer. However, there is typically no legal obligation on behalf of the corporation to consult the employee's lawyer prior to an internal interview or to allow the employee's lawyer to sit in on the interview. Depending on the circumstances, though, ethical considerations may warrant dealing with an employee's lawyer rather than with the employee. For instance, if the employee interview is conducted by outside counsel (as opposed to a company employee), the applicable ethical standards arguably require that a communication with that employee proceed through counsel. In these situations, the corporation's lawyer should proceed cautiously to ensure that no one's rights are infringed upon.

E. *Employees' Right of Privacy*

Workplace privacy has been a rapidly developing area of employment law. Privacy concerns arise in a number of different contexts in the employer-employee relationship, such as surveillance and eavesdropping, desk and locker searches, polygraph testing, and inquiries into personal or off-duty behavior and beliefs.

Some states have statutory protections for privacy. For example, the right of privacy is expressly provided for in the California Constitution, Article I, Section 1. The United States Constitution does not explicitly contain a right of privacy but it has been implied.

In the context of an investigation, the employer must not unreasonably invade or intrude into the private affairs and beliefs of its employees. According to the California Supreme Court, a plaintiff alleging an invasion of privacy must establish a legally protected privacy interest, a reasonable expectation of privacy in the circumstances, and conduct by the defendant constituting a serious invasion of privacy.[29] A defendant may prevail in a privacy case by negating any of the three elements or by proving that the invasion of privacy is justified because it substantially furthers one or more countervailing interests. In effect, the courts review the interests or justifications supporting the challenged practice and weigh those interests against the intrusion on privacy.

An employee may rely on his right of privacy to refuse to answer questions in an investigation that do not rationally relate to the subject of the investigation or that seriously intrude on personal or private matters. Investigators should ask relevant questions designed to elicit information helpful for the scope of the investigation and should avoid questions that might embarrass or humiliate the employee or that seek only private information.

Courts have also started to protect employees whose work areas are searched if there is a reasonable expectation of privacy. Generally, the expectation of privacy may arise if the employee is permitted to lock the desk or locker and to keep the key. Additionally, the expectation of privacy will be greater in purses and wallets and possibly briefcases than in employer-provided desks and working areas. In an investigation, an employer is obviously entitled to obtain all of its employees' work papers even if they are contained in a locked desk. One of the ways to manage this situation is to require the employee to unlock the desk or locker so that it can be searched in the presence of the employee. If an employee refuses to unlock the desk or locker after a reasonable request and assurance that personal items such as a purse or wallet will not be searched, the employer will probably be within its rights in disciplining the employee for refusing the reasonable search.

---

29. Hill v. National Collegiate Athletic Ass'n, 7 Cal. 4th 1, 39-40 (1994).

Most private employers are now restricted in using polygraph tests for current employees, pursuant to the Employee Polygraph Protection Act of 1988.[30] There are three limited exceptions for private employers: (1) investigations conducted by employers who are authorized to manufacture, distribute or dispense certain controlled substances; (2) employers whose primary business purpose is to provide security personnel to protect facilities or operations having a significant impact on public health or safety or who are involved in currency, precious commodities, negotiable securities or proprietary information; and (3) investigations of theft or other instances resulting in economic loss to the employer, provided that the employer has a reasonable suspicion that the employee was involved and gives certain required statutory written notice. Some states also have restrictions on use of polygraphs.[31]

Finally, the employer's rights to monitor or search an employee's electronic communications is restricted by the Electronic Communications Privacy Act of 1986 (ECPA).[32] The ECPA prohibits individuals and employers from intercepting wire, oral or electronic communications of others. The ECPA is not violated if the person who intercepts the communication is a party to the communication or if one of the parties to the communication has given prior consent. States may have similar laws.[33]

In an investigation, the investigator must determine whether the e-mail messages and voice mail messages can be reviewed in compliance with ECPA. If the company's policies on computers and other electronic systems (e.g., e-mail and voice mail) provide that such systems are company property and are not for personal use, and are subject to monitoring and review, then the company has probably obtained the consent of the employee for such review.

F. *Employees' Rights Under the Fair Credit Reporting Act*

If the employer hires a third party to conduct an investigation regard-

---

30. 29 U.S.C. § 2001 et seq.

31. CAL. LAB. CODE § 432.2 prohibits a private employer from requiring an employee to submit to a polygraph test as a condition of continued employment.

32. 18 U.S.C. §§ 2510-2720.

33. For example, California has an Invasion of Privacy Act, CAL. PENAL CODE §§ 631-633.

ing an employee for employment purposes, such as an investigation into whether the employee engaged in sexual harassment, then the Fair Credit Reporting Act (FCRA), as amended,[34] may apply. The FCRA provides fairly broad rights to employees during an investigation if the employer uses an outside "consumer reporting agency," rather than conducting the investigation in-house.[35] If an investigation into an employee's conduct is subject to the act, the investigation may be conducted only after advance written notice to the employee, and no adverse action may be taken against the employee unless a copy of any report of the investigation is first provided to the employee.[36] If the investigation includes interviews, even more stringent disclosure and authorization requirements apply, including a requirement that the employer certify, in writing, to the "consumer reporting agency" that the employer has made the required disclosures and will honor the employee's right to disclosure of the nature and scope of the investigation.[37]

Under an expansive reading of the FCRA, a private investigator or law firm that regularly conducts investigations of alleged workplace misconduct may qualify as a "consumer reporting agency" subject to the FCRA. "The term 'consumer reporting agency' means any person which, for monetary fees, dues or on a cooperative nonprofit basis, regularly engages in whole or in part in the practice of assembling or evaluating consumer credit information *or other information* on consumers for the purpose of furnishing consumer reports to third parties, and which uses any means or facility of interstate commerce for the purpose of preparing or furnishing consumer reports."[38] The Federal Trade Commission, which has the power to enforce the FCRA, has taken the position, albeit reluctantly, that a "private investigator or law firm" that "regularly conducts

---

34. 15 U.S.C. §§ 1681 *et seq.*

35. 15 U.S.C. §§ 168la(d)(2)(A)(i), 168la(f).

36. 15 U.S.C. §§ 168lb(2)(A), 168lb(3)(A).

37. FCRA provides: "The term 'investigative consumer report' means a consumer report or portion thereof in which information on a consumer's character, general reputation, personal characteristics, or mode of living is obtained through personal interviews. . . ." 15 U.S.C. § 1681a(f). Section 606 of the act, 15 U.S.C. § 1681d, imposes several additional strictures on "investigative consumer reports." *See* 15 U.S.C. § 1681d(a)(1), (a)(2), (b), (d)(1). For instance, a consumer notified that he or she is the subject of an investigative consumer report has the right to request a written "disclosure of the nature and scope of the investigation." *Id.* § 1681d(b).

38. 15 U.S.C. § 1681a(f) (emphasis added).

investigations of alleged workplace misconduct" qualifies as a "consumer reporting agency."[39]

The FCRA does not apply, however, if the investigative report does not fall within the definition of a "consumer report." The FCRA defines a consumer report as "any written, oral, or other communication of any information by a consumer reporting agency" that (1) "bear[s] on a consumer's credit worthiness, credit standing, credit capacity, character, general reputation, personal characteristics, or mode of living" and (2) "is used or expected to be used or collected in whole or in part for the purpose of serving as a factor in establishing the consumer's eligibility for ... employment purposes."[40]

Although the act's language is seemingly broad in scope, at least one federal district court has taken a restrictive reading of whether an investigative report bears on an employee's credit history, character, reputation, personal characteristics, or mode of living. In *Hartman v. Lisle Park District*,[41] the court dismissed plaintiff's FCRA claim because, inter alia, the investigative report did not constitute a consumer report. The plaintiff, an employee of the Lisle Park District, alleged she was fired because she spoke to the county attorney's office and testified before the grand jury regarding alleged misuse of public funds by the district's director.[42] The district hired an outside law firm to conduct an investigation on plaintiff.[43] Plaintiff sued, alleging that the district violated the FCRA because it did not notify her of the investigation, obtain her consent prior to the investigation, or provide her with a copy of the report.[44] The court held that "nothing in [plaintiff's] complaint indicates that [the law firm's) investigation and its report concerned [plaintiff's] credit history, her character, her general reputation, or her personal characteristics or mode of living. Rather, it appears to be undisputed that [the law firm's] investigation and report concerned [plaintiff's] dealings with the District."[45]

---

39. *Prepared Statement of the Federal Trade Commission before the House Banking and Financial Services Committee, Subcommittee on Financial Institutions and Consumer Credit,* May 4, 2000, p. 2 (*Prepared Statement of the FTC*). This document is available at www.ftc.gov.

40. 15 U.S.C. § 1681a(d)(1).

41. 158 F. Supp. 2d 869 (N.D. Ill. 2001).

42. *Id.* at 872.

43. *Id.*

44. *Id.* at 872-73.

45. *Id.* at 875.

The second requirement for a report to be a consumer report is that it must be used or expected to be used in whole or in part for employment purposes. The act provides that "[t]he term 'employment purposes' when used in connection with a consumer report means a report used for the purpose of evaluating a consumer for employment, promotion, reassignment or retention as an employee."[46] Although there is little case law on what constitutes "employment purposes," it seems clear that an investigative report prepared for the purpose of providing legal advice on issues unrelated to employment falls outside the act's scope. One court has stated that the FCRA does not apply to an investigative report prepared by outside counsel because, inter alia, the report "was prepared in order to provide legal advice to the company, and not for the purpose of evaluating [the employee] and taking 'adverse action' against him."[47]

The question then arises whether an investigation conducted by outside counsel would result in a "consumer report" if its primary purpose is to investigate allegations of wrongdoing, but the investigation ultimately results in employee discipline, such as termination or demotion of employees found to have engaged in impropriety. A literalistic reading of the FCRA might conclude that it applies even to such investigations, in light of the FCRA's express provision that it applies to consumer reports collected even "*in part* for employment purposes."

Noting that such an interpretation could hamstring internal investigations in a manner not intended by Congress, the Federal Trade Commission has recommended that Congress amend the FCRA to exempt "investigations of alleged or suspected workplace illegality" from various of the act's requirements, including advance notice to implicated employees and the requirement that affected employees be provided a copy of any report of the investigation before adverse action is taken.[48] In light of the same concerns, Congressman Pete Sessions has introduced a bill to exempt workplace misconduct investigations from the FCRA's scope. As of the printing of this book, this bill had not yet been passed by Congress.

Even if a report qualifies as a consumer report, the FCRA is not implicated if the report contains "information solely as to transactions or experiences between the consumer and the person making the report."[49] In

---

46. 15 U.S.C. § 1681a(h).

47. Robinson v. Time Warner, Inc., 187 F.R.D. 144, 148 n.2 (S.D.N.Y. 1999).

48. *Prepared Statement of the FTC, supra* note 39, at p. 4.

49. 15 U.S.C. § 1681a(d)(2)(A)(i).

Hartman v. Lisle Park District, supra, the court stated that "[a]n attorney is the agent of his client.... When an attorney conducts for an employer/client an investigation of an employee's dealings with the employer, he is acting as the client, just as would be the case if the employer had one of its employees conduct the investigation."[50] Thus, the court held, "a report prepared by an attorney about an employee's transactions or experiences with the attorney's client (the employer) qualifies as a 'report containing information solely as to transactions or experiences between the consumer and the person making the report'... even though the report is prepared by an entity other than the employer."[51] If this reasoning—which is contrary to the FTC's reading of the act—were adopted, an investigative report by outside counsel would never be subject to the FCRA. It is too soon to tell whether other courts will adopt the *Hartman* court's novel rationale of treating the employer's outside counsel as the employer under the act.

Although the *Hartman* court's reasoning appears strained, it seems clear that the FCRA was not intended to apply to workplace investigations of alleged illegality, in which employee discipline is at most a by-product of the investigation rather than its goal. The FCRA was not enacted with such investigations in mind, but—as the act's very name makes clear—with respect to more commonplace investigations into consumer credit matters. When it enacted the FCRA, Congress noted: "It is the purpose of this title to require that consumer reporting agencies adopt reasonable procedures for *meeting the needs of commerce for consumer credit,* personnel, insurance, and other information in a manner which is fair and equitable to the consumer...."[52] As the FTC has observed, applying the FCRA outside the context of such routine credit investigations would extend the act beyond its intended scope and would severely hamstring investigations into alleged employee criminality and other misconduct, a result not envisioned by Congress. Courts considering whether the FCRA applies to such investigations should find, consistent with the act's underlying purpose and intended scope, that the FCRA does not apply to them.

The question of whether the FCRA applies to a particular workplace investigation is not merely academic. Any person who "willfully fails to comply with any requirement imposed under [the FCRA] with respect to any [employee]" is liable to that employee for (1) actual damages sus-

---

50. Hartman, 158 F. Supp. 2d at 876-77.
51. *Id.* at 876.
52. 15 U.S.C. § 1681(b) (emphasis added).

tained as a result of noncompliance with the FCRA of not less than $100 and not more than $1,000; (2) punitive damages as the court may allow; and (3) the costs of the civil action and reasonable attorneys' fees.[53] Any person who "is negligent in failing to comply" with the FCRA with respect to any employee is liable to that employee for (1) actual damages and (2) the costs of the action and reasonable attorneys' fees.[54]

IV. COMPANY RIGHTS IN AN INTERNAL INVESTIGATION

A. *Terminating Employees for Failing to Cooperate*

One of the most controversial issues in an internal investigation is whether the company may discharge an employee for failing to cooperate in the investigation. The ability to terminate for noncooperation with an internal investigation varies with state law, the employee's contract, and the facts of each case. Yet, as internal investigations become more frequent, more companies and company counsel will be faced with this dilemma.

In some states, employment for an unspecified duration is "at-will" and an employee can be terminated for any reason that does not violate a statute. Other states use a variety of factors, such as personnel policies, handbooks, longevity, and promotions, to imply a "good cause" requirement for discharge. Many states, even those adhering to at-will employment, permit an employee to sue for discharge in violation of a fundamental public policy.[55] Finally, there are a variety of state and federal laws that prohibit employers from discriminating against employees because of the employee's race, age, sex, national origin, etc., or the employee's whistle-blowing activities.

In the case of an employee who refuses to cooperate in an internal investigation, the company must determine whether the state law requires good cause or prohibits a discharge in violation of public policy, and whether there is any special protection, such as a whistle-blower protection statute, that might apply.

Good cause depends upon the circumstances of the individual em-

---

53. 15 U.S.C. § 1681n.
54. 15 U.S.C. § 1681o.
55. *See, e.g.*, Foley v. Interactive Data Corp., 47 Cal. 3d 654, 765 P.2d 373 (1988); TOBIAS, LITIGATING WRONGFUL DISCHARGE CLAIMS, chs. 4 and 5 (1991).

ployee, the employee's actions, and the company's actions. For example, an internal auditor who refuses to discuss audit findings in an investigation has probably breached the duty to cooperate and a subsequent discharge would be for "good cause."

"Good cause" is an elusive concept, not subject to an exact definition, although it was defined as "a fair and honest cause or reason, regulated by good faith on the part of the party exercising the power" by one court.[56] An employer has "good cause" if the termination is not for any arbitrary, capricious, or illegal reason and was based on substantial evidence, especially after an adequate investigation that includes a chance for the employee to respond to the claimed misconduct.[57] Arbitrators under collective bargaining agreements often examine the following tenets in deciding whether good cause existed for termination:

- Did the employee know that his or her conduct would be subject to discipline?
- Was the rule the employee violated reasonably related to the safe, efficient, or orderly operation of the business?
- Did the company investigate to discover whether the employee violated the rule?
- Did the company conduct a fair and objective investigation?
- Did the company obtain significant evidence of a violation?
- Was the decision nondiscriminatory?
- Was the discipline related to the seriousness of the offense and the prior record of the employee?[58]

Additionally, some employers set forth specific rules or standards of conduct in handbooks, which specify the types of offenses that justify termination. Examples of offenses include insubordination, fighting, unsatisfactory job performance, possession of illegal drugs, excessive tardiness, violation of safety rules, theft, and unexcused absences. Some courts will recognize these offenses as constituting good cause.[59]

---

56. Pugh v. See's Candies, Inc., 116 Cal. App. 3d 311, 330, 171 Cal. Rptr. 917, 928 (1981).

57. Cotran v. Rollins Hudig Hall Int'l Inc., 17 Cal. 4th 93, 108 (1998).

58. TOBIAS, *supra* note 55, § 9.09 (1991); *West Virginia Pulp & Paper Co.*, 45 L.A. 515 BNA (1965).

59. *See* Leikvold v. Valley View Community Hosp., 141 Ariz. 544, 688 P.2d 170

For the common-law public policy cause of action, the employee must establish (1) a relevant public policy, (2) that the termination violated the public policy, such as a termination in retaliation for engaging in protected activity or for refusal to participate in illegal activity, and (3) resulting damages. The public policy probably must relate to an important duty that inures to the benefit of the public at large rather than to a particular employee. The employee may also have to show that public interests predominate over private interests.[60]

In a public policy claim, the employee must establish the key elements set forth above. The company then has the burden of coming forth with evidence that it was not so motivated, but rather had a legitimate business reason for the discharge. The jury ultimately determines whether the employer was properly motivated. The employee can prevail if the forbidden motive is a substantial factor or a contributing factor.[61]

In deciding whether the employee's refusal to cooperate in the internal investigation constitutes a legitimate business reason, a court may consider several factors, including the seriousness of the investigation; the importance of the employee's information in relation to the investigation; other alternative means of discovering the information; the corporation's intent in questioning the employee; the employee's position in the company; the employee's reason for withholding the information; the company's treatment of similarly situated employees; and any other relevant facts.[62]

Under the right circumstances, consequently, the corporation may terminate an employee for refusing to participate, i.e., for insubordination. However, before terminating the reluctant witness, the company should advise the employee in writing of the duty to cooperate in the investigation and the possible discipline for failure to cooperate.

Although an employer may be entitled to discharge an employee for not participating in an internal investigation, a company should consider the potential adverse effects of these actions. A company's goal in performing an internal investigation is to perform an exhaustive inquiry into

---

(1984); Austin's Rack, Inc. v. Austin, 396 So. 2d 1161 (Fla. App. 1981); Toussaint v. Blue Cross & Blue Shield of Mich., 408 Mich. 579, 623, 292 N.W.2d 880, 897 (1980).

60. Tobias, *supra* note 55, § 5.21 (1991); Foley v. Interactive Data Corp., 47 Cal. 3d at 661-71; Green v. Ralee Eng'g Co., 19 Cal. 4th 66 (1998) (administrative regulations can be the source of the public policy).

61. Tobias, *supra* note 55, § 5.23.

62. *See, e.g.*, Blaney v. Commonwealth of Pennsylvania, *supra* note 4.

the subject matter of the investigation. By terminating an employee who is unwilling to participate in an internal investigation, a company might be alienating the one person with the knowledge of the facts required to perform the investigation.

Often, it is better to attempt to alleviate the employee's concerns by helping the employee obtain separate counsel who can properly apprise and protect the employee's rights, while allowing the company to ascertain the facts so it can determine its potential liability. Moreover, starting the interviews with threats of termination and overbearing stances could have a chilling effect on other employees' participation in the interview process, and thereby negatively impact the investigation.

B. *Discipline or Termination of Whistle-Blowers*

Special care must be taken in disciplining a whistle-blower who refuses to participate in the investigation. Again, whistle-blowers are protected from retaliation by federal and state laws. The rights granted by these statutes may conflict with the employer's desire to conduct a full investigation.

The company has the right to interview employees about their knowledge of work-related activities, and also to protect itself from threatened lawsuits, by taking steps such as interviewing employees and obtaining work-related documents from them. Finally, the company has the right to discipline or terminate a whistle-blower who refuses to obey the lawful reasonable requests of the employer. In the event of this discipline, however, the whistle-blower almost certainly will argue that the discipline was because of the whistle-blowing activities, and not because of refusals to obey reasonable requests of the company. The whistle-blower will search for evidence of being treated differently from other employees who refused to cooperate fully. Ultimately, the jury will decide whether retaliation was a motivating or contributing factor.

The surrounding circumstances may dictate whether the company will discipline or terminate the unwilling whistle-blower. For example, if the whistle-blower demands that a lawyer be present for an interview, the company might have a more difficult time convincing a jury that the discipline was imposed not for retaliation, but for insubordination. The goal of the investigation is to learn as much information as possible to protect the company's interests. The presence of the whistle-blower's lawyer will not necessarily hinder that goal, and a jury may second-guess a decision to terminate the whistle-blower under these circumstances.

Similarly, the company may have the right to force the whistle-blower to disclose what was said to the grand jury or to the law enforcement agency.[63] The company may need that information to take corrective action, if necessary, as soon as possible. On the other hand, if the whistle-blower describes all of the facts supporting the allegations, but refuses to discuss the grand jury testimony or the conversation with the law enforcement agency, the company's subsequent termination may appear to be retaliatory.

A company may have a better chance of convincing a jury it was not motivated by retaliation if it can establish that the whistle-blower was a knowing participant in the alleged wrongdoing and that all knowing participants were similarly terminated. The whistle-blower protections of various federal acts were undoubtedly not intended to protect an employee who willfully, and without compulsion, violates a law.[64] The whistle-blower may argue, however, that he or she tried to stop the alleged wrongdoing but was precluded from doing so by upper management. The company should investigate these claims before disciplining the whistle-blower. Finally, on occasion, whistle-blowers have used unlawful means to establish a case of illegal or unlawful conduct by the company. For instance, whistle-blowers may "steal" privileged attorney-client documents or proprietary, confidential data to support the allegation of illegality. It is doubtful that Congress intended to protect employees who engage in criminal conduct to prove a case of wrongdoing.

In summary, the risks in terminating a whistle-blower are quite high: back pay, front pay, compensatory damages, and possibly punitive damages. The company must have strong evidence to support a termination and should ensure that the whistle-blower cannot point out another person who engaged in similar conduct and was not terminated.

C. Termination While Asserting Right Against Self-Incrimination

During the investigation, an employee may refuse to cooperate by asserting the right against self-incrimination. This right should not apply

---

63. The government cannot prevent witnesses from discussing their grand jury testimony. *See* FED. R. CRIM. P. 6; *In re* Vescovo Special Grand Jury, 473 F. Supp. 1335, 1336-37 (C.D. Cal. 1979).

64. The whistle-blower protection section of the False Claims Act refers to "lawful acts," 31 U.S.C. § 3730(h). Other whistle-blower protections do not protect employees who deliberately cause a violation of the law. *See, e.g.,* Energy Reorganization Act, 42 U.S.C. § 5871(g).

to private employers unless there is state action or a special state statute. Even if the right does apply, the company may still terminate the employee if the evidence establishes that the employee was involved in an improper activity.

A company that is in the preliminary stages of its investigation should not immediately terminate an employee who asserts a right against self-incrimination. Instead, the company should warn the employee that there is an expectation of cooperation and that disciplinary action will result for a refusal to cooperate. The company should continue its investigation and attempt to independently determine the involvement of the recalcitrant employee. The company must then weigh the strength of the evidence of wrongdoing against the employee, the need for the information from the employee, whether the employee is actually a target of an investigation by law enforcement, and the extent of the employee's refusal to cooperate. Under these circumstances, an employee's failure to discuss work-related events should constitute good cause for termination. Even where there is state action or a state statute, the fact that the employee asserts a right against self-incrimination should not change the result.

The company also should ensure that it is treating the employee in a similar fashion as other employees who have refused to cooperate in an investigation. Evidence of disparate treatment may be used by the employee to state claims of discrimination on the basis of race, age, sex, national origin, whistle-blowing activities, or similar protected categories.

V. COMPANY DUTIES IN AN INTERNAL INVESTIGATION

A. *Warnings to Employees*

It is imperative that at the outset of every interview, the lawyer give employees certain admonitions. Although a debate exists about the exact scope of these warnings, at a minimum, warnings prior to the interview should include the following:

- A short, concise statement of the purpose and nature of the interview should be made. Generally, the interview is conducted to assist management in responding to the particular pending or anticipated litigation matter, and to provide legal advice.
- The lawyers present are representing the company, not any past, present, or future employees.

- Management believes that the interviews are being conducted subject to the company's (not the employee's) lawyer-client communication privilege and lawyer work product doctrine.
- Management might voluntarily or intentionally elect to disclose anything said during the interview to others in the company or to third parties in its own best interest, but pending this decision, the communications are intended to be privileged.
- The employee should not discuss the interview with anyone, including fellow employees, because disclosure could inhibit the company's ability to assert the aforementioned privileges and may taint the fact-finding investigation.
- The employee should tell the truth.

These warnings are given at the outset of the interview to apprise employees of their rights and to preserve the privileges of the corporation. Of course, during the interview, company counsel must be careful to determine whether any statements made by the employee indicate that the employee could be the subject of criminal charges. If, during the course of the interview or investigation, it appears reasonably possible that criminal allegations against the individual may result, company counsel should consider advising the employee to retain private counsel.

Although the company wants to obtain the full cooperation of its employees, the company may also want to ensure employees that its goal is investigation, not prosecution. The company may offer to assist an employee in selecting counsel and, under some circumstances, may want to wait until counsel is selected before continuing with the interview. On the other hand, the company may have an immediate need to punish wrongdoers to convince the government that those responsible for the illegal activity are no longer employed. The company should consider its approach to this issue at the beginning of its investigation to reduce the risk of disparate treatment of similarly situated employees.

B. *Duty to Pay Fees of Employees' Counsel*

A matter of great concern to any employee involved in an internal investigation is whether the company will reimburse the employee for the costs of retaining separate counsel. As with other areas of the law regarding employee rights in an internal investigation, the question of whether a company can or should reimburse employees for participating in an internal investigation is unresolved.

A company's ability to indemnify its employees for attorneys' fees incurred from participating in an internal investigation is controlled by the applicable state law and the bylaws of the corporation. Many states have statutes that require mandatory reimbursement of fees once the employee has been successful on the merits in defense of any action in which the employee is a party because of activities as an employee.[65] These mandatory statutes, however, do not address whether an employee is entitled to recover attorneys' fees for participating in an internal investigation.

Most states, however, also have statutes that give permissive discretion to corporations to reimburse employees for other actions. For example, Delaware Corporate Code section 145 states:

INDEMNIFICATION OF OFFICERS, DIRECTORS, EMPLOYEES AND AGENTS; INSURANCE—(A) A corporation may indemnify any person who was or is a party or is threatened to be made a party to any threatened, pending or completed action, suit or proceeding, whether civil, criminal, administrative or investigative (other than an action by or in the right of the corporation) by reason of the fact that he is or was a director, officer, employee or agent of the corporation, or is or was serving at the request of the corporation as a director, officer, employee or agent of another corporation, partnership, joint venture, trust or other enterprise, against expenses (including attorneys' fees), judgments, fines and amounts paid in settlement actually and reasonably incurred by him in connection with such action, suit or proceeding if he acted in good faith and in a manner he reasonably believed to be in or not opposed to the best interest of the corporation, and, with respect to any criminal action or proceeding, he had no reasonable cause to believe his conduct was unlawful. The termination of any action, suit or proceeding by judgment, order, settlement, conviction or upon a plea of nolo contendere or its equivalent,

---

65. *See, e.g.*, Cal. Corp. Code § 317(d), which states:

To the extent that an agent of a corporation has been successful on the merits in defense of any proceeding referred to in subdivision (b) or (c) or in defense of any claim, issue or matter therein, the agent shall be indemnified against expenses actually and reasonably incurred by the agent in connection therewith.

shall not, of itself, create a presumption that the person did not act in good faith and in a manner which he reasonably believed to be in or not opposed to the better interest of the corporation, and, with respect to any criminal action or proceeding, had reasonable cause to believe that his conduct was unlawful.

This statute allows corporations to indemnify their employees for certain proceedings. It defines proceedings as "any threatened, pending or completed action or proceeding, whether civil, criminal, administrative or investigative." The statute does not further define the terms "administrative" or "investigative." "Administrative" most likely refers to proceedings before federal, state, and local agencies, while "investigative" probably refers to investigative actions instituted by government agencies or other third parties. Under this definition, a corporation would be entitled to reimburse employees for fees incurred in an internal investigation prompted by a government or third-party investigation, but not necessarily in an internal investigation prompted purely by the company's internal concerns.

While there does not seem to be any case authority on this issue, one commentator has argued that the term "investigative," in a similar California statute, does not apply to this latter category of purely internal investigations.[66] As the commentator wrote:

[I]f the term investigative was interpreted to also include internal investigations by a corporation into its own affairs, this would likely result in employees asserting a right to indemnification for expenses (such as attorneys' fees) incurred in participating in such corporate self-investigations. That result would no doubt chill corporations from undertaking such investigations, and there is no indication on the face of the statute or its legislative history that this was the intended result.

Most courts would probably interpret the statute in the manner the commentator suggests unless the statute and legislative history support the

---

66. *See Advising Employers on Indemnifying Their Agents: The Impact of Corporations Code Section 317 and Labor Code Section 2809*, Los Angeles Lawyer (April 1988) (article examining Cal. Corp. Code § 317, which is identical to the Delaware statute).

opposite result. Therefore, the corporation generally has no duty to advance fees for an internal investigation.

A corporation, however, may still be able to reimburse an employee for attorneys' fees, even in a purely internal investigation. Many states allow corporations to indemnify employees by amending the corporation's articles and bylaws or through a vote by the board of directors. For example, Delaware Corporate Code section 145(f) states:

> The indemnification and advancement of expenses provided by, or granted pursuant to, the other subsections of this section shall not be deemed exclusive of any other rights to which those seeking indemnification or advancement of expenses may be entitled under any bylaw, agreement, vote of stockholders or disinterested directors or otherwise, both as to action in his official capacity and as to action in another capacity while holding such office.

This statute allows the corporation to enter into agreements, either through employment contracts or by passing bylaws, that allow the corporation to reimburse employees for the costs incurred for participating in internal investigations. Naturally, each employee's situation will be different depending on the employment contract, the articles and bylaws of the corporation, and the state laws governing whether permissive reimbursement or advancement of fees is allowed.

Certain states also have broad statutes within their labor codes that arguably could require the corporation to indemnify its employees for costs and fees incurred in participating in purely internal investigations. For example, California Labor Code section 2802 states:

> An employer shall indemnify his employee for all the employee necessarily expends or loses in direct consequence of the discharge of his duties as such, or of his obedience to the directions of the employer, even though unlawful, unless the employee, at the time of obeying such directions, believed them to be unlawful.

Although no case has determined whether this statute would allow an employee to recover costs incurred during an internal investigation, a California court has ruled that it requires a corporation to reimburse an employee for attorneys' fees arising out of a lawsuit. In *Douglas v. Los*

Angeles Herald-Examiner,[67] an investigative reporter for the now-defunct Herald-Examiner newspaper was sued by the target of an article he wrote regarding the alleged unlawful activities of a real estate company. The Herald-Examiner refused to defend Douglas and subsequently refused to indemnify him for the costs and attorneys' fees of his successful defense in his suit for indemnification. The California Appellate Court ruled that the Herald-Examiner owed a duty to indemnify when the employee was required to defend the lawsuit solely because of acts that he performed within the course and scope of the employee's employment.

Because of the broad language of the statute and the holding in *Douglas*, an argument exists, at least in California, that an employee who acts within the scope of employment and faces potential liability should be reimbursed for costs and fees incurred in participating in the internal investigation. Although this argument is tenuous, corporations should expect employees to assert similar arguments under expansive reimbursement statutes.[68]

In an internal investigation, it will be difficult to determine whether the employee has a potential liability at the outset of the investigation to be made a party to a legal proceeding. It may be beneficial for the corporation to advance the fees subject to a later determination of whether the employee will be reimbursed. The company should require the employee to provide adequate assurance that all advanced fees will be refunded if it is ultimately determined that the employee is not entitled to indemnification.[69] Additionally, any advances generally must be specifically approved

---

67. 50 Cal. App. 3d 449, 123 Cal. Rptr. 683 (1975).

68. *See* Grissom v. Vons Co., Inc., 1 Cal. App. 52 (1991) (appellate court held that Labor Code § 2802 required an employer to indemnify an employee "for all that the employee necessarily expends or loses in direct consequence of the discharge" of the employee's duties, which could arguably include the cost of attorney's fee in an internal investigation); Devereaux v. Latham & Watkins, 32 Cal. App. 4th 1571, 1583 (1995) (Labor Code § 2802 requires indemnity for legal expenses only when the expenses are related to conduct within the course and scope of employment).

69. A sample clause pertaining to the advancement of fees between a corporation and the employee that should be included in an agreement should provide:

> Advancement of Expenses. The Company shall advance all expenses incurred by Indemnitee in connection with the investigation, defense, settlement or appeal of any civil or criminal action, suit or proceeding (but not amounts actually paid in the settlement of any action, suit or proceeding). Indemnitee hereby undertakes to repay such amounts advanced only if, and to the extent that, it shall ultimately be determined that the Indemnitee is not entitled to be indemnified by the Company

by the board of directors or its designee before a commitment to the employee is made by corporate counsel.[70] If a lawyer is not known, the corporation can and should recommend someone to represent the employee. Naturally, because of ethical considerations, the corporation should ensure that the recommended lawyer is not presently representing the corporation and is not "captive counsel" for conflicts of interest purposes.

VI. JOINT DEFENSE OR COMMON-INTEREST PRIVILEGE

Many internal investigations involve a situation that could lead to civil or criminal litigation. In certain situations, it is beneficial for the potential defendants, including the company, to coordinate their efforts by pooling information and sharing tactics among co-counsel and their similarly situated clients.[71] This relationship will necessarily result in some shared work product and communication among the lawyers and their clients. The lawyers performing the internal investigation and the employees' lawyers should make every effort to ensure that these communications are protected by the joint defense privilege.[72]

In internal investigations, the joint defense privilege provides an opportunity to protect communications between parties with a similar interest. Although the courts are still struggling to define the parameters of "similar interest,"[73] it generally applies to internal investigations. A "similar interest" was defined by one court as where two parties have an identical legal interest with respect to the subject matter of a communication between a lawyer and client concerning legal advice.[74] Most joint

---

as authorized hereby. The advances to be made hereunder shall be paid by the Company to the Indemnitee within twenty (20) days following delivery of a written request therefore by Indemnitee to the Company.

70. *See e.g.*, DEL. CORP. CODE § 145(e).

71. This pooling may involve an assignment of responsibility for interviewing witnesses, collecting documents and other evidence, hiring and preparing experts, and researching and arguing various legal positions depending on the circumstances of the case.

72. Also known as the "common interest privilege."

73. *See* Continental Oil Co. v. United States, 330 F.2d 347 (9th Cir. 1964).

74. *See* United States v. Zolin, 809 F.2d 1411, 1417 (9th Cir. 1987), *vacated in part on other grounds*, 842 F.2d 1135 (9th Cir. 1988) (en banc), *affirmed in part, vacated in part*, 491 U.S. 554, 109 S. Ct. 2619, 105 L. Ed. 2d 469 (1989); Duplan Corp. v. Deering Milliken Inc., 397 F. Supp. 1146 (D.S.C. 1975).

defense arrangements involving internal investigations should fit this definition.

When the parties have a similar or common interest, the joint defense privilege protects confidential communications passing from one party to the lawyer for another party where a joint defense arrangement exists.[75] Only those communications, however, made in the course of an ongoing joint defense arrangement and intended to further the arrangement are protected.[76]

The joint defense privilege is particularly important in internal investigations because it has been held to apply even when no litigation exists. As one court stated, "the need to protect the free flow of information from client to lawyer logically exists whenever multiple clients share a common interest about a legal matter, and it is therefore unnecessary that there be actual litigation in progress for the common-interest rule of the attorney-client privilege to apply."[77] Neither is it necessary for the lawyer representing the communicating party to be present when the communication is made to the other party's lawyer.[78] A claim resting on the joint defense privilege, however, requires a showing that the communication in question was given in confidence and the client reasonably understood it to be given.[79]

Another important aspect of the joint defense privilege is that it has been extended to both oral and written communications. In *Continental Oil Company v. United States*,[80] the Ninth Circuit prevented discovery of certain memoranda and recorded interviews with employees of the Standard Oil and Continental Oil Companies, which had been subpoenaed by the grand jury. Counsel for each company had exchanged their respective memoranda in confidence and in an effort to prepare effectively for an-

---

75. *See* United States v. Bay State Ambulance & Hosp. Rental Serv., Inc., 874 F.2d 20, 28 (1st Cir. 1989); United States v. Schwimmer, 892 F.2d 237 (2d Cir. 1989), *cert. denied*, 493 U.S. 1071 (1990).

76. Eisenberg v. Gagnon, 766 F.2d 770, 787 (3d Cir.), *cert. denied*, 474 U.S. 946, 106 S. Ct. 342, 88 L. Ed. 2d 290 (1985); Matter of Bevill, Bresler & Schulman Asset Management Corp., 805 F.2d 120 (3d Cir. 1986).

77. *See* Zolin, 809 F.2d at 1417.

78. *See* Matter of Grand Jury Subpoena, 406 F. Supp. 381 (S.D.N.Y. 1975); Hunydee v. United States, 355 F.2d 183 (9th Cir. 1985).

79. *See* United States v. Keplinger, 776 F.2d 678, 701 (7th Cir. 1985), *cert. denied*, 476 U.S. 1183, 106 S. Ct. 2919, 91 L. Ed. 2d 548 (1986); Kevlik v. Goldstein, 724 F.2d 844, 849 (1st Cir. 1984).

80. Continental Oil, *supra* note 73.

ticipated litigation involving the various individual and corporate clients. The court concluded that this exchange had not destroyed the confidential nature of those documents.

Lawyers should be cautious, however, about the joint defense privilege. Although the courts have been receptive, the privilege is still evolving and remains largely undefined. This uncertainty appears especially in waiver of the privilege. Some courts have concluded that a party to joint defense communications may waive the attorney-client privilege by disclosing the confidential information to persons outside the scope of the joint defense relationship.[81] Additionally, courts have held that a party to joint defense communications may waive the work product privilege by disclosing privileged information to third parties in a manner inconsistent with the purpose of maintaining the confidential nature of the information.[82]

Other courts have concluded that a waiver of a privilege relating to information shared in joint defense communications by one party will not constitute a waiver by any other party to the communications.[83] The court reasoned that this limitation was necessary to ensure that joint defense efforts are not inhibited or even precluded by the fear that one party may unilaterally waive the privileges of all participants, either inadvertently or purposely, in an effort to exonerate himself.[84]

The government has recently argued for the disqualification of defense counsel, based upon a conflict of interest arising from the receipt of privileged information from parties to a joint defense agreement. In *United States v. Anderson*,[85] the government argued that defendant's counsel

---

81. *See* Wilson P. Abraham Constr. Corp. v. Armco Steel Corp., 559 F.2d 250, 253 (5th Cir. 1977); United States v. Blasco, 702 F.2d 1315, 1329 (11th Cir. 1983), *cert. denied*, 464 U.S. 914; 104 S. Ct. 275, 78 L. Ed. 2d 256; United States v. Melvin, 650 F.2d 641, 646 (5th Cir. 1981).

82. *See* Permian Ct. v. United States, 665 F.2d 1214, 1219 (D.C. Cir. 1981); United States v. American Tel. & Tel. Co., 642 F.2d 1285, 1299 (D.C. Cir. 1980); Stix Prods., Inc. v. United Merchants & Manufacturers, Inc., 47 F.R.D. 334, 338 (S.D.N.Y. 1969); Transmirra Prods. Corp. v. Monsanto Chem. Co., 26 F.R.D. 572, 578 (S.D.N.Y. 1960); Western Fuels Ass'n, Inc. v. Burlington Northern Ry. Co., 102 F.R.D. 201 (D. Wyo. 1984).

83. *See* Ohio-Sealy Mattress Mfg. Co. v. Kaplan, 90 F.R.D. 21, 29 (N.D. Ill. 1980), *aff'd in part, rev'd in part on other grounds*, 745 F.2d 441 (7th Cir. 1984), *cert. denied*, 471 U.S. 1125 (1985).

84. *Id.* at 32.

85. 790 F. Supp. 231 (W.D. Wa. 1992).

learned privileged information of the co-defendants through the joint defense agreement. Since these co-defendants entered plea agreements and became government witnesses, the government argued that a conflict of interest existed because the defendant's counsel would be required to cross-examine the co-defendants from whom it learned privileged information through the joint defense agreement. Counsel was prevented from using the confidential information even though the information might help the client. As a result, the government requested a hearing to determine if a conflict existed to an extent that counsel should withdraw from the case. The court granted the government's motion and ordered a hearing on this issue to determine if counsel should be forced to withdraw from the case.

Thus, even though the joint defense privilege offers many advantages, some potential problems exist. Counsel for the company, consequently, should consider the matter very carefully before establishing or formalizing a joint defense arrangement. Especially where a joint defense arrangement is offered, the advisability of the agreement and of admitting each proposed member of the cooperating group should be carefully scrutinized. Otherwise, the corporation may ultimately find that it gave away more than it bargained for in the agreement.

VII. CONCLUSION

The law regarding employees' rights and obligations in corporate internal investigations is still evolving. Corporate counsel, consequently, must be aware of the rights of the employees in performing their internal investigations. However, they should not lose sight of their goal—to perform a thorough and exhaustive inquiry.

The Practitioner's Guide to Parallel Proceedings

by Judah Best & Scott N. Auby*

*Judah Best is a senior partner in the Washington, D.C. office of Debevoise & Plimpton. Scott N. Auby is his colleague in that office. This chapter is based on an earlier version authored by Mr. Best and D. Annette Fields. In turn, that version is heavily reliant on the lengthy paper "Follow the Yellow Brick Road," first conceived in the 1980s and authored by Mr. Best and Marc S. Gromis. Messrs. Best and Auby wish to thank Jocelyn Bramble, a 2001 summer associate with the Washington office of Debevoise & Plimpton, for her assistance with the preparation of this chapter.

201

I. INTRODUCTION

THIS CHAPTER FOCUSES UPON the multiple legal actions—so-called parallel proceedings—a company may face upon the discovery and disclosure of improper and potentially unlawful activity within its employee ranks. Given the vast and ever-increasing network of federal, state, and local legislation and regulation governing the business community, it is not surprising that a violation of one law can lead to the institution of numerous proceedings by various governmental authorities at all levels, as well as by private individuals or classes of individuals.

To cite one example: an allegation of price-fixing or bid-rigging can, and often does, trigger multiple, simultaneous inquiries from both federal and state agencies, and from private parties. Parallel proceedings may include:

- a lengthy federal grand jury investigation;
- a lengthy criminal trial for charges involving the Sherman Act, Mail Fraud, False Statements, and RICO (the maximum statutory fine for one Sherman Act offense alone is $1 million);
- a treble-damage action by the federal government as a purchaser under 15 U.S.C. § 15;
- a private treble-damage action by consumers of the product under 15 U.S.C. § 15;
- suspension and debarment proceedings by both state and federal procurement agencies.

There are many other examples where simultaneous, or seriatim, proceedings flow from what one might consider a single act or transaction. Those coming quickly to mind include proceedings related to violations of federal procurement laws, securities laws, environmental laws, and banking laws. In each instance, a single "violation" can result in multiple federal and state criminal prosecutions, civil damage suits, and injunctive actions, as well as local, state, and federal administrative proceedings.

While each substantive area has its own distinct body of law and policy, parallel proceedings present complex legal issues that are common in all contexts. The following are just a few of the many concerns counsel must address:

- May the civil action be stayed by court order pending resolution of a pending parallel criminal investigation or proceeding?
- If the civil proceeding is not stayed, will Fifth Amendment invocations be admitted as "adverse inferences" in the civil proceeding?
- Should a company discipline employees for their misconduct, or will the discipline be seen as proof of wrongdoing?
- Can company counsel represent not only the company but all or some of its employees?

The outcome of any single proceeding can dramatically impact the well-being of a company; in addition, the combined impact of defending against a number of parallel proceedings can be crippling. Because of the enormous stakes involved in defending corporate interests in multiple arenas, it is of utmost importance that company counsel have a fundamental understanding of the existence of, and interplay among, the federal and state laws and regulations pertinent to the particular circumstances faced by the corporate client accused of misconduct. In undertaking an internal investigation, counsel must take care to advise its corporate client that disclosure of any material misconduct discovered in the course of the investigation may trigger a variety of actions from a number of fronts—criminal and civil, state and federal, private and governmental.

In the following pages, some of the more important issues confronting the practitioner involved in parallel proceedings are set out and discussed. Each issue is a subject unto itself and easily justifies a much fuller discussion than permitted here. Issue identification and characterization, however, is critical in this area of the law, and it is hoped that the comments provided will enable counsel for the company to better anticipate and advise the client regarding the potential landmines in the path through parallel proceedings.

II. RECURRING ISSUES IN PARALLEL PROCEEDINGS

A. *Stays of Parallel Civil Actions*

The fact that there is an ongoing criminal investigation ordinarily will not defer or delay proceedings in a parallel civil or administrative case, even though evidence obtained in the civil proceeding may be incriminating in the criminal action. Indeed, generally speaking, unless a party can demonstrate that her rights will be substantially prejudiced if the civil proceeding continues, the courts will not stay it while the criminal matter works its way to completion.[1] In particular, the Supreme Court has long recognized the government's right to pursue criminal and civil proceedings "simultaneously or successively" based on the same underlying set of facts.[2]

For example, the D.C. Circuit in *SEC v. Dresser Industries, Inc.*[3] affirmed the trial court's order compelling Dresser to comply with an outstanding Securities and Exchange Commission (SEC) subpoena and rejected Dresser's argument that compliance would impermissibly allow the government to use information gained during civil discovery to promote the criminal case. The court concluded that:

> Effective enforcement of the securities laws requires that the SEC and Justice be able to investigate possible violations simultaneously. . . . The SEC cannot always wait for Justice to complete the criminal proceedings if it is to obtain the necessary prompt civil

---

1. SEC v. Dresser Indus., Inc., 628 F.2d 1368, 1374 (D.C. Cir.), *cert. denied*, 449 U.S. 993 (1980); *see also* SEC v. Musella, No. 83 Civ. 342, 1983 WL 1297, at *1 (S.D.N.Y. Apr. 4, 1983) ("[C]oncrete examples of circumstances sufficient to suspend the usual rule [allowing parallel proceedings] are few and far between.").

2. Standard Sanitary Mfg. Co. v. United States, 226 U.S. 20, 52 (1912); *see also* United States v. Kordel, 397 U.S. 1, 11 (1970) ("It would stultify enforcement of federal law to require a governmental agency . . . to choose either to forgo recommendation of a criminal prosecution once it seeks civil relief, or to defer civil proceedings pending the ultimate outcome of a criminal trial.").

3. 628 F.2d at 1377.

remedy; neither can Justice always await the conclusion of the civil proceeding without endangering its criminal case.[4]

The court held that, absent "special circumstances," it would not block concurrent, parallel investigations by the SEC and the Department of Justice (DOJ).[5]

What, then, are the "special circumstances" that would permit a stay of a civil proceeding until after the completion of a companion criminal proceeding? The *Dresser* court noted in dicta that if a party is under indictment for a serious offense and is required simultaneously to defend against a civil action involving the same underlying issues, the non-criminal proceeding, if not deferred, could (1) undermine the party's Fifth Amendment privilege against self-incrimination; (2) expand criminal discovery far beyond the limits of Federal Rule of Criminal Procedure 16(b); (3) disclose the party's criminal defense to the prosecution; or (4) otherwise prejudice the case. However, the court qualified this dictum by recognizing that any deferral of the non-criminal proceeding would be justified only if the delay would not seriously injure the public interest.[6]

Cases handed down since *Dresser* involving defendant stay requests generally have not been encouraging for defense counsel facing parallel proceedings. Courts often begin their analysis of a defendant's stay request by citing *Dresser* for the proposition that while courts have discre-

---

4. *Id.* at 1377; *see also* Gellis v. Casey, 338 F. Supp. 651, 653 (S.D.N.Y. 1972) (denying stay of SEC administrative action when the same transactions were the subject of a potential grand jury investigation, noting that "the SEC, as the agency charged with administering the Securities Acts to protect investors, is merely conducting an ordinary and proper administrative proceeding in good faith").

5. *See also* SEC v. First Fin. Group, Inc., 659 F.2d 660, 666-67 (5th Cir. 1981) (upholding denial of a stay of civil discovery in SEC enforcement action despite pendency of a federal grand jury criminal investigation into the transactions at issue).

6. Dresser, 628 F.2d at 1375-76; *see also* Kordel, 397 U.S. at 11 (suggesting in dicta that a stay may be appropriate if (*i*) the government pursues the civil action solely to obtain evidence for a criminal prosecution, (*ii*) the government fails to inform the defendant in the civil case that it plans further criminal proceedings, or (*iii*) the defendant lacks counsel or reasonably fears prejudice from adverse pretrial publicity or other unfair injury); Afro-Lecon, Inc. v. United States, 820 F.2d 1198, 1203 (Fed. Cir. 1987) (recognizing that "parallel proceedings may result in the abuse of discovery" by impermissibly expanding the scope of "highly restricted" criminal discovery to the broad scope of civil discovery).

tion to stay a civil proceeding pending the outcome of a criminal action, they are not required to do so.[7] In balancing the varying interests implicated by a defendant's request for a stay,[8] courts have been solicitous of the concerns of private plaintiffs[9] and the public[10]—arguably to the detriment of defendants' Fifth Amendment rights. Stays generally have been granted only if a defendant can demonstrate that parallel civil and criminal proceedings involve substantially the same facts,[11] and the court con-

---

7. *See, e.g.*, Federal Sav. & Loan Ins. Corp. v. Molinaro, 889 F.2d 899, 902 (9th Cir. 1989); *see also* Metzler v. Bennett, No. 97-CV-0148 (RSP/GJD), 1998 U.S. Dist. LEXIS 5441, at *17 (N.D.N.Y. Apr. 15, 1998) (noting that staying a civil case "is an extraordinary remedy"); *In re* Par Pharm., Inc. Secs. Litig., 133 F.R.D. 12, 13 (S.D.N.Y. 1990) (same).

8. *See* Landis v. North Am. Co., 299 U.S. 248, 254-55 (1936) (stating that a request for a stay of proceedings requires a court to balance the competing interests involved).

9. *See, e.g.*, Wilson v. Olathe Bank, No. 97-2458-KHV, 1998 U.S. Dist. LEXIS 5509, at *22 (D. Kan. Mar. 2, 1998) (stay of class action denied due to risk of "substantial prejudice to the . . . named plaintiffs and the class"); Transatlantic Reins. Co. v. Ditrapani, No. 90 Civ. 2240 (CSH), 1991 U.S. Dist. LEXIS 872, at *10 (S.D.N.Y. Jan. 28, 1991) ("that defendants' conduct also resulted in a criminal charge . . . should not be availed of by [them] as a shield against a civil suit and prevent plaintiffs from expeditiously advancing [their] claim") (quotation omitted); Arden Way Assocs. v. Boesky, 660 F. Supp. 1494, 1497 (S.D.N.Y. 1987) ("It is plainly ludicrous for Mr. Boesky to argue that it is 'unfair' to compel him to face the civil law suits against him which are the creations of his own alleged misconduct. . . . Surely it would be anomalous to suspend plaintiffs' rights in these civil litigations because they deal with Mr. Boesky's misconduct."); Fidelity Bankers Life Ins. Co. v. Wedco, Inc., 586 F. Supp. 1123, 1126 (D. Nev. 1984) ("The long period remaining before the statute of limitations will expire, and any criminal prosecution will be terminated, together with the need by Fidelity for an expeditious resolution of the issues . . . outweigh the impairment of the . . . defendants' ability to put on as complete a defense as they might but for their apprehension of self-incrimination.").

10. *See, e.g.*, First Fin. Group, 659 F.2d at 667 ("Protection of the efficient operation of the securities markets and the financial holdings of investors . . . may require prompt civil enforcement which cannot await the outcome of a criminal investigation.") (citing *Dresser*, 628 F.2d at 1375).

11. *See* Koester v. American Republic Invs., Inc., 11 F.3d 818, 823 (8th Cir. 1993) ("to warrant a stay, defendant must make a strong showing . . . that the two proceedings are so interrelated that he cannot protect himself at the civil trial by selectively invoking the Fifth Amendment privilege") (citation omitted); Bennett, 1998 U.S. Dist. LEXIS 5441, at *18 ("If there is no overlap [between the issues in the civil and criminal proceedings], then there would be no danger of self-incrimination and no need for

cludes that granting a stay is not likely to harm the public interest by interfering with civil governmental enforcement actions or depriving private plaintiffs of an opportunity to pursue legitimate civil claims.[12]

Brock v. Tolkow[13] is an illustrative and frequently cited case. In *Tolkow*, the district court entered a protective order staying "all discovery" in a Department of Labor ERISA civil suit pending the outcome of a parallel criminal investigation.[14] The court accepted the defendants' contention that "the criminal prosecution may be based on the same facts as the complaint in the [civil] case"[15] and noted that the defendants were not seeking to stay the entire case, but rather sought only to have discovery deferred pending the outcome of the criminal investigation.[16] Finally, and perhaps most important, the *Tolkow* court minimized the harm to the public interest that would result from a stay of the civil discovery, observing that "[p]ossible mismanagement of a pension fund simply does not present the same danger to the public interest as violations that other courts have found to warrant denial of a motion for a stay."[17] The court premised this conclusion on the lack of prejudice to the public that would result from delaying the civil proceeding before it. Unlike *Dresser*, where delaying the civil proceeding would have prejudiced the public's interest in timely regulation of the securities markets, and *Kordel*, where granting the stay would have impeded the government's efforts to stop distribution of mislabeled drugs, there was little or no risk that the pension fund's ability ultimately to meet its obligations to its beneficiaries would be endangered

---

a stay."); Trustees of the Plumbers & Pipefitters Nat'l Pension Fund v. Transworld Mechanical, Inc., 886 F. Supp. 1134, 1139 (S.D.N.Y. 1995) ("The first question to be resolved is the extent to which the issues in the criminal case overlap with those present in the civil case, since self-incrimination is more likely if there is a significant overlap.") (citations omitted).

12. It also should be noted that courts consistently recognize that a stay of a civil action is appropriate to remedy bad faith by the government in pursuing parallel civil and criminal proceedings. *See, e.g.*, Kordel, 397 U.S. at 10-11; Dresser, 628 F.2d at 1375.

13. 109 F.R.D. 116 (E.D.N.Y. 1985).

14. *Id.* at 121.

15. *Id.* at 118.

16. *Id.* at 119-20 ("Rather, they ask only that discovery therein be deferred pending the outcome of the criminal investigation; in all other respects the civil case will go forward.") (footnote omitted).

17. *Id.* at 120.

by a stay of discovery.[18] Thus, the *Tolkow* court's decision to grant the stay seems largely based on the conclusion that doing so would not cause substantial harm to the public interest or to civil enforcement efforts; these interests could still be effectively served despite the delay.

Similarly, in *United States v. Certain Real Property & Premises*,[19] the court stayed discovery in a civil forfeiture action brought by the United States pending the outcome of the criminal proceedings against the defendants. The court concluded that the government had not shown that deferring the civil action would injure the public interest.[20] As in *Tolkow*, the court distinguished *Dresser* and *Kordel* as having involved civil governmental enforcement actions brought to protect important public interests that "could be jeopardized by *deferral* of the action."[21]

Counsel should note that a defendant's odds of obtaining a stay of civil proceedings are typically greater after a formal indictment has issued. Granted, in *Certain Real Property*, one of the defendants had not been indicted,[22] and in *Tolkow*, the defendants had received grand jury subpoenas, but had not been indicted.[23] Still, courts have noted that the argument for a pre-indictment stay is "'a far weaker one,'"[24] and notwithstanding the stays in *Certain Real Property* and *Tolkow*, courts generally

---

18. *Id.* ("[The *Dresser* and *Kordel*] cases, unlike the present one, involve a tangible threat of immediate and serious harm to the public at large. While the allegations in this case are indeed serious, there is no indication that plan beneficiaries are suffering or will suffer any irreparable injury if civil discovery is stayed.").

19. 751 F. Supp. 1060 (E.D.N.Y. 1989).

20. *Id.* at 1062.

21. *Id.* (emphasis added). The fact that a stay would not be adverse to the public interest has been crucial to most cases in which a stay of a parallel governmental civil proceeding has been granted. *See, e.g.*, United States v. Armada Petroleum Corp., 700 F.2d 706, 709 (Temp. Emer. Ct. App. 1983); United States v. U.S. Currency, 626 F.2d 11, 17 (6th Cir.), *cert. denied*, 449 U.S. 993 (1980); United States v. $557,933.89, More or Less, in U.S. Funds, No. 95 -CV-3978 (JG), 1998 U.S. Dist. LEXIS 22252, at *12 (E.D.N.Y. Mar. 9, 1998).

22. Certain Real Property, 751 F. Supp. at 1063 (granting stay as to both indicted and non-indicted defendants, noting that the possibility that the non-indicted defendant would be forced to incriminate herself in the course of defending the civil action was "neither 'fanciful' nor 'imaginary'").

23. Tolkow, 109 F.R.D. at 119 n.2 (noting that lack of an indictment "does not make consideration of the stay motion any less appropriate").

24. Molinaro, 889 F.2d at 903 (quoting Dresser, 628 F.2d at 1376).

have been reluctant to grant stays in pre-indictment situations.[25] In fact, some courts have held that the fact that an indictment has not been issued is dispositive in favor of rejecting a defendant's stay request.[26] Likewise, courts appear more sympathetic to the interests of civil plaintiffs seeking discovery in situations where criminal proceedings have not yet been initiated, in part because the courts are reluctant to stay civil actions in the face of an open-ended criminal investigation.[27]

Taken together, the post-*Dresser* cases provide helpful guidance to defense counsel who are considering whether to seek a stay of a parallel civil proceeding. Short of establishing government misconduct in connection with the simultaneous prosecutions, the cases suggest that a stay is more likely to be granted if (1) an indictment has been returned against the defendant who is seeking the stay; (2) the civil and criminal cases involve substantially the same facts; (3) the parallel civil action is not an enforcement action brought by the government to protect important public interests that would be jeopardized by the requested stay; (4) the relief requested is carefully circumscribed, involving only postponing civil discovery to some parties for a limited time, rather than staying an entire civil action;[28] and (5) the two actions involve the same statutory or regulatory

---

25. *See, e.g.*, Trustees of Plumbers Pension Fund, 886 F. Supp. at 1139 ("stays will generally not be granted before an indictment is issued"). Indeed, even the *Tolkow* court noted that the fact that an indictment has not yet been returned "may be a factor counseling against a stay of civil proceedings." Tolkow, 109 F.R.D. at 120 n.2.

26. *See* United States v. Private Sanitation Indus. Ass'n, 811 F. Supp. 802, 805 (E.D.N.Y. 1992) (holding that "since [the defendant] has yet to be indicted by any grand jury, his motion to stay may be denied on that ground alone"); *see also In re* Par Pharmaceutical, 133 F.R.D. at 13 ("[C]ourts will stay a civil proceeding when the criminal investigation has ripened into an indictment . . . but will deny a stay of the civil proceeding where no indictment has issued.") (collecting cases, citations omitted). *But see* Walsh Secs. Inc. v. Crisco Prop. Mgmt. Ltd., 7 F. Supp. 2d 523, 527 (D.N.J. 1998) (stating that stay can be granted although an indictment has not yet been returned, and granting stay in such a case); $557,933.89, More or Less, in U.S. Funds, 1998 U.S. Dist. LEXIS 22252, at *12-*13 (granting stay despite lack of indictment); Wilson, 1998 U.S. Dist. LEXIS 5509, at *21 ("While the lack of any ongoing criminal proceedings is a factor for the Court to consider, it is not determinative.").

27. *See, e.g.*, Fidelity Bankers Life, 586 F. Supp. at 1125-26 ("Delay of these proceedings [for as much as three years] would be unfair to the other parties. . . [who] cannot control the timing of any criminal proceedings.").

28. Courts are generally hesitant to grant a "total stay" of a parallel civil proceeding, *see, e.g.*, Golden Quality Ice Cream Co., Inc. v. Deerfield Specialty Papers, Inc., 87 F.R.D. 53, 58-59 (E.D. Pa. 1980); *see also* Weil v. Markowitz, 829 F.2d 166, 175 n.17

scheme and will vindicate the same or substantially the same public interests.[29] Unless most of these factors are present, a court is not likely to stay a parallel civil action.[30] And even if they are present, substantial prejudice to the public interest or the private litigant against whom the stay would operate may result in a denial or lifting of the stay.[31]

In circumstances where a stay of the civil action is deemed inappropriate, the court may be open to entering a protective order to keep arguably incriminating testimony from being used against the defendant in a

---

(D.C. Cir. 1987) ("A total stay of civil discovery pending the outcome of related criminal matters is an extraordinary remedy appropriate for extraordinary circumstances."), *cert. denied*, 498 U.S. 821 (1990), and are more likely to approve a stay that is narrowly tailored to protecting the legitimate interests of the defendant, *see, e.g.*, Sidari v. Orleans County, 180 F.R.D. 226, 231 (W.D.N.Y. 1997) (staying civil discovery as to issues on which criminal and civil cases overlapped but refusing to stay entire civil matter); SEC v. Rehtorik, 755 F. Supp. 1018, 1019 (S.D. Fla. 1990) (granting stay only as to accounting procedure that arguably raised Fifth Amendment concerns).

29. *See In re* Par Pharmaceutical, 133 F.R.D. at 14 (denying stay because indictments had not been returned and distinguishing *Tolkow* as involving civil and criminal charges that "arise from the same remedial statute" and were brought for "vindication of the same or substantially the same public interest," making the grant of a pre-indictment stay "particularly appropriate"). Courts are also more inclined to grant a stay if the individual would face default or automatic summary judgment in the civil proceedings by invoking the Fifth Amendment. *See* United States v. Lot 5, 23 F.3d 359, 364 (11th Cir. 1994) (citation omitted), *cert. denied*, 513 U.S. 1076 (1995); Vardi Trading Co. v. Overseas Diamond Corp., No. 85 Civ. 2240 (CSH), 1987 WL 17662, at *2 (S.D.N.Y. Sept. 23, 1987).

30. *See also* Keating v. Office of Thrift Supervision, 45 F.3d 322, 325 (9th Cir. 1995) (identifying the following five factors in connection with consideration of a motion to stay: "(1) the interest of the plaintiffs in proceeding expeditiously with this civil litigation or any particular aspect of it, and the potential prejudice to plaintiffs of a delay; (2) the burden which any particular aspect of the proceedings may impose on defendants; (3) the convenience of the court in the management of its cases, and the efficient use of judicial resources; (4) the interests of persons not parties to the civil litigation; and (5) the interest of the public in the pending civil and criminal litigation"), *cert. denied*, 516 U.S. 827 (1995); Private Sanitation Indus. Ass'n, 811 F. Supp. at 805 (same); Golden Quality Ice Cream, 87 F.R.D. at 56 (same).

31. *See In re* Phillips, Beckwith & Hall, 896 F. Supp. 553, 559 (E.D. Va. 1995) (lifting stay after government established prejudice, holding that "[a] party is not entitled to delay resolution of a civil action, even to accommodate her Fifth Amendment interests, if her adversary's case will deteriorate as a result of the stay").

criminal proceeding.[32] Counsel should keep in mind, however, that protective orders may be overturned or modified; thus, there can be no guarantee that testimony provided pursuant to a protective order will not ultimately be disclosed to and used by the government in a subsequent criminal prosecution.[33]

Even if obtaining a stay is unlikely, criminal defense lawyers may be well advised to attempt to have a parallel civil action stayed. Seeking a stay or protective order from the court supervising the parallel civil litigation, even if the effort is unsuccessful, may preserve a defendant's right to appeal a subsequent criminal conviction based on incriminating statements made during discovery in the civil litigation.[34] Thus, losing the "battle" over the stay request in the civil proceeding may provide ammunition in the "war" against liability in the parallel criminal proceeding.

B. *Fifth Amendment Invocations by Company Employees*

If the civil proceeding is not stayed, will invocations by company employees of their Fifth Amendment self-incrimination rights[35] become the subject of "adverse inferences" in the civil proceeding? Failure to obtain a stay of a parallel civil proceeding often can result in a difficult dilemma for defendants. As noted above, statements made during civil discovery can be used as evidence against a defendant in a parallel criminal case. On the other hand, if a defendant refuses to testify in the civil case by asserting his Fifth Amendment privilege against self-in-

---

32. *See, e.g.*, Dresser, 628 F.2d at 1376; Digital Equip. Corp. v. Currie Enters., 142 F.R.D. 8, 12 (D. Mass. 1991); Waldbaum v. Worldvision Enters., Inc., 84 F.R.D. 95, 97-98 (S.D.N.Y. 1979).

33. *See* Andover Data Servs. v. Statistical Tabulating Corp., 876 F.2d 1080, 1083 (2d Cir. 1989); *see generally* Ajit V. Pai, Comment, *Should a Grand Jury Subpoena Override a District Court's Protective Order?*, 64 U. CHI. L. REV. 317 (1997) (discussing the varying approaches taken by the federal circuits in determining whether a grand jury subpoena overrides a civil court's protective order).

34. *See* Mid-America's Process Serv. v. Ellison, 767 F.2d 684, 686 (10th Cir. 1985) ("We believe that by seeking postponement or a protective order from the district court supervising the civil proceeding, on the basis of a reasonable fear of self-incrimination, [the defendants] have adequately preserved their right to object to a subsequent criminal conviction based on their own incriminating statements made during civil discovery.").

35. "No person . . . shall be compelled in any criminal case to be a witness against himself. . . ." U.S. CONST. amend. V.

crimination, courts permit the civil finder of fact to "infer by such refusal that the answers would have been adverse to the witness' interest."[36] The same result obtains even if the plaintiff in the civil action is the government.[37]

Although it is well established that liability in a civil case cannot be imposed based solely upon a defendant's assertion of the Fifth Amendment privilege,[38] the practical effect on a jury upon hearing a defendant's assertion of the privilege is quite substantial—and can be devastating.[39] The courts have not been particularly sympathetic to defendants facing

---

36. Brink's Inc. v. City of New York, 717 F.2d 700, 707 (2d Cir. 1983) (quoting district court's jury instruction); *see* Baxter v. Palmigiano, 425 U.S. 308 (1976); SEC v. Graystone Nash, Inc., 25 F.3d 187, 190 (3d Cir. 1994); *see also* National Acceptance Co. v. Bathalter, 705 F.2d 924, 929 (7th Cir. 1983) ("After *Baxter* there is no longer any doubt that at trial a civil defendant's silence may be used against him, even if that silence is an exercise of his constitutional privilege against self-incrimination.").

37. *See, e.g.*, SEC v. Tome, 638 F. Supp. 629, 632 (S.D.N.Y. 1986).

38. *See* Baxter, 425 U.S. at 317; Lefkowitz v. Cunningham, 431 U.S. 801, 809 n.5 (1977); *see also* LaSalle Bank Lake View v. Seguban, 54 F.3d 387, 390 (7th Cir. 1995) ("Silence is a relevant factor to be considered in light of the proffered evidence, but the direct inference of guilt from silence is forbidden."). This is also true when a civil defendant asserts the Fifth Amendment as the basis for refusing even to deny the allegations in a civil complaint, Bathalter, 705 F.2d at 932 ("It is our best judgment, in the light of *Baxter*, that even in a civil case a judgment imposing liability cannot rest solely upon a privileged refusal to admit or deny at the pleading stage."), as well as in the context of defending against a motion for summary adjudication, Seguban, 54 F.3d at 394; Mount Airy Ins. Co. v. Millstein, 928 F. Supp. 171, 174 (D. Conn. 1996) (stating that adverse inference would not be enough to establish that facts were undisputed and warrant summary judgment). *But see* United States v. Rylander, 460 U.S. 752, 761 (1983) (stating that an invocation of the Fifth Amendment "is not a substitute for relevant evidence"); United States v. 4003-4005 5th Ave., 55 F.3d 78, 83 (2d Cir. 1995) ("[A] claim of privilege will not prevent an adverse finding or even summary judgment if the litigant does not present sufficient evidence to satisfy the usual evidentiary burdens in the litigation."). Similarly, punitive damages may not be premised solely upon a defendant's invocation of the Fifth Amendment. *See* Koester v. American Republic Invs., Inc., 11 F.3d 818, 823-24 (8th Cir. 1993).

39. Indeed, even subsequent acquittal in a criminal case involving the same facts will not invalidate an adverse inference based upon the assertion of the Fifth Amendment privilege in a civil case. Pagel, Inc. v. SEC, 803 F.2d 942, 947 (8th Cir. 1986) (refusing to invalidate retroactively adverse inference in SEC administrative action after a defendant testified at a criminal trial and was acquitted).

this dilemma.[40] As one court noted, "[t]he choice may be unpleasant, but it is not illegal and must be faced."[41]

Corporations, of course, have no Fifth Amendment privilege against self-incrimination,[42] so one might reasonably assume that they would be spared the adverse inference dilemma. Ironically, however, this issue can be particularly troublesome for corporations. A leading case, *Brink's, Inc. v. City of New York*,[43] illustrates the problem. In *Brink's*, company employees asserted their Fifth Amendment privilege at trial and declined to testify; the jury found for the city of New York after being instructed by the trial judge that it was permissible to assume that had the employees testified, their testimony would have been unfavorable to their employer.[44]

This problem for corporations is compounded by the fact that it is not confined to assertions of the privilege by present employees. Consider the following example: A corporate employer, in an effort to respond appropriately to employee misconduct, dismisses an employee who, without authorization, had violated the law. Parallel civil and criminal proceedings subsequently arise out of the employee's misconduct. The former employee asserts her right against self-incrimination in discovery in the

---

40. *See, e.g.*, SEC v. Grossman, 121 F.R.D. 207, 210 (S.D.N.Y. 1987) (refusing to grant a stay of a civil action by defendants who feared that negative inferences would be drawn against them if they asserted their Fifth Amendment privilege in civil litigation).

41. SEC v. Musella, 1983 WL 1297, at *2; *see also* Keating v. Office of Thrift Supervision, 45 F.3d 322, 326 (9th Cir.) ("A defendant has no absolute right not to be forced to choose between testifying in a civil matter and asserting his Fifth Amendment privilege."), *cert. denied*, 516 U.S. 827 (1995).

42. Curcio v. United States, 354 U.S. 118, 122 (1957) ("It is settled that a corporation is not protected by the constitutional privilege against self-incrimination"); *In re* Two Grand Jury Subpoenae Duces Tecum, 769 F.2d 52, 57 (2d Cir. 1985) ("There simply is no situation in which the Fifth Amendment would prevent a corporation from producing corporate records, for the corporation itself has no Fifth Amendment privilege.").

43. 717 F.2d 700 (2d Cir. 1983).

44. *Id.* at 707; *see also, e.g.*, Chariot Plastics, Inc. v. United States, 28 F. Supp. 2d 874, 877 n.1 (S.D.N.Y. 1998) ("An officer's or director's invocation of the Fifth Amendment is admissible as an adverse inference against the corporation."). There must be a nexus, however, between the inference to be drawn against the corporation and the subject matter to which the employee's invocation of the Fifth Amendment relates. *See* Veranda Beach Club Ltd. Partnership v. Western Surety Co., 936 F.2d 1364, 1374 (1st Cir. 1991); Data General Corp. v. Grumman Sys. Support Corp., 825 F. Supp. 340, 352 (D. Mass. 1993), *aff'd and remanded on other grounds*, 36 F.3d 1147 (1st Cir. 1994).

civil litigation involving the corporate employer. In this situation, the trier of fact is permitted to draw an adverse inference against the corporate employer—even though the employee has been dismissed.[45] Not surprisingly, commentators have questioned the practice of permitting adverse inferences to be drawn in these circumstances, particularly "if the employee was fired or departed on unfriendly terms."[46] Nonetheless, courts have held that admitting a former employee's invocation of the Fifth Amendment as evidence is not per se reversible error.[47]

Counsel to the corporation may argue that assertions of privilege by non-parties should not be allowed as admissible evidence. As the dissent in *Brinks* observed, the silence that results from the invocation may (1) lack any real probity under Federal Rule of Evidence 403 because no reliable "answer" may be inferred from it (that is, the unanswered question becomes the evidence)[48] and (2) leave the corporate defendant with no effective ability to cross-examine the non-party asserting the privilege.[49] Courts, however, have been less than fully receptive to these arguments.[50] Rather, courts ultimately look to whether the adverse influence drawn from the non-party's invocation "is trustworthy under all of the circumstances and will advance the search for the truth."[51]

---

45. *See* Rad Servs. Inc. v. Aetna Cas. & Sur. Co., 808 F.2d 271 (3d Cir. 1986); *see also* Federal Deposit Ins. Corp. v. Fidelity & Deposit Co., 45 F.3d 969, 978 (5th Cir. 1995) (permitting adverse inference against an employment fidelity bond surety from invocations by witnesses who had relationships with an allegedly fraudulent employee of the insured).

46. *See* Rad Servs., 808 F.2d at 275 (quoting *Adverse Inferences Based on Non-Party Invocations: The Real Magic Trick in Fifth Amendment Civil Cases*, 60 Notre Dame L. Rev. 370, 386 (1985)); *see also* Michael M. Baylson, *The Fifth Amendment in Civil Antitrust Litigation: Overview of Substantive Law*, 50 Antitrust L. J. 837, 844 (1982) ("An adverse inference is clearly improper against a defendant which has no 'control' over a witness who invokes the privilege or other relationship with the witness sufficient to warrant association of the witness with the party.").

47. Rad Servs., 808 F.2d at 277; *cf.* Cerro Gordo Charity v. Fireman's Fund Am. Life Ins. Co., 819 F.2d 1471, 1481 (8th Cir. 1987) ("we find that the fact that [defendant] may not be presently involved with [the trust] in an official capacity presents no bar to requiring him assert [*sic*] the privilege before the jury").

48. Brink's, 717 F.2d at 715 (Winter, J., dissenting).

49. *Id.* at 716.

50. *See, e.g.*, Cerro Gordo Charity, 819 F.2d at 1482.

51. LiButti v. United States, 107 F.3d 110, 123-24 (2d Cir. 1997) (stating that non-exclusive factors to be considered are (1) the nature of the relevant relationships, (2) the

C. *Double-Jeopardy Clause Protection*

Does the Double Jeopardy Clause[52] protect against the imposition of both criminal and civil penalties for the same alleged misconduct? Can the practitioner successfully argue that prior criminal sanctions against a defendant preclude the government from imposing civil penalties on that defendant for the same transaction, and vice versa? In light of the Supreme Court's decision in *Hudson v. United States*,[53] the answer in all but the rarest of contexts would appear to be a resounding "no."

In its decision in *United States v. Halper*,[54] the Supreme Court had provided defense counsel with solid, but narrow, support for arguing that contemporaneous or successive governmental civil and criminal actions that both resulted in sanctions offended the Double Jeopardy Clause of the Constitution. In *Halper*, the Court ruled that the federal government could not collect a civil penalty in an action for Medicare fraud after having obtained a criminal conviction of the defendant (and imprisonment and fine) based on the same subject matter. The Court noted the enormous disparity between the government's actual loss and the civil fines assessed against the defendant, and concluded that "[t]he Government may not criminally prosecute a defendant, impose a criminal penalty upon him, and then bring a separate civil action based on the same conduct and receive a judgment that is not rationally related to the goal of making the Government whole."[55] As a practical matter, the Court's holding provided defense counsel with the ability—albeit highly circumscribed[56]—to argue that there were limits to the government's right to impose civil penalties that could be characterized as "punishment" against a defendant already sanctioned under the criminal law.[57]

---

degree of control of the party over the non-party witness, (3) the compatibility of their interests in the litigation's outcome, and (4) the role of the non-party witness in the litigation).

52. "No person shall . . . be subject for the same offense to be twice put in jeopardy of life or limb." U.S. CONST. amend. V.

53. Hudson v. United States, 522 U.S. 93 (1997).

54. United States v. Halper, 490 U.S. 435 (1989).

55. Halper, 490 U.S. at 451.

56. *See id.* at 449 ("What we announce now is a rule for the rare case . . . where a fixed-penalty provision subjects a prolific but small-gauge offender to a sanction overwhelmingly disproportionate to the damages he has caused.")

57. *See also id.* at 448-49 ("We therefore hold that under the Double Jeopardy Clause a defendant who already has been punished in a criminal prosecution may not

In *Hudson*, the Supreme Court disavowed the analysis in its *Halper* decision and, according to Justice Scalia, "put the Halper genie back in the bottle."[58] In 1989, the Office of the Comptroller of the Currency (OCC) had brought administrative charges against the defendants in *Hudson* for alleged violations of the federal banking laws. In October of that year, the defendants entered into a consent order with the OCC that resolved the administrative charges in exchange for the defendants' agreement to payment of fines and debarment from the banking industry.[59] In August 1992, nearly three years later, the defendants were indicted on charges of conspiracy, misapplication of bank funds, and making false bank entries based on the same transactions that formed the basis for the 1989 consent order. The defendants challenged their indictment, arguing that it violated their right not to be placed in jeopardy twice for the same offense.[60]

The Supreme Court held that the Double Jeopardy Clause did not prohibit the defendants' criminal prosecution because the administrative proceedings were civil, not criminal.[61] In so doing, the Court refocused the double-jeopardy analysis by stating that the Double Jeopardy Clause "does not prohibit the imposition of any additional sanction that could, 'in common parlance,' be described as punishment"; rather, only multiple *criminal* punishments for the same offense are constitutionally proscribed.[62] In this regard, the Court noted that its analysis in *Halper* had improperly "bypassed the threshold question" of whether a successive punishment was a *criminal* punishment and proceeded directly to determining whether the civil sanction "was so grossly disproportionate to the harm caused as to constitute 'punishment.'"[63]

The *Hudson* Court provided fairly clear guidance to lower courts faced with determining whether civil penalties may be said to be "criminal punishments" that implicate double-jeopardy concerns. First, "[w]hether a particular punishment is criminal or civil is, at least initially, a matter of statutory construction. . . . A court must first ask whether the legislature,

---

be subjected to an additional civil sanction to the extent that the second sanction may not fairly be characterized as remedial, but only as a deterrent or retribution.")

58. *See* Hudson, 522 U.S. at 106 (Scalia, J., concurring).
59. Hudson, 522 U.S. at 97.
60. *Id.* at 97-98.
61. *Id.* at 96.
62. *Id.* at 98-99.
63. *Id.* at 101.

'in establishing the penalizing mechanism, indicated either expressly or impliedly a preference for one label or the other.'"[64] Second, even where the legislature indicates its intention that a penalty be civil, courts are to inquire further "whether the statutory scheme [is] so punitive either in purpose or effect. . . as to transform what was clearly intended as a civil remedy into a criminal penalty."[65] The Court stated that the following factors, set forth in its decision in *Kennedy v. Mendoza-Martinez*,[66] "provide useful guideposts" in performing this latter analysis:

> (1) whether the sanction involves an affirmative disability or restraint; (2) whether it has historically been regarded as a punishment; (3) whether it comes into play only on a finding of scienter; (4) whether its operation will promote the traditional aims of punishment-retribution and deterrence; (5) whether the behavior to which it applies is already a crime; (6) whether an alternative purpose to which it may rationally be connected is assignable for it; and (7) whether it appears excessive in relation to the alternative purpose assigned.[67]

The Court, however, placed two significant restrictions on use of the *Kennedy* factors to override legislative intent; the Court stated that "'these factors must be considered in relation to the *statute on its face*'. . . and '*only the clearest proof*' will suffice to override legislative intent and transform what has been denominated a civil remedy into a criminal penalty."[68]

Applying these principles to the case before it, the Court held that criminal prosecution of the defendants would not violate the Double Jeopardy Clause.[69] The Court found it "evident" that Congress intended the

---

64. *Id.* at 98-99 (citations omitted).

65. *Id.* at 99 (citations omitted).

66. 372 U.S. 144, 168-69 (1963).

67. Hudson, 522 U.S. at 99-100.

68. *Id.* at 100 (emphasis added, citations omitted). The Court criticized the *Halper* decision for addressing the nature and effect of the actual sanctions imposed rather than limiting the inquiry to the statute on its face. *Id.* at 101. In a concurrence joined by Justice Ginsberg, Justice Breyer opined that inquiring beyond the face of the statute to determine the effect of the sanctions on the individual defendant might be appropriate in some circumstances, and disagreed with the notion that "only the clearest proof" could transform a civil remedy into criminal punishment. *Id.* at 115-17 (Breyer, J., concurring).

69. Hudson, 522 U.S. at 103.

OCC monetary and debarment sanctions to be civil in nature.[70] As for the *Kennedy* factors, the Court found "little evidence, much less the clearest proof that we require, suggesting that either OCC money penalties or debarment sanctions are 'so punitive in form and effect as to render them criminal despite Congress' intent to the contrary.'"[71] In particular, the Court stated that neither form of penalty had been viewed historically as punishment; that the penalties did not involve imprisonment, so as to impose on the defendants an "affirmative disability or restraint"; that neither sanction required a finding of scienter; that the fact that the conduct for which the OCC sanctions were imposed may also be criminal was insufficient to render the sanctions criminally punitive; and that the mere fact that the sanctions could serve deterrence goals did not alter their civil nature.[72] In short, the Double Jeopardy Clause presented no obstacle to trying the defendants criminally.[73]

By criticizing *Halper* as a "deviation from longstanding double jeopardy principles [that] was ill-considered," and as having articulated a test that "proved unworkable,"[74] the *Hudson* decision effectively returned the law to its pre-*Halper* state.[75] Indeed, the lower courts have read *Hudson* to mean precisely what it says: Absent the "clearest proof" of extreme punitiveness under the *Kennedy* factors, a remedial scheme designated as "civil" by the legislature will not implicate the Double Jeopardy Clause. Accordingly, SEC civil fines and disgorgements have been held not to trigger double-jeopardy rights,[76] and so have IRS civil penalties and tax additions,[77] broker application denials and debarment orders of the CFTC,[78]

---

70. *Id.*

71. *Id.* at 104.

72. *Id.* at 104-05.

73. *Id.* at 105. Justice Stevens concurred in the result but disagreed with the Court's abandonment of *Halper. Id.* at 106-07 (Stevens, J., concurring).

74. Hudson, 522 U.S. at 101-02.

75. *Cf. id.* at 106 (Scalia, J., concurring) (stating that the Court's opinion "return[s] the law to its state immediately prior to *Halper"*).

76. United States v. Perry, 152 F.3d 900, 903-04 (8th Cir. 1998), *cert. denied*, 525 U.S. 1168 (1999); *see also* SEC v. Palmisano, 135 F.3d 860, 864-86 (2d Cir.) (noting that the fact that scienter is required to prove a violation of the securities laws is not dispositive under *Hudson*), *cert. denied*, 525 U.S. 1023 (1998).

77. Louis v. Commissioner, 170 F.3d 1232, 1234-35 (9th Cir. 1999) (additions to tax for fraud), *cert. denied*, 528 U.S. 1115 (2000); Bickham Lincoln-Mercury, Inc. v. United States, 168 F.3d 790, 794-95 (5th Cir. 1999) (civil penalties).

78. Vercillo v. Commodity Futures Trading Comm'n, 147 F.3d 548, 558 (7th Cir. 1998) (citing Ryan v. Commodity Futures Trading Comm'n, 145 F.3d 910, 913-14

"instance-by-instance" administrative fines under OSHA,[79] civil forfeiture proceedings following convictions for false statements to customs officials,[80] civil penalties for violations of the Food Stamp Act,[81] and FDIC civil proceedings requesting punitive damages.[82]

While it may be tempting to view *Hudson* as a seismic shift in the legal landscape surrounding contemporaneous or successive governmental civil and criminal prosecutions, this would overstate the case for the efficacy of *Halper* as a defense tool. Although the *Hudson* court granted certiorari "because of concerns about the wide variety of novel double jeopardy claims spawned in the wake of *Halper*,"[83] as a practical matter, *Halper* had provided relatively little assistance to the practitioner seeking to bar a criminal prosecution based on an earlier civil sanction (or vice versa).[84] In addition, it should be noted that more traditional modes of constitutional attack on the propriety of civil penalties—due process, equal protection, and the Eighth Amendment's proscription against excessive civil fines and forfeitures—survive *Hudson* intact.[85]

D. *Collateral Estoppel*

To what extent does a final judgment in one action preclude a party from relitigating in another action issues that have been decided against her as part of the judgment? Under the doctrine of collateral estoppel, or issue preclusion, "a final judgment on the merits in a prior suit precludes subsequent relitigation of issues actually litigated and determined in the prior suit, regardless of whether the subsequent suit is based on the same cause of action."[86] In litigating or settling a criminal or civil action in the

---

(7th Cir. 1998); Cox v. Commodity Futures Trading Comm'n, 138 F.3d 268, 274 (7th Cir. 1998); LaCrosse v. Commodity Futures Trading Comm'n, 137 F.3d 925, 932 (7th Cir. 1998); Grossfeld v. Commodity Futures Trading Comm'n, 137 F.3d 1300, 1302-03 (11th Cir. 1998).

79. S.A. Healy Co. v. Occupational Safety & Health Review Comm'n, 138 F.3d 686, 687-88 (7th Cir. 1998).

80. United States v. $273,969.04 U.S. Currency, 164 F.3d 462, 465 (9th Cir. 1999).

81. Traficanti v. United States, 227 F.3d 170, 177 (4th Cir. 2000).

82. United States v. Ely, 142 F.3d 1113, 1122 (9th Cir. 1997).

83. Hudson, 522 U.S. at 98 & n.4 (collecting cases).

84. *Id.* at 108-09 (Stevens, J., concurring).

85. *See* Hudson, 522 U.S. at 102-03.

86. I.A.M. Nat'l Pension Fund v. Industrial Gear Mfg. Co., 723 F.2d 944, 947 (D.C. Cir. 1983); *see also* Parklane Hosiery Co. v. Shore, 439 U.S. 322, 327 n.5 (1979) ("Under

face of actual or potential parallel proceedings, counsel must be cognizant of the potential adverse consequences that can arise from the application of collateral estoppel in a subsequent action.[87]

For example, a criminal judgment against a defendant will operate as an estoppel in any subsequent civil and administrative proceedings as to the specific issues resolved as part of the criminal prosecution.[88] Thus, the government has long been able to use a criminal conviction to collaterally estop defendants from relitigating their guilt, and thus their liability, in subsequent civil proceedings.[89] In addition, a criminal conviction can adversely impact the disposition of private lawsuits involving the same subject matter as the criminal conviction. This is because issue preclusion does not require "mutuality of parties"—that is, it is not necessary that the

---

the doctrine of collateral estoppel, . . . the judgment in the prior suit precludes relitigation of issues actually litigated and necessary to the outcome of the first action.").

87. Under the broader doctrine of res judicata, or "claim preclusion," "a final judgment on the merits bars further claims by parties or their privies based on the same cause of action." Montana v. United States, 440 U.S. 147, 153 (1979). Claim preclusion has little applicability in the context of parallel proceedings involving governmental civil or criminal prosecutions. First, courts have typically rejected the argument that claim preclusion bars the government from bringing, in a subsequent civil proceeding, claims that arguably could have been pursued in a prior criminal prosecution. *See, e.g.,* United States v. Barnette, 10 F.3d 1553, 1561 (11th Cir.), *cert. denied,* 513 U.S. 816 (1994); United States v. Moffitt, Zwerling & Kemler, P.C., 875 F. Supp. 1190, 1196 (E.D.Va. 1995), *rev'd in part on other grounds,* 83 F.3d 660 (4th Cir. 1996), *cert. denied,* 519 U.S. 1101 (1997); *see also* 47 AM. JUR. 2D *Judgments* § 732 (1999) ("a judgment in a criminal proceeding has no *res judicata* effect"). Second, since res judicata only bars "parties and their privies" from relitigating claims that could have been pursued, the government typically is not barred from pursuing causes of action against a corporation that were previously pursued by a private party (and vice versa). *See* Montana, 440 U.S. at 153.

88. *See, e.g.,* Gelb v. Royal Globe Ins. Co., 798 F.2d 38, 43 (2d Cir. 1986), *cert. denied,* 480 U.S. 948 (1987) & 502 U.S. 1005 (1991); *see also* United States v. Uzzell, 648 F. Supp. 1362, 1363-65 (D.D.C. 1986) (criminal conviction of conspiracy after trial operates as estoppel on all underlying facts). A criminal conviction can operate as an estoppel even if the conviction is on appeal. *See* United States v. International Bhd. of Teamsters, 905 F.2d 610, 621 (2d Cir. 1990).

89. *See* Emich Motors Corp. v. General Motors Corp., 340 U.S. 558, 568 (1951) ("It is well established that a prior criminal conviction may work an estoppel in favor of the Government in a subsequent civil proceeding."); United States v. Killough, 848 F.2d 1523, 1528 (11th Cir. 1988).

party attempting to estop the opponent from raising or contesting an issue (previously decided against the opponent) be a party to the prior proceeding.[90] A criminal conviction of the corporation, therefore, may be used offensively in subsequent civil actions by strangers to the original prosecution.[91]

Under federal law, a guilty plea in a criminal action is generally accorded the same preclusive effect in a subsequent civil action as a criminal conviction.[92] A party may, however, be able to escape the collateral effect of a guilty plea by pleading *nolo contendere* instead.[93] By its terms, a plea of *nolo contendere* applies only to the case in which it is entered and cannot be used in any subsequent civil lawsuit based on the same conduct.[94] Of course, whether a *nolo contendere* plea will be available to the corporation will lie within the discretion of the trial judge, and the

---

90. *See* Parklane Hosiery, 439 U.S. 322; McLaughlin v. Bradlee, 803 F.2d 1197, 1201 (D.C. Cir. 1986). Notably, however, nonmutual collateral estoppel may not be utilized to preclude the federal government from litigating an issue on which it has previously been unsuccessful. *See* United States v. Mendoza, 464 U.S. 154 (1984); *see also* Hercules Carriers, Inc. v. Florida, 768 F.2d 1558, 1579 (11th Cir. 1985) (applying *Mendoza's* prohibition against nonmutual collateral estoppel to state governments).

91. Gelb, 798 F.2d at 43-44; Wolfson v. Baker, 623 F.2d 1074, 1080 (5th Cir. 1980), *cert. denied*, 450 U.S. 966 (1981).

92. United States v. Podell, 572 F.2d 31, 35 (2d Cir. 1978) ("It is well-settled that a criminal conviction, whether by jury verdict or guilty plea, constitutes estoppel in favor of the United States in a subsequent civil proceeding.") (citations omitted); *see also* McCarthy v. United States, 394 U.S. 459, 466 (1969) ("a guilty plea is an admission of all the elements of a formal criminal charge"); United States v. 415 E. Mitchell Ave., 149 F.3d 472, 476 (6th Cir. 1998) (affirming application of collateral estoppel in civil forfeiture proceeding based on defendant's guilty plea). *But see* 47 Am. Jur. 2d *Judgments* § 734 (1999) (collecting cases holding that a guilty plea may not serve as the basis for collateral estoppel in a subsequent civil action).

93. *See* Fed. R. Crim. P. 11(b) & Advisory Comm. Note (1974 amends.) ("Unlike a plea of guilty, . . . [a nolo contendere plea] cannot be used against a defendant . . . in a subsequent criminal or civil case."); Doherty v. American Motors Corp., 728 F.2d 334, 337 (6th Cir. 1984).

94. Fed. R. Crim. P. 11(b) & Advisory Comm. Note (1974 amends.); Ranke v. United States, 873 F.2d 1033, 1037 n.7 (7th Cir. 1989). *But see* United States v. Fredrickson, 601 F.2d 1358, 1365 n.10 (8th Cir.) (finding nolo contendere plea admissible as "other crimes" evidence under Federal Rule of Evidence 404), *cert. denied*, 444 U.S. 934 (1979).

prosecutor may well argue that such a plea deprives the public of its interest in a definitive resolution of the criminal matter.[95]

Can court findings during the sentencing phase of a criminal matter have a preclusive effect in parallel civil proceedings? According to a 1999 decision of the Second Circuit, the answer in most cases would appear to be no. In *SEC v. Monarch Funding Corp.*,[96] the SEC sought to collaterally estop a defendant in a civil case from litigating its liability for violations of the federal securities laws, based on sentencing findings in a criminal matter in which the defendant was found liable for obstruction of justice.[97] The district court applied collateral estoppel and granted the SEC a permanent injunction against future violations.[98]

The Second Circuit reversed. It declined to "adopt a per se rule against extending the doctrine of offensive collateral estoppel to sentencing findings,"[99] but held that "precluding relitigation on the basis of such findings should be presumed improper."[100] In particular, the court found that applying estoppel in the case before it would be neither fair nor efficient. Unlike other contexts, where determinations that can be inferred from necessary findings can form the basis of an estoppel, fairness required that the sentencing finding sought to be used be "legally necessary to the final sentence."[101] As to the efficiency of giving preclusive effect to sentencing findings, the court noted that the district court's examination of the collateral estoppel issue "required considerable effort—in all probability more effort than would have been required for a summary adjudication . . . or even for a trial."[102] The court concluded with the following guidance:

> [I]n determining whether to apply collateral estoppel to sentencing findings in the future, district courts should start by making a threshold assessment of whether it will be efficient to do so. Given the potential unfairness associated with extending collateral es-

---

95. FED. R. CRIM. P. 11(b) ("Such a plea shall be accepted by the court only after due consideration of the views of the parties and the interest of the public in the effective administration of justice.") & Advisory Comm. Note (1974 amends.).

96. 192 F.3d 295 (2d Cir. 1999).

97. *Id.* at 298.

98. *Id.*

99. *Id.* at 303.

100. *Id.* at 306.

101. *Id.* at 307.

102. *Id.* at 310.

toppel to sentencing findings generally, if the court reasonably determines that the doctrine will not promote efficiency, it should feel free to deny preclusion for that reason alone.[103]

Civil judgments and findings can also produce collateral estoppel consequences in simultaneous or subsequent civil and administrative proceedings in which the corporation is involved. Of course, in certain instances, the corporation may be able to argue successfully that its victory in a prior civil lawsuit is entitled to preclusive effect in a subsequent civil case. These instances are effectively limited, however, to actions where the party against whom the estoppel is sought was also a party (or privy to a party) in the prior proceeding, for the simple and obvious reason that nonparties to the prior action cannot be deprived of a "full and fair opportunity to litigate" the issues previously decided in the corporation's favor.[104] In addition, if the corporation litigates an issue in a civil case and loses, the principle of collateral estoppel will permit foreigners to the case to utilize the determination offensively in a separate action involving the corporation.[105]

Unlike collateral use of criminal convictions in subsequent civil proceedings, however, a judgment rendered against a corporation in a civil or administrative proceeding will not ordinarily produce collateral estoppel effects in an ongoing or subsequent criminal prosecution brought against the company. This is chiefly because of the different levels of proof required in these proceedings—an ultimate finding "by a preponderance of the evidence" that certain acts have occurred does not conclusively establish that the conduct could have been proven "beyond a reasonable doubt" in a criminal case.[106] This rule, however, has as its corollary the proposi-

---

103. *Id.; see also* New York v. Julius Nasso Concrete Corp., 202 F.3d 82, 87 (2d Cir. 2000) (affirming district court's refusal to estop antitrust defendants on issue of causation based on sentencing findings in prior RICO trial).

104. *See* Resolution Trust Corp. v. Keating, 186 F.3d 1110, 1114 (9th Cir. 1999) (stating that the following are necessary elements of nonmutual offensive collateral estoppel against a party: (1) the party was afforded a full and fair opportunity to litigate the issue in the prior action; (2) the issue was actually litigated and necessary to support the judgment; (3) the issue was decided against the party in a final judgment; and (4) the party was a party, or a privy to a party, in the prior proceeding).

105. *See* Parklane Hosiery, 439 U.S. at 331-32.

106. *See* United States v. Meza-Soria, 935 F.2d 166, 169 (9th Cir. 1991); United States v. General Dynamics Corp., 828 F.2d 1356, 1361 n.5 (9th Cir. 1987); United States v. Beery, 678 F.2d 856, 868 n.10 (10th Cir. 1982); United States v. Konovsky, 202 F.2d 721, 726-27 (7th Cir. 1953).

tion that a defendant cannot use a criminal acquittal as a bar to later civil proceedings initiated by the government.[107]

Application of the doctrine of collateral estoppel to preclude a defendant from relitigating an issue requires courts to determine exactly what was decided in the prior action.[108] Accordingly, courts deciding the collateral estoppel effects of a prior judgment will examine the totality of the record in the prior proceeding, including pleadings, evidence submitted, jury instructions, and any court opinions, to determine whether an issue on which preclusion is sought was "directly put in issue and directly determined" in the prior suit.[109] This fact should be kept in mind by counsel for the corporation facing parallel proceedings in which a judgment or settlement in one action has the potential for collateral consequences in another. It may be possible to structure the terms of any plea agreement or consent order in a manner that corrals the issues precluded, or to clarify in the record the basis (preferably limited) for any unfavorable civil judgment or criminal conviction.

E. *Disciplining Employees for Misconduct*

Should a company discipline employees for their misconduct, or will this action be seen as proof of wrongdoing? In the course of an internal investigation or subsequent proceedings that follow, it may become evident that certain employees engaged in conduct violating company policy, or state or federal law. Upon making this discovery, management and counsel may wish to consider the issue of discipline and the related question of sanctions.

These issues should not be lightly undertaken, for any discipline may be subsequently considered as an admission of misconduct, and will at a minimum provide a road map for the prosecutor in any future criminal proceeding against the company. A somewhat more subtle concern should be that sanctions of differing severity can provide useful and otherwise unavailable insights into the company's own analysis of the misconduct.

One cannot intelligently assess the issue of sanctions without a full appreciation of (1) the advantages, if any, that will surface in the ongoing

---

107. *See* Helvering v. Mitchell, 303 U.S. 391, 397 (1938).

108. *See* Brown v. Felsen, 442 U.S. 127, 139 n.10 (1979) ("collateral estoppel treats as final only those questions actually and necessarily decided in a prior suit").

109. *See* Uzzell, 648 F. Supp. at 1363-64 (citing Emich Motors Corp., 340 U.S. at 569).

civil and criminal actions, (2) the risks associated with taking such a step, and (3) whatever salutary benefits the company may gain as a corporate citizen. Some prosecutors may view employee discipline as truly commendable—an act of corporate citizenship—while others may find it distasteful, if not reprehensible—an unconscionable attempt to shift blame to loyal employees. In particular, swift action to terminate, suspend or transfer an employee responsible for ongoing misconduct can stop the misconduct and thereby prevent further harm to the company.

Thus, the issue of whether to impose sanctions is among the more difficult concerns facing the company in the aftermath of an internal investigation. Without doubt, sanctions are often unnecessary in achieving any legitimate corporate goal and will almost certainly provide government counsel with direct or inferential information it would not otherwise have. Yet, there are times when sanctions are highly appropriate and can be useful in protecting the company.[110]

For the company that has carefully considered all the implications and chooses to embark upon disciplining select employees, several suggestions are in order. To provide maximum possible protection for this decision and action, corporate counsel should undertake the task of notifying the employee of the punishment and explaining the ramifications of the employee's conduct underlying the sanctions. Management should resist the temptation to assign this unpleasant task of discipline to the personnel department. A delegation of this nature virtually ensures that no claim of confidentiality will be successful. While counsel may consider explaining, in writing, the basis for its decision, any such memorialization should be written as though you would expect it to be published on the front page of *The New York Times*.

In addition to the criminal law ramifications of disciplining employees, counsel representing corporations in parallel proceedings should consider the risk that these actions can prompt civil litigation. For example, disclosure of employee misconduct resulting in serious damages or lost economic opportunities for the corporation may trigger shareholder de-

---

110. The SEC has encouraged companies to take "immediate and decisive corrective action" to head off ongoing misconduct. *See In re* Cooper Cos., Exchange Act Release No. 35,082, 58 SEC Docket 591, 596 (Dec. 12, 1994) (investigation report) (criticizing the directors for failing to act swiftly to protect the shareholders in the face of serious indications of management fraud by high-ranking corporate officers).

rivative suits seeking to recover those losses for the corporation.[111] The risk of activating shareholder derivative actions is highest when public companies that are subject to SEC reporting requirements impose disciplinary sanctions on senior managers. In some instances, such as disciplinary action resulting in the resignation of a director, SEC rules may require disclosure of the action taken.[112]

Even if public disclosure of disciplinary action is not required by law, it may be a practical necessity in some cases. Highly regulated enterprises such as banks, insurance companies, and securities firms may be well-advised to take appropriate disciplinary action promptly after discovery and confirmation of employee misconduct, and to disclose the action taken.[113] This action can benefit the corporate entity by defusing regulatory hostility and restoring public confidence that management is prepared to take appropriate corrective action.[114]

In short, employee discipline issues must be considered carefully in each case, with due regard to the collateral consequences of disciplinary

---

111. *See* FED. R. CIV. P. 23.1. For an in-depth treatment of shareholder derivative litigation, *see* RALPH C. FERRARA ET AL., SHAREHOLDER DERIVATIVE LITIGATION (1995).

112. *See* SEC Form 8-K, Item 6 ("Resignations of Registrant's Directors"); *see also* SEC Rule 12b-20 ("Additional Information"), 17 C.F.R. § 240.12b-20.

113. Counsel should be aware that such disclosure may subject the company to a defamation lawsuit by the disciplined employee. *See, e.g.*, Pearce v. E.F. Hutton Group, Inc., 664 F. Supp. 1490 (D.D.C. 1987) (a former employee who was implicated in wrongdoing in an internal investigation report prepared by outside investigatory counsel sued both outside counsel and his former employer for libel). The employee's suit against outside investigative counsel in *Pearce* was ultimately unsuccessful at trial. *See* Pearce v. E.F. Hutton Group, Inc., Civ. No. 87-0008, 1989 WL 4969, at *1 (D.D.C. Jan. 10, 1989).

114. In contrast, the regulatory and reputational effects of waiting to respond to information suggesting misconduct can be devastating. *See, e.g.*, *In re* John H. Gutfreund et al. [1992 Transfer Binder], FED. SEC. L. REP. (CCH) ¶ 85,067 (Dec. 3, 1992) (three executives and general counsel of Salomon Brothers who delayed for several months in investigating or disciplining head of Government Trading Desk for submission of $3.15 billion false bid in treasury auction resigned upon ultimate disclosure of the problem to the press; the three executives were barred or suspended from the securities industry, and the general counsel informed the SEC of his intent not to work in the industry in the future); *cf. also* Micheline Maynard, *Kidder Conducts Major Inquiry in Trading Scandal*, USA TODAY, Apr. 28, 1994, at 2B (reporting that one Kidder Peabody official was fired and six others were suspended pending the outcome of an internal investigation, and quoting an executive as saying that "[t]here's an enormous desire for scalps in the press").

actions. Counsel should weigh both the impact of employee discipline on other pending or threatened legal proceedings and the effect of this action on the perceptions of the company held by prosecutors, regulators, and, for public companies, investors and securities analysts.

Most important, counsel should remember that a lawyer's involvement in the disciplinary process does not necessarily "place a cloak of secrecy around all the incidents of such transaction."[115] The mere fact that it was counsel who recommended the sanctions or who notified the employee of them does not automatically render the event privileged. As is often the case, all facts and circumstances surrounding the sanctions and notification are relevant to determining whether the government or third parties are permitted to obtain discovery of the employee sanctions. Of course, where the company is cooperating with the government, voluntary disclosure follows as a matter of course, but disclosure may be required even in situations where the company is *not* in a cooperative posture.

A decision to discipline an employee premised upon the advice of counsel provides a more legitimate basis for corporate officials to refuse to answer questions regarding the process, the deliberations, and the results. A company official may limit any response to an inquiry by answering that the decision to impose the sanction was arrived at through legal advice.[116]

A final, troublesome issue concerns the employee who voluntarily has disclosed to an outside authority the existence of improper or illegal conduct. A special problem exists with disciplining the employee because of state and federal "whistle-blower" statutes, such as those contained in the False Claims Act[117] and in the Victim and Witness Protection Act of 1982.[118] These statutes and regulations are intended to protect individuals

---

115. United States v. Freeman, 619 F.2d 1112, 1119-20 (5th Cir. 1980) (quoting *In re* Fischel, 557 F.2d 209, 212 (9th Cir. 1977)), *cert. denied*, 450 U.S. 910 (1981); *accord In re* Grand Jury Subpoenas, 803 F.2d 493, 496 (9th Cir. 1986), *corrected by* 817 F.2d 64 (9th Cir. 1987).

116. *See* F.C. Cycles Int'l, Inc. v. Fila Sports, S.p.A, 184 F.R.D. 64, 71 (D. Md. 1998); *In re* Grand Jury Subpoena Duces Tecum, 731 F.2d 1032, 1036-38 (2d Cir. 1984); SCM Corp. v. Xerox Corp., 70 F.R.D. 508, 516-17 (D. Conn.), *appeal dismissed*, 534 F.2d 1031 (2d Cir. 1976).

117. *See* 31 U.S.C. § 3729.

118. *See* 18 U.S.C. § 1512 (codification of Victim and Witness Protection Act of 1982).

who alert the government to potential wrongdoing, and any discipline may be considered retaliation, which can be penalized.

F. *Government Lawyers'* Ex Parte *Interviews of Employees*

Government investigators may seek to gain relevant information about the corporation through *ex parte* contacts with present or former corporate employees. Company counsel should be aware of this possibility and, to the extent possible, formulate official policies and procedures to minimize and control these contacts. In so doing, counsel will find support both in case law and in applicable disciplinary rules.

For example, Disciplinary Rule 7-104(A)(1) of the American Bar Association (DR 7-104(A)(1)) and Rule 4.2 of the ABA Model Rules of Professional Conduct (Model Rule 4.2) limit the circumstances when a lawyer ethically can communicate with parties represented by another lawyer. Both "no contact" rules expressly prohibit communications concerning the subject of the representation. Specifically, DR 7-104(A)(1) forbids a lawyer, or one acting at the lawyer's behest, from communicating with a party who the lawyer knows is represented by another lawyer. Similarly, Model Rule 4.2 prohibits lawyer communications with persons known to be represented by counsel in the matter. Both DR 7-104(A)(1) and Model Rule 4.2 permit communications where counsel representing the opposing party permits or where "authorized by law," and Model Rule 4.2 (as amended in February 2002) also permits comunications that are authorized by "a court order."

Although the ethical proscriptions contained in DR 7-104(A)(1) and Model Rule 4.2 have been held to apply to government lawyers engaged in criminal prosecutions,[119] the extent to which prosecutors are subject to these rules—and their "as adopted" permutations and interpretations in various jurisdictions—have been a source of considerable debate over the past 12 years between the Justice Department and the defense bar.

---

119. *See* United States v. Ryans, 903 F.2d 731, 735 (10th Cir.), *cert. denied*, 498 U.S. 855 (1990) ("It is now well settled that DR 7-104(A)(1) applies to criminal prosecutions as well as to civil litigation.") (collecting cases, quoting United States v. Jamil, 707 F.2d 638, 645 (2d Cir. 1983): "DR 7-104(A)(1) may be found to apply in criminal cases . . . to government attorneys [and] to non-attorney government law enforcement officers when they act as the alter ego of government prosecutors.").

The opening salvo in this debate came in the form of a 1989 Justice Department internal memorandum, dubbed the "Thornburgh Memorandum." In the Memorandum, the Department of Justice (DOJ) took the position that *ex parte* interviews are not improper when conducted during the investigatory phase of a criminal or civil case.[120]

The Thornburgh Memorandum asserted that defense lawyers have broadly interpreted the anti-contact ethical rules "in an effort to prohibit communications by law enforcement personnel with the target of a criminal investigation, whether or not a constitutional right to counsel has attached."[121] The Memorandum stated:

> It is the clear policy of the Department that in the course of a criminal investigation, an attorney for the government is authorized to direct and supervise the use of undercover law enforcement agents, informants, and other cooperating individuals to gather evidence *by communicating with any person who has not been made the subject of formal federal criminal adversarial proceedings arising from that investigation, regardless of whether the person is known to be represented by counsel....* Routine contacts with witnesses, even when not done undercover, are an integral part of federal law enforcement, even where a lawyer may represent the witness. Traditionally, local bar rules have not been thought to prohibit such contact, and any attempt to use the rules in this way runs afoul of the Supremacy Clause.[122]

Although the Memorandum focused on the applicability of the anti-contact rules in pre-indictment situations, it contained sweeping (and, in the defense bar's mind, inflammatory) language that at the least implied that DOJ attorneys were not constrained by state or court-adopted ethical rules against *ex parte* contacts, even in *post*-indictment situations. In particular, the Memorandum stated:

> In sum, it is the Department's position that contact with a represented individual *in the course of authorized law enforcement*

---

120. Memorandum from Richard Thornburgh, Attorney General, to All Justice Department Litigators, dated June 8, 1989 (*reprinted in* In the Matter of John Doe, 801 F. Supp. 478 (D.N.M. 1992)).

121. John Doe, 801 F. Supp. at 489.

122. *Id.* at 492 (emphasis added).

activity does not violate DR 7-104. The Department will resist, on Supremacy Clause grounds, local attempts to curb legitimate federal law enforcement techniques. . . . [A]n attorney employed by the Department, and any individual acting at the direction of that attorney, is authorized to contact or communicate with any individual *in the course of an investigation or prosecution* unless the contact or communication is prohibited by the Constitution, statute, Executive Order, or applicable federal regulation.[123]

Indeed, in *United States v. Lopez*, DOJ attempted to rely on the Thornburgh Memorandum to exempt a prosecutor who engaged in post-indictment contacts with a represented party from court-adopted no-contact rules.[124] In *Lopez*, the prosecutor had conducted *ex parte* meetings with a criminal defendant and concealed those contacts from the defendant's lawyer in an effort to reach a plea bargain and cooperation agreement with the defendant and a co-defendant (the co-defendant's lawyer did participate in the meetings).[125] The response of the district court to DOJ's invocation of the Thornburgh Memorandum was, to say the least, unreceptive. The district court flatly rejected the policy set forth in the Thornburgh Memorandum, noting that "[e]ven a cursory examination of the authority cited by the Attorney General reveals that the cases do not support the policy articulated in the Memorandum."[126] In fact, the court was unable to find any authority supporting the proposition that the ethical rules against *ex parte* contacts do not apply to a government lawyer who communicates with a represented individual under indictment.[127] Based upon the longstanding ethical norm prohibiting communications with represented parties and the courts' consistent rulings that the prohibi-

---

123. *Id.* at 493 (emphasis added).

124. 765 F. Supp. 1433 (N.D. Cal. 1991).

125. *Id.* at 1438-44. The meetings took place after the prosecutor obtained an in camera hearing before a magistrate judge in which the defendant, after being advised of his rights, executed a written waiver of his right to have his counsel present during the plea negotiations. *Id.* at 1442. The district court found that the government had materially misled the magistrate, *id.* at 1460, but on appeal the Ninth Circuit, while agreeing that the magistrate had not been fully informed, remanded the case to resolve the conflicts in testimony regarding the meeting with the magistrate. United States v. Lopez, 4 F.3d 1455, 1462 (9th Cir. 1993).

126. Lopez, 765 F. Supp. at 1446.

127. *Id.* at 1447.

tion applies to prosecutors, the court held that "[t]o the extent that the Memorandum purports to authorize DOJ attorneys to disregard an ethical rule which has been adopted by this court pursuant to its Local Rules, the Memorandum instructs federal prosecutors to violate federal law."[128] The court dismissed the indictment, relying upon its supervisory powers.[129]

The Ninth Circuit subsequently vacated the district court opinion, holding that the dismissal of the indictment was an improper remedy.[130] Importantly, though, the Ninth Circuit noted that "[t]he government, on appeal, has prudently dropped its dependence on the Thornburgh Memorandum . . . , and has thereby spared us the need of reiterating the district court's trenchant analysis of the inefficacy of the Attorney General's policy statement."[131] In addition, the Ninth Circuit rejected DOJ's argument that the State Bar of California's anti-contact rule, which had been adopted by the district court through its local rules, did not apply to its prosecutors, relying on state court precedents.[132] The Ninth Circuit similarly dismissed DOJ's contention that *ex parte* contacts by a prosecutor fall within the "authorized by law" exception to the no-contact rules, holding that the statutes relied on by DOJ in arguing that its post-indictment contacts were not prohibited did not support DOJ's position.[133]

In 1994, after the Ninth Circuit's opinion in *Lopez*, DOJ largely codified its Thornburgh Memorandum position in regulations contained at 28 C.F.R. § 77.1-12. According to the regulations:

> Except as otherwise provided in this part, an attorney for the government may communicate, or cause another to communicate, with a represented person in the process of conducting an investigation, including, but not limited to, an undercover investigation.[134]
>
> Communications with represented parties and represented persons pursuant to this part are intended to constitute communications that are 'authorized by law' within the meaning of Rule 4.2 . . . [and] DR 7-104(A)(1). . . . In addition, this part is intended to preempt and supersede the application of state laws and rules and

---

128. *Id.* at 1450.
129. *Id.* at 1464.
130. Lopez, 4 F.3d at 1464.
131. *Id.* at 1458.
132. *Id.* at 1459-61.
133. *Id.* at 1461.
134. 28 C.F.R. § 77.7 (1994) (repealed).

local federal court rules to the extent that they relate to contacts by attorneys for the government, and those acting at their direction or under their supervision, with represented parties or represented persons in criminal or civil law enforcement investigations or proceedings; it is designed to preempt the entire field of rules concerning such contacts.[135]

In 1998, the Eighth Circuit considered and rejected these regulations as outside the scope of DOJ's rule-making authority.[136] In *United States v. McDonnell Douglas Corp.*, the government appealed the district court's order directing DOJ to cease *ex parte* contacts with employees of McDonnell Douglas and provide discovery of information already obtained from such contacts. The government contended that its regulations superseded the local rules of the district court (which incorporated Missouri's anti-contact rule), or, in the alternative, that *ex parte* contacts by government attorneys and agents fall within the "authorized by law" exception of Rule 4.2.[137] The Eighth Circuit upheld the district court order and affirmed the district court's holding that the DOJ's regulations, and specifically section 77.10(a),[138] were beyond the statutory authority of the Attorney General to enact. In addition, the court refused to adopt the DOJ's position that its regulations preempted local court rules.[139]

In October 1998, Congress entered the fray by enacting the Citizen's Protection Act of 1998 (also known as the McDade Amendment).[140] The Act, which became effective in April 1999 despite the vigorous efforts of the Justice Department to delay its implementation or eliminate it altogether,[141] provides that lawyers for the federal government are subject to

---

135. *Id.* § 77.12 (1994) (repealed).

136. *See* United States v. McDonnell Douglas Corp., 132 F.3d 1252 (8th Cir. 1998).

137. *Id.* at 1254.

138. "A communication with a current employee of an organization that qualifies as a represented party or represented person shall be considered to be a communication with the organization for purposes of this part only if the employee is a controlling individual. A 'controlling individual' is a current high-level employee who is known by the government to be participating as a decision maker in the determination of the organization's legal position in the proceeding or investigation of the subject matter." *Id.* (quoting 28 C.F.R. § 77.10(a) (1994) (repealed)).

139. *Id.* at 1257 & n.4.

140. *Congress Enacts Statute that Subjects Federal Prosecutors to State Laws and Rules*, 64 Crim. L. Rep. (BNA) 70 (Oct. 28, 1998).

141. *See* Bill Moushey, *Justice, Hatch Fight Law Aimed at Overzealous Prosecutors*, Pittsburgh Post-Gazette, Mar. 26, 1999, at A-1.

the ethical rules of the states and courts in which they engage in their duties, and "to the same extent and in the same manner" as other lawyers.[142] As was required by the Act, the Justice Department has issued implementing regulations that provide that:

> In all criminal investigations and prosecutions, in all civil investigations and litigation (affirmative and defensive), and in all civil law enforcement investigations and proceedings, attorneys for the government shall conform their conduct and activities to the state rules and laws, and federal local court rules, governing attorneys in each State where such attorney engages in that attorney's duties, to the same extent and in the same manner as the other attorneys in that State.[143]

Notably, the regulations subject government lawyers to state and court ethics rules regardless of whether a matter has ripened into a formal proceeding,[144] and do not conceive of an exception where application of the rules would merely conflict with federal law enforcement policy.[145] In addition, Justice Department lawyers are instructed not to direct investigative agents acting under their supervision to engage in conduct that would violate their own ethical obligations (although good-faith provision of legal advice or guidance on request is not prohibited).[146] Finally, to determine which state or states government lawyers may be deemed to be "engaged in their duties," the regulations look to whether a case is pending. If a case has been instituted, government lawyers are subject to the rules of the state or federal court in which the case is pending; alternatively, where there is no case pending, government lawyers are subject to the rules of their states of licensure.[147]

As of the date of this writing, attempts to modify or eliminate the duties placed upon government lawyers by the Citizen's Protection Act have failed. In 1999, Senator Orrin Hatch (R.-Utah) sponsored legislation

---

142. 28 U.S.C. § 530B(a).

143. 28 C.F.R. § 77.3.

144. *Id.* & § 77.2(c).

145. *See id.* § 77.1(b) (28 U.S.C. § 530B "should not be construed in any way to alter federal substantive, procedural, or evidentiary law or to interfere with the Attorney General's authority to send Department attorneys into any court in the United States").

146. *Id.* § 77.4(f).

147. *Id.* § 77.2(j)(1).

that would have significantly restricted the Act's limitations on the actions of Justice Department lawyers. Senator Hatch's bill, entitled the Federal Prosecutor Ethics Act, would have exempted federal prosecutors from state ethics rules wherever application "interferes with the effectuation of Federal law or policy, including the investigation of violations of Federal law."[148] Commentators rightly noted that this exemption was so broad that virtually any contact with a represented party could be justified by reference to an ill-defined federal "policy" of vigorously investigating violations of the law.[149] The measure failed to generate sufficient support and was never enacted. Also in 1999, Senator Patrick Leahy (D.-Vermont) proposed a bill entitled the "Professional Standards for Government Attorneys Act," which sought to authorize the Judicial Conference to create a set of national rules governing *ex parte* communications, together with a national system for judicial discipline that would have had priority over the actions of state ethics boards.[150] This bill, too, failed to garner support and died in committee.[151]

In addition, the Justice Department has attempted to negotiate with the American Bar Association for revisions to Model Rule 4.2 that would ease the potential restrictions placed on prosecutorial conduct under that rule. Proposed revisions placed on the initial agenda of the ABA's August 1999 House of Delegates meeting would have permitted government lawyers to authorize investigative agents to contact represented persons prior to the filing of formal criminal charges or a civil proceeding.[152] However, these revisions would not have permitted government

---

148. *See* Robert Morvillo, *Restrictions on Law Enforcement Contact with Corporate Employees*, N.Y. LAW J., Oct. 5, 1999, at 3; *see also Senate Bill Seeks to Preempt, Revamp New Law on Federal Prosecutors' Ethics*, 64 CRIM. L. REP (BNA) 337 (Feb. 3, 1999).

149. *See* Morvillo, *supra* n.148.

150. *The Professional Standards for Government Attorneys Act of 1999*, S. 855, 106th Cong. (1999).

151. In the wake of the events of Sept. 11, 2001, Sen. Leahy attempted to resurrect the Professional Standards for Government Attorneys Act as part of the federal anti-terrorism legislation. Although the Senate's package included the measure, the House of Representatives' package did not, perhaps because of pressure from the ABA, the ACLU, and other legal and civic groups. Thus, the Citizen's Protection Act survived the USA Patriot Act of 2001 intact. *See* Elkan Abramowitz & Barr Bohrer, *In the Name of Counter Terrorism*, N.Y.L.J., Nov. 6, 2001, at 3.

152. ABA House of Delegates 1999 Annual Meeting Recommendation 122B.

lawyers to contact represented persons directly and would have required prosecutors to take steps to ensure that agents did not seek privileged information, induce a represented person to forgo representation, or engage in settlement or plea negotiations.[153] In addition, comments to the revision would have allowed government lawyers to communicate with employees of organizational clients who voluntarily decided to talk to the government concerning a criminal or civil investigation and did not want the organization's lawyer present during the communication.[154] Finally, the comments also would have authorized "investigative activities of lawyers representing government entities prior to an arrest or filing of a formal criminal charge or civil complaint in the matter, when there is applicable judicial precedent that either has found the activity permissible under this Rule [4.2] or has found this Rule inapplicable."[155] The proposal was stricken from the agenda when Justice failed to provide final approval of the amendments prior to the ABA's August 1999 meeting.[156] In addition, a recent ABA Commission of the Evaluation of the Rules of Professional Conduct report on proposed amendments to the Model Rules considered and rejected amendments to Model Rule 4.2 that would have liberalized the application of that rule to federal prosecutors, stating that the existing rule "strikes the proper balance between effective law enforcement and the need to protect client-lawyer relationships that are essential to the proper functioning of the justice system."[157] In February 2002, the ABA reaffirmed the protections contained in Model Rule 4.2, including the Comment to the Rule, that "[t]he fact that a communication does not violate a state or federal constitutional right is insufficient to establish that the communication is permissible under this Rule."[158]

---

153. *Id.* & cmt. 8.

154. *Id.*, cmt. 3.

155. *Id.*, cmt. 6; *see also* nn. 178-81 and accompanying text, *infra*, for a discussion of the judicial precedent regarding pre-indictment *ex parte* contacts by government attorneys.

156. Nancy Ritter, *Feds reopen talks with ABA on ex parte prohibition*, N.Y.L.J., Oct. 18, 1999, at 5; *Ex Parte Contacts Rule Proposal Put on Hold at ABA Meeting after DOJ Opts Out*, 13 CRIM. PRAC. REP. 312 (Aug. 11-25, 1999).

157. ABA, COMMISSION ON THE EVALUATION OF THE RULES OF PROFESSIONAL CONDUCT, REPORT WITH RECOMMENDATION TO THE HOUSE OF DELEGATES (Aug. 2001).

158. MODEL RULES OF PROF'L CONDUCT R. 4.2 cmt. 3 (Feb. 2002).

The gravamen of all this for the corporate client is that whether a government lawyer's *ex parte* contacts with corporate employees will run afoul of ethical constraints will be determined by reference to the state or court ethical rules applicable to the lawyer's conduct, and which set of rules applies will depend on whether a proceeding has been instituted or not.[159] For this reason, attention to detail in reviewing the various aspects of the ethical rules of the pertinent jurisdiction or jurisdictions will become critical in any attempt to challenge prosecutorial misconduct in this regard. Such a review is beyond the scope of this chapter, but several key considerations should be kept in mind.

First, which employees of an organization are "off limits" to government lawyers? The official comment to Model Rule 4.2, as restated in February 2002, makes it clear that when a company is the client, opposing counsel shall not communicate with:

> a constituent of the organization who supervises, directs or regularly consults with the organization's lawyer concerning the matter or has authority to obligate the organization with respect to the matter or whose act or omission in connection with the matter may be imputed to the organization for purposes of civil or criminal liability. Consent of the organization's lawyer is not required for communication with a former constituent.[160]

In interpreting the no-contact rules adopted in various jurisdictions, the vast majority of courts have taken the position that current upper management and some, but probably not all, low- and mid-level employees are within the reach of the rule. Currently, there are at least four standards for identifying employees who are covered by the no-contact rule.[161] One school of thought reads the rule as covering management and employees who have legal authority to speak on behalf of the company (in

---

159. *See, e.g.*, United States v. Colorado Supreme Court, 189 F.3d 1281, 1284 (10th Cir. Sept. 1, 1999) (holding state ethical rule restricting ability of prosecutors to subpoena attorneys for information about clients in criminal proceedings applicable to federal prosecutors, as "the McDade Act . . . conclusively establish[es] that a state rule governing attorney conduct is applicable to federal attorneys practicing in the state").

160. MODEL RULES OF PROF'L CONDUCT R. 4.2 cmt. 6 (Feb. 2002).

161. *See* Baisley, 708 A.2d at 932-33 (surveying the various interpretations of the no-contact rule); Brown, 148 F.R.D. at 253-54 (same).

the sense that their statements constitute admissions under federal evidentiary rules[162]). In this widely held "managing-speaking" view,[163] the no-contact rule applies to few low-level employees.[164] A variation on the "managing-speaking" theory, known as the "alter-ego" test, extends the rule against *ex parte* contacts to cover employees whose acts or omissions in the matter can be imputed to the company for purposes of liability, as well as those employees who are acting on the advice of or to assist corporate counsel in connection with its representation of the company.[165] This increasingly popular interpretation[166] places more non-management-level employees under the *ex parte* prohibition, but (like the "managing-speaking" view) does not reach employees who are merely fact witnesses to the events at issue.[167]

Notably, a third construction, the "scope-of-employment" theory, reads the no-contact rule as reaching witness-employees, even if they are not

---

162. *See* FED. R. EVID. 801(d)(2)(C) (hearsay exception providing for admission of a statement against a party if the statement was made "by a person authorized by the party to make a statement concerning the subject").

163. *See* Brown, 148 F.R.D. at 254 (explaining that the "managing-speaking" and "alter ego" tests have "achieved the widest acceptance").

164. *See* Wright v. Group Health Hosp., 691 P.2d 564, 568-69 (Wash. 1984) (en banc) (announcing the "managing-speaking" test); *see, e.g.*, Chancellor v. Boeing Co., 678 F. Supp. 250, 253 (D. Kan. 1988) (adopting the "managing-speaking" test); Fulton v. Lane, 829 P.2d 959, 960 (Okla. 1992) (same); Weider Sports Equip. Co. v. Fitness First, Inc., 912 F. Supp. 502, 510 (D. Utah 1996) (apparently adopting the "managing-speaking" test).

165. *See* Niesig v. Team I, 558 N.E.2d 1030, 1035 (N.Y. 1990) (enunciating "alter ego" test); *see, e.g.*, Cole v. Appalachian Power Co., 903 F. Supp. 975, 979 (S.D. W. Va. 1995) (adopting "alter ego" test); Bouge v. Smith's Mgmt. Corp., 132 F.R.D. 560, 570 (D. Utah 1990) (same); Strawser v. Exxon Co., 843 P.2d 613, 621 (Wyo. 1992) (same). Under the "alter ego" interpretation, the no-contact rule would cover (for example) a truck driver whose involvement in an accident led to a lawsuit against his employer. The truck driver is not a manager, nor is he authorized to speak on behalf of the company. However, his admission regarding his own action can be used against the company. *See* 2 GEOFFREY C. HAZARD JR. & W. WILLIAM HODES, THE LAW OF LAWYERING: A HANDBOOK ON THE MODEL RULES OF PROFESSIONAL CONDUCT § 4.2:105, at 740 (2d ed. Supp. 1998).

166. *See* Strawser, 843 P.2d at 621 ("alter ego" test is gaining support).

167. Some of the state courts that have adopted the "alter ego" view and rejected the "scope-of-employment" view (discussed below) have done so because the state has no rule of evidence providing for admission of hearsay statements made by employees during and within the scope of their employment (*i.e.*, analogous to FED. R. EVID. 801(d)(2)(D)). *See, e.g.*, Niesig, 76 N.E.2d at 1035.

authorized to speak on behalf of the company.[168] This broad interpretation draws upon the rule of agency law that a current employee's statements may bind his employer if those statements were made within the scope of his employment.[169] This "scope-of-employment" view does not necessarily lead to the conclusion that all current employees fall within the ambit of the rule, but some courts have reached this conclusion nonetheless.[170] Finally, some courts have engaged in a case-by-case analysis, balancing opposing counsel's need for information from a company against the company's need to avoid damaging evidentiary admissions.[171] Courts using this approach often exclude many low-level employees from the scope of the no-contact rule.

Due to the diversity of approaches employed to decide whether and which current employees are within the scope of the no-contact rule, counsel is advised to study the precedents from the relevant jurisdiction(s) carefully. Moreover, due to the complexity of these approaches and the unsettled nature of the case law, counsel should expect that the applicability of the rule to the facts presented will be a matter of ex post interpreta-

---

168. *See, e.g.*, McCallum v. CSX Transp., Inc, 149 F.R.D. 104, 111 (M.D.N.C. 1993) (apparently adopting the "scope of employment" test); Palmer v. Pioneer Hotel & Casino, 19 F. Supp. 2d. 1157, 1162 (D. Nev. 1998); *cf., e.g.*, B.H. v. Johnson, 128 F.R.D. 659, 662, 663 (N.D. Ill. 1989) (purporting not to adopt a specific test, but prohibiting *ex parte* contact with employees whose statements could bind their employer as admissions under FED. R. EVID. 801(d)(2)(D)).

169. Under federal evidentiary rules, an employee's statement may be an evidentiary admission against the company simply because he spoke about a matter that was within the scope of his employment. *See* FED. R. EVID. 801(d)(2)(D) (hearsay exception allowing admission of a statement against a party if the statement was made by the party's employee during and within the scope of his employment). Although this means that low-level employees can bind the employer, the subject matter of such admissions is limited. A statement will not be imputed to the employer unless the employee's job function had something to do with it. *See* Palmer, 19 F. Supp. 2d. at 1164; McCallum, 149 F.R.D. at 111.

170. *See, e.g.*, Cagguila v. Wyeth Lab., Inc., 127 F.R.D. 653, 654 (E.D. Pa. 1989) (prohibiting the use of the statement of a non-managerial employee, which apparently was to be offered as a scope-of-employment admission). *But see* Palmer, 19 F. Supp. 2d at 1162 (explaining that the scope-of-employment view does not work "a blanket ban" on *ex parte* communications with all employees).

171. *See, e.g.*, Morrison v. Brandeis Univ., 125 F.R.D. 14, 17 (D. Mass. 1989); Mompoint v. Lotus Dev. Corp., 110 F.R.D. 414 (D. Mass. 1986); Frey v. Department of Health & Human Servs., 106 F.R.D. 32, 36 (E.D.N.Y. 1985).

tion—with resulting ex ante unpredictability for both sides on the subject of who may be contacted.[172]

Second, do the ethical rules proscribe *ex parte* contacts with former as well as current employees? Although defense counsel representing a corporate employer can argue persuasively that the no-contact rules apply to communications with *present* employees whose acts or omissions are binding on the corporation or are imputed to it for liability purposes, it is more difficult for counsel to argue that prosecutors and their investigative agents should not be permitted to communicate *ex parte* with *former* employees of the corporation.[173] In particular, the American Bar Association Standing Committee on Ethics and Professional Responsibility has opined that counsel to a party adverse to a corporation may communicate about the subject matter of the representation with a former employee without the consent of the corporation's counsel, as long as the former employee is not separately represented.[174] This position also was recently reflected in the official comments to the February 2002 amendments to Model Rule 4.2.[175]

---

172. *See* Morvillo, *supra* n.148.

173. *See* Aiken v. Business & Indus. Health Group, 885 F. Supp. 1474, 1477 ("Notwithstanding some case law to the contrary, the clear majority of courts interpreting Rule 4.2 have held ... that [it] does not apply to communication with former employees of an organizational party who no longer have any relationship with the organization") (collecting cases) (D.Kan. 1995); *see also* H.B.A. Mgmt., Inc. v. Estate of Schwartz, 693 So. 2d 541, 546 (Fla. 1997) (holding that Florida's version of Model Rule 4.2 "neither contemplates nor prohibits an attorney's *ex parte* communications with former employees of a defendant-employer"); Terra Int'l, Inc. v. Mississippi Chem. Corp., 913 F. Supp. at 1315 (only barring *ex parte* contact with former employees still represented by former employer's counsel); Hanntz v. Shiley, Inc., 766 F. Supp. 258, 265 (D.N.J. 1991) ("Ordinarily, it cannot be assumed the corporation's counsel represents the former employees.") (citations omitted). *But see* Olson v. Snap Prods., Inc., 183 F.R.D. 539, 544-45 (D. Minn. 1998) (rejecting a per se rule permitting contacts with former employees in favor of a "flexible approach" that assesses the likelihood that the contact will invade the corporation's attorney-client privilege); Roy Simon, *Interviewing Former Employees of an Adversary*, N.Y.L.J., Nov. 9, 2001, at 16 (outlining differing jurisdictional approaches to whether *ex parte* contacts with former employees are permissible).

174. ABA Standing Comm. on Ethics and Professional Responsibility, Formal Op. 91-359 (1991).

175. MODEL RULES OF PROFESSIONAL CONDUCT R. 4.2, cmt. 6 (Feb. 2002) ("Consent of the organization's lawyer is not required for communications with a former constituent.") *But see id.*, Reporter's Observations, cmt. 6 ("Rule 4.4 precludes the use of methods of obtaining evidence that violate the legal rights of the organization.").

Critical steps can and should be taken, however, to protect the corporation's interest in the testimony of its former employees. Upon discovery of or notice that an investigation may commence, company counsel immediately should identify and locate all former employees who may be witnesses. Counsel should then seek to conduct face-to-face interviews with the potential witnesses and memorialize their recollection of relevant events. While actual or potential conflicts of interest may prevent company counsel from also representing individual former employees, counsel can inform the former employees of the investigation and assist them in retaining separate counsel if they desire to do so.[176] Representation of former employees by capable counsel is often the best means of ensuring that the rights of both the corporation and its employees are not compromised by aggressive government investigators. Finally, it may be possible to obtain court-imposed conditions on governmental contacts with former employees, including requiring the government to maintain lists of the former employees contacted and to make all memoranda prepared as a result of those contacts available for inspection upon request.[177]

Third, to what extent are government lawyers subject to no-contact rules in the investigative phase of a matter—that is, prior to a criminal indictment or the initiation of formal civil proceedings? The official comment to Model Rule 4.2 states that the rule applies to "any person whether or not a party to a formal adjudicative proceeding, contract or negotiation, who is represented by counsel concerning the matter to which the communication relates."[178] Accordingly, a literal interpretation of the rule would prohibit *ex parte* contacts by government prosecutors regardless of whether a formal criminal proceeding is under way. However, courts have gener-

---

176. State corporate law and the corporation's bylaws may require the company to indemnify employees for their legal fees or even to advance legal fees prior to a decision respecting indemnification. *See, e.g.,* DEL. CODE ANN. tit. 8, § 145. The costs involved can be substantial. It therefore is generally in the corporation's best interests for company counsel to be involved from the outset in the selection and retention of separate counsel for employees and, where possible, to suggest multiple representation as a cost-saving measure.

177. *See, e.g.,* McDonnell Douglas, 132 F.3d at 1257-58 (upholding district court's imposition of these restrictions).

178. MODEL RULES OF PROF'L CONDUCT R. 4.2 cmt. 5 (Feb. 2002). Note that Rule 4.2 originally prohibited contacts with represented "parties," but was amended in 1995 to clarify that the pendency of a formal proceeding to which the client is a "party" is not prerequisite to ethical proscriptions against *ex parte* contacts. *Id.* (Legal Background, "Parties" vs. "Persons") (1995).

ally concluded that the ethical prohibition against contacts with represented defendants is co-extensive with the Sixth Amendment right to counsel and, therefore, does not constrain non-custodial prosecutorial contacts prior to a criminal indictment.[179] Notably, however, the Second Circuit has held that the anti-contact rules may apply in certain pre-indictment situations, principally because tying the application of ethical proscriptions to the timing of an indictment simply places too much power in a prosecutor's hands.[180] The Ninth Circuit recently agreed with the case-by-case analysis favored by the Second Circuit.[181]

In light of the complexity of this area of the law, and of the multiple jurisdictions whose law may be in play under the Citizen's Protection Act and the implementing regulations, it is highly recommended that counsel check the most recent decisions involving multiple representation, conflicts, and *ex parte* communications prior to advising their clients. In addition, we have set forth several suggestions below.

179. *See, e.g.,* United States v. Balter, 91 F.3d 427, 436 (3d Cir.), *cert. denied*, 519 U.S. 1011 (1996); United States v. Powe, 9 F.3d 68, 69 (9th Cir. 1993); United States v. Heinz, 983 F.2d 609, 614 (5th Cir. 1993) ("The dullest imagination can comprehend the devastating effect that [a rule limiting pre-indictment contacts] would have on undercover operations."); Ryans, 903 F.2d at 740; United States v. Sutton, 801 F.2d 1346, 1366 (D.C. Cir. 1986); United States v. Dobbs, 711 F.2d 84, 86 (8th Cir. 1983).

180. United States v. Hammad, 858 F.2d 834, 838-40 (2d Cir. 1988) (only extending rule to pre-indictment stage based on "egregious misconduct" by the prosecutor and "urg[ing]" restraint in applying the rule to [pre-indictment] criminal investigations"). *But see* Grievance Comm. v. Simels, 48 F.3d 640, 649 (2d Cir. 1995) ("It is significant that since *Hammad*, neither this Court nor any reported district court decision considering an alleged violation of DR 7-104(A)(1) has found that the Rule had been violated."); United States v. Joseph Binder Schweizer Emblem Co., 167 F. Supp. 2d 862, (E.D.N.C. 2001) ("no district court in the Second Circuit applying *Hammad* appears to have found a violation of the disciplinary rule") (citations omitted).

181. United States v. Talao, 222 F.3d 1133, 1139 (9th Cir. 2000) (finding that although California's no-contact rule governed prosecutor's pre-indictment contacts with employee of corporation represented by counsel, there was no violation of the rule under the circumstances). The ABA's February 2002 comments to amended Model Rule 4.2 provide that communications "authorized by law . . . *may*" include investigative activities of government lawyers and their agents "prior to the commencement of criminal or civil enforcement proceedings," and that when communicating with "the accused in a criminal matter, a government lawyer must comply with this rule in addition to honoring the constitutional rights of the accused." MODEL RULES OF PROF'L CONDUCT R. 4.2, cmt. 3 (Feb. 2002) (emphasis added).

First of all, company counsel should inform all employees early on that federal agents may approach them and ask to interview them, outside the presence of company counsel. The employees should be further informed that while the decision to be interviewed is a matter of choice for the employees, they have the right to be interviewed in the presence of company counsel, and that the company will make arrangements if asked for such an accompanied interview to take place during normal business hours. Suggesting that employees have the choice to refrain from *ex parte* interviews will minimize the risk of harmful admissions under Federal Rule of Evidence 801(d)(2)(D), at a time when the company has not been informed of the nature of the charges against it and has not had adequate opportunity to consider its defenses.

Additionally, at the outset of the criminal investigation, company counsel may wish to inform government counsel that it anticipates representing all present and former company employees, unless ethically prohibited from doing so on grounds of conflict, and that all contacts with employees should be initiated through company counsel. By so doing, government counsel is placed on notice that any attempt to interview employees will be viewed as an *ex parte* contact of an opponent's client and thus ethically proscribed. Company counsel also should contact the former employees most likely to have relevant information, and thus most likely the subject of *ex parte* contacts, and offer the services of company counsel in providing legal advice and possible representation. Finally, because employees may or may not choose to follow this advice, counsel should carefully screen from them all sensitive or strategic nonessential information, for fear that the information may be disclosed during an *ex parte* contact.

G. *Internal Investigations and the Fair Credit Reporting Act*

Attorneys conducting internal investigations should be aware of the potential application of the Fair Credit Reporting Act, 15 U.S.C. §§ 1681 *et seq.* (FCRA) to their activities. In April 1999, a staff attorney with the Federal Trade Commission (FTC) took the position in an advisory letter (now commonly known as the "Vail Letter") that "outside organizations" conducting investigations that would provide information used in making decisions regarding a client's employees must comply with the complex disclosure and accuracy provisions of FCRA or face significant liability.[182]

Applying this position to a lawyer conducting an internal investigation[183] would have troubling ramifications.[184] One of the most potentially troublesome FCRA provisions would require the lawyer to disclose all the information in an individual's file upon request.[185] Another would require the client to disclose the "nature and scope" of the investigation under certain circumstances.[186] Furthermore, if the report would be used for "employment purposes," the employer could not take any employment-related adverse action without first providing the consumer with "a copy of the report."[187]

---

182. Letter from Christopher W. Keller to Judi A. Vail (Apr. 5, 1999) ("Vail Letter"). The FTC has authority to enforce FCRA, but is not authorized to issue regulations. 15 U.S.C. § 1681s. It does, however, issue non-binding letters that interpret various provisions of FCRA. The liability associated with FCRA violations includes private suits for negligent or willful noncompliance, *id.* §§ 1681n-o, administrative enforcement by the FTC and state attorneys general, *id.* §§ 1681s(a), (c), and criminal liability for "knowingly and willingly" obtaining information from a consumer-reporting agency under false pretenses, *id.* § 1681q.

183. Although the Vail Letter does not explicitly mention outside counsel investigations, it was requested by an attorney. *See* Vail Letter, *supra* n.182. Moreover, other advisory letters issued by the FTC suggest that it would not recognize any exceptions or apply special rules based on the attorney-client relationship. *See, e.g.,* Letter from William Haynes to Sylvia Sum (Sept. 15, 1999) (law firm that performs criminal background checks on prospective employees is subject to FCRA.).

184. *See generally* Michael Delikat, *Sexual Harassment Update*, 6506 PLI/Lit. 373, 491-96 (June 2001).

185. Upon request, consumer-reporting agencies must clearly and accurately disclose to the consumer "[a]ll information in the consumer's file at the time of the request." 15 U.S.C. § 1681g(a)(1).

186. If the report is an "investigative consumer report" (*i.e.*, one based on information acquired through personal interviews with people having knowledge of the subject), the entity that "procures" or "causes [the report] to be prepared" must disclose to the consumer the fact that a report may be prepared within three days of the report being requested. *Id.* §§ 1681a(e), 1681d(a). If the consumer makes a written request, that entity must "make a complete and accurate disclosure of the nature and scope of the investigation" to the consumer. *Id.* § 1681d(b). The FTC has stated that by the plain terms of the statute, no information at all can be redacted from the disclosure required under this provision. *See* Vail Letter, *supra* n.182.

187. 15 U.S.C. § 1681b(b)(3)(A). "Employment purposes" is defined as "evaluating a consumer for employment, promotion, reassignment or retention as an employee." *Id.* § 1681a(h). In the employment context, "adverse action" is defined as "a denial of

The Vail Letter's position would not be possible without the considerable breadth that pervades the definitions in FCRA. In particular, FCRA applies when a "consumer reporting agency" provides a "consumer report" to a third party for certain specified purposes, including employment purposes. A "consumer" is simply an individual.[188] A "consumer report" is "any written, oral or other communication of any information ... bearing on a consumer's credit worthiness, credit standing, credit capacity, character, general reputation, personal characteristics, or mode of living which is used or expected to be used or collected in whole or in part" for certain specified purposes, including "employment purposes."[189] And a "consumer reporting agency" is any entity which "regularly engages in whole or in part in the practice of assembling or evaluating" such information in exchange for a fee.[190] Thus, under a literal reading of the statute, any lawyer who assembles or evaluates any information on individuals employed by a client could arguably be subject to FCRA.

Although no case law directly addresses this issue, the FTC's Vail Letter could be interpreted as taking the position that investigating attorneys would be subject to FCRA. The letter, dated April 5, 1999, concerned the application of FCRA to sexual harassment investigations mandated by Title VII.[191] The Vail Letter expressly stated that "outside organizations utilized by employers to assist in their investigations of harassment claims" are consumer-reporting agencies and subject to the provisions of FCRA.[192] This reasoning, if applicable to investigating lawyers, would extend to counsel conducting other types of investigations as well.

Applying the Vail Letter's position to lawyers investigating alleged corporate wrongdoing would conflict with both the legislative intent behind the statute and general principles of common sense. The Congres-

---

employment or any other decision for employment purposes that adversely affects any current or prospective employee." *Id.* § 1681a(k)(1)(B)(ii).

188. *Id.* § 1681a(c).

189. *Id.* § 1681a(d)(1).

190. *Id.* § 1681a(f).

191. *See* Vail Letter, *supra* n.182.

192. In response to a subsequent letter detailing the problems associated with such an approach, the FTC stated that it was "sympathetic to the practical problems that exist in applying the FCRA to investigations by third parties of workplace misconduct," but nevertheless affirmed its position, noting that "any changes or exceptions must come from Congress." Letter from David Medine to Susan R. Meisinger (Aug. 31, 1999).

sional Findings and Statement of Purpose strongly suggest that the statute was intended to apply to the narrow area of credit reporting in a banking context.[193] Moreover, courts have noted that the statute was passed to remedy the abuses of the credit-reporting industry, not to provide an absolute right of individual privacy.[194]

Furthermore, the fact that the statute is entirely silent on some of the obvious issues that would arise in the event it were applied to investigating attorneys strongly indicates that it was not intended to do so. The most glaring omission is the failure of the statute to address privilege issues in any respect. As noted above, if FCRA applied, lawyers would have to turn over the consumer's entire file upon request, and in the case of an "investigative consumer report," the employer would have to make a full disclosure about that "nature and scope of the investigation." Such disclosures would inevitably include privileged information, and the Vail Letter states that, under the plain language of the statute, no information at all can be redacted.[195] It is unlikely that Congress would have enacted a statute intended to apply to investigating attorneys that completely fails to address this crucial and complex topic. Moreover, and perhaps most important, applying FCRA to investigating attorneys would inhibit the self-investigation and analysis that the government has strongly encouraged in recent years.[196] It is extremely unlikely that Congress intended this result.

---

193. "Congressional findings and statement of purpose. . . . The Congress makes the following findings: (1) The banking system is dependent upon fair and accurate credit reporting. Inaccurate credit reports directly impair the efficiency of the banking system, and unfair credit reporting methods undermine the public confidence which is essential to the continued functioning of the banking system. (2) An elaborate mechanism has been developed for investigating and evaluating the credit worthiness, credit standing, credit capacity, character, and general reputation of consumers. (3) Consumer reporting agencies have assumed a vital role in assembling and evaluating consumer credit and other information on consumers. (4) There is a need to insure that consumer reporting agencies exercise their grave responsibilities with fairness, impartiality, and a respect for the consumer's right to privacy." 15 U.S.C. § 1681.

194. *See, e.g.*, Henry v. Forbes, 433 F. Supp. 5, 9 (D. Minn. 1976).

195. *See* Vail Letter, *supra* n.182.

196. *See* Karen Buck Burgess et al., *Recent Legislative Developments Affecting the Work of the Securities and Exchange Commission*, 1234 PLI/Corp 797 (SEC Speaks, March 2001); David B. Fein & Suzanne E. Wachsstock, *Compromising Compliance: FTC Opinion Undercuts Corporations' Ability to Unearth Workplace Problems*, LEGAL TIMES, Sept. 20, 1999, at S34.

Even assuming, however, that the FTC's position accurately states the law with respect to investigating attorneys, several possible defenses to application of FCRA could be available. First, it could be argued that the lawyer does not meet the definition of "consumer reporting agency" because he or she does not "regularly engage" in investigations or in furnishing employment-related information to third parties. The phrase "regularly engage" is not defined in the statute, and there is little case law on the issue. The authority that does exist indicates that "regularly engage" basically means to perform the activity in question as part of one's normal business operations.[197] The strength of this argument would likely turn on the particular facts of a given case, with the possible odd result that experienced investigating attorneys—that is, lawyers who are more likely to have "regularly engaged" in the activity in question—would be subject to FCRA, while less experienced lawyers would not.[198]

Second, assuming that the investigation is a general one, not undertaken specifically for "employment purposes," it might be possible for a lawyer to argue that investigatory work does not meet the definition of "consumer report" because it was not prepared for one of the purposes specifically listed in the definition. This argument may be viable in certain circumstances, but is somewhat problematic. Ambiguous and confusing language in two related provisions of the statute has spawned a great deal of confusion over what the specified purposes are and how they relate to the overall definition of consumer report.[199] Moreover, FCRA defines "con-

---

197. *See, e.g.,* Hodge v. Texaco, Inc., 975 F.2d 1093, 1097 (5th Cir. 1992) (holding that a doctor who performed a drug test was not subject to the act because the test was a "one-time referral," and that the purpose of the "regularly engage" language is to protect individuals who might engage in conduct covered by FCRA on a "casual, one-time basis"); *see also* H.R. 102-692, 102d Cong., 2d Sess. (1992) ("The bill modifies the definition of 'consumer reporting agency' to establish that an organization must be 'in the business' of compiling and furnishing consumer reports in order to be covered by the definition. This modification is not intended to narrow the definition of 'consumer reporting agency' to mean only any person that is primarily in the business of preparing and furnishing consumer reports. Furnishing and preparing consumer reports need be only a component or commercial function of a person's trade or business. This provision is intended to limit those situations whereby an entity that provides credit information (deemed to be a consumer report) to others on rare occasions may inadvertently become a consumer reporting agency.").

198. *See* Fein & Wachsstock, *supra* n.196.

199. The problem is that section 1681a provides that a consumer report is one that is "used or expected to be used or collected" to determine a consumer's eligibility for

sumer report" as one that is "used or expected to be used or collected in whole or in part" for one of the specified purposes. As the Eleventh Circuit has noted, that language has three components: "ultimate use," "expectation of use," and "reason for compilation."[200] Thus a communication falls within the definition of "consumer report" if (1) it is ultimately used for one of the specified purposes; (2) either the requestor or the reporting agency expects that it will used for one of those purposes; *or* (3) the information was originally compiled for one of those purposes.

To maximize this argument's chances of success, investigating attorneys and their clients would need to make it clear to each other that the report is being prepared for reasons other than the ones specified in sections 1681a and 1681b, and would not be able to use any information that has been collected for any of these specified purposes. The profound impact such a precaution could have is illustrated by a comparison of two Eleventh Circuit decisions involving similar facts. In *Yang v. Government Employees Insurance Company*[201] and *Hovater v. Equifax*,[202] insurance companies ordered credit reports on claimants because they suspected fraud. The insurance companies argued that the reports were not "consumer reports" as defined in FCRA because they were not prepared for one of the purposes enumerated in sections 1681a and 1681b. In *Yang*, the court held that the report was a "consumer report" because even though the report was *used* solely to review the insurance claim, the facts showed that the reporting agency *expected* that it would be used for one of the specified purposes, that of evaluating the consumer's credit.[203] In *Hovater*, however, the court held that the report was not a "consumer report" because the facts showed that all parties were aware that the report was being compiled solely for use in evaluating the insurance claim.[204]

Third, depending on the circumstances, a lawyer's work could meet the requirements of the "direct experience" exception to the definition of "con-

---

"credit or insurance," "employment purposes" or *"any other purpose authorized under section 1681b of this title."* 15 U.S.C. § 1681a(d) (emphasis added). Section 1681b, however, adds little or nothing to the definition of a "consumer report" because it merely lists the circumstances under which a consumer-reporting agency may furnish such a report.

200. Yang v. Government Employees Ins. Co., 146 F.3d 1320, 1324 (11th Cir. 1998).

201. 146 F.3d 1320 (11th Cir. 1998).

202. 823 F.2d 413 (11th Cir.), *cert. denied*, 484 U.S. 977 (1987).

203. Yang, 143 F.3d at 1325.

204. Hovater, 823 F.2d at 417.

sumer report." Under 15 U.S.C. § 1681a(d)(2)(A)(I), the term "consumer report" does not include "any report containing information solely as to transactions or experiences between the consumer and the person making the report." Courts have applied this exception in cases where a laboratory conducts a drug test on an employee and reports the results to the employer,[205] as well as to the administrator of a polygraph examination.[206] At least with respect to investigative contacts with the employee ("consumer"), then, counsel might be able to argue that its "report" is based on direct experience with the "consumer" and thus outside the scope of FCRA.

The troublesome implications of the Vail Letter have not gone unnoticed.[207] In November 1999, Representative Pete Sessions introduced H.R. 3408, which would have created a blanket exemption of most third-party workplace investigations from the reporting and notification provisions of the FCRA. The bill languished in committee and died with the 106th Congress.[208] In April 2001, Representative Sessions reintroduced the bill as H.R. 1543, the Civil Rights and Employee Investigation Clarification Act.[209] The Act, which at the time of this writing is pending in the House Banking Committee's Subcommittee on Financial Institutions and Consumer Credit, would exempt communications that otherwise would be deemed "consumer reports" under the FCRA as long as they are made to an employer in connection with an investigation of suspected employment misconduct or with attempts to comply with federal state or local laws or regulations, the rules of a self-regulatory organization (e.g., the NASD), or preexisting written employer policies.[210] However, if any adverse employment action were taken as a result of the communication, the em-

---

205. *See, e.g.,* Hodge, 975 F.2d at 1096-97; Chube v. Exxon Chem. Am., 760 F. Supp. 557, 561-62 (M.D. La. 1991).

206. Peller v. Retail Credit Co., 359 F. Supp. 1235, 1237 (N.D. Ga. 1973), *aff'd without op.,* 505 F.2d 733 (5th Cir. 1974).

207. Indeed, on March 31, 2000, the chairman of the FTC, writing "at the direction of the Commission," acknowledged that the FCRA created "unanticipated conflicts between the aims of the [FCRA] and the public policy favoring prompt, objective investigations of workplace misconduct," and stated that the FTC "strongly endorse[d] a targeted amendment tailored to those specific provisions of the Act that may genuinely impede workplace investigations by third parties." Letter from Robert Pitofsky to Hon. Pete Sessions, dated March 31, 2000 ("Pitofsky Letter").

208. *See* Amy Payne, Note, *Protecting the Accused in Sexual Harassment Investigations,* 87 VA. L. REV. 381 at n.166 & accompanying text (Apr. 2001).

209. H.R. 1543 (107th Congress, 1st Session).

210. *Id.* § 2(b).

ployer would be required to disclose to the employee "a summary containing the nature and substance of the communication upon which the adverse action is based."[211] Depending on the meaning of the phrase "nature and substance," this formulation could still require the disclosure of privileged communications between counsel and the employer.[212]

H. *Providing Counsel for Employees*

A company can properly provide legal representation for those employees called as witnesses or named as defendants in the course of parallel proceedings.[213] Payment of attorney's fees by the employer does not create a per se conflict of interest or require disqualification of counsel who has accepted such a fee arrangement.[214] Indeed, most state business codes expressly authorize employers to indemnify employees and/or advance fees and expenses incurred in connection with legal proceedings.[215]

Employers can also pay for employees to be represented by the employer's own counsel.[216] Corporations often prefer one law firm to represent all interested parties because it can significantly lessen the amount of legal fees. Additionally, it usually leads to more efficient representation. Both defense counsel and the company benefit from the centraliza-

---

211. *Id.*

212. See Pitofsky Letter n.8 ("we do not believe that generalized or conclusory statements would constitute a good-faith disclosure of the nature and substance of a report").

213. *See, e.g.,* United States v. Smith, 186 F.3d 290, 295 (3d Cir. 1999) (no conflict found where employer paid for employee's counsel), *abrogation by rule on other grounds recognized by* United States v. Diaz, 245 F.3d 294 (3d Cir. 2001); Bucuvalas v. United States, 98 F.3d 652, 656-57 (1st Cir. 1996) (same).

214. *Smith*, 186 F.3d at 295; Bucuvalas, 98 F.3d at 656-57. There is, however, a potential for conflict of interest in this situation. *See* Wood v. Georgia, 450 U.S. 261, 268-69 (1981) ("Courts and commentators have recognized the inherent dangers that arise when a criminal defendant is represented by a lawyer hired and paid by a third party, particularly when the third party is the operator of the alleged criminal enterprise."); *see also* MODEL RULES OF PROF'L CONDUCT R. 1.8(f) (a "lawyer shall not accept compensation for representing a client from one other than the client unless: (1) the client consents after consultation; (2) there is no interference with the lawyer's independence of professional judgment or with the client-lawyer relationship; and (3) information relating to representation of a client is protected as required by Rule 1.6.").

215. *See, e.g.,* DEL. CODE ANN. tit. 8, § 145.

216. *See, e.g.,* United States v. Finlay, 55 F.3d 1410, 1415 (9th Cir.) (no conflict of interest found where corporation and chief executive officer of corporation were represented by the same lawyer), *cert. denied*, 516 U.S. 871 (1995).

tion of information and the natural advantages flowing from one counsel having overall responsibility for the case. Counterproductive debates over defense strategy are often avoided when the company and its employees are jointly represented. Joint representation also avoids the tension that inevitably results from an employee having separate counsel. Moreover, the company retains greater control over the proceedings when only one law firm is retained.[217]

Joint representation, however, does create a significant potential for conflict of interest. This potential can mature into claims of non-compliance with professional ethics rules, the prospect of disqualification at various stages of the proceeding, exposure to claims of ineffective assistance of counsel, and the possible appearance of impropriety.

Model Rule of Professional Conduct 1.7(b) prohibits joint representation unless "the lawyer reasonably believes the representation will not be adversely affected, and . . . the client consents after consultation."[218] Thus, the Model Rules require the lawyer to make an objective evaluation of the potential for conflict of interest and to obtain each client's informed consent to the arrangement.[219] While impermissible conflict of interest is a serious risk inherent in joint representation in any type of legal proceeding,[220] the commentary to Rule 1.7(b) notes that in criminal proceedings,

---

217. For an analysis of the advantages and disadvantages of multiple representation, *see* Teresa Stanton Collett, *The Promise and Perils of Multiple Representation*, 16 REV. OF LITIG. 567 (Summer 1997).

218. MODEL RULES OF PROF'L CONDUCT R. 1.7(b) ("A lawyer shall not represent a client if the representation of that client may be materially limited by the lawyer's responsibilities to another client or to a third person, or by the lawyer's own interests, unless: (1) the lawyer reasonably believes the representation will not be adversely affected; and (2) the client consents after consultation. When representation of multiple clients in a single matter is undertaken, the consultation shall include explanation of the implications of the common representation and the advantages and risks involved.").

219. According to the comments to Rule 1.7(b), when a "disinterested lawyer would conclude that the client should not agree to the representation," the lawyer cannot ethically ask the client to consent or provide any representation based on that consent. The critical questions the lawyer must consider are "the likelihood that a conflict will eventuate and, if it does, whether it will materially interfere with the lawyer's independent professional judgment in considering alternatives or foreclose courses of action that reasonably should be pursued on behalf of the client." *Id.*

220. The comments to Rule 1.7(b) list some examples of situations in which an impermissible conflict of interest might arise: where there is a "substantial discrepancy in the parties' testimony," where there is "incompatibility in positions in relation

the "potential for conflict of interest . . . is so grave that ordinarily a lawyer should decline to represent more than one codefendant."[221]

Even if a lawyer determines that joint representation is appropriate under the applicable professional ethics rules, he or she may still be subject to disqualification at various stages of the proceeding on grounds of conflict of interest.[222] Courts have broad discretion to disqualify lawyers on the grounds of actual, or even serious potential, conflict,[223] although the conflict must be explicit and specific to justify disqualification[224] and

---

to an opposing party," or when "there are substantially different possibilities of settlement of the claims or liabilities in question." *Id.* Furthermore, an obvious conflict of interest exists if the lawyer's judgment may be influenced by concern over future employment by the corporation. *See* United States v. Rodriguez, 929 F.2d 747, 749 (1st Cir. 1991); United States v. Allen, 831 F.2d 1487, 1496-97 (9th Cir.), *cert. denied*, 487 U.S. 1237 (1988); United States v. Bernstein, 533 F.2d 775, 788 (2d Cir.), *cert. denied*, 429 U.S. 998 (1976).

221. *See also* Cuyler v. Sullivan, 446 U.S. 335, 348 (1980) (noting that a "possible conflict inheres in almost every instance of multiple representation").

222. *See* United States v. Malpiedi, 62 F.3d 465, 470 (2d Cir. 1995) ("The government can itself seek to disqualify defense counsel because of a conflict. Indeed, it frequently does so.") (citations omitted). This is true even though disqualification proceedings may be subject to tactical manipulation. *See* United States v. Register, 182 F.3d 820, 833 (11th Cir. 1999) (although "[s]trategic maneuvering by the government to disqualify defense attorneys" is a possibility, district court still given broad discretion to decide the issue), *cert. denied*, 530 U.S. 1250 (2000).

223. Wheat v. United States, 486 U.S. 153, 164 (1988) (although "[t]he District Court must recognize a presumption in favor of petitioner's counsel of choice, . . . that presumption may be overcome not only by a demonstration of actual conflict but by a showing of a serious potential conflict"). This standard applies to both the pre-indictment and post-indictment stages of a proceeding. *See, e.g., id.* at 162 (post-indictment); United States v. Moscony, 927 F.2d 742, 750 (3d Cir.) (same), *cert. denied*, 501 U.S. 1211 (1991); *In re* Grand Jury Proceedings, 859 F.2d 1021,1024 (1st Cir. 1988) ("Although *Wheat* involved the Sixth Amendment rights of a criminal defendant, we believe that the standards enunciated in *Wheat* may also apply in the grand jury context, at least to some extent . . . . The showing that must be made in order to burden a grand jury witness's right to choose certain counsel *need be no greater* than when the question is one of restricting the Sixth Amendment rights possessed by criminal defendants.") (citation omitted, emphasis added); *In re* Feb. 1977 Grand Jury, 581 F.2d 1262, 1264 (7th Cir. 1978) ("[I]n the context of a grand jury proceeding, a disqualification motion may be granted without proof of the existence of an actual conflict of interest . . . when the possibility of a conflict becomes great enough. . . . ").

224. *See In re* Grand Jury Proceedings, 859 F.2d at 1026 (reversing district court's disqualification order where the court "did not identify any *specific* conflict, actual *or* potential. . . . Our concern is that . . . a court could make the requisite *Wheat* finding

the government bears a "heavy burden" in this regard.[225] Furthermore, disqualification may occur even where a client has knowingly waived the right to conflict-free counsel.[226] As the Supreme Court has stated, "The district court must be allowed substantial latitude in refusing waivers of conflict of interest not only in those rare cases where an actual conflict may be demonstrated before trial, but in the more common cases where a potential for conflict exists which may or may not burgeon into an actual conflict as the trial progresses."[227] Finally, in the post-indictment context, Federal Rule of Criminal Procedure 44(c) requires the district court to make an independent inquiry into the possibility of a conflict of interest in cases of joint representation and to "take such measures as may be appropriate to protect each defendant's right to counsel,"[228] including, where necessary, ordering that co-defendants be separately represented.[229]

Even if a lawyer is not disqualified, it should be kept in mind that multiple representation may be the basis for later claims of ineffective assistance of counsel under the Sixth Amendment.[230] Although multiple representation is not an automatic violation of the defendant's Sixth Amendment right to effective assistance of counsel, a defendant may make an ineffective assistance of counsel claim where, for example, similar concessions are achieved for all clients, even though some clients are less culpable than others.[231]

---

solely on tenuous inferential relationships. We believe that this is contrary to the holding in *Wheat*, and that generally there must be a direct link between the clients of an attorney—or at least some concrete evidence that one client . . . has information about another client . . . —before the right to counsel of choice is barred by disqualification.") (emphasis in original). *But see* United States v. Lanoue, 137 F.3d 656, 664 (1st Cir. 1998) ("Although the facts of this case may well reach the outer limits of 'potential conflict,' the potential for conflict is a matter that is uniquely factual and presents a special dilemma for trial courts.").

225. *Id.*

226. *See, e.g.,* Wheat, 486 U.S. at 162; United States v. Coleman, 997 F.2d 1101, 1104 (5th Cir. 1993), *cert. denied*, 510 U.S. 1077 (1994); *Moscony*, 927 F.2d at 750.

227. Wheat, 486 U.S. at 163.

228. Fed. R. Crim. P. 44(c). The Advisory Committee Notes to Rule 44(c) state that the inquiry is necessary even though attorneys are ethically required to make an independent and objective evaluation of the conflict issues.

229. *See* Wheat, 486 U.S. at 161.

230. Holloway v. Arkansas, 435 U.S. 475, 482-83 (1978).

231. *See, e.g.,* United States v. Swartz, 975 F.2d 1042, 1046 (4th Cir. 1992) (actual conflict of interest existed where defense counsel argued at sentencing hearing that

Furthermore, prosecutors typically are mistrustful of multiple representation. Particularly when the corporation's in-house lawyer, regular outside counsel or outside counsel conducting an internal investigation defends both the company and its employees, prosecutors may not view such counsel as independent, and may even view the common representation as perpetuation of the conspiracy they are investigating. This may make it difficult to negotiate with the prosecutors on settlement or any other matter. In addition, the government may exacerbate the situation by issuing "target letters" indicating that some—but not all—of the employees represented by a single lawyer are targets of the investigation and likely to be indicted. This will require a reshuffling of the representation, with all of the stresses attendant to such an endeavor—including whether the lawyer will be able to cross-examine a former client, can utilize privileged information obtained prior to the reshuffling, or may even face rule 44(c) disqualification entirely. These considerations make multiple representation potentially unattractive and require a careful examination of the relative legal positions of the affected employees *before* deciding which ones may safely be represented by the same lawyer.

Finally, should the corporation choose to advance the costs of legal representation for its individual employees requiring representation in parallel proceedings, great care should be taken before deciding to discontinue the payments. An arrangement whereby representation ceases once an employee chooses to cooperate with the government may well be viewed as coercive.[232]

---

both clients were equally culpable); Thomas v. Foltz, 818 F.2d 476, 478 (6th Cir.) (lawyer who persuaded three clients to plead guilty in order to satisfy a prosecutor's "package deal only" policy rendered constitutionally ineffective assistance to an arguably less culpable member of the trio), *cert. denied*, 484 U.S. 870 (1987); *see also* Allen, 831 F.2d at 1497 ("[N]o one should be represented by an attorney who is making him the 'fall guy' by design.") (citation omitted). Because of this possibility, it has been recommended that counsel for the corporation represent employees only after interviews and a determination as to potential culpability. Gary G. Lynch & Douglas M. Fuchs, *Conducting Internal Investigations of Possible Corporate Wrongdoing*, 943 PLI/Corp. 615, 628 (June 1996).

232. *See* Pirillo v. Takiff, 341 A.2d 896, 903 (Pa. 1975) (criticizing the Fraternal Order of Police for hiring attorney who would withdraw from representation of police officers once they appeared to be considering cooperation with the government), *cert. denied*, 423 U.S. 1083 (1976).

I. *Joint Defense Agreement and Protection of Confidential Exchanges*

Where several defense counsel represent multiple parties in criminal or civil proceedings, counsel should be aware of the protection afforded by what is commonly called the joint defense doctrine.[233] The joint defense doctrine is essentially an exception to the rule that no privilege is available for material shared with a third party.[234] It arises most frequently when criminal co-defendants agree to coordinate their defenses, but it has been applied to civil litigants as well.[235] The joint defense privilege generally reflects a tension between two competing interests: the confidentiality needed to protect the sanctity of the attorney-client relationship and society's countervailing right to hear "everyman's evidence" to assist the judicial system in its truth-seeking role.[236] In examining the availability of the joint defense doctrine, courts attempt to balance these two concerns.[237]

---

233. *See* Continental Oil Co. v. United States, 330 F.2d 347 (9th Cir. 1974); Hunydee v. United States, 355 F.2d 183 (9th Cir. 1965); *see also* United States v. Schwimmer, 892 F.2d 237 (2d Cir. 1989), *cert. denied*, 502 U.S. 810 (1991); United States v. McPartlin, 595 F.2d 1321 (7th Cir.), *cert. denied*, 444 U.S. 833 (1979); *In re* Grand Jury Subpoena Duces Tecum, 406 F. Supp. 381 (S.D.N.Y. 1975). Some courts indicate that the joint defense privilege is "more properly identified as the 'common interest rule.'" *See, e.g.,* Schwimmer, 892 F.2d at 243. Other courts have distinguished between the terms, with the joint defense privilege as a specific version of a more general "common interest" privilege. *See In re* Sealed Case, 29 F.3d 715, 719 (D.C. Cir. 1994).

234. *In re* Regents of the Univ. of Cal., 101 F.3d 1386, 1390-91 (Fed. Cir. 1996), *cert. denied*, 520 U.S. 1193 (1997); *In re* Grand Jury Subpoenas, 902 F.2d 244, 248-49 (4th Cir. 1990).

235. *See In re* Grand Jury Subpoenas, 902 F.2d at 248-49 (noting extension of joint defense privilege to various situations including co-litigants in civil case; information shared by companies summoned before a grand jury; plaintiffs pursuing lawsuits in different jurisdictions; and defendants sued in separate actions); *see also In re* Regents of the Univ. of Cal., 101 F.3d at 1390-91 (extending privilege to patent prosecution); United States v. DeNardi Corp., 167 F.R.D. 680, 686 (S.D. Cal. 1996) (privilege can apply "whether the jointly interested persons are defendants or plaintiffs, and whether the litigation or potential litigation is civil or criminal") (citations omitted).

236. *In re* Grand Jury, 406 F. Supp. at 386.

237. *See, e.g., In re* Grand Jury Subpoena Duces Tecum, 112 F.3d 910, 918-23 (8th Cir.), *cert. denied*, 521 U.S. 1105 (1997); Hewlett-Packard Co. v. Bausch & Lomb, Inc., 115 F.R.D. 308, 309 (N.D. Cal. 1987), *aff'd in part and vacated in part on other grounds*, 882 F.2d 1556 (1989); *In re* Grand Jury, 406 F. Supp. at 385-86.

The decisional law on joint defense agreements flows from the seminal case of *Continental Oil Co. v. United States*.[238] In that case, counsel for employees of Continental and Standard Oil Companies debriefed their clients after they testified before a grand jury, and then exchanged the information in an effort to discern the nature and scope of the grand jury probe. Upon learning of the memoranda, the government subpoenaed both the companies and their lawyers.[239] The Ninth Circuit rejected the government's argument that any privilege the material might have enjoyed was lost following the exchange among counsel.[240] The court further rejected the government's assertion that a joint defense privilege applies only to post-indictment proceedings.[241]

Subsequently, in *Hunydee v. United States*,[242] the Ninth Circuit spelled out the cornerstone of the doctrine:

> [W]here two or more persons who are subject to possible indictment in connection with the same transactions make confidential statements to their attorneys, these statements, even though they are exchanged between attorneys, should be privileged to the extent that they concern common issues and are intended to facilitate representation in possible subsequent proceedings.[243]

Hunydee involved a husband and wife who were being prosecuted for income tax evasion.[244] At a joint conference, the husband agreed to plead guilty and take all the blame for the crime.[245] He later sought to have this statement excluded at his trial on the grounds of attorney-client privilege.[246] The government tried to argue that the material exchanged among co-defendants should not receive the benefits of the joint defense doctrine as articulated in *Continental Oil*, because it did not concern "trial strategy or defenses."[247] The court rejected the government's argument on the

---

238. 330 F.2d 347 (9th Cir. 1964).
239. *Id.*
240. *Id.* at 350.
241. *Id.*
242. 355 F.2d 183 (9th Cir. 1965).
243. *Id.* at 185.
244. *Id.* at 184.
245. *Id.*
246. *Id.*
247. *Id.* at 184.

grounds that the information exchanged in *Continental Oil* was "general information which was needed ... in order to facilitate representation [in grand jury proceedings]," and was not limited to "trial strategy or defenses," and held that the husband's admissions remained privileged under the joint defense doctrine.[248]

These principles have been affirmed in subsequent cases, including the oft-cited *United States v. Schwimmer*.[249] In *Schwimmer*, the court recognized that the joint defense privilege extends to communications made in confidence to an accountant hired by a co-defendant's lawyer. The court held that the joint defense privilege "serves to protect the confidentiality of communications passing from one party to the attorney for another party where a joint defense effort or strategy has been decided upon and undertaken. . . ."[250]

Continental Oil and its progeny define the core elements of the joint defense privilege: (1) the parties (usually co-defendants) must share a *common interest*; (2) the information must have been exchanged in order *to facilitate their representation*; and (3) the material must be *confidential*.[251]

1. Necessity for a Common Interest

This element is the heart of the joint defense doctrine. The parties must be pursuing a common or mutual legal goal in order for the doctrine to apply. It is, however, unlikely that co-defendants or co-litigants will have interests that are identical in every respect. This prong, therefore, requires an examination into how diverse and potentially conflicting the parties' interests are.

Parties seeking the protection of the joint defense privilege can find comfort in the formulation of "common" interest announced by the Seventh Circuit in *United States v. McPartlin*:[252] "[t]he privilege protects pooling of information for any defense purpose common to the participating

---

248. *Id*. at 185.

249. 892 F.2d 237 (2d Cir. 1989), *cert. denied*, 502 U.S. 810 (1991).

250. *Id*. at 243 (citing United States v. Bay State Ambulance & Hosp. Rental Serv., Inc., 874 F.2d 20, 28 (1st Cir. 1989)).

251. Some cases have stated the third element somewhat differently as "the privilege has not been waived." *See, e.g., In re* Bevill, Bresler & Schulman Asset Mgmt. Corp., 805 F.2d 120, 126 (3d Cir. 1986).

252. 595 F.2d 1321 (7th Cir.), *cert. denied*, 444 U.S. 833 (1979).

defendants."[253] The *McPartlin* court found that the defendants' mutual interest in discrediting a government witness constituted a common interest, even though the defendants' various strategies diverged in other respects.[254] Consequently, statements made by one defendant to the investigator[255] for another defendant were protected by the attorney-client privilege, and the defendant could not introduce the co-defendant's confidential statement at their joint trial.[256] The significance of *McPartlin* is its conclusion that some common interest is enough to satisfy the joint defense doctrine—the strategies of the co-defendants need not be uniform to be "common."[257]

Certain courts have found "common" interests, despite recognizing that the co-parties' interests could erupt into litigation in the future.[258] This is so because the inquiry focuses upon the relationship of the parties at the time the material is exchanged, not on subsequent events.[259] As a result, courts have acknowledged that while holders of a joint defense privilege may make for "unsteady bedfellows,"[260] this is not a basis for withholding the privilege.

Nonetheless, no common interest will be found to exist—and no joint defense privilege is available—if the parties' interests are so antagonistic that they are, in reality, adversaries—such as when counsel for one defendant elicits a confession from a co-defendant, exonerating the first.[261] Fur-

---

253. *Id.* at 1337.

254. *Id.* at 1336.

255. The court found that the investigator was the agent of the co-defendant's lawyer, and that communications to the investigator therefore fell within the ambit of the attorney-client privilege. *Id.* at 1337.

256. *Id.*

257. *See also In re* Mortgage Realty & Trust, 212 B.R. 649, 653 (C.D. Cal. Bankr. 1997) (finding common interest between debtor and committee of unsecured creditors); Eisenberg v. Gagnon, 766 F.2d 770, 787-88 (3d Cir.) ("Communications to an attorney to establish a common defense strategy are privileged even though the attorney represents another client with some adverse interests."), *cert. denied*, 474 U.S. 946 (1985).

258. *In re* Grand Jury, 406 F. Supp. at 392.

259. *See* John Morrell & Co. v. Local Union 304A, 913 F.2d 544, 555-56 (8th Cir. 1990), *cert. denied*, 500 U.S. 905 (1991); *In re* LTV Sec. Litig., 89 F.R.D. 595, 604-05 (N.D. Tex. 1981).

260. *See, e.g., In re* Grand Jury, 406 F. Supp. at 392; *see also* Eisenberg, 766 F.2d at 787; McPartlin, 595 F.2d at 1336.

261. *See* North River Ins. Co. v. Columbia Cas. Co., No. 90 Civ. 2518 (MJL),1995 WL 5792, at *4 (S.D.N.Y. Jan. 5, 1995) (communications between parties with antago-

ther, no common interest will be found where one party's alleged interest is vague or generic.[262]

2. Exchange of Information to Facilitate Representation

This second prong of the joint defense doctrine assesses the parties' motives for pooling their confidential information.[263] This requirement is perhaps best phrased in the negative: the information must not have been exchanged "for the purpose of allowing unlimited publication and use, but rather, ... for the limited purpose of assisting in their common cause."[264] Realistically, the self-interest of co-defendants would seem to make this requirement superfluous. Perhaps all the courts truly seek is an assurance that the cooperation was motivated by legal rather than purely commercial concerns.[265]

---

nistic interests not privileged); *see also* Government of the Virgin Islands v. Joseph, 685 F.2d 857, 862 (3d Cir. 1982) (distinguishing *McPartlin* on the amount of antagonism present and noting that in *Hunydee,* the co-defendant had made the statement in question to his own lawyer, whereas in the instant case, the defendant communicated directly with his co-defendants' counsel).

262. For example, the Eighth Circuit held during the Clinton Administration that Hillary Clinton and the White House as an institution did not share a common interest for purposes of the joint defense doctrine. *In re* Grand Jury Subpoena Duces Tecum, 112 F.3d at 922-23. The court noted that Ms. Clinton's interest was in avoiding prosecution, while the White House had only its asserted interest in avoiding misunderstandings and not leaking information, which does not satisfy the requirements of the doctrine. *Id.*

263. *See, e.g.,* Hunydee, 355 F.2d at 185 (information relating to grand jury proceedings protected by the joint defense doctrine to the extent that it is "intended to facilitate representation in the possible subsequent proceedings").

264. Wilson P. Abraham Constr. Corp. v. Armco Steel Corp., 559 F.2d 250, 253 (5th Cir. 1977); Burton v. R.J. Reynolds Tobacco Co., 167 F.R.D. 134, 139 (D. Kan. 1996) (citation omitted).

265. *See In re* Subpoena Duces Tecum, No. M 8-85 MHD, 1997 WL 599399, at *4 (S.D.N.Y. Sept. 26, 1997) ("it appears that [parties] must possess not merely a common commercial interest, but 'a common legal interest'") (citations omitted); *see also* United States v. Aramony, 88 F.3d 1369, 1392 (4th Cir. 1996) (privilege not applicable to development of defense for individual defendant that would also protect organization's reputation because "preservation of one's reputation is not a legal matter"), *cert. denied,* 520 U.S. 1239 (1997).

Few parties lose the joint defense privilege solely for failing to meet this prong.[266] That is not to say, however, that defendants never lose the privilege for want of this element.[267] Accordingly, parties to a joint defense agreement should manifest their intent that the sole purpose for exchanging information is to facilitate their joint representation.

3. Requirement of Confidentiality

Because the joint defense doctrine is an application of the attorney-client privilege,[268] the requirement of confidentiality is critical to its successful assertion.[269] Where there is consultation among defense counsel and their respective clients, allied in a common legal cause, it may be reasonably inferred that the discussions and any corollary disclosures are intended to be confidential within the group. If this is the case and counsel can demonstrate that the disclosures would not have been made except for the purpose of obtaining or advancing legal representation, then it is

---

266. *See, e.g.,* Aramony, 88 F.3d at 1392 (without discussing requirement that the exchange facilitate representation, court declined to apply privilege because no common interest); United States v. Keplinger, 776 F.2d 678, 701 (7th Cir. 1985) (without discussing requirement that the exchange facilitate representation, court declined to apply joint defense privilege because defendant failed to meet common interest and confidentiality prongs), *cert. denied,* 476 U.S. 1183 (1986); Government of the Virgin Islands, 685 F.2d at 862 (same); SCM Corp. v. Xerox Corp., 70 F.R.D. at 513 (distinguishing *Continental*'s finding that the exchange had been intended to facilitate representation on the grounds that the present defendants lacked a common interest).

267. *See* Bay State Ambulance, 874 F.2d at 29 (holding that one can infer that a document is not prepared as part of joint defense if defendant did not consult or even inform his own lawyer of its existence or transmittal to co-defendant); Polycast Tech. Corp. v. Uniroyal, Inc., 125 F.R.D. 47, 50 (S.D.N.Y. 1989) (declining to apply the joint defense privilege because defendants had failed to demonstrate that they reasonably believed their statements were made "in furtherance[] of their joint defense") (quoting *In re* Grand Jury, 406 F. Supp. at 389).

268. While the joint defense privilege is an extension of the attorney-client privilege, it also may be invoked in connection with the work-product doctrine. Haines v. Liggett Group, Inc., 975 F.2d 81, 94 (3d Cir. 1992) (citation omitted). Like the attorney-client privilege, the joint defense privilege does not apply in certain instances, *e.g.,* the crime-fraud exception. *Id.* at 94-95.

269. Bay State Ambulance, 874 F.2d at 28 (citations omitted).

likely that a claim of privilege will be upheld.[270] As one court stated, a communication will be found privileged "if it is intended to remain confidential and was made under such circumstances that it was reasonably expected and understood to be confidential."[271]

The case law in connection with the confidentiality element shows that the courts engage in two lines of inquiry. The first analysis is subjective and asks whether the co-defendants intended the pooled information to remain confidential. The second line of reasoning looks at the objective circumstances surrounding the materials' purported confidentiality.[272] For a party to succeed on both the subjective and objective prongs, it must demonstrate a "conscious and conscientious joint defense undertaking."[273]

The subjective inquiry into the confidentiality element presents another area in which a written joint defense agreement might prove helpful in memorializing the parties' intent that all information exchanged should remain confidential, thereby showing at least a "conscious" undertaking. The more important aspect of the confidentiality requirement is the objective manifestations of the parties' intent and the surrounding circumstances as indicia of "conscientiousness." Courts will almost certainly pay more attention to what the co-defendants do rather than what they say, regardless of whether they say it in an executed agreement.[274] Courts place

---

270. McPartlin, 595 F.2d at 1335-37 (the defendant's statements to an investigator who was acting as an agent for a co-defendant's lawyer were inadmissible because of joint defense privilege); Hunydee, 355 F.2d at 185 (confidential statements made by two or more persons to their lawyers where such persons are subject to possible indictment in connection with the same transactions should be privileged to the extent that such statements concern common issues and are intended to facilitate representation and possible subsequent proceedings); *Continental Oil,* 330 F.2d at 350 (exchange of debriefing memoranda between counsel of employees interviewed after their appearance before the grand jury did not destroy the privilege).

271. United States v. Melvin, 650 F.2d 641, 645 (5th Cir. 1981); *see also* Government of Virgin Islands, 685 F.2d at 862 (employing this analysis).

272. *See* Bay State Ambulance, 874 F.2d at 28 ("In addressing whether a given communication was meant to be confidential, what 'the client *reasonably* understood' is the 'key question.'") (citation omitted, emphasis in original).

273. *In re* Grand Jury, 406 F. Supp. at 391.

274. *See, e.g., In re* Regents of the Univ. of Cal., 101 F.3d at 1390 (finding joint defense privilege despite absence of written agreement to that effect); SIG Swiss Indus. Co. v. Fres-Co Sys., USA, Inc., No. Civ. A 91-0699, 1993 WL 82286, at *1 (E.D. Pa. Mar. 17, 1993) (same).

significant emphasis on the reasonableness of the parties' beliefs and actions.[275]

Given that parties seeking protection under the joint defense doctrine may make for "unsteady bedfellows,"[276] signatories to joint defense agreements should be aware that if they face co-defendants in a subsequent civil suit, the possibility exists that information previously exchanged pursuant to the doctrine may lose some of its protection from disclosure. It is therefore possible that the pooled information could be used by a co-defendant against a former co-defendant in future civil litigation,[277] even though the information would remain privileged from disclosure to strangers.[278] As one commentator has stated,

> [t]he traditional rule with regard to the joint defense doctrine is that the privilege does not prevent one former joint defendant from disclosing statements made by another former joint defendant in a suit . . . between those two parties. The statements remain protected vís-a-vìs "strangers"; but they are not protected in a suit between the co-defendants themselves.[279]

With the exception of this *inter sese* context, the joint defense privilege cannot be waived without the consent of all of its holders.[280]

---

275. *See, e.g.,* Sheet Metal Workers Int'l Ass'n v. Sweeney, 29 F.3d 120, 124 (4th Cir. 1994) (no reasonable expectation of confidentiality where defendant's actions were inconsistent with attorney-client relationship, as, for example, when defendant asked his supposed attorney to leave the room during a meeting with the government); *see also Melvin,* 650 F.2d at 645-46 (disclosure of confidential material in the presence of third party who has not joined the "defense team" contravenes reasonable expectation of confidentiality).

276. *In re* Grand Jury, 406 F. Supp. at 392.

277. *See, e.g.,* Ageloff v. Noranda, Inc., 936 F. Supp. 72, 76 (D.R.I. 1996) ("The law is well-settled that a joint defense privilege is waived in a subsequent controversy between the joint defendants.") (citations omitted); United States v. Moscony, 697 F. Supp. 888, 894 (E.D. Pa. 1988), *aff'd,* 927 F.2d 742 (3d Cir.), *cert. denied,* 501 U.S. 1211 (1991); *In re* Grand Jury, 406 F. Supp. at 389.

278. Query the value of the privilege as against third parties, however, if the material is revealed in open court.

279. John E. Sexton, *A Post-Upjohn Consideration of the Corporate Attorney-Client Privilege,* 57 N.Y.U. L. Rev. 443, 512 (1982).

280. *E.g.,* John Morrell & Co., 913 F.2d at 556.

4. Remedies for Breach of Joint Defense Privilege

In *United States v. Melvin*,[281] notwithstanding a pre-trial breach of the joint defense privilege by one defendant, the court concluded that absent prejudice, a breach will not result in the dismissal of the other defendants. In that case, one of the defendants participated in joint meetings with co-defendants and lawyers after agreeing to become an informant for the prosecution. The defendant provided privileged information to the government prosecution, including tapes of strategy sessions among defense lawyers and their clients. The district court found a violation of the Sixth Amendment and dismissed the indictment. The Fifth Circuit reversed, concluding that the co-defendants were not entitled to any remedy absent a showing of "prejudice." According to the court, even if the co-defendants could demonstrate prejudice, the trial judge should fashion a remedy short of dismissal, such as suppression of the evidence obtained as a result of the breach.[282]

Because of this limited protection, defense counsel should seek ways to prevent, limit, or highlight a breach of the joint defense privilege. If counsel discovers that a co-defendant has become a government witness, it is important to flag this issue immediately. Counsel can seek an order impounding any privileged material in the possession of the co-defendant or the lawyer. Counsel can also list all information being shared so that if a breach occurs, evidence to suppress can be readily identified. Finally, counsel should request a hearing to determine the extent to which privileged information has already been utilized or may be utilized in a subsequent proceeding.

J. *Protection Against Disclosure*

In the course of parallel proceedings, counsel should remain aware of the possibility that information provided to a government agency either voluntarily or in response to a subpoena, as well as information subpoenaed by a grand jury, could potentially be disclosed to various entities.

---

281. 650 F.2d 641 (5th Cir. 1981).

282. *Melvin*, 650 F.2d at 644; *see also Schwimmer*, 892 F.2d at 245 (remanding case and implying that some form of remedy or sanction is available if prejudice is shown).

1. Information Provided to Government Agencies

At the beginning of a government agency investigation, the agency will subpoena documents or request the corporation and/or its employees to turn the documents over voluntarily. In deciding whether to challenge the subpoena or disclose documents voluntarily, counsel and corporate officers must consider the freedom with which the agency will share the information with other agencies, private parties, or a grand jury.

As a general matter, information provided to one agency, whether voluntarily or pursuant to summons or subpoena, generally will be made available to other agencies, including state agencies, or to law enforcement agencies such as the DOJ upon request.[283] It is well-nigh impossible to obtain agreements from any agency officials that would prevent the transfer of information between law enforcement agencies, or to even require notice to the submitter that a transfer has taken, or will take, place. Certain government agencies have established specific procedures for addressing requests for confidential treatment of submitted information. Counsel should always check the rules and procedures for an agency that requests or subpoenas information and documents. Generally, government agencies are limited by statute in their ability to obtain information. Moreover, in order to enforce any subpoenas, the agency must first file an action in federal district court.

Counsel should also keep in mind that private parties can request agency information under the Freedom of Information Act (FOIA).[284] Federal agencies promulgate regulations implementing procedures under FOIA with respect to granting third parties access to information provided to the agency. The SEC's FOIA regulations are particularly illustrative.[285] The two SEC FOIA provisions that are most important for maintaining the confidentiality of corporate records submitted to a government agency are Exemption 4, covering confidential "commercial or financial information," and Exemption 7, covering "investigatory records compiled for law enforcement purposes."[286] Counsel should be mindful that the latter exemption ceases to have effect at the conclusion of an investigation,[287]

---

283. For a full treatment of this issue, the reader should review chapter 8, "Disclosure of Results of Internal Investigation to the Government or to Other Third Parties."
284. 5 U.S.C. § 552.
285. *See* Confidential Treatment Procedures Under FOIA, 17 C.F.R. § 200.83.
286. 5 U.S.C. §§ 552(c)(4), (c)(7).
287. *In re* Subpoenas Duces Tecum, 738 F.2d 1367, 1374 (D.C. Cir. 1984).

and the former exemption becomes more difficult to assert as time passes. Accordingly, it is always wise to attempt to have the agency return materials submitted by the corporation (and any copies that have been made) promptly at the conclusion of the investigation.

Finally, a grand jury can issue a subpoena for government agency material. Subpoenas issued by the grand jury can be broad, and standards of relevance or materiality, which may have some application in civil discovery, do not apply.[288] Consequently, a grand jury can obtain the information and documents in possession of the government agency independently through the use of a subpoena.[289] An equally important consideration is whether testimony provided in a civil deposition—pursuant to a protective order—can be obtained by the grand jury. The answer, according to the Fourth, Ninth, and Eleventh Circuits, is in the affirmative: A civil protective order cannot be used to shield discovery materials that are sought by a grand jury subpoena.[290] The Second Circuit, however, has declined to adopt this per se rule; instead, it has stated that the government must establish "some extraordinary circumstance or compelling need" to obtain materials subject to an existing protective order.[291] The First Circuit rejects both these approaches in favor of a rule providing that a grand jury subpoena ordinarily trumps a civil protective order "unless the person seeking to avoid the subpoena can demonstrate the existence of exceptional circumstances that clearly favor subordinating the subpoena to the protective order."[292]

---

288. *See* United States v. Dionisio, 410 U.S. 1, 9-13 (1973); Branzburg v. Hayes, 408 U.S. 665, 688 (1972).

289. Counsel must be mindful that a failure to continue objections to a grand jury subpoena may result in a court later ruling that materials disclosed pursuant to that subpoena were voluntarily revealed. *See* Westinghouse Elec. Corp. v. Republic of Philippines, 951 F.2d 1414, 1427 n.14 (3d Cir. 1991).

290. *In re* Grand Jury Subpoena, 62 F.3d 1222, 1226 (9th Cir. 1995); *In re* Grand Jury Proceedings, 995 F.2d 1013, 1015 (11th Cir. 1993); *In re* Grand Jury Subpoena (Under Seal), 836 F.2d 1468 (4th Cir.), *cert. denied*, 487 U.S. 1240 (1988).

291. Martindell v. International Tel. & Tel. Corp., 594 F.2d 291, 296 (2d Cir. 1979). The Second Circuit reaffirmed its approach in *In re* Grand Jury Subpoenas Duces Tecum, 945 F.2d 1221, 1225 (2d Cir. 1991). Relatedly, the Second Circuit has held that an unwilling non-party witness cannot be forced to testify in reliance on a protective order. Andover Data Servs. v. Statistical Tabulating Corp., 876 F.2d 1080, 1084 ("[a] court in a civil action is simply without the means to fashion a sufficiently durable safeguard for the full protection of the fifth amendment rights of a reluctant non-party witness. . . . ").

292. *In re* Grand Jury Subpoena, 138 F.3d 442, 445 (1st Cir.), *cert. denied*, 524 U.S. 939 (1998).

2. Information Obtained by Grand Juries

Another primary concern for corporate counsel is whether information provided to the grand jury will be released to the public or to another federal or state agency. The requirement of grand jury secrecy is embodied in rule 6(e) of the Federal Rules of Criminal Procedure, which provides that grand jurors and those who work with the grand jury "shall not disclose matters occurring before the grand jury, except as otherwise provided for in these rules."[293]

In theory, this rule of secrecy makes it very difficult to legitimately transfer grand jury material to administrative agencies. Federal Rule of Criminal Procedure 6(e)(3)(A), however, provides for disclosure to: "(i) an attorney for the government for use in the performance of such attorney's duty; and (ii) to such government personnel . . . as are deemed necessary by an attorney for the government to assist an attorney for the government in the performance of such attorney's duty to enforce federal criminal law." Rule 54(c) defines "attorney for the government" as "the Attorney General, a United States Attorney, [and] an authorized assistant of the United States Attorney. . . ." The Advisory Committee Notes (Notes) make clear that the Assistant Attorney General and other Justice Department lawyers also are included within this definition.[294]

The August 1985 amendments to rule 6(e) permit the disclosure of grand jury materials to appropriate state or municipal officials for the purpose of enforcement of state criminal statutes "when permitted by a court at the request of an attorney for the government, upon a showing that such matters may disclose a violation of state criminal law. . . ."[295] This amendment did away with the standard of "particularized need" previously required of state officials for access to grand jury materials.[296] However, according to the Notes, it is the policy of the DOJ to seek disclosure on behalf of state officials under rule 6(e)(3)(C)(iv) only upon approval of the Assistant Attorney General in charge of the Criminal Division. The

---

293. Fed. R. Crim. P. 6(e)(2).

294. Note that federal administrative attorneys, including attorneys at the SEC, are not considered "attorneys for the government" under these provisions. Bradley v. Fairfax, 634 F.2d 1126, 1130 (8th Cir. 1980); *In re* Grand Jury Investigation, 414 F. Supp. 74, 76 (S.D.N.Y. 1976).

295. Fed. R. Crim. P. 6(e)(3)(C)(iv).

296. *See* Illinois v. Abbott & Assoc., Inc., 460 U.S. 557 (1983) (district court must weigh whether the need for disclosure to a governmental body is greater than the need for continued secrecy).

Notes state: "There is no intention, by virtue of this amendment, to have federal grand juries act as an arm of the state."

Although this amendment relaxes the standards for the release of grand jury materials to state officials pursuing criminal actions, it does not affect access to those materials in civil cases. In *United States v. Sells Engineering, Inc.*,[297] the Supreme Court held that rule 6(e)(3)(A)(i) does not entitle Civil Division lawyers in the DOJ to automatic disclosure of matters occurring before a grand jury for use in a civil suit. The Court in *Sells* upheld the "strong showing of a particularized need" standard enunciated in *Illinois v. Abbott*.[298] The Court concluded that in order to gain access to rule 6(e) material, the Justice Department lawyers would have to obtain a court order under paragraph (C)(i) of the rule after making such a showing.[299]

However, a lawyer who conducts a criminal prosecution may make continued use of materials received as a result of a grand jury investigation during the civil phase of the same dispute without obtaining a court order under rule 6(e). In *United States v. John Doe, Inc.*,[300] the Supreme Court held that rule 6(e) forbids only the "disclosure" of material by the government attorney, and when the same attorney is involved in the civil phase of a dispute, a review of the material does not constitute a disclosure.[301]

With respect to disclosure of grand jury materials to private parties, the Supreme Court has held that the party seeking disclosure must show that (1) the material is needed to avoid a possible injustice in another judicial proceeding; (2) the need for disclosure is greater than the need for continued secrecy; and (3) the request is structured to cover only material so needed.[302] Given the public interest in maintaining the secrecy of grand

---

297. 463 U.S. 418, 443 (1983).

298. *Id.* at 420; *accord In re* Grand Jury Proceedings, 851 F.2d 860, 865 (6th Cir. 1988); *In re* Sealed Case, 801 F.2d 1379 (D.C. Cir. 1986).

299. Sells Eng'g, 463 U.S. at 420.

300. 481 U.S. 102 (1987).

301. *Id.* at 107-08; *see* Pilon v. United States, 73 F.3d 1111, 1120 (D.C. Cir. 1996) (emphasizing the limited scope of the holding in *John Doe*); *see also* DiLeo v. Commissioner, 959 F.2d 16, 21 (2d Cir.) (permitting IRS agent to attend civil trial and citing *John Doe* for the proposition that "a government employee who has participated in a criminal prosecution may participate in the civil phase of the dispute without obtaining a court order to do so under Rule 6(e)"), *cert. denied*, 506 U.S. 868 (1992).

302. *See* Sells, 463 U.S. at 443; Douglas Oil Co. v. Petrol Stops N.W., 441 U.S. 211, 222 (1979). *But see In re* Grand Jury Proceedings, 813 F. Supp. 1451, 1466 n.11 (D. Colo. 1992) ("there is no indication that Rule 6(e) contemplates disclosure to the public").

jury proceedings, this showing must be made regardless of whether the grand jury's operations are ongoing or have terminated.[303] It also should be noted that at least one circuit has held that the government may "seek release of grand jury materials on behalf of others, including private litigants."[304]

Several circuits have held that rule 6(e)'s limitations upon disclosure are not applicable if release of the documents would not reveal what transpired with the grand jury. For example, in *United States v. Stanford*,[305] FBI agents showed interviewees copies of certain documents that previously had been presented to the grand jury. The court held that the disclosure fell outside the scope of rule 6(e) because the documents had been created for purposes other than the grand jury, and the disclosures were made for legitimate purposes unconnected with the grand jury investigation to persons legitimately connected with the documents.[306] The same result was reached in *United States v. Interstate Dress Carriers, Inc.*[307] In that case, the court upheld the granting of a DOJ application to allow Interstate Commerce Commission representatives to examine records that had been obtained by grand jury subpoena because "testimony or data [was] sought for its own sake—for its intrinsic value in the furtherance of a lawful investigation—rather than to learn what took place before the grand jury. . . ."[308] Courts have noted, however, that the disclosure of grand jury transcripts provides a greater "degree of exposure" into the grand

---

303. Douglas Oil Co., 411 U.S. at 222.

304. United States v. Nix, 21 F.3d 347, 351 (9th Cir. 1994).

305. 589 F.2d 285, 291 (7th Cir. 1978), *cert. denied*, 440 U.S. 983 (1979).

306. *Id.* at 291. *See also* United States v. Reiners, 934 F. Supp. 721, 723 (E.D. Va. 1996) (Financial records submitted to grand jury could be disclosed to financial institutions seeking to trace payments made to perpetrators of fraud in order to recover from perpetrator's assets, since request was not made for the purpose of determining what took place before the grand jury and disclosure would not reveal any secret aspect of the grand jury's deliberations.).

307. 280 F.2d 52, 54 (2d Cir. 1960).

308. *Id.*; *accord* United States v. Dynavac, Inc., 6 F.3d 1407, 1411-12 (9th Cir. 1993); SEC v. Dresser Indus., Inc., 628 F.2d 1368 (D.C. Cir.), *cert. denied*, 449 U.S. 993 (1980); *see also* DiLeo, 959 F.2d at 19 (reaffirming that *Interstate Dress* "remains the law in this circuit regarding the proper interpretation of Rule 6(e)"); *In re* Grand Jury Subpoenas Duces Tecum, 904 F.2d 466, 468 (8th Cir. 1990) (permitting release of grand jury materials to Internal Revenue Service for use in tax court proceeding).

jury process than disclosure of the documents divulged to the grand jury would.[309]

As the foregoing discussion illustrates, in determining whether disclosure of grand jury materials is permissible, a court must make the threshold determination that the materials sought to be disclosed are in fact "matters occurring before the grand jury" that come within the purview of the secrecy rule.[310] This question arises whenever a party seeks only documents that were subpoenaed by the grand jury, rather than a transcript of grand jury testimony. Courts have adopted four different approaches. Some courts hold that documents are never "matters occurring before the grand jury" and thus can be disclosed.[311] Other courts hold that documents are always "matters occurring before the grand jury" and can never be disclosed without a showing of particularized need.[312] Still others hold that there is a rebuttable presumption that documents subpoenaed by the grand jury are "matters occurring before the grand jury" and therefore protected.[313] The majority of courts, however, apply an "effects" test, which focuses on whether disclosure will provide a view of some secret part of the grand jury deliberations.[314]

---

309. *See, e.g.*, *In re* Grand Jury Proceedings Relative to Perl, 838 F.2d 304, 306 (8th Cir. 1988); *In re* Sealed Case, 801 F.2d at 1381; *cf.* United States v. Weinstein, 511 F.2d 622, 627 n.5 (2d Cir.) ("it is questionable whether Rule 6(e) applies to documents"), *cert. denied*, 422 U.S. 1042 (1975). Courts have also considered whether to distinguish between a transcript of grand jury testimony and a summary of what a witness divulged to an investigator outside the jury room. *Compare* Anaya v. United States, 815 F.2d 1373, 1378 (10th Cir. 1987) (finding a distinction and permitting the latter to be discovered) *with In re* Potash Antitrust Litig., 896 F. Supp. 916, 918 (D. Minn. 1995) (finding Rule 6(e) applicable to both documents) *and* United States v. Armco Steel Corp., 458 F. Supp. 784, 790 (W.D. Mo. 1978) (same).

310. *See* Brian L. Porto, *What Are "Matters Occurring Before Grand Jury" Within Prohibition of Rule 6(e) of the Federal Rules of Civil Procedure?* 154 A.L.R. FED. 385 (1999).

311. *See, e.g.,* Interstate Dress Carriers, 280 F.2d at 54; *see also* United States v. OMT Supermarket, Inc., 995 F. Supp. 526, 532 (E.D. Pa. 1997) (documents that "exist independently of the grand jury process" are not matters occurring before the grand jury for purposes of Rule 6(e)).

312. *See, e.g.,* Texas v. United States Steel Corp., 546 F.2d 626, 629 (5th Cir.), *cert. denied*, 434 U.S. 889 (1977).

313. *See, e.g., In re* Grand Jury Proceedings, 851 F.2d at 867.

314. *See, e.g, In re* Grand Jury Subpoena (Under Seal), 920 F.2d 235, 241 (4th Cir. 1990); *In re* Grand Jury Proceedings Relative to Perl, 838 F.2d at 306; Senate of Puerto Rico v. United States, 823 F.2d 574, 582 (D.C. Cir. 1987); *Anaya*, 815 F.2d at 1379; *In*

Because the material would have already been revealed, an improper disclosure under rule 6(e) is difficult to remedy, but courts have made efforts to do so, usually by attempting to limit further disclosure of the material.[315]

K. *Debarment and Suspension Proceedings*

Parallel proceedings can have serious economic consequences for corporations that contract with the federal government. Contracts with executive agencies, including the Department of Defense and the General Services Administration, are governed by the Federal Acquisition Regulation (FAR), which includes provisions for suspension and debarment of government contractors.[316] The suspension and debarment provisions of the FAR contain traps for the unwary government contractor and should not be overlooked by counsel guiding a corporation with government contracts through a parallel proceeding.

A government contractor can be suspended from working with the federal government "upon adequate evidence" of certain specified offenses, including "any . . . offense indicating a lack of business integrity or business honesty that seriously and directly affects the present responsibility of a Government contractor or subcontractor."[317] The FAR thus gives government officials broad discretion to suspend contractors "pending the completion of investigation or legal proceedings."[318] Moreover, a

---

re Special March 1981 Grand Jury, 753 F.2d 575, 578 (7th Cir. 1985); *In re* Grand Jury Matter, 682 F.2d 61, 63 (3d Cir. 1982).

315. *See* Sells, 463 U.S. at 422 n.6 ("We cannot restore the secrecy that has already been lost but we can grant partial relief by preventing further disclosure."); United States v. Smith, 123 F.3d 140, 154 (3d Cir. 1997) ("[E]ven if grand jury secrets are publicly disclosed, they may still be entitled to at least some protection from disclosure."); *see also* Nix, 21 F.3d at 352 (remanding case for a remedy and suggesting possible options); United States v. Coughlan, 842 F.2d 737, 740 (4th Cir. 1988) (indicating that grand jury materials should be suppressed if government cannot demonstrate particularized need for the testimony on remand).

316. *See* 48 C.F.R. subpart 9.4. In addition, some individual agencies have promulgated their own supplemental regulations to implement the FAR. *See, e.g., id.* subpart 209.4 (Department of Defense supplemental Debarment, Suspension, and Ineligibility regulations). These supplemental regulations may impose additional burdens on entities facing debarment or suspension proceedings.

317. *Id.* § 9.407-2(a)(7).

318. *Id.* § 9.407-1(b)(1).

suspension can apply to all subsidiaries and divisions of a contractor[319] and generally is effective throughout the executive branch of the government.[320] The FAR provides that suspension is to be imposed for a "temporary period pending the completion of investigation and any ensuing legal proceedings,"[321] and cannot extend beyond eighteen months unless legal proceedings have been initiated within that period.[322]

The provisions for debarment of government contractors also can be implicated by a parallel proceeding. A government contractor can be debarred "for a conviction of[[323]] or a civil judgment for" (among other things): fraud in connection with obtaining, attempting to obtain, or performing a public contract; embezzlement, theft, forgery, bribery, falsification or destruction of records, making false statements, tax evasion, or receiving stolen property; or "any other offense indicating a lack of business integrity or business honesty that seriously and directly affects the present responsibility" of the contractor.[324] Like suspension, debarment may apply to all subsidiaries or divisions of a contractor[325] and generally is government-wide, applying throughout the executive branch.[326] The FAR further provides that debarment "shall be for a period commensurate with the seriousness of the cause(s)" and generally should not exceed three years.[327]

In addition to the FAR, a "Common Rule" promulgated by twenty-eight federal agencies (with various modifications by each agency) provides for suspension, debarment or exclusion from participation in federal

---

319. *See id.* § 9.407-1(c).

320. *See id.* § 9.407-1(d). The suspension also may be extended to any affiliate of the contractor. *See id.* § 9.407-1(c).

321. *See id.* § 9.407-4(a).

322. *See id.* § 9.407-4(b).

323. A criminal conviction constitutes grounds for suspension and debarment regardless of whether it is entered upon a verdict, guilty plea, or plea of nolo contendere. *See id.* § 9.403.

324. *Id.* § 9.406-2(a). Although the FAR gives government officials broad discretion to suspend and debar contractors, *see id.*, the FAR specifically provides that suspension or debarment may be imposed "only in the public interest for the Government's protection and not for purposes of punishment," *id.* § 9.402(b).

325. *See id.* § 9.406-1(b).

326. *See id.* § 9.406-1(c).

327. *Id.* § 9.406-4(a)(1).

non-procurement programs and activities.[328] Pursuant to 1995 amendments, suspension and debarment under the Common Rule and the FAR are reciprocal and government-wide.[329] As a result, suspension or debarment from either procurement or non-procurement transactions with one agency means that the entity is suspended or debarred from both non-procurement and procurement transactions with a wide range of agencies. Accordingly, suspension or debarment of an entity in one context can have far-reaching effects on the entity's other business interests.[330]

As one commentator has observed, "[t]he debarment or suspension from government contracting of a major defense contractor is an economic event of catastrophic proportions to the corporation involved."[331]

---

328. *See* 53 Fed. Reg. 19,161 (1988) (Common Rule on nonprocurement suspension and debarment); *see, e.g.*, 24 C.F.R. pt. 24 (HUD version of the Common Rule); 40 C.F.R. pt. 32 (EPA version of the Common Rule). Federal nonprocurement programs covered by the Common Rule include grants, cooperative agreements, contracts of assistance, loans, loan guarantees, subsidies, insurance, and other financial and nonfinancial transactions. *See, e.g.*, 24 C.F.R. § 24.110(a)(1) (HUD regulation defining "covered transaction" under the Common Rule); 40 C.F.R. § 32.110(a)(1) (EPA regulation defining "covered transaction").

329. *See* 48 C.F.R. § 9.401 (FAR provision providing for reciprocal, government-wide debarment and suspension); 60 Fed. Reg. 33,037, passim (1995) (amending the Common Rule to provide for reciprocal, government-wide debarment and suspension); *see, e.g.*, 24 C.F.R. § 24.110(c) (HUD reciprocal provision); 40 C.F.R. § 32.110(c) (EPA reciprocal provision).

330. Some federal statutes also provide for debarment from contracting with particular agencies as a result of particular kinds of offenses. *See, e.g.*, 10 U.S.C. § 2408(a) (providing for the debarment of individuals convicted of certain felonies arising out of Department of Defense contracts); 41 U.S.C. § 354(a) (ineligibility for future contracts as a result of violations of the Service Contract Act of 1965); 33 U.S.C. § 1368 (providing for debarment for violations of certain provisions of the Clean Water Act); 42 U.S.C. § 7606 (providing for debarment for violations of certain provisions of the Clean Air Act). These statutes typically are very specific and limited in scope. Further, many state and municipal governments also have disqualification procedures comparable to the FAR provisions. *See, e.g.*, FLA. STAT. ANN. § 287.133 (Florida debarment statute); MASS. GEN. L. ANN. ch. 29 § 29F (Massachusetts debarment statute).

331. Frank J. Hughes, *The Fall and Rise of Global Settlements: How Will They Fare in an Age of Voluntary Disclosure?*, ARMY LAW., Jan. 1988, at 4; *accord*, Steven D. Gordon, *Suspension and Debarment From Federal Programs*, 23 PUB. CONT. L.J. 573, 604 (1994) (referring to debarment or lengthy suspension as "an economic 'death penalty'"); Michael J. McCarthy, *How One Firm Tracks Ethics Electronically*, WALL ST.

The same can be said of other enterprises that rely heavily upon government contracts for their economic livelihood. The reach of the suspension and debarment provisions is extended by the fact that even unauthorized actions of employees, if on behalf of a contractor or with the contractor's knowledge, can be imputed to the entire corporation and result in suspension or debarment.[332] Efforts to challenge the suspension and debarment process in the federal courts generally have not been successful.[333] Counsel retained to represent a corporation in parallel proceedings involving civil fraud allegations or criminal charges should ascertain whether government contracts are at risk. In a society where government is a major consumer of the goods and services supplied by the business sector, defense counsel must be prepared to defend not only against government charges of misconduct, but also against the resulting loss of a client's valuable government contracts.

L. *Achieving a Global Settlement*

For counsel representing a party to parallel proceedings, it may be unrealistic to expect complete victory on all fronts. A more attainable goal

---

J., Oct. 21, 1999, at B1 (quoting a Martin-Marietta official as saying that debarment would be "death for this company").

332. Gordon, *supra* n.331, at 586-88.

333. These efforts fail largely due to the deferential standard of review that federal courts employ when determining whether a debarment or suspension was warranted. *See* Shane Meat Co. v. United States Dep't of Defense, 800 F.2d 334, 336 (3d Cir. 1986) (explaining that the standard for reviewing a suspension or debarment is whether the decision to suspend or debar was "arbitrary, capricious, an abuse of discretion or otherwise not in accordance with law"); *see, e.g.*, Marshall v. Cuomo, 192 F.3d 473, 480 (4th Cir. 1999) (holding that debarment was not arbitrary or capricious, nor an abuse of discretion); IMCO, Inc. v. United States, 97 F.3d 1422, 1427 (Fed. Cir. 1996) (same); Kisser v. Cisneros, 14 F.3d 615, 618-19, 621-22 (D.C. Cir. 1994) (same); Wellham v. Cheney, 934 F.2d 305, 309 (11th Cir. 1991) (same). However, challenges to suspension or debarment may be successful if the agency failed to follow the proper procedures in reaching the decision to suspend or debar, *see, e.g.*, Humphreys v. DEA, 96 F.3d 658, 664 (reversing revocation by DEA because the agency failed to consider defendant's primary defense), *motion to vacate denied*, 105 F.3d 112 (3d Cir. 1996), or applied the incorrect legal standard in deciding whether the suspension or debarment was warranted under the relevant regulations, *see, e.g.*, Novicki v. Cook, 946 F.2d 938, 942 (D.C. Cir. 1991) (reversing suspension of individual when it appeared that the agency may have applied an incorrect legal standard, and remanding for further proceedings).

is to strive for a "global settlement" that will resolve all pending and threatened proceedings on terms acceptable to the client. A leading practitioner has defined a global settlement as "one in which the criminal, civil and administrative disposition, with particular regard to sanctions, are negotiated in a single bargain."[334] Although easy to seek in theory, global settlements are difficult to obtain in practice.[335]

In most parallel proceedings situations, the principal impediment to obtaining a global settlement is the autonomy of the various government authorities who are involved.[336] In the context of a criminal investigation, for example, a United States Attorney in one district is not likely to accept language in a plea agreement that could be construed as binding on other districts or other agencies, such as the Internal Revenue Service.[337] In addition, prosecutors may be hesitant to negotiate global settlements be-

---

334. Presentation of (now Judge) Paul Friedman titled, "The Law and Tactics of Global Settlements," presented at an American Bar Association program on Procurement Fraud Prosecutions and Debarment (Washington, D.C., Feb. 20-21, 1986).

335. Counsel should consider, however, that even seeking to negotiate a global settlement can affect the dynamics of a parallel proceedings case. "By indicating a willingness to negotiate, counsel runs the risk that the government may demand more than it would in separate dispositions, or that the case is perceived to be more significant than otherwise thought, or that information divulged during the course of negotiations may create an unexpected synergism." Stephen Wilson & A. Howard Matz, *Obtaining Evidence for Federal Economic Crime Prosecutions, excerpted in* PARALLEL GRAND JURY AND ADMINISTRATIVE AGENCY INVESTIGATIONS 956 (Neil Kaplan et al. eds., 1981).

336. Agencies also may have policies that deter efforts to achieve a global settlement. For example, the Enforcement Division of the SEC has a policy of not negotiating settlements of civil actions that involve disposition of criminal proceedings. *See* 17 C.F.R. § 202.5(f). Although there are exceptions to this policy, in general, the SEC staff will decline to address potential criminal charges in a civil settlement. *See* Peter Morrison, *SEC Criminal References, reprinted in* Kaplan, *supra* n.335, at 161-63.

337. The Department of Justice "cannot bind independent regulatory agencies, such as [the] SEC, and plea bargains do not exclude possible civil action by those agencies, unless they specifically concur in that agreement." Marvin Pickholz, *Parallel Civil Cases and Global Settlements, excerpted in* Kaplan, *supra* n.335, at 987. *See also* U.S. v. Killough, 848 F.2d 1523, 1526 (11th Cir. 1988) (promise by assistant U.S. attorney in criminal proceedings not a bar to subsequent False Claims Act case); Johnson v. Lumpkin, 769 F.2d 630, 634 (9th Cir. 1985) (promise by federal prosecutor cannot bind state authorities).

cause of a "legitimate fear of being charged with improper conduct and abuse of the criminal process."[338]

Since most complex criminal cases involve conduct occurring in more than one judicial district and subject to enforcement action by more than one federal agency, a settlement with a single authority is not likely to resolve the matter. Similarly, coordinating a settlement involving two or more government agencies with competing policy objectives, such as in a procurement fraud case involving the Department of Defense and the DOJ, can be particularly arduous.

Notwithstanding these impediments, obtaining a global resolution can be essential to a successful resolution of a case. The importance of obtaining a global settlement cannot be overstated. Debarment or suspension from government contracting can have disastrous economic consequences. Bringing together the DOJ and the Department of Defense to obtain an acceptable global settlement can be a "tortuous task"[339] in which counsel may find themselves "in the awkward position of serving as a 'broker' between the various parts of the government in order to achieve the desired [global settlement] result."[340] Despite these difficulties, in the procurement fraud area, because there are enormous stakes involved—loss of economic livelihood for a company that is dependent on government contracts—defense counsel must either obtain a satisfactory global settlement or litigate with the government.[341]

Similar pressure to obtain a global settlement can exist in other kinds of parallel proceedings. A settlement with the Enforcement Division of the SEC is not of great benefit to a client if it significantly increases the client's exposure to damages in private securities class-action litigation.[342]

---

338. *See* Friedman, *supra* n.334, at 2 (citing United States v. Litton Sys., Inc., 573 F.2d 195 (4th Cir.), *cert. denied*, 439 U.S. 828 (1978)).

339. *Id.* at 30.

340. *Id.* at 33.

341. "[A]bsent special circumstances, no defense contractor is likely to enter a guilty plea without the assurance that it will not be debarred." *Id.* at 32.

342. In such cases, counsel may seek a settlement with the administrative agency that includes establishment of a "restitution fund" to compensate private plaintiffs. The SEC, for example, has increasingly used this vehicle in settling cases involving insider trading and other securities violations. *See* F. Daniel Bell III, *Recent State Enforcement Initiatives*, 981 PLI/CORP. 69 (Mar. 1997) (discussing funds established in cases involving Drexel Burnham Lambert, Salomon Brothers, Prudential Securities, and PaineWebber).

Similarly, a civil settlement with the Federal Election Commission is not beneficial if it leaves open the possibility of criminal prosecution for election law violations. These situations require overall resolution—not piecemeal, reactive defense efforts.

The key to a favorable global resolution of parallel proceedings often is a matter of timing. Even if separate government agencies cannot be brought together into a single, comprehensive global settlement, defense counsel may be able to orchestrate a settlement through which an arrangement with one adversary lays the foundation for settlement with another, leading to successful resolution of all proceedings. For example, a favorable settlement with the SEC, perhaps involving a delicately drafted consent to carefully negotiated regulatory violations that do not include fraud allegations, can serve as the catalyst for an early, favorable settlement of private shareholder litigation. Similarly, in a criminal case, negotiating a favorable plea agreement in one judicial district, which usually provides for cooperation with the government, can provide a basis for similar agreements with other districts or agencies. Still, if separate settlements are sought, it is often difficult to get different agencies to settle within the same window of time.

Further, the practitioner seeking to use the settlement of a criminal matter to set the stage for the favorable resolution of parallel proceedings will find that a substantial impediment is presented by the DOJ's inclination, of recent vintage, to demand waiver of the attorney-client privilege and work product doctrines as a condition of reaching a plea agreement.[343] Indeed, this inclination is now stated DOJ policy. In a June 16, 1999, memorandum entitled "Federal Prosecution of Corporations," the DOJ indicated that prosecutors considering whether to charge corporations

---

343. *See* Ursula Himali, *Treating Doctors Like Mobsters*, INVESTOR'S BUS. DAILY, Apr. 20, 1999, at A1 (discussing Baptist Medical Center's waiver of the privilege in connection with a settlement with DOJ and noting the "trend among prosecutors to gut" the privilege by seeking waiver as a condition of settlement); Janet Novak, *First, Indict All the Lawyers*, FORBES, Jan. 25, 1999, at 62 ("Companies that wish to settle with the government . . . are increasingly being pressed to waive [the attorney-client] privilege."); Breckinridge L. Willcox, *Lawyers as Defendants: Where Is the Government Going and Why Have Rules Changed?*, 5 BUS. CRIMES BULL. 2 (Nov. 1998) ("Waivers of attorney-client privilege from settling entities will likely become commonplace. . . ."); *see also* Steve Miletich, *State Tobacco Suit Comes Down to Crunch Time*, SEATTLE POST-INTELLIGENCER, Sept. 22, 1998, at A1 (discussing waiver of privilege by Liggett Group in connection with global settlement with state attorneys general).

should consider its "willingness to cooperate in the investigation of its agents, including, if necessary, the waiver of the corporate attorney-client and work product privileges."[344] One "carrot" that accompanies the "stick" of waiver is the potential that a guilty plea will result in favorable treatment under the Federal Sentencing Guidelines.[345] In addition, the economic consequences of a criminal conviction may be so dire that waiver of the privilege seems a small price to pay to settle the matter.[346]

In the context of parallel proceedings, the government doubtless seeks waiver of the privilege for the purpose of eliminating any restrictions on the government's access to, and use of, corporate information in a parallel civil matter. However, because information typically loses its privilege when disclosed to third parties,[347] the ramifications of waiving the privilege in the DOJ's favor can be felt in proceedings not involving the DOJ— for example, in civil investigations or proceedings by other government agencies, or even in litigation between private parties. Even if the DOJ would be willing to agree to maintain the confidentiality of privileged information disclosed, the prospects for success in arguing that such an agreement maintains the privileged quality of the information are dubious at best.[348] Further, waiver of the privilege in the plea agreement may turn

---

344. *See Justice Department Guidance on Prosecutions of Corporations*, 66 CRIM. L. REP. (BNA) 189 (Dec. 8, 1999); *see also generally* Ronald C. Minkoff, *A Leak in the Dike: Expanding the Doctrine of Waiver of the Attorney-Client Privilege*, 107 PLI/ NY 359 (Aug. 2001); David M. Zornow & Keith D. Krakaur, *On the Brink of a Brave New World: The Death of Privilege in Corporate Criminal Investigations*, 37 AM. CRIM. L. RPTR. 147 (Spring 2000).

345. *See* U.S.S.G. § 8C2.5(g); *see also* Willcox, *supra* n.343 ("The government is aggressively pushing corporate entities who wish to benefit from the 'cooperation' credit under the Federal Sentencing Guidelines to waive their attorney-client privilege and work-product protection. . . .").

346. *See, e.g.*, Himali, *supra* n.343 (noting that a Medicare provider's conviction on kickback charges results in a five-year debarment and "can sound a company's death knell").

347. *See, e.g.*, United States v. El Paso Co., 682 F.2d 530, 540 (5th Cir. 1982), *cert. denied*, 466 U.S. 944 (1984).

348. Most courts have held that providing information to the government destroys its confidentiality and, hence, the applicability of the privilege. *See, e.g.*, United States v. Massachusetts Inst. of Tech., 129 F.3d 681, 685-86 & n.3 (1st Cir. 1997) (collecting cases). *But see* Thomas Holliday & Charles Stevens, *Disclosure of Results of Internal Investigations to the Government or Other Third Parties, in* INTERNAL CORPORATE INVESTIGATIONS 186, 197 (ABA Lit. Sec. 1992) (discussing "limited waiver" theory fashioned by some courts for disclosures to governmental agencies).

the lawyer defending the corporation's interests in the criminal case into a key opposition witness in parallel proceedings.[349]

There simply are no hard and fast rules that apply in attempting to obtain a favorable global settlement, and there is no "checklist" for counsel to follow in this area. Instead, defense counsel must be guided by a realistic assessment of the client's exposure—which is usually impossible without a thorough internal investigation—and a carefully conceived strategic defense plan for an orderly resolution of all pending and threatened proceedings.

III. CONCLUSION

Lawyers are seeing more and more parallel proceedings being initiated, particularly in the areas of securities, banking, government contracts, and insurance; this trend seems likely to continue. As the issues raised in this chapter illustrate, company counsel must pay very close attention to every detail during an internal investigation in order to ensure protection for the corporation from the potentially devastating consequences of any subsequent parallel proceedings.

---

349. *Cf.* Novak, *supra* n.343 (noting that waiver of attorney-client privilege by settling company "exposes the lawyers to prosecutorial scrutiny").

Disclosure of Results of Internal Investigations to the Government or Other Third Parties

8

by Thomas E. Holliday & Charles J. Stevens*

---

* Thomas E. Holliday is a partner in the law firm of Gibson, Dunn & Crutcher in Los Angeles, California, and a member of the firm's Business Crimes and Investigations Group. Mr. Holliday also is a Fellow in the American College of Trial Lawyers. Charles J. Stevens is a founding partner of Stevens & O'Connell LLP in Sacramento, California, and a former United States Attorney for the Eastern District of California. Mr. Stevens is a former partner in the law firm of Gibson, Dunn & Crutcher. Bradley A. Benbrook of Stevens & O'Connell LLP assisted with the updating of this chapter. The authors wish to dedicate this chapter to the memory of Mary Laura "Chee" Davis, a cherished partner of Gibson, Dunn & Crutcher.

279

I. INTRODUCTION

A COMPANY CONDUCTING AN internal investigation inevitably must decide whether information gathered in the course of the investigation should be disclosed to the government or other third parties. This issue raises two initial questions. First, the company must analyze whether nondisclosure of information suggesting criminal conduct within the company constitutes independent unlawful conduct or violates an applicable statute or regulation imposing a duty to disclose. Second, the company must consider whether, even if there is no affirmative disclosure obligation, disclosure of information learned in the investigation would nonetheless be prudent.

Assuming the company intends to disclose, counsel should carefully analyze the implications of such disclosure for the company. In particular, counsel should consider the impact of disclosure on the attorney-client privilege and the work product doctrine. The law governing waiver of these privileges is, in many respects, unclear and constantly in a state of flux. Although there is no guaranteed way to guard against waiver in connection with a disclosure, counsel and the company can take some steps to minimize the risk of this result.

Once a company has decided to disclose, it must also determine the mechanics of the disclosure. Counsel needs to consider:

- Who should make the disclosure?
- To whom should it be made?
- When should the disclosure be made?
- Should the disclosure be written or oral?

In this chapter we explore each of these questions. None has a simple answer, and each depends upon the unique circumstances of the situation confronting counsel and company management.[1]

---

1. Because of the possible ramifications of a disclosure of criminal wrongdoing to the company's business and future, senior management should be included in the decision-making process. In addition, those involved in the decision-making process should, to the maximum extent possible, be free of any involvement in the underlying misconduct.

II. REQUIRED DISCLOSURE

A. *Common-Law Rule*

The threshold question regarding disclosure is whether the company risks criminal liability when it uncovers evidence of criminal conduct but does not report its knowledge to the appropriate authorities. The general rule is that a company is not required to report knowledge of criminal conduct to authorities or to disclose evidence of that conduct voluntarily.[2] For example, the federal misprision of felony statute is violated only if (1) an individual has actual knowledge of the commission of a felony by someone else; (2) the individual fails to notify authorities; and (3) the individual deliberately takes an *affirmative step to conceal the crime.*[3]

In light of the affirmative step requirement, courts have on the one hand held that "'[mere] silence, without some affirmative act, is insufficient evidence' of the crime of misprision of felony," even if there is first-hand knowledge of a crime.[4] On the other hand, the giving of an untruthful statement to investigating authorities is a sufficient act of concealment to sustain a conviction for misprision of felony.[5] It has been held that it is not misprision to disclose some knowledge of a crime to an investigating agent and intentionally withhold other relevant information.[6] However, because partial disclosure could in some cases mislead the investigating agents and therefore possibly constitute an act of obstruction or concealment, companies and their counsel should use extreme care in making partial disclosures.

Based upon the rules just described, agents of the company may not

---

2. 18 U.S.C. § 4; United States v. Baez, 732 F.2d 780 (10th Cir. 1984); United States v. Sampol, 636 F.2d 621 (D.C. Cir. 1980); United States v. Hodges, 566 F.2d 674 (9th Cir. 1977); Neal v. United States, 102 F.2d 643, 646 (8th Cir. 1939).

3. Neal v. United States, 102 F.2d at 646.

4. United States v. Ciambrone, 750 F.2d 1416, 1418 (9th Cir. 1984); Lancey v. United States, 356 F.2d 407, 410 (9th Cir.), *cert. denied,* 385 U.S. 922 (1966); United States v. Hodges, 566 F.2d 674, 675 (9th Cir. 1977); United States v. Pittman, 527 F.2d 444, 445 (4th Cir. 1975), *cert. denied,* 424 U.S. 923 (1976).

5. *See, e.g.,* Hodges, 566 F.2d at 675; Pittman, 527 F.2d at 445; Lancey, 356 F.2d at 410.

6. Ciambrone, 750 F.2d at 1418 (holding that truthful but partial disclosure of knowledge of a counterfeiting operation is not misprision of a felony because investigating agents could not have been misled by truthful statements and there is no obligation to disclose the information voluntarily).

actively conceal the wrongdoing from investigators or intentionally mislead them. Indeed, if the affirmative step requirement of the misprision statute is satisfied, criminal liability will likely arise under several other statutes as well.[7] For example, an individual violates the federal accessory-after-the-fact statute if that individual has knowledge that another has committed a crime and proceeds to assist the perpetrator with the purpose of hindering the perpetrator's apprehension.[8] Likewise, impeding certain types of government auditors in their attempt to complete an audit examination or investigation constitutes a crime.[9]

A question that can arise is whether the destruction of company records, not yet subpoenaed, constitutes a separate criminal offense. Certainly the intentional destruction of documents known to be sought by a grand jury can constitute the crime of obstruction of justice.[10] It would also certainly constitute misprision of a felony for an individual to destroy documents or other evidence for the purpose of "covering up" criminal conduct.

Not every decision to discard incriminating documents, however, constitutes misprision or obstruction. Thus, lawyers conducting internal investigations are frequently asked by management whether the company may discard documents pursuant to the company's policy of periodic document destruction (for example, some companies regularly discard documents after a certain period of time has elapsed from their creation). In addition to the misprision and obstruction concerns outlined above, counsel must consider that the federal witness-tampering statute also precludes the destruction of documents (even if the documents were subject to a claim of privilege) if the purpose of the destruction was to impair a

---

7. 18 U.S.C. § 2 (accessory after the fact); 18 U.S.C. § 1503 (obstruction of justice); 18 U.S.C. § 1505 (destruction or concealment of documents to be used in certain administrative proceedings). *See also* 18 U.S.C. § 1512 *and* 18 U.S.C. §§ 1516, 1517. There may also be state statutes implicated by the conduct.

8. United States v. Elkins, 732 F.2d 1280 (6th Cir. 1984) (destruction of contraband while investigators attempting to search for same); United States v. Mills, 597 F.2d 693 (9th Cir. 1979); United States v. Barlow, 470 F.2d 1245 (D.C. Cir. 1972).

9. *See, e.g.,* 18 U.S.C. §§ 1516, 1517.

10. *See, e.g.,* United States v. Walasek, 527 F.2d 675 (3d Cir. 1975) *and* United States v. Solow, 138 F. Supp. 812 (S.D.N.Y. 1956).

11. 18 U.S.C. § 1512. For an analysis of § 1512 and its relationship to other obstruction statutes, see United States v. Kulczyk, 931 F.2d 542 (9th Cir. 1991). For a complete discussion of the witness-tampering statute, see chapter 4, "Perjury, Obstruction of Justice, and the Victim and Witness Protection Act."

judicial proceeding.[11] Note, too, that this statute applies even if a judicial proceeding is not pending at the time of the destruction. Accordingly, allowing document destruction to proceed in the ordinary course (assuming no grand jury subpoena or agency request for documents has been received or is anticipated) is acceptable. If, however, the destruction is in any way linked to a concern about future discovery, counsel's safe choice is to advise the client to hold off on the destruction program.

In sum, agents of a company who communicate with government investigators, auditors, or regulators conducting an inquiry of the company should bear in mind the principles noted above. Simply stated, a false or misleading statement may qualify as an affirmative act of concealment under the misprision of felony statute or lead to a charge of obstruction of justice.

B. *Statutory Disclosure Requirements*

Although federal criminal statutes generally do not compel the disclosure of criminal conduct, certain highly regulated industries are subject to special statutory disclosure requirements. For example, the Anti-Kickback Enforcement Act of 1986 requires government contractors to report in writing to the Inspector General of the contracting agency whenever there are "reasonable grounds" to believe that a kickback may have occurred between upper- and lower-tier government contractors.[12] In a similar vein, federally insured banks are subject to provisions that require the submission of a written report to the Office of Comptroller of the Currency if there is cause to believe that the bank has been defrauded.[13] Indeed, regulators of financial institutions generally require outside counsel to conduct an internal investigation of the financial institution and to provide the regulators (e.g., Office of Comptroller of the Currency or Federal Deposit Insurance Corporation) with the report. The financial institution is generally required to sign a Supervisory Agreement providing for the report, or else the institution will be taken over by a conservator or receiver.

In addition to industry-specific statutes, all public companies are subject to the disclosure requirements of the federal securities statutes and

---

12. 41 U.S.C. § 57. Similarly, states may impose broad disclosure obligations upon government contractors. *See, e.g.*, CAL. PUB. CONT. Code § 10282 (subcontractor or agent or employee of contractor may be guilty of felony for failing to report knowledge of work being performed in violation of government contract).

13. *See, e.g.,* 12 C.F.R. § 21.11 (1989).

rules. For example, in each annual report on Form 10-K, an issuer must disclose whether any of its officers or directors is or has been, within the previous five years, "a named subject of a pending criminal proceeding."[14] More generally, the filing of certain registration statements under the Securities Act of 1933 and periodic reports under the Securities Exchange Act of 1934 requires the disclosure of various "material" facts.[15] "Materiality" is an elusive concept for issuers seeking comfort that a decision to refrain from disclosure is safe.[16] Counsel conducting investigations relating to potential environmental problems should take note that the securities laws impose special disclosure obligations relating to environmental proceedings.[17] Given the complexity of the securities laws' disclosure requirements and the pervasive risk of shareholder lawsuits, public companies should consult securities counsel prior to making a disclosure decision with respect to information gathered in an investigation.

Even when disclosure of criminal conduct is not required by statute, a company must still be careful not to commit new crimes by incorporating or acting upon the prior misconduct in the course of its regular business. For example, if a company learns that an employee failed to perform certain product inspections required by a government contract, it would be unlawful for the company to certify in writing that the contract has been fully performed or even to accept payment on the contract where an

---

14. *See* Reg. S-K, Item 401(f)(2).

15. *See, e.g.,* Reg. S-K, Item 303(a)(3)(ii) (MD&A disclosure shall include description of "any known trends or uncertainties that have had or that the registrant reasonably expects will have a material ... unfavorable impact" on registrant's business).

16. The basic standard for determining "materiality" is whether "there is a substantial likelihood that a reasonable shareholder would consider [the information] important" in deciding how to proceed. TSC Industries, Inc. v. Northway, Inc., 426 U.S. 438, 449 (1976) (applying test to proxy statements); Basic Inc. v. Levinson, 485 U.S. 224 (1988) (applying TSC Industries standard in § 10(b) and Rule 10b-5 context). "[T]o fulfill the materiality requirement 'there must be a substantial likelihood that the disclosure of the omitted fact would have been viewed by the reasonable investor as having significantly altered the "total mix" of information made available.'" Basic, 485 U.S. at 231-32 (quoting TSC Industries, 426 U.S. at 449).

17. *See* Reg. S-K, Item 101(c)(xii) ("[a]ppropriate disclosure ... shall be made as to the material effects that compliance with [environmental regulations] may have upon the capital expenditures, earnings and competitive position of the registrant").

implicit premise for the payment is full compliance with the agreement.[18] Even keeping records in the company files implying that the inspections were completed can cause additional criminal exposure.[19] Similarly, criminal liability may be premised on the dissemination of documents that incorporate or adopt material statements from earlier documents that are known to be false by the time of the republication.[20]

Thus, although mere silence regarding previous unlawful conduct does not normally constitute an independent crime, such silence coupled with other conduct may well provide a basis for criminal liability under other statutes.[21] As a consequence, disclosure of past misconduct (at least at some level) may be the only means of avoiding additional future liability.[22]

C. *Problems Arising from Counsel's Knowledge of Criminal Conduct*

One of the most troubling risks confronting counsel performing an internal investigation is the risk that the lawyer will become involved in what is perceived to be an obstruction of the government's ability to investigate. This problem can arise either in the guise of an obstruction charge[23] or as part of what is alleged to be a conspiracy under the *Klein* doctrine.[24] A *Klein* conspiracy is a conspiracy that impairs, impedes, or obstructs an agency of the United States government from performing its lawful function.

---

18. *See, e.g.,* United States v. Milton-Marks Corp., 240 F.2d 838 (3d Cir. 1957).

19. *See, e.g.,* 18 U.S.C. §§ 1001 and 1516. *See also* United States v. Rutgard, 108 F.3d 1041, 1057-58 (9th Cir. 1997) (affirming conviction under 18 U.S.C. § 1001 of doctor who maintained patient files falsely stating medical necessity of treatment).

20. *See, e.g.,* United States v. Natelli, 527 F.2d 311 (2d Cir. 1975), *cert. denied,* 425 U.S. 934 (1976) (accountants held criminally liable because proxy statement contained materially misleading statements derived from previously prepared financial statements that accountants knew or should have known were false).

21. *See, e.g.,* 18 U.S.C. § 287 (false claim), § 1341 (mail fraud), § 1343 (wire fraud), § 1344 (bank fraud), § 1001 (false statement to government agency).

22. One way of dealing with inaccurate documents that are supposed to be maintained (*e.g.,* test results) is to note on the document that it is inaccurate, and any questions should be directed to counsel or an appropriate person in management.

23. *See, e.g.,* 18 U.S.C. § 1512.

24. 18 U.S.C. § 371; United States v. Klein, 247 F.2d 908 (2d Cir. 1957), *cert. denied,* 355 U.S. 924 (1958). *See also* Haas v. Henkel, 216 U.S. 462 (1910); Hammerschmidt v. United States, 265 U.S. 182 (1924); Tanner v. United States, 483 U.S. 107 (1987).

In the modern regulatory state, it is often difficult to discern the difference between advocacy on behalf of a client that is the subject of investigation, on the one hand, and impairing, impeding, or obstructing an agency in connection with that investigation, on the other. For example, in dealing with regulators in the health care fraud arena, company lawyers frequently find themselves on "the front line" arguing and advocating a particular position against the government's regulators. However, the regulators may perceive that the government has an absolute right to the information it is seeking and may view the advocacy of the lawyer as misleading and obstructionist. For example, if defense counsel responds negatively to a government agent's inquiry as to whether the corporate client has conducted a private audit of alleged overbilling when, in fact, such an audit was performed by the client (and it documented overbilling), the government would likely accuse counsel of participating in a conspiracy to obstruct when it discovers the private audit.

An even more difficult problem arises under the *Klein* doctrine when company employees seek advice from counsel on the company's options after an investigation has uncovered legal problems with potential criminal ramifications. From the lawyer's perspective, a myriad of options for responding to the problem could exist in the abstract and be discussed in that light. Some of these options might, after due consideration, be viewed as improper or illegal and rejected by counsel. But complications arise when employees choose to exercise one of those options rejected by counsel. For example, an employee might destroy documentation of overbilling that falls within the scope of a grand jury subpoena, even after counsel gave advice to the contrary. In such cases, the government will contend that the seeking of advice from counsel in connection with a crime or fraud means the communications between counsel and the client are no longer privileged.[25] This result would obtain even if the lawyer is innocent of any wrongdoing and is an unknowing participant in a discussion that really is intended to further or advance a crime or fraud.[26] At best, the lawyer becomes a chief witness against the company and its employees. At worst, the lawyer becomes a defendant in a criminal prosecution.

In sum, it is imperative that counsel weigh every action and reaction carefully while proceeding through the course of an investigation and

---

25. United States v. Zolin, 905 F.2d 1344 (9th Cir. 1990); United States v. Hodge & Zweig, 548 F.2d at 1347 (9th Cir. 1977).

26. United States v. Hodge & Zweig, 548 F.2d at 1354 (9th Cir. 1977).

while dealing with a government agency. It is far safer to make clear to government representatives at the outset of an internal investigation that company counsel is in an advocate's position with respect to disclosure (thus provoking the government's skepticism and wrath) than to allow the government to believe that counsel intended to fully cooperate with the government's investigation—subsequent events will inevitably demonstrate that this was not the case. It is equally important for counsel to monitor closely all of the employees involved in the investigation and in the interaction with government representatives in order to ensure that counsel's advice is being followed.

III. VOLUNTARY DISCLOSURE

A. *The Benefits*

Even if a company concludes that it is not legally required to disclose information learned in the course of an internal investigation, the company should consider the potential benefits of voluntarily disclosing the information. For example, in some circumstances, voluntary disclosure may increase the likelihood of convincing the government that legal or equitable factors weigh against prosecution or a harsh sentence. Similarly, the company may be able to avail itself of a formal voluntary disclosure program (i.e., a program adopted pursuant to formal agency guidelines) that, if properly complied with, would insulate the company from criminal prosecution.

It should be said, however, that many practitioners believe that the benefits of voluntary disclosure are greatly overstated, except as discussed below, in the context of the Sentencing Guidelines and disclosure pursuant to formal agency guidelines. The primary arguments in favor of disclosure are that disclosure demonstrates the integrity of the company, especially if coupled with prompt and effective corrective action, and that displays of such integrity may persuade the government to decline indictment and focus on less forthright companies.[27] This theory, however, is

---

27. Attempting to demonstrate this integrity through disclosure seems particularly important for government contractors; indeed, failing to make disclosures before the government discovers the facts may call into question the contractor's "responsibility" and right to bid on and perform government contracts. And, even if criminal prosecution is inevitable, voluntary disclosure may still help government contractors in administrative debarment or suspension proceedings.

articulated by government lawyers more often than it is proven correct. Instead, many defense attorneys believe that the benefit of voluntary disclosure is largely illusory, and that any pre-indictment presentation that implicitly concedes guilt serves only to convince the prosecutor that prosecution is warranted.

Voluntary disclosure may, however, afford other potential benefits. It enables a company to bring exculpatory evidence to the prosecutor's attention, to articulate the corresponding legal defenses, and to correct errors or misunderstandings on the part of the investigators reporting to the prosecutor. These benefits are sometimes real and occasionally successful. In complicated investigations, prosecutors commonly overlook defenses and misapprehend facts due, among other reasons, to incomplete or inaccurate investigative reports. Assuming that the disclosure could conceivably preclude an indictment, it is generally beneficial to remedy these problems with a pre-indictment submission. Most successful pre-indictment presentations are premised on these potential benefits, rather than the hope that a company's demonstrated integrity will enable it to avoid indictment. It should be noted, likewise, that it is probably impossible to make a candid and complete disclosure that enables a company to reap these benefits if an internal investigation has uncovered evidence of criminal conduct.

Another potential benefit of voluntary disclosure may be found in the federal Sentencing Guidelines for organizations, which became effective November 1, 1991.[28] These guidelines set forth the fine calculation for organizations convicted of violating almost all federal laws. As discussed in greater detail below, the methodology for calculating fines under the guidelines can be dramatically altered based upon a voluntary disclosure by the company. Accordingly, a decision not to disclose carries with it substantial economic risks in the form of a fine, as well as terms and conditions of probation.

As with the sentencing guidelines for individuals, the organizational guidelines establish base penalties—fines in the case of organizations—that are determined by the nature of the offense committed and its economic effect. In order to arrive at a base fine, a sentencing court begins by looking at the guideline tables to determine the offense level of the misconduct in the same manner as for an individual whose conduct led to the

---

28. *See* UNITED STATES SENTENCING GUIDELINES, ch. 8.

corporation's conviction. Under the organizational guidelines, the base fine is then deemed to be the greatest of (1) the amount stated for the crime in the offense-level table just discussed; (2) the organization's pecuniary gain resulting from the criminal conduct; or (3) the pecuniary loss to others caused by the organization "to the extent the loss was caused intentionally, knowingly, or recklessly."[29]

This base fine is then modified by the court by use of a culpability score that takes into account a variety of facts and circumstances. The culpability score determines the multiplier factor that is to be used in adjusting the base fine. A culpability score of 10, for example, requires the sentencing court to multiply the base fine by a multiplier of no less than 2 and no greater than 4. Under these circumstances, a base fine of $10 million would become an actual fine of between $20 million and $40 million (as determined by the sentencing court). On the other hand, a culpability score of 5 reduces the multiple range to between 1 and 2, with a corresponding decrease in the fine exposure.

An organization's voluntary disclosure of wrongdoing tends to reduce its culpability score, and thus its multiplier and actual fine. More specifically, if the organization:

- voluntarily discloses the offense to the government *before disclosure is threatened or a government investigation begins,*
- fully cooperates in the subsequent government investigation, and
- clearly recognizes and accepts responsibility for its conduct before trial (i.e., pleads guilty),

then five points will be subtracted from the culpability score.

The effect of this five-point reduction on the multiplier will depend upon where on the culpability score range an organization finds itself, which in turn depends upon the other factors that go into the culpability score calculus.[30] However, as noted above, a reduction in the culpability score from 10 to 5 would result in the court using a multiplier between 1 and 2, rather than between 2 and 4.

Finally, there exists the possibility that a company may be able to take advantage of an agency's formal voluntary disclosure program and avoid

---

29. UNITED STATES SENTENCING COMMISSION, GUIDELINES MANUAL § 8C2.4(a).

30. These factors include, but are not limited to, the involvement of high-level personnel in the crime and the organization's prior criminal history.

prosecution entirely. Certain of these disclosure programs represent a commitment by the government to strongly consider a declination of prosecution if the company voluntarily comes forward with incriminating information. The Department of Justice and other agencies, such as the Department of Defense, the Environmental Protection Agency, and the Internal Revenue Service, provide written guidelines for voluntary disclosure in such programs.[31] Each of these programs carries with it a common theme—that the disclosure must be truly voluntary. This means that the disclosure must not in any way be prompted by a fear that the unlawful activity will be discovered.

Not surprisingly, a company considering a formal voluntary disclosure program often doubts whether it will be treated fairly once the disclosure is made. Moreover, once disclosure commences under such a program, there is rarely an opportunity to turn back. And, with rare exceptions,[32] participation by a company does not protect individual employees who committed the wrongdoing; their fate will be determined without regard to the credit given for a voluntary disclosure by the company.[33] Therefore, counsel should engage in careful and thorough analysis with a company prior to participating in a voluntary disclosure program.

In light of the enhanced penalties caused by the Sentencing Guidelines, it may be that disclosure under a formal program is truly beneficial. At the initial stage, the company has the argument that it should not be

---

31. *See* UNITED STATES ATTORNEY'S MANUAL 9-42.430; Department of Justice Antitrust Division Corporate Leniency Policy (Aug. 10, 1993); "Factors in Decisions on Criminal Prosecutions for Environmental Violations in the Context of Significant Voluntary Compliance or Disclosure Efforts by the Violator," Department of Justice (July 1, 1991); "Incentives for Self-Policing: Discovery, Disclosure, Correction and Prevention of Violations," Environmental Protection Agency (Dec. 22, 1995) (regarding potential civil violations); Environmental Protection Agency Office of Criminal Enforcement, Forensics and Training Memorandum (Oct. 1, 1997) (regarding potential criminal violations); Office of Inspector General "Operation Restore Trust" Voluntary Disclosure Program (May 3, 1995). *See also* United States v. Rockwell, 924 F.2d 928 (9th Cir. 1991).

32. For an example of the risks associated with a good-faith disclosure, see *United States v. Rockwell*, 924 F.2d 928 (9th Cir. 1991).

33. Significantly, the Antitrust Division's Corporate Leniency Policy does provide for the non-prosecution of company employees. *See* Corporate Leniency Policy, Section C; Department of Justice, "The Corporate Leniency Policy: Answers to Recurring Questions" (April 1, 1998).

indicted at all given its efforts in bringing the wrongdoing to the attention of the government. Second, if an indictment and conviction should result, the cooperation should prove beneficial to the company with respect to the amount of the fine ultimately imposed at sentencing.

B. *The Risks*

The risks of voluntary disclosure (whether pursuant to a formal program or otherwise) are real and serious. First, the information disclosed might be used directly against the company in a subsequent criminal case, unless a formal voluntary disclosure program or a written agreement precludes this use. There is even some risk that the government may attempt to use representations by defense counsel on the theory that counsel's statements are admissions under Rule 801(d)(2)(C) of the Federal Rules of Evidence.[34] Second, an opposing party in a civil case may use the information against the company in parallel civil litigation. Even if not used directly, the information may provide the government or opposing parties with a virtual road map of leads, such as names of witnesses and the existence of documents containing relevant information.

Moreover, disclosure may "educate" the government about previously unknown trial issues and defenses, thus permitting the government to explain these problems and counter the defenses, whether in drafting an indictment or at trial. Finally, it is possible that voluntary disclosure to the government will have a chilling effect on the willingness of employees to disclose knowledge of wrongful conduct. If employees believe their candid responses to the internal company investigators will be disclosed to the government, they may fear criminal liability, or that their employment is at risk.

The risks of voluntary disclosure are illustrated by the common scenario of a company discovering that an employee has engaged in criminal conduct without the knowledge of anyone in management, and contrary to company policy. Many erroneously believe that this situation does not expose the company itself to criminal prosecution and that the responsible course of conduct is to report the errant employee to the authorities. Under the federal rule of corporate vicarious liability, however, the com-

---

34. *See, e.g.,* United States v. Valencia, 826 F.2d 169 (2d Cir. 1987). For this reason, care should be taken to ensure that the purposes for which the disclosure may be used are expressly agreed upon (*e.g.,* settlement purposes only, pursuant to Fed. R. Evid. 408 and 410 or plea negotiations under Fed. R. Crim. P. 11.).

pany is criminally liable for the employee's unlawful act unless that act was outside the scope of the individual's employment—which courts have not often found to be the case.[35] Thus, to disclose unlawful conduct by an employee is often to "serve the company on a platter" to a prosecutor. In many cases, whether the company is indicted will turn purely on the prosecutor's appetite.

Still, there may be circumstances in which the company will benefit by disclosing the illegal acts of its employees. If the responsible employees work at low levels within the company, and if the company itself did not benefit from the wrongdoing, the government might decide not to prosecute the company. In addition, disclosure and subsequent prosecution of the employee could deter other employees from committing future illegal acts. Finally, the benefits offered by the Sentencing Guidelines should not be underestimated, and, if the company faces potential jeopardy, any decision to refrain from disclosure should carefully consider the cost of defending against prosecution and the magnitude of potential fines.

C. *Disclosure Effects on Attorney-Client Privilege and Work Product Doctrine*

Another more general problem associated with voluntary disclosure is the probability that disclosure will effect a waiver of the attorney-client privilege, which applies to corporations as well as individuals,[36] and protection of the work product doctrine.

A number of recent decisions have considered whether and to what extent a prior voluntary disclosure constitutes a waiver of the attorney-client privilege.[37] As a general rule, disclosure of a communication protected by the attorney-client privilege completely waives the privilege

---

35. *See, e.g.,* United States v. Hilton Hotels Corp., 467 F.2d 1000 (9th Cir. 1972), *cert. denied,* 409 U.S. 1125 (1973); United States v. Basic Construction Co., 711 F.2d 570 (4th Cir.), *cert. denied,* 464 U.S. 956 (1983); United States v. Beusch, 596 F.2d 871 (9th Cir. 1979); Standard Oil Co. of Texas v. United States, 307 F.2d 120 (5th Cir. 1962).

36. *See, e.g.,* Upjohn v. United States, 449 U.S. 383, 389 (1981).

37. *See In re* the Leslie Fay Cos. Inc. Sec. Litig., 161 F.R.D. 274 (S.D.N.Y. 1995); *In re* Kidder Peabody Sec. Litig., 168 F.R.D. 459 (S.D.N.Y. 1996); *In re* Woolworth Corp. Sec. Class Action Litig., 1996 WL 306576 (S.D.N.Y. 1996); *In re* Subpoena Duces Tecum Served on Willkie Farr & Gallagher, 1997 WL 118369 (S.D.N.Y. 1997); *see also Developments in the Law – Privileged Communications,* 98 HARV. L. REV. 1450, 1650-59 (1985).

with respect to that communication. A few courts, however, have recognized that public policy concerns may argue in favor of allowing a company that has voluntarily conducted an internal investigation to disclose the results of that investigation without completely waiving the attorney-client privilege.[38] The weight of authority indicates that such cases are fairly rare exceptions to the general rule of waiver.

Because protection of documents under the work product doctrine is

---

38. *See, e.g., In re* Woolworth Corp., 1996 WL 306576 (S.D.N.Y. 1996). In *Woolworth*, plaintiffs in a securities class-action suit, filed after the announcement of allegations by corporate treasurer of accounting irregularities, sought counsel's internal notes and memoranda generated during the investigation of the company's alleged misreporting. Despite the fact that counsel met with the SEC and publicly released their investigation report, the privilege prevented discovery of the lawyers' materials:

> Strong public policy considerations . . . militate against finding a waiver of the privilege. A finding that publication of an internal investigative report constitutes waiver might well discourage corporations from taking the responsible step of employing outside counsel to conduct an investigation when wrongdoing is suspected.

Id., at *2.

In addition, some courts have adopted a "limited waiver theory" under which a company's disclosure does not constitute a blanket waiver. *See* Diversified Indus. v. Meredith, 572 F.2d 596, 606 (8th Cir. 1977); Pritchard-Keang Nam Corp. v. Jaworski, 751 F.2d 277, 284 (8th Cir. 1984), *cert. dism.*, 472 U.S. 1022 (1985). Nonetheless, several courts have explicitly rejected the limited waiver doctrine and have held that the disclosure of information gathered in an internal investigation constitutes a waiver of the privilege for purposes of subsequent proceedings. *See, e.g.,* Westinghouse Elec. Corp. et al. v. The Republic of Philippines et al., 951 F.2d 1414 (3d Cir. 1991) (voluntary disclosure to the SEC and the Justice Department constitutes waiver of attorney-client and work product privileges); *In re* Subpoena Duces Tecum (Fulbright & Jaworski), 738 F.2d 1367, 1369 (D.C. Cir. 1984) (voluntary submission to SEC constitutes waiver of attorney-client and work product privileges); *In re* John Doe Corp. (Southland), 675 F.2d 482 (2d Cir. 1982) (disclosure of investigative report to insurance underwriter's attorney waives the privilege). The courts rejecting the limited waiver approach have done so on the theory that a party should not be able to "pick and choose among his opponents" because the privilege "is not designed for such tactical employment." Fulbright & Jaworski, 738 F.2d at 1370.

It is not necessarily the case that a complete waiver of the attorney-client privilege also constitutes a waiver of the work product privilege. There are circumstances under which the work product privilege may remain even though the attorney-client privilege has been waived. *Id.*; United States v. AT&T, 642 F.2d 1285, 1299 (D.C. Cir. 1980).

based on a different premise than the attorney-client privilege, and because the protection of the doctrine is in some ways broader, the waiver issues with respect to work product are slightly different. Courts have generally held that not all voluntary disclosures constitute a waiver of the protection afforded by the doctrine.[39] Instead, courts look to a number of factors to determine whether work product protection is waived. These include:

- whether the party claiming the privilege seeks to use it in a way that is not consistent with the purpose of the privilege—namely, the promotion of an attorney's preparation in representing a client;[40]
- whether waiver of the privilege in the circumstances would tread on policy elements inherent in the privilege;
- whether the party had a reasonable basis for believing that the disclosed materials would be kept confidential by the governmental agency to which disclosure was made; and
- whether the disclosure was voluntary or involuntary.[41]

Given the uncertainty in the law and the flexibility of tests that courts have applied to waiver issues, it is impossible for company counsel to guarantee that the company's investigation report and materials will remain privileged. Nonetheless, there are a number of steps that can be taken to maximize the application of the privileges and protect against their waiver.[42]

At the outset of any investigation, the corporation should, through its management, make clear that counsel is directed to conduct an investigation to render *legal advice* concerning the matter at issue, rather than to simply report the facts, render business advice or help with a potential

---

39. Fulbright & Jaworski, 738 F.2d at 1372.

40. Recent decisions have highlighted the importance of this factor. One court concluded that work product did not protect the investigating attorneys' materials underlying a previously disclosed report because the investigation was conducted "primarily for business reasons. Therefore the ancillary existence of ongoing litigation does not shield their investigatory documentation from discovery." *In re* Leslie Fay, 161 F.R.D. at 280; *see also In re* Kidder Peabody, 168 F.R.D. at 462-67; *In re* Wilkie Farr & Gallagher, 1997 WL 118369 at *2.

41. *See* Marmaro, *Protecting the Results of Internal Corporate Investigations,* WHITE COLLAR CRIME REPORTER, July/August 1987.

42. Some of these steps are discussed in more detail in Marmaro, *supra* note 41.

public relations problem.[43] The request for advice should make clear that counsel is charged with obtaining information from all corporate employees whose jobs provide them access to relevant facts. Management should also instruct all employees to cooperate with counsel, and advise the employees of the purpose of the inquiry, as well as its confidential nature. Finally, management should authorize counsel to make use of outside consultants or accountants who will assist in rendering legal advice and act under counsel's direction and control. These actions will lay the proper foundation for subsequent exercise of the attorney-client and work product privileges.

Throughout the course of the investigation, counsel should mark all relevant documents with the heading "privileged and confidential." Counsel's notes and memoranda of employee interviews should not be read back to, signed, adopted or approved by the employee.[44] The investigative documentation should be maintained in the custody of the lawyer and should not be made part of the corporate files. Counsel should also conduct the interviews in person wherever possible, and reiterate to interviewed employees the privileged and confidential nature of the information exchanged, and the risks of inadvertent disclosure.[45]

If a report or other materials are voluntarily disclosed to a government agency, the company should seek to obtain a confidentiality agreement or a protective order from that agency. The agreement should provide, in clear terms, that the information disclosed is not to be made available to other government agencies or members of the public without the company's prior consent. To be sure, many agencies will be reluctant to agree to this limitation, and the extent of any agreement will undoubtedly turn upon the specific situation and the relative bargaining power of the parties. (Since there are presumably other advantages that prompt a company to consider voluntary disclosure, the government agency may feel there is

---

43. For example, counsel should spell this out in any retainer agreement and initial correspondence with the client.

44. Such an action could make these "statements" under 18 U.S.C. § 3500 (Jencks Act) and Rule 26.2 of the FED. R. CRIM. P. and therefore discoverable if the employee testifies for the company at trial. In those circumstances in which an employee's "statement" is truly desired, the writing should expressly recite the fact that it is the statement of the employee.

45. Counsel should also establish the nature of the relationship with the employer (*i.e.,* not the employee's personal lawyer) and make clear that the company, and not the employee or counsel for the company, is the holder of the privilege.

no need to grant the company's confidentiality request in order to obtain the materials. Conversely, the government agency may have a particular need for the information and be amenable if an agreement speeds the disclosure.) In any case, there would appear to be no theoretical bar to the enforcement of a well-drafted[46] confidentiality agreement accepted by the government agency with respect to disclosure, both to other government agencies and to third parties.[47]

D. *The Mechanics of Disclosure*

Care should also be exercised with respect to the mechanics of informal disclosure. If the disclosure is made pursuant to one of the recognized voluntary disclosure programs, the mechanics of disclosure should be spelled out in the terms of the program. If, however, the disclosure is not made pursuant to a formal agency program, a number of practical issues arise. First is the question of *who* should make the disclosure—the corporation's counsel, a business representative, or both. Generally, the most prudent course is to effect disclosure through counsel. Counsel is generally in the best position to convey the information in an unemotional manner, and to refrain from saying or doing things that may undermine the effectiveness of a privilege or applicable confidentiality, or narrow its scope. Moreover, most government agencies, especially the Department of Justice, feel more comfortable dealing with lawyers than with individuals who might be viewed as percipient witnesses, or even targets.

The next issue to consider is *when* disclosure should be made. Company management should be very careful not to make any disclosure until the investigation has been completed and all the facts are under-

---

46. In drafting such an agreement, defense counsel should consider including the following points:

- that statements in a disclosure report will be deemed to be made for settlement purposes under FED. R. EVID. 408 and 410;
- that any statements in the report should not constitute a waiver of the attorney-client privilege or any work product protection that may apply to underlying witness interviews, notes, or documents upon which the statements were based.

47. *Cf.* Permian Corp. v. United States, 665 F.2d 1214, 1215-16 (D.C. Cir. 1981) (upholding SEC's agreement to notify corporation before disclosure to other government agencies).

stood. Credibility is the most valuable asset to a party that voluntarily discloses potentially incriminating information; repeated corrections and additions to previous disclosures will destroy a company's credibility, as well as annoy the government. The piecemeal approach to disclosure has little to commend it.

Finally, a company must decide on the *form* of the disclosure. Should it be written, oral, or both? Although each situation requires particularized consideration, it is fair to say that ordinarily the best approach is to make disclosure in the form of a written submission, which then may be followed up by an oral appearance (preliminary decisions to set the stage for the written report should have already taken place). This approach allows the company to avoid inadvertent waivers of the applicable privileges. The company should thoroughly review the written disclosure document prior to disclosure to ensure its accuracy and to determine whether any facts require further development or investigation. Again, thorough and accurate disclosure enhances the company's ability to maintain its credibility.

IV. CONCLUSION

The complexity of decision-making for company counsel conducting an internal investigation into alleged wrongdoing by company employees has increased dramatically in light of the government's voluntary disclosure programs, the Sentencing Commission Guidelines, and the increased likelihood that disclosure effects a waiver of the attorney-client privilege or the work product doctrine, thus making the counsel's investigative work available to hostile third parties. Given this complexity, the most prudent course of action is for company counsel to analyze at the outset the nature and scope of the investigation to be conducted and the course of action that will be taken at the end of the investigation, depending upon the conclusions reached. In other words, before company counsel starts to walk down an investigative path, counsel and the client should clearly understand what the company will do when the end of the path is reached.

The Special Litigation Committee Investigation: No Undertaking for the Faint of Heart

9

by Lawrence J. Fox*

* Lawrence J. Fox is a partner at Drinker, Biddle & Reath. He wishes to acknowledge the able assistance of his former colleagues at Drinker, Biddle & Reath: Joanne Lahner, Sinclair Ziesing, and Bernard Diggins.

IN THE SPECIAL world of lawyer-conducted investigations, no undertaking calls for more finesse, diplomacy, independence, care, and judgment than acting as counsel for a special litigation committee. Not unlike the raising of mushrooms, the parties must conduct the process in the dark, manage it to inspire confidence that sanitary conditions have been maintained, and produce a perfect product that can withstand the most careful scrutiny of any number of skeptical inspectors. The lawyer who fails to handle it wisely and well can end up not with the sought-after opaque pearlescent mushrooms, but with nothing more than large quantities of mushroom "soil."

I. THE SETTING

How many times have the shouts "Strike suit!" "Plaintiffs' lawyers" or just plain "@#$%*#$ lawyers" reverberated through the corporate board rooms of America? There are few experiences to match that shocking combination of dismay and self-righteous outrage when the titans of our industrial and financial establishment learn that some self-appointed private attorney-general has commenced litigation "on behalf of" the corporation, typically against these very directors. "How dare someone institute litigation over that decision?" "How could anyone suggest that we have acted other than in the best interests of our corporation?" "How are you going to get officers and directors of our stature to serve the corporations of America if frivolous suits like this can be brought at the drop of a hat?"

When the shrill notes are but a lingering echo, the directors will calm down long enough to learn that lawyers not only have created the problem but also can provide, in certain circumstances, an appropriate approach for dealing with the problem—the establishment of a Special Litigation Committee (SLC, or the Committee) of the board. It is the purpose of this chapter to provide counsel to the SLC with guidelines for the conduct of the SLC's work, particularly the required investigation that lies at the heart of the SLC's responsibilities.

II. THE THEORETICAL FOUNDATION FOR A SPECIAL LITIGATION COMMITTEE

As a general proposition, the decision whether a corporation should proceed with any given litigation matter, like the decision to issue subordinated debentures or to hire a new chief executive officer, is a business decision for the corporation's board.[1] Accordingly, since a derivative action purports to be and, if pressed, is in fact brought on behalf of the corporation, at least in certain instances[2] and as an initial matter,[3] it is the corporation's full board of directors that is entitled to make the decision whether it is in the best interests of the corporation to pursue the derivative claims. As a result, the requirement has been established that, in certain circumstances, a shareholder who wishes to bring a derivative suit must first make a formal demand upon the board of directors that may, as a matter of business judgment, determine that it is not in the best interests of the corporation for the litigation to go forward. Assuming a board with capacity to so decide, if the decision is not to proceed, that is the end of the matter.

---

1. *See, e.g.*, Joy v. North, 692 F.2d 880, 887 (2d Cir. 1982) (decision to bring lawsuit normally corporate business decision for board) (citing United Copper Securities Co. v. Amalgamated Copper Co., 244 U.S. 261 (1917) (same)), *cert. denied*, 460 U.S. 1051 (1983); Spiegel v. Buntrock, 571 A.2d 767, 772-73 (Del. Super. Ct. 1990) (decision to litigate is management decision made by board, not shareholders) (citing Zapata Corp. v. Maldonado, 430 A.2d 779, 782 (Del. Super. Ct. 1981) (same)); American Law Institute, *Principles of Corporate Governance: Analysis and Recommendations* (hereinafter ALI Principles) § 7.05(a) (1994) ("The Board has the authority to dismiss the derivative action as contrary to the best interests of the corporation." (Pennsylvania became the first jurisdiction to adopt the ALI Principles in *Cuker v. Mikdauskas*, 547 Pa. 600, 692 A.2d 1042 (1997)).

2. Beyond the scope of this chapter is an extensive discussion of when the matter is taken out of the hands of the corporation entirely. *See generally* BLOCK, BARTON & RADIN, *infra* note 8.

3. See the discussion at *supra* note 8 relating to when courts are permitted to second-guess the Committee's judgment.

However, under other circumstances, the courts have held, applying various tests, that the demand requirement is excused as futile.[4] In the demand-excused setting, the full board must recognize an unpleasant fact: because of the nature of the charges and/or the identity of the defendants, the board is disabled from reaching the decision not to proceed with the derivative claim.[5] At that point, the board must either permit the suit to go forward or try to identify from among its members (or even add to its membership) board members who are not so disabled. If the board can find a sufficient number of disinterested directors within its own ranks or if the board can add more directors (with due regard to state corporate law and corporate bylaw requirements as to the number of directors required to act in the name of the board and the method for adding new directors), the board can constitute a special litigation committee of the board.[6] It then becomes the responsibility of the full board to pass an appropriate resolution delegating to the board committee full authority to act in the name of the board with respect to the putative derivative claims. It is important that this resolution clearly provide that final authority rests with the SLC and that the SLC is not simply making a recommendation back to

---

4. *See, e.g.,* Aronson v. Lewis, 473 A.2d 805, 814 (Del. Super. Ct. 1984) (standard for determining whether demand is futile is reasonable doubt that "directors are disinterested" or that transaction was "a valid exercise of business judgment"); Barr v. Wackman, 329 N.E.2d 180, 188 (1975) (demand excused by allegations of board "participation in and approval of active wrongdoing"); ALI Principles § 7.03 ("Demand on the Board will only be excused if the plaintiff makes a specific showing that irreparable injury to the corporation would otherwise result.") *See also* Kamen v. Kemper Fin. Serv., Inc., 500 U.S. 90, 92 (1991) (rejects "universal demand" requirement under federal common law).

5. Beyond the scope of this chapter is a discussion of when it is desirable to forgo forming an SLC even though enough disinterested directors are available. The decision to pursue an SLC is not always the recommended course of action.

6. *See, e.g.,* Rosengarten v. Buckley, 613 F. Supp. 1493, 1499 (D. Md. 1985) (adopts majority rule that interested board has power to appoint special committee of independent directors to review derivative action (citing Zapata, 430 A.2d at 785 (one shareholder should not have power to incapacitate entire board)); ALI Principles § 7.05(b)("The Board has the authority to delegate its authority to take any action specified in § 705(a) to a committee of directors or request the court to appoint a special panel in lieu of a committee of directors.") *But see* Miller v. Register and Tribune Syndicate, Inc., 336 N.W.2d 709 (Iowa 1983) (adopts minority rule that when all or nearly all directors are named defendants, no power to add or appoint new directors to special committee).

the disabled full board for final action.[7] A typical board resolution is annexed hereto as Appendix A.

III. DERIVATIVE PLAINTIFF'S COUNSEL

From the beginning, the SLC must guide all its conduct by the overriding expectation that, unless the SLC decides the derivative claim should go forward, plaintiff's counsel will challenge on all available fronts the recommendation of the SLC to terminate litigation. Included will be challenges to the independence of the Committee, the independence of counsel, the adequacy of the investigation, the objectivity of the investigation and, in those jurisdictions where it is available, a challenge that the final decision by the SLC violates the business judgment rule.[8] Thus, counsel must guide the entire SLC investigative process with one eye firmly fixed on the possibility and content of these challenges and the process by which the challenges will be mounted (i.e., likely discovery, anticipated testimony, the contents of the final Committee report).

IV. THE TOTAL CONTEXT

While the Committee is established in the context of a derivative claim

---

7. *See, e.g.*, Zapata, 430 A.2d at 786 (express provision of Delaware statute allows for delegation of full board authority to special committee by resolution).

8. *Id.* at 788-89 (under Delaware approach, court has discretion in demand—excused cases to apply own independent business judgment to special committee's decision not to file suit even after it is found committee is independent, acted in good faith, and conducted reasonable investigation). *See also* D. BLOCK, N. BARTON & S. RADIN, THE BUSINESS JUDGMENT RULE 522 (4th ed. 1993) (*Zapata* approach followed by federal courts construing Connecticut, Georgia, Maryland, and Virginia law) [hereinafter BLOCK, BARTON & RADIN]. For an excellent discussion of the continued vitality of *Zapata*'s two-step approach to SLC decisions (Was the investigation fair? Is the result reasonable?), *see* G. Varallo, W. McErlean, E.R. Silberglied, *From Kahn to Carlton: Recent Developments in Special_Committee Practice*, 33 BUS. LAW. 397 (1998). *But see* Auerbach v. Bennett, 393 N.E.2d 994, 1000-02 (1979) (under New York approach, court inquires into committee's good faith and independence; once found, business judgment rule shields decision of committee from further scrutiny). The American Law Institute, in its *Principles of Corporate Governance*, adopts the *Auerbach* approach except in cases in which the claim is the defendant committed a knowing and culpable violation of law in a control transaction or a tender offer, where the court can determine whether the grounds warrant reliance.

pending alone, it is equally likely that the derivative claim will arise as the companion to (or be spawned by) a related class action brought in the name of the shareholders of the corporation against both the putative defendants in the derivative action and the corporation itself. This companion action will allege that the same conduct which gave rise in the derivative context to the alleged corporate injury also directly injured the shareholders of the corporation. For example, the situations abound in which a shareholder brings a securities fraud class action alleging a failure to timely disclose some negative information that, when disclosed, resulted in a large drop in the price of a corporation's shares. At the same time, a shareholder might bring a derivative claim against the corporation's officers and directors alleging that their conduct caused the corporation great injury, to wit the need to pay the class significant dollar damages in the class action.

Thus, it is not at all uncommon that as the SLC and its counsel conduct their work, they will have to be mindful of the impact their meetings, deliberations, investigation, decisions, and subsequent report, if any, will have upon companion class-action litigation. Similarly, different counsel will be retained to defend the class-action litigation. Accordingly, the structuring and coordination of the relationship between class-action defense counsel and SLC counsel will require diplomacy and due regard for the often disparate interests or goals of the corporation in each piece of litigation.

V. SELECTION OF COUNSEL

The SLC's first act should be to select counsel to provide legal services to the Committee. While no one should ever select counsel in a casual manner, in this instance, the Committee must look beyond the usual credentials one would seek in counsel (skill, experience, personality, etc.). The Committee must conduct a thorough review of counsel's "independence" and consider whether that independence will withstand the strict scrutiny that will necessarily follow the completion of the Committee's work. It is the job of the Committee members not only to explore that issue, but also to require candidates for the assignment to explore it themselves before "tossing their hats into the ring."

The matters that the Committee should investigate in this context go beyond the usual conflict of interest analysis. Indeed, some possible candidates for the assignment, like present outside corporate counsel, who could "clear the conflict" without even "looking it up," are particularly unsuitable to act as counsel to the SLC simply because they are so involved with the corporation and its present officers and directors that their independence would be subject to substantial challenge.[9] Possible connections between putative counsel's firm colleagues and the defendants in the derivative action that would be irrelevant for conflict purposes (membership in the same clubs, service on common boards, etc.) may have an impact on whether the courts eventually view counsel as independent.[10] Thus, the search for independent counsel may be an arduous one, but one well worth the effort if the courts are to give the work of the Committee full effect. Regardless of the Committee's decision, if counsel is eventually found not to be independent, the Committee's work will be for naught, and the decision whether to pursue the claim will be entirely in the hands of derivative plaintiff and his or her counsel.

VI. THE INDEPENDENCE OF THE COMMITTEE

Once counsel is retained, the Committee should conduct a reciprocal independence analysis of its members. While one would hope that the board thoroughly explored these issues when the Committee was first formed by the board, it is not unusual for the Committee to make these appointments in haste, at a time of frenzy in the corporate board room, on a superficial basis (Jack's not named as a defendant; let's put him on the committee), or for precisely the wrong reason (Mary and I serve on the electric company board; I know I can trust her). In any event, a second check on independence is certainly in order, and, at a minimum, it will give counsel for the Committee an early opportunity to provide the SLC

---

9. *See, e.g.*, Kahn v. Tremont, 694 A.2d 422 (Del. 1997) (criticism of lawyer for special litigation committee who was recommended by counsel for the corporation); Maldonado v. Flynn, 485 F. Supp. 274, 283 (S.D.N.Y. 1980) (shareholder challenged independence of committee on basis of appointment of committee member's law firm as special counsel), *aff'd in part, rev'd in part on other grounds*, 671 F.2d 732 (2d Cir. 1982). *See also* E. BRODSKY & M.P. ADAMSKI, LAW OF CORPORATE OFFICERS AND DIRECTORS; RIGHTS, DUTIES AND LIABILITIES § 9:09, 42 (1984 & Supp. 1989) [hereinafter BRODSKY & ADAMSKI] (special counsel should be without any regular relationship with corporation or management).

10. *See, e.g.*, Kaplan v. Wyatt, 499 A.2d 1184, 1190 (Del. Super. Ct. 1985) (committee's good faith challenged on basis of appointment of special counsel who was former defendant in unrelated litigation prosecuted by shareholder's counsel).

with counsel's own independent assessment of whether a court will ultimately view the Committee as independent. After all, no special litigation committee is ever free from an attack on the grounds of independence. By definition, the Committee members serve on the board with, or know, the officers or directors who are the defendants in the derivative action because they are directors.

This charge of cronyism is as inevitable as the search by derivative plaintiff's counsel for fees. But it is the other connections, such as those mentioned in the discussion on independence of counsel (Did the president and a member of the special litigation committee room together in college? Is officer A related to SLC member B?), that the Committee and SLC counsel must carefully explore.[11] It is far too late to be surprised by such disclosures when derivative plaintiffs' counsel takes the depositions of the Committee members after the work of the Committee is complete.

Similarly, counsel must warn the Committee in the strongest possible terms to maintain its independence while its investigation is ongoing.[12] The Committee members, as board members, by definition will be meeting with their fellow "interested" board members at the regular meetings of the board. In addition, one can never overstate how nervous the putative derivative action defendants will be regarding the work of the Committee. Reciprocally, the Committee members will want to provide some assurances to their fellow directors if, as, and when it becomes likely that the Committee's work will result in a recommendation to drop the derivative claims. However, the Committee must avoid any of these pre-final report discussions lest plaintiff's counsel use them at a later date to prove that the Committee either acted too hastily or was otherwise biased or lacked independence.

---

11. *See, e.g., In re* MAXXAM, 1997 WL 187317 (Del. Ch. Apr. 4, 1997) (questioning independence of committee members); Lewis v. Fugua, 502 A.2d 962, 967 (Del. Ch. 1985) (sole director SLC member "should like Caesar's wife, be above reproach"); Bach v. National Western Life Ins. Co., 810 F.2d 509 (5th Cir. 1967) (plaintiffs challenged independence of SLC members on basis of prior meeting at resort of SLC and defendant director's counsel, among other connections); ALI Principles § 7.09(1)("The board/committee should be composed of two or more persons, no participating member of which was interested in the action, and should as a group be capable of objective judgment in the circumstances.").

12. *See, e.g.,* Abella v. Universal Leaf Tobacco Co., 546 F. Supp. 795, 800 (E.D. Va. 1982) (one factor in holding committee was independent was delegation of full board authority to committee without right of review by board); Spiegel v. Buntrock, 571 A.2d 767, 776 n.18 (Del. Super. Ct. 1990) (formation of committee isolates board from information during investigation and decision-making).

Human nature being what it is, the need to deliver warnings regarding this type of conduct repeatedly and in the strongest terms is manifest.

VII. THE DILEMMA INHERENT IN THE COMMITTEE'S WORK

Once the Committee and counsel are in place, the work of the Committee can progress. As with the selection process itself, the Committee must conduct every phase of its work with great care, under the guidance, but not the control, of outside counsel.

Why such sensitivity? It is because in conducting its work, the Committee is negotiating a minefield, with potential jeopardy to the effectiveness of the Committee's work at every juncture. On the one hand, the Committee wants to conduct a full and independent investigation, including examining privileged materials, interviewing key people, and following leads wherever they may go. On the other, as already noted, it is more common than not that during the investigation, the corporation is a defendant in a class action arising out of the same set of facts. Thus, the Committee and SLC counsel must do everything to ensure that the work of the Committee, if at all possible, does not enhance class-action plaintiffs' case against the corporation by providing plaintiffs' counsel with a road map, waiving the privilege, or otherwise creating a situation where the corporation ends up with a pyrrhic victory—a splendid claim against present or former directors or officers who have few or no assets, coupled with a multimillion-dollar liability for the corporation vìs-a-vìs its shareholders. The Committee thus must be sure to keep its work as confidential as possible, attempting to protect the attorney-client and attorney work product privileges. Above all, the Committee must make sure its work does not result in greater costs to the corporation than if it had never been formed.[13] For these reasons, not only the guidance of counsel (who are sensitive to these issues) but also the participation of counsel (who may provide an attorney work product or attorney-client privilege protection) is essential.

---

13. While beyond the scope of this paper, an issue that must be recognized is that there are certain situations in which the creation of an SLC, though technically possible, simply makes no sense because the risks inherent in it are too great to assume. The fact that the Committee conducts an investigation and produces a report always carries with it the possibility that discovery in related litigation will include inquiry into the working of the Committee and disclosure of its work product.

VIII. IT IS THE COMMITTEE'S INVESTIGATION

At the very first meeting, the Committee must decide upon the allocation of responsibility between counsel and Committee. As important as counsel's role is, one thing is certain: The investigation must be that of the Committee, not counsel, if it is to survive scrutiny.[14] Thus, the Committee must establish early some mechanism to meet regularly, perhaps monthly, with counsel. While counsel may make recommendations as to where the investigation should lead, these should be only in the form of suggestions. The Committee members must ratify those suggestions and have ample opportunity to make their own suggestions. If choices are required, those choices must be those of the Committee, not of counsel.

Similarly, while the Committee members presumably do not have the time, inclination, or ability to conduct interviews or search through what are typically thousands of documents, the Committee should establish a mechanism for reporting progress to counsel for evaluating the substance of what is being revealed. There may even be an understanding at this early juncture that, while counsel will do the "grunt work" for the Committee, the Committee itself, before it reaches a final conclusion, will either conduct or observe counsel conducting several key interviews or review key documents that counsel views as pivotal.

The tension here is obvious and inevitable. The more the Committee itself does, the less likely it may be viewed as a privileged undertaking; the less the Committee does, the more likely it is that the investigation will be viewed as a "counsel investigation" and, thus, not entitled to full effect. Good judgment requires that counsel and the Committee, in full recognition of this additional dilemma, reach a balance that makes sense under the circumstances.

---

14. *See, e.g.*, Kahn v. Tremont Corp., 694 A.2d at 426 (lack of participation by some members "severely limited the exchange of ideas and prevented special committee as a whole from acquiring critical knowledge of essential aspects of purchase"); *In re* MAXXAM, 1997 WL 187317, at *21 (member of committee cannot recall details, opening position or how many registration meetings were held); Watts v. Des Moines Register & Tribune, 525 F. Supp. 1311, 1328 (S.D. Iowa 1981) (substantial participation of committee members in investigation, though advised by special counsel, supported holding that committee itself made reasonable investigation). *See also* BRODSKY & ADAMSKI, *supra* note 9, § 9:09 at 42 (although special counsel may make recommendations to committee, active involvement and supervision of investigation by committee is essential).

IX. COMMITTEE INTERVIEWS

Since the Committee's investigation will inevitably include interviews with employees of the corporation, it is wise for the Committee to adopt a protocol as to how these interviews will be conducted. The role of the special litigation committee and the implications of the investigation it conducts are confusing even to the sophisticated. Because the Committee is a committee of the corporate board, and because counsel are employed by the Committee, interviewees may view counsel as their own lawyer and assume the results are confidential, when in fact just the opposite is the case. Lest any interviewee be misled, counsel should draft a protocol speech similar to the one annexed hereto as Appendix B for the Committee, and the SLC should adopt a resolution stating that no interviews will be conducted without the interviewee first hearing "the speech."

X. MINUTES OF COMMITTEE MEETINGS

The question of recording the work of the Committee is also one that counsel and the Committee must explore at the first meeting. It is best, of course, if only official notes of the Committee meeting exist. Individual handwritten notes that reflect different styles and levels of attention can often be grist for the plaintiffs' counsel's deposition mill when the Committee's work meets its inevitable challenge.

Counsel should prepare the official minutes in the expectation that privilege will not attach to them. The minutes should be written in such a way that Committee members can quickly recall what was discussed, without providing the kind of detail that might come back to haunt all if the court determines the minutes are required to be turned over to plaintiffs' counsel. The minutes ought to reflect the fact that the Committee controlled the investigation, yet the writer should purge the minutes of all tentative conclusions or working hypotheses formed along the way. There will be time and opportunity enough to document the work of the Committee and the reasons for its decision when a final report, if any, is written.

The level of detail the author thinks is appropriate is reflected in the hypothetical Committee meeting minutes attached hereto as Appendix C. While the minutes tell the reader who attended and how long the meeting lasted, and give a report on past activities, a preview of future activities, a tentative timetable for completion of the work, and a full discussion of all these matters, in the final analysis the minutes contain nothing that would provide fodder for plaintiff's counsel.

XI. RELATIONSHIP WITH OTHER INSIDE AND OUTSIDE COUNSEL

Once the board launches the investigation, how does counsel begin? The derivative complaint is a start; thus, counsel can identify some early interviewees and relevant documents at the initial meeting. But the first fact of life that counsel for SLC will quickly learn is that they are dependent on the cooperation of inside counsel and, if there is parallel class-action litigation, counsel for the corporate defendant in that matter. Counsel have no subpoena power, no right to take depositions, no entitlement to see privileged documents, though they probably have free rein otherwise over corporate documents. Counsel also do not want to re-invent the wheel. If counsel wish to review relevant documents and lawyers for the class-action corporate defendant are already gathering the same documents for production to class-action plaintiffs' counsel, it does not make sense for the same corporate entity to pay two different firms to undertake this initial canvassing of corporate records. Thus, counsel for the SLC must to some extent coordinate its work with both of these other counsel.

However, there are two other forces at work that complicate this need to coordinate. First, counsel for the SLC must remain independent and also maintain the appearance of independence from other counsel. Counsel for the SLC should never place themselves in a position in which either inside counsel or counsel for class-action defendants are directing or limiting the scope of the investigation. Suggestions, cooperation, and assistance are appropriate, if not required; meddling, direction, and scope limitations are not. In the foregoing example, then, while it was satisfactory to depend on class-action defense counsel to gather the universe of documents, it would be unacceptable for SLC counsel to accept class-action defense counsel's representation that the documents in a given group were the only relevant ones.

Second, inside counsel and counsel for the class-action defendant are vitally interested in the work of the Committee, and frankly hope that the Committee's work will reach a conclusion favorable to incumbent management. These counsel will express their anxiety in many forms; even while recognizing fully that they do not want to sully the independence of the Committee, they will be tempted to intervene.

The Committee and SLC counsel must manage this uneasy alliance with diplomacy. Surely the cooperation of regular outside counsel is a treasured thing; there is no reason not to listen to what they have to say. But the investigation should follow a path mandated by the Committee, not general counsel, and Committee members and counsel should keep confidential reports on the course of the investigation, not share them with nervous general counsel who may be putting intense pressure on SLC counsel.

In this context, SLC counsel may and indeed should share with other counsel matters uncovered in the SLC investigation that directly and significantly impact the class-action litigation. Similarly, SLC counsel should share with class-action defense counsel SLC counsel's views on the credibility of witnesses or the likelihood that any particular defense would prevail. After all, counsel are all seeking to act in the best interests of the corporation, which includes mounting the best possible defense to the plaintiff's class action. If SLC counsel has a second opinion or special insights, the parties should encourage an exchange of this information as entirely consistent with counsel's independent role. And if inside counsel has a special need to get an expedited reading from the SLC on a particular charge or employee because of some pressing business reason (for example, a derivative defendant may be about to be promoted to executive vice president and management is attempting to avoid later embarrassment), the parties should agree to communicate that request to the SLC for it to exercise its independent business judgment in balancing the need for independence and the corporation's need for an early answer.

But at the end of the day, while SLC counsel wants to be able to testify that he received full cooperation from these other lawyers, that the corporation granted complete access to documents, that it arranged all interviews that were required, and that other counsel otherwise provided all necessary assistance, SLC counsel also must be able to testify, under what may be the withering cross-examination of derivative plaintiff's counsel, that the Committee was the sole guide for the investigation.

XII. APPEARANCE OF COUNSEL FOR DERIVATIVE PLAINTIFF

Counsel also must decide with the Committee what role plaintiff's derivative counsel should play in the investigation. After all, it is plaintiff's allegations that are the starting place for the work of the Committee. At a minimum, SLC counsel should invite plaintiff's counsel to submit in writing any presentation plaintiff's counsel wishes the Committee to consider. Though more risky, and perhaps not likely to provide anything more than aesthetics, SLC counsel may invite plaintiff's counsel to meet with SLC counsel or even address the Committee on his or her clients' concerns. The effect of all of this can be quite disarming—it is plaintiff's counsel who may ultimately challenge the Committee's action. Certainly part of that challenge can be blunted if the Committee has considered the views of plaintiff's counsel, and, even more so, if the Committee has followed the leads supplied or suggestions offered by plaintiff's counsel. Moreover, if plaintiff's counsel fails to take advantage of this offer, SLC counsel can feel more comfortable in limiting the investigation to the allegations of the complaint—allegations that are often inartfully crafted and lacking in real substance.

XIII. PROTECTING THE PRIVILEGE

Perhaps the most critical part of the investigation for counsel is dealing with documents that are subject to the attorney-client privilege and attorney work-product doctrine. In the context of an SLC investigation, each of these privileges exists on two different levels. On the first level, there are communications between SLC counsel and the Committee that, if properly handled, qualify for the attorney-client privilege.[15] For example, counsel's opinion to the Committee members on the likelihood of their being deemed independent would come within this doctrine. There is also the work of SLC counsel that—again, if properly handled—should come within the attorney work-product doctrine.[16] Examples of this would in-

---

15. *See, e.g.*, Dennis J. Block & Nancy E. Barton, *Internal Corporate Investigations: Maintaining the Confidentiality of a Corporate Client's Communications with Investigative Counsel*, 35 Bus. Law 5, 9-13 (1979) [hereinafter Block & Barton] (attorney-client privilege extends to communications between client and counsel if purpose for retention is legal advice rather than investigation). *See also* chapter 2, "Implications of the Attorney-Client Privilege and the Work-Product Doctrine," and chapter 11, "Report of the Investigation."

16. *See, e.g.*, Block & Barton, *supra* note 15, at 21-23 (work-product doctrine protects documents prepared by counsel in anticipation of litigation absent de-

clude counsel's interview notes, counsel's analyses of documents and counsel's working hypotheses regarding the possibility that the corporation might have a claim. Because all of this work is conducted in anticipation of litigation (either a motion to have the derivative claim dismissed based on the Committee's work and business judgment or the actual prosecution of a claim on behalf of the corporation), it is not a stretch to argue that the attorney work-product doctrine should apply.

On a second level, there is the review by SLC counsel and the Committee of documents created by other counsel, their experts, or corporate employees that qualify for the attorney-client and/or attorney work product privileges. For example, the SLC counsel may review privileged documents created by general counsel at the time the corporation made an important decision whether to disclose a potentially material fact in filing its report on Form 10-k. Or SLC counsel may review, as part of the SLC investigation, witness notes created by counsel defending the companion class action. Protection of these two privileges is the subject of a separate chapter in this book, and the principles outlined therein apply with equal vigor here. And because counsel for the SLC is simply another counsel for the corporation, SLC counsel's review of the second-level documents subject to the attorney-client and attorney work product privileges should not, if analyzed properly, act as a break or waiver of either.

However, there is one aspect of the SLC investigatory and report process that has special impact on both privileges, at both levels. The Committee must reach a decision. If it is a decision not to proceed with the derivative claim, the SLC must be prepared to demonstrate in some way or other that it reached its decision after a thorough investigation, after numerous interviews, after the review of all relevant documents by an independent committee that met regularly, guided by independent counsel, and, in some jurisdictions, that the decision fits well within the business judgment rule. It also must be prepared to resist an inevitable challenge from the derivative plaintiff's counsel to all of the foregoing. This means that discovery will occur into the work of the Committee and its counsel.

Anticipating the probable scope of this discovery has an inevitable effect on the scope of the Committee's investigation. If the Committee's report mentions a particular document, regardless of its privileged charac-

---

monstrated substantial need by plaintiff). *See also In re* LTV Sec. Litig., 89 F.R.D. 595, 620 (N.D. Tex. 1981) (work product of special counsel to audit committee protected because investigation and report required legal acumen and expertise).

ter, derivative plaintiff's counsel certainly will seek and likely receive it in discovery.[17] Similarly, if the Committee relies on privileged material to reach its conclusion, the Committee can expect that plaintiff's counsel will succeed in discovering those documents despite their confidential character. However, mere review of privileged material by counsel for the Committee should not have the effect of acting as a waiver. Nonetheless, all of the foregoing suggests that the SLC and its counsel should take care in deciding what to review.

While it might at first appear that the SLC would benefit from appearing to have had its members or counsel review the universe of available documents, there might be situations in the area of privileged documents where it is better to avoid reviewing them—for example, if the Committee or SLC counsel can elicit factual information in a different way. (Why look at counsel's notes of a key interview when the interviewee can be reinterviewed by SLC counsel?) Moreover, while it is clearly helpful, if not necessary, for counsel to have access to underlying privileged documents as well as privileged documents created in connection with the parallel class-action litigation, counsel does not want this access to result in disclosure to derivative plaintiff's counsel. Thus, SLC counsel must make judgments at every step of the way when it comes to privileged documents—whether SLC counsel should review the documents, whether SLC counsel should share the documents with the Committee, whether the documents should play a role in the conclusions reached by the Committee, and whether the final report should reference the documents.

The fine line that must be drawn is exemplified by *Zitin v. Turley*.[18] After the plaintiffs had filed their derivative suit, the corporation created an SLC to investigate their demands. The SLC (with assistance of counsel) produced a report recommending against the action. The company then used the report as a basis for its summary judgment motion.

The plaintiffs thereafter sought drafts of the report, any documents reviewed in preparing the report, and any communications between counsel

---

17. *See, e.g.*, *In re* Matter of Continental Illinois Sec. Litig., 732 F.2d 1302, 1314 (7th Cir. 1984) (report prepared by committee to evaluate derivative claims is discoverable, since it was admitted into evidence to support motion to terminate claims) (citing Joy v. North, 692 F.2d 880, 893 (2d Cir. 1982) (committee reports used in adjudicative stages of derivative litigation are discoverable; protected only if confidentiality is maintained)).

18. No. Civ. 89-2061-PHX-CAM, 1991 U.S. Dist. LEXIS 10084 (D. Ariz. June 25, 1991).

and the committee. The court held that all of the documents requested were protected by the attorney-client or work product privileges.[19] However, the court held that by disclosing the report, "the Corporation has waived any claims of privilege and work product immunity to the extent that counsel communicated the information or documents to the committee."[20]

Farber v. Public Service Co.[21] is also instructive. In preparation for expected derivative suits, the corporation in *Farber* created an SLC, which then produced a report. The report was subsequently filed in one of the pending derivative suits. The plaintiffs then sought the disclosure of all documents reviewed, the notes of the SLC members, and any communications to or from SLC members. Examining the corporation's work product claims, the court held that to permit such broad categories of discovery would militate against common sense and undermine the work-product doctrine.[22] The court permitted disclosure of any documents reviewed, but protected the SLC members' notes and the communications to or from SLC members.[23]

XIV. THE INVESTIGATION

Describing how the actual investigation should be conducted is about as elusive a topic as how to defend litigation. All investigations are fact-specific, and the conscientious and imaginative lawyer must structure and complete the necessary work in an appropriate manner. Nonetheless, there are a few rules that SLC counsel should apply, given the special characteristics of the SLC and the goal of counsel to see the SLC's ultimate decision given full effect.

First, since it is known that plaintiff's counsel will mount an inevitable challenge to the scope of the SLC's investigation in reaching its decision, it may be that counsel will want to extend its work beyond what the normal cost/benefit analysis might suggest was appropriate in other contexts.[24]

---

19. *Id.* at 10-11.

20. *Id.* at 15.

21. Civ. No. 89-0456 JB/WWD, 1991 U.S. Dist. LEXIS 18051 (D.N.M. Apr. 4, 1991).

22. *Id.* at *3.

23. *Id.* at *3-4.

24. *See, e.g.,* Zapata Corp. v. Maldonado, 430 A.2d 779, 788 (Del. Super. Ct. 1981) (under Delaware approach, corporation must prove "reasonable investigation" con-

While it is almost unavoidable that at least one witness will be left uninterviewed and one box of documents unreviewed, the ability to say that counsel extended the investigation beyond normal limits could be helpful.

Second, the Committee and SLC counsel should leave no reasonable leads (regardless of their anticipated value) unfollowed. If witness A insists that witness B was a key participant, it is far better to interview B to put that allegation to rest rather than to reject A's suggestion on the basis of other information available to counsel.

Third, the Committee and SLC counsel should thoroughly investigate and evaluate any information supplied by derivative plaintiff's counsel. There is no more likely challenge to the Committee's work than that plaintiff's counsel's allegations were ignored as part of a "cover-up."

Fourth, if at all possible, the Committee and SLC counsel should interview each derivative claim defendant. Confronting the alleged perpetrators of the injury to the corporation lends a credibility to the investigation that will carry great weight later.

Fifth, SLC counsel should not hesitate to hire an expert to help the Committee evaluate any technical or arcane factual issues that are beyond the expertise of counsel and the Committee members. For example, if the allegation is that pre-release tests should have revealed an inherent defect in a particular product, the SLC should retain an expert to assist with the physics or chemistry in order to enhance its work.[25]

Finally, it should be remembered that in determining whether it is in the best interests of the corporation to pursue derivative litigation, the Committee must evaluate more than the merits of the claim.[26] The Com-

---

ducted before motion to dismiss will be granted); Auerbach v. Bennett, 393 N.E.2d 994, 1000-02 (N.Y. 1979) (under New York approach, court may look at methodologies and procedures of investigation; if restricted in scope, shallow in execution or pro forma, question of good faith raised). The views of Chancellor Allen in *Carlton Invs. v. Beatrice Int'l Holdings, Inc.*, 1997 WL 38130, at *5 (Del. Ch. Jan. 29, 1997) are instructive: "[T]o be reasonable in getting information doesn't mean to be perfectly informed," even if the investigation does not locate a "smoking gun."

25. Experts should meet the test of independence as well. *See* Kahn v. Tremont, 694 A.2d 422, 426 (Del. 1997) (challenge to an investment adviser to a special transaction committee who had earned fees from affiliates of majority shareholder).

26. *See, e.g.*, Auerbach, 393 N.E.2d at 1002 (decision to file suit involves "weighing and balancing legal, ethical, commercial, promotional, public relations, fiscal and other factors familiar to the resolution of . . . corporate problems."). *See also* Abella v.

mittee also must add into the equation (a) the likely disruption to the corporation that will result from such a suit going forward, and (b) the likely recovery to the corporation if the corporation were successful. With respect to the former, the investigation should focus on the value of the putative defendants to the ongoing operations of the business, the effect of pursuing the litigation on the putative defendants' ability to continue to operate as effective officers or directors, and the effect on other employees' morale of the corporation's suing the putative defendants. With respect to the latter, the investigation must explore the likely cost in legal fees, expert witnesses, and other litigation costs to pursue the claim; the personal wealth of the putative defendants; and the availability of insurance coverage for any of the claims. The Committee or SLC counsel should explore each of these matters independently.

XV. CONCLUSION

The Special Litigation Committee investigation is one of the more challenging and gratifying assignments counsel can be retained to undertake. From start to finish, the tasks involved must be undertaken with conscientious and finely honed skills, ever mindful of the traps for the unwary that lie at every step along the way. If successfully completed, the result will permit the SLC to implement fully its well-considered decision as to how the Corporation should treat a derivative claim whose initial filing was undoubtedly met with a mixture of scorn and dismay. Counsel who fulfill the assignment conscientiously will have empowered the client in a meaningful way, acting in the finest traditions of the profession.

Universal Leaf Tobacco Co., 546 F. Supp. 795, 801 n.3 (E.D. Va. 1982) (factors considered in weighing costs against benefits included large attorney's fees, loss of time and energy by management, reduction in morale of employees and management, adverse consequences to insurance coverage, and adverse reaction by customers, banker, and stock market). *Cf.* Joy, 692 F.2d at 892 (court may initially weigh attorney's fees, expenses of litigation, and mandatory indemnification of directors and officers, but may not consider existence of insurance; if court then finds no substantial net return compared to shareholder's equity, court may consider impact to key personnel and lost profits from trial publicity).

APPENDIX A

Resolution Establishing a Special Litigation Committee

WHEREAS a class action has been instituted against the Company, its present and former directors and officers as well as a derivative action on behalf of the Company against the same present and former directors and officers; and

WHEREAS it would be proper for the Board of Directors of the Company to delegate to a Special Litigation Committee the responsibility for determining whether it is in the best interests of the Company to pursue any of the claims alleged in the derivative action;

NOW THEREFORE, the following resolution is adopted by the Board of Directors of the Company:

RESOLVED that, pursuant to the Bylaws of the Company, a Special Litigation Committee shall be appointed by the Executive Committee to be ratified by the full Board of Directors; further, it is

RESOLVED that the Special Litigation Committee is authorized to exercise all lawful authority of the Board of Directors in determining what action, if any, the Company should take with respect to the above-referenced derivative litigation and any similar suits that have been or may be filed on the Company's behalf.

APPENDIX B

Advice to Witnesses

As you may know, litigation has been instituted against the Company by a shareholder purporting to represent a class claiming that the Company overstated earnings in the years 1984 and 1985, thereby allegedly defrauding shareholders who bought the Company's stock in those years. The Company's Board of Directors has now received a demand from a shareholder of the Company requesting that the Company institute litigation against those who were already responsible for the alleged overstatement of earnings. A derivative lawsuit on behalf of the Company has also been filed that makes the same demand to recover from these individuals any damages the Company may be forced to pay in the class action.

Because the decision to institute litigation is, like any other business action, subject to the business judgment of the Board, and because some of the present Board members were on the Board at the time of the allegedly inflated earnings reports, the Board has delegated to a three-member Committee of the Board, all of whom joined the Board since 1986, the decision whether it is in the best interests of the Company to pursue litigation against anyone for any conduct associated with these financial statements.

In reaching its decision, the Committee will investigate the facts and circumstances surrounding the issuance of the financial statements to determine whether those in positions of responsibility properly fulfilled their duties in issuing the financial statements. The Committee, of course, recognizes that disclosures that were made in good faith and involved no actionable conduct may appear incorrect with the benefit of hindsight. On the other hand, it is the responsibility of the Committee to determine whether all concerned acted in a manner consistent with their duties to the corporation and its shareholders.

The Committee, in turn, has retained our law firm to be counsel to the Committee to assist the Committee in the conduct of its investigation. It is in that role that we have asked for an opportunity to interview you. It is important that you understand that our firm neither represents the Company generally nor do we represent you. Our only client is the three-member independent Committee to whom we shall report the results of this, as well as our other interviews, so that the Committee can fulfill its important responsibilities.

APPENDIX C

Confidential Attorney-Client and Attorney Work Product Privilege

Minutes of the Special Litigation Committee Meeting of June 1, 2001.

The Special Litigation Committee of X Corporation met on June 1, 2001. All members of the Special Litigation Committee were present as well as Michael Burns and Bobbi Miller, counsel to the Committee. The Chairman of the Committee asked Mr. Burns to keep the minutes of the meeting.

1. The minutes of the previous meeting were reviewed and approved.

2. Counsel reported on the most recent interviews with the Controller and the Chief Financial Officer of the Company. The Committee discussed whether the Committee ought to meet with the CFO at some future date.

3. A review of the due diligence files of the Company conducted by counsel for the Special Litigation Committee was described.

4. Counsel shared her research into the independence of the members of the Special Litigation Committee.

5. A preliminary investigation by counsel into questions of available coverage under the Company's Directors and Officers Liability policy was discussed.

6. A preliminary chronology of key events was circulated.

7. Counsel provided members of the Committee with a schedule of upcoming interviews as well as an explanation of why counsel had selected this particular order for the interviews.

8. Counsel explained the basis for their fees for the last month and a budget for completing counsel's work was discussed.

The next meeting of the Committee was scheduled for July 17, 2001.

Unique Problems Associated with Internal Investigations in Environmental Cases

10

by Michele C. Coyle & Christopher H. Buckley, Jr.*

*   Michele C. Coyle is a partner in the Los Angeles office of Hogan & Hartson L.L.P. Christopher H. Buckley, Jr., is a partner in the Washington, D.C., office of Gibson, Dunn & Crutcher LLP. They wish to thank Robert E. Postawko, an associate with Hogan & Hartson L.L.P., for his assistance.

I. INTRODUCTION

INTERNAL CORPORATE INVESTIGATIONS in the environmental area often begin in response to contact by a government agent or agency. Service of a search warrant on company employees is becoming a more frequent occurrence, and one that triggers an internal investigation in less than ideal circumstances.

Most companies in these instances are shocked by the onslaught of numerous agents executing a search warrant, particularly since company managers usually have no idea that there are any environmental problems within the company. Investigators may seize documents or attempt to make unannounced interviews—all of which are likely to take company officers or employees by surprise. Sometimes government agents arrive unannounced at a company with a demand to review and photocopy documents that relate to environmental permits held by the company. In other instances, a company may simply receive a notice of violation or some other type of citation that should warn the company it may have problems. In all of these circumstances, the government contacts usually prompt a reactive internal company investigation.

More recently, many companies have begun to conduct voluntary internal investigations, often called "environmental audits." Because many companies have various government permits, which are necessary to carry on their business, environmental audits more and more are seen as a prudent way to ensure the company is in compliance with its permits. Voluntary environmental audits, however, present problems different in some respects from those encountered in a reactive internal investigation.

This chapter first discusses some of the unique aspects of reactive investigations, particularly those triggered by some government action, and provides suggestions in conducting such investigations. The second part of this chapter focuses on voluntary environmental audits. Because many companies now conduct voluntary internal investigations, the discussion of voluntary, proactive investigations focuses on the advantages and disadvantages of these investigations and some of the unique problems they present, rather than on the nuts and bolts of conducting them.

II. REACTIVE INVESTIGATIONS

Reactive investigations are those triggered by some defining event, such as an industrial accident, a pollution incident, or the announcement of a government investigation of the company. This type of investigation is more difficult than the routine internal investigation because the company must deal not only with the often complex underlying technical issues, but also with internal and external pressure to resolve the matter quickly, the crisis atmosphere that usually develops within the company, the siege mentality that usually develops relative to those outside the company, and, often, issues of internal company politics and career preservation. In short, the company must cope with a technical problem and, simultaneously, the trauma flowing from the ramifications of the incident.

A. *Search Warrants*

One of the most difficult types of reactive investigations for a company to respond to is that triggered by the execution of an administrative or criminal search warrant at the company. Unfortunately, search warrants are commonly used by investigators in the environmental area. In the environmental context, investigators tend to believe that search warrants are essential and more beneficial than subpoenas. Significantly, environmental investigators can be expected to take samples during the execution of a search warrant, as well as to seize all documents relating to environmental procedures before evidence can be altered or destroyed.

Environmental search warrants are often executed by a SWAT team of numerous law enforcement officers. Some of these officers are dressed in "moonsuits" and take samples during the search. Other officers are assigned to go through all the company's documents and confiscate everything that is reasonably responsive to the search warrant, which is typically very broad in scope. And some officers will attempt to segregate employees into offices and interview them in this terrifying atmosphere. These tactics can have an intimidating and paralyzing effect on management and other personnel present at the time the warrant is executed. Obviously, the manner in which the company deals with a search warrant is part of, and will be essential to, the subsequent internal investigation that will immediately follow.

A few simple steps can minimize disruption and potential harm of the search and enhance any subsequent internal investigation.[1] All companies should designate a senior person to serve as the contact with government investigators. If law enforcement agents appear on the premises and announce their intention to execute a search warrant, the pre-designated person should talk to the officers, identify which agent is heading the search warrant, and read it carefully. Normally, valid objections during the course of a search warrant arise only if the agents go beyond the scope of the warrant. Otherwise, the company must cooperate with the search or risk possible allegations of obstruction of justice.

Always ask the agents executing the warrant if they could either return after business hours to avoid disrupting the business or at least wait until its attorney arrives. Not surprisingly, the agents may object to the delay. For this reason, it is important that the pre-designated senior employee be familiar with counsel experienced with search warrant and criminal matters, so the company can contact its outside counsel immediately. The presence of an experienced lawyer will protect against inadvertent waivers of constitutional rights and procedural protections. The company should advise the lawyer of all details of the warrant, including the regulatory agencies involved, the areas to be searched under the provisions of the warrant, and the types of evidence to be seized.

If the agents insist on proceeding with the search warrant, the company representative should inform them that, due to the disruption, conducting business will be impossible and therefore employees will be sent home. The agents may object, but a search warrant for documents and tangible evidence should not authorize the detainment of employees at the company beyond the brief time necessary to secure the premises and conduct the search.[2]

If members of the news media are present, politely and firmly ask them to leave. Do not engage in any behavior that would make a bad

---

1. Attached as an Appendix is a short checklist of things to do in response to a search warrant.

2. *See, e.g.,* United States v. Photogrammetic Data Svcs., Inc., 259 F.3d 229, 238-40 (4th Cir. 2001); Daniel v. Taylor, 808 F.2d 1401, 1403-05 (11th Cir. 1986); United States v. Rowe, 694 F. Supp. 1420, 1423-25 (N.D. Cal. 1988); United States v. Stevens, 543 F. Supp. 929, 942-43 (N.D. Ill. 1982) (distinguishing the detaining of individuals pursuant to a search warrant for contraband as opposed to a search warrant for documents and evidence.).

impression, such as ducking, hiding, blocking cameras, or using force to remove them. Portrayal of this conduct in newspapers or on television could prejudice prospective jurors and harm the company's reputation in the community.

Do not consent to a warrantless search or to a search beyond the scope of the warrant. Even though the company may have nothing to hide, there is little gained by giving government investigators carte blanche to rummage through company records in an attempt to conjure up damaging evidence.

Likewise, because search warrants are often executed in a circus atmosphere, which terrifies company employees, interviews conducted under intimidating circumstances can lead to inaccurate statements that must be clarified at a later date. Accordingly, it is prudent to advise employees that they do not have to talk to the investigators, that it is entirely their decision to talk to anyone, and that if they choose to speak with investigators, the company will make counsel available prior to the interview if they so desire. Do not, however, instruct the employees not to cooperate. This could lead to allegations of obstruction of justice. In other words, companies should advise employees that they do not have to talk to investigating officers unless they so choose, but the company should not develop a policy or make statements prohibiting employees from talking to the investigators.

The company should monitor the search to ensure that it is proceeding within the proper scope. If the investigators insist on interviewing employees on company premises during the execution of the search warrant, the company should object to interviews being conducted on company time and company premises, at least until the employees can be advised of their rights with regard to the interviews and counsel can be provided. A representative of the company should follow the investigators to the extent permitted and note carefully what the investigators take. The company will receive at the end of the search a detailed receipt of the property seized, but the receipt can be confusing and not particularly helpful. Therefore, a detailed list of seized documents prepared by a company employee is normally more helpful in conducting a subsequent internal investigation.

The company representative also should observe whether any physical items are seized and whether any soil or other samples are taken. If the agents take samples, the company should request "split" samples right away. Certain chemicals must be tested within limited time periods to ensure the validity of the results. Also, if photographs or videotapes are taken, the company will want copies; and if employees are interviewed, someone should list all employees interviewed so the company can follow up in its own investigation.

The company also should make arrangements with the investigators to obtain copies of all seized documents as quickly as possible. During the subsequent internal investigation, the company will want to know precisely what the investigators have in their possession.

It is also essential to get an environmental consultant involved quickly. Indeed, it is desirable to get the consultant to the premises during the course of the search warrant, if possible. The consultant can then observe the agents taking samples and the manner in which they are taken. Of course, one of the most serious problems for the investigating agency is the failure of the agents during the seizure of evidence to follow required procedures for the taking of samples. Improper sampling as well as improper testing of those samples may result in fatal flaws to the investigators' case.[3]

Finally, a search warrant should cause a company to believe it may have serious problems. A search warrant is obtained by going to a court with an affidavit showing sufficient cause to permit the court to sign off on the search warrant. It is a serious matter for investigators and should be treated accordingly by the company. Consequently, as soon as the officers leave the premises, the company should begin its own internal investigation. If the suggestions above have been followed, the internal investigation may run smoothly.

B. *Agency Demands to Review and Photocopy Documents*

Often an agency that has an ongoing regulatory inspection function at a company will arrive and demand to view and photocopy documents pursuant to a permit issued to the company. This procedure can also cause confusion. Although it is not as confrontational as the execution of a search warrant, a government demand for documents provides the requesting agency with just as much information in terms of volume and detail as a wide-ranging search warrant. Agency demands for documents should serve as a high-level warning that the company may have environmental prob-

---

3. *See, e.g.,* People v. Mobil Oil Corp., 143 Cal. App. 3d 261 (1983).

lems. Presumably, the regulatory agency is there to review and photocopy documents in the civil context, not as part of a criminal investigation. A criminal investigation requires a search warrant.[4]

In response to a demand to review and photocopy documents, the company should read the request carefully. Again, it is advisable to consult experienced counsel. The company representative should be present at all times to observe what is being reviewed and photocopied. The company representative should take notes of what occurs during the regulatory agents' visit, and should request copies of all documents the regulatory agency photocopies. The prudent company will perceive this investigation to be a very serious matter and will conduct an ensuing investigation of its own.

C. *Notices of Violations*

A notice of violation, citation, or other document indicating a problem with the facility is typically served on a lower-level employee. Companies should set up an in-house procedure to ensure that the notice of violation is reported immediately to management.

In the past, companies have often allowed lower-level employees to handle these notices with the agencies, only to find themselves later embroiled in civil or criminal litigation with the agency. The notice or citation should state on its face the problem perceived by the agency. However, the absence of a criminal warning on the citation itself does not mean the investigation will not someday turn into a criminal enforcement action. In a time of increasing public pressure for environmental compliance and of increased use of the government's criminal enforcement power, these notices should be treated seriously by the company—both because of the immediate administrative problems and because of the potential civil or criminal enforcement actions. Usually, a consultant should be called in immediately and an internal investigation should begin.

D. *Conducting a Reactive Internal Investigation*

One of the most unique aspects of conducting an internal investiga-

---

4. *See, e.g.*, United States v. Utecht, 238 F.3d 882, 886-87 (7th Cir. 2001); Salwasser Mfg. Co. v. Municipal Ct., 94 Cal. App. 3d 223, 156 Cal. Rptr. 292 (1979); People v. Todd Shipyards Corp., 192 Cal. App. 3d Supp. 20, 238 Cal. Rptr. 761 (1987); Los Angeles Chem. Co. v. Superior Ct., 226 Cal. App. 3d 703, 276 Cal. Rptr. 647 (1990) (interpreting federal search and seizure law).

tion in the environmental area is the importance of an expert or consultant. Technical issues, such as the improper taking or testing of samples, can be critically fatal to the prosecutor's criminal case. Even in a civil dispute with a regulatory agency, technical problems with data can often force the regulatory agency to reach a more beneficial settlement in favor of the company. Finally, an outside consultant brings to the investigation the benefit of a fresh perspective and the objectivity of being independent of the company. Therefore, it is a tremendous advantage for the company to have an experienced engineer or specific consultant on its team.[5]

The company's outside counsel and the consultant should execute a written agreement as soon as possible. This establishes that the consultant is an agent of, works with, and reports to the lawyer. This procedure protects the consultant's work on attorney-client privilege and work product theories.[6]

The consultant can also serve an essential role during the interviews of company employees due to the importance of technical issues in these cases. The consultant may attend some of the employees' interviews with the lawyer to help explore and clarify these critical issues.

Many of the aspects of an internal environmental corporate investigation—interviewing employees, preparing interview memoranda, advising employees of their rights, and reporting to management—are conducted in much the same manner as described above and in other chapters of this book. One significant difference, however, may be the speed at which it is often necessary to conduct an internal environmental investigation. This is partly due to concerns that the company could be hit quickly with a parallel administrative proceeding.

Although the EPA generally does not favor parallel proceedings, at the state level they are very common. For example, when a company is served with a warrant or notice of violation regarding effluent to the sewer, a criminal investigation typically has already been or soon will be referred to a prosecutor, who could take several months to prepare a case and determine if criminal prosecution is appropriate. On the other hand, if there is a problem with effluent to the sewer line, the agency that has

---

5. Although investigators and regulatory agencies are steadily improving in their technical expertise, it should be noted that very few of the regulatory or investigative agents are engineers or Ph.Ds.

6. This "privilege" aspect of an internal investigation is discussed in detail in a prior chapter of this book and therefore will not be belabored here.

issued a sewer permit to the company probably will order the company to appear in the near future at a hearing to show why the sewer line should not be severed. If the sewer line is severed, it could put the company out of business. Thus, the company is caught in an unpleasant squeeze between trying to keep the sewer line open and avoiding admissions that might damage the defense of a subsequent criminal case. Therefore, reactive internal investigations should be conducted soon after government action such as service of a search warrant or a notice of violation so that strategic decisions can be made as quickly as possible.

III. VOLUNTARY ENVIRONMENTAL INTERNAL INVESTIGATIONS

Voluntary environmental internal investigations typically are performed for one of two reasons: (1) to ascertain the status of the company's compliance with the environmental statutes and regulations to which the company is subject; and (2) to investigate conditions existing on real estate the company contemplates selling.

The latter is part and parcel of environmental due diligence investigations undertaken by both parties to a real estate transaction or corporate rearrangement, and can be more fully addressed in a treatise focusing on these transactions. Therefore, the following material focuses on compliance audits.

A. *Reasons for Environmental Compliance Audits*

The need for environmental compliance audits is triggered by the fact that many companies and industries are regulated by environmental laws to varying degrees. At minimum, many companies have permits that are provided by one or more agencies and that are necessary to conduct business. These permits not only authorize the agencies to visit and inspect the company periodically, but also to prepare and submit reports and other technical documents to the agencies. In this growing arena of required permits and documentation, many companies now deem it prudent to conduct internal environmental audits to ensure compliance with all the regulatory requirements.

Internal audits of environmental documentation are becoming more critical as regulatory agencies and prosecutorial offices proceed against companies failing to maintain required documentation. Many permit violations are now misdemeanors carrying strict liability. In this atmosphere of strict liability, the regulated community has ever-greater incentives to routinely conduct their own audits.

In addition to audits of environmental permits and documentation, other factors encourage companies to conduct voluntary internal investigations. Audits can be conducted facility-by-facility and building-by-building to survey all environmental issues. Internal audits can review the company's discharge, storage, and disposal practices, and can examine disposal equipment, printouts, and other technical aspects of the facility to ensure that there are no hidden equipment or operational deficiencies. Also, audits can look at the potential exposure of employees to harmful substances and reveal whether all proper safeguards are in place and that required disclosures are being made to employees. Companies should not underestimate the OSHA implications of operations subject to environmental regulation, especially now that OSHA matters are being enforced in their own right.[7]

Environmental audits can also be beneficial in discovering and deterring possible criminal prosecutions based on illegal disposals by rogue employees. For example, in large companies, one department may be in charge of all incoming materials; a different department may be in charge of manifesting hazardous waste and hauling it off. If a rogue employee is illegally disposing of hazardous waste, the company may be caught in a situation where the left hand does not know what the right hand is doing. In other words, no one will realize that, given the materials coming into the company and the manufacturing process, much more hazardous waste should be manifested and hauled off. An environmental audit looking at the big picture will likely discover this problem.

B. *Importance of Periodic Audits by Outside Consultants*

Although most routine audits are conducted by the company's own staff, periodic audits conducted by independent technical experts or consultants together with lawyers should be considered by companies. The consultant can identify the areas of vulnerability for the company, such as whether the focus should be on air issues, discharges to sewers or waterways, underground tanks, asbestos, or a host of other potential concerns.

---

7. For example, the district attorney for the County of Los Angeles, California, has a department titled Environmental Crimes/OSHA Division.

This work, however, should be done under a lawyer's supervision, and for the purpose of providing legal advice to the company, to attempt to protect the work from disclosure absent a state audit privilege statute.

C. *Problems Posed by Audits*

Environmental audits should not be conducted cavalierly. At first blush, it seems that an environmental audit is always desirable; however, there are serious problems that can be presented by an internal investigation. For example, what if the environmental audit discovers unknown problems on the premises? Many cases of spills require immediate reporting. If an audit uncovers a recent spill that was not reported to management, it would open the door to problems with regulatory agencies. An audit might also discover a historic problem that did not trigger immediate reporting requirements. Nevertheless, a historic problem would have to be reported at a sale of the property. If the discovered contamination in any way affects groundwater, the company might have to advise a regulatory agency. Once the regulatory agent is advised of a problem, costly preliminary sampling, reports, and subsequently expensive remediation could be required. Although these concerns do not commend an avoidance of auditing, the company should be aware of ramifications that might flow from the result of the audit, and be committed to taking corrective measures if problems are discovered.

Another serious concern presented by an environmental audit is the possible necessity to disclose the findings at a subsequent date. For example, if the company ends up in civil or criminal litigation over environmental issues, the opposing party probably will serve a document request or subpoena *duces tecum* demanding any and all environmental audits conducted by the company. While the company will attempt to protect these documents under various arguments of privilege, including any statutory privilege under state law, a voluntary environmental audit may be more difficult to protect than a consultant's investigation pursuant to a reactive internal company investigation. It is very difficult to persuade a court that a voluntary environmental audit was done in anticipation of litigation and is therefore work product. With regard to attorney-client privilege, it is also difficult to protect pure facts contained in an audit report. The company should therefore realize at the outset that a voluntary environmental audit does not have absolute protection from disclosure.

As a final thought, it should be noted that the Department of Justice continues to evaluate the issue of how to exercise prosecutorial discretion when the violator company has conducted an environmental audit or has disclosed the violations to the government. In short, an environmental audit is perceived by the Department of Justice as an important mitigating factor in favor of the company, especially if all necessary corrective action recommended by the audit has been implemented by the company.[8]

D. *Audit Privilege Laws*

In order to address some of the uncertainties related to auditing, more than twenty states have enacted environmental audit privilege laws.[9] Most state laws provide a privilege for an environmental audit report under certain circumstances, and usually require any environmental violation to be corrected in order for the privilege to apply. In addition, many state laws also provide qualified penalty immunity for voluntary disclosures of violations discovered during an environmental audit. These laws significantly limit the risk of performing environmental audits and then disclosing violations to the regulatory agency.

Companies should be careful when using state privilege and immunity laws, since EPA believes it is not bound by these laws and it is possible that a violation that is voluntarily disclosed under a state law may still be subject to enforcement actions by EPA. Companies may also want to consider using EPA's audit policy when disclosing violations of environmental laws, although the policy does not provide a privilege for audit reports and provides limited penalty immunity.[10]

IV. CONCLUSION

In a quickly changing world, all companies that have any exposure to environmental issues should be keenly aware of the increasing role of

---

8. *See, e.g.,* June 3, 1991 Memorandum of U.S. Dept. of Justice from Richard B. Stewart, Asst. Attorney General, to all U.S. Attorneys.

9. At this time, the following states have enacted such laws: Alaska, Arkansas, Colorado, Idaho, Illinois, Indiana, Iowa, Kansas, Kentucky, Michigan, Minnesota, Mississippi, Montana, Nebraska, Nevada, New Hampshire, New Jersey, Ohio, Oregon, Rhode Island, South Carolina, South Dakota, Texas, Utah, Virginia, and Wyoming.

10. Incentives for Self-Policing: Discovery, Disclosure, Correction and Prevention of Violations, 65 Fed. Reg. 19,618, (Apr. 11, 2000).

regulatory agencies and prosecutorial offices in environmental compliance. Companies should have procedures in place to react quickly to any aggressive move by an agency, such as a search warrant, demand to review documents, or notices of violation. The company's quick response to initial indications of environmental problems will greatly enhance a subsequent internal investigation. To avoid environmental problems with regulatory agencies and prosecutorial offices, companies are turning more and more to internal environmental audits. Although there are positive and worthwhile reasons to conduct environmental audits and, indeed, companies should be encouraged to do so, certain areas of concern may arise from unfavorable findings in an environmental audit. Nevertheless, as criminal and civil prosecution by regulatory agencies increases and private-party litigation over contamination escalates, prophylactic environmental audits will undoubtedly increase in importance.

APPENDIX
SEARCH WARRANT CHECKLIST

Following is a short checklist of things to do if a search warrant is served on your place of business.

1. Identify who is heading the group executing the warrant.
2. Obtain and read a copy of the search warrant.
3. Call your lawyer with the following information:
   - the fact of the warrant
   - the law enforcement and regulatory agencies involved
   - the areas to be searched under the provisions of the warrant
   - the types of evidence to be seized under the warrant
4. Ask whether employees may be sent home.
5. Observe the course of the search, but do not interfere with it.
6. Note the type of evidence seized, including:
   - documents
   - physical items
   - soil or other samples
   - photographs and/or videotapes
   - interviews of individual employees
   - audio recordings of interviews
7. If possible, designate one employee to deal with the agents and to take notes during the search.
8. Advise employees not to interfere with the search.
9. Advise employees about their rights concerning interviews by investigators.
10. Obtain a detailed receipt for all of the evidence seized.

Report of the Investigation **11**

Edwin G. Schallert & Natalie R. Williams*

* Edwin G. Schallert is a partner at Debevoise & Plimpton in New York, New York. Natalie R. Williams is deputy chief of the civil rights bureau of the Office of the New York State Attorney General in New York, New York.

I. INTRODUCTION

AT FIRST GLANCE, A WRITTEN investigative report may seem an indispensable conclusion to an internal corporate investigation. One might conclude, for example, that there is no better way to persuade corporate officials of the necessity of remedial action, or government lawyers of the legality of your position, than a well-reasoned, comprehensive statement in writing. To some, a written report is preferable to purely oral discussions between counsel and client for any of the following reasons:

- Often providing detailed information about questionable business activities and their legal implications, the report can be a valuable aid for corporate management in deciding what steps, if any, to take in addressing the matter.
- If wrongdoing is identified, a report offers tangible evidence that an internal corporate investigation has been performed and that corrective action is under way. This may forestall a more intrusive government investigation and can be used in settlement negotiations with government agencies.
- Government agencies may require the preparation of a written report and access to it, or at least a summary of the report.
- When not required by government counsel, a detailed report of fact and law may be an important tool in persuading government lawyers that misconduct did not occur and that criminal or civil proceedings should not be brought.
- In the context of a derivative action, a written report may be used as evidence in support of a motion by the board of directors to terminate a lawsuit.

Yet these benefits are accompanied by a variety of risks, all quite serious.

- A written report may contain "smoking-gun" evidence that, if discovered in later litigation, may spawn or strengthen lawsuits against the client that commissioned the report.
- Production of a report to a government agency may result in the loss of all legal privileges associated with preparing the report, opening up virtually all underlying files in the agency investigation, as well as later, related private litigation.

- Production to government lawyers may result in the affirmative use by the agency and possibly civil litigants of any "admissions" within the report, under Federal Rule of Evidence 801(d)(2).

- The conceptual inconsistencies that surround application of established privileges can make these documents susceptible to discovery by a host of adverse parties. Consider several actual examples:

  — Shareholders in a securities fraud action were granted discovery of an internal investigative report prepared by company counsel pursuant to a consent decree with the Securities and Exchange Commission.[1]

  — An internal investigative report commissioned by a company to investigate allegations of fraudulent business dealings on the part of corporate employees was initially held to be not exempt from disclosure to a civil litigant.[2]

  — Third parties were granted access to internal investigative reports that had been voluntarily disclosed to government agencies.[3]

  — On the basis of an internal investigative report prepared while a lawyer in private practice, former Attorney General Griffin Bell was sued for libel by an employee identified in the report as having knowingly assisted in the orchestration of a multimillion-dollar check-kiting scheme.[4]

  — Lawyers conducting an internal investigation found that when the allegations underlying the investigation later resulted in a lawsuit, they were unable to act as trial counsel because opposing counsel designated them as fact witnesses at trial.[5]

---

1. Osterneck v. E.T. Barwick Indus., 82 F.R.D. 81, 87 (N.D. Ga. 1979).

2. Spectrum Sys. Int'l Corp. v. Chemical Bank, 157 A.D.2d 444, 558 N.Y.S.2d 486 (1st Dept.,1990), rev'd, 78 N.Y.2d 581, N.E.2d 1055, 575 N.Y.S.2d 809 (1991).

3. In re Subpoena Duces Tecum (Fulbright & Jaworski), 738 F.2d 1367 (D.C. Cir. 1984) (disclosure to SEC implied waiver of both attorney-client and work-product privileges); In re Sealed Case, 676 F.2d 793, 818 (D.C. Cir. 1982) ("selective disclosure for tactical purposes waives the privilege"); Permian Corp. v. United States, 665 F.2d 1214 (D.C. Cir. 1981).

4. Pearce v. E.F. Hutton Group, 664 F. Supp. 1490 (D.D.C. 1987).

5. See Burton, *Baxter Fails to Quell Questions on Its Role in the Israeli Boycott,* WALL ST. J., Apr. 25, 1991, at A10.

In short, internal investigative reports can cause disputes as well as resolve them. And, not infrequently, lawyers and clients have wished the reports had never been prepared.

In light of the serious risks that attend its preparation, a written report should be avoided where possible in favor of an oral report to select corporate officers, special committees, or members of the board of directors. The oral report minimizes many, though not all, of the risks associated with conducting an investigation, since the primary documents used in making the presentation, counsel's notes, are afforded virtual absolute protection under the work-product doctrine.[6] An oral report provides needed flexibility to investigative counsel if ever compelled to testify about the investigation and its findings. Conversely, a written report necessarily confines later testimony to the expressed statement of facts, opinions, and conclusions found within the report. Furthermore, without a written analysis, adverse parties have no rule 801(d)(2) admissions and no road map on which to rely later.

In instances when a written report is considered essential, either as a means of dissuading government action or of spurring remedial action within the company, the issue then becomes how best to structure the report and the underlying internal investigation to minimize the risks of discovery and liability for counsel.

This chapter focuses on the most significant problems surrounding the written internal investigative report and suggests methods for minimizing those problems. First, the chapter examines the courts' application of the attorney-client and work-product doctrines in the context of the internal investigative report. Next, the issue of libel liability for counsel preparing the report is addressed, analyzing the applicability of the "opinion" and common-law qualified, "interest-related" privileges to the written report. Finally, the chapter recommends strategies for structuring the investigation and reporting to the company, whether orally or in writing.

---

6. Counsel's notes and other investigative information are generally characterized as "opinion work product." *See infra* notes 20-25 and accompanying text. *See also* Upjohn Co. v. United States, 449 U.S. 383, 399 (1980) ("[f]orcing an attorney to disclose notes and memoranda of witnesses' oral statements is particularly disfavored because it tends to reveal the attorney's mental processes").

II. DISCOVERABILITY OF THE INTERNAL INVESTIGATIVE REPORT

The attorney-client privilege and the work-product doctrine have been the principal legal devices used to protect corporate internal investigative reports and their underlying documentation from discovery. Unfortunately, the protection afforded to investigative reports by these privileges has been neither complete nor wholly predictable.[7]

A. *Attorney-Client Privilege*

The attorney-client privilege exists to "encourage full and frank communication between attorneys and their clients . . . [since] sound legal advice or advocacy serves public ends and . . . depends upon the lawyer's being fully informed."[8] Because the privilege is concerned with protecting the relationship between the lawyer and the client,[9] a critical element of a successful claim of privilege is that the contested communications be for the purpose of securing legal advice.

1. Ensuring Privilege Entails Rendering Legal Advice

If the lawyer conducting an internal investigation was hired to render legal advice and the report in fact reflects this advice, it should be privileged. Some courts, however, take the narrow view that a lawyer's investigation of the facts makes the lawyer more like a private eye than a lawyer and the report is not privileged. This view confuses the state of the law and undercuts a lawyer's rightful function.

Most courts have examined both the context of the internal investigation and the resulting report to determine whether a lawyer was em-

---

7. The discussion of the attorney-client privilege and work-product doctrine within this chapter is not intended as a comprehensive treatment of the law in this area; instead, it is provided to remind the lawyer conducting the investigation that the inadvertent discovery of a written report can likely be avoided when counsel keeps uppermost in mind basic principles of privilege. For a complete discussion of these legal doctrines, see chapter 2.

8. Upjohn v. United States, 449 U.S. 383, 389 (1981).

9. United States v. United Shoe Mach. Corp., 89 F. Supp. 357 (D. Mass. 1950).

ployed to render legal advice or mere investigative services.[10] Courts have considered the circumstances of the lawyers' initial engagement in the matter, the tasks performed during the course of the investigation, and the content of the investigative report, focusing on whether the document contained "legal" opinions or "business" recommendations. The mere fact that lawyers were employed to conduct the investigation has not guaranteed a successful claim of privilege under the attorney-client doctrine.[11]

One court has concluded that the participation of lawyers in an internal investigation provided prima facie evidence that the purpose of the communications was to secure legal advice.[12] *Diversified* involved an internal investigation into an alleged "slush fund" maintained by the company allegedly to bribe purchasing agents, including the plaintiff. The board of directors of Diversified commissioned Wilmer, Cutler & Pickering to conduct an internal investigation into the matter. After a preliminary review, Wilmer Cutler prepared a memorandum stating that it would examine relevant records and recommend that the corporation engage an independent accounting firm to assist in the investigation. The final report, which the plaintiff sought through discovery, included the substance of statements made by interviewees, the findings of the accountants, and recommendations by both the firm and the accountants. While a panel of the court originally determined that Wilmer Cutler "was employed solely for the purpose of making an investigation of facts and to make business recommendations with respect to the future conduct of Diversified" and that the work done by Wilmer Cutler "could have been performed just as readily by nonlawyers aided to the extent necessary by a firm of public accountants," the Court of Appeals for the Eighth Circuit sitting en banc reasoned that, while accountants and lay investigators could have just as easily interviewed the employees, "neither would have had the training, skills, and background necessary to make the independent analysis and recommendations which the Board felt essential to the future welfare of the corporation."[13] The en banc court further observed that "the applica-

---

10. *See In re* Grand Jury Subpoena Duces Tecum, 731 F.2d 1032, 1037-38 (2d Cir. 1984).

11. *See In re* Grand Jury Subpoena, 599 F.2d 504, 511 (2d Cir. 1979) ("[p]articipation of the general counsel does not automatically cloak the investigation with legal garb").

12. Diversified Indus., Inc. v. Meredith, 572 F.2d 596 (8th Cir. 1977) (en banc).

13. *Id.* at 608, 610.

tion of the attorney-client privilege to this matter and others like it will encourage corporations to seek out and correct wrongdoing in their own house and to do so with lawyers who are obligated by the Code of Professional Responsibility to conduct the inquiry in an independent and ethical manner."[14]

Other courts have reacted differently. Noting that a lawyer's particular expertise in interviewing witnesses and compiling and evaluating data makes the lawyer an ideal candidate for performing an internal investigation, courts have often reasoned that the use of such skills in an internal investigation does not mean that the lawyer was employed for his legal expertise or for the purpose of securing legal advice.[15]

For example, in *Spectrum Systems Int'l Co. v. Chemical Bank*,[16] an internal investigative report prepared by an outside law firm to examine allegations of fraudulent business dealings between certain bank employees and the company's outside vendors was sought in civil suit. An intermediate appellate court held the report was not exempt from disclosure to a civil litigant in a suit for nonpayment of consulting services. The court reasoned that outside counsel's role was that of investigator as opposed to legal advisor.[17] On appeal, New York's highest court reversed, concluding that the report was made primarily to give legal advice.[18]

2. Required Report May Not Be Privileged

Courts have also considered the "voluntariness" of the corporation's decision to conduct an internal investigation. In *Osterneck v. E. T.*

---

14. *Id.*

15. Osterneck v. E. T. Barwick Indus., 82 F.R.D. at 85; *see also In re* Grand Jury Subpoena, 599 F.2d at 510-11 (documents resulting from an internal investigation conducted by senior management and general counsel into alleged foreign bribes were not within scope of attorney-client privilege).

16. 78 N.Y.2d 371, 581 N.E.2d 1055, 575 N.Y.S.2d 809 (1991).

17. 157 A.D. 2d 444, 588 N.Y.S.2d 486 (1st Dept. 1990). The court also noted that no standard legal tasks, such as legal research, had been performed by the lawyers in course of the investigation.

18. 78 N.Y.2d 371, 581 N.E.2d 1055, 575 N.Y.S.2d 809. Investigative reports prepared by inside counsel have been subjected to even greater scrutiny because these individuals often provide business as well as legal advice. *See In re* Grand Jury Subpoena, 599 F.2d at 510-11.

Barwick Industries,[19] an internal investigative report prepared by outside counsel was held discoverable by shareholders in an action alleging securities fraud. The court reasoned that the lack of "voluntariness" in the corporation's decision to conduct the investigation—the internal investigation was commissioned pursuant to a consent decree with the SEC—indicated that counsel engaged to perform the investigation had been employed solely "to investigate and report."[20] The court specifically stated that it could take notice of the fact that "the decision to set up the [Special Review Committee] and hire special counsel was not reached independently or voluntarily." A better reasoned opinion reached a different result, recognizing a "hybrid" privilege in connection with investigations by special counsel hired pursuant to an SEC consent decree.[21]

3. The Better Rule

The assessment in these cases of the lawyer's role in the internal corporate investigation is questionable. First, because the lawyer's task often involves compiling relevant facts to form a legal opinion, the distinction between investigative and legal activities suggested in these cases is typically blurred. Second, in the corporate context, the demarcation between business advice and legal advice is especially fuzzy. The corporate lawyer's role is often to ascertain how, within the constraints of relevant legal obligations, the corporation should structure its business to achieve desired objectives. Moreover, in the context of the internal investigation, it is the suspected violation of a *legal* obligation that typically triggers the investigation. In these instances, the strands of business and legal advice cannot be easily disentangled.

Some courts also fail to consider perhaps the most important policy behind maintaining confidentiality of the internal investigative report: the promotion of corporate self-policing.[22] Uncertainty as to whether the in-

---

19. 82 F.R.D. 81 (N.D. Ga. 1979).

20. *Id.* at 85.

21. *See In re* LTV Civ. Litig., 89 F R.D. 595, 618-22 (N.D. Tex. 1981).

22. However, the suspicion that "many internal probes are really velvet-coated cover-ups" may cause the courts to be skeptical of invocations of this policy. One article notes that many legislators believe that after "the company's lawyers have framed the issues and defined the events, [the] written report can serve as a road map to help corporate officials orient their stories." Strasser, *Dicey Dilemmas: Corporate Probe Use Expanding*, NAT'L L.J., Jan. 9, 1989, at 1.

ternal investigative report is protected by the attorney-client privilege can only serve as a disincentive to corporations deciding whether to commission an internal investigation.

B. *Work-Product Doctrine: A More Certain Refuge*

The purpose of the work-product doctrine is to promote the adversarial system by protecting a lawyer's preparation on behalf of his or her client from discovery. Codifying the doctrine set forth in *Hickman v. Taylor*,[23] Rule 26(b)(3) delineates the elements of the work product protection for the federal courts and provides that documents or tangible things, prepared in anticipation of litigation or for trial, by or for another party or by or for that party's representative, are protected against discovery unless the party seeking disclosure can demonstrate substantial need, and that it would experience undue hardship about discovery.

1. Internal Investigations "in Anticipation of Litigation"

The "in anticipation of litigation" requirement has not posed a significant barrier to the protection of internal investigative reports from discovery. Most courts have recognized that once the suspicion of wrongdoing rises to the level where an internal investigation is commissioned, litigation is virtually inevitable, particularly where the investigation confirms wrongdoing. This recognition applies to a variety of actions, whether brought by shareholders, governmental agencies, or other parties.[24]

---

23. 329 U.S. 495 (1947).

24. *See In re* Grand Jury Investigation, 599 F.2d 1224, 1228-30 (3d Cir. 1979) (when internal investigation was prompted by suspected criminal violations, "litigation of some sort was almost inevitable"); *In re* LTV Sec. Litig., 89 F.R.D. 595, 612 (N.D. Tex. 1981) ("[i]nvestigation by a federal agency presents more than a remote prospect of future litigation and gives grounds for anticipating litigation sufficient for the work product rule to apply"); United States v. Lipshy, 492 F. Supp. 35, 44 (N.D. Tex. 1979) (bribery allegations and a simultaneous IRS investigation "rendered the prospect of litigation sufficiently likely"); *but see* Litton Sys., Inc. v. American Tel. & Tel. Co., 27 Fed. R. Serv. 2d 819, 821 (S.D.N.Y. 1979) (internal investigation concerning allegedly illegal activity by employees suggested only a "remote possibility" of litigation, insufficient to trigger work product immunity). *See also* cases cited *infra* at 48-49.

2. Reports That Receive Protection from Discovery

The qualified work-product doctrine can be overcome in some circumstances by a showing of substantial need and undue hardship. Opinion work product, defined as material that reveals the lawyer's opinions, conclusions, and mental impressions, receives near-absolute protection.[25] By contrast, ordinary work product, inherently factual in nature and not reflective of the lawyer's mental processes, is provided markedly less protection.[26]

The concept of opinion work product offers substantial assistance in efforts to protect internal investigative reports from discovery: the more the report reflects the lawyer's evaluative tasks, as opposed to mere factual findings, the greater the likelihood that the report, or substantial portions of it, will be characterized as opinion work product.[27] Indeed, some

---

25. Parties seeking disclosure of documents defined as opinion work product must make a showing of extraordinary need. As the Supreme Court noted in *Upjohn*, "a far stronger showing of necessity and unavailability . . . would be necessary to compel disclosure" of opinion work product. 449 U.S. at 401-02. The Court, however, declined to decide whether such materials were entitled to absolute protection. Some lower courts, however, have held that opinion work product is afforded absolute protection. *In re* Martin-Marietta Corp., 856 F.2d 619, 626 (4th Cir. 1988), *cert. denied*, 109 S. Ct. 1655 (1989) ("First and most generally, opinion work product is to be accorded great protection by the courts. While certainly actual disclosure of pure mental impressions may be deemed waiver, and while conceivably there may be indirect waiver in extreme circumstances, we think generally such work product is not subject to discovery."). *In re* Grand Jury Investigation (Sturgis), 412 F. Supp. 943, 949 (1976) ("[interview notes] are so much a product of the lawyer's thinking and so little probative of the witness's actual words that they are absolutely protected from disclosure."); *In re* Grand Jury Proceedings (Duffy), 473 F.2d 840, 848 (8th Cir. 1973) (while "statements prepared or signed by the interviewee" may be discovered upon a showing of good cause, "attorney's personal recollections, notes, and memoranda" may not).

26. Though the determination of whether the particular circumstances merit discovery of ordinary work product is made on a case-by-case basis, courts have considered the nature of the materials requested, the effort entailed in compiling the information, the availability of alternative sources of information, the relevance of the materials to the issues presented, and the procedural posture in which the claim arises in making this evaluation.

27. Often, in analyzing claims of privilege under the work-product doctrine, the courts will perform an in camera review of the documents in order to better evaluate the requesting party's need or undue hardship. If the requesting party carries its burden of

statements, seemingly factual in nature, may be protected as opinion work product if by discovery the adverse party would be able to ascertain counsel's thought processes or line of reasoning. Consequently, where the report is written in a way that minimizes verbatim statements by interviewees and provides as much of the information as possible in the form of opinion or evaluation, the report is more likely to receive near-total protection from discovery.[28] One should keep clearly in mind, however, that the greater the reliance on subjective opinion and mental impressions, the greater the harm should the report be discovered through inadvertent waiver.

While the foregoing doctrines offer substantial assistance to clients desiring to protect internal investigative reports from discovery, a more tailored framework in which to evaluate these claims would be the privilege of self-critical analysis.[29]

C. *Expanding the Privilege of Self-Criticism*

Although the nascent self-criticism privilege has generally protected only corporate materials prepared for required government reports, the rationale behind this privilege is consistent with that favoring protection of internal investigative reports of corporate wrongdoing from discovery: promoting the public interest in encouraging institutional self-policing. As a result, the self-criticism privilege offers perhaps a more appropriate analytical framework than either the attorney-client privilege or work-product doctrine.

---

demonstrating substantial need and undue hardship, the in camera review will enable the courts to excise those parts constituting opinion work product.

28. In some cases, however, the court has granted discovery of opinion work product where it was impossible to redact the contested documents "in such a way as to allow production of the needed facts without disclosing a lawyer's mental impression, opinions, or legal theories." *See* AMERICAN BAR ASSOCIATION, THE ATTORNEY-CLIENT PRIVILEGE AND WORK-PRODUCT DOCTRINE, at 109 (1989), *discussing* Xerox Corp. v. Int'l Bus. Mach. Co., 64 F.R.D. 367 (S.D.N.Y. 1974).

29. As one commentator noted, if the goal of courts analyzing discovery attempts of internal investigative reports and underlying documentation was to encourage corporate self-investigation, the selection of the "attorney-client privilege and work product immunity as the vehicles for protecti[on]" was not the best. Note, *Discovery of Internal Corporate Investigations*, 32 STAN. L. REV. 1163, 1177 (1980).

1. Self-Criticism Privilege Encourages Open Exchange

First fashioned in *Bredice v. Doctor; Hospital, Inc.*,[30] the privilege of self-criticism was held to protect from discovery in a malpractice suit the minutes and reports of a hospital investigative committee charged with the task of improving hospital care. The *Bredice* court reasoned that since confidentiality was critical to the committee's evaluative task, disclosure would greatly diminish the frank and open exchange necessary for effective internal review; the important public interest in health care required that these discussions be encouraged. Balancing the public interest in improved health care against the individual's need for discovery, the court denied discovery of the committee minutes.

2. Self-Criticism Privilege Offers Uncertain Haven

In the corporate context, the self-criticism privilege, rooted in the *Bredice* public interest rationale, has protected internal corporate reports examining equal employment opportunity practices.[31] Though no clear guidelines have been articulated, documents qualifying for protection under the self-criticism privilege have satisfied the following criteria: (1) the document has resulted from a critical self-analysis undertaken by the party desiring protection; (2) the public has a strong interest in maintaining the free flow of information of the type sought; and (3) the information is of the type whose flow would be stifled without protection.[32] Unfortunately, courts have defined the scope of the privilege in terms of subjective or evaluative materials reminiscent of a distinction found in the context of the work product doctrine.[33] The self-

---

30. 50 F.R.D. 249 (D.D.C. 1970), *aff'd*, 479 F.2d 920 (D.C. Cir. 1973).

31. *See* Banks v. Lockheed-Georgia Co., 53 F.R.D. 283 (N.D. Ga. 1971); O'Connor v. Chrysler Corp., 86 F.R.D. 211 (D. Mass. 1980). While a few courts have expressly rejected the self-criticism privilege, a number of courts have approved its rationale. *See* Note, *Criticizing the Self-Criticism Privilege*, 1987 ILL. L. REV. 675, 679-80 (1984).

32. Note, *The Privilege of Self-Critical Analysis*, 96 HARV. L. REV. 1083, 1086 (1983).

33. Lloyd v. Cessna Aircraft Co., 74 F.R.D. 518 (E.D. Tenn. 1977) (product list not protected); O'Connor v. Chrysler Corp., 86 F.R.D. 211, 218 (D. Mass. 1980) (facts upon which self-evaluative report is based are discoverable); Roberts v. National Detroit Corp., 87 F.R.D. 30, 32 (E.D. Mich. 1980) (while statistical information is discoverable, evaluation of institutional goals is not); Wright v. Patrolmen's Benevolent Ass'n, 72 F.R.D. 161, 164 (S.D.N.Y. 1976) (witnesses' names and statements are not protected).

criticism privilege has also been held inapplicable against government entities.[34]

Despite the broad range of documents ostensibly meeting these criteria, the courts have been hesitant to grant the privilege broad application given its undefined scope.[35] The Court of Appeals for the Seventh Circuit, for example, has expressly declined to recognize a privilege of self-critical analysis for internal corporate investigations examining suspected corporate improprieties.[36] In a case implicating not the self-criticism privilege but rather its principal rationale—the encouragement of free, frank evaluations concerning matters in which the public has an interest—the Supreme Court refused to recognize a qualified privilege shielding tenure peer review materials from disclosure, reasoning, in part, that the "chilling effect" on frank evaluation of academics by their colleagues caused by the absence of such a privilege, was, at best, speculative.[37] Judicial apprehension about a broad self-criticism privilege may stem from the Supreme Court's admonitions against the expansion of existing, and the creation of new, privilege doctrines.[38] However, this privilege would avoid some of

---

34. Federal Trade Comm'n. v. TRW, 628 F.2d 207, 211 (D.C. Cir. 1980); United States v. Noall, 587 F.2d 123, 126 (2d Cir. 1978), *cert. denied*, 441 U.S. 923 (1979).

35. Rule 501 of the Federal Rules of Evidence leaves the formulation of new privileges to the courts. It states, in relevant part:

> Except as otherwise required by the Constitution of the United States or provided by Act of Congress or in rules prescribed by the Supreme Court . . . the privilege of a witness . . . shall be governed by the principles of the common law as they may be interpreted by the courts of the United States in the light of reason and experience.

FED. R. EVID. 501.

36. *In re* Continental Illinois Sec. Litig., 732 F.2d 1302, 1315 (7th Cir. 1984) ("There is no general privilege, analogous to the fifth amendment's protection against self-incrimination, that protects against disclosure of information that may lead to civil liability.").

37. University of Penn. v. EEOC, 110 S. Ct. 577, 587-88 (1990). Reasoning that the asserted injury to the academic freedom was "speculative," the Court stated: "Although it is possible that some evaluators may become less candid as the possibility of disclosure increases, others may simply ground their evaluations in specific examples and illustrations in order to deflect potential claims of bias or unfairness."

38. *See, e.g.*, University of Penn. v. EEOC, 110 S. Ct. at 588 (Supreme Court is reluctant to recognize constitutional privileges of uncertain scope and application); Wei v. Bodner, 127 F.R.D. 91, 100 (D.N.J. 1989) (*Bredice* rationale is "questionable" in

the difficulties raised by placing corporate entities within the scope of privileges established for the individual, while advancing the public interest in corporate self-policing.

III. PROTECTING THE REPORT: SHAREHOLDER ACTIONS AND DISCLOSURE TO GOVERNMENT AGENCIES

A. *Shareholder Actions*

Shareholder suits, whether derivative or stockholder class actions, present a conceptual dilemma for the attorney-client privilege due to the fiduciary relationship that exists between the corporation and its shareholders. Because the corporation exists for the benefit of the shareholders, allowing the corporation free rein to assert the privilege against these same shareholders appears anomalous. On the other hand, the corporation will need to seek legal advice free from fear of disclosure to individual shareholders who may not represent the best interests of the majority of stockholders.

1. Company May Not Own the Privilege or Report

To strike an appropriate balance between the interests of shareholders and those of the corporation, several courts have incorporated a "good-cause" exception into the attorney-client privilege. The good-cause exception holds that the corporation maintains the right to assert the privilege in a shareholder suit "subject to the right of the stockholders to show cause why it should not be invoked in the particular instance."[39]

---

light of Supreme Court decisions in *United States v. Nixon*, 418 U.S. 683, 710 (1974) (stating "these exceptions to the demand for every man's evidence are not lightly created nor expansively construed, for they are in derogation of the search for truth"), and *Herbert v. Lando*, 441 U.S. 153, 175 (1979) (stating that "[e]videntiary privileges in litigation are not favored")).

39. Garner v. Wolfinbarger, 430 F.2d 1093, 1104 (5th Cir. 1970), *cert. denied*, 401 U.S. 974 (1971). The following factors were deemed relevant in making the "good cause" assessment:

[T]he number of shareholders and the percentage of stock they represent; the bona fides of the shareholders; the nature of the shareholders' claim and whether it is obviously colorable; the apparent necessity or desirability of the sharehold-

If discoverable by shareholders, the internal investigative report could provide damning evidence of corporate wrongdoing, thereby laying the foundation for shareholders' claims. Moreover, facts revealed in the internal investigative report could spawn lawsuits not previously contemplated. Given the threat of these consequences, corporations will be less likely to undertake internal investigations and to document those findings in a written report.

Recognizing the "great injury to the corporate interest in self investigation,"[40] courts have imposed a temporal limitation on the application of the good-cause exception. The exception has been held not to apply to postevent communications concerning offenses already completed."[41] This

---

ers having the information and the availability of it from other sources; whether, if the shareholders' claim is of wrongful action by the corporation, it is of action criminal, or illegal but not criminal, or of doubtful legality; whether the communication related to past or to prospective actions; whether the communication is of advice concerning the litigation itself; the extent to which the communication is identified versus the extent to which the shareholders are blindly fishing; the risk of revelation of trade secrets or other information in whose confidentiality the corporation has an interest for independent reasons.

Garner has been an influential decision, with some courts extending its rationale to fiduciary relationships outside the shareholder derivative context, as well as situations where the fiduciary relationship did not exist at the time of the communication. *See, e.g.*, Quintel Corp. v. Citibank, 567 F. Supp. 1357 (S.D.N.Y. 1983) (*Garner* applied to fiduciary relationship between bank and its client in context of a real estate transaction); Cohen v. Uniroyal, 80 F.R.D. 480, 484 (E.D. Pa. 1978) (*Garner* applied although no fiduciary relationship existed at the time communications were made). In light of these expansions of the *Garner* doctrine and their concomitant effect on the corporation's ability to assert the attorney-client privilege, some courts have criticized *Garner*'s logic and attempted narrowly to confine its scope. *See, e.g.*, Shirvani v. Capital Investing Corp., Inc., 112 F.R.D. 389, 390-91 (D. Conn. 1986) ("[t]he *Garner* problem is perhaps that the shareholder or other owed a duty of trust becomes too readily and artificially recognized as the 'client' for purpose of privilege."); Weil v. Investment/Indicators Research & Mgmt., Inc., 647 F.2d 18 (9th Cir. 1981) (refusing to extend *Garner* outside the context of shareholder derivative actions); Ward v. Succession of Freeman, 854 F.2d 780, 785 (5th Cir. 1988) ("clear that *Garner* did not establish an absolute exception to the attorney-client privilege rule"); *but see In re* Int'l Sys. & Controls Corp. Sec. Litig., 693 F.2d 1235, 1239 n.1 (5th Cir. 1982) (rejecting Ninth Circuit's limitation of the *Garner* doctrine solely to shareholder derivative actions).

40. *In re* LTV Sec. Litig., 89 F.R.D. 595, 608 (N.D. Tex. 1981).
41. *Id.* at 607.

distinction stems from a recognition that, after wrongdoing is complete, management will need to seek assistance from counsel. The internal investigative report, generally a postevent examination and evaluation of allegedly improper corporate practices, seems to fall within this category of protected postevent communications.

Whatever the status of the corporation's attorney-client privilege against its own shareholders, the work product protection should be available. It exists to protect information in the context of anticipated or pending litigation—exactly when shareholders seek information. Rejecting the application of the *Garner* good-cause exception in the context of the work product doctrine, the Court of Appeals for the Fifth Circuit, in *In re International Systems & Controls Corp.*,[42] reasoned that once there was a sufficient anticipation of litigation to trigger work product immunity, the "mutuality of interest" upon which the *Garner* exception is predicated is destroyed.

2. Affirmative Use Requires Production to Dissident Shareholders

The internal investigative report commissioned by a special litigation committee to evaluate the merits of a shareholder derivative action is in a different class. If the report is being used to support a motion by the board of directors to dismiss the action, courts have held that it is freely discoverable by shareholders and other third parties. In *Joy v. North*,[43] the Second Circuit Court of Appeals ruled that the corporation could not use the attorney-client privilege to shield its investigative report from shareholders when it sought to assert the report as evidence in support of its motion to terminate. In *In re Continental Illinois Securities Litigation*,[44] a newspa-

---

42. 693 F.2d 1235, 1239 (5th Cir. 1982). In that case, the corporation, desiring to enroll in the SEC's voluntary disclosure program, appointed a special audit committee to commission an internal investigation that was conducted by an outside law firm, assisted by independent accountants. Subsequently, a consent decree was negotiated with the SEC. A derivative action shortly followed, and the stockholders sought access to certain information found in the accountants' binders. The court held that the *Garner* doctrine should not be extended to the work product doctrine, because once the threshold of "anticipation of litigation" sufficient to trigger work product immunity has been reached, the "mutuality of interest" between corporation and shareholders no longer exists.

43. 692 F.2d 880, 894 (2d Cir. 1982), *cert. denied*, 460 U.S. 1051 (1983).

44. 732 F.2d 1302 (7th Cir. 1984).

per covering a shareholder suit was granted access to an internal investigative report that had been placed into evidence to support a motion to terminate the derivative action.[45]

B. *Disclosure to Government Agencies*

Disclosure of the internal investigative report to government agencies[46] may be beneficial, particularly if the internal investigation has uncovered evidence of wrongdoing. Providing government lawyers with a written analysis of fact and law may be, in counsel's mind, the only realistic means available of avoiding prosecution. By submitting the report to government agencies, the corporation may forestall a disruptive agency investigation and perhaps negotiate a favorable settlement. Despite these advantages, disclosure of the report to government entities may constitute a waiver of the privilege for a potentially damaging document, as well as all underlying documentation, to other agencies and to third parties.

1. "Limited" Waiver Usually Total Waiver

In accordance with a principal objective of both the work product and attorney-client privileges, the maintenance of confidentiality, disclosure of privileged documents or communications generally constitutes a waiver of the privilege.[47] However, in the context of voluntary corporate

---

45. 732 F.2d at 1314. Noting the Second Circuit's decision in *North* holding that disclosure of an investigative report in support of a motion to dismiss waived the privilege, the court reasoned that although it would not go so far as to rule the privilege waived upon disclosure, it nonetheless "attach[ed] less weight to the public interest in the attorney-client privilege and work product immunity ...than in a case where absolute confidentiality had been maintained."

46. This topic—Disclosure to Government Agencies—is treated at length in chapter 8. Here, the authors discuss it briefly because of its obvious relevance to the present topic. Not infrequently, written reports are prepared for the very purpose of dissuading government action, and thus counsel may choose to provide the report to government lawyers, in whole or in summary.

47. Under the attorney-client privilege, voluntary disclosure waives the privilege. *United States v. American Tel. & Tel.*, 642 F.2d 1285, 1299 (D.C. Cir. 1980). In contrast, under the work product doctrine, disclosure to parties "with common interests on a particular issue against a common adversary" generally does not constitute a waiver. *Id.* Indeed, some courts have suggested that disclosure of work product to a governmental agency under a confidentiality agreement *may* protect the contested work product. *See In re* Subpoena Duces Tecum, 738 F.2d at 1372-74 (reasoning "that parties did not have

disclosures of internal investigative findings to government agencies, a few courts have protected documents from discovery in subsequent proceedings under the concept of "limited" waiver.[48] First articulated in *Diversified*, the limited waiver theory recognizes the potential "chilling effects" a doctrine of total waiver would have on corporate cooperation in voluntary government disclosure programs and holds that disclosure of documents to a government agency does not effect a complete waiver of the privilege. This notion of "limited waiver" has encountered sharp criticism in both legal and academic circles.[49] Because the doctrine creates risks of encouraging tactical selective disclosure by corporations while offering speculative benefits,[50] most courts have rejected the limited waiver theory with respect to both the attorney-client and work product privileges, holding that disclosure of internal investigative reports and related documentation to government agencies waives the privilege in subsequent proceedings.[51]

---

any proper expectations of confidentiality which might mitigate" fairness considerations raised by disclosure). *In re* Sealed Case, 676 F.2d at 823 ("[c]orporations may protect their privileges . . . simply by being forthright with their regulators and identifying material as to which they claim privilege at the time they submit their voluntary disclosure reports."); *see also* Teachers Ins. & Annuity Ass'n v. Shamrock Broadcasting Co., 521 F. Supp. 638, 644-45 (S.D.N.Y. 1981) ("Disclosure to the SEC should be deemed a complete waiver of the attorney-client privilege unless the right to assert the privilege in subsequent proceedings is specifically reserved at the time disclosure is made.").

48. *See Diversified Indus.*, 572 F.2d at 611, 606 (since the company disclosed contested documents "in a separate and nonpublic SEC agency investigation, only a limited waiver of the privilege occurred"); *In re* LTV, 89 F.R.D. at 620-21 ("The voluntary disclosure of information to an agency, as part of an agency enforcement proceeding, often is viewed as only a partial waiver of the attorney-client privilege."); Byrnes v. IDS Realty Trust Co., 85 F.R.D. 679, 687-89 (S.D.N.Y. 1983) (supporting *Diversified*'s "limited waiver" theory).

49. *See, e.g.*, Note, *Discovery of Internal Corporate Investigations*, 32 Stan. L. Rev. 1163 (1980); Note, *The Limited Waiver Rule: Creation of an SEC-Corporation Privilege*, 36 Stan. L. Rev. 789 (1984).

50. *See Permian Corp.*, 665 F.2d at 1221, n.13 ("We cannot see how the developing procedure of corporations to employ independent outside counsel to investigate and advise them would be thwarted by telling a corporation that it cannot disclose the resulting reports to the SEC if it wishes to maintain their confidentiality.").

51. *See In re* Subpoena Duces Tecum (Fulbright & Jaworski), 738 F.2d at 1370 ("[f]or the purposes of the attorney-client privilege, there is nothing special about another federal agency in the role of potential adversary as compared to private party

2. Disclosure May Waive Protection of All Papers

Disclosure of the internal investigative report to government agencies presents the further problem of waiving the privilege for the report's underlying documentation. In *In re Sealed Case*, a grand jury sought information that had not been disclosed to the SEC when the company submitted its final report to the agency. Rejecting the corporation's argument that disclosure would thwart voluntary corporate cooperation with the government, the court upheld the grand jury's subpoena for the documents, giving special consideration to the following factors: (1) the final report had emphasized that it was based on a review of all relevant files; (2) the corporation had misrepresented the completeness of the file when it granted the SEC access to the records; and (3) the documents were particularly significant because they shed doubt on the truth of the final report.[52] Similarly, in *In re Martin Marietta Corp.*,[53] the court held that the corporation had waived the attorney-client privilege for materials that formed the basis for information disclosed to the U.S. Attorney.

These cases illustrate that courts will not accept uncritically generalized arguments based on the need to encourage corporate self-examination and cooperation. Particularly where courts sense that a corporation is trying to deceive or manipulate the government, they will not tolerate the use of a privilege as both a shield and a sword.

---

litigants acting as adversaries"); *In re* Sealed Case, 676 F.2d at 822-23 (while recognizing that the purposes of the work product doctrine were not inconsistent with selective disclosure, concluded that a corporation that decides that the benefits of participation in voluntary disclosure program outweigh the benefits of confidentiality "forgoes traditional protections of the adversary system . . . to avoid some of the traditional burdens"); Permian Corp. v. United States, 665 F.2d at 1221 ("client cannot be permitted to pick and choose among his opponents, waiving the privilege for some and resurrecting the claim of confidentiality to obstruct others, or to invoke the privilege as to communications whose confidentiality he has already compromised for his own benefit . . . the attorney client privilege is not designed for such tactical employment.").

52.   676 F.2d at 817-22.

53.   856 F.2d at 623-24. The *Marietta* court, noting that the Fourth Circuit had not adopted *Diversified*'s "limited waiver" concept, reasoned that since the contested material or its underlying documentation had already been disclosed to the government, attorney-client privilege protection was lost.

IV. LIBEL

A. *Written Reports May Invite Libel Claims*

In order for the written report to be a useful tool in ferreting out and addressing wrongdoing, it must be both meticulous and frank. Candor usually requires that the responsible parties be identified and their allegedly "questionable" activities be detailed. These descriptions may be tantamount to the accusation of a crime, or at least of dishonesty and untrustworthiness. Assessments may have a devastating impact on the professional and personal lives of the individuals so identified.[54] Consequently, the written investigative report, pitting the individual's reputational interest[55] against the corporation's interest in self-policing, provides fertile ground for possible libel actions.

Defamation generally consists of unprivileged false statements of fact, of and concerning the plaintiff, that are defamatory and published to third parties.[56] In some jurisdictions, the construction of the term "publication" may allow the internal investigative report to fall outside the boundaries of defamation liability altogether. Predicated on agency principles, a significant minority of jurisdictions has held that wholly intracorporate communications among employees within the scope of their employment do not constitute publication. Under this view, such communication is "simply

---

54. As one commentator noted:

Very few defamatory statements carry more potential for devastating harm to the victim than false and defamatory evaluations of an employee's work performance. Careers may turn on such evaluations and courts are thus faced with a power conflict between protecting the substantial social interest in candid and honest appraisals of an employee's competence and the equally substantial interest in safeguarding the employee from undeserved injury.

R. Smolla, *Law of Defamation* 8-27 (1986) [hereinafter *Law of Defamation*].

55. As the Supreme Court noted in *Rosenblatt v. Baer,* "[s]ociety has a pervasive and strong interest in preventing and redressing attacks upon reputation." 383 U.S. 75, 86 (1966). Given society's significant interest in addressing attacks on reputation, the law of defamation is "aimed at preventing wrongful disruption of the relational interest that an individual has in maintaining personal esteem in the eyes of others." *See Law of Defamation, supra* note 54, at 1-15 (1986). In the pre-*New York Times v. Sullivan* era, defamation law's recognition of this interest consisted largely of strict liability tort rules highly favorable to the plaintiff.

56. *See* RESTATEMENT (SECOND) OF TORTS § 558 (1977).

the corporation talking to itself.[57] However, most jurisdictions have not recognized this exception for corporate actors, reasoning that the "no publication" view rests upon a confusion of the publication issue with the existence of a common-law privilege.[58]

Nonetheless, other avenues of protection exist for defamatory statements contained in the investigative report. Modern defamation law is characterized by an array of constitutional and common-law doctrines designed to balance competing reputational and free speech interests. Countervailing free speech interests have been given legal significance in part through the doctrine of privileged communications.[59] Both absolute and qualified privileges have been developed to immunize otherwise actionable defamatory statements because of the type of speech involved,

---

57. Luttrell v. United Tel. Sys., Inc., 683 P.2d 1292, 9 Kan. App. 2d 620 (Kan. App. 1984), aff'd, 695 P.2d 1279, 236 Kan. 710 (Kan. 1985); see, e.g., Johnson v. Delchamps, 715 F. Supp. 1345 (D. La. 1989) (no publication where results of a polygraph test that resulted in plaintiff employee's dismissal were only disseminated among employees during termination decision); Wilson v. Southern Med. Ass'n, 547 So. 2d 510 (Ala. 1989) (no publication occurred, since memorandum containing allegedly defamatory statements was read only by executive director's secretary, plaintiff, and plaintiff's supervisor); Washington v. Thomas, 778 S.W.2d 792 (Mo. App. 1989).

58. See Law of Defamation, supra note 54, at 15-7 to 15-8; Loughry v. Lincoln Bank, 67 N.Y.2d 369, 377, 502 N.Y.S.2d 965 (Ct. App. 1986) (rejecting defendant corporation's "no publication" claim, reasoning that it was "clear that a false and malicious utterance by one employee to another c[ould] be actionable"); Heselton v. Wilder, 496 A.2d 1063 (Me. 1985) (communication by plaintiff's supervisor to loss-prevention department may have been privileged but still constituted publication); Cashio v. Holt, 425 So. 2d 820 (L.A. App. 1982) (publication of plaintiff's termination occurred when copies were provided to six principal managers); Bander v. Metropolitan Life Ins. Co., 313 Mass. 337, 47 N.E.2d 595 (Mass. 1943) (no good reason exists to immunize defamation communicated by one corporate agent to another); Arsenault v. Allegheny Airlines, Inc., 485 F. Supp. 1373, aff'd, 636 F.2d 1199 (1st Cir. 1981), cert. denied, 454 U.S. 821 (1981) (Massachusetts rejects the proposition that there can be no publication of an intracorporate communication); Jones v. Britt Airways, Inc., 622 F. Supp. 389 (N.D. Ill. 1985) (discussions between managerial employees and several low-level employees constituted publication where statements revealed that investigation as to allegations that plaintiff had embezzled corporate funds had been commenced, and where low-level employees were outside the scope of such investigation).

59. Constitutional fault standards have also been developed to promote the public interest in robust, rich public debate.

the status of the speaker, the forum in which the speech occurs, or the relationship between the publisher and third parties.[60]

The privileges of particular import for the investigative report are the "opinion" and the common-law "interest-related" privileges. However, these privileges are mired in uncertainty, with reviewing courts employing different standards to determine their contours and applicability. As a result, defamation liability, as well as the costs associated with defending these actions, should be a source of concern for both investigative counsel and the client.

B. *Example of Libel Claims against Counsel*

Vividly illustrating the investigative report's "libel potential" is the case of *Pearce v. E.F. Hutton Group*.[61] *Pearce* involved a libel suit against former Attorney General Griffin Bell and the Hutton Group on the basis of an internal investigative report prepared by Bell while a lawyer in private practice. The Hutton report concluded that the plaintiff had participated knowingly in an unlawful check-kiting scheme. At issue in the suit were Bell's assessments that "no reasonable person could have believed that this conduct was proper," "[plaintiff's conduct was] so aggressive and egregious as to warrant sanctions," and "[plaintiff had] actually engaged in wrongdoing" and was "a moving force in improprieties."[62] Bell sought to protect the statements through the invocation of various constitutional and common-law doctrines, including the absolute opinion privilege, the common-law interest-related privileges, the fair-comment privilege, and the constitutional "actual malice" fault standard.

Applying the "totality of the circumstances test" articulated in *Ollman v. Evans*,[63] one of several different tests used to distinguish "opinion" from "fact,"[64] the court in *Pearce* ruled that the alleged defamatory statements were not sheltered by the absolute opinion privilege.[65] The court further declined to find that a qualified "interest-related" privilege even initially attached to the statements.[66] The court rejected the notion that the

---

60. *See generally* R. SACK, LIBEL, SLANDER & RELATED PROBLEMS 267-339 (1980).

61. 664 F. Supp. 1490 (D.D.C. 1987).

62. *Id.* at 1501.

63. 750 F.2d 970, 974-75 (D.C. Cir. 1984).

64. *See infra* notes 72-79 and accompanying text.

65. 664 F. Supp. at 1500-03.

66. *Id.* at 1504-06. The court reasoned that "there [was] little likelihood that [refusing to recognize a qualified privilege would] have a chilling effect on speech. Future investigative reports are unlikely to be deterred as they are motivated by profit."

standard of fault should be "actual malice"—a knowing or reckless false-hood—and applied a negligence standard.[67] The case was then sent to the jury on the issue of compensatory damages, where Bell and Hutton ultimately prevailed.[68]

This case highlights the risks presented by the written report and the uncertainty surrounding judicial application of the relevant privileges. Investigative counsel's task therefore becomes the fine art of drafting the document in a manner that places the report as securely as possible within the scope of these somewhat confused doctrines.

C. *Opinion and Qualified Interest Privileges*

1. Opinion Privilege

With the pronouncement that "there is no such thing as a false idea," the Supreme Court, in *Gertz v. Robert Welch, Inc.*,[69] appeared to elevate the well-established, common-law fact-opinion distinction, which found its expression under the aegis of the fair comment privilege,[70] to constitutional stature.[71] However, by failing to articulate an approach to

---

67. The plaintiff's claims for punitive damages were dismissed because the court deemed sufficient evidence had not been adduced to support a finding that counsel had published the report knowing that it was false or with reckless disregard as to its truth or falsity. 664 F. Supp. at 1509-19. This portion of the court's holding reflected the rule established in *Gertz v. Robert Welch Inc.*, 418 U.S. 323, 349 (1974) (discussed *infra* note 95), where the Supreme Court held that "states may not permit recovery of presumed or punitive damages, at least when liability is not based on a showing of knowledge of falsity or reckless disregard for the truth."

68. Ladd, *Bell Suit Fallout: Outside Probers Want Protection*, LEGAL TIMES, June 27, 1988, at 8.

69. 418 U.S. 323, 339 (1974).

70. The fair comment privilege protected only statements of opinion; as should have been anticipated, distinguishing between fact and opinion was an exceptionally arduous, if not impossible, task that led to a hodgepodge of results. *See* Note, *The Fact-Opinion Distinction in First Amendment Law: The Need for a Bright-Line Rule*, 72 GEO. L.J. 1817, 1820 (1984).

71. Specifically the Court stated:

We begin with the common ground. Under the First Amendment there is no such thing as a false idea. However pernicious an opinion may seem, we depend for its correction not on the conscience of judges and juries but on the competition of other ideas. But there is no constitutional value in false statements of fact.

be employed in making the all crucial fact-opinion distinction, *Gertz* spawned the development of a flurry of tests by the lower courts.

2. Applicable Tests for Libel

Some courts have chosen a "provable as false" standard to determine whether a statement is protected.[72] Several courts, adopting a "reasonable reader" standard as the inquiry's focal point, have deemed privileged statements depicted as "rhetorical hyperbole" such that no reasonable reader could perceive as fact.[73] Others have adopted the *Restatement (Second) of Torts* method, which focuses on the adequacy of the factual presentation made by the author.[74] Premised upon the common-law rationale that stated facts provide a basis upon which the reader can evaluate the soundness of the opinion, the *Restatement* approach protects a statement if it "does not

---

Lower courts and the RESTATEMENT (SECOND) OF TORTS had interpreted this language as requiring absolute protection for statements of opinion. *See, e.g.*, Ollman v. Evans, 713 F.2d 838, 840-41 (D.C. Cir. 1983) (Robinson, C.J., concurring); Bose Corp. v. Consumers Union of United States, Inc., 692 F.2d 189, 193-94 (1st Cir. 1982); Church of Scientology of California v. Cazares, 638 F.2d 1272, 1286 (5th Cir. 1981); Avins v. White, 627 F.2d 637, 642 (3d Cir. 1980), *cert. denied*, 449 U.S. 982 (1980); RESTATEMENT (SECOND) OF TORTS § 566 (1977), stating defamation actions for "pure" expressions of opinion are unconstitutional in light of *Gertz*. However, the Supreme Court's opinion in *Milkovich v. Lorain Journal Co.*, 110 S. Ct. 2695, 2707 (1990), held that no "additional separate constitutional privilege for 'opinion' is required to ensure the freedom of expression guaranteed by the First Amendment." This case has been interpreted as rejecting only the notion that *Gertz* established an absolute privilege for statements of opinion, limiting opinion protection to those statements not provable as false and those that cannot be reasonably interpreted as assertions of fact. *See The Supreme Court—Leading Cases: Libel Law-Opinion Privilege*, 104 HARV. L. REV. 219 (1990).

72. *See, e.g.*, Liberty Lobby, Inc. v. Anderson, 746 F.2d 1563, 1572 (D.C. Cir. 1984), *vacated and remanded on other grounds*, 477 U.S. 242 (1986); Buckley v. Littell, 539 F.2d 882, 895 (2d Cir. 1976), *cert. denied*, 429 U.S. 1062 (1977). *See also* Milkovich v. Lorain Journal Co., 110 S. Ct. 2695, 2701-07 (1990), discussed *infra* notes 80-89 and accompanying text.

73. Pring v. Penthouse Int'l Ltd., 695 F.2d 438, 443 (10th Cir. 1983), *cert. denied*, 462 U.S. 1132 (1983); Pease v. Telegraph Publishing, Inc., 121 N.H. 62, 65, 426 A.2d 463, 465 (N.H. 1981).

74. Avins v. White, 627 F.2d 637 (3d Cir. 1980), *cert. denied*, 449 U.S. 982 (1980); Bruno v. New York News, Inc., 89 A.D.2d 260, 264, 456 N.Y.S.2d 837, 840 (3d Dept. 1982); Holy Spirit Ass'n for Unification of World Christianity v. Sequoia Elsevier Publishing Co., 75 A.D.2d 523, 426 N.Y.S.2d 759, 760 (1st Dept. 1980); Braig v. Field Communications, 456 A.2d 1366, 310 Pa. Super. 569 (Pa. Super. 1983).

imply the existence of undisclosed defamatory facts."[75] Some courts have employed contextual analyses in making the determination. The "totality of the circumstances" test assesses "all relevant factors including: the surrounding words, any cautionary language, and the surrounding circumstances such as the medium used and the audience addressed."[76] Despite the wealth of choice, each of these tests suffers from problems of vagueness and ambiguity. In "reasonable reader" jurisdictions, no guidance is offered as to how to measure the "reasonable reader's" perceptions.[77]

The mechanical *Restatement* test, with its full disclosure requirement, fails to define what constitutes a "fact" and to offer any clear method of ascertaining when a statement implies undisclosed facts.[78] The contextual approaches, similar to the "reasonable reader" test, place the prospective defendant in the position of determining what circumstances will be deemed legally significant.[79]

3. Supreme Court's Decision Provides Little Clarity

The Supreme Court's decision in *Milkovich v. Lorain Journal Co.*[80] did little to bring clarity to this area. Rejecting a categorical absolute privilege for "opinion," the *Milkovich* Court held that statements not suscep-

---

75. *The Fact-Opinion Distinction, supra* note 70, at 1826. Although the common law never resolved the fundamental problem of how to discern whether a statement implies defamatory facts, this approach was adopted by the RESTATEMENT (SECOND) OF TORTS, which subdivided "opinions" into two categories: pure opinion, based upon stated facts or "clearly" based on facts known or assumed by the audience, and mixed opinion, not based on stated or assumed facts, therefore implying the existence of undisclosed defamatory facts. Under the RESTATEMENT view, expressions of pure opinion are absolutely protected, while expressions of "mixed opinion" may be actionable. Though the RESTATEMENT offers clarifying examples, these hypotheticals fail to grapple with the critical question, especially trying in the usual complex factual background found in fact-opinion cases: *how* to decide *when* a statement implies no undisclosed defamatory facts.

76. Comment, *Statement of Facts, Statements of Opinion and the First Amendment*, 74 CALIF. L. REV. 1001, 1015 (1984); *see, e.g.,* Lewis v. Time, Inc., 710 F.2d 549 (9th Cir. 1983); Information Control Corp. v. Genesis One Computer Corp., 611 F.2d 781, 784 (9th Cir. 1980); Gregory v. McDonnell-Douglas Corp., 17 Cal. 3d 596, 601-03, 552 P.2d 425, 428-29 (1970).

77. *The Fact-Opinion Distinction, supra* note 70, at 1831-32.

78. *Id.* at 1827-29.

79. *Id.* at 1836-39.

80. 110 S. Ct. 2695 (1990).

tible of being proved as false are protected opinion, thereby making only those statements that may reasonably be interpreted as asserting a verifiable fact capable of forming the basis for a defamation action.[81] Despite this attempt to define protectible "opinion," the Court's articulation of the "provable as false" standard essentially reiterates the principal thrust of the tests applied by the lower courts for years.

The continued viability of the test most favorable to the investigative report, the *Restatement* test, is more doubtful in light of dicta in the majority opinion. Writing for the *Milkovich* majority, Justice Rehnquist posed the following hypothetical:

> If a speaker says, "In my opinion John Jones is a liar," he implies a knowledge of facts which lead to the conclusion that Jones told an untruth. Even if the speaker states the facts upon which he bases his opinion, if those facts are either incorrect or incomplete, or if his assessment of them is erroneous, the statement may still imply a false assertion of fact.[82]

The investigative report, presenting conclusions based upon the investigation's factual findings, provides a classic example of "deductive opinion."[83] Fully disclosing the underlying factual basis for its "opinion," the investigative report would be nonactionable, even if false, under the *Restatement* test. The language in *Milkovich*, however, suggests that a statement will be actionable, though it does not imply the existence of defamatory facts, if the author's conclusion as to the meaning of those facts is erroneous.[84]

Consequently, the post-*Milkovich* "opinion" privilege is not a sure "safe haven" for the investigative report. The uncertainty surrounding *Milkovich*'s "provable as false" and "reasonable reader" standards is high-

81. 110 S. Ct. at 2701-07.

82. 110 S. Ct. at 2705-06.

83. "An opinion is deductive if it implies or deduces misconduct or a disparaging fact about the plaintiff on the basis of true information supplied to the public or already generally known to the public." *Law of Defamation, supra* note 54, at 6-19, discussing the opinion classifications set forth in W. PROSSER & W. KEETON, THE LAW OF TORTS § 113 A, 813-14 (5th ed. 1981).

84. *Leading Cases, supra* note 71, at 226, n.72. *See also* Goodale, *Milkovich: Modest Loss for the Press*, NEW YORK L.J., June 27, 1990, at 1, stating that "[a]fter *Milkovich* there will be liability for statements of opinion complicating facts about public officials or public figures when made recklessly or without knowledge that the facts are false."

lighted by the divergent outcomes reached by the majority and the dissent in their respective applications of the tests.[85] Similarly, as illustrated in *Pearce*, the contextual analysis tends to favor a finding of fact, not opinion, when examining an investigative report.[86]

Although *Milkovich* rejected the existence of an absolute "opinion" privilege under the First Amendment, state courts, invoking state constitutional law, may still afford expressions of "opinion" heightened protection.[87] The New York Court of Appeals, reconsidering a pre-*Milkovich* case on remand from the Supreme Court, affirmed its decision that the statements at issue were protected "opinion" on both federal and independent state law grounds.[88] Noting the "expansive language" of the state's

---

85. The majority found the statement, "Anyone who attended the meet. . . knows in his heart that Milkovich and Scott lied at the hearing after each having given his solemn oath to tell the truth," implied that Milkovich committed perjury and was "sufficiently factual to be susceptible of being proved true or false." 110 S. Ct. at 2707. In contrast, Justice Brennan in dissent declared that, assessing the column in context, "[n]o reasonable reader could understand [the reporter] to be implied asserting—as fact—that Milkovich lied." Milkovich v. Lorain Journal Co., 110 S. Ct. at 2711-12 (Brennan, J., dissenting).

86. In *Pearce*, a case expressly involving a libel claim based on an internal investigative report, the court, employing the *Ollman* test, deemed the opinion privilege inapplicable. In its analysis of the four factors, the court reasoned that the professional nature of the report, the purpose of the underlying investigation, the content of the contested statements, and the surrounding context of the internal investigation led to the conclusion that the statements were assertions of fact and not opinion. The final two prongs of the inquiry, the immediate and broader social context queries, posed particular problems for the report. The court found that both elements suggested the Hutton investigative report was factual rather than opinion-based. The report's use of cautionary language, such as "we conclude" or "we think" was deemed inconclusive, as the context of this particular report made the language seem "more akin to a summary of facts than a subjective analysis of them." 664 F. Supp. at 1502. Incorporating the RESTATEMENT test into the immediate context inquiry, the court found that because "the challenged statements set forth plaintiff's culpability, they impl[ied] the existence of damaging, undisclosed facts beyond the mere description of the chaining and overdrafting activities given in more detailed sections of the Hutton report." *Id.* Without much discussion, the *Pearce* court found that the broader social context—an investigative report into illegal corporate activities prepared by independent counsel who was a former attorney general and federal judge—"would cause the reasonable person to view [the statements] as fact, not opinion." *Id.*

87. *See* Goodale, *Modest Loss, supra* note 84.

88. Immuno v. Jan-Moor Jankowski, No. 264 (N.Y. Jan. 15, 1991) (LEXIS, N.Y. library, *Cases* file).

constitutional guarantee of freedom of expression, manifested in its "exceptional history and rich tradition" of jurisprudence in that area, the court of appeals concluded that it was appropriate to decide the matter on independent state law grounds as well as on federal First Amendment bases.[89] In light of the diminished significance of the constitutional opinion privilege in the context of the written investigative report, the qualified or conditional common-law privileges assume greater importance.

4. Qualified Interest-Related Privileges

In recognition of the need for frank communication regarding matters in which the parties have an interest or duty, qualified privileges exist to immunize otherwise actionable statements. These privileges have been recognized for statements made in the interests of the publisher, the recipient, third parties, the public, and persons sharing a common interest.[90]

The qualified privilege does not sanction all defamatory statements cloaked with the requisite interest. Critical to the successful invocation of this doctrinal shield is the publisher's "good faith," evidenced by the publisher's motivations in making the statements, the nexus between the statement's content and the proffered purpose, and the degree to which "malice," "ill-will," or "spite" played a factor in publication. The qualified privilege is thus subject to loss for "abuse."

The employer's traditional qualified privilege for critical statements concerning former and current employees communicated to persons having a corresponding interest or duty provides a particularly apt analytical framework for shielding written investigative reports from defamation liability. This privilege initially attaches to communications made by em-

---

89. The court of appeals reasoned that the Supreme Court in *Milkovich* applied an analysis similar to the *Ollman* contextual inquiry, differing primarily on the construction of the last two prongs of the *Ollman* test—the immediate and broader social context inquiries. The court reasoned that these inquiries focused on the "type of speech" at issue, and that the Supreme Court ostensibly intended absolute protection to apply only to "loose, figurative hyperbolic language"; in contrast, "statements that contain[ed] or impl[ied] assertions of provably false fact w[ould] likely be actionable." Concluding that its decision could rest on state constitutional law, the court expressed its "concern[ ] that if indeed the type of speech is to be construed narrowly—insufficient protection may be accorded to the central values protected by the law of this State."

90. B. Sanford, Libel & Privacy: The Prevention and Defense of Litigation 413-24 (1985).

ployers[91] or agents such as private investigators hired to make employee evaluations.[92] This is of great assistance since in many instances, as demonstrated by *Pearce*, the defamation plaintiff will be an employee criticized in the report.[93]

Some confusion arises as to when the privilege is lost through abuse. The employer's qualified privilege may be forfeited by a showing of "excessive publication," publication for purposes other than those giving rise to the privilege, malice in both its common law and constitutional sense, bad faith, recklessness, and negligence.[94] Clearly, excessive publication and publication for purposes unrelated to those giving rise to the privilege will lose the qualified privilege. However, it is unclear what standard of fault—negligence or a more culpable standard—is necessary to overcome the privilege.

A negligence standard is inappropriate. Since negligence is already a minimum constitutional standard for fault liability,[95] a determination that

---

91. Note, *Employer Defamation: The Role of Qualified Privilege*, 30 WM. & M. L. REV. 469, 471 (1989), *citing* RESTATEMENT (SECOND) OF TORTS § 595 (1977) and 50 AM. JUR. 2D, *Libel and Slander* § 275 (1970).

92. Campbell v. Willmark Serv. Sys., 123 F.2d 204 (3d Cir. 1941); Roscoe v. Schoolitz, 105 Ariz. 310, 464 P.2d 333 (1970); Freeman v. Mills, 97 Cal. App. 2d 161, 217 P.2d 687 (Cal. App. 19-50); Dierson v. Robert Griffin Investigations, 92 Nev. 605, 555 P.2d 843 (Nev. 1976).

93. Even if the plaintiff is not an employee, a qualified privilege, based either on self-interest, common interest, or the furtherance of another's interest, should still apply. Moreover, if the plaintiff is a public figure, as may occur, e.g., in the context of an investigative report examining alleged violations of the Foreign Corrupt Practices Act, the report may enjoy the enhanced protection of the "actual malice" constitutional standard.

94. *Employer Defamation, supra* note 91, at 488.

95. Constitutionalizing much of modern defamation law, *New York Times Co. v. Sullivan,* 376 U.S. 254 (1964), and its progeny established the principle that the First Amendment requires a finding of fault, ranging from "actual malice" in public figure cases to negligence in private-figure cases involving "matters of public concern," be made before liability is imposed for libel. Curtis Publ'g Co. v. Butts, 388 U.S. 130 (1967) ("actual malice" standards governs public figures); Associated Press v. Walker, 388 U.S. 130 (1967) ("actual malice" governs public figures); Gertz v. Robert Welch, Inc., 418 U.S. 323 (1974) (no liability without fault); Dun & Bradstreet, Inc. v. Greenmoss Builders, Inc., 105 S. Ct. 2939 (1985) (presumed and punitive damages restricted to cases that "do not involve matters of public concern"). Predicated on the status of the plaintiff and the type of speech involved, these fault standards operate in much the same fashion as privileges, providing varying safe harbors for speech in which the public has an interest.

a showing of negligence defeats the qualified privilege renders the privilege meaningless. Fortunately, the negligence "abuse" standard is the minority rule,[96] with most jurisdictions opting for some standard of malice, either in its constitutional or common-law forms.[97] Thus, the employer's qualified privilege should provide substantial protection for the investiga-

---

In *Gertz*, the Court reaffirmed *New York Times Co. v. Sullivan*'s holding that public officials and public figures were required to demonstrate actual malice and ruled that with respect to private figure plaintiffs, states could devise their own standard of liability as long as no liability was imposed without a showing of fault. 418 U.S. at 348. *Gertz* appeared to require a showing of at least negligence in all defamation actions, and lower courts accordingly interpreted *Gertz*'s fault requirement as establishing a minimum culpability standard of negligence. However, in a dramatic retreat from *Gertz*, the Court in *Dun & Bradstreet* ruled that *Gertz*'s restriction of punitive and presumed damage awards to cases in which actual malice is shown does not apply to defamatory statements that "do not involve matters of public concern." The task of discerning what constitutes "public concern" has been left largely to the lower courts; the *Dun & Bradstreet* plurality opinion articulated no clear guidelines or benchmarks, simply stating that "whether . . . speech addresses a matter of public concern must be determined by [the statement's] content, form, and context . . . as revealed by the whole record"—basically holding that courts must consider everything.

Dun & Bradstreet thus called into question at least some aspect of the applicability of the *Gertz* "no liability without fault" rule for speech not involving matters of public concern. This decision potentially permits the states to revitalize early strict liability standards for their defamation actions involving private figure plaintiffs and no public issues.

Consequently, three standards of fault—negligence, actual malice, and strict liability—conceivably govern modern defamation law, turning on the status of the plaintiff and the subject matter at issue. The vast majority of jurisdictions tend to follow the "negligence" rule for private figure plaintiff cases, while a few states have adopted an actual malice standard. Other states, notably New York, have developed some intermediate standard for private figure plaintiffs. *See Law of Defamation, supra* note 54, at 3-28.

96. *See, e.g.*, Schneider v. Pav'n Save Corp., 723 F.2d 619 (Alaska 1986).

97. Actual malice is defined as "knowledge of falsity or reckless disregard for the truth," Dun & Bradstreet, 105 S. Ct. at 2941, while common-law malice envisions actual "spite" or "ill-will." *See Law of Defamation, supra* note 54, at 3-28. *See, e.g.*, Lewis v. Equitable Life Assurance Soc'y, 389 N.W.2d 876, 891 (Minn. 1986) (common-law malice); Stuempages v. Parke, Davis & Co., 297 N.W.2d 252, 257 (Minn. 1980) (common-law malice); Hoesl v. United States, 451 F. Supp. 1170, 1179 (N.D. Cal. 1978) (actual malice); Marchesi v. Franchino, 283 Md. 131, 387 A.2d 1129 (Md. App. 1978) (actual malice); Roemer v. Retail Credit Co., 3 Cal. App. 3d 368, 83 Cal. Rptr. 540 (Cal. App. 1978) (actual malice).

tive report, provided the report is disclosed only to essential parties and the prior investigation is thorough and complete.

D. *Strategies for Minimizing Liability for Defamation*

1. Emphasize Opinions

While the "opinion" privilege is of limited value for the investigative report, investigative counsel should still attempt to use the protections of this privilege to the greatest extent possible by explicitly detailing the factual basis for the report's conclusions about individual culpability. Cautionary language, though possessing no automatic power to turn factual statements into protected opinion, should be used when practicable.

2. Avoid Overstatement and Loosely Formed Conclusions

Because the most important vehicle of protection will be the qualified privilege and particularly the employer's qualified privilege, both the investigation and the report should be carefully done. To ensure the report is not negligently prepared[98] and that it is not "knowingly" or "recklessly false," the underlying investigation should be thorough, supporting facts and sources should be verified, and the conclusions drawn should be reasonably justified by the facts. Lawyers should refrain from the use of caustic, hyperbolic, and otherwise colorful language.

---

98. The reasonable person standard governs the negligence inquiry. In making this determination, courts generally will examine such issues as "the cost of further investigation and further delay in publishing, and the importance of the interests being promoted by the speech measured against the probability of foreseeable harm to the plaintiff's reputation, including the reliability of sources . . . the seriousness of the defamatory charges, and their inherent plausibility." *Law of Defamation, supra* note 49, at 3-73. Negligence problems can arise as a result of the lawyer's "failure to pursue further investigation; unreasonable reliance on sources; unreasonable formulation of conclusions, inferences or interpretations; errors in note-taking and quotation of sources; misuse of legal terminology; mechanical or typographical errors; unreasonable screening or checking procedures; and the failure to follow established internal practices and policies." *Id.* at 3–75.

3. Avoid Unnecessary Publication

Since excessive publication will negate the common-law privilege, lawyers and the corporation should be especially careful in disseminating the report. Disclosure of the report pursuant to a corporation's participation in a voluntary disclosure program should not be fatal since the government agency, in all probability, would be deemed a party with a corresponding interest in the communication. Likewise, disclosure of the report to the direct supervisors of the persons named in the report should not constitute excessive publication. Outside this audience, however, disclosure of the report should be curtailed. As *Pearce* demonstrates, widespread disclosures (a public news conference in that case) are hazardous and may prompt reviewing courts to refuse to recognize even the existence of the privilege.[99]

4. Consider Indemnification

Finally, investigative counsel should consider an indemnification clause within the engagement contract. While the qualified privilege generally will safeguard both counsel and the corporation from liability, the costs of defending defamation actions are quite substantial.[100] Given that in most instances of suspected corporate wrongdoing, an internal investigation and concluding report will be in the corporation's best interest, indemnification clauses should not pose any substantial threat to the internal investigation practice area.[101]

---

99. The unusual circumstances surrounding the Hutton report, most notably the fact that the investigation was commissioned after settlement had been reached with the Department of Justice and was designed to calm public furor generated by the settlement agreement, appeared to play a pivotal role in the court's decision, particularly on the qualified privilege issue. *See* Pearce, 449 F. Supp. at 1504-06.

100. *See Bell Suit Fallout: Outside Probers Want Protection, supra* note 68, discussing the indemnification debate among lawyers specializing in internal corporate investigations in the aftermath of the Bell suit. Many practitioners in the field, including Bell, have decided to ask for indemnification clauses in their engagement contracts. Others believe that such a condition may be seen as compromising the impartiality and independence of investigative counsel, and have chosen not to seek it.

101. As one lawyer noted: "Most of these companies won't be in a position to decide against an investigation simply because they are going to have to assume a contingent liability." *Id.*

V. CONCLUSION

A. *Summary*

As must be clear by now, the preparation of a written report of the internal investigation is fraught with danger. It may subject the author to a lawsuit in which exemplary damages are sought; it may be turned against the client by the very agency counsel is seeking to appease; it may be disclosed in later litigation and admissions within; it may prove quite harmful; and its disclosure, intended or not, may result in disclosure of all underlying records.

Given the range of uncertainties accompanying the preparation of a report, one might well conclude that *no* good reason exists to create a written document. As this chapter suggests, oral reports are far preferable to a written record. More fundamentally, one might ask whether the reasons arguing against the creation of a written report argue just as strongly that no investigation take place at all. For, whether the ultimate product of the investigation—the report—is oral or written, the fact remains that in the course of the investigation considerable information is collected by counsel; and some of that information, perhaps much, will damage the company once disclosed.

Yet, the option of beginning an investigation, or of rendering only an oral report may not always be available to counsel. The client may insist on the investigation and insist on the preparation of a thorough, detailed written analysis, believing that nothing short of that will accomplish its purposes. Or, the lawyer may conclude that a well-reasoned statement of fact and law is essential to dissuading government lawyers from prosecution. Finally, the preparation of the report—indeed the convening of the investigation itself—may be imposed by government regulation or made a predicate to settlement.

B. *Minimizing Risks*

In view of these competing considerations, how can counsel best minimize the many risks associated with undertaking the corporate investigation, while still fully probing into the conduct giving rise to the investigation in the first place? This is not an easy task, but the following guidelines may be helpful in walking this fine line.

1. Strictly Observe Legal Privileges

While the privilege of self-criticism would provide a more appropriate protection for the internal investigative report than the attorney-client or work product protections, courts have been reluctant to accept it. Hence, a lawyer preparing a report should structure both the investigation and written report to obtain the full protection of the established privileges. It is certainly more prudent to attempt to keep the protection of the privileges so the client will have the option of waiving them rather than to lose them by inadvertence. In this regard, counsel must never forget that *any* disclosure of the report beyond the company may result in some degree of waiver, whether complete or partial, of both the contents of the report and of underlying work papers. By understanding this distinct possibility—in a sense, expecting the worst—counsel can more intelligently go about the task of accumulating the facts and reporting the results.

2. Begin with Prepared Engagement Letter

Since the analysis of the attorney-client privilege depends on content, the initial engagement letter between the corporation and its counsel should frame the representation in accordance with the Supreme Court's decision in *Upjohn*[102] and should explicitly state that counsel is being engaged for the purpose of securing legal advice. Where possible, the report should recite that the investigation is undertaken in anticipation of litigation. Moreover, using outside rather than inside counsel increases the chances for protection because it avoids the argument that in-house lawyers often provide business advice. It will be a more difficult task, in the event of a discovery dispute, to demonstrate that inside counsel acted solely in its "legal capacity" in the course of the investigation. Finally, counsel may wish to include an indemnification clause.

---

102. According to *Upjohn*, to come within the privilege, the following circumstances must be present: (1) the communications by employees to corporate counsel are to secure legal advice for the company; (2) the employees are cooperating with corporate counsel at the direction of corporate superiors; (3) the communications concern matters within the employees' scope of employment; and (4) the information is not available from upper-echelon management. Upjohn Co. v. United States, 449 U.S. 383 (1981).

3. Enlist Independent Audit Committee or Outside Directors

If the various "self-policing" rationales are to have any force, appearance must be a critical concern in every aspect of the internal investigation. To convey credibility, the supervisory body, as well as the investigators and the investigation, must possess a significant degree of independence. Particularly in matters involving complex and wide-ranging schemes, where a colorable claim of high-level knowledge and participation can be made, the corporate board of directors should not be in charge of supervising the investigation. In most cases, an independent audit committee of the board of directors or a specially appointed committee comprising outside directors should be assigned this task.[103] In certain circumstances, for example, investigations triggered by suspicions of wrongdoing by low-level employees, supervisory authority exercised by executive management or the board is appropriate.

In all instances, however, the role played by corporate personnel in structuring the investigation, including the persons interviewed, the documents reviewed, and the avenues pursued, should be strictly advisory and facilitative, not decisive. Investigative counsel alone should be in charge of the investigation, though its scope should be articulated and ostensibly formulated by the board of directors or senior management in the initial engagement letter.

4. Act as Legal Counsel

Courts have denied claims of privilege and protection to those reports in which counsel provided investigative services only, or rendered business advice alone. Thus, the report should plainly indicate that the lawyer was hired to provide legal advice with respect to certain matters and explain what the lawyer did to provide the advice. To ensure coverage by both the attorney-client and work product privileges, the lawyer's analysis of the factual findings and their legal implications should be reflected throughout the document. The actual investigative report should consist of a statement of the objective of the investigation, the investigation's factual findings, the lawyer's analysis of these findings,

---

103. *See* Mueller, *Practical Considerations in Conducting an Internal Business Investigation, in* PLI, THE ROLE OF OUTSIDE COUNSEL IN THE BUSINESS INVESTIGATION, No. 279, 163, 170-71 (1985).

and a list of recommendations. The lawyer's recitation of the facts should be structured so as to reveal the reasoning. Furthermore, the statements of persons interviewed and other primarily factual information should be summarized in order to fall more comfortably under the rubric of opinion work product and to avoid the problem of legal "admissions." The report should indicate that it is the lawyer's views of the witnesses' statements that enable conclusions to be drawn.

5. Express Limitations

Both for purposes of accuracy and protection in the event of subsequent disclosure, the report should make clear its limitations. Frequently, a discussion of methodology and procedures followed will help achieve this. Where recollections or documents are ambiguous or in conflict, they should be conveyed. Where assumptions have been made, they should be stated. A report that presents a balanced appraisal of events will best serve the client and its authors.

6. Match Conclusions with Facts

Finally, to maximize the protections afforded by constitutional and common-law privilege against libel suits, the report should be distributed to a limited, relevant audience; should carefully explain the factual bases for its conclusions; and should attempt to characterize its ultimate conclusions as subjective opinions and recommendations.

Internal Investigations for Government Contractors

12

by Michael Waldman*

---

　　* Michael Waldman is a partner at the law firm of Fried, Frank, Harris, Shriver & Jacobson in Washington, D.C. He gratefully acknowledges the assistance of Andrew Skowronek in connection with this chapter.

373

THE U.S. GOVERNMENT is the world's largest purchaser of goods and services. Numerous businesses rely heavily on their contracts with the government, ranging from the neighborhood doctor providing medical services to Medicare/Medicaid patients to the large defense contractor supplying multimillion-dollar weapons systems to the U.S. military. For all government contractors regardless of size, internal corporate investigations are especially important. Unlike other commercial businesses, government contractors cannot simply treat a potential criminal or civil problem in isolation. Rather, the government contractor has a more complex task: the contractor must ensure that it continues to maintain the confidence and good favor of its government customer throughout the investigatory process. In addition, the detailed statutory and regulatory framework in which government contractors operate greatly complicates any internal investigation. While the techniques used by the lawyer for identifying the potential legal problem, gathering documents, and interviewing witnesses are generally common to all internal investigations, this chapter highlights some of the special considerations that must be analyzed when conducting an internal corporate investigation for a government contractor.[1]

I.   WHO ARE GOVERNMENT CONTRACTORS?

It is important for a lawyer to determine early on whether the client is a government contractor, since this will likely affect the subsequent approach to the internal investigation. Recognizing that the client is a government contractor is not always easy. Because of the pervasive role of the federal government, many companies have contractual ties to the government that one would not expect. A lawyer also needs to be aware that a company may be the supplier of parts or services to a customer who, in

---

1. This chapter does not attempt to address the basic techniques and procedures for conducting internal corporate investigations, which are set out elsewhere at length in this book.

turn, is providing an end-product to the U.S. government. In these circumstances, the subcontractor also is generally subject to the statutory and regulatory rules applicable to the prime contractor.

A. *Suppliers to the Federal Government*[2]

When one typically thinks of government contractors, major military suppliers such as Lockheed Martin, Northrop Grumman, and Raytheon immediately come to mind. The U.S. government, however, purchases much more than B-2 bombers and Patriot missiles. There is almost no product that the U.S. government does not purchase in substantial quantities—in almost all instances it is the largest purchaser in the world.[3] The General Services Administration maintains a vast schedule from which government offices around the country can purchase wastepaper baskets, furniture, office supplies, and the like. Government agencies also contract out (or, in the popular parlance, "outsource") broad varieties of services, from fixing equipment to maintaining parks and grounds to the running of certain prisons. The massive highway bill passed by Congress in 1998 also will be a font of federal contracting of all types for years to come. Lawyers must be aware that no matter how mundane or unusual the company's product or service, the U.S. government may be a major customer.

In particular, it should be noted that computer hardware and software are among the largest and fastest-growing areas of federal government procurements. Like private businesses, the federal government is attempting to increase productivity through technology innovations. Almost every major department and agency has been purchasing new computers or upgrading its present capacity. The government also is pouring billions of dollars into integration and software services. Counsel for companies involved in these aspects of the information industry should be especially prudent when surveying any potential contractual relationships with the United States.

---

2. This chapter will focus on suppliers to the federal government. It should be noted that the same issues and problems generally apply at the state and local government levels. In fact, many states have enacted their own false claims statutes. *See, e.g.,* John T. Boese, *Civil False Claims and Qui Tam Actions,* ASPEN LAW & BUSINESS 2d ed., ch. 6 and Appendices I-X (collecting false claims statutes for various states).

3. One distinguished government contracts lawyer tells the story, perhaps an apocryphal, of his representation of a maker of musical instruments. This attorney asserted that, through the numerous military bands, the U.S. Department of Defense was the world's largest single purchaser of musical instruments.

B. *Health Care Providers*

The passage of Medicare and Medicaid in 1965 also led to the U.S. government playing a major role in the health care industry.[4] The federal government spends countless billions of dollars on Medicare and Medicaid spending. Few hospitals, nursing homes, home health companies or laboratories can function without some Medicare and Medicaid patient funding. Individual doctors also are frequently dependent on the payment from patients covered by these federal programs. While many criticize the incentives and paperwork involved in Medicare and Medicaid, few health care providers can stay in business without participating in these programs. Stamping out fraud in these federal health care programs has become the top priority of federal law enforcement. As a result, when conducting an internal investigation of a health care provider, a lawyer should consider as a matter of course the potential liabilities to the United States.

C. *Other Government Contractors*

There also exist other companies that have significant dealings with the federal government, yet in more unconventional ways. For example, there have been a number of false claims lawsuits against the major oil and gas companies based on alleged violations of their federal land leases.[5] In other instances, the United States or its whistle-blower proxy have filed civil false claims actions against tugboat operators for improper waste dumping[6] and against a well-known clothing retailer for allegedly false customs declarations.[7] While not strictly government contractors, these companies perform in a regulatory framework that subjects their businesses to many of the same onerous fines and penalties as government contractors. As one judge wrote:

> In this day of pervasive government regulation of both public and private conduct, it is impossible even to estimate the number of times each day, each month, or each year that private citizens

---

4. Medicare is codified primarily at 42 U.S.C. §§ 1395-139511. Medicaid is codified primarily at 42 U.S.C. §§ 1396-1396p.

5. *See, e.g.,* United States *ex rel.* Johnson v. Shell Oil Co. et al., 183 F.R.D. 204 (E.D. Tex. 1998).

6. Pickens v. Kanawha River Towing, 916 F. Supp. 702 (S.D. Ohio 1996).

7. United States *ex rel.* American Textile Mfrs. Inst., Inc. v. The Limited, Inc., Case No. C2-97-776, 1997 U.S. Dist. LEXIS 18142 (S.D. Ohio Nov. 13, 1997).

create or submit some type of document required by the government or subject to government review or the number of times that such a document, if not completely accurate, could lead to the filing of a False Claims Act case.[8]

II. BEGINNING OF THE INVESTIGATION

When a lawyer is considering performing an internal investigation of a government contractor, he or she needs to understand the basic history and peculiarities of the specific business in question. Defending Lockheed Martin presents very different issues than if you are representing a local ambulance company. Each operates against a different regulatory background, and each will be faced with different government strategies to combat fraud. Nevertheless, there are certain fundamental similarities that implicate and organize the internal investigation of all government contractors.

The lawyer may first learn of the potential problem in a myriad of ways. The first appearance of trouble may be the typical type of notice of a government investigation: the grand jury subpoena for documents, the FBI agent interviewing employees, the search warrant. The issues raised by learning of the existence of a government investigation, and the possible responses, are addressed elsewhere in this book and need not be repeated here. It is important to recognize, however, that several government investigative tools are unique to government contractors.

A. *Subpoenas*

1. Inspector General Subpoena

The inspector general (IG) subpoena is an administrative subpoena that may be used by investigators from federal agencies to require the production of information, documents, reports, answers, records, accounts, papers, and other data and documentary evidence necessary for the performance of the Inspector General's duties. The Inspectors Gen-

---

8. *Id.* at 26. Although that court rejected such an expansive view of False Claims Act liability, there is no doubt that such false statements made in a regulatory context subject the company or individual to criminal liability under 18 U.S.C. §1001 as well as possible administrative sanction.

eral of federal departments or agencies are charged with fighting "fraud, waste and abuse" related to that department or agency. Although the IG subpoena has historically been documentary only, the Inspector General of the Department of Health and Human Services (HHS) has recently used this subpoena to take oral testimony as well as collect documentary evidence. However, counsel may be present for an oral interview made pursuant to an IG subpoena, and a court order must be obtained to compel its enforcement. The evidentiary threshold that must be met before an IG subpoena may be served is equivalent to a grand jury subpoena— "nothing more than official curiosity" is enough to justify its enforcement against a contractor.[9] Additionally, the IG subpoena lacks the secrecy requirement found in Rule 6(e) of the federal grand jury, thereby providing IG investigators with increased flexibility.[10] As a result, the government— especially HHS in health care investigations—makes frequent use of the IG subpoena.

2. Civil Investigative Demand

A civil investigative demand (CID) is another specialized tool that allows the Attorney General to obtain information crucial to a fraud investigation without the necessity of seeking a grand jury subpoena. Like a grand jury subpoena, a CID may be used to obtain oral testimony, in addition to documentary materials and written interrogatory answers. Congress has only authorized the issuance of CIDs for specific violations of the law, and a CID cannot be issued after the commencement by the government of a civil suit. The information obtained with a CID usually can only be disclosed to government agents within the scope of the authorized inquiry, and ordinarily cannot be disclosed to a qui tam relator suing under the False Claims Act[11] or to law enforcement agencies.[12] Moreover, the person authorized to issue a CID, usually the Attorney Gen-

---

9. *See, e.g.,* United States v. Morton Salt Co., 338 U.S. 632, 643, 652 (1950) ("Even if one were to regard the request for information in this case as caused by nothing more than official curiosity, nevertheless law enforcing agencies have a legitimate right to satisfy themselves that corporate behavior is consistent with the law and the public interest.").

10. *See* Pamela Bucy, *Health Care Fraud*, LAW JOURNAL SEMINARS PRESS, 1998, at ¶ 6.04.

11. *See* 31 U.S.C. §§ 3729 *et seq.*

12. *See id.*

eral, cannot delegate that authority. Like an IG subpoena, a person who receives a CID may refuse to comply in the first instance—a CID does not carry contempt sanctions, and the Attorney General must obtain a separate court order to compel enforcement of a CID.[13] The Justice Department frequently uses CIDs to gather documents and testimony to assist in determining whether to intervene in a qui tam complaint or (if no such qui tam action has been filed) to file its own lawsuit.

3. DCAA Request

The defense contracting audit agency (DCAA) is the Department of Defense's (DoD) auditor and has extensive audit rights over virtually all DoD contracts. Congress granted DCAA the power to subpoena those records it already has a contractual right to review, but which a contractor has refused to turn over. Congress's grant of this limited subpoena power was not meant to expand the scope of DCAA's authority to review documents, and in most circumstances the power amounts to the right to compel disclosure of a contractor's cost and pricing data. However, companies must be cognizant of the fact that a DCAA request can indicate that the agency has identified a problem with a specific aspect of a contractor's accounting.

4. Medicare Fiscal Intermediary Request

The fiscal intermediaries (FIs) are private companies that process Medicare claims for the federal government. As part of this task, the government has directed these FIs to actively seek to root out fraud by those Medicare providers submitting bills to the FI. Accordingly, one must be aware that on occasion the FIs' specific requests for information may relate to possible mischarging allegations.

B. *Internal Discovery*

A company may also learn of a potential problem through internal means. All responsible government contractors, as well as many other types of companies, now have internal "hotlines" to handle complaints

---

13. CIDs have been authorized for investigations concerning the Racketeer Influenced and Corrupt Organizations Act, antitrust violations, false claims investigations, and certain enumerated violations of the health care laws. *See* 18 U.S.C. § 1968 (RICO); 15 U.S.C. § 1312 (antitrust); 31 U.S.C. § 3733 (false claims).

by employees. Some employees will call these hotlines anonymously to report fraudulent activities by coworkers. Other employees may come forward to their supervisor or the legal department with possible problems. In addition, internal audits may reveal anomalies that demand further investigation.

The need for internal investigations in these circumstances is readily apparent. However, a key difference exists concerning what government contractors and non-government contractors may choose to do with the results of such an internal investigation. Government contractors generally have the option of applying for admission to the formal voluntary disclosure programs at the Department of Defense and the Department of Health and Human Services. There are advantages and disadvantages in engaging in such a voluntary disclosure. While it is beyond the scope of this chapter to discuss the calculus that must go into any voluntary disclosure decision, it is important that an attorney recognize from the outset that a voluntary disclosure is a possible strategy, and in some cases may be an obligation,[14] when faced with a possible fraud discovered internally and of which the government has no knowledge.

C. *The Qui Tam Telephone Call*

A government contractor also may first learn of a fraud allegation by receiving a telephone call from a lawyer from the Department of Justice or the U.S. Attorney's Office. In these telephone calls, the government attorney will likely disclose that a civil false claims action has been filed by a qui tam relator against the contractor under seal, that the United States intends to or is seriously considering joining the lawsuit, and that the United States is willing to hear arguments from the contractor or consider settlement. This type of a telephone call is unique to government contractors.

The Civil False Claims Act (FCA) is perhaps the government's oldest, yet most modern, weapon against government fraud.[15] Originally enacted in the Civil War, the FCA allows the government or a private party on behalf of the United States to bring suit against any persons or companies who present a false claim to the government. The FCA provides for the United States to recover treble damages as well as penalties of $5,500 to

---

14. For example, government contractors are required by law to report violations of the Anti-Kickback Act, 41 U.S.C. § 51 *et seq.*

15. 31 U.S.C. § 3729 *et seq.*; originally codified at Ch. 67, 12 Stat. 696-98.

$11,000 per false claim. This statute also contains a qui tam provision, which allows the whistle-blower suing on behalf of the United States to share in the recovery awarded the United States, up to 30 percent. The whistle-blower or qui tam relator also can pursue the lawsuit even if the government does not wish to intervene in the litigation. The qui tam relator must initially file his or her lawsuit under seal and without serving the defendant in order to give the United States an opportunity to investigate the allegations in secret and determine whether to join the relator in the lawsuit.

Because qui tam lawsuits must be filed under seal, the government contractor may not become aware that a qui tam claim has been filed against it until well after both the relator and the government have completed significant investigation. In fact, because of the under-seal provisions, the contractor's first indication that it is the subject of an FCA claim may not occur until the Department of Justice (DOJ) contacts the contractor "to discuss" the qui tam complaint. The common practice is that the DOJ will first obtain a court order for a "partial unsealing" of the qui tam complaint to allow the department to disclose the existence and nature of the complaint to the defendant. The government attorney in charge of the investigation will then telephone the defendant, inform it of the complaint, and offer it an opportunity to address the allegations.

At that point, the contractor generally has two options: 1) try to convince the United States that the case is without merit and that it should not intervene in the lawsuit, or 2) begin settlement discussions to resolve the matter. The government lawyer may indicate directly or indirectly whether the first option is a realistic possibility at this point in the government's review. In many instances, the government has already reached its decision to intervene and does not even profess to still being open-minded on this issue. It may be that, given the government's firmly held view as to liability or the results of your own investigation, the contractor may wish to pursue settlement. A settlement reached prior to the formal unsealing may allow the client to suffer only a one-time hit of bad publicity relating to the fraud.

If the contractor has a strong defense, however, defense counsel may wish to explain to the government why it should not waste government resources in joining the relator in a losing lawsuit. This presentation may take the form of an oral presentation to the government attorney handling the case or a formal written response with extensive citation to legal authority. This initial presentation may be the most important of the case. The government's intervention in a qui tam claim should be avoided if at all possible. Unlike most relators, the United States boasts significant resources and institutional expertise in these matters. In addition, the prestige of the United States has an impact on both judges and juries. Persuading the government to stay out of the case will sometimes be followed by a quick capitulation by relator's counsel unwilling to bear the time and expense of litigating alone. Moreover, even if the government should ultimately elect to intervene, an effective presentation by the company as to the problems with the government's theory may set the stage for reasonable settlement demands by the government and/or narrow the issues for discovery and trial.

If a contractor receives this phone call, its counsel must aggressively pursue an internal investigation in order to obtain the data necessary to take advantage of any meeting with the Department of Justice. There is, after all, often only one opportunity to influence the government's thinking on the issue of whether or not to intervene in a qui tam suit.

III. RESPONDING TO A FRAUD INVESTIGATION: BASIC PRINCIPLES FOR GOVERNMENT CONTRACTORS

A. *Unique Features of Fraud Investigations Faced by Government Contractors*

1. The Qui Tam Suit

As the previous section makes clear, one of the unique features with which legal counsel for a government contractor must contend is the qui tam lawsuit. The qui tam provisions of the False Claims Act—whereby a private party (the relator) stands in the shoes of the United States and sues government contractors for fraud on behalf of the United States in return for a percentage of the recovery—raise a host of unusual and distinctive issues. These issues range from the broad constitutionality and standing issues posed by having "bounty hunters" bring suit in the name of the United States to the narrow statutory issues relating to the definitions of "public disclosure" and "original source" under the statute. The False Claims Act has special provisions or case law addressing virtually every aspect of litigation, from the procedure for the initial filing by the qui tam relator under seal to the procedures for settling of the lawsuit by the United States and/or relator. It is essential for the attorney for government contractors to be knowledgeable about this unique body of law and to take it into account in identifying issues and conducting any internal investigation.[16]

2. Complex Structure of Parties

In any fraud investigation by the United States against a government contractor, there will typically be at least two, and often three, distinct and separate "parties" on the government side. One is the Justice Department or U.S. Attorney's Office, which is the government's law firm responsible for running the investigation and legal action. The other is the government agency that contracted with the company and that arguably was defrauded. This government agency is, in theory, the "client/victim" of the Justice Department. In the case of qui tam lawsuits, there is a third party on the government side, since the relator has a financial interest and a statutory right to participate as a party to the litigation against the government contractor.[17] Quite obviously, this unusual proliferation of parties has the potential to create a dynamic and complex interrelationship between the various interests.

The relationship among these parties on the government side will change as the suit progresses, but at any given moment they may well have differing, and even conflicting, views of the case. The relator may wish to litigate aggressively, either in the hope of seeking to win a big payday or due to personal animus arising from the whiste-blower's often former employment relationship with the contractor.

The government agency that is supposedly the victim may have a very different view, and is often more sympathetic to the contractor. Many times the government contractor has a longstanding and ongoing relationship performing services for the government agency, which makes the agency reluctant to seek harsh measures against the company. It is not unheard of, for instance, for employees of the contractor's customer to testify favorably for the defendant.

The Justice Department, on the other hand, often finds itself in the middle between the wishes of its client, the "defrauded" government

---

16. For the definitive treatise on the subject, *see* JOHN T. BOESE, CIVIL FALSE CLAIMS AND *QUI TAM* ACTIONS (Aspen Law & Business 2d ed.).

17. 31 U.S.C. § 3730(c) & (d).

agency, and the relator's desire for a large monetary settlement. In addition, the Justice Department itself is often conflicted between its institutional imperative of enforcing the laws and ensuring that the United States receives the largest damages and fines possible and, in contrast, its need to balance the broader policy impact and precedent created by any single case.

The key point is that there are a number of interested parties on the government side of any investigation or lawsuit against a government contractor. The different interests on the other side presents problems and opportunities for the company's attorney. At every stage, the attorney for the government contractor must keep all these stakeholders in mind and conduct his or her work accordingly, taking advantage of the different vantage points and interests on the government side wherever possible.

3. Regulations and Oversight

A government contractor, unlike many commercial concerns, is always subject to an intricate web of detailed regulations and elaborate performance verification and oversight. These rules will likely consist of highly specific statutes, regulations or contracts governing interactions with the relevant government agency. For example, many investigations involve fraud or wrongdoing in obtaining government contracts, so the rules governing private companies in such federal procurements would be the lengthy and highly technical Federal Acquisition Regulations (FAR). Similar comprehensive regulatory schemes control a contractor's dealings with virtually every agency or department of the government, whether DoD, HHS, EPA, GSA or another government agency. These regulations will invariably be very complicated—and potentially very helpful. In the event that a contractor's lawyer becomes aware of the existence of a fraud investigation, whether qui tam or government initiated, it will be necessary to gain a thorough understanding of the applicable regulations as quickly as possible.

It is impossible to overstate the importance of finding and learning the applicable regulations. Government contracts fraud cases frequently turn on the interpretation of the complicated regulatory scheme. In many instances, the lawyers handling the investigation from the Justice Department or U.S. Attorney's Office are not expert in the specialized fields, such as defense contracting or billing for health care services, and government contractors can succeed in having investigations ended or cases dropped by educating the government about its own arcane and technical rules. Learning the applicable regulatory scheme better than the government is essential to any internal investigation for government contractors.

By understanding the regulatory scheme, the lawyer also will be in a better position to find and know the controlling documents. In a case based on a government procurement or grant, one should find, and then study, the contract or grant documents and study them. In a health care case, identify and review the key patient or billing records or physician agreements. These documents will often solve the case for the contractor or, at least, clarify the issues and frame the internal investigation. Also, the attorney for the government contractor should search for documents or testimony showing that individuals from the government agency involved in the contract approved, or at least knew of, the contractor's contested conduct. Government investigations and lawsuits can often be derailed by demonstrating that government officials reviewed and acquiesced in the contractor's actions. Although "government knowledge" is not an absolute defense, it goes far to demonstrating good faith and lack of wrongful intent on the part of the contractor;[18] as a practical matter, it goes far toward ending the United States' interest in a matter.

4. Parallel Criminal Proceedings

Whenever the government is pursuing a civil fraud investigation, it should be assumed that the government also will be conducting a parallel criminal investigation into any allegations of wrongdoing. Because of the numerous quasi-criminal investigators from the IG and other law enforcement groups involved in government contracts matters, and because of the priority given to health care fraud and other government contracts fraud among the "Public Integrity" units at the Justice Department and U.S. Attorney's Offices, there is a high probability that any allegations against a government contractor will be reviewed for possible criminal prosecution.

While such a parallel criminal investigation does not always ensue, the lawyer for a government contractor faced with allegations of possible wrongdoing is best advised to always assume that there may be a parallel criminal investigation.

---

18. *See, e.g.,* Wang v. FMC Corp., 975 F.2d 1412, 1420 (9th Cir. 1992); United States *ex rel.* Butler v. Hughes Helicopter Co., 1993 U.S. Dist. LEXIS 17844, *41 (C.D. Cal. Aug. 25, 1993), *aff'd,* 71 F.3d 321 (9th Cir. 1995).

5. Waiver of Privilege

As discussed above, one of the key differences between government contractors and non-government contractors is that the government contractor may elect to avail itself of a formal voluntary disclosure program offered by the government agency or department with which the company contracted.[19] This approach may be beneficial to the contractor by allowing it to maintain ongoing good relations with the government agency for which it works and receives contracts. Voluntary disclosure also may allow the company to avoid some of the harsher criminal or administrative punishments by demonstrating the contractor's good faith and cooperation. As part of demonstrating the contractor's good faith and cooperation, however, the government often requires that the contractor waive its attorney-client and work product privileges in connection with the subject matter of the disclosure. Therefore, while conducting any internal investigation of potential government fraud, lawyers for the government contractor should be aware that there may well be some form of voluntary disclosure of their own activities and work product. Attorneys for the government contractor must perform their internal investigation with the recognition that their own communications and work product may ultimately end up with the Justice Department and may even become available to the general public.

Even where the contractor does not make a voluntary disclosure, the lawyer should be prepared to have the government obtain his or her privileged materials. Often the contractor's best chance to escape indictment or the government's intervention in a qui tam lawsuit is to make a fulsome presentation to the government attorneys as to why the allegations against the contractor are incorrect. To be successful, this presentation will necessarily need to be detailed in drawing on the results of the contractor's internal investigation. A significant collateral effect of making such a presentation to the government, however, is the potential waiver of both the attorney-client privilege and the work-product doctrine.[20]

---

19. *See supra*, Section II.B.

20. It has been argued, and one court has adopted the position, that disclosure to the United States in this situation should not result in a general waiver of either privilege. *See* Diversified Indus., Inc. v. Meredith, 572 F.2d 596, 610 (8th Cir. 1977). Other courts have specifically rejected this argument, however, and the law in this area remains unsettled. *See* Westinghouse Elec. Corp. v. Republic of the Philippines, 951 F.2d 1414 (3d Cir. 1991); Permian Corp. v. United States, 665 F.2d 1214 (D.C. Cir. 1981).

The contractor's attorney should attempt to obtain a confidentiality or a non-disclosure agreement with the Department of Justice in which it agrees not to deem such a presentation to be a waiver and not to disclose to the relator any materials obtained from the report or the presentation. The Justice Department may or may not be willing to enter into such an agreement. Although the D.C. Circuit has upheld a particular confidentiality agreement, other courts have not found their existence dispositive of the waiver issue.[21] Because the law is this area is either unsettled or generally unfavorable, the most effective way to mitigate this potential consequence of a waiver of privilege is to presume its inevitability and to plan your internal investigation from the outset with such a possible waiver in mind.

IV. CONCLUSION

In many respects, the principal objectives in conducting an internal investigation for a government contractor are basically the same as for any other corporate client. First, one wants to be in a position to convince the ultimate finder of fact—whether it be a civil jury or a U.S. Attorney deciding whether to indict—of the strength of the company's position. In the government contractor context, there often is a special wrinkle because of the False Claims Act's procedure whereby whistle-blowers file qui tam lawsuits under seal and the Justice Department then decides whether to intervene. As a result, lawyers for government contractors often find themselves conducting investigations aimed toward convincing the DOJ lawyers why the whistle-blower is mistaken and why intervention in the qui tam lawsuit is not warranted.

The other objective common to all internal investigations is to follow the maxim of the medical profession: "do no harm." The response to the government investigation should not cause the company to be in deeper trouble than before. For attorneys, this usually entails preventing the company employees from destroying documents, lying to investigators, or otherwise obstructing justice. Retaliating against the suspected whistle-

---

21. *See* Westinghouse Electric Corp. v. Republic of the Philippines, 951 F.2d 1414, 1427 (3d Cir. 1991) ("Even though the DOJ apparently agreed not to disclose the information, under traditional waiver doctrine a voluntary disclosure to a third party waives the attorney-client privilege even if the third party agrees not to disclose the communications to anyone else.").

blower is another common temptation that must be resisted by government contractors. In addition, the lawyer should not create new evidence that can be used against the company—a concern where the waiver of attorney-client and attorney work product privileges is a real possibility.

In one important respect, the government contractor has a very different objective. In addition to being the putative plaintiff against the company, the government also is a valuable customer. For this reason, the government contractor strives to remain on good terms with its customer throughout the litigation. In addition to the primary objective of avoiding criminal and civil liability, the lawyer for the government contractor must also conduct his or her activities with a view toward mitigating or eliminating any potential damage to the company's ongoing relationship with the government department or agency with which it does business. Avoiding the administrative sanction of debarment (i.e., no longer being eligible for additional government contracts) is often the contractor's primary goal; to many companies who rely heavily on government contracts, debarment is the equivalent of the corporate death penalty. In this context, a scorched-earth litigation strategy is rarely in the contractor's best interest. Rather, understanding the regulatory scheme and convincing the government (or, if necessary, the court) of the contractor's good faith are usually more useful approaches for the attorney representing the government contractor.

No Security: Internal Investigations into Violations of the Securities Laws

13

by Michael Shepard*

---

* Michael Shepard is a partner at Heller Ehrman White & McAuliffe LLP in San Francisco, California.

ANY INTERNAL INVESTIGATION calls upon the lawyer to negotiate between Scylla and Charybdis: the risks of exposing the corporation to increased liability by failing to inquire sufficiently into possible wrongdoing, and the risks of exposing the company to increased liability by developing evidence of that wrongdoing that can later be used against the corporation. Internal investigations into violations of the securities laws add two twists that heighten the challenge: the complexities created by various obligations to disclose wrongdoing, and the pressures generated by the likelihood of parallel proceedings. The existence of these two twists means that internal investigations into potential violations of the securities laws put a premium on the speed and accuracy that is desirable in all internal investigations.

This chapter begins by briefly identifying the most typical securities violations that generate internal investigations. It then describes the duties to disclose and the risks of parallel proceedings inherent in such violations, and offers some principles to assist in making the challenging decisions inherent in such investigations.

I. OVERVIEW OF SECURITIES VIOLATIONS

Securities violations that might prompt an internal investigation come in many forms. For publicly traded companies, the most common violations are financial frauds, such as misstatements of earnings or failure to disclose adequately some material news,[1] violations of the Foreign Corrupt Practices Act,[2] and insider trading.[3]

---

1. Section 10(b) of the Securities Exchange Act of 1934, 15 U.S.C. § 78j(b); *In re Sensormatic Electronics Corp.*, Rel. No. 33-7518 (misstated earnings); S.E.C. v. *Fries et al.*, Lit. Rel. No. 14263, Rel. No. AE-604 (materially overstated results of operations); S.E.C. v. *Time Energy Sys.*, Lit. Rel. No. 11,106, Rel. No. AE-99 (misstated net and retained earnings).

2. Section 13(b)(2) of the 1934 act, 15 U.S.C. § 78m(b)(2); Exchange Rules 13b2-1 and 13b2-2, 17 C.F.R. §§ 240.13b2-1 and 240.13b2-2; S.E.C. v. *Moskowitz et al.*, Lit. Rel. No. 11,849 (misleading statements to auditors); S.E.C. v. *Cali Computer Sys., Inc., et al.*, Lit. Rel. No. 11,733, Rel. No. AE-190 (false and misleading statements to auditors concerning performance of its franchise contract obligations and opening of franchise centers using its products); S.E.C. v. *Hermetite Corp., et al.*, Lit. Rel. No. 9756 (violation of books and records, and internal control provisions of the FCPA).

3. Under the "classical" theory of insider trading, a corporate insider who trades in

Corporations generally are held responsible for employees who engage in these financial frauds and corrupt practices.[4] Insider trading can be unique because a corporation is liable for a civil penalty for the insider trading of an employee only if the corporation "knew or recklessly disregarded the fact" that the employee was likely to engage in insider trading and "failed to take appropriate steps to prevent such act or acts before they occurred."[5] While these limits may affect the need for and conduct of an internal investigation,[6] they do not free the corporation from all liability. For example, a lesser standard applies to the imposition of liability other than civil penalties, ranging from disgorgement to injunctive relief and from private civil damage remedies to delisting.[7] There also are stock

---

the securities of his corporation on the basis of material, nonpublic information violates section 10(b) of the 1934 act and Rule 10b-5, 17 C.F.R. § 240.10b-5. United States v. O'Hagan, 117 S. Ct. 2199, 2207 (1997). Under the misappropriation theory of insider trading, a person who misappropriates confidential information and trades on the basis of that information, in breach of a duty owed to the source of the information, violates section 10(b) and Rule 10b-5. *Id.* While the classical theory is based on the insider's breach of a fiduciary duty owed to the corporation's shareholders, the misappropriation theory is based on the trader's deception of those who entrusted him with access to the confidential information. *Id.*

4. A corporation may be liable for the violations of its employees under theories of respondeat superior. Hollinger v. Titan Capital Corp., 914 F.2d 1564, 1576-78 (9th Cir. 1990). In addition, under the controlling person standard of section 20(a) of the 1934 act, 15 U.S.C. § 78t(a), the defendant bears the burden of proving that it acted in good faith and did not induce the violation by the controlled person. *Id.* at 1575.

5. *See* section 21A(b)(1)(A) of the Securities Exchange Act of 1934, 15 U.S.C. § 78u-1(b)(1)(a). This provision specifies the standard for corporate liability for a civil penalty as a "controlling person" of an inside trader. *See* section 21A(a)(1), 15 U.S.C. § 78u-1(a)(1) (civil penalty may be imposed on a person who "directly or indirectly controlled the person who committed the violation"). Liability would of course attach if the trading was conducted for the benefit of the corporation.

Section 21A(b)(2), 15 U.S.C. § 78u-1(b)(2), further specifies that a penalty may not be imposed on an employer on the basis of respondeat superior and that the controlling person standard of section 21A(b)(1) must be met.

6. *See* page 403.

7. Section 21A(b)(2) provides that the general controlling person standard set forth in section 20(a) of the 1934 act, 15 U.S.C. § 78t(a), does not apply to actions *for civil penalties* for insider trading under section 21A(a). However, section 21A does not specify the standard for liability of a controlling person for an employee's insider trading in other contexts, such as SEC actions for disgorgement or private actions for damages. In these contexts, the general standard for controlling person liability set forth in section 20(a) of the 1934 act, 15 U.S.C. § 78t(a), still applies. Under section

exchange rules broad enough to permit the delisting or expulsion of an issuer for the insider trading of its employees, but it does not appear that either the NYSE or the NASD has ever taken such action against an ongoing, established business.[8]

Brokers and dealers[9] face an even wider range of potential liability in

---

20(a), "[e]very person who, directly or indirectly, controls any person liable under any provision of this chapter or of any rule or regulation thereunder" is jointly and severally liable for the controlled person's violation, "unless the controlling person acted in good faith and did not directly or indirectly induce the act or acts constituting the violation or cause of action." Section 21A(b)(2).

8. Although no reported cases against major firms exist, NYSE Rule 499 provides: "Securities admitted to the list may be suspended from dealings or removed from the list at any time." Rule 499.10 states that the numerical criteria (such as number of publicly held shares and aggregate market value of publicly held shares) for listing on the NYSE are not exclusive criteria and that the NYSE may consider other factors, such as "the failure of a company to make timely, adequate, and accurate disclosures of information to its shareholders and the investing public or to observe good accounting practices in reporting of earnings and financial position; other conduct not in keeping with sound public policy; unsatisfactory financial conditions and/or operating results; inability to meet current debt obligations or adequately to finance operations; abnormally low selling price or volume of trading; unwarranted use of company funds for the repurchase of its equity securities; any other event or condition which may exist or occur that makes further dealings and listing of the securities on the Exchange inadvisable or unwarranted in the opinion of the Exchange."

Similarly, NASD Rule 4300 provides that Nasdaq "may deny initial inclusion or apply additional or more stringent criteria for the initial or continued inclusion of particular securities or suspend or terminate the inclusion of particular securities based on any event, condition, or circumstance which exists or occurs that makes initial or continued inclusion of the securities in Nasdaq inadvisable or unwarranted in the opinion of Nasdaq, even though the securities meet all enumerated criteria for initial or continued inclusion in Nasdaq." NASD Rule 4330 provides that Nasdaq may "deny inclusion or apply additional or more stringent criteria for the initial or continued inclusion of particular securities or suspend or terminate the inclusion of an otherwise qualified security if:... (3) Nasdaq deems it necessary to prevent fraudulent and manipulative acts and practices, to promote just and equitable principles of trade, or to protect investors and the public interest."

9. The term "broker" is defined in section 3(a)(4) of the Securities Exchange Act of 1934 to mean "any person engaged in the business of effecting transactions in securities for the account of others...." The term "dealer" is defined in section 3(a)(5) of the Securities Exchange Act of 1934 to mean "any person engaged in the business of buying and selling securities for his own account, through a broker or otherwise... or any person insofar as he buys or sells securities for his own account,

the event their registered or unregistered employees defraud customers, breach any fiduciary duties owed to customers (for example, by recommending unsuitable securities to a customer),[10] trade excessively in a customer's account for the purpose of generating commissions,[11] or manipulate the market through activity such as front-running.[12] The SEC has sought to impose liability on firms and individuals based on the failure to provide reasonable supervision over the actions of their employees. The SEC and self-regulatory organizations (SROs) have increasingly sought to impose such liability,[13] which can be avoided by proof that (1) there

---

either individually or in some fiduciary capacity, but not as a part of regular business." This chapter refers to brokers and dealers collectively as "broker-dealers."

10. *In re* Hampton, Exchange Act Rel. No. 35,570 (Apr. 5, 1995); *In re* Grosby, Exchange Act Rel. No. 34,805 (Oct. 7, 1994); *In re* Sela, Exchange Act Rel. No. 33,789 (Mar. 21, 1994).

11. *In re* Parodi, Exchange Act Rel. No. 27,299, 44 S.E.C. Docket (CCH) 1111 (Sept. 27, 1989) (broker churned accounts); Mihara v. Dean Witter & Co., Inc., 614 F.2d 814, 820 (9th Cir. 1980) (churning is when "a securities broker engages in excessive trading in disregard of his customer's investment objectives for the purpose of generating commission business. . . .").

12. A broker or dealer front-runs when he or she trades in anticipation of a large block transaction of one of his or her customers. The broker or dealer benefits from the price change in the security expected to follow the block transaction.

13. S.E.C. v. Citron, et al., Civil Action No. SA CV 96-0074 AHS (E. Ex.) (C.D. Cal.), Lit. Rel. No. 14792 (Jan. 24, 1996); *In re* Credit Suisse First Boston Corp., Jerry Nowlin and Douglas Montague, 1998 WL 30378 (S.E.C.), Rel. No. 34-39,595, 66 S.E.C. Docket 807. *See also John H. Gutfreund*, Exchange Act Rel. No. 31,554, 52 S.E.C. 2849 (Dec. 3, 1992) (sanctions imposed on Salomon Brothers executives based on their failure to take any action on learning that the head of the firm's Government Trading Desk had committed what amounted to a criminal act by purposely submitting a false $3.15 billion bid for U.S. Treasury securities); *see also Patricia A. Johnson*, Exchange Act Rel. No. 35,698, 59 S.E.C. 618 (May 10, 1995) (branch manager ignored numerous warnings signs that broker was misappropriating customer funds and committing other fraudulent acts); *Dan A. Druz*, Exchange Act Rel. No. 35,203, 58 S.E.C. 1526 (Jan. 9, 1995) (branch office manager ignored repeated indications that broker was defrauding customers by executing unauthorized trades); *Prudential Bache Securities*, Exchange Act Rel. No. 35,698, 59 S.E.C. 618 (May 10, 1995) (sanctions imposed on a branch manager for failure to follow numerous supervisory and compliance procedures designed to detect and prevent violations of the law); *Frank J. Custable*, Exchange Act Rel. No. 33,324, 55 S.E.C. 1794 (Dec. 10, 1993) (manager failed to follow firm's compliance procedures, including maintaining customer contact log, and reviewing employee's customer book); *Nicolas A. Boccella*, Exchange Act Rel. No. 26,574, 42 S.E.C. 1388 (Feb. 27, 1989) (manager failed to "police compliance" with

were established procedures to prevent and detect the violation, and (2) the broker or dealer implemented the procedures without cause to believe that they were not being followed.[14]

---

firm procedures relating to hand delivery of checks to customers by sales brokers and identification and proper designation of employee-related accounts); *Steven P. Sanders and Daniel M. Porush*, Exchange Act Rel. No. 34-40,600, 68 S.E.C. Docket 745 (Oct. 26, 1998) (head trader employed by broker-dealer engaged in excessive and fraudulent mark-ups; SEC sustained sanctions imposed by NASD against president of broker-dealer for his failure to supervise head trader); *Stuart K. Patrick*, Exchange Act Rel. No. 34-32,314, 51 S.E.C. 419 (May 17, 1993) (floor trader employed by broker-dealer committed violations in connection with trades in firm's proprietary account; SEC sustained NYSE's sanctions against Patrick, the chief executive officer and president of the firm, where Patrick failed to establish systems and procedures and failed to provide supervision over trader).

14. Securities Exchange Act § 15(b)(4)(E); 15 U.S.C. § 78o(b)(4)(E). Section 15(b)(4)(E) is a "safe harbor" provision, and a broker-dealer may comply and avoid sanctions for failure to supervise by having and enforcing procedures as specified in that section. *See In re Lehman Bros., Inc.*, Rel. No. 34-37,673, 1996 WL 519914, *7 n.11 (Sept. 12, 1996); *In re Goldman, Sachs & Co.*, Rel. No. 34-33,576, 1994 WL 29479, *6 (Feb. 3, 1994).

Section 15(b)(4)(E) does not specify that establishing and following such procedures is the *only* way that a firm can satisfy its supervision obligations. However, several SEC opinions have emphasized the importance of formal written procedures, especially for large firms, and have indicated that, if violations occur, the absence of adequate procedures is likely to result in a finding that the firm did not provide reasonable supervision. *See In re Smith Barney, Inc.*, Rel. No. 34-39,118, 1997 WL 583802, *5 (Sept. 23, 1997) ("The responsibility of broker dealers to supervise their employees by means of effective, established procedures is a critical component in the federal investor protection scheme regulating the securities market."; firm liable for failure to supervise because absence of written procedures "or other institutionally-recognized practice" resulted in failure to detect violations by firm's municipal derivatives banker) (citations omitted); *In re Lehman Bros., Inc.*, Rel. No. 37,673, 1996 WL 519914, *8 (Sept. 12, 1996) (firm liable for failure to supervise where firm had insufficient policies or procedures designed to prevent excessive mark-ups); *In re Goldman, Sachs & Co.*, Rel. No. 34-33,576, 1994 WL 29479, *6 (Feb. 3, 1994) ("It is essential . . . not only that a system of controls adequate to meet the problems inherent in a large and scattered organization be established but also that such controls be effectively enforced by those in authority"; firm was not entitled to protection of safe harbor provision where firm had general policy regarding execution of trades to realize tax· losses, but policy was not committed to writing, firm did not articulate criteria explaining general rule, and firm had no procedures for detecting violations of policy) (citations omitted); *In re Smith Barney, Harris Upham & Co.*, Rel. No. 21,813, 1985 WL

Insider trading issues for brokerage firms are even more complex. While not automatically liable for insider trading of their employees, brokerage firms can be responsible for such trading on a lesser standard than a corporation: liability may arise from the firm's failure to have in place and enforce written policies and procedures reasonably designed to prevent insider trading violations.[15] This concern is highlighted by the ability of integrated firms to offer a range of financial services from investment banking to retail sales, which results in the presence of insider information in one portion of the firm and a special need to ensure that trading decisions are not made by employees in possession of material nonpublic information.[16]

II. OBLIGATIONS TO UNCOVER AND REPORT VIOLATIONS

Publicly traded companies and brokers and dealers involved in potential

---

61318, *7 (Mar. 5, 1985) ("Broker-dealers must not only adopt effective procedures but also ensure that their branch managers and compliance personnel fully understand and follow their job requirements and firm compliance procedures."; firm had inadequate procedures for detecting improper sales of uncovered options).

15. S.E.C. v. First Boston Corp., Lit. Rel. No. 11,092 [1986-1987 Transfer Binder] CCH Fed. Sec. L. Rep. ¶ 92,712 (S.D.N.Y. May 5, 1986); S.E.C. v. Kidder, Peabody & Co., Lit. Rel. No. 11,452, 38 S.E.C. Docket 647 (S.D.N.Y. June 4, 1987). Section 21A(b)(1)(B) of the 1934 act provides that a civil penalty may be imposed on a broker or dealer or investment adviser that "knowingly or recklessly failed to establish, maintain, or enforce any policy or procedure required under section 78o(f) of this title [section 15(f) of the Exchange Act] or section 80b-4a of this title [section 204A of the Investment Advisers Act of 1940] and such failure substantially contributed to or permitted the occurrence of the act or acts constituting the violation." Section 15(f) of the Exchange Act and section 204A of the Investment Advisers Act of 1940, referenced in section 21A(b)(1)(B), require brokers, dealers, and investment advisers to establish "written policies and procedures reasonably designed" to prevent insider trading violations.

16. Rule 14e-3(b) creates a "safe harbor" by acknowledging the use of "ethical walls" and restricted trading lists as effective defenses to firm liability for insider trading by firm employees. "Ethical walls" typically consist of written policies restricting the dissemination of material, non-public information within the firm. Restricted lists prohibit trading in the identified security while material, non-public information exists within the firm about the security. *In re Merrill, Lynch, Pierce, Fenner & Smith*, Exchange Act Rel. No. 8459 [1967-1969 Transfer Binder] CCH Fed. Sec. L. Rep. ¶ 77,629 at 83,350.

violations of the securities laws must assess not only their own liability for such violations, but also the extent to which they have an obligation to report the violation in a public filing or to a stock exchange, or to investigate the violation for purposes of making a report. The existence of these obligations impacts the necessity for conducting an investigation and the decision whether to disclose the results to prosecutors and/or the SEC. In addition, these obligations affect the process of conducting the investigation, and particularly the process of protecting any written report of the investigation.

This section describes the obligations of publicly traded companies and of brokers and dealers to investigate and report wrongdoing; the next section addresses the issues created by such investigations and reports in the context of parallel proceedings, where the results of investigations and reports can be turned against the corporation or firm.

A. *Publicly Traded Companies*

In the early stages of the discovery of possible wrongdoing, the rules and principles that may compel publicly traded companies to disclose wrongdoing are unlikely to require a public disclosure. But there are circumstances in which a disclosure may be required, even at an early stage.

1. Duties of Disclosure

While a corporation need not disclose information of wrongdoing unless there is a specific duty to do so,[17] there are at least two situations in which a specific duty to disclose information exists.[18] For information that is material: (1) a corporation must disclose it when required by a specific SEC rule; (2) and, even in the absence of a specific

---

17. *See, e.g.,* Roeder v. Alpha Industries, Inc., 814 F.2d 22, 27 (1st Cir. 1987) (no general affirmative duty to disclose material information where "there is no insider trading, no statute or regulation requiring disclosure, and no inaccurate, incomplete, or misleading prior disclosures"); United States v. Yeaman, 987 F. Supp. 373, 377-78 (E.D. Pa. 1997) (same); United States Securities & Exchange Comm'n v. Fehn, 97 F.3d 1276, 1289 (9th Cir. 1996) (section 10b-5 imposes liability only for misstatements or omissions that are misleading; "in the case of an omission [of material fact], silence, absent a duty to disclose, is not misleading") (quoting McCormick v. Fund American Cos., 26 F.3d 869, 875 (9th Cir. 1994) (quoting Basic, Inc. v. Levinson, 485 U.S. 224, 239 n.17 (1988)) (internal quotation marks omitted).

18. In addition, anyone who trades on inside information must disclose that information to persons with whom he trades or abstain from trading. *See* Chiarella v. United States, 445 U.S. 222, 227-29 (1980).

SEC rule, when a corporation discloses information, it must also disclose such further information as is necessary to ensure that its disclosure is not inaccurate, incomplete, or misleading.

a. SEC Rules Requiring Specific Disclosures Regarding Actual or Potential Wrongdoing

The SEC's Regulation S-K, 17 C.F.R. Part 229, sets forth specific information that must be disclosed in the periodic and other reports filed with the SEC by publicly traded companies. *See generally* 17 C.F.R. Part 229; *United States v. Crop Growers Corp.*, 954 F. Supp. 335, 347 (D.D.C. 1997). Regulation S-K includes three provisions that may require a corporation to disclose specific information about actual or potential wrongdoing by the corporation or its directors or officers: (1) Item 103, 17 C.F.R. § 229.103, governing the disclosure of legal proceedings involving the corporation; (2) Item 401(f), 17 C.F.R. § 229.401(f), governing the disclosure of legal proceedings involving directors, nominees to become directors, and executive officers; and (3) Item 303, 17 C.F.R. § 229.303, concerning management's discussion and analysis of the corporation's financial condition and results of operations.

Item 103: Legal Proceedings Involving the Corporation. Item 103 requires disclosure of certain pending legal proceedings.[19] It does not on its face require disclosure of matters that are under investigation, either by the government or internally. Rather, Item 103 requires disclosure only of legal proceedings that are actually pending or that are "known to be contemplated by governmental authorities."[20]

---

19. Section 229.103 (Item 103) provides:

Describe briefly any material pending legal proceedings, other than ordinary routine litigation incidental to the business, to which the registrant or any of its subsidiaries is a party or of which any of their property is the subject. Include the name of the court or agency in which the proceedings are pending, the date instituted, the principal parties thereto, a description of the factual basis alleged to underlie the proceeding and the relief sought. Include similar information as to any such proceedings known to be contemplated by governmental authorities.

20. For SEC investigations, it is not clear whether proceedings are "known to be contemplated" when the SEC requests a Wells submission, when the Commission actually authorizes an action against the corporation, or at some other point.

Accordingly, the mere allegation of securities violations (or other wrongdoing) does not require disclosure. *See Bolger v. First State Financial Services,* 759 F. Supp. 182, 194 (D.N.J. 1991) (in the context of proxy disclosures under SEC Rule 14a-9, 17 C.F.R. § 240.14a-9, corporation was not required to disclose mere allegations of illegal conduct and mismanagement by officers and directors); *Levine v. NL Industries, Inc.,* 717 F. Supp. 252, 255 (S.D.N.Y. 1989) (where corporation had knowledge of possible violations of environmental statutes and knowledge that such violations could *possibly* result in legal proceedings by state regulators, but no information that regulators were actually contemplating such proceedings, Item 103 did not require disclosure of this knowledge on a Form 10-K). Neither Item 103 nor its instructions, nor subsequent judicial decisions, specify at what point beyond the existence of mere allegations it can be said that a corporation *knows* that legal proceedings are contemplated. While its holding is suspect, one court has stated that Item 103 does not require disclosure even if the corporation has received a target letter. *See Crop Growers,* 954 F. Supp. at 347 (citing *In re Browning-Ferris Indus., Inc. Shareholder Derivative Litig.,* 830 F. Supp. 361, 369 (S.D. Tex. 1993), *aff'd mem.,* 20 F.3d 465 (5th Cir. 1994)).[21] Moreover, a

---

In addition to the cases discussed in the text, two SEC releases have discussed this issue. The first, Securities Act Release No. 5949, *Uniform and Integrated Reporting Requirements,* 1978 WL 14845, *11 (July 28, 1978), which extended the obligation to disclose proceedings "known to be contemplated by government authorities" to quarterly reports on Form 10-Q, was of little help. Commentators argued extending the obligation in this fashion "would increase costs and risks of error because companies would be required to determine on a more or less continuous basis what the government was contemplating." *Id.* The SEC responded to this argument by stating that "only 'material' proceedings 'known' by the registrant to be contemplated need be reported. It appears to the Commission that these qualifications sufficiently assure the reasonableness of the requirement." *Id.*

Second, in *In re Occidental Petroleum Corp.,* Exchange Act Release No. 16,950, 1980 WL 121345, *4 (July 2, 1980), the government had informed a subsidiary of Occidental that a criminal action against the subsidiary for environmental violations was likely, but negotiations between the subsidiary and the government were still continuing. The SEC stated that Occidental should have disclosed this matter as a proceeding "known to be contemplated" by the government. *Id.*

21. *Crop Growers* cites *Browning-Ferris* as holding that receipt of a target letter is insufficient to trigger a disclosure obligation under Item 103. *See* Crop Growers, 954 F. Supp. at 347. However, *Browning-Ferris* held that receipt of a target letter by a director nominee did not trigger a disclosure obligation under Item 401(f), which governs disclosure of legal proceedings involving directors, officers, and director nominees,

company may initiate an investigation into the allegations without automatically triggering a disclosure obligation. In *Bolger*, the court held that because the corporation was not obligated to disclose mere allegations of wrongdoing, it also was not obligated to disclose "whatever preliminary steps it took in response to those allegations." *Id.*

Item 401(f): Legal Proceedings Involving Directors, Director Nominees, or Executive Officers. Item 401(f), 17 C.F.R. § 229.401(f), governs the obligation to disclose information about legal proceedings involving directors, persons nominated to become directors, or executive officers of the corporation. Like Item 103, Item 401(f) is also focused on more advanced stages of proceedings than the start of a government or internal investigation.[22]

By all accounts, Item 401(f) does not require disclosure of uncharged criminal conduct. *See, e.g., United States v. Matthews*, 787 F.2d 38, 43-44, 47 (2d Cir. 1986) (Item 401(f) only required disclosure of convictions and pending criminal proceedings and did not require disclosure of fact that director was the named subject of a criminal investigation); *Crop Grow-*

---

rather than under Item 103. Browning-Ferris, 830 F. Supp. at 368-70. Moreover, *Browning-Ferris* did not address whether a target letter received in a currently pending investigation would trigger a duty of disclosure. In *Browning-Ferris*, the court held that the corporation was not obligated to disclose in a proxy statement a target letter received by the director nominee three years earlier, in connection with an investigation that did not result in an indictment and that was no longer pending at the time the proxy statement was issued. *Id.*

22. With respect to civil violations of federal or state securities laws or federal commodities laws, Item 401(f) requires disclosure only after a court or the SEC or CFTC has actually made a finding that the director, nominee, or executive officer committed a violation. *See* 17 C.F.R. § 229.401(f)(5) and (6). With respect to criminal proceedings, Item 401(f) requires disclosure only when the director, nominee, or executive officer was "convicted in a criminal proceeding" or "is a named subject of a pending criminal proceeding." See 17 C.F.R. § 229.401(f)(2). Item 401(f) requires public companies to: "Describe any of the following events that occurred during the past five years and that are material to an evaluation of the ability or integrity of any director, person nominated to become a director or executive officer of the registrant: . . . (2) Such person was convicted in a criminal proceeding or is a named subject of a pending criminal proceeding (excluding traffic violations and other minor offenses)." Item 401(f) also requires disclosure if a director, nominee, or executive officer was found by a court in a civil action or by the SEC or CFTC to have violated federal or state securities laws or federal commodities laws, and such finding has not been reversed, suspended or vacated. *See* 17 C.F.R. § 229.401(f)(5) and (6).

ers, 954 F. Supp. at 347 (Item 401(f) did not require disclosure of uncharged criminal conduct); *Browning-Ferris*, 830 F. Supp. at 369 (Item 401(f) did not require disclosure of the fact that a target letter was sent to director nominee in an investigation that was no longer pending).

Item 303: Management's Discussion and Analysis (MD&A). Item 303 of Regulation S-K is potentially the broadest and the least easily defined disclosure provision. It requires a public company to provide management's discussion and analysis of the company's "financial condition, changes in financial condition, and results of operations." 17 C.F.R. § 229.303. Comment 3 to Item 303(a) requires the corporation to discuss "material events and uncertainties known to management that would cause reported financial information not to be necessarily indicative of future operating results or of future financial condition. This would include descriptions and amounts of (A) matters that would have an impact on future operations and have not had an impact in the past, and (B) matters that have had an impact on reported operations and are not expected to have an impact on future operations." Interpreting this requirement, the SEC stated in an August 1988 Release that government *inquiries* into questionable conduct must be disclosed if the issuer reasonably expects the investigation to have a material impact on the company's business practices or financial condition.[23]

The SEC has interpreted the financial disclosure provisions of Rule 303 as requiring a corporation to disclose illegal conduct that has a material impact on its financial condition *and* to disclose the *cessation* of illegal conduct when the cessation has a material impact on the corporation's financial condition. For example, in *In re E.F. Hutton & Co.*, Litigation Release No. 10915, 1985 WL 61025 (1985), the SEC charged E.F. Hutton (Hutton) with improperly failing to disclose illegal conduct in the MD&A sections of two Forms 10-K. In 1985, E.F. Hutton pleaded guilty to 2,000 counts of mail and wire fraud in connection with checking account practices allegedly designed to obtain interest-free use of bank funds. *Id.* at *1. The SEC filed and settled a complaint charging Hutton with, among other things, improperly failing to discuss this misconduct in the MD&A sections of its 1981 and 1982 Forms 10-K. *Id.* at *3-4. In the complaint, the SEC contended that Hutton should have disclosed that the increased

---

23. Exchange Act Rel. No. 25,951 (Aug. 2, 1988).

use of the illegal practices in 1981 was a material cause of the material increase in Hutton's net interest income from 1980 to 1981 and that the decreased use of such practices in 1982 was a material cause of the material decrease in Hutton's net interest income from 1981 to 1982. *Id.*

b. Rules 10b-5 and 12b-20: The Duty to Disclose Information Necessary to Ensure That Prior Disclosures Are Not Misleading

If none of the SEC's specific disclosure rules require a corporation to disclose a particular item of information pertaining to corporate or managerial wrongdoing, the corporation may still be required to disclose the information to ensure that any prior disclosures it has made are not misleading under Rule 10b-5[24] and Rule 12b-20.[25]

Rules 10b-5 and 12b-20 permit the imposition of liability for failure to disclose information about corporate or managerial wrongdoing. For example, in *Securities & Exchange Comm'n v. Fehn*, 97 F.3d 1276, 1280 (9th Cir. 1996), a corporation and the individual who served as its president and CEO committed securities violations in connection with the corporation's initial public offering. The corporation subsequently filed several Forms 10-Q that did not mention contingent liabilities stemming from the prior securities violations. *Id.* at 1281. The Ninth Circuit held that, because the Forms 10-Q included required financial information supplied by the corporation's accountants, the failure to disclose contingent liabilities stemming from the prior securities violations rendered the required financial information misleading. *Id.* at 1289-90.

---

24. Rule 10b-5 requires the disclosure of information necessary to ensure that any disclosure, whether it was mandatory or voluntary, is not misleading. Securities & Exchange Comm'n v. Fehn, 97 F.3d 1276, 1290 n.12 (9th Cir. 1996); *see In re* Par Pharmaceuticals, Inc. Securities Litig., 733 F. Supp. 668, 675 (S.D.N.Y. 1990) ("Under [Rule 10b-5], even though no duty to make a statement on a particular matter has arisen, once corporate officers undertake to make statements, they are obligated to speak truthfully and to make such additional disclosures as are necessary to avoid rendering the statements made misleading."). A statement is misleading if "a reasonable investor, in the exercise of due care, would have received a false impression from the statement." Par Pharmaceuticals, 733 F. Supp. at 677; *see* Levine v. NL Indus., Inc., 717 F. Supp. 252, 254 (S.D.N.Y. 1989), *aff'd*, 926 F.2d 199 (2d Cir. 1991).

25. Rule 12b-20, 17 C.F.R. § 240.12b-20 provides: "In addition to the information expressly required to be included in a statement or report, there shall be added such further material information, if any, as may be necessary to make the required statements, in the light of the circumstances under which they are made, not misleading."

A second example is *Par Pharmaceuticals*, 733 F. Supp. at 672-74, in which the defendants allegedly bribed FDA officials to obtain FDA approvals for drug products and subsequently made claims in Forms 10-K and 10-Q and other public documents about their ability to obtain speedy FDA approvals. Rejecting in part a motion to dismiss in a civil case, the court held that a jury could find these disclosures misleading under Rule 10b-5 because the disclosures gave investors the false impression that the defendants' success in obtaining FDA approvals stemmed not from bribery but from expertise constituting a legitimate competitive advantage. *Id.* at 678; *see also Yeaman*, 987 F. Supp. at 380 (where Form 10-K provided incomplete and misleading information about defendant's prior securities violation, Rule 12b-20 required the inclusion of corrective information in the 10-K); *Ballan v. Wilfred American Educational Corp.*, 720 F. Supp. 241, 249 (E.D.N.Y. 1989) (where educational corporation allegedly violated federal student aid regulations and then made disclosures about its financial condition without disclosing facts about the alleged violations that might materially affect the corporation's financial condition, jury could find such disclosures materially misleading under Rule 10b-5).[26]

---

26. There is a dispute over whether this general disclosure duty is sufficient to support *criminal* liability for non-disclosure of uncharged criminal conduct. Two cases hold that the due process clause limits the government's ability to impose criminal liability for failing to disclose uncharged prior criminal conduct. *See* Matthews, 787 F.2d at 49 (holding that "at least so long as uncharged criminal conduct is not required to be disclosed by any rule lawfully promulgated by the SEC, nondisclosure of such conduct cannot be the basis of a criminal prosecution," and noting "the obvious due process implications that would arise from permitting a conviction to stand in the absence of clearer notice as to what disclosures are required in this uncertain area"); Crop Growers, 954 F. Supp. at 346 (due process dictates that, if defendant does not receive fair notice that specific conduct is prohibited, that conduct cannot be prosecuted; rejecting application of general requirements of Item 303 and Rule 12b-20 as bases for criminal liability). In addition, *Matthews*, which involved an individual defendant, stated that its holding was "buttressed by concerns about the self-incrimination implications" of permitting imposition of criminal liability for failure to confess uncharged criminal conduct. Matthews, 787 F.2d at 49. But it is generally not an excuse in civil cases to rely on the Fifth Amendment to justify a non-disclosure, *see, e.g.,* Fehn, 97 F.3d at 1293; Par Pharmaceuticals, 773 F. Supp. at 675 n.8, and other courts have distinguished *Matthews* and *Crop Growers* even in criminal cases. In *Yeaman*, a criminal case, the court held that Rule 12b-20 can be the basis for the imposition of criminal liability for the failure to disclose wrongdoing. The *Yeaman* court stated that *Crop Growers* had rejected the application of Rule 12b-20

c. A Duty to Investigate?

None of the SEC rules on their face create a duty to investigate, but principles developed in civil cases do impose such a duty under certain circumstances. Numerous civil cases have held that a failure to investigate signs of illegal conduct by employees may constitute recklessness and subject a corporation to liability for failure to disclose those violations. *See Hollinger v. Titan Capital Corp.,* 914 F.2d 1564, 1569-70 (9th Cir. 1990) (recklessness requires a "highly unreasonable omission" constituting an "extreme departure from the standards of ordinary care, and which presents a danger of misleading buyers and sellers that is either known to the defendant or is so obvious that the actor must have been aware of it"; broker-dealer did not act recklessly in failing to disclose registered representative's 11-year-old forgery conviction) (citations omitted). The failure to investigate adequately and the resulting failure to uncover wrongdoing can constitute recklessness if the defendant ignored clear warning signs. *See, e.g., In re Leslie Fay Companies, Inc.,* 871 F. Supp. 686, 698 (S.D.N.Y. 1995) (if, as complaint alleged, accountants recklessly ignored "red flags" indicating that issuer's employees were falsifying issuer's books, accountants could be held liable under Rule 10b-5; accountants' alleged conduct supported inference that accountants acted with intent and deliberately disregarded warning signs to avoid antagonizing issuer).

No court has yet imposed a duty to conduct an internal investigation

---

"because that rule cannot, in the first instance, impose a duty to speak where none otherwise existed" but held that, where Regulation S-K specifically requires particular disclosures, Rule 12b-20 requires the disclosure of additional information necessary to render the disclosed information not misleading. Yeaman, 987 F. Supp. at 381 n.7. In *Fehn,* a civil case, the Ninth Circuit noted that *Matthews* involved the disclosure requirements for proxy statements under Rule 14a-9, 17 C.F.R. § 240.14a-9, rather than Rule 10b-5, and stated that Rule 10b-5 imposes liability for failure to make corrective disclosures even where no specific regulation requires disclosure of the omitted information. Fehn, 97 F.3d at 1290 n.12.

One case has applied similar due process principles to prohibit criminal prosecution for nondisclosure even when the nondisclosure is based on more specific obligations such as Item 303. In *Crop Growers,* 954 F. Supp. at 347-48, the court held that Item 303's requirement to disclose "any known trend or uncertainty" likely to influence the registrant's liquidity or operational results did "not provide sufficient notice that a particular disclosure is required to allow criminal liability for the alleged non-disclosure." *Id.* at 348. No case has applied the principles of *Crop Growers* outside the context in which the government is seeking to prosecute the nondisclosure criminally.

per se, but the Delaware Chancery Court took a giant step down that road in *In re Caremark International Inc. Derivative Litigation*, 698 A.2d 959, 970 (Del. Ch. Ct. 1996). By imposing an obligation to create "information and reporting systems to keep track of the corporation's compliance with law," *Caremark* not only emphasized the corporation's duty to keep informed, but also required the creation of a system that will identify allegations of wrongdoing and effectively compel the corporation to investigate them or face charges that it recklessly avoided learning about the misconduct. The obligation to investigate allegations of wrongdoing is heightened by the obligation to disclose matters covered by Item 303, which inherently implies some duty to gather—or at least not to ignore—potential matters to be disclosed. Eventually this set of obligations creates a dog chasing its tail: The corporation receives an allegation that does not on its face require disclosure. It then investigates, and if it reports a violation to the government and the government takes on the case, the corporation as a result of its own inquiries and statements may end up with a required disclosure under the SEC's rules or other principles.

2. Materiality

All of the theories imposing liability for a corporation's failure to disclose wrongdoing in its SEC filings require proof that the information was material. *Levine v. NL Industries, Inc.*, 926 F.2d 199, 202 (2d Cir. 1991). An omitted fact is material if there is a substantial likelihood that a reasonable investor would consider it important in making an investment decision. *See Basic, Inc. v. Levinson*, 485 U.S. 224, 231-32 (1988). There must be a "'substantial likelihood that the disclosure of the omitted fact would have been viewed by the reasonable investor as having significantly altered the "total mix" of information made available.'" *Id.* (quoting *TSC Industries, Inc. v. Northway, Inc.*, 426 U.S. 438 (1976)). The materiality of an event that is "contingent or speculative" in nature "'will depend at any given time upon a balancing of both the indicated probability that the event will occur and the anticipated magnitude of the event in light of the totality of the company activity.'" *Basic*, 485 U.S. at 238 (quoting *SEC v. Texas Gulf Sulphur Co.*, 401 F.2d 833, 849 (2d Cir. 1968) (en banc)).[27]

---

27. The SEC's disclosure rules, such as Items 103 and 401(f), also incorporate the requirement of materiality. Under Item 103, pending legal proceedings involving the

Avoiding disclosure based on an asserted lack of materiality is a risky proposition. Not only is such a determination "peculiarly one[] for the trier of fact," *Basic*, 485 U.S. at 231-32, but the assessments are "delicate." *Id.* While there are cases holding that mere allegations of wrongdoing are not automatically material, *see Bolger v. First State Financial Services*, 759 F. Supp. 182, 194 (D.N.J. 1991); *GAF Corp. v. Heyman*, 724 F.2d 727, 739 (2d Cir. 1983), the case law is mixed at best. Because materiality is a fact-intensive inquiry, courts are reluctant to decide as a matter of law that the failure to disclose certain information about corporate misconduct was not material. *E.g., Ballan*, 720 F. Supp. at 249-50 (declining to dismiss complaint alleging that defendants failed to disclose policies that violated federal regulations).

In judging the likelihood that the event will occur—that alleged corporate wrongdoing will result in harm to the corporation—most courts appear to give the corporations some room, recognizing that the "outcome of legal proceedings is inevitably uncertain," *Ballan*, 720 F. Supp. at 248, and not requiring management to "characterize its behavior in a pejorative manner." *Id.* at 249; *see Amalgamated Clothing and Textile Workers Union, AFL-CIO*, 475 F. Supp. 328, 330-31 (S.D.N.Y. 1979), *vacated as moot*, 638 F.2d 7 (2d Cir. 1980) (per curiam) (rejecting contention that proxy solicitation was fraudulent where it disclosed specific la-

---

corporation need not be disclosed if they are "routine" and "incidental to the business" of the corporation. *See* 17 C.F.R. § 229.103; *id.*, Instruction 1; Bolger, 759 F. Supp. at 194. In addition, proceedings that "involve[] primarily a claim for damages" need not be disclosed if the amount involved does not exceed 10% of the current assets of the corporation and its subsidiaries. *See* 17 C.F.R. § 229.103, Instruction 2. If several actions that are pending or known to be contemplated involve the same legal and factual issues, the amounts involved in those proceedings must be added together in computing the percentage under Instruction 2. *See* 17 C.F.R. § 229.103, Instruction 2.

Under Item 401(f), the corporation is only required to disclose criminal convictions or charges that occurred within the last five years and that are "material to an evaluation of the ability or integrity" of the director, nominee, or executive officer. The SEC has stated that the five-year period specified in Item 401(f) is intended only as a "guide" and that "events occurring outside this period should be disclosed." *See* Securities Act Release No. 5949, 1978 WL 14845, *8 (July 28, 1978); Securities Act Release No. 5758, 1976 WL 15989, *2 (Nov. 2, 1976). One court, however, has rejected the SEC's interpretation as inconsistent with the plain language of Item 401(f), holding that Item 401(f) requires disclosure only of events occurring within the last five years. United States v. Yeaman, 987 F. Supp. 373, 384 (E.D. Pa. 1997).

bor litigation in which the corporation was involved and specific findings of labor violations but did not disclose that nominees for directorships "had participated in a concerted effort to thwart the labor laws of this country"). In addition to harm resulting from the imposition of legal proceedings, corporations also must consider the harm resulting from the cessation of the activities. *See In re E.F. Hutton & Co.,* Lit. Rel. No. 10915, 1985 WL 61025 (1985) (SEC charged that firm should have disclosed fact that reduced use of illegal checking account practices was a material cause of a material decrease in firm's interest income). In either case, while not necessarily requiring disclosure of the fact of an investigation, some courts have required disclosure of "facts showing that [the corporation's] management or employees committed specific acts or permitted specific practices that an informed investor would consider as potentially endangering its future financial performance." *Ballan,* 720 F. Supp. at 249.

In judging the "magnitude of the event," there is authority establishing that wrongdoing with little or no impact on earnings need not be disclosed. *See, e.g., Levine v. NL Industries,* 717 F. Supp. 252, 253 (S.D.N.Y. 1989), *aff'd,* 926 F.2d 199 (2d Cir. 1991) (where defendant corporation was contractually entitled to indemnification for all expenses incurred in complying with environmental laws, corporation's environmental violations could have no effect on corporation's financial condition and were therefore immaterial and did not have to be disclosed). At the same time, any conduct that could undermine a corporation's license to do business, *Securities & Exchange Comm'n v. Joseph Schlitz Brewing Co.,* 452 F. Supp. 824, 830 (E.D. Wis. 1978), or its ability to obtain government contracts, *Cooke v. Teleprompter Corp.,* 334 F. Supp. 467, 470-71 (S.D.N.Y. 1971), may have a sufficient impact on earnings to require disclosure no matter how small an amount of money may initially be implicated.

These cases, described by commentators as "quantitative materiality" cases, present a standard that, while difficult, has been applied with some predictability. *See, e.g., Schlitz,* 452 F. Supp. at 830 (alleged bribes to retailers, although relatively small in amount, were material because they posed a threat to the company's ability to retain its licenses to sell beer, which were essential to the company's continued operations and prosperity). But other courts have added a second concept requiring disclosure: "qualitative materiality." "Qualitative materiality" rests on the notion that acts of wrongdoing that in and of themselves are insignificant to the corporation's bottom line could still have "vast economic implications" in that they might call into question the "competency of management" in putting the corporation at risk, or might otherwise undermine the integrity of management, making the corporation less attractive to investors. *See Roeder*, 814 F.2d at 25-26 (bribes paid by corporation to obtain subcontracts created risk that corporation could lose its ability to obtain future government contracts).

This principle is potentially boundless, but not all courts have read it so expansively. In determining when "qualitative" disclosures regarding the integrity of management are required, courts generally have held that management misconduct is not material if it does not involve self-dealing and does not affect the corporation's financial condition. In *Gaines v. Haughton*, 645 F.2d 761, 776-79 (9th Cir. 1981), *overruled in part on other grounds*, *In re McLinn*, 739 F.2d 1395, 1397 (9th Cir. 1984), the court held that the corporation was not required to disclose in a proxy statement its payments to foreign officials, which payments had been made prior to the enactment of the Foreign Corrupt Practices Act. The court drew "a sharp distinction... between allegations of director misconduct involving breach of trust or self-dealing the nondisclosure of which is presumptively material and allegations of simple breach of fiduciary duty/ waste of corporate assets the nondisclosure of which is never material for § 14(a) purposes." *Id.* at 776-77; *see Maldonado v. Flynn*, 597 F.2d 789, 796 (2d Cir. 1979) (finding that alleged self-dealing by corporate directors could be material under proxy solicitation disclosure rules, as "the circumstances surrounding corporate transactions in which directors have a personal interest are directly relevant to a determination of whether they are qualified to exercise stewardship of the company"). A few cases go even farther and reject the theory that "qualitative" materiality requires disclosure of matters bearing on management ethics and integrity, stating that courts "almost universally have rejected efforts to require that management make qualitative disclosures that were not at least implicit in the Commission's rules." 787 F.2d at 48.

B. *Brokers and Dealers*

Brokers and dealers face additional reporting requirements to their exchanges. In certain circumstances, these requirements go so far as to compel reports of the details of, progress of, and results of internal investigations. While the penalties have not necessarily been severe, proceedings have been brought to sanction violators.

Both the New York Stock Exchange (NYSE)[28] and the National Association of Securities Dealers (NASD)[29] require members to report violations of the securities laws committed by them or by their employees.[30] The NYSE rules also require each member to review securities trades effected for the account of the member (proprietary trades) or its employees (employee trades), to investigate any trades that may be in violation of the securities laws or regulations or Exchange rules, and report to the

28. NYSE Rule 351(a)(1) requires that members or member organizations report to the Exchange whenever they or any of their employees has "violated any provision of any securities law or regulation, or any agreement with or rule or standards of conduct of any governmental agency, self-regulatory organization, or business or professional organization, or engaged in conduct which is inconsistent with just and equitable principles of trade or detrimental to the interests or welfare of the Exchange." Rule 351(a)(1). The remaining provisions of Rule 351(a) require members and member organizations to report customer complaints of theft or forgery, proceedings against the member or its employees for violations of the securities laws, settlement of civil actions, criminal indictments and convictions, and other information. Rule 351(a). Rule 351(b) requires that each member associated with a member organization and each employee of a member or member organization report the same information "to the member or member organization with which such person is associated."

29. NASD Rule 3070(a)(1) requires each member to report to the NASD whenever the member or a person associated with the member "has been found to have violated any provision of any securities law or regulation, any rule or standard of conduct of any governmental agency, self-regulatory organization, or financial business or professional organization, or engaged in conduct which is inconsistent with just and equitable principles of trade; and the member knows or should have known that any of the aforementioned events have occurred." Rule 3070(a)(1). Like NYSE Rule 351(a), the balance of NASD Rule 3070(a) requires disclosure of customer complaints of theft or forgery, proceedings against the member or its employees for violations of the securities laws, settlement of civil actions, criminal indictments and convictions, and other information. Rule 3070(b) requires each person associated with a member to report the same information to the member. Rule 3070(b). However, any "member subject to substantially similar reporting requirements of another self-regulatory organization of which it is a member is exempt from the provisions of" Rule 3070. *See* Rule 3070(e).

30. If an event is reportable, the member must file a Disclosure Reporting Page (DRP) with the Central Registration Depository (CRD), a computer system operated by NASD that maintains registration information regarding broker-dealers and their registered personnel. *See generally Broker-Dealer Registration and Reporting*, Release No. 34-31,660, 1992 WL 395541, *1-3 (Dec. 28, 1992). The DRP becomes part of the broker-dealer's or registered employee's record in the CRD. The event reported to the CRD may become the subject of an investigation, and possibly an enforcement action, by the SEC or by one or more SROs.

Exchange the results of its reviews and investigations.[31] Each quarter, members and member organizations must either report that there is no cause to believe a violation occurred or provide details of any questionable trades and the internal investigations into them.[32]

The NASD does not have a similar rule specifically requiring reviews and/or investigations of proprietary and employee trades to identify trades that may violate securities laws and exchange rules pertaining to insider trading and manipulative and deceptive devices. However, NASD Rule 3010, which specifies the supervisory responsibilities of NASD members, contains a more general provision requiring NASD members to conduct annual internal inspections that are "reasonably designed to assist in detecting and preventing violations of and achieving compliance with applicable securities laws and regulations, and with the Rules of [the NASD]."[33]

---

31. NYSE Rule 342.21 requires members and member organizations to: "(a) Subject trades in NYSE listed securities and in related financial instruments which are effected for the account of the member or member organization or for the accounts of members, allied members or employees of the member or member organization and their family members (including trades reported by other members pursuant to Rule 407) to review procedures that the member or member organization determines to be reasonably designed to identify trades that may violate the provisions of the Securities Exchange Act of 1934, the rules under that act or the rules of the Exchange prohibiting insider trading and manipulative and deceptive devices, and (b) Conduct promptly an internal investigation into any such trade that appears that it may have violated those laws and rules in order to determine whether it did violate those laws and rules."

32. NYSE Rule 351(e).

33. NASD Rule 3010(c) provides:

Each member shall conduct a review, at least annually, of the businesses in which it engages, which review shall be reasonably designed to assist in detecting and preventing violations of and achieving compliance with applicable securities laws and regulations, and with the Rules of this Association. Each member shall review the activities of each office, which shall include the periodic examination of customer accounts to detect and prevent irregularities or abuses and at least an annual inspection of each office of supervisory jurisdiction. Each branch office of the member shall be inspected according to a cycle which shall be set forth in the firm's written supervisory and inspection procedures. In establishing such cycle, the firm shall give consideration to the nature and complexity of the securities activities for which the location is responsible, the volume of business done, and the number of associated persons assigned to the location. Each member shall retain a written record of the dates upon which each review and inspection is conducted.

The NYSE has brought actions against brokers and dealers for failure to report violations required to be reported under its rules.[34] For example, in *Sutro & Co., Inc.,* 1997 WL 594193, *1 (N.Y.S.E.) (Exchange Hearing Panel Decision 97-105) (1997), an Exchange Hearing Panel approved a Stipulation of Facts and Consent to Penalty entered into by the NYSE's Division of Enforcement and the securities firm Sutro. The stipulation stated that Sutro had violated Rule 351(a) by failing to report at least 80 reportable events and failing to promptly report at least 74 reportable events. *Id.* at *2-3. The unreported events included customer complaints, settlements, and arbitration awards. *Id.* The stipulation further provided that Sutro violated Exchange Rule 342 by failing to "maintain appropriate procedures of supervision and control, and a system of follow-up and review, with respect to its obligation to promptly report matters to the Exchange as required by Exchange rules." *Id.* at *4. Sutro consented to a censure, a $115,000 fine, and an undertaking to have a review done of its reporting system and procedures by "a person or entity not unacceptable to the Exchange." *Id.* at *6.[35]

III. PARALLEL PROCEEDINGS

Of all the cases in which internal investigations are conducted, violations of the securities laws are perhaps the most likely to lead to parallel pro-

---

34. NASD Rule 3070, which took effect on September 8, 1995, has not yet been the subject of any reported NASD proceedings.

35. In other cases, the NYSE has imposed penalties on firms that violated Rule 351 by failing to file reports or by filing late reports. *See, e.g.,* Smith Barney, Inc., 1997 WL 431496 (N.Y.S.E.) (Exchange Hearing Panel Decision 97-73) (1997) (approving stipulation and consent providing that Smith Barney violated Exchange rules by filing numerous late reports pertaining to the termination of registered employees and the initiation and settlement of customer complaints and arbitrations; firm consented to censure, $125,000 fine, and requirement to maintain centralized tracking system for reportable events); Oppenheimer & Co., Inc., 1997 WL 219814 (N.Y.S.E.) (Exchange Hearing Panel Decision 97-32) (1997) (firm violated Rule 351(a) and other rules by failing to promptly report information pertaining to registered employees, customer complaints, commencement of arbitrations, and dispositions of matters including settlements, awards, and dismissals; firm violated Rule 342 by failing to maintain adequate supervisory systems to ensure compliance with reporting requirements; NYSE imposed censure, $60,000 fine, and required review of firm's procedures designed to ensure compliance with reporting requirements).

ceedings. In addition to the active plaintiffs securities bar, any willful violation of the securities laws is a crime,[36] and the SEC possesses and exercises considerable jurisdiction to review violations.[37]

The SEC's enforcement powers were codified eight years ago with the passage of the Remedies Act.[38] The SEC may seek civil money penalties in enforcement actions in federal district court and in administrative actions,[39] cease and desist orders restraining violation of the securities laws,[40] and bars from service as officers or directors of publicly traded companies.[41] The expanded powers under the Remedies Act have increased the complexity and duration of case investigations, settlement negotiations, and other case dispositions.[42]

---

36. *See* 15 U.S.C. § 77x (Securities Act of 1933); 15 U.S.C. § 78ff (Securities Exchange Act of 1934); 15 U.S.C. § 80b-17 (Investment Advisers Act of 1940); 15 U.S.C. § 80a-48 (Investment Company Act of 1940).

37. *See* 15 U.S.C. § 77v; 15 U.S.C. § 78aa; 15 U.S.C. § 80b-14; 15 U.S.C. § 80a-43.

38. The Securities Enforcement Remedies and Penny Stock Reform Act of 1990, Pub. L. No. 101 - 429, 104 Stat. 931 (codified in various sections of 15 U.S.C.). The SEC may pursue administrative proceedings against regulated entities, 15 U.S.C. §§ 80a-9(d), 80a-42(e), 80(b)-3(i), and 80(b)-9(e), or may pursue actions in federal district court, 15 U.S.C. §§ 77t, 78u, 78u-1. The SEC has broad authority to investigate past, ongoing or potential violations and to order the production of documents and appearance of witnesses regarding the subject of its investigation. 15 U.S.C.A. §§ 78u, 77t, 77u, 80b-9, 80a-41.

39. 15 U.S.C. §§ 77t(d), 78u(d)(3), 77u-1, 80a-41(e), 80b-9(e), 78u-2.

40. 15 U.S.C. § 78u-3. The SEC may order the corporation to take specific steps to come into compliance within a set period of time, and may initiate proceedings to extract a civil penalty if the corporation does not comply. See 15 U.S.C. § 78u(d)(3)(A).

41. 15 U.S.C. § 77t-(e) and § 78u(d).

42. *See generally* Arthur B. Laby and W. Hardy Callcott, *Patterns of SEC Enforcement Under the 1990 Remedies Act: Civil Money Penalties,* 58 ALB. L. REV. 5 (1994); *Committee on Federal Regulation of Securities, Report of the Task Force on SEC Settlements,* 47 BUS. LAW. 1083 (1992). Furthermore, there is often no limited time frame under which the SEC must pursue actions. Many courts have ruled that no statute of limitations applies to certain SEC civil enforcement actions. *See, e.g.,* SEC v. Rind, 991 F.2d 1486 (9th Cir. 1993) (no statute of limitations bars Commission's enforcement proceedings seeking injunctive relief under the Securities Act or Exchange Act, though court could consider remoteness of violations in deciding whether to grant equitable relief); SEC v. Lorin, 869 F. Supp. 1117 (S.D.N.Y. 1994) (citing other decisions). *But see* Johnson v. SEC, 87 F.3d 484 (D.C. Cir. 1996) (imposing five-year statute of limitations on Commission-initiated proceedings where penalties are sought). *See also* Matthew Scott Morris, *The Securities Enforcement Remedies and Penny Stock Reform Act of 1990: By Keeping Up with the Joneses, the SEC's Enforcement Arsenal*

Brokers and dealers are subject to the same SEC sanctions—injunctions, disgorgement, and civil penalties—as others who violate the securities laws. In addition, as persons subject to licensing and registration requirements, brokers and dealers are subject to sanctions imposed administratively by the Commission, which include monetary penalties[43] and restrictions on acting as brokers or dealers.[44]

While many SEC offices now ask a company to respond informally to allegations of wrongdoing, often within two weeks of the events, more formal inquiries often still proceed on a somewhat slower track. In addition, since the passage of the Private Securities Litigation Reform Act of 1995, the plaintiffs securities bar seems to be waiting longer—and perhaps conducting longer investigations themselves—before filing suit.[45]

Is Modernized, 7 ADMIN. L.J. AM. U. 151, 195-196 (Spring 1993) (noting that the Remedies Act does not contain a provision for the automatic termination of a cease and desist order issued without prior notice, and that the order may remain in effect indefinitely).

43. Section 21B(a) of the 1934 act, 15 U.S.C. § 78u-2(a), authorizes the SEC to impose a civil penalty on a broker-dealer in an administrative proceeding if the SEC finds that such a penalty is in the public interest and that the broker-dealer: (1) willfully violated a provision of the federal securities laws or regulations; (2) willfully aided, abetted, counseled, commanded, induced, or procured such a violation by any other person; (3) willfully made a false or misleading statement in an application or report required to be filed with the SEC or certain other regulatory agencies, or omitted to state a material fact required to be stated therein; or (4) failed reasonably to supervise, with a view to preventing violations of the securities laws and regulations, another person who commits such a violation, if such other person is subject to the broker-dealer's supervision.

44. Section 15(b)(4) of the 1934 act empowers the Commission to censure, place limitations on the activities of, deny, suspend or revoke the registration of a broker or dealer. The ultimate sanction the Commission may administratively impose is an order barring the individual for life from associating with any registered broker or dealer. Subsections (A) through (F) of section 15(b)(4) enumerate the grounds on which the Commission may impose such sanctions. Section 15(b)(4)(D) is a catch-all that allows the Commission to revoke or suspend a broker's license if he or she violates any of the statutes under the Commission's jurisdiction.

45. Joseph A. Grundfest, Michael A. Perino, *Ten Things We Know and Ten Things We Don't Know About the Private Securities Litigation Reform Act of 1995,* 1015 PLI/CORP. 1015, 1090 (September 1997); Joseph A. Grundfest, Michael A. Perino, *Securities Litigation Reform: The First Year's Experience,* 1015 PLI/CORP. 955, 959-66 (September 1997). In their most recent article, the authors add that there has been a "steady upward trend" in filings since the passage of the Reform Act after an initial slowdown.

As a result, there may be a narrow window within which the corporation can conduct its internal investigation before parallel proceedings begin and make that investigation more difficult. Such events can include subpoenas to or interviews of individuals that cause them to retain separate and potentially uncooperative counsel, or seizures of documents necessary to prepare a defense.

But while the investigation must therefore be conducted swiftly, it also must be conducted with an eye toward three issues that are likely to arise as parallel proceedings develop and progress: maintaining work product and other privileges protecting the information gathered in the investigation, either from the government or, more likely, from third-party plaintiffs; managing the risk of potential assertions by employees of their Fifth Amendment privilege; and assessing the possibility of staying either the SEC investigation and/or the private securities action.

A. *Using the Investigation to Assist in Dealing with the Government Without Waiving the Privilege*

One dilemma repeatedly presented in parallel proceedings is maintaining the privilege for reports or other records of an internal investigation while still using the investigation to obtain a favorable result in negotiations with the government. There are many potential advantages to the corporation in disclosing the results of or information from an internal investigation to federal prosecutors or to the SEC. Such disclosures may facilitate an earlier settlement; especially absent a report, the government is traditionally unwilling to settle promptly out of a fear that by doing so it will miss a material aspect of the wrongdoing, and a disclosure of an internal investigation can speed the government's ability to obtain a full understanding or the events. Disclosure also serves the purpose of demonstrating proper corporate governance to the market. In cases with the potential for criminal prosecution, disclosures provide the benefit of supporting an argument that the corporation should not be charged in light of its corrective actions and in light of the impact on innocent shareholders; even if this argument fails, disclosure may allow the corporation

---

Joseph A. Grundfest, Michael A. Perino, Paul Lomio, Erika V. Wayne, and Rilla Reynolds, *Securities Class Action Litigation in Q1 1998: A Report to NASDAQ from the Stanford Law School Securities Class Action Clearinghouse*, 1070 PLI/CORP 69, 74 (September-October 1998).

to seek a reduced punishment under the sentencing guidelines.[46] These arguments are often needed given the relative ease within which corporations can be found liable for the wrongdoing of their employees.[47] In any event, even if it were not often beneficial to the corporation to supply its internal investigation results to the government, increasing numbers of prosecutors are demanding the waiver of privileges and the production of reports as a precondition to settlement or a declination of prosecution.

This is not to say that disclosure is always the correct approach. An early disclosure may result in the government learning and prosecuting wrongdoing of which it otherwise would have been unaware,[48] and disclosure inherently places the corporation in a position adverse to individual employees who may face career-threatening penalties or even jail as a result of the disclosures.[49] But discovery of the wrongdoing is often inevitable, and many corporations subordinate the interests of their employees—especially those who stand accused of wrongdoing—to the enhancement of short-term shareholder value.

As a result, a pivotal factor in evaluating whether to make a disclosure to the government is that it may waive the attorney-client and/or work-product privileges and thereby prompt, or at least impair the corporation's ability to defend against, shareholder suits, derivative actions or other civil cases. There is some support for the notion that the privileges can be waived selectively for information disclosed to the government or government agencies,[50] but most prevailing authority refuses to provide such

---

46. *See* United States Sentencing Guidelines (U.S.S.G.) § 8C2.5(g).

47. *See* Hollinger, *supra* note 4.

48. It is also possible that a report to the government, especially if protected by some sort of settlement privilege, *see* note 56, *infra*, may mean that the investigation will be viewed as a contemplated legal proceeding for purposes of Item 103.

49. 15 U.S.C. §§ 77t-(e) and 78u(d) (prohibiting persons from serving as officers or directors); 15 U.S.C. §§ 77x, 78ff, 80b-17, and 80a-48, and U.S.S.G. § 2F1.1 (penalty and sentencing provisions).

50. *See* Diversified Industries v. Meredith, 572 F.2d 596 (8th Cir. 1977) (en banc); United States v. Shyres, 898 F.2d 647, 657 (8th Cir. 1990); *In re* LTV, 89 F.R.D. 595, 615 n.13 (N.D. Tex. 1981); *In re* Grand Jury Subpoena Dated July 13, 1979, 478 F. Supp. 368, 372-73 (E.D. Wis. 1979); Byrnes v. IDS Realty Trust, 85 F.R.D. 679, 685-89 (S.D.N.Y. 1980); The Triax Co. v. United States, 11 Cl. Ct. 130, 133 (1986); M & L Business Machine Co., Inc. v. Bank of Boulder, 161 B.R. 689, 697 (D. Colo. 1993). *See also* Anne C. Flannery & Katherine M. Polk, *Between a Rock and a Hard Place: Internal Corporate Investigations and the Attorney-Client Privilege,* 963 PLI/CORP. 585 (October/November 1996); Anne C. Flannery & Jennifer S. Milano, *The Confusion*

protection.[51] Nor is there much backing for the argument that internal reports could be separately protected by a self-evaluative privilege. [52]

Continues: Protection of Internal Corporate Investigation Materials Under the Attorney-Client Privilege and Work Product Doctrine, Revisited, 1023 PLI/CORP. 519 (November 1997).

51. *See* Permian Corp. v. United States, 665 F.2d 1214 (D.C. Cir. 1981); *In re* Martin Marietta Corp., 856 F.2d 619 (4th Cir. 1988); Westinghouse Electric Corp. v. Republic of Philippines, 951 F.2d 1414 (3d Cir. 1991); Neal v. Honeywell, Inc., 1995 U.S. Dist. LEXIS 14488 (N.D. Ill. 1995); *In re* Kidder Peabody Securities Litigation, 168 F.R.D. 459 (S.D.N.Y. 1996); Genentech, Inc. v. United States Internat'l Trade Comm'n, 122 F.3d 1409, 1417 (Fed. Cir. 1997); *In re* Steinhardt Partners, L.P., 9 F.3d 230, 235 (2d Cir. 1993); McMorgan & Co. v. First California Mortgage Co., 931 F. Supp. 703 (N.D. Cal. 1996). It should be noted, however, that many of these decisions are premised on the voluntary nature of the disclosure. *See In re* Subpoenas Duces Tecum, 738 F.2d 1367, 1373 (D.C. Cir. 1984) ("there may be less reason to find waiver in circumstances of involuntary disclosure. . . ."); Bank of Boulder, 161 B.R. at 696-97 (limited waiver where bank's cooperation with U.S. Attorney was in compliance with mandatory duties under Federal Reserve System procedures, unlike SEC's voluntary disclosure program); Westinghouse, 951 F.2d at 1427 n. 14 (Westinghouse's disclosure to the DOJ was voluntary even though it was prompted by a grand jury subpoena because Westinghouse withdrew its motion to quash the subpoena and produced documents pursuant to a confidentiality agreement); Boston Auction Co., Ltd. v. Western Farm Credit Bank, 925 F. Supp. 1478 (D. Haw. 1996) (bank's disclosures to the FCA not voluntary because FCA has federal authority to access all files).

52. The "self-evaluative" privilege, designed to encourage self-criticism by protecting self-evaluative materials, initially seemed to be a promising basis on which a corporation could withhold internal reports. *See, e.g.,* Allen & Hazelwood, *Preserving the Confidentiality of Internal Corporate Investigations,* 12 J. CORP. L. 355 (1987); Crisman & Mathews, *Limited Waiver of Attorney-Client Privilege and Work-Product Doctrine in Internal Corporate Investigations: An Emerging Corporate 'Self-Evaluative' Privilege,* 21 AM. CRIM. L. REV. 123 (1983); Note, *Discovery of Internal Corporate Investigations,* 32 STAN. L. REV. 1163 (1980). However, there has been much confusion about the privilege, and it has been applied only seldom and in limited contexts. *See* Dowling v. American Hawaii Cruises, Inc., 971 F.2d 423, 426 n. 1 (9th Cir. 1990). The application in the context of internal corporate investigations is rare. *See, e.g.,* FTC v. TRW, Inc., 628 F.2d 207, 210-11 (D.C. Cir. 1980). Furthermore, courts have refused its application where documents are sought by a government agency, *see* United States v. Dexter, 132 F.R.D. 8, 9 (D. Conn. 1990), or by a grand jury, *In re* Grand Jury Proceedings, 861 F. Supp. 386 (D. Md 1994), while many find no self-evaluative privilege under federal law at all, Spencer Savings Bank v. Excell Mortgage Corp., 960 F. Supp. 835 (D.N.J. 1997). However, the public policy reasons that supported the privilege are now frequently weighed by courts in deciding whether a corporation has waived the attorney-client or work product privilege by providing internal investiga-

This potential inability to gain absolute protection for the report means first that the effects of dissemination must be added in balancing whether to prepare a report and whether to disclose the report to the government at all. It also means that careful attention must be paid to the steps that might be taken to try to maintain the privilege while still producing the report.

A leading case addressing steps designed to maintain privilege is *In re Steinhardt Partners, LP*, 9 F.3d 230 (2d Cir. 1993). The SEC had asked Steinhardt for documents relating to allegations of wrongdoing in the securities markets, and later asked for a memorandum addressing legal theories applicable to the facts of the case. Steinhardt supplied the information, adding the "confidential treatment requested" stamp common to SEC productions.[53] As is typical, the SEC did not respond to or acknowledge the request. Later, civil suits were filed and the plaintiffs asked for all documents previously produced to the government. Steinhardt refused to produce its memorandum, but the district court granted the plaintiffs' motion to compel.

The Second Circuit's affirmance explicitly recognized the "Hobson's choice" between disclosing information in an effort to avoid an SEC sanction on the one hand, and protecting the privilege against private litigants on the other, but went off on the notion that *voluntary* disclosure of work product to an *adversary* waived the privilege. Underscoring the significance of those circumstances, the court explained that waiver might not occur where "the SEC and the disclosing party have entered into an explicit agreement that the SEC will maintain the confidentiality of the disclosed materials." *Id.* at 236.

This decision suggests several steps that can be taken to increase the chance that disclosure of a report to the government will not result in waiver of the privilege.[54] While none of these steps guarantee protection,

---

tions to third parties like government agencies. *See, e.g., In re* Kidder Peabody Secs. Litig., 168 F.R.D. 459 (S.D.N.Y. 1996); *In re* Woolworth Corp. Secs. Class Action, No. 94 Civ. 2217, 1996 WL 306576 (S.D.N.Y. June 7, 1996); Picard Chemical Inc. Profit Sharing Plan v. Perrigo Co., 951 F. Supp. 679 (W.D. Mich. 1996).

53. This legend, based on 17 C.F.R. § 200.83, seeks protection from disclosure under the Freedom of Information Act.

54. While auditors can lend considerable credibility and suport to an investigation, the use of auditors—as opposed to independent consultants hired by lawyers—should be approached with caution. Auditors generally have duties not to disclose the confidential information of their clients. *See, e.g.,* Checkosky v. SEC, 23 F.3d 452 (D.C. Cir. 1994). However, there are several situations in which information discovered by or

proposing them has little downside risk. First, especially when it will not undermine an attempt to claim the benefits of voluntary disclosure,[55] a subpoena can be requested. Second, a confidentiality agreement can be

---

disclosed to an auditor must or may be disclosed to other parties. Most significantly, the 1995 Reform Act implemented procedures for reporting the discovery of potential illegal acts. 15 U.S.C. § 78j-1. If an independent public accountant determines that an illegal act may have occurred, the accountant must make certain findings and report such findings to the audit committee or board of directors, unless the illegal act is clearly inconsequential; if the accountant concludes that there is a failure to take remedial action, it must report its conclusions to the board of directors. *Id.* The issuer whose board of directors receives such a report must immediately inform the Commission of the report. If the accountant does not receive confirmation that such notice has been given, the accountant must resign from the engagement, or furnish the Commission with documentation of its report; even if the auditor resigns, it must furnish to the Commission a copy of its report. *Id. See generally* Andrew W. Reiss, *Powered by More Than GAAS: Section 10A of the Private Securities Litigation Reform Act Takes the Accounting Profession for a New Ride*, 25 HOFSTRA L. REV. 1261 (1997). Additionally, even apart from these provisions in the Reform Act, parties in litigation may have access to information about corporations generated by or in the possession of accountants because there is no confidential accountant-client privilege under federal law. *See* United States v. Arthur Young & Co., 465 U.S. 805, 817 (1984) (ordering production of accountants' tax accrual workpapers). The relationship of a client with an auditor does not give rise to the same privileges as does the relationship with an attorney because "the independent auditor assumes a public responsibility transcending any employment relationship with the client." *Id.* at 817-18. An exception to this rule arises where information is disclosed to an accountant for the purpose of obtaining legal advice from a lawyer. *See* United States v. Kovel, 296 F.2d 918, 922 (2d Cir. 1961) (privilege applies where the client first consults with a lawyer who retains an accountant, or if the client consults a lawyer with his own accountant present, but not where the client communicates first to his accountant, even though the client later consults an attorney on the same matter); Grand Jury Proceedings Under Seal v. United States, 947 F.2d 1188, 1190-91 (4th Cir. 1991) (same). However, statements to accountants that are not related to the corporation's seeking of legal advice are not privileged. *See, e.g.,* John Doe Corp. v. United States, 675 F.2d 482, 488 (2d Cir. 1982). *See also In re* Subpoena Duces Tecum Served on Willkie, Farr & Gallagher, No. M8-85(JSM), 1997 WL 118369 (S.D.N.Y. 1997) (documents generated during an internal investigation were no longer protected under the attorney-client privilege once they were revealed to company's outside auditors).

55. These benefits can be the result of informal appeals to the discretion of the SEC or prosecutors, and the result of the more formal benefits provided by the Sentencing Guidelines. *See, e.g.,* U.S.S.G. § 8C2.5(g). In some cases, claiming such benefits while still requesting a subpoena might be accomplished by making a more informal, unwritten voluntary disclosure in advance of the production of the report.

sought. While there is growing authority that a protective order in a civil case cannot trump a grand jury subpoena,[56] at a minimum a protective order can be of utility in opposing a civil discovery request.[57] Another possibility is to seek the benefits of the protections for settlement discussions contained in Federal Rule of Evidence 408 by declaring (and obtaining agreement) that the submission is made for purposes of settlement.[58]

---

56. *In re* Grand Jury Subpoena, 836 F.2d 1468 (4th Cir. 1988); *In re* Grand Jury Subpoena, 62 F.3d 1222 (9th Cir. 1995); *In re* Grand Jury Proceedings, 995 F.2d 1013 (11th Cir. 1993). However, some circuits hold that a protective order prevents disclosure notwithstanding a grand jury subpoena, under certain circumstances. *See In re* Grand Jury Subpoena Duces Tecum Dated April 19, 1991, 945 F.2d 1221 (2d Cir. 1991); *In re* Grand Jury Subpoena, 138 F.3d 442 (1st Cir. 1998). Courts indicate that a mere confidentiality agreement is less compelling than a protective order entered by the court. *See, e.g.,* Grand Jury Subpoena Duces Tecum Dated October 29, 1992 v. Doe, 1 F.3d 87, 94 n. 4 (2d Cir. 1993); *In re* Grand Jury Subpoena Duces Tecum Dated April 19, 1991, 945 F.2d at 1225; *In re* Grand Jury Subpoena, 836 F.2d at 1474.

57. *See, e.g.*, Florida State Bd. of Admin. v. Waste Mgmt. Inc., No. 98 L 6034 (Circuit Court of Cook County, Ill., April 2, 1999) (in an unreported opinion, Illinois trial court upholds confidentiality agreement between company and SEC relating to internal investigation report, without prejudice to civil plaintiffs' opportunity to seek the material later in the case).

58. However, FRE 408 provides only limited protections. Courts routinely find that FRE 408 addresses only the admissibility of documents at trial and does not limit the disclosure of a document for other purposes. *See* NAACP Legal Defense Fund and Educ. Fund, Inc. v. U.S. Dep't of Justice, 612 F. Supp. 1143, 1146 (D.D.C. 1985) ("Although the intent of FRE 408 is to foster settlement negotiations, the sole means used to effectuate that end is a limitation on the admission of evidence produced during settlement negotiations for the purpose of proving liability at trial. It was never intended to be a broad discovery privilege"); Morse/Diesel, Inc. v. Fidelity and Deposit Co. of Maryland, 122 F.R.D. 447, 449 (S.D.N.Y. 1988) (Rule 408 "only applies to the admissibility of evidence at trial and does not necessarily protect such evidence from discovery"). In the event that the government suggests that proceedings are not far enough advanced to be "settled," then it might be amenable to agreeing that the corporation is not yet an adversary, so that an exception to the waiver analysis in *Steinhardt* is available. Especially given the SEC's unwillingness to advise anyone whether they are a subject of a target, this approach might be stretched into an argument that the corporation and the SEC have common interests in corporate governance and therefore fall within a common interest privilege. Steinhardt, 9 F.3d at 236, *citing In re* Sealed Case, 676 F.2d 793, 817 (D.C. Cir. 1982) and *In re* LTV Secs. Litig., 89 F.R.D. at 614-15. But this argument appears to have gained little or no acceptance: as *Steinhardt* itself indicates, the fact that production of a report to the SEC is voluntary and that formal enforcement proceedings have not begun is not enough to make the SEC and

Many of these approaches depend on support from or agreement by the government and, as a result, rest on the ability to convince the government to assist in maintaining the privilege.[59] In urging this position on the government, the now-rejected arguments in favor of the critical self-analysis privilege can come in handy: The government's task can be made easier, and corporations can be encouraged to police wrongdoing and assist the government, if doing so does not lay the corporation bare to the claims of private plaintiffs, who will be seeking further recovery on top of the punishment that the government deemed appropriate under the circumstances.

In response to this urging, the SEC has agreed to enter into confidentiality agreements. An affidavit from the Commission's Associate Director of the Division of Enforcement submitted in an amicus brief supporting a confidentiality agreement challenged by civil plaintiffs reported that the SEC agreed to something less than ten confidentiality agreements between 1996 and 1999. These agreements, which provide that the SEC will not disclose the documents to third parties except in certain limited circumstances (generally disclosures required by federal law or in furtherance of the Commission's discharge of its duties and responsibilities), were based on the corporation's agreement to turn over work product and the SEC's determination that the work product was reliable, would significantly benefit the SEC's investigation, and could not otherwise be obtained. *See* Affidavit of Thomas C. Newkirk in Support of the Brief of

---

the corporation "non-adversaries" so that the common-interest privilege applies. Steinhardt, 9 F.3d at 234. *See also In re* Subpoenas Duces Tecum, 738 F.2d at 1372 (no common interest between law firm and SEC as to materials provided as part of voluntary disclosure program). *Cf.* Bank of Boulder, 161 B.R. at 694 (Bank's and U.S. Attorney's "purported joint interest in prosecuting federal banking crimes is too abstract to permit the Bank to benefit from the common interest exception").

59. No such approval can be granted by the SEC for a so-called Wells procedure, which provides a process allowing for a party facing potential charges to submit a written argument to the commissioners setting forth the reasons why charges should not be filed. The Wells procedure does not permit confidentiality. *See* 17 C.F.R. § 200.83 (specifying that parties submitting information to the SEC may request confidential treatment under the Freedom of Information Act but that such a request does not affect the SEC's right or obligation to disclose information in any other context). There are cases in which the SEC has agreed to notify a party before disclosure. Permian v. United States, 665 F.2d 1214, 1215-16 (D.C. Cir. 1981). The government's ability to consent to nondisclosure may be limited by obligations such as those under *Brady v. Maryland*, 373 U.S. 83 (1963).

United States Securities and Exchange Commission as Amicus Curiae, *Florida State Board of Administration v. Waste Management, Inc.*, No. 98L6034 (Circuit Court of Cook County, Illinois, March 30, 1999).

Despite the possibility that the SEC might later agree to confidentiality and a court might uphold the agreement, the potentially severe consequences of the disclosure to private plaintiffs of internal investigation materials counsel that each step in the process of creating and/or producing to the government any written investigation materials should be carefully examined. First, a written record of an internal investigation should not always be viewed as an inevitable part of the assignment. Management or the board of directors may view a written record as necessary for the discharge of their responsibilities,[60] and the government may regard the written report as a useful step in the corporation's acceptance of responsibility. But where management, the board, and the government can do without a written report, the benefits of eliminating the risk of disclosure to the plaintiff should not be ignored.

Second, even when some written record is maintained, not all of it needs to be circulated.[61] However, most attempts to limit the waiver when a report has been provided to the government have been unsuccessful.[62]

---

60. *Cf. In re* Caremark Int'l Inc. Derivative Litig., 698 A.2d 959, 970 (Del. Ch. Ct. 1996). In *Caremark*, following the company's guilty plea, the court evaluated whether corporate directors violated their duty of care and were thus responsible for the corporation's non-compliance with applicable legal standards. The court held that to satisfy their obligations to be reasonably informed about the corporation, corporate boards must "assur[e] themselves that information and reporting systems exist in the organization that are reasonably designed to provide to senior management and to the board itself timely, accurate information sufficient to allow management and the board, each within its scope, to reach informed judgments concerning both the corporation's compliance with law and its business performance."

61. Another option would be for the corporation to generate a written report and keep it in counsel's possession. However, if the court were to find a waiver of the attorney-client privilege, this act alone would probably not be sufficient to protect the document. *Cf.* Fisher v. United States, 425 U.S. 391, 403 (1976) ("[t]his Court and the lower courts have thus uniformly held that pre-existing documents which could have been obtained by court process from the client when he was in possession may also be obtained from the attorney by similar process following transfer by the client in order to obtain more informed legal advice.").

62. Once a court finds a waiver of the privilege with respect to an investigative report, there is a danger that it will also find a waiver as to the materials underlying the report. *See, e.g., In re* The Leslie Fay Companies, Inc. Secs. Litig., 161 F.R.D. 274, 283

No cases yet have squarely addressed the issue whether the fact that a disclosure is required for the reasons set forth in Section II above means that the protection of investigation materials provided by the attorney-client privilege and the work product doctrine will inevitably be lost.[63] While the attorney-client privilege in other contexts has been limited when the client instead understands that the material will be revealed to others in reports or disclosures,[64] even this principle has been distinguished and the privilege has been maintained in cases more analogous to internal investigations in which the information is communicated with the understanding that the lawyer has discretion about whether to include the information in a report to be made public.[65]

(S.D.N.Y. 1995) (production of report to public and use in litigation waived privilege as to documents underlying the report); Neal v. Honeywell, Inc., 1995 U.S. Dist. LEXIS 14488 (N.D. Ill. 1995) (upholding magistrate judge's opinion that production of report to government agency constituted subject matter waiver, but noting that Seventh Circuit had not ruled on the issue); *In re* Kidder Peabody Secs. Litig., 168 F.R.D. 459 (S.D.N.Y. 1996) (ordering Kidder to produce factual summaries of witness statements and other documents that formed the basis of a report given to the SEC and the public).

   63.   One court held that no privilege exists when a report was required pursuant to a consent decree with the SEC. Osterneck v. E.T. Barwick Indus., 82 F.R.D. 81 (N.D. Ga. 1979). *But see In re* LTV Civ. Litig., 89 F.R.D. 595, 618-22 (N.D. Tex. 1981).

   64.   *See In re* Grand Jury Investigation, 557 F. Supp. 1053, 1056 (E.D. Pa. 1983); United States v. (Under Seal), 748 F.2d 871 (4th Cir. 1984) (privilege held not to protect any information disclosed with the understanding that it will be revealed to others and applying holding also to "the details underlying the data which was to be published," including the communications relating the data, any document to be published containing the data, all preliminary drafts of the document, attorney's notes containing material necessary to the preparation of the document, and even copies of other documents, the contents of which were necessary to the preparation of the published document). Accordingly, courts have held that if a client communicates information to an attorney with the understanding that the information will be revealed to others in reports or disclosures, the information is not protected by the attorney-client privilege. *See, e.g.,* United States v. Lawless, 709 F.2d 485, 487-88 (7th Cir. 1983) (information transmitted for use on tax return); United States v. Oloyede, 982 F.2d 133, 141 (4th Cir. 1993) (information for use in filing citizenship application); Grand Jury Investigation, 557 F. Supp. at 1056-57 (information on attorney's accident report sheets that "will, in almost all circumstances, have been either disclosed to third parties, a matter of public record, or intended by the client to be disclosed by the attorney in filing claims, instituting litigation, or investigating the accident").

   65.   This is a significant limitation given that, even when disclosure is required, what is required to be disclosed is likely to be far less than the report and all the

Finally, these risks and waivers put a premium on careful articulation of what appears in the report and in any other written materials that might be required to be produced. The report and any other written materials should contain only so much material critical of the corporation as is necessary to satisfy the board's obligations and any concerns by the government, without resolving unnecessary issues. In addition, they should be written to avail themselves as much as possible of the safe harbor given by most courts to opinion work product.[66]

B. *Fifth Amendment Assertions*

While assertions of the Fifth Amendment privilege meet a few restrictions in investigations of violations of the securities laws, many opportunities remain for the assertion of the privilege by individuals, and each use of the privilege raises issues for the company.

Of course, only individuals can assert the Fifth Amendment privilege, but even individuals can face restrictions on and sanctions for their exer-

---

supporting documentation created by counsel. *See generally* United States v. Threlkeld, 241 F. Supp. 326 (W.D. Tenn. 1965) (some privilege maintained for information provided to attorney in course of preparation of tax return); *see also In re* Grand Jury Subpoena (Dorokee Co.), 697 F.2d 277, 280 (10th Cir. 1983). Moreover, in United States v. (Under Seal), 748 F.2d 871, 875-76 (4th Cir. 1984), the Fourth Circuit held that if a client communicates information to an attorney not so the attorney can file a public document but so that the attorney can research the *possibility* of filing a public document, such information remains privileged unless the information actually is disclosed. *See also* United States v. Schlegel, 313 F. Supp. 177, 179 (D. Neb. 1970) (waiver limited to whatever is finally sent to the government).

Similarly, the work product doctrine may be limited by the view that no privilege applies to internal investigation report prepared not only in anticipation of litigation but also in order to fulfill the corporation's disclosure or reporting obligations. If documents "would have been prepared independent of any anticipation of use in litigation (*i.e.*, because some other purpose or obligation was sufficient to cause them to be prepared), no work product protection can attach." First Pacific Networks, Inc. v. Atlantic Mut. Ins. Co., 163 F.R.D. 574, 582 (N.D. Cal. 1995) (documents prepared in order to satisfy statutory and contractual obligation to provide information to insurance carrier and to try to persuade carrier to provide coverage were not protected by work product doctrine); *see* Fox v. California Sierra Fin. Svcs., 120 F.R.D. 520, 528-29 (N.D. Cal. 1988) (securities opinion letter, which counsel was required by regulations to prepare in connection with public offering, was not protected by work product doctrine).

66. *See, e.g., In re* Martin Marietta Corp., 856 F.2d 619, 626 (4th Cir. 1988).

cise of the privilege: The privilege is inapplicable to requests to brokers and dealers for records they are required by the SEC to maintain.[67] In addition, while brokers and dealers can assert the privilege in response to requests for other documents or for testimony, they face sanctions for doing do.[68]

Frequently individuals will lose some of the benefit of asserting the privilege by agreeing to answer the company's questions at the outset of an internal investigation and then seeing the company volunteer that information to the government (or, in some instances with broker-dealers, tender the information to the Exchange as required—and thereby hand it over to the government). While this does not mean that the individual has waived the privilege,[69] the individual will have impaired her ability in any subsequent criminal case to keep her defense a secret until after seeing the government's case, and may have created impeaching material in the event she chooses to testify at trial. But no court has yet held that the relation-

---

67. Production of other documents may be compelled under the Fifth Amendment's "required records" exception, if: (1) the government's inquiry is essentially regulatory rather than criminal; (2) the requested records contain information the party ordinarily would keep; and (3) the documents have assumed public aspects analogous to public documents. *See, e.g.,* Grosso v. United States, 390 U.S. 62, 67-68 (1968); Smith v. Richert, 35 F.3d 300 (7th Cir. 1994). Objections to producing such records based on not betraying confidences to customers, McMann v. SEC, 87 F.2d 377 (2d Cir. 1937), and the disruption such production would cause to the business, SEC v. Brigadon Scotch Distributing Co., 480 F.2d 1047 (2d Cir. 1973) have been rejected.

68. Rule 8210 of the National Association of Securities Dealers (NASD) Procedural Rules requires any person associated with a member firm, or subject to NASD jurisdiction, to testify under oath when requested by the NASD for the purpose of an investigation, complaint, examination or proceeding. NASD Manual Rule 8210, p. 7241. Similarly, the rules of the New York Stock Exchange provide that members and employees are required to cooperate with investigators and may be expelled, suspended, fined or barred for failure to comply with a request by the NYSE for documents, testimony or other information. Rule 476(a) of the New York Stock Exchange, Inc. Disciplinary Rules. The imposition of such sanctions has been upheld. *In re* Application of Frank W. Leoneseio, Exchange Act Release No. 34-23,524 (Aug. 11, 1986); 36 S.E.C. Dkt. 328, 331; *In re* Application of Daniel C. Adams, Exchange Act Release No. 34-19,915 (June 27, 1983), 28 S.E.C. Dkt. 245 (refusal to provide information based on assertion of privilege against self-incrimination "[w]ould not affect the right of a self-regulatory organization, such as the NASD, to sanction [the broker] for that refusal, since such organizations are not part of the government.").

69. *See, e.g.,* United States v. Housand, 550 F.2d 818, 821 n.3 (2d Cir. 1977).

ship between the government and the company gathering the information pursuant to a compliance program and internal investigation created in response to the Sentencing Guidelines is sufficiently close to call the company an agent of the government, so that the statement to the company should be suppressed absent *Miranda* warnings.[70]

Many individuals provide information to the company in its internal investigation because they are, or feel, obligated to do so as employees of the company; some refuse entirely; and others represented by counsel at the time the company knocks on their door agree to provide the information only pursuant to a joint defense agreement providing, among other things, that the information cannot be disclosed without the consent of the employee.[71] Whether it is in the company's interest to accept such a limitation can be a difficult choice. The employee may have leads or other information vital to the company's ability to learn the facts and defend itself, but a restriction on disclosure can crimp any presentation to the government and cause the government to conclude that the company's cooperation has been less than full.

Once the company survives any hurdles created by Fifth Amendment assertions in its own investigation, the problem may only get worse. In civil cases, the trier of fact will be asked to draw adverse inferences against an employer on the basis of an employee's or former employee's assertion of the privilege against self-incrimination. In determining whether to draw adverse inferences from a non-party's assertion of the Fifth Amendment privilege, courts may consider the circumstances of the particular case. In *LiButti v. United States*, 107 F.3d 110, 123-24 (2d Cir. 1997), the Second Circuit identified non-exclusive factors to guide a trial court in making this determination: (1) the nature of the relationship between the party and the non-party; (2) the degree of control of the party over the non-party witness; (3) the compatibility of the interests of the party and the non-party witness in the outcome of the litigation; and (4) the role of the nonparty witness in the litigation. In evaluating these and other relevant factors, the "overarching concern is fundamentally whether the adverse inference is trustworthy under all of the circumstances and will advance the search for the truth." *Id.* at 124.

---

70. *See* Estelle v. Smith, 451 U.S. 454, 466 (1981); *see also* United States v. Roston, 986 F.2d 1287, 1292 (9th Cir. 1993).

71. *See, e.g., In re* Grand Jury Subpoenas, 902 F.2d 244, 248 (4th Cir. 1990).

There are substantial arguments against drawing the inference. First, the employee's assertion of the privilege provides little basis to conclude that the employee, let alone the employer, engaged in criminal wrongdoing.[72] Second, especially in the current world of high employee mobility, some employees—and many former employees—are disgruntled enough not to mind that their assertion of the privilege discredits the employer, *see, e.g., FDIC*, 45 F.3d 969, 978, thereby undermining the premise on which drawing an adverse inference is based: that "an employee's self-interest would counsel him to exculpate the employer if possible." *RAD*, 808 F.2d at 275.

Nonetheless, the inference is often allowed. *See, e.g., Brink's, Inc. v. City of New York*, 717 F.2d 700, 707-10 (2d Cir. 1983) (when corporate plaintiff's former employees asserted Fifth Amendment privilege in response to questions about whether they stole parking meter revenues, jury was properly instructed that it could draw adverse inferences against plaintiff); *RAD Servs., Inc. v. Aetna Casualty & Surety Co.*, 808 F.2d 271, 275-77 (3d Cir. 1986) (trial court properly permitted jury to draw adverse inference against plaintiff when current or former employees of plaintiff asserted the Fifth Amendment in response to questions about environmental violations; it was uncertain whether witnesses were current or former employees because witnesses asserted Fifth Amendment privilege when asked that question).

Indeed, some courts have stated that the employee-employer relationship presents the strongest case for drawing adverse inferences against a party based on a non-party's assertion of the Fifth Amendment privilege. In *RAD*, 808 F.2d at 275, the court stated that the rationale for admitting statements of employees as vicarious admissions of a corporation under Federal Rule of Evidence 801(d)(2)(D) also justifies informing the trier of fact when the corporation's agent invokes the Fifth Amendment privilege. In addition to reasoning that the employee would want to exculpate the employer, the court explained that the employer "could rebut any adverse inference that might attend the employee's silence, by producing contrary

---

72. *See, e.g.*, Slochhower v. Board of Higher Educ., 350 U.S. 551, 557 (1956) ("We must condemn the practice of imputing a sinister meaning to the exercise of a person's constitutional right under the Fifth Amendment."); State Farm Life Ins. Co. v. Gutterman, 896 F.2d 116, 119 (5th Cir. 1990) ("the assertion of the privilege, particularly on the advice of counsel, is an ambiguous response"); *In re* Stelweck, 86 B.R. 833, 850-51 (Bankr. E.D. Pa. 1988), *aff'd*, 108 B.R. 488 (E.D. Pa. 1989).

testimonial or documentary evidence." *Id.; see also Federal Deposit Ins. Corp. v. Fidelity & Deposit Co. of Maryland (FDIC)*, 45 F.3d 969, 978 n.4 (5th Cir. 1995) ("The fact of present employment serves primarily to reduce the chance that the employee will falsely claim to have engaged in criminal conduct for which the defendant employer is liable.").

Even assertions of the privilege by former employees or other non-parties have been used in some cases against the employer. *See, e.g., Brink's*, 717 F.2d at 707-10 (former employees); *RAD*, 808 F.2d at 275-77 (former employees). In *FDIC*, the court held that it was permissible for the trier of fact to draw adverse inferences against a loan officer on the basis of Fifth Amendment assertions by loan recipients with whom the officer dealt. 45 F.3d at 978. In reaching this conclusion, the court discussed the propriety of drawing adverse inferences against a party based on Fifth Amendment assertions by former employees. *Id.*

Acknowledging that not all former employees would remain loyal, the court stated that any "factors suggesting that a former employee retains some loyalty to his former employer—such as the fact that the employer is paying for his attorney—" would reduce the chance that the former employee would falsely cast blame on the former employer and justify use of the adverse inference.[73]

C. *Stays of Parallel Civil and SEC Proceedings*

It is now well settled that the due process clause does not require the government to choose between proceeding criminally and civilly,[74] and the SEC and federal prosecutors often investigate the same case[75]—sometimes in a coordinated fashion and sometimes not.[76] In addition, private plaintiffs have causes of action parallel to those of the SEC.

---

73. *Id.* at 978 n.4. This reasoning is curious given that the corporation may be paying the fees solely as a result of a legal obligation to do so. *See, e.g.,* CAL. LAB. CODE § 2802.

74. United States v. Kordel, 397 U.S. 1 (1970).

75. The only exception, rarely if ever found to exist but perhaps used as a basis to seek limited discovery, is if the civil proceeding was designed solely to gather evidence for the criminal case. *See, e.g.,* United States v. LaSalle National Bank, 437 U.S. 298 (1978); United States v. Gel-Spice Co., Inc., 773 F.2d 427 (2d Cir. 1985); United States v. Cahill, 920 F.2d 421 (7th Cir. 1990); United States v. Aero-Mayflower Transit Co., 831 F.2d 1142 (D.C. Cir. 1987).

76. Coordination, including full access for prosecutors to SEC files, is permitted at the discretion of SEC supervisors. *See* 17 C.F.R. § 200. 30-4(A)(7). Investigations that

In the event that parallel proceedings develop and a corporation addresses the prospect of a stay of civil proceedings, the corporation must first decide whether it would be benefited by discovery or whether the protections of a stay would be desirable, and then evaluate its ability to win either the right to take discovery or the protection of a stay in the event the government or other parties take a contrary position.

While in most instances it will be in the interests of a corporation, as well as in the interests of its individual employees, to stay civil discovery in the face of a criminal investigation, there may be some cases in which the corporation or its employees would achieve a net gain by engaging in discovery. Among the factors affecting this balance are the relative significance of the criminal case compared to any civil matters; the extent of discovery already gained by the government; and the existence of pivotal adverse witnesses whom the company would otherwise not have an opportunity to question before they appear as prosecution witnesses in a criminal case. When the potential civil liability is relatively small, the government has already questioned most or all of the company's employees, and the pivotal prosecution witnesses refuse to be interviewed, the balance could tip in favor of pursuing discovery, even if doing so exposes the corporation and its employees to the adverse inferences in subsequent civil proceedings resulting the assertion of a of Fifth Amendment privilege by employees.[77] But for the most part, the knowledge and tactical assistance gained by the thorough discovery will be outweighed by the costs, the difficulties of deciding on a defense and on the exercise of Fifth Amendment privileges before the government's case is fully known, and the benefits to the government of additional discovery.

If a stay is sought, the law of stays in parallel proceedings is difficult to reconcile except based on the notion that the government usually gets what it wants. The traditional factors considered by courts in deciding

---

proceed on an uncoordinated basis allow opportunity for informal discovery. For example, when the SEC sends a Wells notice, 17 C.F.R. 202.5(c), the staff in response to a request will often describe the evidence it has gathered, even if by doing so it reveals matters that prosecutors conducting a grand jury investigation have not yet disclosed. Alternatively, prosecutors are often willing to address at the outset what is being investigated, while the SEC may be refusing to respond to similar inquiries.

77. *See, e.g.,* SEC v. Chestman, 861 F.2d 49 (2d Cir. 1988); *In re* Boesky, 128 F.R.D. 47 (S.D.N.Y. 1989).

stay motions are the effect on the plaintiff's interest,[78] the effect on the defendant's interests,[79] the convenience to the courts,[80] and the public interest.[81] In the event that the defense seeks a stay and that request is contested by the government, the stay is usually denied on the theory that "effective enforcement of the securities laws requires that the SEC and Justice be able to investigate possible violations simultaneously,"[82] and that "the public's interest in the integrity of the stock market" is advanced by swift resolution of SEC complaints.[83]

No case has ever stayed a criminal investigation or proceeding. There is language suggesting that civil cases, including those brought by the SEC, can be stayed until the end of the companion criminal proceeding based on "special circumstances,"[84] but such special circumstances are rarely found when it is the defendant who makes the request.[85] An argument based on special circumstances would start with the burdens placed upon the defendant by parallel discovery and attempts to magnify them

---

78. Typical interests in prompt resolution for plaintiffs are fading memories of witnesses, loss or destruction of evidence, and dissipation of assets. *See, e.g.,* Connecticut vs. BPS Petroleum Distribution, 1991 U.S. Dist. LEXIS 13951 (D. Conn. 1991).

79. *See* discussion below.

80. This factor usually translates into judicial economy—avoiding duplication by staying a civil case that might be resolved or limited substantially by the disposition of a criminal case. Some courts have discounted this factor when no criminal case is pending. *See In re* Mid Atlantic Toyota Antitrust Litig., 92 F.R.D. 358, 359 (D. Md. 1981).

81. One case distinguished a large group of individuals—beneficiaries of a pension plan—from the general public. Brock v. Tolkow, 109 F.R.D. 116, 120-21 (E.D.N.Y. 1985).

82. *See, e.g.,* United States v. Kordel, 397 U.S. 1 at 12, n.27 (1970).

83. *See, e.g.,* SEC v. Grossman, Fed. Sec. L. Rep. ¶ 93,184 (S.D.N.Y. 1987); *see* Connecticut v. BPS Petroleum Distribution Inc., 1991 U.S. Dist. LEXIS 13951 (D. Conn. 1991).

84. SEC v. Dresser Indus., Inc., 628 F.2d 1368, 1375 (D.C. Cir. 1980). The authority for a stay appears to be based on the All Writs Act, 28 U.S.C. § 1651(a). *See* United States v. Birrell, 276 F. Supp. 798, 812 (S.D.N.Y. 1967).

85. *See, e.g.,* Arden Way Assoc. v. Boesky, 660 F. Supp. 1494, 1497 (S.D.N.Y. 1987) ("It is plainly ludicrous for Mr. Boesky to argue that it is 'unfair' to compel him to face the civil lawsuits against him which are the creations of his own alleged misconduct."). Outside the securities context there are a few cases staying parallel proceedings, but these opinions turn on the perceived lack of public interest in prompt resolution of the civil case, a perception unlikely to be applicable to an SEC proceeding. *See, e.g.,* Brock v. Tolkow, 109 F.R.D. 116 (E.D.N.Y. 1985).

based on the facts of the case. Among these burdens are undermining the Fifth Amendment privilege of the individuals by forcing them to choose between the privilege and protecting themselves in civil proceedings; expanding discovery available to the prosecution beyond that permitted by Federal Rule of Criminal Procedure 16; and prematurely disclosing theories of defense.[86] Another possibility is that adverse publicity from a civil trial (as opposed to the discovery, which can be conducted under a protective order) would deprive the defendant of a fair trial and therefore require a stay.[87]

The timing of the various proceedings appears to have an effect on how the stay motion is received. When the defendant is actually under indictment, the burdens of parallel proceedings on the Fifth Amendment and discovery are magnified.[88] When a defendant is under indictment, there are cases in which discovery has been stayed when the defendant requests it and the SEC is not a party. *See, e.g., Perry v. McGuire*, 36 F.R.D. 272 (S.D.N.Y. 1964). By contrast, where there is no known criminal investigation, there is no chance to obtain a stay.

In the event that the government seeks a stay when the defense tries to avail itself of civil discovery, the same traditional factors are generally turned against the defendant. The defendant's interest in obtaining discovery—and in being able to supply a prompt and vigorous defense to allegations filed against him—is generally found to be outweighed by the public interest. It could be argued that the public interest in a speedy disposition is unaffected by who asks for a stay, and that in seeking a stay the government is not advancing the public interest and is instead advancing a tactical litigation advantage, but this argument is generally not accepted. Instead, the "public interest" is allowed to be determined by "a government policy determination of priority." *See Campbell v. Eastland*, 307 F.2d 478, 487 (5th Cir. 1962). Nonetheless, a few cases outside of securities violations have accepted the argument and denied a stay of discovery sought by the government. *See, e.g., United States v. Banco Cafetero Int'l*, 107 F.R.D. 361, 366 (S.D.N.Y. 1985), *aff'd on other grounds*, 797 F.2d 1154 (2d Cir. 1986).

---

86. Dresser, 628 F.2d at 1376.

87. SEC v. Dresser Industries, Inc., 628 F.2d 1374, 1375 (D.C. Cir. 1980). The authority for a stay offer to be based on the All Writs Act, 28 U.S.C. § 1651(a). *See* United States v. Birrell, 276 F. Supp. 798, 812 (S.D.N.Y. 1962).

88. *See* DeVita v. Sills, 422 F.2d 1172 (3d Cir. 1970).

IV. CONCLUDING LESSONS

The challenges of investigating securities violations, heightened by obligations to disclose wrongdoing and by exposure to parallel proceedings, yield to no easy answers. Eschewing an investigation entirely is generally no answer given the existence of obligations to investigate and disclose wrongdoing. The only possible exception is in response to allegations of insider trading by employees, which corporations often do not investigate on the theory that only individuals potentially face liability for such conduct. But even this approach is a bit of an oversimplification, and an inquiry should be conducted into matters such as whether management or the company is implicated in any insider trading, and whether there is any procedural failure by the corporation leading to the trading that requires correction.

Once the investigation is commenced, speed is vital in order to gather information in the narrow window before the government takes action, increasing the chance that access to witnesses and documents will be lost. But amidst the speed, the investigation must carefully avail itself of each opportunity to avoid recording anything more than is necessary to fulfill the purposes of the investigation, and to maximize any available protection against disclosure of what is recorded.

Internal Investigations in Health Care: Unique Enforcement Environment and the Dilemma of Disclosure

14

by Stacy L. Brainin*

---

* Stacy Brainin is a partner in Haynes & Boone, L.L.P. in Dallas, Texas, where she is a member of the White Collar Defense and Antitrust Practice Group.

I. INTRODUCTION

INVESTIGATIVE COUNSEL FACE TRULY unique challenges in conducting internal audits of health care providers. In recent years, the whirlwind of enforcement activity within this industry has complicated the role of legal counsel immensely, and created a set of challenges rarely found in more traditional audits. The Health Insurance Portability and Accountability Act of 1996 (HIPAA) created so-called "health care fraud crimes" and changed existing laws affecting providers in significant ways. With its passage, prosecuting health care fraud became a top enforcement priority. Dramatically enhanced funding and manpower are committed to investigating and prosecuting health care fraud and formulating new enforcement strategies. Beyond public enforcement, the False Claims Act allows qui tam actions by private citizens on the government's behalf. Corporate compliance programs are increasingly common among providers, and corporate integrity agreements are routinely imposed in any settlement of government claims. These compliance programs and the information they generate in turn pose troublesome issues of mandatory or voluntary disclosure.

To be sure, internal audits of health care providers proceed much like legal audits in many other industries. Familiarity with applicable privileges, employee rights, and interview techniques is essential. This chapter will not revisit these more familiar topics, but will instead focus on the complex statutory environment in which health care providers operate, the prominent role of corporate compliance programs within the industry, and the thorny issue of voluntary or mandatory disclosure.

II. HEALTH CARE ENFORCEMENT ENVIRONMENT

Over the years, federal enforcers have punished health care fraud under a wide variety of federal administrative, civil, and criminal statutes. With the enactment of the Health Insurance Portability and Accountability Act

(HIPAA) came legislative manifestation of the initiative to end health care fraud. The act created a new category of crimes called "health care fraud crimes." What follows is an overview of the laws that have historically affected health care providers in the past and an introduction to some of the important provisions of the HIPAA.

A. *Civil and Administrative Enforcement*

In the civil context, the Civil False Claims Act is particularly dangerous to health care providers because, in addition to treble damages, a fine of $5,000 to $10,000 per false claim may be imposed.[1] Because health care providers typically generate huge volumes of small claims, this statute carries potentially astronomical sanctions. Perhaps the most devastating sanction of all is an administrative sanction—exclusion from Medicare. Title 42 requires mandatory exclusion from the Medicare program of any provider convicted of a crime related to delivery of an item of service or neglect or abuse of patients.[2] The same statute also contains permissive exclusion provisions under which a provider may be excluded for various grounds. Finally, Title 42 also authorizes imposition of civil monetary penalties and places limitations on certain physician referrals.[3]

B. *Criminal Enforcement*

In the criminal context, the Anti-Kickback Statute prohibits illegal remuneration arrangements based on referrals under Medicare or state health care programs.[4] In addition to existing criminal and administrative penalties, the Balanced Budget Act of 1997 amended section 1320a-7a to create a civil monetary penalty for anti-kickback violations. Title 42 also prohibits the intentional making of a false statement in order to qualify for Medicare or Medicaid; the intentional charging or acceptance of excess Medicaid payments; and the intentional violation of participating physician or supplier agreements in the Medicare program.[5]

---

1. *See* 31 U.S.C. § 3729 *et seq.*
2. *See* 42 U.S.C. § 1320a-7.
3. *See* 42 U.S.C. §§ 1320a-7a; 1395nn.
4. *See* 42 U.S.C. § 1320a-7b(b).
5. *See* 42 U.S.C. §§ 1320a-7b(a), (c), (d), (e). In addition to these Title 42 crimes, the government still uses various Title 18 criminal statues, when applicable, to prosecute health care providers. These include mail fraud (§ 1341), wire fraud (§ 1343), conspiracy to defraud (§ 371), money laundering (§§ 1956, 1957), obstruction of jus-

HIPAA was a dramatic step in the government's fight against health care fraud. By creating comprehensive new laws and broadening old ones, the act expanded the government's power to investigate and prosecute health care fraud beyond public programs to fraud affecting private plans. The act provided for increased funding for investigating health care fraud, new investigative tools for the DOJ, rewards to individuals who report Medicare fraud, and expanded Medicare exclusions.[6]

Most significantly, HIPAA created five new federal crimes specifically directed at health care fraud. Importantly, under HIPAA, criminal penalties now extend beyond federal programs to private insurers as well. HIPAA prohibits knowingly and willfully executing or attempting to execute a scheme or artifice to defraud any "health care benefit program."[7] HIPAA also prohibits false statements relating to health care matters.[8] Other statutes under HIPAA prohibit theft or embezzlement in connection with health care; obstruction of criminal investigations of health care offenses; and disposing of assets in order to qualify for Medicaid.[9]

HIPAA also expanded the Attorney General's investigative and enforcement powers in very significant ways. It authorized the Attorney General to: (1) seek injunctive relief to stop ongoing federal health care offenses or prevent prospective ones; (2) bring suits to freeze assets; and (3) seek forfeiture of property that constitutes or is derived from the proceeds of the commission of a federal health care offense.[10] In addition,

---

tice (§ 1505), RICO (§§ 1961 *et seq.*), aiding and abetting (§ 2), forgery (§ 494), misprision of felony (§ 4), false claims (§ 287), conspiracy to defraud by false claims (§ 286), theft or bribery concerning federally funded programs (§ 666), and fraud or false statements (§ 1001).

6. HIPAA also authorized the Department of Health & Human Services to issue comprehensive and complex rules regarding the privacy of patient information, which went into effect April 14, 2001. 65 Fed. Reg. 82,798-82,829 (Dec. 28, 2000). Although it is beyond the scope of this chapter, counsel conducting an internal investigation involving patient information must be familiar with these restrictions, which may affect the provider's ability to disclose covered information.

7. 18 U.S.C. § 1347. A "health care benefit program" is defined as: "[A]ny public or private plan or contract, affecting commerce, under which any medical benefit, item, or service is provided to any individual, and includes any individual or entity who is providing a medical benefit, item, or service for which payment may be made under the plan or contract." 18 U.S.C. § 24(b).

8. 18 U.S.C. § 1035.

9. 18 U.S.C. § 669; 18 U.S.C. § 1518; 42 U.S.C. § 1320a-7b(a)(6).

10. 18 U.S.C. §§ 1345(a)(1); 1345(b)(2); 982(a)(6).

the act created a new investigative demand procedure for use in "any investigation relating to any act or activity involving a Federal health care offense."[11] Accordingly, the Department of Justice has administrative subpoena authority to require the production of documents and records and the testimony of their custodians in health care fraud investigations.

III. CORPORATE COMPLIANCE PROGRAMS

As the above discussion illustrates, health care providers face an array of civil and criminal statutes that can impact the provider's ability to conduct business. In the face of these laws and their harsh consequences, health care providers have increasingly turned to corporate compliance programs. This trend has been spurred by three realities facing health care providers: (1) the Federal Sentencing Guidelines and their strong incentives to adopt compliance programs; (2) the OIG's Model Plans for the health care industry; and (3) Corporate Integrity Agreements, often required when settling governmental actions.

A. *Federal Sentencing Guidelines*

The Federal Sentencing Guidelines unequivocally laud the benefits of corporate compliance programs.[12] Experience suggests, however, that true benefits under the guidelines are many times illusory. To begin, by mandating seven requirements for an "effective" compliance program, the guidelines all but prescribe failure.[13] To make matters worse, these

---

11. 18 U.S.C. § 3486.

12. A three-point reduction in culpability level is available if "the offense occurred despite an effective program to prevent and detect violations of law." U.S. SENTENCING COMMISSION, GUIDELINES MANUAL (USSG), § 8C2.5(f) (Nov. 1999).

13. According to the guidelines, "[t]he hallmark of an effective program . . . is that the organization exercised due diligence in seeking to prevent and detect criminal conduct. . . ." At a minimum, the corporation must have met seven requirements to claim due diligence:

- The corporation did not "delegate substantial discretionary authority" to somebody who it should have known has a "propensity to engage in illegal activities."
- The corporation established "standards and procedures" that are "reasonably capable of reducing the prospect of criminal conduct."

requirements are vague and strict, and a failure to meet even one may eliminate any benefit whatsoever. And even when all seven requirements are met, a reduction in fine can be obtained only if additional conditions exist. A company may receive no credit for its compliance program if any "high-level personnel participated in, condoned, or was willfully ignorant of the offense" or if it failed to report violations without "unreasonable delay."[14] To many, these exceptions swallow any potential benefit. As discussed below, self-reporting or voluntary disclosure is a thorny dilemma.

In short, the guidelines speak aspirationally of effective compliance programs and consequent benefits. Experienced counsel may well recommend the implementation of such programs, but in doing so will likely look to the obvious value of detection and self-correction rather than to any perceived reduction in sentence.

B. *OIG Model Plans*

The most valuable source of information on the characteristics of an effective compliance program are the model compliance plans issued by the Department of Health and Human Services, Office of Inspector General (OIG). These Model Plans or "Compliance Program Guidance," as they are now called, are important not only because they apply specifically to the health care industry, but also because they constitute the OIG's opinion of what is required for an "effective" program. OIG has issued

---

- The corporation assigned specific "high-level personnel" to take "overall responsibility to oversee" the compliance program.
- The corporation took steps "to communicate effectively its standards and procedures" to its employees and agents.
- The corporation took "reasonable steps to achieve compliance" such as utilizing reasonably designed "monitoring and auditing systems" and establishing and "publicizing a reporting system" that eliminates "fear of retribution."
- The corporation "consistently enforced" the standards through "appropriate disciplinary mechanisms," including "adequate discipline" of both "individuals responsible for an offense" and "individuals responsible for failure to detect an offense."
- The corporation took "all reasonable steps to respond appropriately" to offenses detected and "prevent further similar offenses," including modifications to its program.

See USSG § 8A1.2(k).
  14. USSG § 8C2.5(f).

Compliance Program Guidance for Clinical Laboratories; Hospitals; Home Health Agencies; Third-Party Medical Billing Companies; Durable Medical Equipment, Prosthetics, Orthotics and Supply Industry; Hospices; Nursing Facilities; Medicare+Choice Organizations; and Individual Physicians and Small Group Practices. The model plans are posted on the OIG's Web site at www.dhhs.gov/progorg/oig and published in the *Federal Register.*

The Model Plans are basically more detailed renditions of the Sentencing Guidelines' seven requirements, adapted for particular segments of the health care industry. The Model Plans are an invaluable elaboration on the requirements of the Federal Sentencing Guidelines because they identify specific conduct that the OIG considers necessary to maintaining an effective compliance program.

For example, the OIG's Compliance Program Guidance for Hospitals provides specific guidance on investigating and reporting detected violations.[15] According to the OIG, whenever there is a report or reasonable indication of suspected noncompliance, the compliance officer "should initiate prompt steps to investigate the conduct" to determine whether there has been a material violation of applicable law or the requirements of the compliance program.[16] The compliance officer should also take appropriate steps to prevent the destruction of documents or other evidence and should keep records of the investigation, including documentation of the alleged violation, a description of the investigative process, copies of interview notes and key documents reviewed, and the results of the investigation.[17] In addition, if there is reason to believe that the integrity of the investigation may be affected by the presence of certain employees under investigation, those employees should be removed from their current work activity until the investigation is completed.

---

15. *See* Compliance Program Guidance for Hospitals, Department of Health and Human Services, Office of Inspector General (Compliance Guidance for Hospitals), 63 Fed. Reg. 8987, 8997-98 (Feb. 23, 1998).

16. Depending on the circumstances, such steps may include an immediate referral to criminal and/or civil law enforcement authorities, a corrective action plan, a report to the government, and the submission of any overpayments. *See* Compliance Guidance for Hospitals, 63 Fed. Reg. at 8997.

17. The OIG acknowledges that "some hospitals should consider engaging outside counsel, auditors, or health care experts" to assist with the investigation. Compliance Guidance for Hospitals, 63 Fed. Reg. at 8997.

A properly functioning compliance program will likely generate damaging allegations, true or false, that may ultimately serve as a road map for adversaries, public or private. Although techniques for protecting such information is beyond the scope of this chapter, it is worth noting that some steps that might seem intuitive in another setting may have unforeseen implications in the context of the OIG's Compliance Program Guidance. As only one example, while it might seem advisable to install in-house counsel as the gatekeeper of the compliance process, the OIG's Compliance Guidance for Hospitals specifically advises against this.[18]

C. *Corporate Integrity Agreements*

Corporate Integrity Agreements are an almost unavoidable component of settlement agreements with the government and thus serve as a useful resource for internal compliance programs. While these agreements are not formally published, copies can be requested through the Freedom of Information Act. Procedures for making such a request and a list of health care providers who are currently subject to these agreements are available on the OIG's Web site at www.dhhs.gov/progorg/oig/cia.

Though mandatory compliance programs implemented through these agreements are similar in form and substance to the guidance found in the Sentencing Guidelines and in the OIG's Model Plans, there are several key differences. The first concerns the audit team itself. Under mandatory programs, much of the monitoring and auditing must be performed by independent professionals or the government itself. Additionally, often the agreements provide that the settling company must allow HHS to examine its records and evaluate its compliance program. Finally, mandatory programs require self-reporting of "material violations" and require annual reporting to OIG. Thus, these agreements, once entered into, necessarily predetermine such crucial judgments as when to conduct an internal investigation, how to define the investigative team, and whether to agree in advance to self-report the results.

---

18. The OIG believes that having a compliance process subordinate to the hospital's general counsel undercuts the independence and objectivity of the process. It is OIG's view that, by separating the compliance function from the general counsel, a system of checks and balances is established to more effectively achieve the goals of the compliance program. *See* Compliance Guidance for Hospitals, 63 Fed. Reg. at 8993 n.35.

IV. SELF-REPORTING: MANDATORY OR VOLUNTARY

Effective compliance programs routinely generate allegations of misconduct, and those allegations will ordinarily be reviewed by investigative counsel.[19] Because of unique disclosure issues faced by health care providers, careful consideration of the potential obligation to disclose the results of the investigation must be taken into account *before* commencing the inquiry. Because self-reporting is contrary to most every instinct and because the risks of voluntary disclosure may outweigh possible benefits, experienced counsel seldom choose this route. Recent developments within the law enforcement community, however, suggest that investigative counsel is wise to undertake a more critical analysis of this issue when representing a health care provider. Considerations that must now be taken into account include: (1) relevant health care statutes; (2) mandatory disclosure provisions of Corporate Integrity Agreements and OIG Model Plans; and (3) the OIG's Provider Self-Disclosure Protocol.

A. *Relevant Statutes*

As a general rule, companies are under no legal obligation to report past misconduct to enforcement authorities. No one would seriously suggest that company counsel is legally obligated to report, for example, past price-fixing behavior within a client organization. However, under the Medicare Fraud and Abuse Statute, it is a felony for anyone "having knowledge of the occurrence of an event affecting his initial or continued right to any benefit or payment" to "conceal or fail to disclose that event."[20] In the Compliance Program Guidance for Hospitals, the OIG warns that failure to repay "overpayments" within a reasonable time may be interpreted as an intentional attempt to conceal the overpayment and may thereby establish an independent basis for criminal liability. This warning would apply not only to a hospital, but also to any involved individual.[21] While there are no reported cases interpreting this statute, some prominent federal prosecutors have suggested that use of the statute will increase in coming years.[22]

---

19. This discussion addresses the disclosure issues when wrongdoing is uncovered in an internal investigation. In the absence of fraud or other violations, repayment issues are ordinarily resolved with the carrier or intermediary.

20. 42 U.S.C. § 1320a-7b(a)(3).

21. *See* Compliance Guidance for Hospitals, 63 Fed. Reg. at 8998.

22. *See* 2 BNA Health Care Fraud Report 167 (March 11, 1998).

Despite this warning, there are sound reasons to question such far-reaching interpretations. First, section 1320a-7b(a)(3) was transposed, in its entirety, from the Social Security Act that makes illegal an entirely different type of conduct (keeping a Social Security check to which one is not entitled). (There is no legislative history indicating its purpose or meaning in the Medicare context.) The statute provides no procedure for disclosure and does not state to whom any disclosure should be made. Further, the statute requires that the failure to disclose be coupled with a criminal intent, "an intent fraudulently to secure benefit or payment either in a greater amount or quantity than is due or when no such benefit or payment is authorized."[23] Additionally, courts interpreting nearly identical statutes in other Title 42 sections have held that the government must prove "that the defendant knew that he was legally obligated to disclose" the information or event in question.[24] Finally, courts have held that the due process clause prohibits punishment of wholly passive conduct.[25] Thus, it would seem that simple knowledge of past misconduct (overpayments) without more would not be seen as criminal.

Another statute counsel should consider on the issue of disclosure is 18 U.S.C. § 1035. Under this HIPAA provision, it is a felony if a provider "in any matter involving a health care benefit program . . . knowingly and willfully falsifies, conceals, or *covers up* a material fact."[26] Although a failure to disclose prior "misconduct" stands in sharp contrast to any practical interpretation of "cover-up," this statute must not be overlooked by the health care practitioner. It is useful to note that the language of section 1035 parallels other Title 18 "false statement" statutes (sections 1001 et seq.), and that it is generally thought that, to establish a false statement violation, federal prosecutors must prove an affirmative act by which a material fact was actively concealed.[27]

---

23. 42 U.S.C. § 1320a-7b(a)(3).

24. *See* United States v. Phillips, 600 F.2d 535, 536 (5th Cir. 1979).

25. *See* Lambert v. California, 355 U.S. 225 (1957).

26. 18 U.S.C. § 1035.

27. *See* United States v. Ford, 797 F.2d 1329, 1334 (5th Cir. 1986); United States v. London, 550 F.2d 206, 212-13 (5th Cir. 1977). Other statutes that could possibly be implicated by a failure to disclose overpayments or refund monies include the new HIPAA health care conversion statute (18 U.S.C. § 669) and the federal money-laundering statute (18 U.S.C. § 1956(c)(7)(F)).

B. *Corporate Integrity Agreements and OIG Model Plans*

As discussed above, if a provider is operating under a Corporate Integrity Agreement pursuant to a settlement with the government, certain disclosures may be mandatory under the terms of that agreement.

Also as discussed above, the OIG's Compliance Program Guidance for Hospitals (so-called Model Plan) states that once there is reason to believe there may have been a violation of criminal, civil, or administrative law, the hospital should promptly report[28] the misconduct to the appropriate governmental authority and provide all evidence relevant to the alleged violation and potential cost impact.[29] The decision to make a voluntary disclosure and the mechanics of that disclosure depend on the totality of the facts and circumstances.[30]

C. *The OIG's Provider Self-Disclosure Protocol*

In 1995, as part of "Operation Restore Trust," federal enforcement authorities (OIG in conjunction with the Department of Justice) instituted a pilot Voluntary Disclosure Program to implement the disclosure provisions of the False Claims Act for health care providers. While the Program eliminated some uncertainty surrounding disclosure, what remained was

---

28. The misconduct must be reported within a reasonable period, but not more than sixty days after determining that there is credible evidence of a violation. *See* Compliance Guidance for Hospitals, 63 Fed. Reg. at 8998.

29. According to the OIG, the prompt reporting of misconduct "will be considered a mitigating factor in determining administrative sanctions (*e.g.*, penalties, assessments, and exclusion), if the reporting provider becomes the target of an OIG investigation." Compliance Guidance for Hospitals, 63 Fed. Reg. at 8998.

30. For example, if the particular incident of noncompliance is merely an unintentional overbilling, disclosure should be made in the form of an overpayment refund to the carrier or fiscal intermediary. The OIG recognizes that "where potential fraud or False Claims Act liability is not involved . . . HCFA regulations and contractor guidelines already include procedures for returning overpayments as they are discovered." Compliance Guidance for Hospitals, 63 Fed. Reg. at 8997. On the other hand, "the OIG believes that some violations are so serious that they warrant immediate notification to government authorities," even prior to commencing an internal investigation. These include any conduct that: (1) is a clear violation of criminal law; (2) has a significant adverse effect on the quality of care provided to program beneficiaries; or (3) indicates a systematic failure to comply with applicable laws, an existing corporate integrity agreement, or other standards of conduct. *See* Compliance Guidance for Hospitals, 63 Fed. Reg. at 8998 n.58.

less than comforting.[31] Response to the pilot program was lukewarm at best, with only twenty applications and fourteen admissions to the program.

In October 1998, the OIG issued a new version of a voluntary disclosure program called the Provider Self-Disclosure Protocol.[32] This newer version was intended to both expand and simplify voluntary disclosure practices. Unlike the pilot program, the Provider Self-Disclosure Protocol (Protocol) is open to all health care providers nationwide, including providers making good-faith disclosures related to matters already the subject of government inquiry.[33] Other advantages of the Protocol over the pilot program are that the Protocol does not require participants to apply for admission or submit pre-acceptance disclosures.

The Protocol basically operates in four steps. First, a provider initiates the process by making a written, certified Voluntary Disclosure Submission to OIG.[34] This initial disclosure should include basic but detailed information about the disclosing provider and the misconduct

---

31. First, providers were not guaranteed acceptance to the program and had to request admission by submitting a written disclosure application giving detailed information about the misconduct, including the names and titles of employees involved. Second, even if a provider's application was approved, the applicant was accepted into the program only if it was willing to enter into a Voluntary Disclosure Program agreement providing that the disclosing party would cooperate fully with OIG's verification of the disclosure and would take appropriate corrective action. Third, participation in the pilot program was limited to providers disclosing matters not already under investigation by or known to federal or state law enforcement authorities. *See* Medicare Compliance Alert Special Document Service: OIG Procedures for Pilot Voluntary Disclosure Program (June 19, 1995).

32. *See* Provider Self-Disclosure Protocol, Department of Health and Human Services, Office of Inspector General (Protocol), 63 Fed. Reg. 58,399 (Oct. 30, 1998); http://www.dhhs.gov/progorg/oig/modcomp/oigdis.pdf.

33. The Protocol is intended only for matters that are potentially violative of federal criminal, civil or administrative laws. It is consistent with the Compliance Guidance for Hospitals in suggesting that matters involving overpayments or simple billing errors should be brought to the attention of the appropriate carrier or intermediary. *See* Protocol, 63 Fed. Reg. at 58,400.

34. Unfortunately, the Protocol requires that all submissions, including the initial disclosure, internal investigation report, and financial self-assessment, contain a certification that the report is truthful "to the best of the individual's knowledge." Protocol, 63 Fed. Reg. 58,399. These requested certifications create additional risk for participating providers.

being reported. Second, the disclosing health care provider is expected to conduct an internal investigation and internal financial assessment and report its findings to the OIG.[35] The Protocol contains Internal Investigation Guidelines requiring the provider to collect and submit specific categories of information identifying and describing the nature and extent of the improper practice and the discovery of and response to it. The Protocol also contains Self-Assessment Guidelines requiring the provider to estimate the monetary impact of the disclosed matter and describing acceptable approaches to the self-assessment process.[36] Third, OIG must verify the information disclosed. The Protocol is vague regarding the verification process but states that "OIG must have access to all audit work papers and other supporting documents without assertion of privileges or limitations on the information produced."[37] Once a provider decides to enter the Protocol, it is imperative that its disclosures be clear and complete. Otherwise, any matters discovered during the verification process unrelated to the matters disclosed will be treated as new matters, and thus outside the Protocol.[38] Fourth, the disclosing health care provider must make appropriate payments. Generally, OIG will not accept reimbursement of presumed overpayments until verification is

---

35. However, when an ongoing fraud scheme is discovered, the Protocol dictates that the provider should contact OIG immediately, before investigating further, to avoid compromising any subsequent investigation by the government. *See* Protocol, 63 Fed. Reg. at 58,400. While the OIG's position is understandable, it is never prudent to cut short an internal review at the risk of reporting unfounded allegations.

36. A provider can either review all the claims affected or calculate the loss through statistical sampling. However the financial assessment is made, the disclosing provider must submit to OIG a work plan describing the self-assessment process. *See* Protocol, 63 Fed. Reg. at 58,402-03.

37. According to the Protocol, verification will not normally impact the attorney-client privilege but may require production of documents or other materials covered by the work product doctrine. *See* Protocol, 63 Fed. Reg. at 58,403.

38. Once a provider enters the Protocol, it is too late to turn back and dangerous to withhold cooperation. "If a provider fails to work in good faith with OIG to resolve the disclosed matter, the lack of cooperation will be considered an aggravating factor when OIG assesses the appropriate resolution of the matter. Similarly, the intentional submission of false or otherwise untruthful information, as well as the intentional omission of relevant information, will be referred to DOJ or other Federal agencies and could, in itself, result in criminal and/or civil sanctions, as well as exclusion from participation in the Federal health care programs." *See* Protocol, 63 Fed. Reg. at 58,403.

completed.[39] Even after verification and payment, it is unclear how a provider is formally removed from the Protocol or what removal means.[40]

D. *Risks and Benefits of Voluntary Disclosure*

1. Risks

Although the Protocol eliminates some flaws of the earlier pilot program, it still suffers from many of the weaknesses inherent in any voluntary disclosure program. First, because there is no amnesty from criminal prosecution or waiver of damages in return for disclosure, the consequences of disclosure are still uncertain.[41] The Protocol makes it clear that "OIG is not bound by any findings made by the disclosing provider under the Provider Self-Disclosure Protocol and is not obligated to resolve the matter in any particular manner ... [and] upon review of the provider's disclosure submission and/or reports, OIG may conclude that the disclosed matter warrants a referral to DOJ for consideration under its civil and/or criminal authorities."[42] Second, regardless of the government's response, the program offers a volunteer no protection whatsoever against

---

39. If OIG does consent to such a payment, the disclosing provider must agree in writing that acceptance of the payment does not constitute the government's agreement as to the amount of losses suffered or affect the government's ability to pursue criminal, civil, or administrative remedies. *See* Protocol, 63 Fed. Reg. at 58,403.

40. Under the pilot program, a provider was not removed from the program until the OIG decided what criminal or civil action should be brought and what administrative sanctions should be imposed and until the provider received written notice that the matter was officially closed. *See* Medicare Compliance Alert Special Document Service: OIG Procedures for Pilot Voluntary Disclosure Program (June 19, 1995).

41. One positive aspect of the Pilot Voluntary Disclosure Program that was not carried forward into the Protocol was the pilot program's specific guidance on the possibility of exclusion from federal programs for violations of fraud and abuse laws. *See* Medicare Compliance Alert Special Document Service: OIG Procedures for Pilot Voluntary Disclosure Program (June 19, 1995). Since the pilot program expired, however, OIG has published specific criteria setting forth the factors taken into consideration in determining whether it is appropriate to exclude a health care provider under 42 U.S.C. § 1320a-7(b)(7). *See* Criteria for Implementing Permissive Exclusion Authority Under Section 1128(b)(7) of the Social Security Act, Department of Health and Human Services, Office of Inspector General, 62 Fed. Reg. 67,392 (Dec. 24, 1997).

42. Protocol, 63 Fed. Reg. at 58,401.

spinoff litigation[43] or against the possibility of waiver of the attorney-client privilege or work product doctrine in subsequent civil litigation as a result of the required disclosure to the government.

2. Benefits

While disclosure under the Protocol requires a certain amount of faith, undoubtedly there is a strong incentive for the government to treat participants fairly and make it less likely that a criminal prosecution will result. In an open letter to the health care community, the OIG identified several ways it would consider lessening the normally rigorous nature of corporate integrity agreements in appropriate self-disclosure cases.[44] Indeed, the OIG went so far as to state that "if a self-disclosing provider has demonstrated that its compliance program is effective and agrees to maintain its compliance program as part of a False Claims Act settlement, the OIG may not even require a corporate integrity agreement."[45]

In addition, there are tangible statutory "benefits" that may be gained from voluntary disclosure. The Federal Sentencing Guidelines have al-

---

43. Disclosure may encourage both private claims and qui tam suits. One step that companies making disclosures can take to avoid qui tam suits is to also make a public disclosure. Once the facts are public knowledge, qui tam actions are jurisdictionally barred. One way for the government to eliminate the disclosure disincentive created by the possibility of a qui tam suit would be to implement a procedure whereby an administrative monetary penalty action is filed in conjunction with every disclosure. False Claims Act § 3730(e)(3) bars actions based on allegations or transactions that are the subject of a civil suit or administrative proceeding in which the government is already a party. Therefore, the government could preempt qui tam suits by filing a formal complaint with a provisional settlement. The OIG, however, has been unwilling to consider such a policy, claiming that it would be improper for it to intentionally undermine the qui tam provision and that it does not have the authority to grant immunity.

44. *See* Open Letter to Health Care Community Urging Providers to Self-Disclose Improper Conduct, Department of Health and Human Services, Office of Inspector General (Open Letter) (March 9, 2000); www.dhhs.gov/oig. In particular, the open letter stated that while typically all Corporate Integrity Agreements include a provision to exclude a provider from participation in the federal health care programs if there is a material breach of the agreement, the OIG may forgo the exclusion remedy in appropriate cases where the provider demonstrates "sufficient trustworthiness." The OIG may also consider alternatives to standard auditing requirements and permit a self-disclosing provider to perform some or all of the billing audits internally. *See* Open Letter (March 9, 2000).

45. Open Letter (March 9, 2000).

ready been addressed above, and counsel must have a clear understanding of the "benefits" of disclosure.[46] Additionally, the False Claims Act includes voluntary disclosure provisions that can reduce the judgment imposed on an offending party.[47]

There are other considerations as well. Voluntary disclosure may well appeal to the considerable discretion of federal prosecutors and trial judges. For example, voluntary disclosure may encourage the Department of Justice to look favorably upon the company, and not insist upon treble damages or civil penalties under the False Claims Act. Disclosure may also encourage civil settlement and reduce the likelihood that criminal charges will be brought in a particular situation. Because exclusion from federal reimbursement programs can be ruinous, voluntary disclosure may assist the provider who seeks to avoid exclusion from Medicare or other federal programs, or at least limit its duration. Finally, voluntary disclosure allows a corporation to *control* the time, place, and manner of disclosing prior misconduct.

---

46. Just as a corporation may earn a three-point reduction in its culpability score for having an effective compliance program, it may earn an additional five-point reduction if it voluntarily and promptly discloses a particular offense to the government, cooperates with the investigation, and accepts responsibility for its conduct. *See* USSG § 8C2.5(g). Moreover, if the corporation does not disclose, it may lose the three-point credit attributable to its compliance program. *See* USSG § 8C2.5(f). Therefore, the decision on disclosure can result in an eight-point swing in the corporation's culpability score.

47. Under the False Claims Act, corporations found liable are subject not only to treble damages but also to a civil penalty of between $5,500 and $11,000 per false claim. *See* 31 U.S.C. § 3729(a). If certain disclosure criteria are met, however, the court may reduce a provider's liability to double damages. *Id.* The basic thrust of the criteria is that there must be a timely, complete, and truly "voluntary" disclosure, rather than simply a belated attempt to mitigate the results of an already ongoing government investigation. The specific criteria are as follows: (1) the disclosure was made to the DOJ; (2) the disclosure was made within 30 days after the information was obtained; (3) the corporation fully cooperated with any government investigation; and (4) at the time the information was furnished to the government, no criminal, civil, or administrative action had commenced with respect to the violation, and the corporation had no knowledge of the existence of an investigation of the violation. *See* 31 U.S.C. § 3729(a).

V. CONCLUSION

Internal investigations in the health care industry are complicated by the current enforcement environment, the prevalence of compliance programs that generate issues to investigate, and the unique dilemma of self-disclosure. A clear understanding of the risks and benefits of an internal investigation is critical at the outset.

An Overview of Internal Investigations from the In-house Perspective

15

by H. Lowell Brown*

* H. Lowell Brown is the former assistant general counsel, Northrop Grumman Corporation, and now practices law in Washington, D.C., and California. The views expressed are those of the author and do not necessarily represent the views of Northrop Grumman Corporation.

449

I. INTRODUCTION

THE INTENT OF THIS CHAPTER is to provide observations (mostly personal) concerning corporate internal investigations from the perspective of in-house counsel. Other chapters address in detail the significant, substantive legal issues that arise in conducting internal investigations. In contrast, the discussion here attempts a broader view of the considerations that go into structuring an internal investigation: why a corporation should undertake an internal investigation; when an investigation should be undertaken and who should conduct it; how the investigation should be organized; and finally, how the investigation should be conducted.

In the present day of frequent litigation and government oversight, in-house counsel must be vigilant in investigating allegations of illegal behavior and serious misconduct by corporate employees. The decision of the Delaware Court of Chancery in the case *In re: Caremark International, Inc. Derivative Litigation*[1] underscored the importance of corporate management, both directors and officers, informing themselves of violations of law that may adversely affect the operation of the corporation's business.[2] The Court of Chancery concluded that a rational director "attempting in good faith to meet an organizational governance responsibility" should take account of the compliance program provisions in the Federal Sentencing Guidelines for organizations[3] and should ensure that the corporation has in place

---

1. 1996 Del. Ch. LEXIS 125 (decided Sept. 25, 1996).

2. Following indictments by grand juries in Minnesota and Ohio, Caremark International, Inc., a provider of patient care and managed health care services, pleaded guilty to mail fraud in connection with payments of "referral fees" and other monetary inducements to physicians. Caremark agreed to pay civil and criminal fines and to make reimbursements to insurers totaling $250 million. Five shareholder derivative actions were filed against Caremark's directors alleging a breach of the director's duty of care by failing to supervise the conduct of Caremark's employees or to otherwise take corrective measures, thereby exposing Caremark to significant criminal and civil liability. A settlement agreement was reached and was submitted to the Delaware Chancery Court for approval. Based on the actions taken by the directors and management to address the issues under investigation, including termination of past practices, issuance of revised policies and procedures, compliance reviews by the internal audit organization, review of the control structure by independent auditors, training, and appointment of the chief financial officer as compliance officer, the court concluded that "there is a low probability that it would be determined that the directors of Caremark breached any duty to appropriately monitor and supervise the enterprise." *Id.*

3. *See* chapter 8, "Sentencing of Organizations," FEDERAL SENTENCING GUIDELINES MANUAL (1995) (Guidelines). Under those guidelines, a corporation can reduce the

an "information and reporting system" that is adequate to ensure that information concerning legal compliance comes to its attention in a timely manner.[4] The court went so far as to suggest that these obligations were elements of a director's duty of care.[5]

Even had *Caremark* not been decided, corporate self-policing, as part

---

applicable fine by having in place "an effective program to prevent and detect violations of law." § 8C2.5(f). The fine can also be reduced by self-reporting, cooperating, and accepting responsibility pursuant to § 8C2.5(g). *See* chapter 8, *infra*. In order to qualify as having an "effective program to prevent and detect violations of law," the corporation must have "exercised due diligence in seeking to prevent and detect criminal conduct by its employees and other agents" including, inter alia, "utilizing monitoring and auditing systems reasonably designed to detect criminal conduct by its employees and other agents. . . ." § 8A1.2 Application Note 3(k). Additionally, the fine can be increased if there is evidence that "high-level personnel" within the corporation "condoned" or were "willfully ignorant of the offense." § 8C2.5(b). Such a person will be considered to have been "willfully ignorant" of the criminal conduct "if the individual did not investigate the possible occurrence of unlawful conduct despite knowledge of circumstances that would lead a reasonable person to investigate whether unlawful conduct had occurred." § 8A1.2 Application Note 3(j). Thus, as Chancellor Allen noted in *Caremark*, the sentencing guidelines for organizations "offer powerful incentives for corporations today to have in place compliance programs to detect violations of law, promptly to report violations to appropriate public officials when discovered, and to take prompt, voluntary remedial efforts," and in light of those incentives, "[a]ny rational person attempting in good faith to meet an organizational governance responsibility would be bound to take into account this development and the enhanced penalties and the opportunities for reduced sanctions that it offers." 1996 Del. Ch. LEXIS 125.

4. In the chancellor's view, it would be a "mistake" for directors to conclude that "the obligation to be reasonably informed" could be satisfied "without assuring themselves that information and reporting systems exist in the organization that are reasonably designed to provide to senior management and to the board itself timely, accurate information sufficient to allow management and the board, each within its scope, to reach informed judgments concerning both the corporation's compliance with law and its business performance." *Id.* Thus, the chancellor considered it "important that the board exercise a good faith judgment that the corporation's information and reporting system is in concept and design adequate to assure the board that appropriate information will come to its attention in a timely manner as a matter of ordinary operations, so that it may satisfy its responsibility." *Id.*

5. As the chancellor stated, "I am of the view that a director's obligation includes a duty to attempt in good faith to assure that a corporate information and reporting system, which the board concludes is adequate, exists, and that failure to do so under some circumstances may, in theory at least, render a director liable for losses caused by non-compliance with applicable legal standards." *Id.*

of an overall program of compliance, makes good business sense. Prompt investigation of alleged misconduct allows the corporation to correct errors and to mitigate their effects before a problem worsens. Prompt investigation and appropriate discipline also send a powerful message to employees that violations of law and company policy will not be condoned.

There are also significant incentives for the corporation to investigate misconduct that may result in exposure to criminal liability. In general, the law permits corporations to be held liable for crimes an employee committed within the scope of the employee's duties with at least some intent to benefit the corporation.[6] Although several courts have suggested that an employee's actions in contravention of established, and rigorously enforced, company policy will not subject the corporate employer to vicarious criminal liability,[7] this is not the majority view.[8] Moreover, because both the intent[9] and collective knowledge[10] of the corporation's

---

6. This has been the law for the better part of this century. *See* New York Central & Hudson River R.R. Co. v. United States, 212 U.S. 481, 494 (1909); United States v. Adams Express Co., 229 U.S. 381, 390 (1913) (joint stock companies); United States v. A.P. Trucking Co., 358 U.S. 121, 124 (1958) (partnerships). "It is," as Learned Hand observed in 1918, "a question upon which the law has always tended towards larger and larger liability." United States v. Nearing, 252 F. 223, 231 (S.D.N.Y. 1918).

7. *See*, e.g., Holland Furnace Co. v. United States, 158 F.2d 2 (6th Cir. 1946); United States *ex rel.* Porter v. Kroger Grocery & Baking Co., 163 F.2d 168 (7th Cir. 1947); Nobile v. United States, 284 F. 253 (3d Cir. 1922); John Gund Brewing Co. v. United States, 204 F. 17 (8th Cir.), *modified*, 206 F. 386 (8th Cir. 1913).

8. *See* United States v. Basic Construction Co., 711 F.2d 570, 573 (4th Cir.), *cert. denied*, 464 U.S. 956 (1983); United States v. Beusch, 596 F.2d 871, 878 (9th Cir. 1979); United States *ex rel.* Porter v. Kroger Grocery & Baking Co., 163 F.2d 168 (7th Cir. 1947); Holland Furnace Co. v. United States, 158 F.2d 2, 5 (6th Cir. 1946); Nobile v. United States, 284 F. 253, 255 (3d Cir. 1922); John Gund Brewing Co. v. United States, 204 F. 17, 23 (8th Cir.), *modified*, 206 F. 386 (8th Cir. 1913).

9. United States v. Portac, Inc., 869 F.2d 1288 (9th Cir. 1989), *cert. denied*, 498 U.S. 845 (1990); United States v. Automated Med. Labs, Inc., 770 F.2d 399 (4th Cir. 1985); United States v. Cadillac Overall Supply Co., 568 F.2d 1078 (5th Cir. 1978); United States v. Hilton Hotels Corp., 467 F.2d 1000 (9th Cir. 1972), *cert. denied*, 409 U.S. 1125 (1973); United States v. Harry L. Young & Sons, Inc., 464 F.2d 1295 (10th Cir. 1972); Standard Oil Co. v. United States, 307 F.2d 120 (5th Cir. 1962); Dollar S.S. Co. v. United States, 101 F.2d 638 (9th Cir. 1939); United States v. Wilson, 59 F.2d 97 (W.D. Wash. 1932).

10. A corporation may be held liable for "knowing" violations of law based on the knowledge of one or more of its employees. For example, in *Apex Oil Co. v. United*

employees will be imputed to the corporate employer, there are circumstances in which the corporation may be held liable when none of its employees would be held individually responsible.[11] Thus, because the

---

States, 530 F.2d 1291 (8th Cir. 1976), a corporation was liable under the Water Pollution Control Act, 33 U.S.C. § 1321(b) (5), for failing to report a "known oil spill." Although it was acknowledged that "no officer or director of the corporation had knowledge of the spill prior to the determination by the Coast Guard of the spill's origin," the court nevertheless held that "the knowledge of the employees is the knowledge of the corporation." 530 F.2d at 1295. Similarly, in *Steere Tank Lines, Inc. v. United States*, 330 F.2d 719, 723 n.3 (5th Cir. 1964), Judge Bell observed that "[k]nowledge affecting the corporation, which has been gained by any officer, agent or employees thereof in the course of his work for the company, is attributed to the corporation, and this includes subordinate employees, such as truck drivers." Knowledge of employees has been attributed to the corporate employer in a variety of circumstances. *See, e.g.*, United States v. Miller, 676 F.2d 359, 362 (9th Cir. 1982) (employees' knowledge of a fraudulent real estate financing scheme was imputed to the lender); United States v. Andreadis, 366 F.2d 423 (2d Cir. 1966) (corporation convicted of fraud in connection with advertising claims that manager knew to be false), *cert. denied*, 385 U.S. 1001 (1967); United States v. Chicago Express, Inc., 273 F.2d 751 (7th Cir. 1960) (truck driver's knowledge that truck did not display required dangerous cargo warnings attributed to corporate employer).

11. For example, in *United States v. Bank of New England*, 821 F.2d 844 (1st Cir.), *cert. denied*, 484 U.S. 943 (1987), the bank was convicted of 31 counts of violating the Currency Reporting Act, 31 U.S.C. §§ 5311-5322, for failing to report cash withdrawals in excess of $10,000 by one of its customers. These withdrawals were effected on 31 occasions between May and July 1983 by the simultaneous presentation of a series of checks, each under $10,000, to a single teller. The bank's argument that it should not be held liable when "one part of the corporation has half the information making up [the total], and another part of the entity has the other half" was rejected. Instead, the court held that:

> Corporations compartmentalize knowledge, subdividing the elements of specific duties and operations into smaller components. The aggregate of those components constitutes the corporation's knowledge of a particular operation. It is irrelevant whether employees administering one component of an operation know the specific activities of employees administering another aspect of the operation. . . .

821 F.2d at 856. *Accord* United States v. T.I.M.E. - D.C., Inc., 381 F. Supp. 730, 738 (W.D. Va. 1974) ("knowledge acquired by employees, within the scope of their employment is imputed to the corporation. In consequence, a corporation cannot plead innocence by asserting that the information obtained by several employees was not acquired by any one individual employee who then would have comprehended its full import. Rather, the corporation is considered to have acquired the collective knowledge of its employees and is held responsible for their failure to act accordingly."); *see also* United

corporation's vicarious criminal liability is, often, strict liability, a corporation, faced with the real possibility of criminal liability, must act expeditiously to analyze its exposure and to frame an appropriate response.

The corporation's prompt response to alleged misconduct can mitigate the consequences to the corporation. For example, the corporation may seek entry into a voluntary disclosure program administered by any of several federal agencies.[12] Admission to a voluntary disclosure program usually results in an agreement by the government not to prosecute the corporation criminally.[13] Admission to such programs ordinarily requires that the disclosure be made before a government investigation has commenced.[14] In the event that the corporation is already the subject of a government investigation, an informal disclosure to the prosecutor may be made in an effort to convince the prosecutor that, in the exercise of prosecutorial discretion, the corporation should not be prosecuted.[15]

Even if the corporation does not escape criminal prosecution altogether, a company's prompt response to allegations of criminal misconduct can be beneficial. As was noted in *Caremark*, the Federal Sentencing

---

States v. LBS Bank-New York, Inc., 757 F. Supp. 496, 501 n.7 (E.D. Pa. 1990) ("[k]nowledge possessed by employees is aggregated so that a corporate defendant is considered to have acquired the collective knowledge of its employees.")

12. For example, the U.S. Department of State has adopted a voluntary disclosure program for violations of the Arms Export Control Act, 22 U.S.C. §§ 2751 *et seq.* (1968) and the International Traffic In Arms Regulations, 22 CFR §§ 120 *et seq.* (1997). The U.S. Department of Justice, Antitrust Division has also instituted an amnesty program, U.S. Department of Justice, Antitrust Division, Corporate Leniency Policy (Aug. 10, 1993). The Justice Department and the U.S. Department of Defense jointly administer a voluntary disclosure program for defense contractors to report instances of fraud, waste, and abuse. Inspector General, Department of Defense, The Department of Defense Voluntary Disclosure Program (April 1990).

13. *See* discussion *infra* at chapter 8.

14. *See, e.g.,* The Department of Defense Voluntary Disclosure Program, *supra* n. 12, at 5 ("[a] matter will be preliminarily accepted to the DoD Voluntary Disclosure Program" if it is determined that "the disclosure was not triggered by the contractor's recognition that the potential criminal or civil fraud matter or the underlying facts were about to be discovered by the government through audit, investigation, contract administration efforts, or reported to the government by third parties. One factor in determining whether the requirement has been met is whether the government had prior knowledge of the matter(s) disclosed").

15. *See* Justice Department Manual, PRINCIPLES OF FEDERAL PROSECUTION, § 230 at 9-505 to 9-506 (voluntary disclosure as factors in the decision whether to pursue criminal charges).

Guidelines for organizational defendants[16] offer "powerful incentives" for organizations to implement what the guidelines refer to as an "effective program to prevent and detect violations of law."[17] An essential element of such a program is the investigation of wrongdoing resulting in prompt remediation, including appropriate discipline.[18] The guidelines also recognize timely self-reporting of violations as a mitigating factor in determining punishment.[19]

Additionally, for corporations in regulated industries, disqualification from conducting business as a result of conviction may be a greater punishment than the fine or probationary term imposed under the sentencing guidelines. For example, corporations doing business with the U.S. government are subject to immediate suspension from contracting with the government if indicted and may be debarred from contracting for up to three years if convicted of offenses reflecting a lack of "present responsibility."[20] Prompt and comprehensive corrective action can position the corporation to argue that it is "presently responsible" to continue government contracting notwithstanding the criminal conviction.

Thus, there are significant benefits to the corporation from timely re-

---

16. *Supra* note 3.

17. 1996 Del. Ch. LEXIS 125.

18. According to the guidelines, the "hallmark" of an effective program is that the organization exercised due diligence in seeking to prevent and detect criminal conduct by its employees and other agents. GUIDELINES, *supra* note 3, § 8A1.2 application Note 3(k). Among the steps required by this due diligence is that "[t]he organization must have taken reasonable steps to achieve compliance with its standards [of conduct] . . . by utilizing monitoring and auditing systems reasonably designed to detect criminal conduct by its employees and other agents . . . " *Id.* Another element of due diligence under the GUIDELINES is that:

> The standards must have been consistently enforced through appropriate disciplinary mechanisms, including, as appropriate, discipline of individuals responsible for failure to detect an offense. Adequate discipline of individuals responsible for an offense is a necessary component of enforcement; however, the form of discipline that will be appropriate will be case specific.

Id.

19. GUIDELINES, *supra* note 3, § 8C2.5(g). The guidelines contemplate "that the organization will be allowed a reasonable period of time to conduct an internal investigation." *Id.* § 8C2.5 application note 10.

20. *See, e.g.*, 48 C.F.R. § 9.406 (1996); Joseph Construction Co. v. Veterans Admin., 595 F. Supp. 448 (N.D. Ill. 1984) (criminal conduct of company's president and sole shareholder was sufficient grounds to warrant debarment of the company).

sponse to employee misconduct. However, in order to obtain those benefits, the corporation must be able to respond quickly to reports of misconduct by aggressively investigating such reports, analyzing the legal consequences, and formulating an appropriate response.

Nevertheless, it must also be recognized that an internal investigation can have significant adverse effects on the organization. The presence of lawyers, the formality of the interview process, and the gathering of documents unavoidably signal to employees that the corporation believes there may be something wrong in the workplace. Employees who may have been involved, however innocently, in the conduct under investigation may feel that they have been singled out and are under suspicion. These employees and their management may fear, often with reason, that investigation of their actions will adversely affect their careers.

None of this diminishes the importance of internal investigations, which are essential to responsible corporate self-governance. But in planning and executing internal investigations, in-house counsel must be mindful of the short- and long-term effects the investigation may have on the corporation, its employees, and its culture.

II. WHEN SHOULD AN INTERNAL INVESTIGATION BE UNDERTAKEN?

An internal investigation should be conducted whenever there is a credible indication of a violation of law or established company policy. These indications may come from a variety of sources, and the corporation's response will depend on the nature and gravity of the violation.

If the corporation has established a mechanism for employees to report possible misconduct without fear of retaliation[21] (e.g., "hotlines" or ombudsmen), all such reports should be followed up. Other sources of information include internal audits, exit interviews with departing employees, reports by outside auditors, press reports or inquiries, and allegations made in employment actions and civil litigation.

As noted in chapter 1, in some instances the corporation must react to

---

21. *See* GUIDELINES, *supra* note 3, § 8A1.2 application note 3(k) (5) (among the "reasonable steps to achieve compliance" with the corporation's standards of conduct is "having in place and publicizing a reporting system whereby employees and other agents could report criminal conduct by others within the organization without fear of retribution").

a government investigation that is already under way. Search warrants, grand jury subpoenas, administrative subpoenas and civil investigative demands are increasingly becoming common "investigative tools" by government prosecutors. Once it learns of a government investigation, the corporation must move swiftly to identify and analyze relevant documents to interview percipient witnesses; to assess the corporation's rights, obligations, and potential liability; and to report conclusions to senior management and the board of directors.

As a general rule, all credible reports of misconduct should be investigated. Obviously, however, not all such reports require the level of investigation described in previous chapters. Once it is decided that an internal investigation should be initiated, the next critical question is who should have responsibility for conducting the investigation.

III. WHO SHOULD CONDUCT THE INVESTIGATION?

As an initial matter, it must be decided who will be responsible for conducting the internal investigation. To a great extent, this will depend on the nature and circumstances of the alleged wrongdoing. Allegations of theft, long lunch hours, and other isolated incidents of erroneous time charging can be appropriately responded to by the corporation's human resources or security organizations. On the other hand, violations of law or significant corporate policy that expose the corporation to criminal or civil liability should be conducted under the direction of lawyers in order to obtain the protections of the attorney-client privilege and work product doctrine against compelled disclosure to third parties. An internal investigation in response to a government inquiry should be conducted under counsel's auspices for the same reason.

Having determined that a matter should be investigated on a privileged basis by counsel, it must then be determined whether to rely on in-house counsel to conduct the investigation or to engage outside counsel. It has been recognized, since the Supreme Court's decision in *Upjohn Company v. United States*,[22] that the attorney-client privilege and work product doctrine apply to corporate internal investigations.[23] It is also settled

---

22. 449 U.S. 383 (1981).

23. *See* United States v. Rowe, 96 F.3d 1294, 1297 (9th Cir. 1996); United States v. Shyres, 898 F.2d 647, 655 (8th Cir. 1990); *In re* Grand Jury Subpoena Dated December

that these protections against forced disclosure attach equally to investigations by both in-house and outside counsel.[24]

Unless the corporation has had a longstanding relationship with a law firm, in-house counsel are usually more familiar with the nature of the company's business. In-house counsel generally have a greater understanding of the corporate culture and organization than their counterparts in private law practice. In-house counsel are also more familiar with the corporation's processes and procedures. In-house counsel may be better prepared to evaluate the significance of documents, or their absence, than counsel from outside the corporation. Finally, in-house counsel may know, at least by reputation, the personalities of the people involved in the matter.

On the other hand, because outside counsel are not "captive" employees of the corporation, they enjoy a greater perception of being independent. Further, because outside counsel are generally not as directly involved in providing business as well as legal advice, there is a stronger presumption that their work for the corporation is within the attorney-client privilege and work product doctrine.[25] Outside counsel are likely to be more familiar with local practices, particularly if in-house counsel is

---

19, 1978, 599 F.2d 504, 510 (2d Cir. 1979); Diversified Indus., Inc. v. Meredith, 572 F.2d 596, 610 (8th Cir. 1979) (en banc); *In re* Woolworth Corp. Sec. Class Action Litig., 1996 U.S. Dist. LEXIS 7773 (S.D.N.Y. 1996); *In re* Leslie Fay Companies, Inc. Sec. Litig. 161 F.R.D. 274, 282 (S.D.N.Y. 1995); *In re* LTV Sec. Litig., 89 F.R.D. 595, 601 (N.D. Tex. 1981). The attorney-client privilege and work product doctrine as they apply to internal corporation investigations are discussed, *infra*, at chapter 2.

24. *See In re* Sealed Case, 737 F.2d 94, 99 (D.C. Cir. 1984); Natta v. Hogan, 392 F.2d 686, 692 (9th Cir. 1968); *In re* LTV Sec. Litig., 89 F.R.D. at 601; O'Brien v. Board of Educ., 86 F.R.D. 548, 549 (S.D.N.Y. 1980); Valiente v. PepsiCo, Inc., 68 F.R.D. 361, 367 (D. Del. 1975); Malco Mfg. Co. v. Elco Corp., 45 F.R.D. 24, 26 (D. Minn. 1968); 8-in-1 Pet Products, Inc. v. Swift & Co., 218 F. Supp. 253 (S.D.N.Y. 1963); Georgia - Pacific Plywood Co. v. United States Plywood Corp., 18 F.R.D. 463, 464 (S.D.N.Y. 1956); United States v. United Shoe Mach. Corp., 89 F. Supp. 357, 360 (D. Mass. 1950).

25. *See e.g.,* United States v. Chevron Corp., 1996 U.S. Dist. LEXIS 4154 (N.D. Cal. 1996) ("[s]ome courts have applied a presumption that all communications to outside counsel are primarily related to legal advice.... In this context, the presumption is logical, since outside counsel would not ordinarily be involved in the business decisions of a corporation. However, the ... presumption cannot be applied to in-house counsel because in-house counsel are frequently involved in the business decisions of a company. While an attorney's status as in-house counsel does not dilute the attorney-client privilege ... a corporation must make a clear showing that in-house counsel's advice was given in a professional legal capacity.") (citations omitted).

located in a distant city, and may enjoy better relationships with local prosecutors. Outside counsel may also have greater resources and expertise in specialized areas of the law relevant to the investigation.

The choice between in-house counsel and outside counsel may be determined by reasons of economy. There may not be sufficient resources for in-house counsel to conduct an internal investigation. Likewise, in-house counsel may lack the background or expertise necessary to conduct internal investigations effectively. Of course, cost is always a consideration, and the corporation may be unwilling to accept the expense of an investigation conducted by someone outside the corporation. There may also be circumstances in which the investigation should be undertaken by someone outside the corporation, as when the conduct of senior management is directly implicated.

In most instances, the most effective approach has proved to be a teaming of in-house and outside counsel. By joining the two, the benefits that both in-house and outside counsel bring to the investigation can be obtained. Additionally, the participation of in-house counsel can facilitate communication with management, who may expect in-house counsel to be involved, as well as with employees, who may be reluctant to confide in "outsiders."

After counsel has been designated to conduct the investigation, there are formalities that should be observed, and issues that should be addressed at the outset of the investigation.

IV. INITIATING THE INVESTIGATION

In order to establish and document the basis for asserting the attorney-client privilege with regard to the internal investigation, as discussed in chapter 2, it is advisable to recognize certain formalities. The first of these is a formal request by corporate management that counsel undertake the investigation of a specific matter for the purpose of providing legal counsel to the management concerning the corporation's rights and obligations. Such a request is often referred to as an *"Upjohn* letter."

This request should describe the subject matter of the investigation with reasonable specificity and should be addressed to the senior in-house lawyer. The recipient of the request may then delegate authority to other counsel to carry out the investigation. Counsel receiving the original request may wish to acknowledge the assignment in a separate document.

Next, the manager requesting the investigation should issue a directive to the employees who may be contacted by counsel during the investigation. This document should inform the employees that counsel has been requested by management to conduct an inquiry and to provide legal advice to the corporation, and that they may be contacted by counsel as part of this inquiry. The employees should be further instructed that they are to provide counsel with any information requested by counsel concerning the performance of the employees' duties and assignments. The purpose of this document is to evidence that counsel is acting at the request of the corporation's management, as set forth in the *Upjohn* letter, and that the information sought and received is in furtherance of that request.

Finally, if outside counsel is to participate in the internal investigation, it is advisable to engage counsel in writing. The letter retaining counsel should also reference management's request as set forth in the *Upjohn* letter. This correspondence will further evidence that counsel is acting pursuant to management's request for legal advice.

V. STRUCTURING THE INVESTIGATION

In addition to the formalities that should be observed at the time the investigation is initiated, a number of important decisions should be made at or near the outset concerning how the investigation is to be conducted. These decisions pertain to the resources necessary to conduct the investigation, the investigative plan, the legal representation of individual employees, and document control and organization.

A. *Assembling the Investigative Team*

Once the composition of the legal team has been established, thought should be given to what additional resources will be necessary to analyze the facts gathered during the investigation. Auditors and forensic accountants may be needed to analyze financial records and data. Engineers, architects, and systems designers may be needed for technical or quality issues. Chemists, hydrologists, and other technicians may be needed in environmental investigations.

Often these resources can be found within the corporation. Indeed, the expertise of operations personnel is in most instances essential to understanding processes and analyzing relevant documents. Similarly, the assistance of internal auditors who are familiar with company practices and procedures is invaluable.

When the necessary expertise cannot be found in the corporation, outside consultants must be engaged. These experts should be brought in as early as possible so that they can assist in structuring and refining the investigation. In some instances, even when the necessary expertise exists within the corporation, it may be advisable to retain an outside expert either to assist in a presentation to the government prosecutor or to provide expert testimony should civil or criminal litigation ensue.

In order to preserve the privileges applicable to these experts' work, it should be documented that this non-legal assistance is being rendered at the request and under the direction of counsel. If resources outside the corporation are being used, they should be retained by outside counsel. If in-house personnel are being used, they should be formally tasked to work at the direction and under the supervision of counsel.

B. *The Investigative Plan*

Once the team has been assembled, it is essential that an investigative plan be developed and agreed upon. The plan should include a clear understanding of the objectives of the investigation as well as the means to be employed in achieving those objectives. The plan should define the specific responsibilities of the individual members of the team and should establish the work product for which each member of the team will be responsible. The plan should also establish a budget for accomplishing each of the principal tasks.

1. Objectives

The plan should identify what it is that the investigation seeks to accomplish. The objective may be as simple as determining whether a discrete allegation of misconduct is well-founded. In contrast, the objective may be as complex as evaluating the legality and effect of a widespread company procedure and, if the procedure is deficient, proposing corrective measures.

An internal investigation can take on a life of its own. Issues may arise that were not anticipated, and leads may develop that must be pursued. For these reasons, it is critical that the objectives of the investigation be understood so that focus is not lost as the investigation unfolds. At the same time, the plan needs to be flexible enough to enable counsel conducting the investigation to adapt to new facts, new leads, and new issues.

In formulating the investigative plan and in formulating the objectives, care should be taken to ensure that the objective of the investigation is consistent with the preservation of the attorney-client privilege and work product doctrine. For example, unless there is a compelling business reason to the contrary, the decision whether to disclose the results of the investigation to third parties should be reserved until the investigation has been completed. Otherwise, an announcement that the results of the investigation will be reported to the government or the public threatens to compromise attorney-client and work product protections.[26]

2. Communication with Management

It is essential that corporate management and the Board of Directors be kept apprised of significant investigations. Indeed, the purpose of an internal investigation is to gather information in order to provide legal advice to the corporation. However, the level of detail that is communicated while the investigation is ongoing is a matter of some delicacy and should be appropriate to the recipient's "need to know." As part of the structuring of the investigation, a mechanism must be established for briefing responsible management periodically during the investigation.

a. The Board of Directors

If the investigation directly implicates the continued viability of the corporation (the so-called "bet-the-company problem"), the board must be actively involved. If the investigation concerns the actions of senior management, the board itself (acting through the independent directors) should oversee the investigation, which in this instance should be conducted by outside counsel engaged by the board.[27] In other serious but not life-threatening matters, the board of directors should be regularly apprised of the status of the investigation.

The corporation's chief legal officer (i.e., the general counsel) is the appropriate person to advise the board of directors of the progress of

---

26. *See, e.g., In re* Kidder Peabody Sec. Litig., 1996 U.S. Dist. LEXIS (S.D.N.Y. 1996) (company's stated intent to disclose the report of an internal investigation to the Securities and Exchange Commission and to the public was evidence that the report was not prepared in anticipation of litigation and therefore the work product doctrine did not apply).

27. *See infra*, chapter 9.

internal investigations. The general counsel should also keep the board advised on the status of government investigations. This can be accomplished as part of the general counsel's regular briefing of significant legal matters.

b. The Chief Executive Officer

Similarly, the general counsel should keep the CEO regularly apprised of the progress of significant investigations. However, in providing information to the CEO, it is important to advise restraint (not something that comes naturally to most CEOs) so that the investigation can run its course. There may be intense pressure from the board or the CEO to put the problem "behind us," and the challenge to the general counsel in those instances is to forestall action until the matter has been investigated and understood.

c. Operations Management[28]

Understandably, operations management will also demand to be informed of investigations involving their areas of responsibility. The success of the investigation—that is, the ability to gather relevant, reliable information quickly—will depend to a great extent on the cooperation of operations management. However, because operations managers are often "can-do" people who thrive on problem solving, extra care—and diplomacy—must be exercised in providing information concerning the investigation.

Operations managers may become witnesses in a government investigation, and care must therefore be taken not to "educate" potential witnesses about information learned in the course of the investigation that was not otherwise known to them. In this connection, it is extremely important to explain the operation of the attorney-client privilege and to preface every briefing with a reminder of the applicability of the privilege.

Equally important, operations managers will often try to "get to the bottom" of the problem. In so doing, unprivileged documents, some of which may be quite damaging to the company's best interest, may be

---

28. As used here, "Operations Management" includes those managers directly involved in the conduct of the company's business (in contrast to overall management), such as division or sector general managers and program managers. These managers may feel that they have the most at stake as the investigation concerns conduct alleged to have occurred in their area of responsibility.

created. The investigators must be attentive to such activities and attempt, insofar as possible, to avoid or truncate them. Good communication, and confidence building between the investigators and the managers, can go a long way in avoiding the problem.

The degree of detail provided to each of these groups must be carefully considered. Any disclosure creates the risk of waiver of the attorney-client privilege or work product doctrine. Further, some of these people, particularly at the operations level, may have a motive to alter or destroy documents because of the investigation. Thus, counsel must exercise good judgment to ensure that the level of information imparted to employees is appropriate under the circumstances.

3. Communication Outside the Corporation

There may be occasions when it is necessary or advisable to communicate with persons outside the corporation concerning the investigation. Obviously, these communications create the greatest risk of waiver of the attorney-client privilege and work product doctrine. Accordingly, a mechanism for effecting these communications should be established as well.

a. The Government

If the corporation does business in a regulated industry, it is often advisable to make contact with the licensing authority at an early stage in an investigation, particularly if the corporate investigation parallels a government investigation. Early contact with the licensing authority may avoid precipitous action by the licensing authority and will provide a predicate for establishing the corporation's "present responsibility" necessary to prevent or mitigate suspension or debarment from the regulated activity.

Additionally, regulatory agencies may require corporations to report investigations of misconduct. Publicly traded companies that are targets of grand jury investigations may be obliged to disclose the pendency of such investigations in filings with the U.S. Securities and Exchange Commission if indictment would have material adverse impact on their operations.[29] In like fashion, bank regulatory authorities require financial institutions to make reports of "known or suspected criminal activity."[30]

---

29. *See* Item 103, SEC Reg. S-K, 17 C.F.R. § 229.103 (1997).

30. *See* 12 C.F.R. §§ 21.11 *et seq.* (1997) (requiring national banks to report known

If the corporate internal investigation is in response to a government investigation, it is also generally advisable to establish communication with the prosecutor assigned to the case. It is usually necessary to negotiate the scope of grand jury subpoenas as well as a schedule for producing responsive documents. Early informal communication with the prosecutor can help refine the issues under investigation (thereby avoiding time-consuming and expensive tangents) and can provide insight into the government's specific concerns. Corporate management will also take some comfort from the knowledge that the company's lawyers are engaged in dialogue with the government.

b. Third Parties

There are also a variety of non-governmental third parties who will seek information concerning the corporation's investigation. Depending on the circumstances, there may be substantial business reasons for communicating with them.

First among these third parties are the corporation's independent auditors. The auditors will request a representation concerning potential "loss contingencies," in accordance with Statement of Financial Accounting Standards No. 5 issued by the Financial Accounting Standards Board, as part of their annual audit of the corporation's financial records. The American Bar Association has provided guidance to counsel responding to such requests.[31] Nevertheless, there are significant risks of waiver of the attorney-client privilege and work product doctrine in providing otherwise privileged information in response to these requests.[32]

If the government's investigation has attracted public notice, counsel should anticipate that there will be requests for information concerning the investigation from other third parties as well. Investment bankers and commercial lenders may seek assurances, as may institutional investors and other shareholders. Customers and suppliers may also seek to be assured that ongoing commercial relationships will not be disrupted. The

---

or suspected criminal violations or transactions related to money-laundering activity or violation of the Bank Secrecy Act); 12 C.F.R. §§ 353.1 *et seq.* (1997) (imposing the same requirements on FDIC-insured state banks).

31. AMERICAN BAR ASSOCIATION, AUDITORS LETTER HANDBOOK (1976).

32. *See, e.g., In re* Subpoena Duces Tecum Issued to Wilkie Farr & Gallagher, 1997 U.S. Dist. LEXIS 2927 (S.D.N.Y. 1997) (disclosure of a report to an internal investigation to the outside auditors in order to obtain an unqualified audit opinion was a waiver of the attorney-client privilege).

financial press, and even the general press, may cover the investigation. Coordination with the corporation's public affairs, banking, and shareholder relations organizations is especially important in responding, if at all, to these requests.

4. Employee Interviews

There should be a clear understanding on the part of the investigators and the company in regard to several issues that routinely arise when employees are interviewed. These issues involve the rights and obligations of employees—first when the employee is interviewed by the company, and second when the government seeks to interview the company's employees.

When the company interviews its own employees as part of an internal investigation, there is often a question whether an employee will be permitted to be accompanied by a representative during the interview. If the employee is covered by a collective-bargaining agreement, the terms of the agreement may control whether a representative can be present. Similarly, if the employee is involved in litigation with the corporation, the subject matter of which is related to the transaction under investigation, company counsel may be ethically constrained from interviewing the employee without the employee's counsel being present. Absent such considerations, it is discretionary whether the company will allow the employee to be represented during an interview by the company's counsel, there being no general right to counsel at a company interview.[33]

A second issue that arises when employees are interviewed in a corporate internal investigation is whether the employee will be subject to adverse personnel action for refusing to cooperate with the investigation. Most, if not all, companies take the position that an element of the employer/employee relationship is the obligation to provide information concerning matters within the scope of employment. Indeed, the memorandum from management to employees advising them of the investigation, discussed earlier, is intended to document management's directive that employees provide information to the investigators pursuant to this employment obligation.

---

33. *See* United States v. Calhoon, 859 F. Supp. 1496, 1498 (M.D. Ga. 1994); TRW, Inc. v. Superior Court of Los Angeles County, 25 Cal. App. 4th, 1834, 31 Cal. Rptr. 2d 460 (1994). An employee's rights in this regard are discussed, *infra*, at chapter 6.

If an employee refuses to cooperate, the company must determine whether to take disciplinary action. Many companies have a policy that failure to cooperate with company counsel is grounds for termination (a so-called "talk or walk" policy). Other companies provide for a range of possible disciplinary actions. In any event, the investigators and the company should agree on the approach to be taken in the event of non-cooperation and, if it is decided that discipline will result from a failure to cooperate, that discipline should be imposed consistently and uniformly.[34]

Very different considerations apply when it is the government that seeks to interview the corporation's employees. First, the employee has a constitutional privilege against self-incrimination that entitles the employee, if he or she chooses, to decline to be interviewed, even though the corporation itself is cooperating with the government's investigation. Second, the corporation must decide whether to advance the fees for the legal representation of the employees interviewed by the government.

There is a tendency among many companies to have company counsel (in-house or outside) represent employees at interviews with government agents, largely for reasons of cost. Although there are circumstances in which representation by company counsel is completely appropriate, it is often a false economy to have the same counsel represent both the corporation and its employees.[35] There is the risk that a conflict of interest can develop between one employee and another or between one or more employees and the company. In that event, counsel would be bound to withdraw from the representation and could face possible disqualification at a critical juncture in the investigation.[36]

Counsel representing one or more individuals often interacts with government investigators differently from company counsel. Counsel for

---

34. *See* discussion, *infra*, at chapter 6.

35. *See* discussion, *infra*, chapter 7.

36. *See* DR5-105 (ABA 1981); Model Rule 1.7(a) (ABA 1989); United States v. Moscony, 927 F.2d 742, 748 (3d Cir. 1991). In this connection, great care must be taken by company counsel at the outset of an interview with an employee to make clear that counsel represents the corporation, not the employee. Counsel should also explain the applicability of the attorney-client privilege to the matters discussed during the interview and should emphasize the importance of maintaining confidentiality. Counsel must also make it clear, however, that the privilege belongs to the corporation, not to the employee, and that the corporation may waive the privilege and disclose the matters discussed in the interview at a future time. These corporate "*Miranda* warnings" are discussed, *infra*, in chapters 3 and 6.

an individual properly may instruct the individual not to be interviewed or, even during an interview, not to answer a particular question. Company counsel cannot give either instruction while at the same time maintaining that the company is cooperating with the government's investigation. Similarly, an individual's counsel may negotiate immunity when company counsel could not.

Alternatively, the corporation may be obliged to make individual counsel available to employees who may become involved in a government investigation. For example, under California state law, an employer is required to indemnify employees for expenses incurred as a consequence of the discharge of the employees' duties.[37] In these circumstances, the corporation should suggest one or more skilled white-collar counsel but should refrain from requiring that the attorney choose a particular lawyer.

When the corporation advances fees for an individual's counsel, it may be necessary to require the individual employee to execute an undertaking that the fees and expenses advanced will be repaid if it is determined that the individual was not entitled to indemnification. Such an undertaking may be required by law,[38] or may be warranted by sound corporate governance. Employees are often confused when confronted

---

37. CAL. LABOR CODE § 2802 provides:

An employer shall indemnify his employee for all that the employee necessarily expends or loses in direct consequence of the discharge of his duties as such, or of his disobedience to the directions of the employer, even though unlawful, unless the employee, at the time of obeying such directions, believed them to be unlawful.

Similarly, CAL. CORP. CODE § 317(d) provides:

To the extent that an agent of a corporation has been successful on the merits in defense of any proceedings... or in defense of any claim, issue or matter therein, the agent shall be indemnified against expenses actually and reasonably incurred by the agent in connection therewith.

The obligation of the employee to advance fees for counsel is discussed, *infra*, in chapter 6.

38. For example, Delaware corporation law establishes a corporation's power to indemnify persons acting on behalf of the corporation (*i.e.*, directors, officers, employees or agents) against attorney's fees and expenses in connection with a civil, criminal, administrative or investigative matter if the individual "acted in good faith and in a manner he reasonably believed to be in or not opposed to the best interests of the corporation, and, with respect to any criminal action or proceeding, had no reasonable cause to believe his conduct was unlawful." DEL. CORP. LAW § 145(a) and (b).

with such an undertaking. They are concerned that the corporation, which has just assured them that counsel would be provided, is now saying that they may have to repay the fees at a later time. As a result, both company counsel and the individual's counsel should each endeavor to explain the import of the undertaking to the individual employee.

Finally, when one or more counsel are engaged to represent individuals, it may be in the best interests of all concerned to enter into an information-sharing and confidentiality agreement. These agreements are also known as "joint defense" agreements. Some government agents and prosecutors have been critical of, if not overtly hostile to, joint defense agreements, but, as discussed in chapters 6 and 7, so long as the independence and loyalty of the attorneys and their clients are recognized and respected, information-sharing agreements are a legitimate response to a government investigation. However, any disclosure of confidential information risks a subsequent finding that the attorney-client privilege and work product doctrine have been waived. Similarly, there may be circumstances in which the corporation may decide that it is inappropriate to ally itself closely with others. Thus, while there are clear benefits to information-sharing agreements, company counsel should carefully consider the disadvantages before entering into such agreements.

5. Maintaining Control Over Documents

Concurrent with and sometimes prior to the interview of knowledgeable employees, documents relevant to the investigation must be identified and analyzed. If the government has made a formal request for the production of documents, by means of subpoena, civil investigative demand or other administrative process, the corporation must act promptly to preserve responsive documents so that they can be collected, reviewed, and produced. Additionally, even before a formal request has been made, it is prudent for the corporation to take the steps necessary to preserve

---

Delaware law further provides:

> Expenses incurred by an officer or director in defending a civil or criminal action, suit or proceeding may be paid by the corporation in advance of the final disposition of such action, suit or proceeding upon receipt of an undertaking by or on behalf of such director or officer to repay such amount if it shall ultimately be determined that he is not entitled to be indemnified by the corporation as authorized in this Section.

DEL. CORP. LAW § 145(e).

relevant documents once the subject matter of the government's investigation is known in order to avoid a later claim of spoliation of evidence, and the attendant negative inference.[39]

The mechanics of gaining control of relevant documents are discussed in chapter 6. However, several points should be kept in mind.

If the corporation has an established document retention program, the destruction of potentially relevant documents must be halted immediately. Employees who reasonably may be expected to have relevant, responsive documents should be given notice of the government's document request and should be specifically instructed to preserve documents. Members of the investigative team should meet with these employees and their supervisors to emphasize the importance of retaining documents and to explain the procedures that will be followed. Frequent monitoring is necessary to ensure that counsel's directives are being followed and that the procedures are being implemented.

As early as possible in the process, a document custodian should be designated to oversee the gathering and production of responsive documents. The document custodian should be familiar with the types of responsive documents that are created by the corporation in the ordinary course of business and with their location. The document custodian should bear principal responsibility for conducting the corporation's search for documents.

On the other hand, company counsel must be responsible for the determination of responsiveness and privilege. Counsel should be assisted in determining what documents are responsive by operations personnel. Thus, when assembling the investigative team, it is often helpful to include persons from the operations who can interpret the relevant documents.

Lastly, a document control center should be established for housing the documents relevant to the subject matter of the investigation, regardless of whether the documents are responsive to the document request or are privileged. The document control center should be under the control of the document custodian. If warranted, use of scanning technology will

---

39. *See, e.g.,* CAL. EVID. CODE § 412 ("[i]f weaker less satisfactory evidence is offered when it was within the power of the party to produce stronger and more satisfactory evidence, the evidence offered should be viewed with distrust") and § 413 ("[i]n determining what inferences to draw from the evidence or facts in the case against a party, the trier of fact may consider, among other things, the party's failure to explain or to deny by his testimony such evidence or facts in the case against him, or his willful suppression of evidence relating thereto, if such be the case").

allow the transformation of the documents at the control center to electronic images accessible by members of the investigative team at remote locations, obviating the need for team members to come to the center to review the documents.

VI. REPORTING THE RESULTS OF THE INVESTIGATION

Once the investigation has been completed, it must be determined what is to be done with the results. Of course, appropriate management, including the board of directors, must be advised of counsel's findings, conclusions, and advice. This information can be given in a series of oral briefings tailored to the manager's need to know. Most commonly, however, the investigative team produces a written report. As discussed in chapter 11, great care must be exercised in reporting counsel's conclusions to preserve applicable privileges and to avoid possible claims of defamation.

Also, as discussed in chapter 8, the corporation must decide whether to disclose the results of the investigation to the government. Such a disclosure may be in the form of a formal voluntary disclosure under the auspices of an established voluntary disclosure program.[40] The disclosure may also be made less formally to the prosecutor in an effort to persuade the prosecutor to decline prosecution. In either event, the disclosure can result in the waiver of the attorney-client privilege and work product doctrine, at least as to the report itself.[41] The consequences of such a waiver, particularly in regard to third-party civil liability, must be carefully weighed.[42]

---

40. *See supra* note 12.

41. See *In re* Steinhardt Partners, L.P., 9 F.3d 230, 236 (2d Cir. 1993) (disclosure to the SEC); Westinghouse Elec. Corp. v. Republic of the Philippines, 951 F.2d 1414, 1427-29 (3d Cir. 1991) (disclosure to the SEC and Department of Justice); *In re* Martin Marietta Corp., 856 F.2d 619, 623-24 (4th Cir. 1988) (disclosure to the U.S. Attorney's Office), *cert. denied,* 109 S. Ct. 1655 (1989); *In re* Subpoena Duces Tecum (Fulbright & Jaworski), 738 F.2d 1367, 1370-75 (D.C. Cir. 1984) (disclosure to the SEC); *In re* Sealed Case, 676 F.2d 793, 817 (D.C. Cir. 1982) (disclosure to the SEC); Permian Corp. v. United States, 665 F.2d 1214, 1219 (D.C. Cir. 1981) (disclosure to the SEC); *In re* Kidder Peabody Sec. Litig., 1996 U.S. Dist. LEXIS 6700 (S.D.N.Y. 1996) (disclosure to the SEC); Isaacson v. Keck, Mahin & Cate, 875 F. Supp. 478, 480 (N.D. Ill. 1994) (disclosure to the SEC and attorney disciplinary committee); *In re* Leslie Fay Co. Sec. Litig., 152 F.R.D. 42 (S.D.N.Y. 1993) (disclosure to the SEC and the U.S. Attorney's Office); United States v. Mierzwicki, 500 F. Supp. 1331, 1334 (D. Md. 1980) (disclosure to the Department of Justice).

Management will expect that the investigation will also result in proposed remedial actions to mitigate any damage that may have resulted. It will also be expected that corrective actions will be proposed to prevent recurrence of similar misconduct in the future.

If recommendations are made, they must be practical and realistically achievable by the corporation. It must also be impressed on management that if the recommendations are adopted, they must be implemented. Otherwise, if they are not, there is the risk that the government will later point to the corporation's failure to follow through as evidence of the corporation's indifference to legal compliance and its intent to violate the law.

VII. CONCLUSION

Although there are clear benefits to the corporation from conducting internal investigations of suspected wrongdoing, the manner in which investigations are conducted can have a decidedly negative effect within the corporation. The role of in-house counsel is critical both to achieve these benefits and to minimize the negative effects of the investigation itself.

Thus, the successful investigation not only gathers and analyzes facts quickly and efficiently, but also responds effectively to the concerns within the corporation. Obviously, that does not mean that individual responsibility for misconduct should not be established without fear or favor. Rather, in structuring and carrying out the investigation along the lines discussed in the previous chapters, it is important that the investigation have clear objectives, that the investigation follow a plan established at the outset, that efforts be made not to disrupt the operation of the company unnecessarily, and that both management and the board of directors be kept advised of the progress and status of the investigation.

---

42. *See* discussion, *infra*, at chapter 8.

Index

E